Blockchain Foundations

Mastering Cryptographic Primitives, Consensus Mechanisms, and the Mathematics Behind Distributed Ledger Technology

Nagnath Savant

Apress®

Blockchain Foundations: Mastering Cryptographic Primitives, Consensus Mechanisms, and the Mathematics Behind Distributed Ledger Technology

Nagnath Savant
Pune, Maharashtra, India

ISBN-13 (pbk): 979-8-8688-2890-4 ISBN-13 (electronic): 979-8-8688-2891-1
https://doi.org/10.1007/979-8-8688-2891-1

Managing Director, Apress Media LLC: Welmoed Spahr
Acquisitions Editor: Shivangi Ramachandran
Editorial Assistant: Jessica Vakili

Cover designed by eStudioCalamar

Cover image designed by Pixabay

Distributed to the book trade worldwide by Springer Science+Business Media New York, 1 New York Plaza, New York, NY 10004. Phone 1-800-SPRINGER, fax (201) 348-4505, e-mail orders-ny@springer-sbm.com, or visit www.springeronline.com. Apress Media, LLC is a Delaware LLC and the sole member (owner) is Springer Science + Business Media Finance Inc (SSBM Finance Inc). SSBM Finance Inc is a **Delaware** corporation.

For information on translations, please e-mail booktranslations@springernature.com; for reprint, paperback, or audio rights, please e-mail bookpermissions@springernature.com.

Apress titles may be purchased in bulk for academic, corporate, or promotional use. eBook versions and licenses are also available for most titles. For more information, reference our Print and eBook Bulk Sales web page at http://www.apress.com/bulk-sales.

The manuscript was prepared with the assistance of Open AI's ChatGPT 5.1 and Google Gemini 3 Pro, 2025 generative AI. Every section was carefully reviewed, revised, and approved by the author(s) to ensure that the text is appropriate concerning content and scientific correctness and maintains the integrity of the original content.

Any source code or other supplementary material referenced by the author in this book is available to readers on GitHub. For more detailed information, please visit https://www.apress.com/gp/services/source-code.

If disposing of this product, please recycle the paper

To my Mother

You never read a line of code.

You read me instead.

That was always enough.

Table of Contents

About the Author xiii

About the Technical Reviewer xv

Acknowledgments xvii

Introduction xix

Part I: Cryptographic Foundations 1

Chapter 1: The Why of Blockchain 3

1.1 Distributed Systems, Trust, and the Byzantine Generals Problem 3

1.1.1 The Problem: Trust in Distributed Systems 4

1.1.2 The Byzantine Generals Problem 7

1.1.3 Early Digital Cash Attempts 11

1.1.4 Digital Cash Evolution 12

1.1.5 Trust Assumptions in Distributed Systems 14

1.1.6 Why the Byzantine Generals Problem Matters 16

1.1.7 Summary 22

1.1.8 Exercises 23

1.1.9 Further Reading 24

Chapter 2: Cryptographic Primitives 25

2.1 Hashes, MACs, CSPRNGs, Merkle Trees, and Patricia Tries 25

2.1.1 Introduction: The Building Blocks of Blockchain 26

2.1.2 Cryptographic Hash Functions 26

2.1.3 Hash Functions in Blockchain: SHA-256 and Keccak 28

2.1.4 Message Authentication Codes (MACs) 35

2.1.5 Cryptographically Secure Random Number Generation 37

2.1.6 Merkle Trees: Efficient Data Verification 40

2.1.7 Patricia Tries: Prefix Trees for Key-Value Storage 46
2.1.8 Merkle-Patricia Tries in Ethereum 47
2.1.9 Summary 52
2.1.10 Exercises 53
2.1.11 Further Reading 54

Chapter 3: Digital Signatures 55

3.1 Public Key Cryptography and Authentication 55
3.1.1 Introduction: Authentication Without Trust 55
3.1.2 Public Key Cryptography Basics 56
3.1.3 RSA Signatures: The Classic Approach 58
3.1.4 Schnorr Signatures: Simplicity and Aggregation 64
3.1.5 EdDSA: Deterministic Signatures with Curve25519 69
3.1.6 Multi-Signatures and Threshold Signatures 72
3.1.7 Summary 76
3.1.8 Exercises 78
3.1.9 Further Reading 78

Chapter 4: Zero-Knowledge Proofs 81

4.1 Advanced Cryptographic Primitives for Privacy and Scalability 81
4.1.1 Introduction: Proving Without Revealing 82
4.1.2 Zero-Knowledge Proofs: Definitions and Properties 82
4.1.3 zk-SNARKs: Succinct Non-Interactive Arguments 86
4.1.4 zk-STARKs: Transparent and Scalable Proofs 93
4.1.5 Bulletproofs: Efficient Range Proofs 95
4.1.6 Commitment Schemes 100
4.1.7 Ring Signatures: Signer Ambiguity 103
4.1.8 Verifiable Random Functions (VRFs) 110
4.1.9 Summary 115
4.1.10 Exercises 117
4.1.11 Further Reading 118

Part II: Consensus Mechanisms 119

Chapter 5: Proof of Work 121

5.1 Mining, Difficulty, and Security Analysis 121

5.1.1 Hash Puzzles: The Foundation of Proof of Work 122

5.1.2 Difficulty Adjustment Algorithms 127

5.1.3 Mining Economics 131

5.1.4 The 51% Attack 136

5.1.5 Selfish Mining 139

5.1.6 Energy Consumption and Sustainability 143

5.1.7 Mining Pools and Centralization 146

5.1.8 Summary 150

5.1.9 Exercises 151

5.1.10 Further Reading 151

Chapter 6: Proof of Stake 153

6.1 Security, Slashing, and Long-Range Attacks 153

6.1.1 From Computation to Capital 154

6.1.2 The Nothing-at-Stake Problem 159

6.1.3 Ethereum's Gasper Consensus 161

6.1.4 Slashing Mechanisms 173

6.1.5 Long-Range Attacks 177

6.1.6 Validator Economics 180

6.1.7 PoS Security Analysis 184

6.1.8 Summary 186

6.1.9 Exercises 187

6.1.10 Further Reading 188

Chapter 7: Byzantine Fault Tolerance 189

7.1 PBFT, HotStuff, and Tendermint 189

7.1.1 Byzantine Agreement Fundamentals 190

7.1.2 PBFT: Practical Byzantine Fault Tolerance 193

7.1.3 HotStuff: Linear Complexity BFT 205

7.1.4 Tendermint Core 212
7.1.5 Synchrony Assumptions and Network Partitions 221
7.1.6 Summary 222
7.1.7 Exercises 224
7.1.8 Further Reading 225

Chapter 8: Novel Consensus Mechanisms 227

8.1 Avalanche, GHOST, and Ouroboros 227
8.1.1 Beyond Classical BFT and Nakamoto Consensus 228
8.1.2 Avalanche Consensus Family 228
8.1.3 GHOST Protocol 237
8.1.4 Ouroboros: Provably Secure Proof of Stake 242
8.1.5 Nakamoto Consensus Variants 247
8.1.6 Finality Models: Probabilistic, Deterministic, and Economic 248
8.1.7 Summary 250
8.1.8 Exercises 252
8.1.9 Further Reading 253

Chapter 9: Consensus Comparison Framework 255

9.1 Systematic Methodology for Evaluating Consensus Mechanisms 255
9.1.1 Why a Framework Matters 256
9.1.2 Security Analysis Framework 257
9.1.3 Performance Metrics 267
9.1.4 Decentralization Measurement 272
9.1.5 Energy Efficiency Comparison 278
9.1.6 Economic Security: Cost of Attack Analysis 279
9.1.7 Applying the Framework: Decision Methodology 281
9.1.8 Summary 282
9.1.9 Exercises 284
9.1.10 Further Reading 285

Part III: Blockchain Architecture and Execution..287

Chapter 10: Data Structures..289

10.1 UTXO vs. Accounts and State Management..289

10.1.1 Two Models of Blockchain State..290

10.1.2 The UTXO Model in Depth..291

10.1.3 The Account Model in Depth..300

10.1.4 State Management with Merkle Proofs..307

10.1.5 State Growth and Sustainability..313

10.1.6 Summary..317

10.1.7 Exercises..318

10.1.8 Further Reading..319

Chapter 11: Virtual Machines..321

11.1 EVM, WASM, and Execution Environments..321

11.1.1 Why Blockchain Needs a Virtual Machine..321

11.1.2 The Ethereum Virtual Machine..322

11.1.3 Gas Mechanics and EIP-1559..336

11.1.4 WebAssembly for Blockchain..339

11.1.5 Parallel Transaction Processing..340

11.1.6 Summary..344

11.1.7 Exercises..345

11.1.8 Further Reading..346

Chapter 12: Transaction Models and MEV..347

12.1 Transaction Lifecycle and Maximal Extractable Value..347

12.1.1 Transaction Lifecycle..348

12.1.2 Maximal Extractable Value (MEV)..356

12.1.3 The MEV Supply Chain: From Searcher to Proposer..364

12.1.4 MEV Mitigation Approaches..368

12.1.5 Quantitative MEV Measurement..369

12.1.6 Summary..371

12.1.7 Exercises..372

12.1.8 Further Reading..373

Chapter 13: Cryptoeconomic Security 375

13.1 Game Theory, Incentive Mechanisms, and Economic Attack Analysis 375

13.1.1 Game Theory in Blockchain Protocols 376

13.1.2 Tokenomics and Monetary Policy 382

13.1.3 Security Budget: The Price of Consensus 386

13.1.4 Optimal Deterrence and Penalty Design 389

13.1.5 Fee Market Dynamics and Security Budget Composition 391

13.1.6 Economic Attacks Beyond Double-Spending 392

13.1.7 Summary 393

13.1.8 Exercises 395

13.1.9 Further Reading 396

Chapter 14: Formal Verification and Security Analysis 397

14.1 Applying Formal Methods to Blockchain Protocol Verification 397

14.1.1 Why Formal Methods Matter for Blockchain 398

14.1.2 Formal Specification with Temporal Logic 398

14.1.3 Model Checking 402

14.1.4 Proof Assistants for Protocol Verification 408

14.1.5 Symbolic Execution for Protocol-Level Security 409

14.1.6 Security Audit Methodology 410

14.1.7 The Gap Between Verification and Security 415

14.1.8 Summary 416

14.1.9 Exercises 417

14.1.10 Further Reading 418

Part IV: Scalability and Advanced Topics 419

Chapter 15: Layer-2 Scaling 421

15.1 Rollups, State Channels, and Plasma 421

15.1.1 The Layer-2 Thesis 422

15.1.2 Optimistic Rollups 423

15.1.3 ZK Rollups 431

15.1.4 State Channels 435

15.1.5 Plasma: Child Chains with Exit Games 441
15.1.6 Validiums and the Data Availability Spectrum 449
15.1.7 Cross-L2 Composability and the Fragmentation Problem 450
15.1.8 Summary 453
15.1.9 Exercises 454
15.1.10 Further Reading 456

Chapter 16: Sharding and Parallel Execution 457

16.1 Data Availability Sharding, Cross-Shard Communication, and Danksharding 457
16.1.1 The Sharding Thesis 458
16.1.2 Execution Sharding vs. Data Availability Sharding 461
16.1.3 Erasure Coding and Data Availability Sampling 464
16.1.4 Cross-Shard Communication 471
16.1.5 Ethereum's Sharding Evolution 476
16.1.6 Practical Sharding Implementations 479
16.1.7 Summary 485
16.1.8 Exercises 486

Chapter 17: Data Availability and Modular Blockchains 489

17.1 The Data Availability Problem and Modular Architecture 489
17.1.1 The Data Availability Problem 490
17.1.2 Data Availability Sampling: The Solution 495
17.1.3 Celestia: Purpose-Built Data Availability 499
17.1.4 The Modular Blockchain Paradigm 504
17.1.5 Restaking and Shared Security 507
17.1.6 The Future of Modular Design 511
17.1.7 Summary 512
17.1.8 Exercises 513
17.1.9 Further Reading 514

Chapter 18: Post-Quantum Cryptography 515

18.1 Preparing Blockchain for the Quantum Computing Era 515
18.1.1 The Quantum Threat to Blockchain 516
18.1.2 Shor's Algorithm: Breaking Public Key Cryptography 518

18.1.3 Grover's Algorithm: Weakening Symmetric Cryptography 522
18.1.4 NIST Post-Quantum Cryptography Standards 529
18.1.5 Migration Strategies 534
18.1.6 Timeline and Urgency 542
18.1.7 Summary 546
18.1.8 Exercises 547
18.1.9 Further Reading 548

Chapter 19: Future Directions and Open Problems 551

19.1 Research Challenges and the Evolution of Blockchain Technology 551
19.1.1 The Scalability Trilemma: Fundamental Law or Engineering Challenge? 552
19.1.2 Privacy and Regulatory Compliance 553
19.1.3 Sustainable Consensus 554
19.1.4 Cross-Chain Interoperability 555
19.1.5 Verifiable Computation 557
19.1.6 Long-Term Open Problems 557
19.1.7 Synthesis: What This Book Has Covered 558
19.1.8 Summary 559
19.1.9 Exercises 560
19.1.10 Further Reading 561

Appendix A: Mathematical Foundations 563

Appendix B: Security Best Practices 587

Appendix C: Formal Security Definitions 597

Appendix D: Exercise Solutions (Selected) 605

Glossary 777

Bibliography 787

Index 793

About the Author

Nagnath Savant is an independent blockchain researcher, technology author, and engineer specializing in cryptocurrency systems, blockchain security, and post-quantum cryptography. He holds a Bachelor of Engineering in Electronics and Telecommunication Engineering and has a strong background in cryptographic protocols, distributed systems, and security-focused system design.

He has previously worked as a faculty member at KIT, Pandharpur, teaching electronics, digital technology, and blockchain technology at the undergraduate level. He continues to actively deliver guest lectures at various colleges, primarily on blockchain technology, decentralized systems, and their real-world applications.

About the Technical Reviewer

Dr. Rahul Konapure is an Assistant Professor in the Department of Electronics and Telecommunication Engineering at Walchand Institute of Technology (WIT), Solapur—one of Maharashtra's leading engineering institutions. He holds a doctoral degree in blockchain technology and specializes in IoT-based traceability systems, pharmaceutical supply chain security, and embedded network design. His research focuses on blockchain and IoT integration for real-time medicine traceability and verification to combat counterfeit medicines. His research and teaching experience in secure communication and system design further enriches his understanding of trust verification, data privacy, and the security of decentralized systems—insights that add significant depth to this work.

Acknowledgments

A book is never the work of one person, and this one is no exception.

The Apress Team

I am deeply grateful to my editor at Apress, **Shivangi Ramachandran**, for her guidance, precision, and patience throughout every stage of this manuscript. To **Deepa Tryphosa**, Project Coordinator, thank you for keeping the production process on track with quiet professionalism. My thanks also go to **Jessica Vakili** and the broader Apress team—copyeditors, layout designers, and production staff—whose craft is visible on every page.

The Technical Reviewer

The technical reviewer **Dr. Rahul Konapure** brought exceptional rigor and genuine engagement to this work, catching errors and sharpening explanations in ways that significantly improved the final manuscript. I am fortunate to have had such careful and expert scrutiny.

My Mentors

I owe a particular debt of gratitude to my mentors: **Dr. Ajit Kanase**, whose belief in this project and whose guidance shaped the way I approach every hard problem; **Dr. Milind Nikalje**, whose example showed me that rigor and curiosity go hand in hand; and **Dr. Aashish Joshi**, whose willingness to help—at any hour, with anything needed—I have never taken for granted.

Friends and Colleagues

Finally, to the friends and colleagues who offered feedback, answered questions, and kept me going through the difficult stretches: thank you. You know who you are.

—Nagnath Savant

Introduction

At some point someone hands you a blockchain system to reason about, and you realize that "it's like a distributed database with cryptography" doesn't get you very far. Not when you need to defend a security assumption in front of people who will push back. Not when you're evaluating whether a consensus protocol actually holds under the adversary model it claims to resist. Not when you're trying to explain why that bridge got drained for the fourth time this year.

That's where this book starts—not with what blockchain *is* in the marketing sense, but with how it actually works. The cryptographic primitives underneath. The consensus protocols built on top of them. The execution environments, the economic incentive structures, and the specific places where all of it comes apart if you get the engineering wrong.

Every chapter is written to give you something concrete: explain why ECDSA's security rests on a discrete logarithm assumption, calculate the cost of a majority-hash attack with real numbers, and reason through why a seven-day optimistic rollup challenge window is the specific tradeoff it is. The goal is technical literacy you can defend—not familiarity you can perform in conversation.

Who This Book Is For

If you write code, can follow mathematics at roughly the level of a first-year graduate course, and want to understand blockchain systems the way you understand other protocols you build on—this book is for you.

Background in distributed systems, cryptography, or networking helps but isn't required. Chapter 1 builds from first principles. What *is* required is willingness to work through formal arguments rather than skip straight to the intuition. The intuition in this field is wrong often enough that it's worth earning.

This book is not an introduction to cryptocurrency as an investment, a DeFi user guide, or an enterprise blockchain pitch. Those books exist. This is the one that puts you in front of the machinery and doesn't move on until you can reason about it yourself.

How This Book Is Structured

Part I: Cryptographic Foundations (Chapters 1–4)

Chapter 1 establishes the core problem—consensus across untrusted machines—through the Byzantine Generals Problem and a survey of pre-Bitcoin digital cash systems. By the end you'll know exactly which trust levers blockchain actually turns down and which ones stay stubbornly on.

Chapter 2 covers the cryptographic primitives everything else rests on: hash functions (SHA-256, Keccak), collision resistance and the birthday bound, Merkle trees, Ethereum's Merkle-Patricia trie, CSPRNGs, and MACs, including HMAC. The chapter is careful about what each primitive actually provides—and what it doesn't—because "just hash it" is a phrase that has cost people money.

Chapter 3 works through digital signatures—RSA, ECDSA, Schnorr with aggregation, EdDSA, and threshold multi-signature schemes—with a running focus on real-world implementation pitfalls. Understanding the math isn't sufficient; the chapter covers where it goes wrong in production.

Chapter 4 introduces zero-knowledge proofs: the distinction between interactive and non-interactive systems, zk-SNARKs, zk-STARKs, Bulletproofs, commitment schemes, ring signatures as used in Monero, and verifiable random functions. The bar is understanding well enough to evaluate a ZK-based system, not to implement one from scratch.

Part II: Consensus Mechanisms (Chapters 5–9)

Chapter 5 covers proof of work—hash puzzles, difficulty retargeting, selfish mining, the majority-hash attack with actual dollar numbers attached, mining pool payout schemes (PPS, PPLNS), and miner game-theoretic equilibria. The energy section works through why naive terawatt-hour comparisons miss the point and why ASIC resistance as a design goal has never held.

Chapter 6 covers proof of stake—the nothing-at-stake problem and the pile of patches that make PoS shippable (slashing, finality gadgets, inactivity leaks), Gasper (GHOST picks the tip, Casper FFG hammers epochs shut), long-range attacks, weak subjectivity, and staking economics, including MEV and recentralization dynamics. The chapter ends with what running a validator actually entails day to day.

Chapter 7 covers Byzantine Fault Tolerance—PBFT's three-phase protocol and its $O(n^2)$ communication problem, the FLP impossibility result, HotStuff's linear-complexity fix via threshold signatures, and Tendermint Core. The chapter is careful about synchrony assumptions: which protocols are safe under any network condition and which are only live when the network eventually cooperates.

Chapter 8 covers the protocols that fit neither the Nakamoto nor the BFT mold: Avalanche-style subsampled voting, DAG-structured ledgers, GHOST fork choice, the Ouroboros formally proven PoS line, and the Nakamoto-descendant family—Bitcoin-NG, PHANTOM/SPECTRE, Prism. The probabilistic versus deterministic finality distinction gets a full treatment because it becomes expensive the moment you build a bridge on top of it.

Chapter 9 provides a comparison framework for consensus protocols. Most published comparisons are somewhere between sloppy and actively misleading—different transaction types, different finality definitions, different adversary models, all presented as if the numbers mean the same thing. This chapter gives you the normalization methodology to cut through that noise and closes with practical guidance for the moment you actually have to pick one.

Part III: Blockchain Architecture and Execution (Chapters 10–14)

Chapter 10 compares Bitcoin's UTXO model and Ethereum's account model across privacy, parallelism, smart contract expressiveness, and formal semantics, with Merkle proof plumbing and state growth covered in full. State growth is a problem that doesn't get nearly the public attention it deserves; blockchains are accumulating state they can never easily discard, and this chapter covers where that leads, including the state rent and expiry proposals that have been argued about for years without resolution.

Chapter 11 covers virtual machines: EVM architecture and the complete opcode set, gas mechanics including EIP-1559 dynamic base fee and EIP-2929 cold/warm storage costs, WebAssembly as an alternative execution environment, parallel execution with conflict detection, and the security vulnerabilities that arise specifically from how execution environments work—reentrancy and stack depth attacks among them.

Chapter 12 follows a transaction from construction through the mempool to final inclusion, covering MEV extraction strategies (DEX arbitrage, sandwich attacks, liquidations, JIT liquidity), Flashbots, MEV-boost, Proposer-Builder Separation, and how MEV is actually measured. What hundreds of millions of dollars extracted annually means for validator centralization incentives is covered here.

Chapter 13 covers cryptoeconomic security—game theory applied to protocol design, when honest behavior is a Nash equilibrium and when it breaks down, tokenomics (issuance schedules, halvings, burn mechanics) as a security variable rather than a marketing story, the issuance-versus-fees split that shapes long-run security budgets, attack cost models with real numbers, and economic stress testing under token price collapse.

Chapter 14 covers formal verification: temporal logic specification (LTL, CTL), model checking, proof assistants (Coq, Isabelle, Lean), symbolic execution, and how to structure a security audit across consensus, cryptography, networking, and economics layers. Common vulnerability patterns are catalogued—reentrancy, integer overflow, oracle manipulation, and flash loan surfaces—and the chapter closes on the uncomfortable gap between "formally verified" and "actually secure," which are not the same thing.

Part IV: Scalability and Advanced Topics (Chapters 15–19)

Chapter 15 covers Layer-2 scaling—optimistic rollups with fraud proofs and seven-day challenge windows, ZK rollups with validity proofs and circuit constraints, state channels with HTLC routing and generalized state, Plasma's exit game and why it lost to rollups, and cross-L2 composability problems including liquidity fragmentation and shared sequencing proposals.

Chapter 16 covers sharding—the single-shard takeover problem and committee rotation as the standard defense, execution versus data availability sharding (and why the entire industry changed its mind about the former), erasure coding, Data Availability Sampling, cross-shard atomicity tradeoffs, and Ethereum's evolution through EIP-4844 to full Danksharding. Real implementations in Zilliqa, NEAR, and Polkadot are analyzed as concrete datapoints on different design bets.

Chapter 17 covers data availability and the modular blockchain thesis—DAS, Celestia's purpose-built DA layer, the modular separation of execution/consensus/DA/settlement, EigenLayer's restaking model and its correlation risks, and the honest tradeoff between monolithic designs (better latency and composability simplicity) and modular ones (better specialization and flexibility). The fat-protocol-to-thin-layers shift in how value accrues is explained here.

Chapter 18 covers post-quantum cryptography—Shor's algorithm and what it breaks (ECDSA, EdDSA, RSA, DH), Grover's and what it weakens (hashes and symmetric crypto lose roughly half their effective bit security), the harvest-now-decrypt-later threat, NIST's three post-quantum signature standards (ML-DSA/Dilithium, FN-DSA/Falcon, SLH-DSA/SPHINCS+), and migration challenges for chains that have been running for a decade. The timeline uncertainty is treated honestly—the engineering schedule for cryptographically relevant quantum hardware is unknown, but data recorded on public chains today can be held and decrypted later. Waiting is not a plan.

Chapter 19 closes with the open problems: the scalability trilemma examined as an engineering constraint rather than a physical law, ZK-based privacy-preserving compliance, sustainable consensus economics under PoS concentration, trust-minimized bridge designs after more than $2.5B in exploits, verifiable computation as the thread connecting scaling and privacy, and the governance and Sybil resistance problems nobody has cracked. The intersections with AI, IoT, and DeFi composability are covered as areas of active collision rather than distant speculation.

The book reads straight through; Parts I and II are the foundation, and each subsequent part builds on them. Readers already familiar with applied cryptography can begin at Chapter 5 or 7. Readers coming from distributed systems will find Chapters 7 and 9 the most direct entry points. Each chapter ends with graded exercises; Appendix D contains worked solutions for a selected set.

PART I

Cryptographic Foundations

CHAPTER 1

The Why of Blockchain

1.1 Distributed Systems, Trust, and the Byzantine Generals Problem

This chapter starts at the foundation—the problem blockchain is actually built to solve. Before any protocol detail makes sense, you need to understand why trust breaks down across a network of strangers, why decades of serious attempts at digital cash kept failing at the same point, and how Bitcoin's combination of proof-of-work and a longest-chain rule finally closed the gap. The Byzantine Generals Problem is not a historical footnote here; it is the precise shape of the consensus challenge that every distributed ledger must answer. By the end of this chapter, you will have covered:

- Why consensus across machines is harder than it sounds (and keeps sounding easy until it isn't)
- The Byzantine Generals story, except it isn't a museum piece—it's the shape of the problem
- Pre-Bitcoin digital cash: what people tried, where it cracked, what that tells you about Bitcoin
- Which trust levers blockchain tries to turn down (and which ones stay stuck)
- How "impossible in theory" turns into "works in production" without anyone cheating the math
- Why PoW ended up being the weird trick that made open networks workable

N. Savant, *Blockchain Foundations*, https://doi.org/10.1007/979-8-8688-2891-1_1

1.1.1 The Problem: Trust in Distributed Systems

Money has always been tangled up with trust. You accept a dollar bill because you trust other people will too. You put money in a bank because you trust the bank to give it back. You send an electronic payment trusting that the intermediaries will actually move the money where it's supposed to go.

In the physical world, these trust arrangements work well enough. Banks get audited. Governments regulate them. Courts enforce contracts. But strip away all those intermediaries and try to create digital money? Things get complicated fast.

At first glance, the problem seems almost trivial. Represent money as digital records. Alice has 10 coins and wants to send 5 to Bob. Update the records. Alice: 5. Bob: 5. Basic accounting, right?

It really, really isn't.

The Double-Spending Problem

Think about the simplest possible attack. Alice has one digital coin. She sends it to Bob. She also sends the exact same coin to Carol. If she times it right, both Bob and Carol might accept the payment before either one finds out about the other transaction.

You can't pull this off with physical cash. Hand someone a dollar bill and it's gone—you don't have it anymore. Physical objects don't clone themselves. But digital information? It copies perfectly. Infinitely. A digital coin is just a string of bits. Nothing stops Alice from duplicating those bits and spending them twice.

```
Time    Alice's Action                Bob's View            Carol's View
--------------------------------------------------------------------------
t0      Alice has 1 coin              -                     -
t1      Sends coin to Bob      --->   Receives coin         -
t2      Sends SAME coin to Carol      Has coin       <---   Receives coin
t3      Both think they own the coin!
```

Figure 1-1. *The Double-Spending Attack*

You might figure cryptographic signatures solve this. Alice signs the transaction to Bob, proving she authorized it. But she can just as easily sign a second transaction sending the same coin to Carol. Both signatures are perfectly valid. Signatures prove who authorized something. They don't prove it only happened once.

***Table 1-1.** What Digital Signatures Do and Don't Provide*

Property	Provided?	Explanation
Authentication	✓ Yes	Proves Alice authorized the transaction
Integrity	✓ Yes	A transaction can't be modified without detection
Non-repudiation	✓ Yes	Alice can't deny signing the transaction
Uniqueness	✗ No	Doesn't prevent Alice from signing multiple transactions
Ordering	✗ No	Doesn't establish which transaction came first

The actual problem comes down to ordering. Which transaction happened first? If Alice-to-Bob came first, that one's valid, and Alice-to-Carol gets rejected. Flip it and the reverse is true.

On a single computer, ordering is trivial—just timestamp everything. In a distributed system with no trusted clock? Figuring out what happened when becomes shockingly difficult.

Why Centralized Solutions Are Inadequate

The obvious answer is: just centralize it. One trusted server handles everything. Alice wants to pay Bob? She asks the server. The server checks the records, confirms Alice owns the coin, transfers ownership to Bob, and rejects any later attempt by Alice to spend it again.

And this works. It's basically how digital payments function today. Your bank keeps a centralized ledger. When you transfer money, the bank updates its records. Double-spending doesn't happen because the bank controls the one authoritative copy.

But centralization comes with its own baggage:

Table 1-2. *Problems with Centralized Payment Systems*

Problem	Impact	Real-World Example
Single point of failure	System stops if server fails	PayPal outages affect millions of merchants
Censorship	Authority can block transactions	WikiLeaks donation blocking (2010)
Privacy loss	All transactions are visible to operator	Financial surveillance programs
Systemic risk	Breaches affect many users	Equifax breach (147M people, 2017)
Counterparty risk	Operator bankruptcy = lost funds	Mt. Gox collapse (850K BTC, 2014)
Operational errors	Database corruption loses money	Knight Capital loss ($440M, 2012)

These aren't hypotheticals. Banks do fail. Payment processors do get hacked. Governments do freeze assets. 2008 showed everyone that even regulated, audited financial institutions can blow up spectacularly.

So here's the question: can you build digital money that works without trusted intermediaries? A system where nobody controls the ledger, but somehow everyone agrees on what transactions are valid and in what order?

That's the problem blockchain is trying to solve.

The Distributed Ledger Concept

What if, instead of one server keeping the ledger, everybody keeps a copy? Alice pays Bob; she broadcasts it to the whole network. Everyone updates their copy. No single point of failure—if some participants go offline, the rest keep things running.

Sounds good until you think about synchronization. Networks have latency. Messages arrive in different orders for different people. Some participants might be offline when a transaction gets broadcast.

And it gets worse. Some participants might be actively trying to cheat. A double-spender could broadcast conflicting transactions to different parts of the network, hoping to confuse things.

This is where distributed systems theory enters the picture. The problem of keeping a consistent shared state across unreliable networks with potentially malicious participants—researchers have been studying this formally for decades. And the results, frankly, aren't encouraging.

1.1.2 The Byzantine Generals Problem

In 1982, Leslie Lamport, Robert Shostak, and Marshall Pease published a paper that put a name to the whole challenge: "The Byzantine Generals Problem." The name comes from a thought experiment about Byzantine army generals, but the implications reach far beyond military coordination.

The Setup

Picture several divisions of the Byzantine army surrounding an enemy city. Each division has a general. They can only communicate through messengers. They need to agree on a plan: attack or retreat. A coordinated attack might win. A coordinated retreat saves lives. But if some attack while others retreat—disaster.

Here's the twist: some generals might be traitors. Traitors can send different messages to different generals. They can refuse to relay messages. They can even coordinate their lies.

Can the loyal generals still reach agreement? That's the question.

Let's keep it simple. Three generals. One is the commander who proposes a plan. The other two are lieutenants deciding whether to follow.

```
Scenario 1: Commander Loyal, One Lieutenant is Traitor
═══════════════════════════════════════════════════════
```

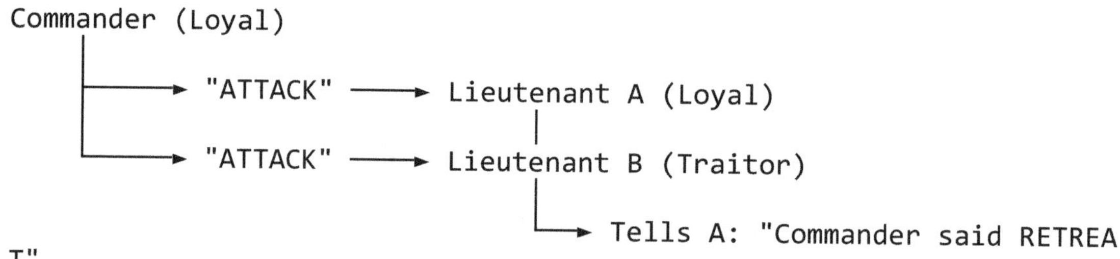


```
Lieutenant A's dilemma:
  • Direct order from Commander: ATTACK
  • Report from Lieutenant B: Commander said RETREAT
  • Cannot determine who is lying!

Scenario 2: Commander is Traitor
═════════════════════════════════
```

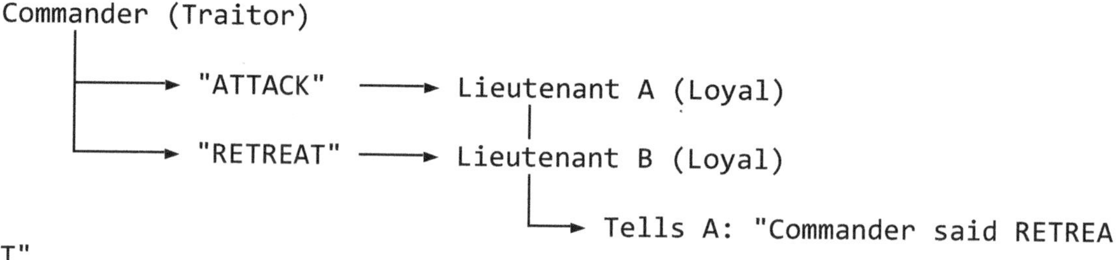


```
From Lieutenant A's perspective:
  • Direct order: ATTACK
  • Lieutenant B reports: RETREAT
  • Indistinguishable from Scenario 1!
```

Figure 1-2. *Byzantine Generals Problem with 3 Participants*

If the commander is loyal and orders "attack," and both lieutenants are loyal too, everyone attacks. Done.

But say one lieutenant is a traitor. The commander sends "attack" to both. The loyal lieutenant gets "attack" and prepares to move. The traitor tells the loyal lieutenant: "The commander said retreat." Now the loyal lieutenant doesn't know who to believe.

Gets even nastier if the commander is the traitor. He tells one lieutenant "attack" and the other "retreat." Each loyal lieutenant has a different order and no way to tell the other got something different.

Formal Statement

If you want it in textbook language, the problem asks for three properties at once:

Agreement: loyal generals don't split and pick different actions.

Validity: when the commander isn't lying, honest players actually follow the order.

Termination: the thing halts. Nobody waits forever in limbo.

Those three lines are doing real work—they line up with what we usually mean by consensus:

- Agreement is the "same state" requirement (consistency, in the usual jargon).
- Validity is the "don't invent fake inputs" requirement (correctness relative to honest senders).
- Termination is the "don't stall" requirement (liveness—something useful happens).

Impossibility Results

Here's where things get discouraging. Under certain conditions, the Byzantine Generals Problem flat out has no solution.

Table 1-3. *Byzantine Fault Tolerance Requirements*

Total Nodes (n)	Max Faulty Nodes (f)	Consensus Possible?	Example
3	1	✗ No	Proven impossible
4	1	✓ Yes	Minimum for f=1
5	1	✓ Yes	Extra redundancy
6	2	✗ No	Violates n > 3f
7	2	✓ Yes	Minimum for f=2
10	3	✓ Yes	Minimum for f=3
31	10	✓ Yes	Minimum for f=10

The general rule: n must be strictly greater than 3f (that's n > 3f).

Result 1: Three participants, one of them faulty? Consensus is impossible.

The proof is actually pretty elegant. Three generals: A, B, C. You want to tolerate one traitor. Consider two scenarios:

> *Scenario 1: A is the loyal commander, B is loyal, C is the traitor. A sends "attack" to both. C tells B that A actually ordered "retreat." B sees one "attack" and one "retreat"—can't tell who's lying.*

> *Scenario 2: A is the traitor commander. A sends "attack" to B and "retreat" to C. C honestly tells B what he received. From B's perspective—identical to scenario 1.*

B can't distinguish these scenarios. Is A honest (and C is lying) or is A the traitor (and C is telling the truth)? No algorithm can help B decide, because the information looks exactly the same.

Result 2: More generally, with n participants and up to f faulty ones, you need n > 3f for consensus.

Want to handle 1 traitor? You need at least 4 participants. 10 traitors? At least 31 participants. The bound is tight—it's both necessary and sufficient, and there are algorithms that actually achieve it.

The implications are serious. If a third or more of participants are malicious, deterministic consensus is provably impossible. This isn't an engineering limitation. It's a mathematical one.

Why This Matters for Blockchain

A blockchain is a shared ledger updated by strangers who don't owe each other loyalty. That's literally the Byzantine setup, just with worse branding.

- Think of miners/validators as the generals (yes, awkward analogy, but it sticks).
- Someone proposes a block—that's the "order" floating around the network.
- Is everyone arguing about which block comes next? That's consensus.
- Double-spenders, censors, and griefers—they're the traitors in the story. Same math, different costumes.

1.1.3 Early Digital Cash Attempts

Bitcoin wasn't the first swing at electronic cash. The table below is a quick tour of who tried what—but right after it, I want to spell out how live systems usually dodge the worst-case impossibility theorems. That "dodge" is load-bearing for everything later.

Table 1-4. *Timeline of Digital Cash Evolution*

Year	System	Creator	Key Innovation	Fatal Flaw
1989	DigiCash	David Chaum	Blind signatures for privacy	Required trusted banks
1998	b-money	Wei Dai	Public key accounts	No consensus mechanism
1998-2005	Bit Gold	Nick Szabo	Proof-of-work for scarcity	No distributed consensus
2008	Bitcoin	Satoshi Nakamoto	PoW + longest chain rule	Solved BFT consensus

Partial synchrony is the big one. Fully asynchronous models let messages stall forever, which is where a lot of impossibility proofs live. Most chains quietly assume the network isn't that hostile—messages show up eventually, within some bound. That's closer to how the internet actually behaves, and it buys you protocols that can ship.

Probabilistic finality is another escape hatch. You stop demanding ironclad certainty on block one. Maybe a payment can theoretically be unwound early on, but the odds drop fast as blocks pile up. After enough depth, reversing stops being a realistic threat.

Economics is the third lever. You don't only engineer around attackers—you price them out. If the attack costs more than the loot, rational actors go hunt easier prey. The question flips from pure safety to incentive compatibility.

None of that "disproves" the classical results. You're just not in the same toy model anymore: probabilistic guarantees, timing assumptions that aren't worst-case forever, and payoffs attached to behavior.

1.1.4 Digital Cash Evolution

Back to history. Before Bitcoin, people weren't clueless—they were stuck on the same missing piece: open participation plus agreement without a referee.

David Chaum's DigiCash (1989)

David Chaum cared a lot about privacy—enough to build a company around it. DigiCash (1989) was the first serious stab at electronic cash that felt cryptographically serious.

Blind signatures were the engine. You mint a random serial, blind it, and send the blinded blob to the bank. The bank signs without seeing the underlying serial, debits you, and you unblind afterward so you hold a coin the bank authenticated.

Privacy actually worked: spending didn't have to deanonymize the withdrawal. A merchant could check the bank's signature without learning which customer originally pulled the coin.

The catch was operational: you still had a bank-shaped object in the middle. Somebody had to sign issuance and track spent coins so the same token couldn't pay twice. Merchants basically called home.

Which meant DigiCash imported all the usual centralized failure modes—downtime, pressure, gatekeeping—plus the cold reality that banks didn't rush to adopt. The company folded in 1998.

Takeaway in one sentence: fancy math can hide balances from counters, but it doesn't remove the need for a party everyone agrees to trust.

Nick Szabo's Bit Gold (1998)

Nick Szabo sketched Bit Gold starting in 1998 and kept poking at it for years. Nobody shipped it, yet a lot of it rhymes with Bitcoin.

PoW was the scarcity engine: puzzles were expensive to solve and cheap to check. Solve one, stamp it, register it—you've minted something that didn't exist a moment ago.

Transfers were supposed to be signed updates to a shared registry. Servers (or something like servers) would make sure each chunk of Bit Gold moved at most once.

Szabo also saw the early-easy/late-hard dynamic as mining showed up—his fix was to price pieces by the work embedded in them.

What stayed fuzzy: who decides the canonical registry if servers disagree? How do you order conflicting spends? How do you stop one actor from puppeting a pile of fake "servers"?

So Bit Gold had the scarcity gadget and still lacked the agreement machinery.

Moral: PoW can manufacture hardness; it doesn't, by itself, manufacture consensus.

Wei Dai's b-money (1998)

Wei Dai's b-money (also 1998) stayed a proposal, not a running network—still worth reading because it tries to imagine money without a crown behind it.

Accounts were public keys; payments were broadcasts plus signatures. That part aged well.

One flavor assumed every participant keeps the full ledger and "just follows" the rules when a tx lands. Cute—until someone doesn't.

Another flavor added server-ish operators with collateral (hash-locked deposits) to punish cheating. The idea points at incentives; the details are hand-wavy.

Neither draft closed the loop on malice. Collateral sounds nice until you ask: how much, held where, and adjudicated how?

Underneath both: no real story for Byzantine agreement on a single world state.

So: public-key money is necessary, not sufficient.

What These Attempts Reveal

If you squint, each precursor contributed something load-bearing:

- DigiCash: privacy tech that actually worked on paper (and in pilots).
- Bit Gold: scarcity from work, not from a mint's pinky promise.
- b-money: the shape of peer-to-peer settlement—keys, broadcasts, replication.

What none of them solved: Byzantine fault-tolerant consensus in an open network where anyone can join and nobody gets special trust.

That's what made Bitcoin genuinely new. Satoshi Nakamoto combined proof-of-work with economic incentives and a longest-chain rule to create the first working solution to distributed consensus in a permissionless network.

1.1.5 Trust Assumptions in Distributed Systems

Every distributed system makes trust assumptions. Getting clear on what those assumptions are is probably the most important thing you can do when evaluating a blockchain.

The Trust Spectrum

On one end of the spectrum: fully trusted systems. Using PayPal means trusting PayPal completely—to keep accurate records, process transactions correctly, not steal your money, and protect your data. If PayPal goes rogue, you're out of luck.

On the other end: truly trustless systems. In a perfectly trustless system, you verify everything yourself. Nobody can cheat you, steal from you, or block your transactions. That's the dream, anyway.

Bitcoin gets called "trustless" a lot. It's not quite accurate. Bitcoin minimizes trust—dramatically—but doesn't zero it out. Understanding what trust remains is how you figure out whether blockchain actually solves the problems people claim it does.

Bitcoin's Trust Model

What you get to stop outsourcing:

You don't have to pick a single company to be the ledger-keeper. Even in a ridiculous extreme where almost every miner vanishes, one honest miner still keeps the lights on (slowly).

You also don't need a blessed clock in the sky. Ordering comes from the chain itself, not from someone stamping "official time" on your tx.

And you don't have to trust strangers' validation if you don't want to: sync the chain, recompute the checks, and stare at the PoW yourself. Painful, yes—optional, also yes.

What you don't get to hand-wave away:

Cryptography isn't magic—it's assumptions with citations. If SHA-256 or ECDSA breaks in the wild, Bitcoin isn't having a bad day; it's done.

Majority hashpower has to stay non-hostile-ish. Cross 50% adversarial power and double-spends stop being theoretical.

Aspect	Traditional Bank	Bitcoin	Analysis
Single Entity Risk	High—must trust bank	Low—distributed across miners	Bitcoin advantage
Censorship Resistance	Low—bank can freeze accounts	High—no central authority	Bitcoin advantage
Privacy	Low—bank sees all transactions	Medium—pseudonymous but traceable	Mixed
Regulatory Compliance	High—legal framework exists	Low—regulatory uncertainty	Bank advantage
Recourse for Errors	Yes—chargebacks, insurance, legal system	No—transactions irreversible	Bank advantage
Technical Complexity	Low—user-friendly	High—manage keys, understand protocol	Bank advantage
Cryptographic Assumptions	Minimal—only for communications	Critical—entire security depends on it	Bank advantage
Network Dependency	Moderate—bank's network	High—need blockchain connectivity	Bank advantage
Majority Attack Risk	N/A	Real—51% attacks possible	Bank advantage
Counterparty Risk	Yes—bank can fail	Minimal—protocol-level security	Bitcoin advantage

So Bitcoin doesn't delete trust; it reroutes it—away from brand names, toward math and miner economics.

In practice that means you're still betting on: hash functions, signatures, honest-ish hashpower, your client not being buggy, your network being reachable, and you not losing your keys to a sticky note disaster.

"Less trust" than what? Compared to retail banking, maybe. Compared to naive "no humans involved" marketing, definitely not.

The trade is familiar: one bank can be leaned on; buying half the hashpower is a different scale of attack, not a non-attack.

Quantifying Security

One thing modern crypto research does well: it tries to put numbers on security instead of treating it as a yes-or-no question.

For proof-of-work systems like Bitcoin, security is basically a cost-benefit calculation. Want to double-spend? You need >50% of mining power. That means either:

1. Buying enough hardware to outpace every other miner (capital cost)
2. Renting hash power from people already mining (operational cost)
3. Somehow compromising enough existing miners (coordination cost)

As long as attacking costs more than what you'd gain, nobody rational will bother. That's why Bitcoin's security scales with its value—more value means more miners means higher attack cost.

Mathematically: let V be what an attacker could steal and C be the cost of pulling off a 51% attack. Bitcoin is economically secure when

$$C > V$$

As of early 2026, C runs into the billions (hardware, electricity, plus the fact that a successful attack would crater Bitcoin's price, making the stolen coins worthless). For most threat models, attacking just doesn't make financial sense.

But there's a big asterisk: this assumes rational attackers. A nation-state might attack for geopolitical reasons, net loss be damned. Someone ideologically motivated might not care about profit. The economic model only holds if everyone's a rational profit-maximizer.

1.1.6 Why the Byzantine Generals Problem Matters

You might be wondering why we spent so many pages on a thought experiment about ancient generals. We're building cryptocurrency, not planning sieges.

The reason: the Byzantine Generals Problem precisely captures the challenge of distributed consensus. Every blockchain faces some version of this problem. Understanding it is how you evaluate whether any proposed solution actually works.

The CAP Theorem and Blockchain

CAP is a different lens on the same bruises (Brewer, 2000; Gilbert & Lynch nailed it down in 2002). Pick two, maybe, of three:

C: everybody agrees on what the latest state is (strong consistency vibe).

A: requests don't hang forever—you get a response (success or failure counts; indefinite limbo doesn't).

P: the world splits in half, and the system doesn't pretend that can't happen.

Partitions happen. So you're usually negotiating a tension between "everyone matches" and "always responds."

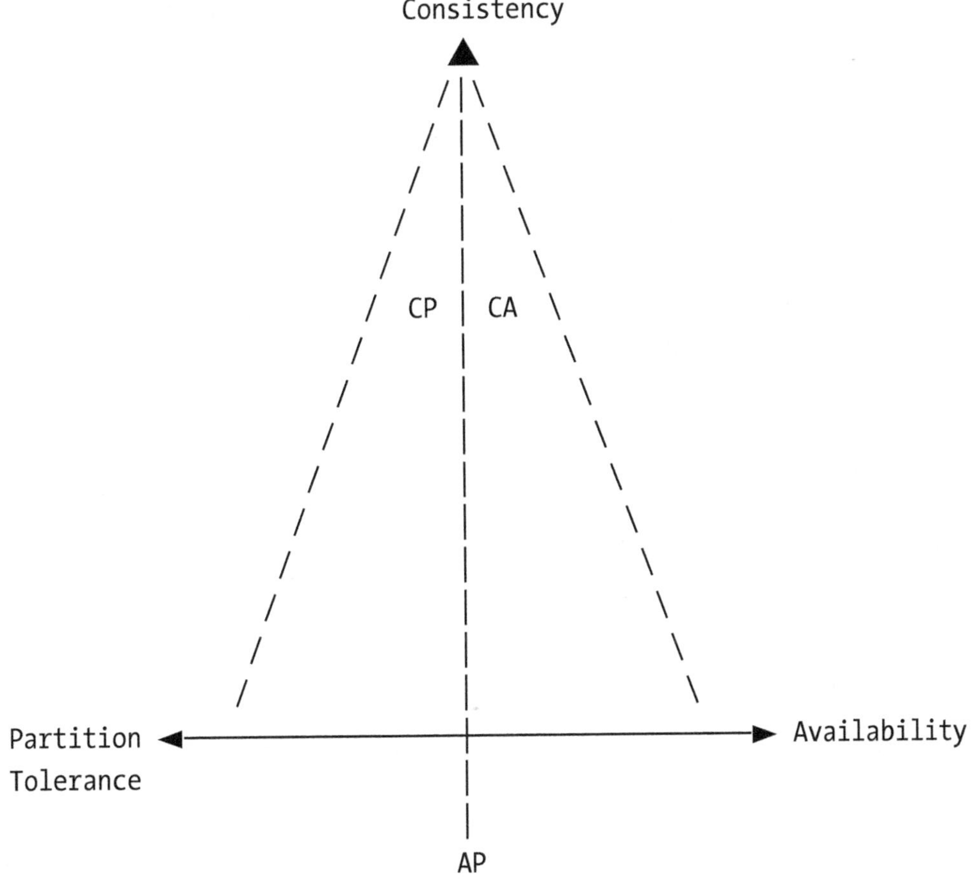

```
CP (Bitcoin): Consistency + Partition Tolerance
CA (Traditional DB): Consistency + Availability (assumes no partitions)
AP (Some eventual consistency systems): Availability + Partition Tolerance
```

Table 1-5. *Blockchain Design Choices in CAP Theorem*

System	Choice	Behavior During Partition	Trade-Off
Bitcoin	CP	Nodes on the minority fork eventually orphaned	Consistency over availability
Ethereum	CP	Similar to Bitcoin with fork choice rules	Consistency over availability
Some permissioned chains	CA	Halt if a partition is detected	Availability only when no partition
Eventual consistency systems	AP	Nodes diverge, reconcile later	Availability over consistency

Bitcoin picks consistency over availability. When the network splits, the longest-chain rule ensures all nodes eventually converge on the same history. But during a partition, some nodes might be building on a fork that'll get abandoned—temporarily reducing availability.

Other blockchains make different bets. Some lean toward availability, accepting that nodes might temporarily disagree about state. Different trade-offs, same underlying impossibility.

Practical Implications

When someone pitches you a chain, I keep coming back to a short checklist:

1. **Adversaries:** How many Byzantine nodes, under what network model? Remember n > 3f for classical BFT—but read the fine print on extra assumptions.

2. **Clocks and Delays:** Do the proof assume messages show up on time? What happens when the internet has a bad day?

3. **Finality Flavor:** Ironclad finality vs. "probably final after k blocks" vs. something weirder.
4. **Progress Guarantees:** Can a motivated attacker freeze the chain or only grief a little?

None of that is trivia—it's where protocols quietly differ.

Code Example: Simulating Byzantine Behavior

Let's write a quick simulation showing the Byzantine Generals' Problem in action. Not a real consensus protocol—just enough to see how malicious behavior messes up agreement.

```
import random
from enum import Enum
from typing import List, Dict

class Action(Enum):
    ATTACK = 1
    RETREAT = 2

class GeneralType(Enum):
    LOYAL = 1
    TRAITOR = 2

class General:
    def __init__(self, id: int, general_type: GeneralType):
        self.id = id
        self.type = general_type
        self.received_orders: Dict[int, Action] = {}

    def send_order(self, order: Action, recipient: 'General', sender_
    id: int):
        """
        Send an order to another general.
        Traitors may send conflicting orders.
        """
```

```
        if self.type == GeneralType.TRAITOR:
            # Traitor sends random orders
            order = random.choice([Action.ATTACK, Action.RETREAT])

        recipient.receive_order(sender_id, order)

    def receive_order(self, sender_id: int, order: Action):
        """Receive an order from another general"""
        self.received_orders[sender_id] = order

    def decide(self) -> Action:
        """
        Decide on action based on majority of received orders.
        If tied, default to RETREAT (safer option).
        """
        if not self.received_orders:
            return Action.RETREAT

        attack_votes = sum(1 for action in self.received_orders.values()
                          if action == Action.ATTACK)
        retreat_votes = len(self.received_orders) - attack_votes

        return Action.ATTACK if attack_votes > retreat_votes else
        Action.RETREAT

def simulate_scenario(num_generals: int, num_traitors: int, commander_
order: Action) -> Dict:
    """
    Simulate the Byzantine Generals Problem.

    Args:
        num_generals: Total number of generals
        num_traitors: Number of traitor generals
        commander_order: The order issued by commander

    Returns:
        Dictionary with simulation results
    """
```

```
# Create generals
generals = []
for i in range(num_generals):
    gtype = GeneralType.TRAITOR if i < num_traitors else
    GeneralType.LOYAL
    generals.append(General(i, gtype))

# Commander (general 0) sends orders to all lieutenants
commander = generals[0]
for i in range(1, num_generals):
    commander.send_order(commander_order, generals[i], i)

# Each lieutenant relays what they heard to other lieutenants
for i in range(1, num_generals):
    for j in range(1, num_generals):
        if i != j:
            # Lieutenant i tells j what commander said
            order = generals[i].received_orders.get(commander.id,
            Action.RETREAT)
            generals[i].send_order(order, generals[j], commander.id)

# Each general decides
decisions = {}
for i, general in enumerate(generals[1:], 1):  # Skip commander
    decisions[i] = general.decide()

# Check if loyal generals agree
loyal_decisions = [decisions[i] for i in range(1, num_generals)
                  if generals[i].type == GeneralType.LOYAL]
consensus = len(set(loyal_decisions)) == 1

return {
    'consensus_reached': consensus,
    'decisions': decisions,
    'loyal_agree_on': loyal_decisions[0] if consensus else None
}
```

```
# Run scenarios
print("Scenario 1: 3 generals, 1 traitor, commander loyal")
result = simulate_scenario(3, 1, Action.ATTACK)
print(f"Consensus: {result['consensus_reached']}")
print(f"Decisions: {result['decisions']}\n")

print("Scenario 2: 4 generals, 1 traitor, commander loyal")
result = simulate_scenario(4, 1, Action.ATTACK)
print(f"Consensus: {result['consensus_reached']}")
print(f"Decisions: {result['decisions']}\n")

print("Scenario 3: 4 generals, 2 traitors, commander loyal")
result = simulate_scenario(4, 2, Action.ATTACK)
print(f"Consensus: {result['consensus_reached']}")
print(f"Decisions: {result['decisions']}")
```

Running it a bunch of times tends to look like this:

1. n=3, f=1: chaos—agreement keeps falling apart.
2. n=4, f=1: usually stabilizes (not a proof, a vibe from the toy sim).
3. n=4, f=2: back to pain—you're below the $n > 3f$ line.

The code is simplified. Actual Byzantine fault-tolerant algorithms are way more involved. But it drives home the core challenge: telling honest messages from dishonest ones when you can't trust the people sending them.

1.1.7 Summary

Pulling the thread: agreement under malice is the whole game. DigiCash-style privacy, Bit Gold-style scarcity, and b-money-style broadcasting—useful, but none of them closed the permissionless consensus loop.

If you want bullets, fine—but they're the same ideas in louder fonts:

- Double-spending is the original sin of digital cash: bits copy cleanly, bills don't.
- Byzantine agreement is the clean formalization; $n > 3f$ is the line in the sand for a big class of settings.

- The pre-Bitcoin experiments mixed great ingredients and still missed the oven: a mechanism everyone could run without appointing a referee.
- “Trustless” is marketing. Enumerate assumptions instead.
- Live chains mostly don’t break impossibility proofs—they walk around them with probability, timing, and money.

Which means your job is skepticism with vocabulary: when a deck claims a miracle, find the changed model.

If you only read one paragraph: strangers updating a shared ledger is Byzantine agreement wearing a hoodie. Signatures authenticate intent; they don’t, by themselves, pick up a global order—you need a coordination story. CAP still bites because networks partition; most chains lean consistency + partition tolerance and pay for it in availability edge cases. DigiCash/Bit Gold/b-money each had a piece (privacy, scarcity, peer-to-peer shape) and still tripped over open-network consensus. Bitcoin’s punchline was PoW plus incentives plus a fork rule people could run. Classical BFT arithmetic: you need $n \geq 3f+1$ (think ~2/3 honest) when you’re in that world—don’t quote meme percentages without checking the model.

Next up: hashes, Merkle trees, signatures—the stuff you can actually implement and test.

1.1.8 Exercises

Problem 1 (Basic): Explain the double-spend issue without hand-waving—why signatures aren’t enough, what has to coordinate beyond them.

Problem 2 (Calculation): Ten-node BFT. Max Byzantine faults? Show $n > 3f$ arithmetic explicitly.

Problem 3 (Design): Four nodes, one Byzantine. Sketch messages round-by-round; say where you rely on $n > 3f$.

Problem 4 (Analysis): CAP: contrast Bitcoin vs. Ethereum vs. a retail bank—who sacrifices what when the network splits?

Problem 5 (Historical): DigiCash shipped tech and died anyway—what lesson is hiding in that story besides “marketing matters”?

Problem 6 (Theory): Prove (or carefully sketch) FLP: no deterministic asynchronous agreement with even one crash fault. Then spell the blockchain-relevant implication—what assumption changes in practice?

Problem 7 (Implementation): Tiny four-node Byzantine sim: one adversary spews contradictions. Does your protocol recover? When?

Problem 8 (Critical Thinking): Defend PoW as wasteful; defend it as not-wasteful. No strawmen.

Problem 9 (Advanced): Invent (on paper) a faster-finality cousin of Nakamoto consensus—then list what you broke.

Problem 10 (Research): Autopsy a 2011-2014 altcoin corpse: cause of death. Could it rise zombie-style today?

(Solutions in Appendix D)

1.1.9 Further Reading

If you want to go deeper on any of this:

Lamport/Shostak/Pease (1982) is still the right starting line—TOPLAS, if you're hunting the canonical citation.

FLP (1985) is the depressing one: one crashly process, full asynchrony, deterministic agreement—nope. CAP in Gilbert/Lynch form (2002) is the "pick your pain" companion read.

Chaum for blind signatures and the 1980s privacy mindset; Szabo for Bit Gold-adjacent essays; Dai's b-money page for dense ideas per kilobyte.

Bitcoin's nine-page PDF is unfairly readable once you know what words like "nonce" are doing. After that, pick up any security analysis paper with an explicit adversary and squint at the model.

I'd ignore decks that "solve Byzantium" in three slides—usually assumptions smuggled in via font size. Same for takes that pretend trust evaporates; it doesn't. It relocates.

CHAPTER 2

Cryptographic Primitives

2.1 Hashes, MACs, CSPRNGs, Merkle Trees, and Patricia Tries

Cryptographic primitives are the load-bearing layer underneath every blockchain. Hashes, Merkle trees, Patricia tries, CSPRNGs, and MACs are not decoration—they are what make integrity, efficiency, and verifiability possible at scale. This chapter walks through each one: what it does, where it sits in the stack, and where the assumptions behind it can snap. By the end, you will be able to explain:

- What hashes are actually doing when we talk about integrity (and what they don't do)
- Why Bitcoin latched onto SHA-256 and Ethereum onto Keccak, and why that split isn't cosmetic
- Why collisions matter and why birthdays ruin your intuition about how hard they are to find
- **Merkle Trees**: The trick that lets you vouch for a huge pile of data with a handful of hashes
- Patricia tries in plain English, and where they save you pain in real systems
- How Ethereum glues a Merkle structure onto a prefix trie so the whole state gets one root hash
- Where CSPRNGs fit (hint: anywhere a guessable bit burns you)
- MACs, especially HMAC, and why "just hash it" isn't authentication

N. Savant, *Blockchain Foundations*, https://doi.org/10.1007/979-8-8688-2891-1_2

2.1.1 Introduction: The Building Blocks of Blockchain

Peel off the apps and the consensus drama, and you're left with a small toolkit: hashes, trees, keyed MACs, and decent randomness. Nobody puts that on a billboard. It's still what keeps the thing from collapsing into trust-me theater.

So what does a distributed ledger need from crypto, really?

Integrity first. If someone sneaks a bit-flip into old history, you want that to show up loud—not as a polite footnote.

Efficiency second. Validators aren't replaying genesis on every new block. They need shortcuts that are still honest.

Uniqueness. Addresses, txids—you can't have accidental twins showing up at a party scale.

Compactness. You want to make strong statements about enormous datasets without shipping the whole dataset every time.

Hashes and Merkle-ish structures are what make those properties negotiable. If you only ever call library functions and never read the threat model, you'll ship something that passes tests and fails reality. Knowing where the math actually snaps matters.

We'll walk from hash basics up through trees. Endgame: watching Ethereum compress "the world state" down to 32 bytes in the header. Still feels a little like a party trick even when you know how it works.

2.1.2 Cryptographic Hash Functions

A hash eats an arbitrary-length input and spits out a fixed-size fingerprint. SHA-256 doesn't care if you hand it one byte or a fat blob. Out comes 256 bits. Always. Thirty-two bytes, clockwork.

```
import hashlib

# Hash a short string
short = hashlib.sha256(b"Hello").digest()
print(f"Hash of 'Hello': {short.hex()}")

# Hash a longer string - still 32 bytes
long_text = b"Hello " * 10000
long = hashlib.sha256(long_text).digest()
print(f"Hash length: {len(long)} bytes")
```

Sounds boring until you count. Infinitely many inputs, only 2^256 outputs—the pigeonhole principle says collisions exist. The whole game is that nobody can find them on demand.

Good cryptographic hashes make collisions exist on paper and stay practically unreachable in practice. That's the load-bearing assumption for half the stack.

Security Properties

Cryptographic hashes aren't "regular" hashes. Roughly three security properties separate the two camps:

Table 2-1. *Hash Function Security Properties*

Property	Definition	Attack Difficulty	Blockchain Use
Preimage Resistance	Given hash h, infeasible to find input x where H(x) = h	2^256 operations for SHA-256	Address generation, proof-of-work
Second Preimage Resistance	Given x_1, infeasible to find $x_2 \neq x_1$ where $H(x_1) = H(x_2)$	2^256 operations for SHA-256	Transaction integrity
Collision Resistance	Infeasible to find any $x_1 \neq x_2$ where $H(x_1) = H(x_2)$	2^128 operations for SHA-256 (birthday bound)	Block linking, Merkle trees

In practice, the three properties feel like this:

Preimage resistance (one-wayness). Someone shows you h; finding any m with H(m)=h should be intractable. Like having a phone number with no directory.

On-chain: Bitcoin addresses lean on hashing the public key. Seeing the address doesn't let you rewind to the key material. That's the privacy model in a nutshell.

Second preimage resistance. You're given m and h=H(m); finding a different m' with H(m')=h should be hard. Otherwise, you could swap payloads after the fact.

Example: Alice signs transaction T1. An attacker wants a different T2 with the same hash to smuggle past verification. Second-preimage hardness is what makes that fantasy stay expensive.

Collision resistance (the strong flavor). Find any pair m, m' with H(m)=H(m'). You don't fix h in advance—you hunt for a matching pair.

Chains care because blocks point at parents by hash. You want that pointer to name one predecessor, not two plausible histories. Weak collisions break that story.

The Birthday Attack and Collision Resistance

Collisions and second preimages sound similar; they're not the same game. Second preimage: you're tied to a specific h from a given input. Collision: you pick both sides of the pair. Extra freedom, better birthday math.

Birthday paradox: 23 people in a room, >50% chance some pair shares a birthday. Sounds wrong—you think you need ~183 people. But you're counting pairs, not matching one fixed date. Pairs grow like n^2; intuition lags.

Same shape for hashes. Rough preimage search against 256-bit output: think ~2^256 work (ignoring constants). Generic collision search: birthday scaling knocks you down toward ~2^128. Still huge—but notice the square-root gap.

```
Hash Output Size    Preimage Difficulty    Collision Difficulty
________________________________________________________________
128 bits            2^128 operations       2^64 operations
256 bits            2^256 operations       2^128 operations  ← Bitco
in/Ethereum
512 bits            2^512 operations       2^256 operations

Security Comparison:
2^64  ~ 18 quintillion         (attackable with modern hardware)
2^80  ~ 1.2 septillion         (marginal security)
2^128 ~ 3.4×10^38              (secure for foreseeable future)
2^256 ~ 1.15×10^77             (more than atoms in universe)
```

Figure 2-1. *Birthday Attack Complexity*

That's why 256-bit outputs stuck around: even after halving the exponent for collisions, you're still in "no hardware on Earth" territory.

2.1.3 Hash Functions in Blockchain: SHA-256 and Keccak

Different chains picked different hashes on purpose—not fashion, but different engineering bets and risk posture.

Table 2-2. Major Cryptographic Hash Functions in Blockchain

Hash Function	Output Size	Block Size	Rounds	Used By	Design Basis	Year
SHA-256	256 bits	512 bits	64	Bitcoin, many others	Merkle-Damgård	2001
SHA-3 (Keccak)	Variable (typically 256)	Variable	24	Ethereum	Sponge construction	2015
BLAKE2	Up to 512 bits	Variable	10 or 12	Some altcoins	HAIFA	2012
RIPEMD-160	160 bits	512 bits	80	Bitcoin addresses	Merkle-Damgård	1996

SHA-256: The Bitcoin Standard

SHA-256: SHA-2 family, NIST standardized in 2001. Bitcoin leaned on it everywhere:

- **PoW**: double-SHA-256 on the 80-byte header (the thing miners grind)
- **Txids**: HASH256(serialized tx)—yes, hashed twice again
- **P2PKH Addresses**: RIPEMD160(SHA256(pubkey))—different hash, still in the family photo

Why SHA256(SHA256(x))? SHA-256 is Merkle-Damgård under the hood; length-extension bites naive MACs. The outer hash isn't superstition—it's plugging a known footgun.

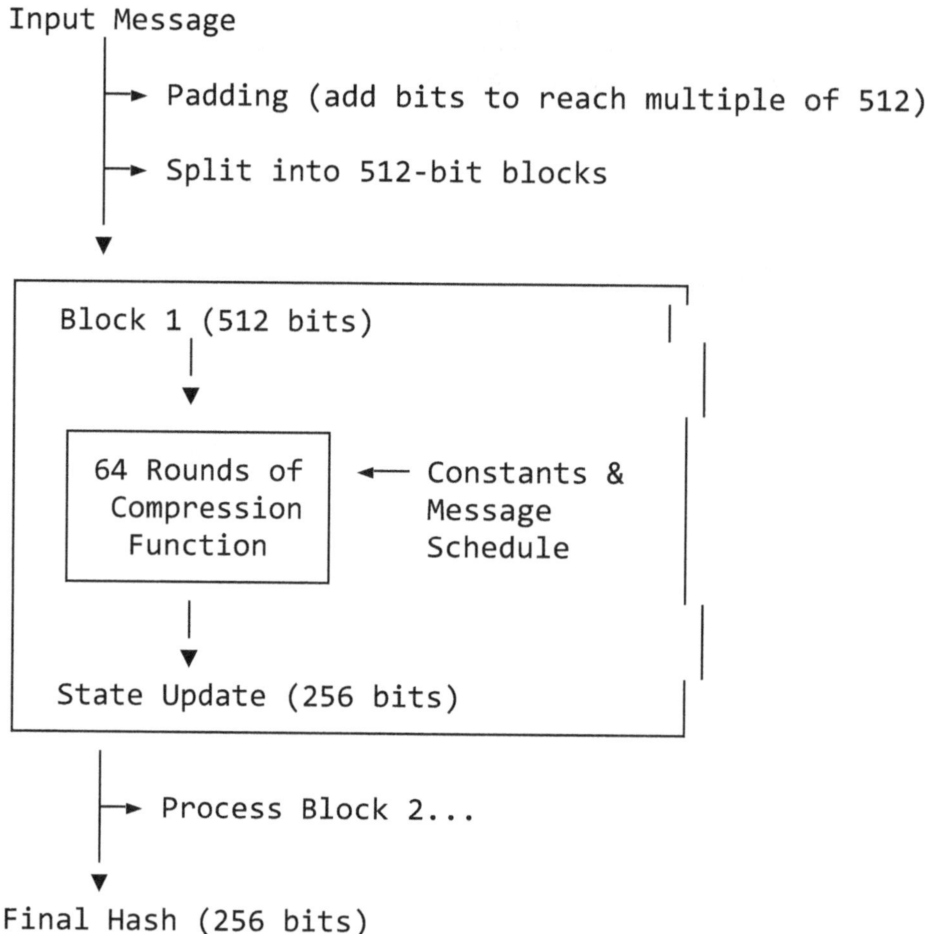

Figure 2-2. *SHA-256 Internal Structure (Simplified)*

Inside the compression function (hand-wavy but true): eight 32-bit registers, a mess of bitwise ops and rotations, round constants from cube roots of primes, a message schedule expanding each 512-bit chunk. The details matter if you implement; if you import hashlib, you mostly care about the interface.

Keccak (SHA-3): The Ethereum Choice

Ethereum went to Keccak-256 (SHA-3 competition winner, 2012). For Keccak-256, the capacity c = 512, so c/2 = 256—giving exactly the 256-bit security level. Annoying detail: on-chain “Keccak” padding isn’t byte-identical to the final NIST SHA-3 tweak—related, not interchangeable. Don’t blindly swap libraries.

Why bother switching families?

1. **Diversity**: Sponge internals aren't Merkle-Damgård. If SHA-2 ever ate a class break, Keccak probably wouldn't copy-paste the same failure mode.
2. **Speed**: On short contract-sized inputs, Keccak often wins in software benchmarks—matters when you meter gas.
3. **Hardware**: Keccak's parallelism plays nice with ASIC/FPGA pipelines if you're building serious gear.

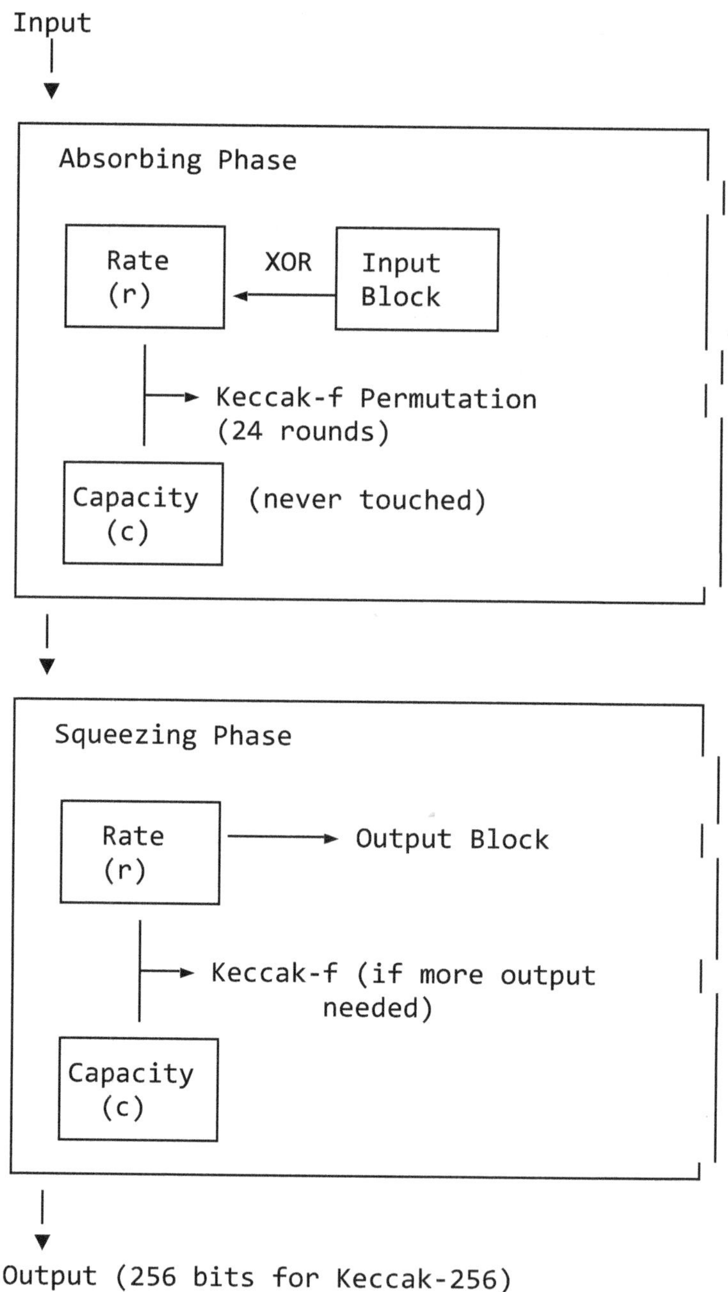

***Figure 2-3.** Keccak Sponge Construction*

Sponge picture: 1600-bit state split into rate r (where inputs get XORed) and capacity c (untouched surface that soaks up security margin). For Keccak-256, think r=1088, c=512 in the usual parametrization.

Security tracks capacity: collision strength tracks like c/2 in the usual sponge analysis. Keccak-256 lines up with 256-bit collision resistance in the standard telling.

Implementation: Computing Hashes

Below is toy code for hashing bytes the way you'd touch it in tooling—nothing exotic, just the API shape.

```
import hashlib
import time

def sha256_hash(data: bytes) -> bytes:
    """Single SHA-256 hash"""
    return hashlib.sha256(data).digest()

def double_sha256(data: bytes) -> bytes:
    """Double SHA-256 hash (Bitcoin style)"""
    return hashlib.sha256(hashlib.sha256(data).digest()).digest()

def keccak256(data: bytes) -> bytes:
    """
    Keccak-256 hash (Ethereum style).
    Note: Standard hashlib doesn't include Keccak,
    but we can simulate it conceptually.
    In practice, use: from Crypto.Hash import keccak
    """
    # For demonstration, we'll use sha3_256
    # Real Ethereum uses: keccak.new(digest_bits=256).update(data).digest()
    return hashlib.sha3_256().digest()

def benchmark_hashes(data_size: int, iterations: int):
    """Compare hash function performance"""
    data = b"x" * data_size

    # SHA-256
    start = time.time()
    for _ in range(iterations):
        hashlib.sha256(data).digest()
    sha256_time = time.time() - start
```

```
    # SHA3-256 (Keccak)
    start = time.time()
    for _ in range(iterations):
        hashlib.sha3_256(data).digest()
    sha3_time = time.time() - start

    return sha256_time, sha3_time

# Example usage
message = b"Block #12345: Alice sends 1 BTC to Bob"
print(f"SHA-256:        {sha256_hash(message).hex()}")
print(f"Double SHA-256: {double_sha256(message).hex()}")
print(f"Keccak-256:     {keccak256(message).hex()}")

# Performance comparison
sha256_t, sha3_t = benchmark_hashes(1000, 10000) #The benchmark results can
change on different systems
print(f"\nPerformance (10k hashes of 1KB):")
print(f"SHA-256:   {sha256_t:.4f}s")
print(f"SHA3-256:  {sha3_t:.4f}s")
```

Table 2-3. *Hash Function Performance Comparison*

Function	Software Speed (MB/s)	Hardware Speed	Power Efficiency	Quantum Resistance
SHA-256	150-400	Excellent (ASICs exist)	High	No
Keccak-256	200-500	Very good	Very high	No
BLAKE2	300-1000	Good	Very high	No
SHA-512	180-450	Good	Moderate	No

Quantum footnote: Grover's search halves effective bit strength against preimage-style games. 256-bit hash ~ 128-bit quantum bucket—still uncomfortable to attack, but long-term people track migration plans.

2.1.4 Message Authentication Codes (MACs)

Hashes alone don't authenticate. Alice sends Bob a file plus H(file). Mallory swaps the file, recomputes the hash, and Bob's check passes—because Mallory could compute H from scratch too. Integrity without a secret is theater.

MACs fix that by keying the tag. No shared secret, no valid tag. Different threat model.

Table 2-4. *Hash vs. MAC vs. Digital Signature*

Property	Hash	MAC	Digital Signature
Integrity	✓	✓	✓
Authentication	X	✓	✓
Non-repudiation	X	X	✓
Secret required	None	Symmetric key	Private key
Public verification	✓	X	✓
Speed	Very fast	Fast	Slow

HMAC: Hash-Based MAC

HMAC is the usual construction: wrap your favorite hash in a keyed sandwich. Same primitives you already ship.

```
HMAC(K, m) = H((K ⊕ opad) ‖ H((K ⊕ ipad) ‖ m))
```

Unpacking HMAC in one breath: key K, message m, hash H, inner pad ipad, outer pad opad, XOR, and concatenation as usual. Details live in the diagram—the point is the structure, not memorizing hex constants.

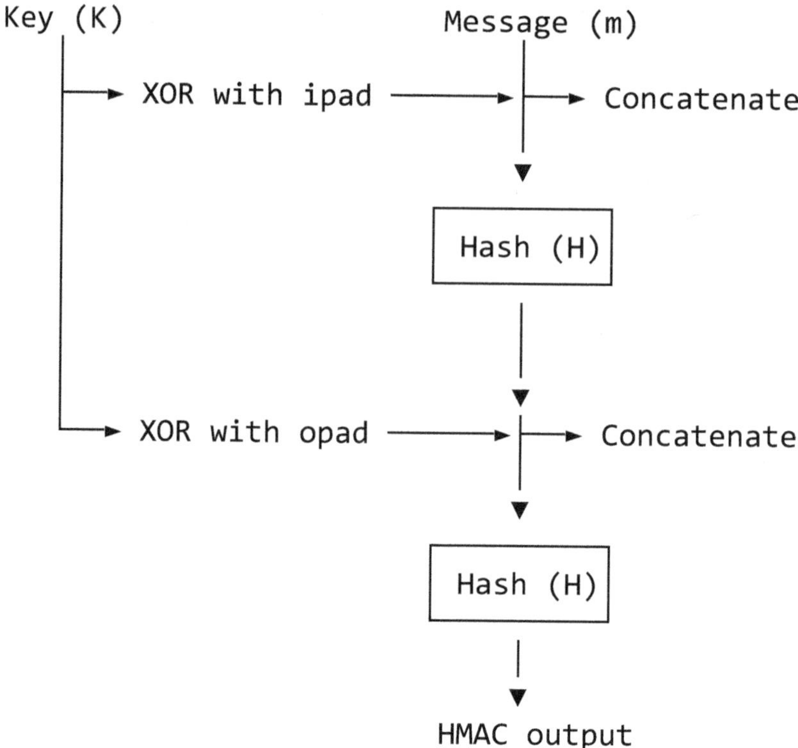

Figure 2-4. *HMAC Construction*

Looks fussy on purpose. H(K||m) and friends invite length-extension games; HMAC's nesting exists to close those lanes.

Implementation: HMAC

```
import hmac
import hashlib

def compute_hmac(key: bytes, message: bytes) -> bytes:
    """Compute HMAC-SHA256"""
    return hmac.new(key, message, hashlib.sha256).digest()

def verify_hmac(key: bytes, message: bytes, mac: bytes) -> bool:
    """Verify HMAC in constant time (prevents timing attacks)"""
    expected = compute_hmac(key, message)
    return hmac.compare_digest(expected, mac)
```

```
# Example usage
key = b"secret_key_for_blockchain_node"
message = b"Transaction: Alice -> Bob, 5 ETH"

mac = compute_hmac(key, message)
print(f"Message: {message}")
print(f"MAC: {mac.hex()}")

# Verification
is_valid = verify_hmac(key, message, mac)
print(f"Valid: {is_valid}")

# Tampered message
tampered = b"Transaction: Alice -> Carol, 5 ETH"
is_valid = verify_hmac(key, tampered, mac)
print(f"Tampered valid: {is_valid}")
```

Where MACs actually show up around chains:

1. P2P session-ish auth when two peers already share a symmetric key—cheaper than full sig verify on every gossip packet.
2. **Wallet Derivation**: BIP32 marches keys forward with HMAC-SHA512 in the mix.
3. **Light-Client Fetch Paths**: MACs can tag replies so tampering doesn't silently pass.

2.1.5 Cryptographically Secure Random Number Generation

If you learn one thing from crypto history, learn this: bad randomness is how keys die. Keys, nonces, salts—predict any of them and someone else will.

PS3 signing disaster: reused ECDSA nonce k across signatures. One repeat is enough to peel the private key; suddenly anyone can sign as Sony. Nightmare scenario, real incident.

Android wallet era: broken SecureRandom meant keys weren't as random as users thought. People lost real coins. RNG bugs aren't theoretical.

True Randomness vs. Pseudorandomness

TRNGs harvest physical noise—thermal jitter, avalanche noise, and sometimes fancier quantum toys. Unpredictable, often slower, hardware-dependent.

PRNGs stretch a seed through a deterministic update function. Fast—and catastrophic if the seed leaks.

CSPRNGs aim for PRNG speed with crypto-grade outputs. Two standard intuitions: next-bit test—after k bits, bit k+1 should still look like a coin flip to any efficient distinguisher; state compromise resistance—even if an attacker snapshots internal state now, past outputs shouldn't rewind cleanly (exact guarantees depend on the construction).

Table 2-5. *Randomness Sources for Blockchain*

Source	Type	Predictable?	Speed	Blockchain Use
/dev/urandom (Linux)	CSPRNG	No (if properly seeded)	Fast	Key generation, nonces
Hardware RNG	TRNG	No	Fast	Seeding CSPRNGs
Current timestamp	Weak	Yes	Instant	✗ Never for keys!
Block hash	Weak for RNG	Partially	N/A	✗ Miners can influence
VRF (Verifiable Random Function)	Strong	No (with proper construction)	Moderate	On-chain randomness

Implementation: Safe Random Generation

```
import secrets  # Cryptographically secure
import os
import hashlib

def generate_private_key() -> bytes:
    """
    Generate a cryptographically secure 256-bit private key.
    Uses os.urandom which draws from OS entropy pool.
    """
    return secrets.token_bytes(32)
```

```python
def generate_nonce() -> bytes:
    """Generate a random nonce for signing"""
    return secrets.token_bytes(32)

def unsafe_random_example():
    """
    NEVER DO THIS! Demonstrates weak randomness.
    Python's random module is NOT cryptographically secure.
    """
    import random
    random.seed(12345)  # Predictable!
    weak_key = random.getrandbits(256)
    return weak_key.to_bytes(32, 'big')

# Generate secure key
private_key = generate_private_key()
print(f"Secure private key: {private_key.hex()}")

# Demonstrate the danger of reusing nonces
# (Don't actually do ECDSA with same nonce - this is illustration)
message1 = b"Transaction 1"
message2 = b"Transaction 2"
k = generate_nonce()  # Nonce

# In real ECDSA, reusing k for different messages exposes private key!
print(f"\nNonce k: {k.hex()}")
print("Using same nonce for multiple signatures = CATASTROPHIC!")

# Proper usage: new nonce for each signature
k1 = generate_nonce()
k2 = generate_nonce()
print(f"Nonce k1: {k1.hex()}")
print(f"Nonce k2: {k2.hex()}")
print("Different nonces = SAFE")
```

Rules that survive audits:

1. Use OS-grade entropy APIs—Python secrets, Go crypto/rand, /dev/urandom class sources. Not rand().
2. **Fresh Nonce Per Signature**: The PS3 story is what happens when "usually" replaces "always."
3. Don't seed security from timestamps or block hashes alone—they're structured, not secret.
4. **Homebrew PRNGs**: If you must, seed from serious entropy. Otherwise, you're decorating determinism.

2.1.6 Merkle Trees: Efficient Data Verification

Without Merkle trees, light clients don't work at phone scale—you'd be dragging whole blocks to check one payment.

The Problem

Say a block carries 100k txs. A phone wants to know if one tx landed. Naive approach:

1. Download every tx in the block (enjoy your bandwidth bill)
2. Hash each candidate leaf yourself
3. Rebuild the Merkle tower and compare it to the header root—still brute force, just fancier

That's gigabytes to vouch for one row. Nobody's paying that bill.

The Solution

Merkle's 1979 idea (patents and all): binary tree of hashes. Leaves hash data; parents hash children; the root commits to everything below. One root, whole dataset.

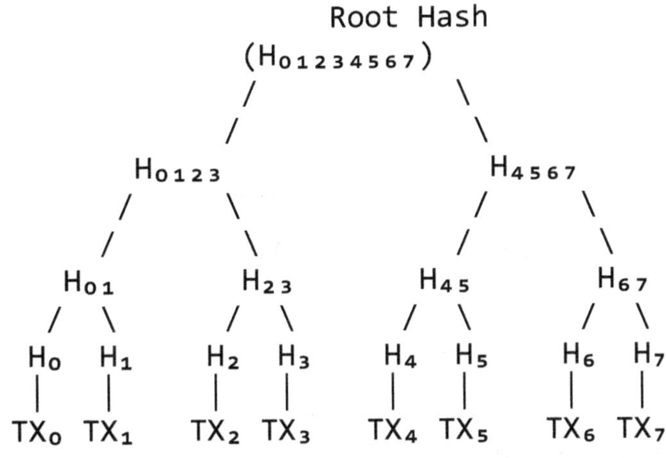


```
Where:
  H0 = Hash(TX0)
  H1 = Hash(TX1)
  H01 = Hash(H0 || H1)
  H0123 = Hash(H01 || H23)
  Root = Hash(H0123 || H4567)
```

Figure 2-5. *Merkle Tree Structure (8 transactions)*

To prove TX3, you don't ship the forest—you ship TX3, sibling hashes up the path, maybe ~log n total. Verifier recomputes toward the root they trust.

Walk upward: hash the leaf, pair with sibling hash, repeat until root. Match? Inclusion holds.

Root matches what you already trust? Then that leaf is in the set. Done.

100k leaves sounds big; the proof path is ~log2(100k) hashes—call it 17 steps. A million leaves? Still ~20. That's the win.

Table 2-6. Merkle Proof Size vs. Data Size

Transactions	Naive Verification	Merkle Proof Size	Reduction Factor
100	100 hashes	7 hashes	14x
1,000	1,000 hashes	10 hashes	100x
10,000	10,000 hashes	14 hashes	714x
100,000	100,000 hashes	17 hashes	5,882x
1,000,000	1,000,000 hashes	20 hashes	50,000x

Implementation: Merkle Tree

```
from typing import List
import hashlib

class MerkleTree:
    def __init__(self, data_blocks: List[bytes]):
        """
        Build a Merkle tree from data blocks.
        Pads with duplicate last element if odd number.
        """
        if not data_blocks:
            raise ValueError("Cannot create empty Merkle tree")

        self.leaves = [self._hash(block) for block in data_blocks]
        self.tree = self._build_tree(self.leaves)
        self.root = self.tree[-1] if self.tree else None

    def _hash(self, data: bytes) -> bytes:
        """Hash a single block"""
        return hashlib.sha256(data).digest()

    def _build_tree(self, level: List[bytes]) -> List[bytes]:
        """Build tree from bottom up"""
        tree = level[:]

        while len(level) > 1:
            # If odd number of nodes, duplicate the last one
```

```
            if len(level) % 2 == 1:
                level.append(level[-1])

            # Compute parent level
            next_level = []
            for i in range(0, len(level), 2):
                parent = self._hash(level[i] + level[i + 1])
                next_level.append(parent)
                tree.append(parent)

            level = next_level

        return tree

    def get_root(self) -> bytes:
        """Get the Merkle root"""
        return self.root

    def get_proof(self, index: int) -> List[tuple]:
        """
        Generate Merkle proof for element at index.
        Returns list of (hash, position) where position is 'left' or
        'right'.
        """
        if index >= len(self.leaves):
            raise ValueError(f"Index {index} out of range")

        proof = []
        level = self.leaves
        pos = index

        while len(level) > 1:
            # Duplicate last element if odd
            if len(level) % 2 == 1:
                level = level + [level[-1]]

            # Find sibling
            if pos % 2 == 0:  # Left child
                sibling = level[pos + 1]
```

```
                proof.append((sibling, 'right'))
            else:  # Right child
                sibling = level[pos - 1]
                proof.append((sibling, 'left'))

            # Move to parent level
            level = [self._hash(level[i] + level[i + 1])
                    for i in range(0, len(level), 2)]
            pos = pos // 2

        return proof

    def verify_proof(self, data: bytes, index: int, proof: List[tuple],
                    root: bytes) -> bool:
        """Verify a Merkle proof"""
        current = self._hash(data)

        for sibling, position in proof:
            if position == 'left':
                current = self._hash(sibling + current)
            else:
                current = self._hash(current + sibling)

        return current == root

# Example usage
transactions = [
    b"Alice sends 1 BTC to Bob",
    b"Carol sends 2 BTC to Dave",
    b"Eve sends 0.5 BTC to Frank",
    b"Grace sends 3 BTC to Henry",
    b"Ivan sends 1.5 BTC to Judy",
    b"Kevin sends 2.5 BTC to Laura",
    b"Mike sends 0.8 BTC to Nancy",
    b"Oscar sends 1.2 BTC to Paul"
]
```

```
# Build tree
tree = MerkleTree(transactions)
root = tree.get_root()
print(f"Merkle root: {root.hex()}\n")

# Generate proof for transaction 3
tx_index = 3
proof = tree.get_proof(tx_index)
print(f"Proof for transaction {tx_index}:")
for i, (hash_val, pos) in enumerate(proof):
    print(f"  Step {i+1}: {hash_val.hex()[:16]}... ({pos})")

# Verify proof
tx_data = transactions[tx_index]
is_valid = tree.verify_proof(tx_data, tx_index, proof, root)
print(f"\nVerification result: {is_valid}")

# Try with wrong data
wrong_data = b"Tampered transaction"
is_valid = tree.verify_proof(wrong_data, tx_index, proof, root)
print(f"Verification with tampered data: {is_valid}")

# Show proof size efficiency
print(f"\n Efficiency:")
print(f"Transactions: {len(transactions)}")
print(f"Full data size: {sum(len(tx) for tx in transactions)} bytes")
print(f"Proof size: {len(proof)} hashes ({len(proof) * 32} bytes)")
```

Security Properties

Why people reach for Merkle trees:

Tiny commitment: 32-byte root names an arbitrarily large set (up to collision bounds).

Cheap verification: O(log n) hashes, not O(n) data movement.

Tamper-evidence: flip a leaf; the path to the root changes unless you break the hash.

2.1.7 Patricia Tries: Prefix Trees for Key-Value Storage

Any serious chain needs a key-value story. Bitcoin tracks UTXO sets; Ethereum maps accounts to balances, code, and storage—a way fatter state.

Patricia tries to keep that kind of keyed state from exploding. The acronym is silly long; think "compressed radix trie that people actually Merkleize."

Trie Basics

Trie = retrieval tree (yes, pronounced "tree"). Paths spell keys; branches split on successive symbols; shared prefixes share path prefixes.

```
Keys: "do", "dog", "dodge", "cat", "car"
```

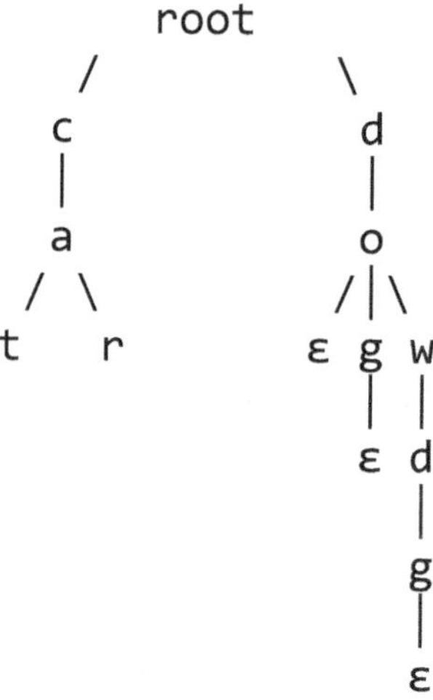


```
Where ε represents end-of-key marker
```

Figure 2-6. *Simple Trie Example*

Upside: lookups scale with key length, not table size; prefix queries fall out naturally.

Downside: one node per symbol can bloat memory; random-looking keys don't share much; tree gets wide and awkward.

Patricia Trie Optimization

Patricia/radix trie collapses long unary chains—edges carry whole string chunks instead of single characters.

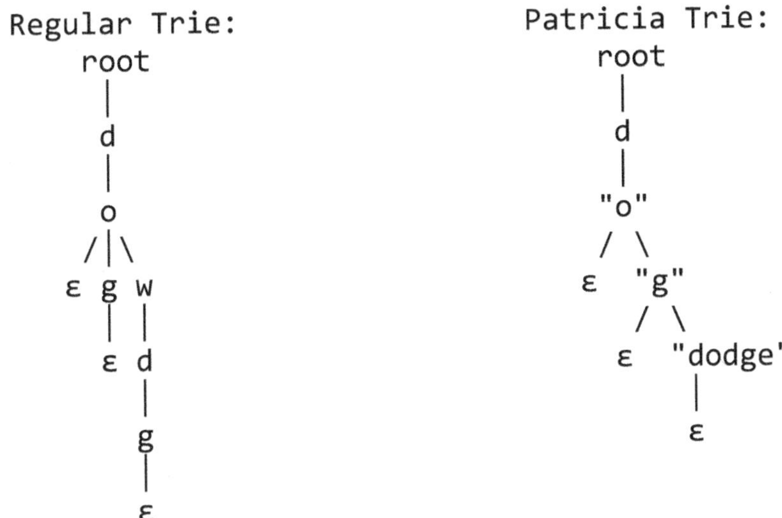

Figure 2-7. *Patricia Trie vs. Regular Trie*

Edges hold strings, not just glyphs—fewer nodes, fewer pointers, less empty scaffolding.

2.1.8 Merkle-Patricia Tries in Ethereum

Merkle gives you proofs; Patricia gives you keyed routing without a naive map scan. Stack them: the Merkle-Patricia trie—Ethereum's big structural bet.

Structure

Ethereum's trie mixes a small zoo of node shapes (branch, extension, leaf)—see the table for the exact typing.

Table 2-7. *Ethereum Merkle-Patricia Trie Node Types*

Node Type	Structure	Purpose
Leaf	[path, value]	Stores actual data at end of key path
Extension	[path, hash]	Compresses non-branching path, points to next node
Branch	[v_0, v_1, …, v_{15}, value]	16 children (for hex digits) plus optional value

```
State:
  0xa7... → {balance: 100, nonce: 5}
  0xa7fa... → {balance: 50, nonce: 2}
  0xb3... → {balance: 200, nonce: 1}

                    Root Hash
                        |
                    Branch Node
                    /          \
                   a            b
                   |            |
              Extension        Leaf
            (path: "7")      (path: "3", value: {200, 1})
                   |
              Branch Node
              /          \
             ε            f
             |            |
            Leaf         Leaf
   (path: "", value: {100, 5})  (path: "a", value: {50, 2})
```

Figure 2-8. *Merkle-Patricia Trie Example*

Hash each node, Merkle-style, and the root commits to the whole keyspace. That's how state proofs attach to headers.

Why This Matters

Full nodes lug the trie; light clients want to live thin:

1. Trust a 32-byte state root from a sync'd header
2. Pull sibling hashes on demand from whoever still has full state
3. Recompute upward locally—no need to mirror every account

Prove balance for 0xa7fa...? Ship the path, sibling hashes level by level; client recomputes upward; matches the trusted root -> belief updates.

Table 2-8. Ethereum State Trie Properties

Property	Value	Impact
Root hash size	32 bytes	Constant-size commitment to entire state
Proof size	~2-5 KB	Logarithmic in state size
Insert/Update time	O(log n)	Efficient modifications
Lookup time	O(log n)	Fast queries
Deterministic	Yes	Same state → same root

Implementation: Simple Patricia Trie

```
from typing import Optional, Dict, List
import hashlib

class PatriciaNode:
    """Base class for Patricia trie nodes"""
    pass

class LeafNode(PatriciaNode):
    def __init__(self, path: str, value: bytes):
        self.path = path
        self.value = value

    def hash(self) -> bytes:
        """Compute hash of this node"""
        data = f"leaf:{self.path}:{self.value.hex()}".encode()
        return hashlib.sha256(data).digest()

class ExtensionNode(PatriciaNode):
    def __init__(self, path: str, next_hash: bytes):
        self.path = path
        self.next_hash = next_hash

    def hash(self) -> bytes:
        data = f"ext:{self.path}:{self.next_hash.hex()}".encode()
        return hashlib.sha256(data).digest()
```

```
class BranchNode(PatriciaNode):
    def __init__(self):
        self.children: Dict[str, bytes] = {}  # hex digit -> child hash
        self.value: Optional[bytes] = None

    def hash(self) -> bytes:
        # Hash all children
        children_str = ",".join(
            f"{k}:{v.hex()}" for k, v in sorted(self.children.items())
        )
        value_str = self.value.hex() if self.value else ""
        data = f"branch:{children_str}:{value_str}".encode()
        return hashlib.sha256(data).digest()

class SimplePatriciaTrie:
    """
    Simplified Patricia trie for demonstration.
    Real Ethereum trie is more complex with RLP encoding.
    """
    def __init__(self):
        self.storage: Dict[bytes, PatriciaNode] = {}
        self.root_hash: Optional[bytes] = None

    def insert(self, key: str, value: bytes):
        """Insert key-value pair"""
        # Convert key to hex string
        hex_key = key.encode().hex()

        # Create leaf node
        leaf = LeafNode(hex_key, value)
        leaf_hash = leaf.hash()
        self.storage[leaf_hash] = leaf

        # For simplicity, just store root as this leaf
        # Real implementation would handle path compression
        self.root_hash = leaf_hash
```

```
    def get_root(self) -> bytes:
        """Get current root hash"""
        return self.root_hash or b"\x00" * 32

    def get_proof(self, key: str) -> List[bytes]:
        """
        Generate Merkle proof for key.
        Returns list of node hashes along path.
        """
        # Simplified: return just the leaf
        hex_key = key.encode().hex()
        proof = []

        for node_hash, node in self.storage.items():
            if isinstance(node, LeafNode) and node.path == hex_key:
                proof.append(node_hash)

        return proof

    def verify_proof(self, key: str, value: bytes,
                     proof: List[bytes], root: bytes) -> bool:
        """Verify Merkle proof"""
        hex_key = key.encode().hex()

        # Simplified: just check if value hashes correctly
        for node_hash in proof:
            node = self.storage.get(node_hash)
            if isinstance(node, LeafNode):
                if node.path == hex_key and node.value == value:
                    return node_hash == root

        return False

# Example usage
trie = SimplePatriciaTrie()

# Insert some account data
accounts = {
    "0xa7": b"balance:100,nonce:5",
```

```
    "0xa7fa": b"balance:50,nonce:2",
    "0xb3": b"balance:200,nonce:1"
}

for addr, data in accounts.items():
    trie.insert(addr, data)

root = trie.get_root()
print(f"State root: {root.hex()}")

# Generate and verify proof
key = "0xa7fa"
value = accounts[key]
proof = trie.get_proof(key)
is_valid = trie.verify_proof(key, value, proof, root)
print(f"\nProof for {key}: {is_valid}")
```

What we coded here is didactic. Mainnet Ethereum adds RLP, gnarlier path encoding, and Keccak everywhere—same ideas, production seasoning.

2.1.9 Summary

That's the bedrock chapter: hashes, MACs, RNG discipline, Merkle, Patricia, then how Ethereum glues them.

Hashes: integrity + IDs + PoW inner loops. SHA-256 in Bitcoin-land, Keccak in Ethereum-land—both beaten on for years in the wild.

MACs add keyed authentication atop hashes; HMAC is the boring default that works; wallet paths lean on it.

CSPRNGs guard keygen and nonces. Slip once—reused nonce, weak seed—and keys walk out the door. No partial credit.

Merkle trees are how thin clients survive: logarithmic proof paths instead of full replay.

Patricia tries to tame state size; Merkleizing them means account data stays provable against a header root.

This isn't trivia for interviews—if you touch protocol or security review, these primitives are the vocabularies.

If you're scanning for bullets, here's the compressed version:

- **Birthdays**: Collision search scales ~2^(n/2), preimage-ish games scale ~2^n (hand-waving constants).
- **Double SHA-256 in Bitcoin**: Length-extension mitigation, not cosplay.
- Nonce reuse in ECDSA (and friends) can key-recover you—PS3 taught that class.
- **Merkle Proofs**: ~log n hashes even when n is obscene (millions/billions).
- Patricia keeps updates localized; Merkle wrapper keeps the state root honest.

Numbers worth remembering without turning into a spreadsheet: SHA-256 ~128-bit collision / ~256-bit preimage strength at the birthday vs. preimage scales (Grover aside); Bitcoin double-SHA, Ethereum Keccak; Merkle proofs ~log n hashes (so ~20 steps at a million leaves—ballpark hundreds of bytes, not megabytes); Patricia compression keeps state traversal from devolving into naive maps; Ethereum's MPT ties account data to headers; RNG failures and ECDSA nonce reuse aren't lore—they're exploit recipes; birthday math means collision work lives near 2^(n/2), not 2^n.

Next chapter: signatures—how we bind messages to keys without meeting in a basement to swap secrets first.

2.1.10 Exercises

Problem 1 (Probability): Approximate P(collision) after 2^128 SHA-256 outputs; argue why grinding that out still isn't a Tuesday project.

Problem 2 (Calculation): Merkle tree, 1e6 leaves—how many sibling hashes in inclusion proof? Rough byte count vs. shipping all leaves?

Problem 3 (Implementation): Build inclusion + exclusion proofs. What extra bookkeeping does exclusion need?

Problem 4 (Storage): Compare the footprint for the full chain vs. roots-only vs. Patricia state—who's the user for each?

Problem 5 (Security): Avalanche effect: tiny input change, huge output change—show how that frustrates near-collision hunting.

Problem 6 (Light Clients): Sketch SPV-ish verification with Merkle proofs—minimal bytes a phone must fetch to believe a tx is in a block.

Problem 7 (Cryptography): Why does HMAC nest hashes? What breaks if you use plain H(K||msg)?

Problem 8 (Proof): Show an n-leaf binary Merkle tree has n-1 internal nodes; tally hash ops to build bottom-up.

Problem 9 (Research): Verkle trees—what problem do they solve vs. MPT on Ethereum's roadmap?

Problem 10 (Challenge): Patricia trie with real prefix compression vs. flat hash map—benchmark realistic Ethereum-shaped keys.

(Solutions in Appendix D)

2.1.11 Further Reading

Hashes: NIST SHA-3 materials are great for comparing families; the Keccak team's writeups explain sponges; Rogaway/Shrimpton if you want definitions of preimage vs. collision formalized.

Merkle: Ralph's old patent prose is oddly readable. Bitcoin SPV deep dives for what light clients actually assume: variants (sum trees, etc.) if you outgrow vanilla binary trees.

Patricia/Ethereum: Yellow Paper for the real spec; Morrison '68 if you want the historical name-drop; geth trie code if you learn by reading implementations.

Randomness: "Mining Your Ps and Qs" for depressing real-world RNG failures; NIST SP 800-90A for what "approved" CSPRNG construction looks like.

Skip: breathless "SHA-256 broken" posts with no citations; DIY crypto tutorials with timestamp seeds; anything reusing nonces for "efficiency."

CHAPTER 3

Digital Signatures

3.1 Public Key Cryptography and Authentication

Every blockchain transaction rests on digital signatures—the mechanism that lets you prove ownership and authorize transfers without handing over the private key that makes it possible. This chapter works through the signature schemes that make that work: RSA, elliptic curve cryptography, ECDSA, Schnorr, and EdDSA, along with multi-signature schemes, threshold cryptography, and the implementation of pitfalls that trip up real systems. By the end, you will have covered:

- How public key cryptography enables authentication without shared secrets
- The mathematical foundations of RSA and elliptic curve cryptography
- Why ECDSA dominates blockchain systems
- The advantages of Schnorr signatures and signature aggregation
- How EdDSA provides deterministic signing with strong security
- Multi-signature schemes and threshold cryptography
- Real-world signature implementation and security pitfalls

3.1.1 Introduction: Authentication Without Trust

Digital signatures solve a fundamental problem: how do you prove you authorized a transaction without revealing the secret that grants you that authority?

N. Savant, *Blockchain Foundations*, https://doi.org/10.1007/979-8-8688-2891-1_3

In the physical world, handwritten signatures provide weak authentication. They're easy to forge, hard to verify, and don't prove intent—I might sign a blank piece of paper, and you could write anything above my signature.

Digital signatures are cryptographically strong. They provide three critical properties:

Authentication: Only the holder of the private key could have created this signature.

Integrity: If even one bit of the signed message changes, the signature becomes invalid.

Non-Repudiation: The signer can't later claim they didn't sign the message (assuming their private key wasn't compromised).

These properties make digital signatures the backbone of blockchain systems. Every transaction is a signed message saying, "I authorize moving funds from my account." Without digital signatures, blockchain would require trusted intermediaries to authorize transactions.

This chapter explores the mathematics and engineering of digital signature schemes, from RSA's factoring-based security to modern elliptic curve systems that achieve equivalent security with much smaller keys.

3.1.2 Public Key Cryptography Basics

Traditional cryptography uses symmetric keys: Alice and Bob share a secret key, using it for both encryption and authentication. This requires establishing shared secrets through secure channels—a chicken-and-egg problem for decentralized systems.

Public key cryptography (also called asymmetric cryptography) solves this elegantly:

Key Pair Generation: Generate two mathematically related keys:—Private key (d): Kept secret, used for signing—Public key (Q): Shared publicly, used for verification

Signing: Create signature σ = Sign(message, d)

Verification: Check Verify(message, σ, Q) = true or false

The mathematical relationship between keys ensures: (1) Signatures created with a private key can be verified with a public key. (2) Computing the private key from the public key is infeasible. (3) Forging signatures without the private key is infeasible.

Table 3-1. *Symmetric vs. Asymmetric Cryptography*

Property	Symmetric (e.g., AES)	Asymmetric (e.g., ECDSA)
Key distribution	Requires a secure channel	Public keys can be shared openly
Speed	Very fast (~GB/s)	Slow (~1–10k ops/s)
Key size	128–256 bits	256–4096 bits
Use case	Bulk encryption	Authentication, key exchange
Blockchain role	Minimal	Critical (all transactions signed)

This asymmetry is what makes the entire blockchain signing model possible: deriving a public key from a private key is trivial, but the reverse is infeasible.

In elliptic curve schemes, the forward direction is repeated point addition on a curve: starting from a known generator point G, compute Q = d × G. The double-and-add method performs this in roughly 256 steps for a 256-bit key. Going backward—given Q and G, recovering the scalar d—is the elliptic curve discrete logarithm problem. No algorithm solves this in fewer than roughly 2^128 steps for a well-chosen 256-bit curve.

In RSA, the forward direction is multiplying two large primes to get their product. A modern CPU multiplies two 1024-bit primes in microseconds. Going backward—decomposing that product into its prime factors—has resisted four decades of algorithmic research.

The mathematical problems underpinning signature schemes share a common structure: one direction of computation is cheap, while reversing it is astronomically expensive. The private key holder possesses a shortcut that makes the reverse direction tractable for them alone.

Think of mixing paint. Combining yellow and blue to get green takes seconds. But separating green paint back into its original yellow and blue components? That is a fundamentally harder problem—one that chemistry offers no efficient solution for. Public key cryptography exploits the same kind of asymmetry, but with number theory instead of pigments.

3.1.3 RSA Signatures: The Classic Approach

RSA (Rivest-Shamir-Adleman, 1977) was the first practical public key cryptosystem. While blockchain systems rarely use RSA for signatures (preferring elliptic curves), understanding RSA illuminates core concepts.

RSA Mathematics

Key generation:

1. Choose two large prime numbers, p and q (typically 1024–2048 bits each)
2. Compute n = p × q (the modulus)
3. Compute φ(n) = (p-1)(q-1) (Euler's totient function)
4. Choose a public exponent e (commonly 65537)
5. Compute private exponent d ≡ e^(-1) mod φ(n)

Public key: (n, e)Private key: d (keep p, q, φ(n) secret too)

Signing:

To sign message m: 1. Hash: h = H(m) 2. Convert hash to integer (with padding) 3. Compute signature: σ = h^d mod n

Verification:

To verify signature σ on message m: 1. Hash: h = H(m) 2. Compute: h' = σ^e mod n 3. Check if h' = h

Why this works: σ^e = ($h^{d)}$e = h^(de) = h^1 = h (mod n), using the fact that de ≡ 1 (mod φ(n)).

Table 3-2. *RSA Signature Security Parameters*

Key Size	Security Level	Factoring Difficulty	Quantum Resistance	Sign Time	Verify Time
1024-bit	~80 bits	2^80 operations	None	5–10 ms	0.5 ms
2048-bit	~112 bits	2^112 operations	None	20–40 ms	1–2 ms
3072-bit	~128 bits	2^128 operations	None	60–100 ms	3–5 ms
4096-bit	~140 bits	2^140 operations	None	150–250 ms	6–10 ms

Why Blockchain Prefers Elliptic Curves Over RSA

1. **Key Size**: 256-bit ECC provides equivalent security to 3072-bit RSA. Smaller keys mean smaller transactions.
2. **Signature Size**: ECDSA signatures are ~64 bytes; RSA signatures match key size (256–512 bytes).
3. **Address Generation**: Bitcoin addresses are hashes of public keys. Smaller ECC keys make addresses more compact.
4. **Performance**: ECC signature generation is faster than RSA for equivalent security.

Table 3-3. *RSA vs. ECC Comparison*

Security Level	RSA Key Size	ECC Key Size	RSA Signature Size	ECC Signature Size	Advantage
80-bit	1024 bits	160 bits	128 bytes	40 bytes	ECC: 6.8x smaller
112-bit	2048 bits	224 bits	256 bytes	56 bytes	ECC: 4.6x smaller
128-bit	3072 bits	256 bits	384 bytes	64 bytes	ECC: 6x smaller
256-bit	15360 bits	512 bits	1920 bytes	128 bytes	ECC: 15x smaller

The following code shows how to generate RSA keys, sign a message, and verify the signature using a standard library. This helps to understand how digital signatures work in practice.

Implementation: RSA Signatures

```
from Crypto.PublicKey import RSA
from Crypto.Signature import pkcs1_15
from Crypto.Hash import SHA256

def generate_rsa_keypair(bits=2048):
    """Generate RSA key pair"""
```

```
    key = RSA.generate(bits)
    private_key = key.export_key()
    public_key = key.publickey().export_key()
    return private_key, public_key

def rsa_sign(message: bytes, private_key_pem: bytes) -> bytes:
    """Sign message with RSA private key"""
    private_key = RSA.import_key(private_key_pem)
    h = SHA256.new(message)
    signature = pkcs1_15.new(private_key).sign(h)
    return signature

def rsa_verify(message: bytes, signature: bytes, public_key_pem: bytes)
-> bool:
    """Verify RSA signature"""
    public_key = RSA.import_key(public_key_pem)
    h = SHA256.new(message)
    try:
        pkcs1_15.new(public_key).verify(h, signature)
        return True
    except (ValueError, TypeError):
        return False

# Example usage
message = b"Transfer 5 BTC to Bob"

# Generate keys
priv, pub = generate_rsa_keypair(2048)
print(f"RSA-2048 private key: {len(priv)} bytes")
print(f"RSA-2048 public key: {len(pub)} bytes")

# Sign
signature = rsa_sign(message, priv)
print(f"Signature size: {len(signature)} bytes")

# Verify
is_valid = rsa_verify(message, signature, pub)
print(f"Signature valid: {is_valid}")
```

```
# Tampered message
tampered = b"Transfer 5 BTC to Eve"
is_valid = rsa_verify(tampered, signature, pub)
print(f"Tampered signature valid: {is_valid}")
```

Curve	Field Size	Order n	Security Level	Signature Size	Used By
secp256k1	256 bits	~2^256	128 bits	64–72 bytes	Bitcoin, Ethereum (legacy)
P-256 (secp256r1)	256 bits	~2^256	128 bits	64–72 bytes	TLS, many systems
secp384r1	384 bits	~2^384	192 bits	96–104 bytes	High-security applications
Curve25519	255 bits	~2^252	128 bits	64 bytes	EdDSA (not ECDSA)

The reverse operation—given the generator G and the result Q, recover the scalar d—is the elliptic curve discrete logarithm problem (ECDLP). For curves like secp256k1 (Bitcoin) and Curve25519 (EdDSA), the best known attack requires approximately 2^128 group operations. At one billion operations per second, this would take roughly 10^22 years.

Repeated addition—computing Q = d × G by adding the generator point G to itself d times—is the forward operation that creates public keys from private keys. The double-and-add method reduces this from d additions to about 256 steps for a 256-bit scalar, making it fast even for huge private keys.

The finite-field version replaces this geometric reasoning with modular slope calculations. For distinct points $P = (x_1, y_1)$ and $Q = (x_2, y_2)$, the slope is $\lambda = (y_2 - y_1) \times (x_2 - x_1)^{-1} \bmod p$. For doubling (P = Q), the slope is $\lambda = (3x_1^2 + a) \times (2y_1)^{-1} \bmod p$. In both cases, the result is $x_3 = \lambda^2 - x_1 - x_2 \bmod p$, $y_3 = \lambda(x_1 - x_3) - y_1 \bmod p$.

The geometric picture over real numbers provides helpful intuition, even though the actual computation uses modular arithmetic. If you place a straight line through two points P and Q on the real-number curve, that line generally intersects the curve at exactly one more point. Negating the y-coordinate of that intersection point gives you the sum P + Q. When P and Q coincide, you use the tangent line at P instead.

What makes these point sets useful is that you can define an addition operation over them that behaves like ordinary addition: it is associative, commutative, has an identity element, and every point has an inverse. This gives the points a group structure, which is the algebraic foundation for all elliptic curve cryptography.

The curves used in cryptography satisfy the Weierstrass equation $y^2 = x^3 + ax + b$, but they are not the smooth curves you might visualize from calculus. Blockchain implementations operate over finite fields—all arithmetic is performed modulo a large prime p, so the "curve" is actually a scattered collection of integer-coordinate points that satisfy $y^2 \equiv x^3 + ax + b \pmod{p}$. There is no continuous line to draw; the structure is algebraic, not geometric.

RSA's key sizes are impractical for blockchains where every transaction carries a public key and signature. A 3072-bit RSA key consumes 384 bytes; a secp256k1 key achieves equivalent security in 33 bytes. This order-of-magnitude difference is why Bitcoin, Ethereum, and virtually every blockchain adopted elliptic curve schemes instead.

The following code demonstrates how ECDSA is used to sign and verify a message. It also shows how hashing is applied before signing, like how it is done in blockchain systems.

Implementation: ECDSA

```
from ecdsa import SigningKey, VerifyingKey, SECP256k1
from ecdsa.util import sigencode_string, sigdecode_string
import hashlib
import secrets

def generate_ecdsa_keypair():
    """Generate ECDSA key pair on secp256k1"""
    private_key = SigningKey.generate(curve=SECP256k1)
    public_key = private_key.get_verifying_key()
    return private_key, public_key

def ecdsa_sign(message: bytes, private_key: SigningKey) -> bytes:
    """Sign message with ECDSA"""
    # Hash message first (Bitcoin-style double SHA-256)
    h = hashlib.sha256(hashlib.sha256(message).digest()).digest()
    signature = private_key.sign_digest(h, sigencode=sigencode_string)
    return signature
```

```
def ecdsa_verify(message: bytes, signature: bytes,
                public_key: VerifyingKey) -> bool:
    """Verify ECDSA signature"""
    h = hashlib.sha256(hashlib.sha256(message).digest()).digest()
    try:
        public_key.verify_digest(signature, h, sigdecode=sigdecode_string)
        return True
    except(ValueError,TypeError);
        return False

def demonstrate_nonce_reuse_vulnerability():
    """
    Demonstrate why nonce reuse is catastrophic.
    DO NOT use this in production!
    """
    # Generate key
    privkey = SigningKey.generate(curve=SECP256k1)
    pubkey = privkey.get_verifying_key()

    # Get private key value (for demonstration)
    d = int.from_bytes(privkey.to_string(), 'big')
    n = SECP256k1.order

    # Sign two different messages with SAME nonce (bad!)
    message1 = b"Transfer 1 BTC to Alice"
    message2 = b"Transfer 1 BTC to Bob"

    # Use a fixed k (simulating nonce reuse - NEVER DO THIS!)
    k = secrets.randbelow(n - 1) + 1  # Fixed k for both signatures

    # Manually compute signatures with same k
    e1 = int.from_bytes(hashlib.sha256(message1).digest(), 'big') % n
    e2 = int.from_bytes(hashlib.sha256(message2).digest(), 'big') % n

    # This would expose the private key!
    # Attack: k = (e1 - e2) / (s1 - s2) mod n
    # Then: d = (s*k - e) / r mod n
```

```
    print("WARNING: Nonce reuse allows private key extraction!")
    print("Always use unique nonces for each signature.")

# Example usage
message = b"Send 10 BTC from Alice to Bob"

# Generate keypair
privkey, pubkey = generate_ecdsa_keypair()
print(f"Private key size: {len(privkey.to_string())} bytes")
print(f"Public key size: {len(pubkey.to_string())} bytes")

# Sign
signature = ecdsa_sign(message, privkey)
print(f"Signature size: {len(signature)} bytes")

# Verify
is_valid = ecdsa_verify(message, signature, pubkey)
print(f"Signature valid: {is_valid}")

# Tampered message fails
tampered = b"Send 10 BTC from Alice to Eve"
is_valid = ecdsa_verify(tampered, signature, pubkey)
print(f"Tampered message valid: {is_valid}")

# Demonstrate nonce reuse danger
print("\n--- Nonce Reuse Vulnerability ---")
demonstrate_nonce_reuse_vulnerability()
```

3.1.4 Schnorr Signatures: Simplicity and Aggregation

Schnorr signatures, proposed by Claus Schnorr in 1989, offer significant advantages over ECDSA. Bitcoin activated Schnorr support (BIP 340) in 2021 via the Taproot upgrade.

Why Schnorr Is Better

Table 3-4. *ECDSA vs. Schnorr Comparison*

Property	ECDSA	Schnorr
Signature size	64–72 bytes (with DER encoding)	64 bytes (fixed)
Linearity	No	Yes
Signature aggregation	No	Yes
Batch verification	No	Yes
Multi-signature complexity	Complex, multiple rounds	Simple, one round
Security proof	Heuristic	Provably secure
Malleability	Vulnerable (needs extra checks)	Not vulnerable

Schnorr Signing

To sign message m with private key d:

1. **Generate nonce**: $k \leftarrow$ random from $[1, n-1]$
2. **Compute R**: $R = k \times G$
3. **Compute challenge**: $e = H(R \| Q \| m)$
4. **Compute s**: $s = k + ed \bmod n$
5. **Return signature**: (R, s)

Schnorr Verification

To verify signature (R, s) on message m with public key Q:

1. **Compute challenge**: $e = H(R \| Q \| m)$
2. **Verify**: Check if $s \times G = R + e \times Q$

Why it works: $s \times G = (k + ed) \times G = k \times G + ed \times G = R + e \times (d \times G) = R + e \times Q$ ✓

Signature Aggregation

The "linearity" property enables elegant multi-signatures. If multiple parties sign the same message:

Naive attempt (insecure): Party i has a keypair (d_i, Q_i)—Each creates a signature (R_i, s_i)—Aggregate: $R = R_1 + R_2 + \ldots$, $s = s_1 + s_2 + \ldots$, $Q = Q_1 + Q_2 + \ldots$

This aggregate signature (R, s) is valid for aggregate public key Q!

Problem: "Rogue key attack"—attacker can choose $Q_2 = Q_2'—Q_1$, causing the aggregate key to equal Q_2' (key they control).

Solution: MuSig protocol adds key aggregation with protection: Use $H(Q_1 \parallel Q_2 \parallel \ldots)$ to derive coefficients—$Q = a_1Q_1 + a_2Q_2 + \ldots$ where $a_i = H(L \parallel Q_i)$ and L is a sorted list of all public keys—Prevents rogue key attack

Benefits: Multiple signatures → one signature (same size as single signature)—Saves blockchain space—Improves privacy (multi-sig looks like single-sig)

```
Traditional Multi-Sig (e.g., 2-of-3):
    Transaction: [Sig₁][Sig₂][PubKey₁][PubKey₂][Script]
    Size: ~200 bytes signatures + script overhead

Schnorr Aggregated (MuSig):
    Transaction: [AggSig][AggPubKey]
    Size: ~96 bytes total

Savings: ~50%+
Privacy: Looks identical to single-sig on blockchain
```

Figure 3-1. *Signature Aggregation Benefits*

Implementation: Schnorr Signatures

```
import hashlib
import secrets
from dataclasses import dataclass

# Simplified Schnorr over secp256k1
# Real implementation should use proper secp256k1 library

@dataclass
class Point:
    """Elliptic curve point"""
    x: int
    y: int
```

```
# secp256k1 parameters (simplified - use library in production)
P = 0xFFFFFFFFFFFFFFFFFFFFFFFFFFFFFFFFFFFFFFFFFFFFFFFFFFFFFFFEFFFFFC2F
N = 0xFFFFFFFFFFFFFFFFFFFFFFFFFFFFFFFEBAAEDCE6AF48A03BBFD25E8CD0364141
Gx = 0x79BE667EF9DCBBAC55A06295CE870B07029BFCDB2DCE28D959F2815B16F81798
Gy = 0x483ADA7726A3C4655DA4FBFC0E1108A8FD17B448A68554199C47D08FFB10D4B8
G = Point(Gx, Gy)

def schnorr_sign_simplified(message: bytes, private_key: int) -> tuple:
    """
    Simplified Schnorr signature (for demonstration).
    Use proper library (e.g., python-bitcoinlib) in production.
    """
    # Generate random nonce
    k = secrets.randbelow(N - 1) + 1

    # R = k × G (point multiplication - simplified here)
    # In reality, use proper point multiplication
    R = k  # Placeholder - actual implementation needs point multiplication

    # Challenge e = H(R || Q || m)
    # Simplified: just hash components
    h = hashlib.sha256(message).digest()
    e = int.from_bytes(h, 'big') % N

    # s = k + e*d mod N
    s = (k + e * private_key) % N

    return (R, s)

def schnorr_verify_simplified(message: bytes, signature: tuple,
                              public_key: int) -> bool:
    """
    Simplified Schnorr verification.
    Real implementation needs proper point operations.
    """
    R, s = signature
```

```
    # Compute e = H(R || Q || m)
    h = hashlib.sha256(message).digest()
    e = int.from_bytes(h, 'big') % N

    # Verify: s*G = R + e*Q
    # Simplified check (real implementation needs point arithmetic)
    # In practice: compute both sides as points and compare

    return True  # Placeholder

# Demonstrate signature aggregation concept
def demonstrate_aggregation():
    """Show how Schnorr enables signature aggregation"""
    print("Signature Aggregation Benefits:")
    print("-" * 50)

    # Single signature
    single_sig_size = 64  # bytes
    print(f"Single Schnorr signature: {single_sig_size} bytes")

    # Traditional multi-sig (2-of-3)
    traditional_multisig = 2 * 64  # Two signatures
    print(f"Traditional 2-of-3 multi-sig: {traditional_multisig} bytes")

    # Aggregated Schnorr
    aggregated_size = 64  # Same as single!
    print(f"Aggregated Schnorr (2-of-3): {aggregated_size} bytes")

    savings = ((traditional_multisig - aggregated_size) / traditional_
    multisig) * 100
    print(f"\nSpace savings: {savings:.1f}%")
    print("Additional benefit: Enhanced privacy")

# Example
demonstrate_aggregation()
```

3.1.5 EdDSA: Deterministic Signatures with Curve25519

EdDSA (Edwards-curve Digital Signature Algorithm) is a modern signature scheme using twisted Edwards curves. It's used by Monero, Stellar, and increasingly by new blockchain projects.

Why EdDSA?

Advantages over ECDSA:

1. **Deterministic Nonces**: Eliminates nonce reuse vulnerability by deriving k from private key and message
2. **Fast**: Faster point operations on Edwards curves
3. **Side-Channel Resistant**: Constant-time operations prevent timing attacks
4. **Secure by Default**: Hard to implement incorrectly
5. **Small Keys and Signatures**: 32-byte keys, 64-byte signatures

Table 3-5. *EdDSA Variants*

Variant	Curve	Key Size	Signature Size	Security Level	Used By
Ed25519	Curve25519	32 bytes	64 bytes	128 bits	Monero, Stellar, Cardano
Ed448	Edwards448	57 bytes	114 bytes	224 bits	High-security applications

Ed25519 Signing

To sign message m with private key (a, A): a = secret scalar (32 bytes)—A = a × G (public key point)

1. **Compute Nonce Deterministically**: $r = H(h_2 \| m)$, where h_2 is the second half of H(private key)
2. **Compute R**: $R = r \times G$
3. **Compute Challenge**: $h = H(R \| A \| m)$

4. **Compute S**: S = (r + h × a) mod ℓ

5. **Return Signature**: (R, S)

No random number generation needed! This eliminates the entire class of nonce-related vulnerabilities.

Ed25519 Verification

To verify signature (R, S) on message m with public key A:

1. **Compute Challenge**: h = H(R || A || m)

2. **Verify Equation**: S × G = R + h × A

Implementation: Ed25519

```
from nacl.signing import SigningKey, VerifyKey
from nacl.encoding import HexEncoder
import hashlib

def generate_ed25519_keypair():
    """Generate Ed25519 key pair"""
    private_key = SigningKey.generate()
    public_key = private_key.verify_key
    return private_key, public_key

def ed25519_sign(message: bytes, private_key: SigningKey) -> bytes:
    """Sign message with Ed25519 (deterministic)"""
    signed = private_key.sign(message)
    # Return just the signature (nacl includes message)
    return signed.signature

def ed25519_verify(message: bytes, signature: bytes,
                   public_key: VerifyKey) -> bool:
    """Verify Ed25519 signature"""
    try:
        public_key.verify(message, signature)
        return True
    except:
        return False
```

```
def compare_signature_schemes():
    """Compare different signature scheme properties"""
    schemes = {
        "RSA-2048": {"key": 256, "sig": 256, "speed": "Slow", "quantum":
        "Vulnerable"},
        "ECDSA secp256k1": {"key": 32, "sig": 64, "speed": "Medium",
        "quantum": "Vulnerable"},
        "Schnorr secp256k1": {"key": 32, "sig": 64, "speed": "Medium",
        "quantum": "Vulnerable"},
        "Ed25519": {"key": 32, "sig": 64, "speed": "Fast", "quantum":
        "Vulnerable"},
    }

    print("Signature Scheme Comparison:")
    print("-" * 80)
    print(f"{'Scheme':<20} {'Key (bytes)':<15} {'Sig (bytes)':<15}
    {'Speed':<10} {'Quantum'}")
    print("-" * 80)
    for name, props in schemes.items():
        print(f"{name:<20} {props['key']:<15} {props['sig']:<15} "
              f"{props['speed']:<10} {props['quantum']}")

# Example usage
message = b"Transfer 100 XLM from Alice to Bob"

# Generate keypair
privkey, pubkey = generate_ed25519_keypair()
print(f"Ed25519 private key: {len(privkey.encode())} bytes")
print(f"Ed25519 public key: {len(pubkey.encode())} bytes")

# Sign (deterministic - same message, same signature every time!)
signature = ed25519_sign(message, privkey)
print(f"Signature: {len(signature)} bytes")

# Sign again - identical signature (deterministic)
signature2 = ed25519_sign(message, privkey)
print(f"Deterministic: {signature == signature2}")
```

```
# Verify
is_valid = ed25519_verify(message, signature, pubkey)
print(f"Signature valid: {is_valid}")

# Tampered message
tampered = b"Transfer 100 XLM from Alice to Eve"
is_valid = ed25519_verify(tampered, signature, pubkey)
print(f"Tampered message valid: {is_valid}")

# Comparison table
print("\n")
compare_signature_schemes()
```

3.1.6 Multi-Signatures and Threshold Signatures

Many blockchain use cases require multiple parties to authorize transactions: corporate wallets, decentralized governance, and security redundancy. Multi-signatures and threshold signatures provide this capability.

Multi-Signature Schemes

Naive approach: Transaction includes multiple signatures—Pro: Simple, works with any signature scheme—Con: Large transaction size (n signatures), poor privacy (reveals number of signers)

Aggregated signatures: Combine multiple signatures into one—Schnorr: MuSig, MuSig2 protocols—BLS signatures: Native aggregation support—Pro: Constant size, better privacy—Con: More complex, requires interactive protocols

Table 3-6. Multi-Signature Comparison

Approach	Size	Privacy	Complexity	Used By
Naive (multiple sigs)	Linear (n × 64 bytes)	Poor (reveals n)	Simple	Bitcoin (early), Ethereum
Schnorr MuSig	Constant (64 bytes)	Excellent	Medium	Bitcoin Taproot
BLS aggregation	Constant (48–96 bytes)	Excellent	Medium	Ethereum 2.0
Threshold ECDSA	Constant (64 bytes)	Excellent	High	Some DeFi protocols

Threshold Signatures

Threshold scheme (t-of-n): Any t out of n parties can create a valid signature, but t-1 or fewer cannot.

Key generation: Use distributed key generation (DKG)—No single party ever knows complete private key—Each party holds a "share" of the private key—t shares can reconstruct signing capability

Signing: Threshold signing protocol—t parties cooperate to create signature—Uses secure multi-party computation (MPC)—Result: standard signature (indistinguishable from single-party signature)

Example: 2-of-3 threshold—Three parties generate key shares via DKG—Each holds one share—Any two can cooperate to sign—One party alone cannot sign—Signature looks identical to a normal signature

Use cases: Corporate wallets (require multiple executives)—Decentralized custody (distribute trust)—Key backup (lose one share, still functional)—Governance (require majority approval)

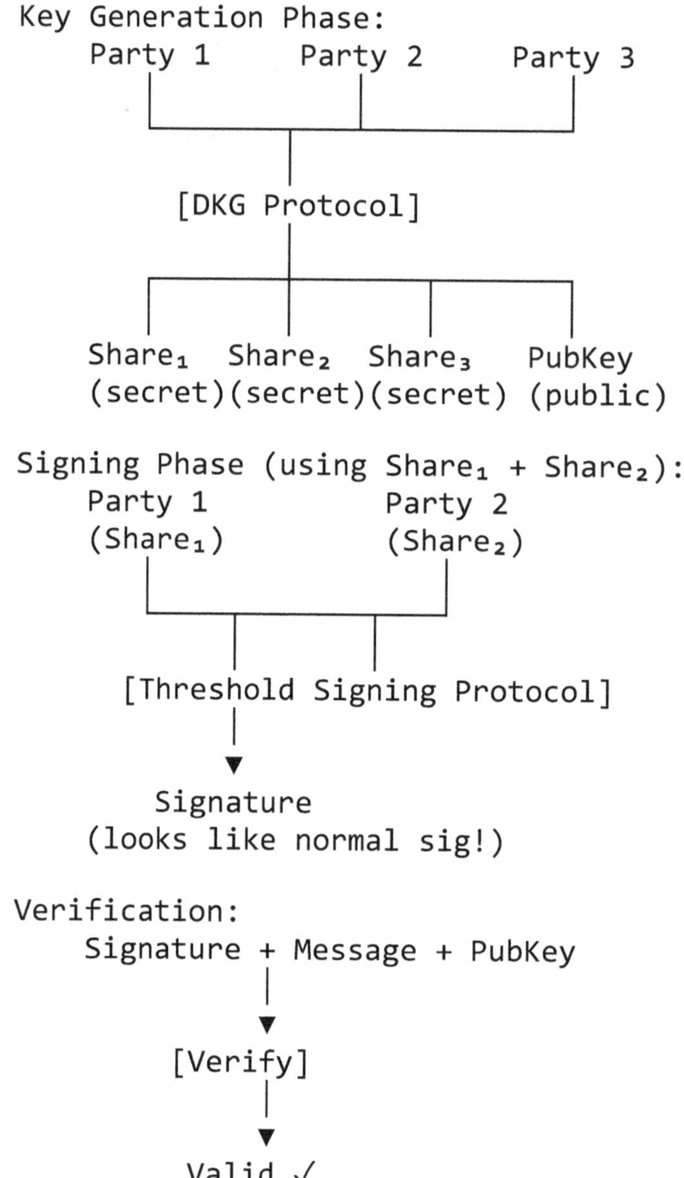

***Figure 3-2.** Threshold Signature (2-of-3) Workflow*

Implementation: Simple Multi-Sig Concept

```
from typing import List
import hashlib

def naive_multisig_verify(message: bytes, signatures: List[bytes],
                          public_keys: List[bytes], threshold: int) -> bool:
    """
    Naive multi-signature verification (NOT space-efficient).
    Requires threshold signatures to match message.
    """
    if len(signatures) < threshold:
        return False

    valid_count = 0
    for i, (sig, pubkey) in enumerate(zip(signatures, public_keys)):
        # In reality, use actual signature verification
        # This is simplified demonstration
        if verify_signature(message, sig, pubkey):
            valid_count += 1
            if valid_count >= threshold:
                return True

    return valid_count >= threshold

def verify_signature(message: bytes, sig: bytes, pubkey: bytes) -> bool:
    """Placeholder signature verification"""
    # In real implementation, use ECDSA/Schnorr/Ed25519 verify
    return True  # Simplified

def demonstrate_multisig_sizes():
    """Show size difference between naive and aggregated multi-sig"""
    print("Multi-Signature Size Comparison (3-of-5 scheme):")
    print("-" * 60)

    n_signers = 5
    threshold = 3
    sig_size = 64  # bytes per signature
    pubkey_size = 33  # bytes per compressed public key
```

```
    # Naive approach
    naive_sigs = threshold * sig_size
    naive_pubkeys = n_signers * pubkey_size
    naive_total = naive_sigs + naive_pubkeys

    print(f"Naive Multi-Sig:")
    print(f"  Signatures: {threshold} × {sig_size} = {naive_sigs} bytes")
    print(f"  Public keys: {n_signers} × {pubkey_size} = {naive_
    pubkeys} bytes")
    print(f"  Total: {naive_total} bytes")

    # Aggregated (Schnorr MuSig or threshold)
    agg_sig = sig_size
    agg_pubkey = pubkey_size
    agg_total = agg_sig + agg_pubkey

    print(f"\nAggregated (Schnorr/Threshold):")
    print(f"  Signature: {agg_sig} bytes")
    print(f"  Public key: {agg_pubkey} bytes")
    print(f"  Total: {agg_total} bytes")

    savings = ((naive_total - agg_total) / naive_total) * 100
    print(f"\nSpace savings: {savings:.1f}%")
    print(f"Privacy improvement: Threshold not revealed on-chain")

# Demonstrate
demonstrate_multisig_sizes()
```

3.1.7 Summary

Digital signatures are the cryptographic backbone of blockchain systems, enabling trustless authentication and authorization. This chapter explored the evolution from RSA's factoring-based security to modern elliptic curve schemes that achieve equivalent security with dramatically smaller keys.

RSA signatures pioneered public key cryptography but require large keys (2048+ bits) and produce large signatures (256+ bytes). While historically important, RSA's inefficiency makes it impractical for blockchain.

ECDSA dominates current blockchain systems (Bitcoin, Ethereum) due to small keys (32 bytes) and signatures (64 bytes). However, ECDSA has drawbacks: no signature aggregation, vulnerability to nonce reuse, and complex multi-signature schemes.

Schnorr signatures offer the same security as ECDSA with crucial advantages: provable security, signature aggregation, simpler multi-signatures, and elimination of malleability issues. Bitcoin's Taproot upgrade activated Schnorr support in 2021.

EdDSA (particularly Ed25519) provides deterministic signing that eliminates nonce reuse vulnerabilities, fast verification, and resistance to side-channel attacks. Monero, Stellar, and Cardano use EdDSA variants.

Multi-signatures and threshold schemes enable complex authorization policies while maintaining security and privacy. Aggregated signatures (Schnorr, BLS) provide constant-size multi-signatures that look identical to single signatures on-chain.

Key Takeaways:

- Never reuse nonces in ECDSA—use deterministic generation (RFC 6979) or EdDSA
- Schnorr aggregation reduces transaction size and improves privacy
- Threshold signatures enable trustless key management and governance
- Choose a signature scheme based on requirements: ECDSA for compatibility, Schnorr for aggregation, and EdDSA for simplicity
- All current schemes are vulnerable to quantum computers (need post-quantum alternatives)

Public key cryptography enables authentication without shared secrets through trapdoor functions—ECDSA dominates blockchain (Bitcoin, Ethereum) due to 32-byte keys vs. 256-byte RSA—Schnorr signatures provide provable security and signature aggregation (Bitcoin Taproot 2021)—EdDSA (Ed25519) offers deterministic signing, eliminating nonce reuse vulnerability—Multi-signature schemes enable m-of-n authorization without revealing the full key set—Threshold signatures split the private key across parties; reconstruction requires t-of-n cooperation—BLS signatures enable constant-size aggregation: 1000 signatures → 1 proof—All current signature schemes are vulnerable to quantum computers (need post-quantum alternatives)

The next chapter explores advanced cryptographic techniques—zero-knowledge proofs, ring signatures, and other privacy-preserving technologies that build on these signature foundations.

3.1.8 Exercises

Problem 1 (Cryptography): Why can't symmetric encryption provide non-repudiation? What property of public-key systems enables this?

Problem 2 (Implementation): Implement ECDSA signing and verification using a cryptography library. Test with malicious signature modification.

Problem 3 (Security): Explain how nonce reuse in ECDSA allows private key recovery. Provide the mathematical derivation.

Problem 4 (Comparison): Create a comparison matrix for ECDSA, Schnorr, and EdDSA across: security proof, aggregation, signature size, speed.

Problem 5 (Application): Design a 2-of-3 multisig wallet using Schnorr signatures. How does this differ from the naive approach?

Problem 6 (Advanced): Implement threshold signature key generation and signing for a 3-of-5 scheme. Test reconstruction.

Problem 7 (Analysis): Bitcoin Taproot uses Schnorr. What privacy and efficiency benefits result from signature aggregation?

Problem 8 (Research): Investigate post-quantum signature schemes (CRYSTALS-Dilithium, Falcon). Which is most blockchain-suitable?

Problem 9 (Cryptanalysis): Why does EdDSA use deterministic nonces while ECDSA uses random? What attacks does each prevent?

Problem 10 (Challenge): Implement BLS signature aggregation. Benchmark verification time: n individual signatures vs. 1 aggregated.

(Solutions in Appendix D)

3.1.9 Further Reading

On Public Key Cryptography: "A Method for Obtaining Digital Signatures and Public-Key Cryptosystems" by Rivest, Shamir, and Adleman (1978)—the original RSA paper—"New Directions in Cryptography" by Diffie and Hellman (1976)—the paper that started public key cryptography—Lecture notes from Dan Boneh's Cryptography course (Stanford) provide excellent modern treatment

On Elliptic Curve Cryptography: "Guide to Elliptic Curve Cryptography" by Hankerson, Menezes, and Vanstone—comprehensive technical reference—SEC 2 standard documents the secp256k1 curve used by Bitcoin—SafeCurves website (`https://safecurves.cr.yp.to`) analyzes security properties of various curves

On Schnorr Signatures: BIP 340 specifies Bitcoin's Schnorr implementation—"Simple Schnorr Multi-Signatures with Applications to Bitcoin" (MuSig paper) by Maxwell, Poelstra, Seurin, and Wuille—"Multi-Signatures in the Plain Public-Key Model and a General Forking Lemma" by Bellare and Neven

On EdDSA: "High-speed high-security signatures" by Bernstein et al.—the Ed25519 paper—RFC 8032 specifies EdDSA for IETF protocols—libsodium documentation provides practical implementation guidance

On Threshold Cryptography: "Practical Threshold Signatures" by Shoup—foundational RSA threshold work—"FROST: Flexible Round-Optimized Schnorr Threshold Signatures"—modern Schnorr threshold scheme—Research on threshold ECDSA by Gennaro and Goldfeder

Avoid: Tutorials that implement cryptography from scratch without security analysis—Claims of "quantum-resistant" signatures using classical schemes (they're all vulnerable)—Advice to use custom curves or parameters instead of standard, well-analyzed curves

CHAPTER 4

Zero-Knowledge Proofs

4.1 Advanced Cryptographic Primitives for Privacy and Scalability

Zero-knowledge proofs are one of the more counterintuitive ideas in applied cryptography: it is possible to convince someone that a statement is true without revealing anything about why it is true. This chapter works through how that holds up mathematically and where it matters in practice—from the zk-SNARKs powering Zcash's private transactions to the zk-STARKs behind StarkNet's rollup architecture, along with Bulletproofs, commitment schemes, ring signatures, and verifiable random functions. By the end, you will have covered:

- How zero-knowledge proofs enable proving statements without revealing information
- The difference between interactive and non-interactive proof systems
- zk-SNARKs and their application in Zcash and other privacy coins
- zk-STARKs and their advantages for blockchain scalability
- Bulletproofs for efficient range proofs
- Commitment schemes and their role in blockchain protocols
- Ring signatures and their use in Monero
- Verifiable random functions (VRFs) for on-chain randomness

N. Savant, *Blockchain Foundations*, https://doi.org/10.1007/979-8-8688-2891-1_4

4.1.1 Introduction: Proving Without Revealing

Here is a scenario that comes up more often than you might think. You walk into a bar. The bouncer needs to know you are over 21. You hand over your driver's license, and in that single gesture you have given away your full name, your home address, your exact date of birth, your license number, and—depending on the state—your height, weight, and whether you need corrective lenses. All the bouncer actually needed was a yes-or-no answer to one question: are you old enough?

Zero-knowledge proofs flip this dynamic on its head. They let you prove a fact about yourself—or about a piece of data or about a computation you performed—without handing over any of the underlying evidence. The bouncer learns "yes, this person is over 21" and nothing else. Not your birthday. Not your name. Nothing.

For blockchains, this idea unlocks capabilities that seemed contradictory before ZK proofs existed:

You can prove you have enough funds to cover a transaction without showing your wallet balance or any part of your transaction history. A rollup operator can compress ten thousand transactions into a single cryptographic proof that fits in a few hundred bytes—and anyone can verify that proof in milliseconds. A regulated institution can demonstrate compliance with anti-money-laundering rules ("none of these funds originated from sanctioned addresses") without exposing customer identities. A blockchain protocol can generate provably fair random numbers without any party being able to predict or manipulate the outcome.

If that sounds too good to be true, you are in good company—the original 1985 paper by Goldwasser, Micali, and Rackoff met considerable skepticism. But the mathematics holds up, and three decades later, ZK proofs have moved from theoretical curiosity to production infrastructure running billions of dollars in transactions.

What follows is a tour through the major ZK proof systems, starting with the core definitions and building up to the specific constructions that power Zcash's private transactions, StarkNet's rollup architecture, and Monero's confidential transaction system.

4.1.2 Zero-Knowledge Proofs: Definitions and Properties

At its core, a zero-knowledge proof is a conversation—or, in the non-interactive variants that blockchains actually use, a monologue—between two roles:

The prover, who knows something and wants to convince someone else of a specific fact about what they know. And the verifier, who starts out skeptical and needs to be persuaded.

For this interaction to qualify as a zero-knowledge proof, three conditions must all hold simultaneously—and the fact that all three can coexist is genuinely surprising:

First, completeness. If the prover is telling the truth and follows the protocol honestly, the verifier will always be convinced. A correct proof never fails to persuade. This sounds obvious, but it rules out protocols where even truthful provers sometimes get unlucky.

Second, soundness. If the prover is lying—if the statement they claim to be true is actually false—then no matter what tricks they try, the verifier will catch them. More precisely, the probability of a dishonest prover fooling the verifier can be made as small as you like by repeating the protocol enough times.

Third, and this is the remarkable one, zero-knowledge itself. The verifier ends the interaction knowing that the statement is true but learns absolutely nothing about why it is true. They could not reconstruct the prover's secret, could not narrow down the space of possible secrets, and could not distinguish this interaction from one that was entirely faked. Formally, anything the verifier sees during the proof could have been generated by a simulator that does not know the secret at all.

Table 4-1. *Zero-Knowledge Proof Properties*

Property	Definition	Intuition	Mathematical Formulation
Completeness	True statements accepted	Honest prover succeeds	Pr[V accepts I statement true, P honest] $\geq$ 1 - ε
Soundness	False statements rejected	Cheating fails	Pr[V accepts I statement false] $\leq \varepsilon$
Zero-Knowledge	No information leaked	Only truth is revealed	∃ Simulator that generates identical distributions

The Classic Example: Graph 3-Coloring

A worked example makes these abstract properties concrete. The classic illustration—the one that appears in nearly every graduate cryptography course—involves coloring a graph.

Suppose you have a graph: a collection of nodes connected by edges. A valid 3-coloring assigns one of three colors (say, red, green, blue) to each node such that no two nodes sharing an edge have the same color. Finding such a coloring is computationally hard in general (it is NP-complete). But if you happen to know a valid coloring, you can prove that fact to someone without revealing a single color assignment. Here is how.

The protocol works in rounds. Each round goes like this:

1. **Prover Commits**: Randomly permute colors, commit to colored graph (e.g., hash each node's color)
2. **Verifier Challenges**: Choose a random edge
3. **Prover Reveals**: Open commitments for the two nodes of the chosen edge
4. **Verifier Checks**: Verify colors are different

Why It Works:

Why does this work? If the prover genuinely knows a valid coloring, then in every round—no matter which edge the verifier picks—the two revealed nodes will have different colors. The prover passes every time. That is completeness. Now suppose the prover is bluffing and no valid coloring exists. Then somewhere in the graph, two adjacent nodes must share a color. If the verifier happens to pick that edge, the prover is caught. The probability of picking that particular edge in a single round might be small (1 divided by the number of edges), but after hundreds of rounds, the probability of never catching a cheater becomes vanishingly tiny. That is soundness.

And zero-knowledge? Each round, the prover randomly permutes the colors before committing. So the verifier sees two colors per round—say, "red and blue"—but those labels are meaningless because the permutation was random. Tomorrow the same edge might reveal "green and red." The verifier accumulates no useful information about the actual coloring. A simulator who does not know the coloring could produce transcripts that look statistically identical.

```
Original Coloring (Prover's Secret):

    (R)-1———————2-(G)
        |       |
        |       |
        3———————4
       (B)     (R)

Round 1:
    Prover: Randomly permute colors (R→B, G→R, B→G)
    Commits: H(B), H(R), H(G), H(B)

    Verifier: "Show me edge 1-2"
    Prover: Opens H(B)=Blue, H(R)=Red
    Verifier: ✓ Different colors

    Knowledge gained: Edge 1-2 has different colors
    Zero-knowledge: Random permutation reveals nothing about actual
coloring

Round 2:
    Prover: New random permutation (R→G, G→B, B→R)
    Commits: H(G), H(B), H(R), H(G)

    Verifier: "Show me edge 3-4"
    Prover: Opens H(R)=Red, H(G)=Green
    Verifier: ✓ Different colors

After n rounds: Verifier convinced (cheating probability = (1 - 1/|e
dges|)^n)
                Verifier learned: Nothing about actual colors!
```

Figure 4-1. *Graph 3-Coloring Zero-Knowledge Proof*

Interactive vs. Non-Interactive Proofs

The graph-coloring protocol is interactive—prover and verifier go back and forth for many rounds. That is fine in a live conversation but terrible for a blockchain, where you need to post a proof once and let thousands of nodes verify it independently, possibly years later. Nobody is sitting around to play challenge-response.

Non-interactive zero-knowledge proofs (NIZKs) solve this by having the prover generate the challenges themselves—but in a way that cannot be manipulated. The standard technique, called the Fiat-Shamir heuristic, replaces the verifier's random challenges with the output of a hash function applied to the prover's own messages. Since hash functions are deterministic and unpredictable, this produces challenges the prover cannot game. The result is a single proof string that anyone can verify at any time without interacting with the prover. Every practical ZK system used in blockchain—SNARKs, STARKs, Bulletproofs—is non-interactive.

Table 4-2. *Interactive vs. Non-Interactive Proofs*

Property	Interactive	Non-Interactive (NIZK)
Rounds	Multiple (e.g., 20-100)	Single proof generation
Verifier role	Active (generates challenges)	Passive (checks proof)
Blockchain suitable	No (can't interact with history)	Yes
Setup	None or public parameters	Often requires trusted setup
Proof size	Varies	Fixed (often succinct)
Examples	Graph 3-coloring, Sigma protocols	zk-SNARKs, zk-STARKs

4.1.3 zk-SNARKs: Succinct Non-Interactive Arguments

The acronym unpacks as "Zero-Knowledge Succinct Non-Interactive Argument of Knowledge," and every word earns its place. These proofs are the workhorse behind Zcash's private transactions, the early ZK rollups on Ethereum, and a growing number of identity and compliance protocols.

Key Properties

Succinct means the proof is tiny—a few hundred bytes regardless of whether the underlying computation involved ten operations or ten million. This is what makes SNARKs practical for blockchains where every byte of on-chain data costs money.

Non-interactive means the prover generates one proof and walks away. The verifier—or ten thousand verifiers—can check it independently.

Argument (as opposed to "proof" in the mathematical sense) signals that soundness holds against computationally bounded adversaries, not against adversaries with unlimited power. In practice this is fine—real attackers do not have infinite computing resources.

Of Knowledge adds the requirement that the prover must actually possess the secret witness, not merely know that one exists somewhere. This distinction matters: in a blockchain context, you want to prove "I know the private key for this address," not just "someone, somewhere, has a private key for this address."

How zk-SNARKs Work (Simplified)

Setup phase (one-time):

1. Define computation as an arithmetic circuit
2. Generate a common reference string (CRS) using a trusted setup ceremony
3. CRS has two parts: proving key and verification key

Proving:

1. Prover has private input (witness) and public input
2. Evaluates arithmetic circuit on inputs
3. Generates proof using a proving key
4. Proof: ~200 bytes

Verification:

1. Verifier has public input and proof
2. Checks proof using verification key
3. Verification: O(1) time, very fast (~few milliseconds)

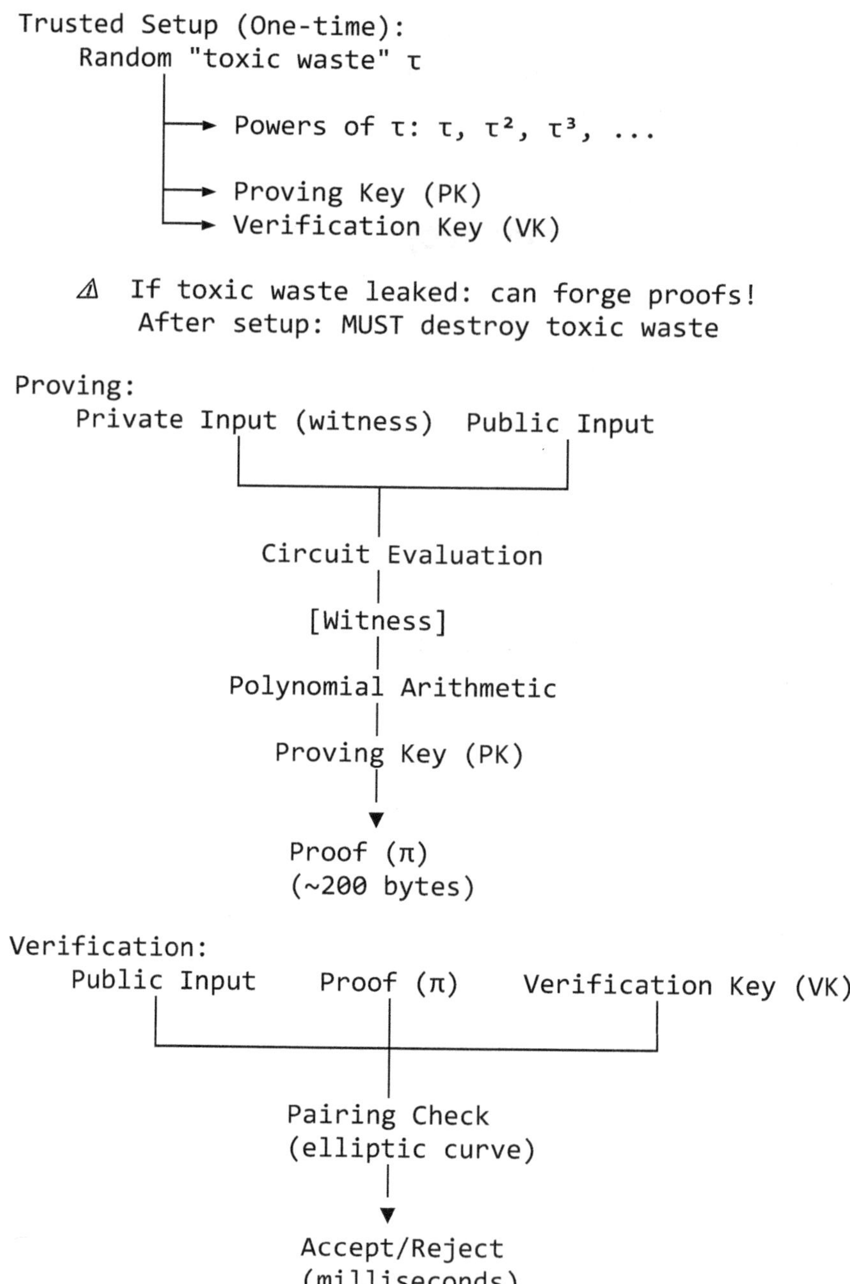

***Figure 4-2.** zk-SNARK Workflow*

The Trusted Setup Problem

There is a catch, and it is a significant one. Before anyone can generate or verify a SNARK proof, someone must run a one-time setup ceremony that produces a pair of keys: one for proving, one for verifying. The setup process involves generating random mathematical parameters—the so-called "toxic waste"—that must be destroyed immediately after the ceremony.

If any participant in the setup retains the toxic waste, they gain the ability to forge proofs. In a privacy coin like Zcash, this means minting unlimited counterfeit coins. In a ZK rollup, it means stealing every asset locked in the rollup contract. The consequences are catastrophic and—because the forged proofs are indistinguishable from legitimate ones—undetectable.

The mitigation is multi-party computation (MPC). Dozens or hundreds of independent participants each contribute their own randomness to the ceremony. The final toxic waste is a combination of all their contributions. The critical insight: as long as even one participant honestly destroys their share, the combined toxic waste is unrecoverable. Zcash's "Powers of Tau" ceremony involved over a thousand participants across six continents. You would have to believe that every single one of them conspired to retain their share—a paranoid assumption that most people find unreasonable.

More recent SNARK constructions—PLONK, Marlin, and their descendants—use a "universal" setup that works for any computation, not just one specific circuit. This means a single ceremony covers every possible application, reducing the trust burden further.

Table 4-3. *zk-SNARK Variants*

Variant	Setup	Proof Size	Verify Time	Prover Time	Used By
Groth16	Trusted, per-circuit	~200 bytes	~1ms	Medium	Zcash, Tornado Cash
PLONK	Universal trusted	~400 bytes	~5ms	Medium	Aztec, Polygon zkEVM
Marlin	Universal trusted	~300 bytes	~3ms	Medium	Aleo
Sonic	Universal trusted	~300 bytes	~10ms	Slow	Research

Zcash: Privacy Through zk-SNARKs

Zcash uses zk-SNARKs to enable private transactions:

Shielded transaction: Sender proves:

1. "I own coins being spent" (without revealing which coins)
2. "I haven't spent these coins before" (without revealing nullifiers)
3. "Input value = output value" (without revealing amounts)
4. "I know private keys for inputs" (without revealing keys)

All this in a ~200-byte proof!

Implementation:

```
# Conceptual zk-SNARK usage (simplified)
# Real implementation uses libsnark, bellman, or similar

class ZcashTransaction:
    def __init__(self):
        self.nullifiers = []  # Prevent double-spending
        self.commitments = []  # New note commitments
        self.proof = None     # zk-SNARK proof

    def create_shielded_transaction(self, private_key, notes_to_spend,
                                    recipients, amounts):
        """
        Create shielded transaction with zk-SNARK proof.

        Public inputs: nullifiers, commitments
        Private inputs (witness): private keys, notes, amounts
        """

        # Compute nullifiers (prevents double-spend)
        for note in notes_to_spend:
            nullifier = self.compute_nullifier(note, private_key)
            self.nullifiers.append(nullifier)

        # Create new note commitments
        for recipient, amount in zip(recipients, amounts):
            commitment = self.compute_commitment(recipient, amount)
            self.commitments.append(commitment)
```

```
        # Generate zk-SNARK proof
        # Proves: I know private key, notes, amounts such that:
        # - Nullifiers correctly computed
        # - Commitments correctly computed
        # - Sum(inputs) = Sum(outputs)
        # - All notes exist in commitment tree

        witness = {
            'private_key': private_key,
            'notes': notes_to_spend,
            'amounts': amounts,
            'merkle_paths': self.get_merkle_paths(notes_to_spend)
        }

        public_inputs = {
            'nullifiers': self.nullifiers,
            'commitments': self.commitments,
            'merkle_root': self.get_merkle_root()
        }

        self.proof = self.generate_snark_proof(witness, public_inputs)

        return self

    def verify(self):
        """Verify zk-SNARK proof"""
        public_inputs = {
            'nullifiers': self.nullifiers,
            'commitments': self.commitments,
            'merkle_root': self.get_merkle_root()
        }

        return verify_snark_proof(self.proof, public_inputs)

    def compute_nullifier(self, note, private_key):
        """Compute nullifier = Hash(note, private_key)"""
        import hashlib
        data = note.encode() + private_key.encode()
        return hashlib.sha256(data).hexdigest()
```

```
    def compute_commitment(self, recipient, amount):
        """Compute commitment = Hash(recipient, amount, randomness)"""
        import hashlib
        import secrets
        randomness = secrets.token_bytes(32)
        data = recipient.encode() + str(amount).encode() + randomness
        return hashlib.sha256(data).hexdigest()

    def generate_snark_proof(self, witness, public_inputs):
        """Generate zk-SNARK proof (placeholder)"""
        # In reality: compile circuit, evaluate, generate proof
        # Using libraries like libsnark, bellman, circom
        return b"snark_proof_bytes"

    def get_merkle_paths(self, notes):
        """Get Merkle authentication paths for notes"""
        return []  # Placeholder

    def get_merkle_root(self):
        """Get current Merkle root of all commitments"""
        return "merkle_root"  # Placeholder

def verify_snark_proof(proof, public_inputs):
    """Verify zk-SNARK proof"""
    # In reality: use verification key, check pairing equation
    return True  # Placeholder

# Example usage
tx = ZcashTransaction()
tx.create_shielded_transaction(
    private_key="secret_key",
    notes_to_spend=["note1", "note2"],
    recipients=["recipient1", "recipient2"],
    amounts=[10, 5]
)
```

```
print(f"Nullifiers: {tx.nullifiers}")
print(f"Commitments: {tx.commitments}")
print(f"Proof size: {len(tx.proof)} bytes")
print(f"Valid: {tx.verify()}")
```

4.1.4 zk-STARKs: Transparent and Scalable Proofs

Where SNARKs require you to trust a setup ceremony, STARKs—Scalable Transparent Arguments of Knowledge—sidestep the issue entirely. Developed primarily by Eli Ben-Sasson and collaborators at the Technion and later at StarkWare, STARKs derive their security from collision-resistant hash functions rather than elliptic curve pairings.

Key Advantages Over SNARKs

The transparency is the headline feature. Every parameter in a STARK proof is derived from public randomness. No secret ceremony, no toxic waste, no trust assumptions beyond the security of the hash function itself.

That hash-function foundation also buys quantum resistance. Since STARKs do not rely on the discrete logarithm problem or elliptic curve pairings, they remain secure against Shor's algorithm. This is a property that no deployed SNARK system currently offers.

All proof parameters are publicly verifiable—no hidden setup, no privileged participants.

The prover's computation scales quasi-linearly with the size of the computation being proven, which means STARKs handle very large computations more gracefully than some SNARK variants.

Trade-Offs

The cost of all these advantages shows up in proof size. A Groth16 SNARK proof is roughly 200 bytes. A STARK proof for comparable computation runs tens to hundreds of kilobytes—anywhere from 100 to 1,000 times larger. For on-chain verification where every byte has a gas cost, this is a meaningful penalty.

Verification is also slower, though still fast in absolute terms—milliseconds to low single-digit seconds rather than the near-instant verification of a SNARK.

Table 4-4. *zk-SNARKs vs. zk-STARKs Comparison*

Property	zk-SNARKs (Groth16)	zk-STARKs
Proof size	~200 bytes	~50-200 KB
Verification time	~1-5 ms	~10-50 ms
Prover time	Medium	Fast (for large computations)
Trusted setup	Required	None
Post-quantum	No (uses pairings)	Yes (uses hashes)
Transparency	Requires trust	Fully transparent
Use case	Privacy (small proofs)	Scalability (large computations)

StarkWare and Ethereum Layer 2s

StarkWare, the company founded by the STARK inventors, has built two major products on this technology:

StarkEx is a transaction-processing engine that powers dYdX (perpetual futures), Immutable X (NFT trading), and Sorare (fantasy sports). It batches thousands of off-chain transactions, generates a STARK proof that all of them were executed correctly, and posts that proof to Ethereum. The gas savings can reach 100 to 1,000 times compared to executing each transaction on L1.

StarkNet is a general-purpose Layer 2 network where developers deploy smart contracts (written in Cairo, a STARK-native language). Execution happens off-chain; proofs of correct execution are posted to Ethereum. It is, in effect, an attempt to build a full programmable blockchain whose security ultimately rests on Ethereum's consensus plus the mathematical soundness of STARK proofs.

How It Works:

1. Users submit transactions to L2
2. Sequencer executes transactions, updates state
3. Prover generates STARK proof: "These transactions were executed correctly"
4. Proof posted to Ethereum L1
5. Anyone can verify proof, ensuring validity

```
Layer 2 (Off-chain):
    User₁ ──► Tx₁ ┐
    User₂ ──► Tx₂ ├──► Sequencer ──► Execute ──► New State
    User₃ ──► Tx₃ │                              (S₁ → S₂)
    User₄ ──► Tx₄ ┘                                  │
                                                     │
    Thousands of transactions                        ▼
                                                 [Prover]
                                                     │
                                           STARK Proof (50 KB)
                                           "S₁ → S₂ correct"
                                                     │
                                                     ▼
Layer 1 (Ethereum):
    ┌──────────────────────────────────────────────┐
    │ Verifier Contract                            │
    │ - Receives proof                             │
    │ - Verifies: proof valid?                     │
    │ - Updates state root: S₁ → S₂                │
    │ - Gas cost: ~500k (vs 50M for raw txs)       │
    └──────────────────────────────────────────────┘

Scaling: 1000× throughput, 1/100 cost
Security: Inherit Ethereum L1 security
```

Figure 4-3. *zk-Rollup with STARKs*

4.1.5 Bulletproofs: Efficient Range Proofs

Bulletproofs occupy a different niche in the ZK landscape. They are not trying to prove arbitrary computations—that is what SNARKs and STARKs do. Instead, Bulletproofs are optimized for a specific, high-value task: proving that a hidden number falls within a specified range. No trusted setup required.

Why Range Proofs Matter

When transaction amounts are hidden behind commitments (as in Monero's confidential transactions), you face a subtle attack. Someone could commit to a negative amount—say, -10 coins—and combine it with a positive output to create coins from thin air. Or they could commit to a value so large it wraps around the integer range, achieving the same effect. Range proofs close this loophole by demonstrating, without revealing the amount, that every committed value is a sensible non-negative number within the expected range.

Without this check, any confidential transaction system is vulnerable to silent inflation—the worst kind of bug because nobody can detect it until the damage is irreversible.

Bulletproof Properties

Bulletproofs need no ceremony, no trusted third party, and no setup whatsoever. Their security rests on standard cryptographic assumptions (the discrete logarithm problem in the same elliptic curve groups used by signatures).

The proof size grows logarithmically with the range being proven. For a 64-bit range (the standard for transaction amounts), a single Bulletproof is roughly 670 bytes. Earlier range proof constructions—the Borromean ring signatures that Monero previously used—required around 5 kilobytes per output. That is an 80% reduction.

Multiple range proofs can be aggregated and verified together, amortizing the cost further when a transaction has several outputs.

Table 4-5. *Range Proof Size Comparison*

Method	Proof Size (64-Bit Range)	Setup Required
Naive (per-bit commitment)	~5 KB	No
Borromean ring signatures	~5 KB	No
Bulletproofs	~670 bytes	No
zk-SNARK (Groth16)	~200 bytes	Yes (trusted)

Monero's Use of Bulletproofs

Monero switched to Bulletproofs in October 2018, and the impact was dramatic:

Average transaction size dropped from roughly 13 kilobytes to under 2 kilobytes. Blockchain growth rate slowed proportionally. Transaction fees fell. Users noticed nothing—from their perspective, transactions simply got cheaper and faster. Under the hood, every output now carries a Bulletproof instead of the older, bulkier range proof, and the chain is better for it.

Implementation Concept

```python
import hashlib
import secrets

class Bulletproof:
    """
    Simplified Bulletproof for range proofs.
    Real implementation requires elliptic curve arithmetic.
    """

    def __init__(self):
        self.commitment = None
        self.proof = None

    def create_commitment(self, value: int, randomness: bytes = None):
        """
        Create Pedersen commitment: C = vG + rH
        where G, H are elliptic curve points
        """
        if randomness is None:
            randomness = secrets.token_bytes(32)

        # Simplified: hash-based commitment
        self.commitment = hashlib.sha256(
            str(value).encode() + randomness
        ).digest()

        return self.commitment, randomness

    def prove_range(self, value: int, randomness: bytes,
                    min_value: int = 0, max_value: int = 2**64):
        """
        Generate Bulletproof that value ∈ [min_value, max_value].

        Real implementation:
        - Converts value to binary
        - Creates commitments for each bit
        - Uses inner product argument for efficiency
```

```
        - Results in O(log n) proof size
        """
        if not (min_value <= value < max_value):
            raise ValueError("Value not in range!")

        # Generate proof (simplified)
        # Real Bulletproof uses:
        # 1. Binary decomposition
        # 2. Pedersen commitments
        # 3. Inner product argument
        # 4. Fiat-Shamir for non-interactivity

        proof_data = {
            'A': secrets.token_bytes(32),  # Commitment to bits
            'S': secrets.token_bytes(32),  # Blinding factors
            't1': secrets.token_bytes(32), # Polynomial commitments
            't2': secrets.token_bytes(32),
            'taux': secrets.token_bytes(32),
            'mu': secrets.token_bytes(32),
            'inner_product_proof': secrets.token_bytes(128)
        }

        self.proof = proof_data
        return proof_data

    def verify_range(self, commitment: bytes, proof: dict,
                     min_value: int = 0, max_value: int = 2**64) -> bool:
        """
        Verify Bulletproof range proof.

        Checks:
        - Commitment matches proof
        - Inner product argument valid
        - Value proven to be in range
        """
        # Real verification involves:
        # 1. Reconstruct challenge using Fiat-Shamir
        # 2. Verify Pedersen commitment relationships
```

```
    # 3. Verify inner product proof
    # 4. Check all equations hold

    # Simplified verification
    required_keys = ['A', 'S', 't1', 't2', 'taux', 'mu',
                    'inner_product_proof']

    return all(key in proof for key in required_keys)

def prove_batch_range(self, values: list, randomnesses: list):
"""
In real Bulletproofs, ALL values are aggregated into ONE single proof.
Proof size grows as O(log(n * bits)) - not O(n).

This demo shows the concept only. Use dalek-cryptography's
bulletproofs library for real aggregation.
"""
# Validate all values are in range before proving
for i, (value, randomness) in enumerate(zip(values, randomnesses)):
    if not (0 <= value < 2**64):
        raise ValueError(f"Value at index {i} is out of range!")

# In real Bulletproofs:
# - All values are committed together: C1, C2, ..., Cn
# - A SINGLE inner product argument covers all of them
# - Final proof size = O(log(n * 64)) - same structure as single proof
# - Verification is also done in one pass

# Simulating what the aggregated proof WOULD contain:
aggregated_proof = {
    'A':  secrets.token_bytes(32),    # Single commitment to all bits
    'S':  secrets.token_bytes(32),    # Single blinding commitment
    't1': secrets.token_bytes(32),    # Polynomial commitment (shared)
    't2': secrets.token_bytes(32),    # Polynomial commitment (shared)
    'taux': secrets.token_bytes(32),
    'mu':   secrets.token_bytes(32),
    'inner_product_proof': secrets.token_bytes(128),  # Covers
    ALL values
```

```
        'n_values': len(values)           # Metadata only
    }

    # KEY POINT: this is ONE dict (one proof) for ALL values
    # NOT a list of n proofs
    return aggregated_proof
# Example usage
bp = Bulletproof()

# Commit to value
value = 1000
commitment, randomness = bp.create_commitment(value)
print(f"Commitment: {commitment.hex()[:32]}...")

# Prove value is in range [0, 2^64)
proof = bp.prove_range(value, randomness)
print(f"Proof size (simplified): {sum(len(v) for v in proof.
values())} bytes")

# Verify
is_valid = bp.verify_range(commitment, proof)
print(f"Proof valid: {is_valid}")

# Batch example
values = [100, 500, 1000, 2000, 5000]
 randomnesses = [secrets.token_bytes(32) for _ in values]
 batch_proofs = bp.prove_batch_range(values, randomnesses)
 print(f"\nBatch proving {len(values)} values")
 print(f"Average proof size: {sum(len(str(p).encode()) for p in batch_
 proofs) / len(values):.0f} bytes")
```

4.1.6 Commitment Schemes

Before diving deeper into the machinery of ZK systems, it is worth pausing on commitment schemes because they are the quiet workhorse underneath almost everything in this chapter. The idea is deceptively simple: you want to lock in a choice now and reveal it later, in a way that prevents you from changing your mind after the fact.

Properties

A good commitment scheme gives you two guarantees. Hiding: looking at the commitment tells you nothing about what was committed. It is like a sealed envelope—you can hold it, weigh it, and shake it, but you cannot read the contents.

And binding: once the envelope is sealed, you cannot swap the contents for something different. When you open it, the value that comes out is the value that went in. No switcheroos.

Two Phases:

1. **Commit**: C = Commit (value, randomness)
2. **Open**: Reveal (value, randomness), verify C = Commit (value, randomness)

Table 4-6. Commitment Scheme Types

Scheme	Construction	Hiding	Binding	Homomorphic	Use Case
Hash-based	C = H(value ll r)	✓	Computational	No	Simple commits
Pedersen	C = vG + rH	✓	Computational	Yes	Confidential transactions
Polynomial	C = Commit(poly)	✓	Varies	No	zk-SNARKs/STARKs
Merkle root	C = MerkleRoot(values)	Partial	✓	No	State commitment

Pedersen Commitments

Pedersen commitments are the construction of choice for blockchain confidential transactions because they have a property that plain hash-based commitments lack: they are homomorphic.

$$C = vG + rH$$

Where: v = value to commit—r = random blinding factor—G, H = elliptic curve generators (with unknown discrete log relationship)

Homomorphic property: $C_1 = v_1G + r_1H$—$C_2 = v_2G + r_2H$—$C_1 + C_2 = (v_1 + v_2)G + (r_1 + r_2)H$

This is the key insight for confidential transactions. A validator can add up all the input commitments and all the output commitments and check that they balance—without ever learning what any individual amount is. The math handles the bookkeeping; the privacy handles itself.

```
Alice's UTXO: 10 BTC (committed)
    C_in = 10G + r₁H

Alice sends: 7 BTC to Bob, 3 BTC change
    C_out1 = 7G + r₂H (Bob)
    C_out2 = 3G + r₃H (Alice change)

Verification:
    C_in = C_out1 + C_out2
    10G + r₁H = (7G + r₂H) + (3G + r₃H)
    10G + r₁H = 10G + (r₂ + r₃)H

    Valid if: r₁ = r₂ + r₃ (Alice proves this)

Verifier sees:
    - Three commitments (random-looking points)
    - Proof that commitments balance
    - NO information about 10, 7, or 3!

Additional: Range proofs ensure values are positive
```

***Figure 4-4.** Confidential Transaction with Commitments*

Implementation

```python
import hashlib
import secrets

def hash_commitment(value: bytes, randomness: bytes = None) -> tuple:
    """Simple hash-based commitment scheme"""
    if randomness is None:
        randomness = secrets.token_bytes(32)

    commitment = hashlib.sha256(value + randomness).digest()
    return commitment, randomness
```

```
def verify_hash_commitment(value: bytes, randomness: bytes,
                           commitment: bytes) -> bool:
    """Verify hash commitment"""
    computed = hashlib.sha256(value + randomness).digest()
    return computed == commitment

# Example: Coin flip commitment
print("=== Commitment-Based Coin Flip ===")

# Alice commits to her choice
alice_choice = b"heads"
commitment, randomness = hash_commitment(alice_choice)
print(f"Alice commits: {commitment.hex()[:32]}...")

# Bob makes his choice (seeing only commitment)
bob_choice = b"tails"
print(f"Bob chooses: {bob_choice.decode()}")

# Alice reveals
print(f"Alice reveals: {alice_choice.decode()}")
is_valid = verify_hash_commitment(alice_choice, randomness, commitment)
print(f"Commitment valid: {is_valid}")

# Alice can't cheat (binding property)
fake_choice = b"tails"
can_cheat = verify_hash_commitment(fake_choice, randomness, commitment)
print(f"Can Alice cheat? {can_cheat}")
```

4.1.7 Ring Signatures: Signer Ambiguity

Ring signatures solve a different privacy problem: not "how much" but "who." When you spend coins on a transparent blockchain like Bitcoin, the transaction explicitly identifies which previous output you are consuming. Anyone watching the chain can trace the flow of funds. Ring signatures break this link.

Properties

The signer picks a group of public keys—the "ring"—that includes their own key plus several decoys drawn from the blockchain. They produce a signature that proves, cryptographically, that someone in the ring authorized the transaction. But the signature gives no indication of which member it was.

Anyone outside the ring cannot produce a valid signature, so unforgeability is maintained.

Unlike multisig or threshold schemes, ring signatures require no coordination among ring members. The other members do not even know they have been included. The signer unilaterally constructs the ring from public data.

How Ring Signatures Work

The mathematical core is an OR-proof: the signer demonstrates knowledge of one private key out of n candidates, without revealing which one. This is related to, but distinct from, the zero-knowledge proofs discussed earlier—a ring signature is specifically designed for authentication rather than general computation.

Construction (simplified):

1. Signer has keypair (d, Q) where Q = dG
2. Signer chooses "ring" of n-1 other public keys Q_1, Q_2, ..., Q_{n-1}
3. Creates proof: "I know private key for one of {Q, Q_1, Q_2, ..., Q_{n-1}}"
4. Anyone can verify signature against the ring

Ring of Public Keys:

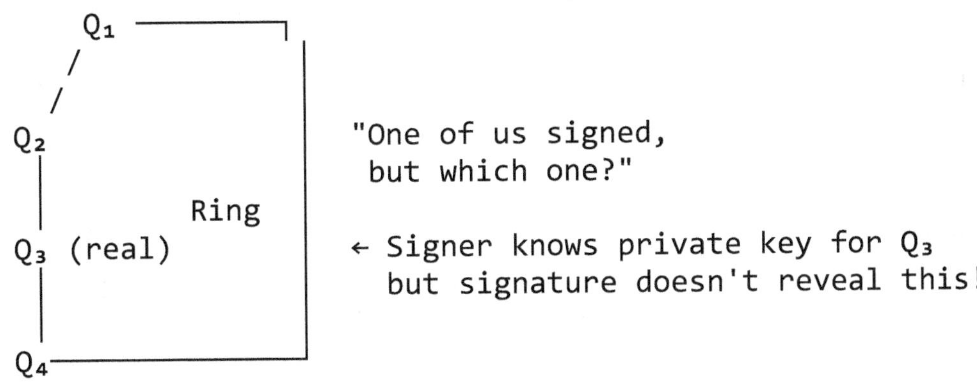

Signature: σ = RingSign(message, d_3, {Q_1, Q_2, Q_3, Q_4})

Verification: RingVerify(message, σ, {Q_1, Q_2, Q_3, Q_4}) = True

Verifier learns: Signature from someone in ring
Verifier doesn't learn: Which key signed

Figure 4-5. *Ring Signature Concept*

Monero's Use of Ring Signatures

Monero builds its transaction privacy on ring signatures as the outermost layer:

Every time you spend an output, your wallet automatically constructs a ring containing your real output plus 15 decoy outputs pulled from the blockchain's recent history. The ring signature proves you own one of the 16 outputs but not which one. An observer—even one with complete access to the blockchain—sees 16 equally plausible candidates and cannot determine the real spender.

Layered on top of this are stealth addresses (so the recipient's public address never appears on-chain) and the Pedersen commitments with Bulletproof range proofs discussed above (so the amount is hidden). The combination covers all three dimensions of a transaction: who sent it, who received it, and how much was transferred.

Table 4-7. Privacy Comparison

Blockchain	Amount Privacy	Sender Privacy	Recipient Privacy	Method
Bitcoin	No	No	No	Transparent
Ethereum	No	No	No	Transparent
Zcash (transparent)	No	No	No	Transparent
Zcash (shielded)	Yes	Yes	Yes	zk-SNARKs
Monero	Yes	Yes (ring sigs)	Yes (stealth addr)	RingCT + Bulletproofs

Implementation Concept

```
import hashlib
import secrets

class RingSignature:
    """
    Simplified ring signature (Borromean ring signature concept).
    Real implementation requires elliptic curve operations.
    """

    def __init__(self):
        self.signature = None

    def sign(self, message: bytes, private_key: int, public_keys: list,
        key_index: int):
    """
    Simplified ring signature - shows correct structure.

    In a real ring signature (e.g. Monero's MLSAG):
    - Responses for decoy members are randomly chosen
    - The real signer's response is computed using their actual private key
      so the ring "closes" mathematically
    - private_key and key_index are essential to this closing step

    Here we simulate the structure clearly so the difference is visible.
    """
```

```
n = len(public_keys)

# Step 1: generate random responses for ALL ring members (including
real signer)
# In reality, decoy responses are random, but the real signer's
response
# is computed as: r[key_index] = k - private_key * c[key_index] mod n
# where k is a random nonce and c is the challenge for that position.
responses = [secrets.token_bytes(32) for _ in range(n)]

# Step 2: compute challenges for each position
# In reality, challenges chain together: c[i+1] = H(message, r[i]*G +
c[i]*Q[i])
# The real signer's position is where this chain is "closed" using
private_key.
message_hash = hashlib.sha256(message).digest()
challenges = []
for i in range(n):
    # Simulated chaining: each challenge depends on message + position
    + response
    # Real version: c[i] = H(message || R_i) where R_i involves elliptic
    curve ops
    c_input = message_hash + i.to_bytes(4, 'big') + responses[i]
    challenges.append(hashlib.sha256(c_input).digest())

# Step 3: mark which position is the real signer (for
illustration only)
# In a real ring signature this is NOT stored – it would break privacy!
# We include it here only so the reader can see how key_index is used.
# Real ring signatures are indistinguishable across all positions.

# Simulate real signer's response being derived from private_key
# Real: r[key_index] = (k - private_key * c[key_index]) % curve_order
# Here: we just show it is derived differently from the decoy responses
real_challenge_int = int.from_bytes(challenges[key_index], 'big')
```

```
    simulated_real_response = (private_key ^ real_challenge_int).to_
    bytes(32, 'big')
    responses[key_index] = simulated_real_response

    ring_data = {
        'public_keys': [pk.hex() if isinstance(pk, bytes) else str(pk)
                       for pk in public_keys],
        'c': challenges,
        'r': responses,
        'message_hash': hashlib.sha256(message).hexdigest()
        # NOTE: key_index is NOT stored - in real ring sigs, signer
        position is hidden
    }

    self.signature = ring_data
    return ring_data

def verify(self, message: bytes, signature: dict) -> bool:
    """
    Verify ring signature.

    Checks that signature was created by someone in the ring,
    without revealing who.
    """
    # Extract components
    public_keys = signature['public_keys']
    challenges = signature['c']
    responses = signature['r']
    message_hash = signature['message_hash']

    # Verify message hash matches
    if message_hash != hashlib.sha256(message).hexdigest():
        return False

    # Real verification:
    # 1. Reconstruct ring using c_i, r_i values
    # 2. Check ring closes properly
    # 3. Verify challenge derivation
```

```
        # Simplified: check basic structure
        return (len(public_keys) > 1 and
                len(challenges) == len(public_keys) and
                len(responses) == len(public_keys))

    def get_ring_size(self, signature: dict) -> int:
        """Get size of ring (anonymity set)"""
        return len(signature['public_keys'])

# Example usage
print("=== Ring Signature Example ===")

# Create ring of public keys
ring_size = 5
public_keys = [secrets.token_bytes(32) for _ in range(ring_size)]
print(f"Ring size: {ring_size}")

# Alice has private key for key #2
alice_private_key = secrets.randbelow(2**256)
alice_index = 2

# Alice signs message
message = b"Transfer 1 XMR to Bob"
ring_sig = RingSignature()
signature = ring_sig.sign(message, alice_private_key, public_keys,
alice_index)

print(f"Signature created")
print(f"Anonymity set: {ring_sig.get_ring_size(signature)} possible
signers")

# Anyone can verify
is_valid = ring_sig.verify(message, signature)
print(f"Signature valid: {is_valid}")

# But nobody knows which key signed!
print(f"\nPrivacy: Observers know signature came from one of {ring_
size} keys")
print(f"Privacy: But cannot determine which one!")
```

4.1.8 Verifiable Random Functions (VRFs)

The last primitive in this chapter addresses a problem that sounds simple but turns out to be devilishly hard on a blockchain: generating a random number that nobody could have predicted or manipulated.

The On-Chain Randomness Problem

You might think you could just use the block hash. Miners can manipulate that—they can discard blocks whose hash does not produce the random outcome they want. Timestamps? Miners have some wiggle room there too. An off-chain oracle like random.org? Now you have introduced a trusted third party, which defeats the purpose of running a decentralized system.

VRF Properties

A VRF takes a secret key and an input and produces two things: a pseudorandom output that looks indistinguishable from random and a proof that the output was computed correctly. The owner of the secret key is the only one who can produce the output, but anyone holding the corresponding public key can verify it.

For any given input and key pair, there is exactly one valid output. You cannot shop around for a more favorable random number.

The proof makes this publicly checkable. Nobody has to trust the VRF evaluator's honesty—the math speaks for itself.

And until the evaluator publishes the output, nobody else can predict what it will be—not even other holders of the same public key, because they lack the secret key.

Table 4-8. *Randomness Generation Methods*

Method	Trust Required	Biasable	Verifiable	Used By
Block hash	Miners	Yes (withhold blocks)	Yes	Early blockchain games
Oracle (Chainlink)	Oracle network	Depends on oracle	Yes	Many DeFi protocols
VRF	None (cryptographic)	No	Yes	Algorand, Cardano
Commit-Reveal	Participants	Yes (last revealer)	Partial	Some protocols
drand (threshold)	Threshold of nodes	No (if threshold honest)	Yes	Some systems

How VRFs Work

Key Generation: Create keypair (sk, pk)

Evaluation: Given input x and secret key sk: Compute y = VRF(sk, x)—Generate proof π that y was correctly computed

Verification: Given input x, output y, proof π, public key pk: Verify proof: VRF_Verify(pk, x, y, π) → True/False

Uniqueness: For given sk and x, only one valid (y, π) pair exists.

```
Validator Selection Using VRF:

Epoch N begins:
    Seed = Hash(Block_{N-1})  ← Public, unpredictable

Each validator generates VRF:
    Validator_i:
        Input: Seed || Validator_ID
        Secret: sk_i

        (y_i, π_i) = VRF(sk_i, Seed || Validator_ID)

        Post: (y_i, π_i) publicly

Selection:
    All validators post their VRFs
    Everyone verifies: VRF_Verify(pk_i, Seed || ID_i, y_i, π_i)

    Leader = Validator with lowest y value

    ✓ Unpredictable (requires sk_i)
    ✓ Unbiasable (unique output for input)
    ✓ Verifiable (anyone can check π_i)
    ✓ Public (deterministic from public info)
```

Figure 4-6. *VRF Usage in Consensus*

Algorand's VRF Usage

Algorand uses VRFs for:

1. **Leader Selection**: Randomly select block proposers
2. **Committee Selection**: Choose validators for Byzantine agreement
3. **Participation Privacy**: Validators prove selection without revealing in advance

Process:
1. Every participant runs VRF with the current seed
2. VRF output determines if a participant was selected
3. Selected participants provide proof
4. Network verifies proof and accepts block/vote

Benefits: No coordination needed—Unpredictable until selection—Cannot bias or manipulate—Cannot target selected validators in advance

Implementation Concept

```
import hashlib
import secrets
from dataclasses import dataclass

@dataclass
class VRFOutput:
    """VRF output and proof"""
    output: bytes  # Pseudorandom output
    proof: bytes   # Proof of correct computation

class VRF:
    """
    Simplified Verifiable Random Function.
    Real implementations use elliptic curves (e.g., ECVRF per RFC 9381).
    """

    def __init__(self):
        self.secret_key = None
        self.public_key = None
```

```
def generate_keypair(self):
    """Generate VRF keypair"""
    self.secret_key = secrets.token_bytes(32)
    # In reality: public_key = secret_key * G (elliptic curve)
    self.public_key = hashlib.sha256(self.secret_key).digest()
    return self.secret_key, self.public_key

def evaluate(self, input_data: bytes) -> VRFOutput:
    """
    Evaluate VRF on input with secret key.

    Real implementation (ECVRF):
    1. Hash input to curve point: H = hash_to_curve(input_data)
    2. Compute gamma = secret_key * H
    3. Derive output: output = hash(gamma)
    4. Generate proof: NIZK that gamma correctly computed
    """
    if self.secret_key is None:
        raise ValueError("Must generate keypair first")

    # Simplified evaluation
    # Real: uses elliptic curve operations
    combined = self.secret_key + input_data

    # Pseudorandom output
    output = hashlib.sha256(combined).digest()

    # Proof (simplified - real uses elliptic curve proof)
    proof = hashlib.sha256(
        self.secret_key + input_data + output
    ).digest()

    return VRFOutput(output, proof)

def verify(self, public_key: bytes, input_data: bytes,
           vrf_output: VRFOutput) -> bool:
    """
    Verify VRF output and proof.
```

```
        Real verification:
        1. Parse proof components
        2. Verify elliptic curve relations
        3. Recompute output from proof
        4. Check output matches
        """

        # Simplified verification
        # Real: verifies elliptic curve equation

        # Check proof structure
        if len(vrf_output.output) != 32 or len(vrf_output.proof) != 32:
            return False

        # In real implementation: verify NIZK proof
        # This ensures output derived from secret key corresponding to
        public_key

        return True  # Simplified

def demonstrate_vrf_leader_selection():
    """Demonstrate VRF-based leader selection"""
    print("=== VRF Leader Selection ===\n")

    # Current block seed (public, unpredictable)
    block_hash = hashlib.sha256(b"previous_block").digest()
    epoch = 12345
    seed = hashlib.sha256(block_hash + epoch.to_bytes(8, 'big')).digest()
    print(f"Epoch {epoch} seed: {seed.hex()[:32]}...")

    # Multiple validators compete
    validators = []
    for i in range(5):
        vrf = VRF()
        sk, pk = vrf.generate_keypair()

        # Each validator computes VRF
        input_data = seed + f"validator_{i}".encode()
        vrf_output = vrf.evaluate(input_data)
```

```
        validators.append({
            'id': i,
            'public_key': pk,
            'vrf_output': vrf_output,
            'vrf_value': int.from_bytes(vrf_output.output, 'big')
        })

        print(f"Validator {i}: VRF = {vrf_output.output.hex()[:16]}...")

    # Leader is validator with lowest VRF output
    leader = min(validators, key=lambda v: v['vrf_value'])
    print(f"\n🏆 Leader: Validator {leader['id']}")
    print(f"   VRF value: {leader['vrf_value']}")

    # Everyone can verify
    vrf_verifier = VRF()
    is_valid = vrf_verifier.verify(
        leader['public_key'],
        seed + f"validator_{leader['id']}".encode(),
        leader['vrf_output']
    )
    print(f"   Proof valid: {is_valid}")

    print("\nProperties:")
    print("✓ Unpredictable (requires secret key)")
    print("✓ Unbiasable (unique output for input)")
    print("✓ Verifiable (anyone can check proof)")
    print("✓ Fair (all validators equal probability)")

# Run demonstration
demonstrate_vrf_leader_selection()
```

4.1.9 Summary

This chapter covered a family of cryptographic tools that share a common thread: they let you prove things about hidden data. Zero-knowledge proofs are the broadest and most powerful member of the family, enabling general-purpose verified computation over private inputs.

We traced the landscape from interactive protocols (interesting in theory, useless on a blockchain) to the three non-interactive systems that matter in practice. SNARKs produce the smallest proofs and the fastest verification, at the cost of a trusted setup ceremony whose failure would be catastrophic. STARKs eliminate the ceremony and add quantum resistance, but their proofs are orders of magnitude larger. Bulletproofs are specialists—optimized for range proofs and deployed in Monero to hide transaction amounts.

Underneath many of these systems sit commitment schemes—Pedersen commitments in particular—whose homomorphic properties enable confidential transactions where validators can check that the books balance without seeing any of the numbers.

Ring signatures provide a complementary form of privacy: not hiding what happened, but hiding who did it. Monero's combination of ring signatures, stealth addresses, and Bulletproof range proofs covers all three privacy dimensions of a payment (sender, receiver, amount).

Finally, VRFs solve the on-chain randomness problem by producing outputs that are simultaneously unpredictable (before generation), deterministic (for a given input and key), and publicly verifiable (anyone can check the proof). Algorand and Cardano use them for validator selection.

Key Takeaways:

- Zero-knowledge proofs enable privacy and scalability simultaneously
- **Trade-Offs Exist**: SNARKs (small proofs, trusted setup) vs. STARKs (large proofs, no setup)
- Range proofs are essential for confidential transactions to prevent inflation
- Ring signatures hide transaction graphs but don't scale as efficiently as zk-SNARKs
- VRFs solve on-chain randomness without trust assumptions

The next chapter shifts from "what can we prove?" to "how do we agree?"—consensus mechanisms that let thousands of mutually distrustful nodes converge on a single transaction history, using the cryptographic tools we have built up over the past four chapters.

4.1.10 Exercises

Problem 1 (Basic): Explain the three properties of zero-knowledge proofs (completeness, soundness, zero-knowledge) using a non-cryptographic analogy. Why is each property necessary for blockchain applications?

Problem 2 (Comparison): Create a comparison matrix for zk-SNARKs (Groth16), PLONK, zk-STARKs, and Bulletproofs across: proof size, verification time, prover time, trusted setup requirement, and quantum resistance. Which is best suited for (a) a privacy coin, (b) an L2 rollup, (c) a range proof system?

Problem 3 (Security): Why do zk-SNARKs require a trusted setup ceremony? What specific attack becomes possible if the toxic waste is compromised? Describe how multi-party computation ceremonies mitigate this risk and what trust assumption remains.

Problem 4 (Implementation): Implement a simplified commitment scheme using SHA-256: commit(value, randomness) = H(value || randomness). Demonstrate the hiding and binding properties. Then implement a Pedersen commitment and show its homomorphic property: C(a) × C(b) = C(a+b).

Problem 5 (Analysis): Zcash uses zk-SNARKs to hide transaction amounts and addresses. Explain the complete flow: how does a sender prove they own the input notes, that the transaction is balanced (inputs = outputs), and that no double-spending has occurred—all without revealing any of these values?

Problem 6 (Design): Design a ZK-based voting system where: (a) each voter can prove eligibility without revealing identity, (b) each voter can vote only once, (c) the final tally is publicly verifiable, and (d) individual votes remain secret. Specify which ZK proof system you would use and why.

Problem 7 (Theory): Explain why zk-STARKs achieve post-quantum security while zk-SNARKs (Groth16, PLONK) do not. What specific mathematical assumptions differ? What is the cost in proof size?

Problem 8 (Application): Monero uses ring signatures for sender privacy and Bulletproofs for amount privacy. Explain how these two primitives work together in a single transaction. What are the limitations?

Problem 9 (Advanced): Implement a simplified interactive zero-knowledge proof for the discrete logarithm problem using the Schnorr identification protocol (commit-challenge-response). Verify that it satisfies completeness and soundness.

Problem 10 (Research): Compare the ZK proof systems used by zkSync (PLONK-based), StarkNet (STARK-based), and Polygon zkEVM (SNARK-based). Document: proof system variant, proof generation time, proof size, on-chain verification cost, and EVM compatibility approach.

(Solutions in Appendix D)

4.1.11 Further Reading

On Zero-Knowledge Proofs: "The Knowledge Complexity of Interactive Proof Systems" by Goldwasser, Micali, and Rackoff (1985)—the foundational paper—"How to Explain Zero-Knowledge Protocols to Your Children" by Quisquater et al.—accessible introduction—Zcash protocol specification for practical zk-SNARK implementation

On zk-SNARKs: "Succinct Non-Interactive Zero Knowledge for a von Neumann Architecture" (Pinocchio) by Parno et al.—Groth16: "On the Size of Pairing-based Non-interactive Arguments" by Jens Groth—PLONK paper: "PLONK: Permutations over Lagrange-bases for Oecumenical Noninteractive arguments of Knowledge"

On zk-STARKs: "Scalable, transparent, and post-quantum secure computational integrity" by Ben-Sasson et al.—StarkWare's blog series on STARK mathematics—Vitalik Buterin's "STARKs" blog series provides accessible explanations

On Bulletproofs: "Bulletproofs: Short Proofs for Confidential Transactions and More" by Bünz, Bootle, Boneh, et al.—Dalek Cryptography's implementation documentation

On Ring Signatures: "How to Leak a Secret" by Rivest, Shamir, and Tauman (2001)—the original ring signature paper—Zero to Monero book—a comprehensive treatment of Monero's cryptography—CryptoNote whitepaper describing RingCT

On Verifiable Random Functions: RFC 9381: "Verifiable Random Functions (VRFs)"—IETF standard—Algorand's technical papers on VRF-based consensus—"Verifiable Random Functions" by Micali, Rabin, and Vadhan (1999)

Avoid: Implementations claiming "quantum-proof" zero-knowledge without specifying which scheme—Tutorials implementing zk-SNARKs from scratch without security analysis—Claims that specific ZK schemes provide unconditional privacy (all have trust assumptions or setup requirements)

PART II

Consensus Mechanisms

CHAPTER 5

Proof of Work

5.1 Mining, Difficulty, and Security Analysis

This chapter covers how Proof of Work functions—hash puzzles, difficulty retargeting, mining economics, 51% attacks, selfish mining, energy costs, and pool dynamics. Finish it, and you should be able to explain:

- Why hash puzzles aren't trivia—they're the whole PoW game
- How difficulty retargeting keeps block times from drifting when hashrate throws a tantrum
- Mining economics for real: rigs, power bills, margins, and why "ASIC resistance" never stays settled
- Selfish mining—when the "honest" playbook leaves money on the table
- The majority-hash attack with numbers attached, not just scary headlines
- What PoW burns in electricity and why knee-jerk TWh comparisons usually miss the point
- Pools: how pay works, why variance matters, and how coordination creeps in
- Miner game theory—equilibria, pool choice, who eats the risk

N. Savant, *Blockchain Foundations*, https://doi.org/10.1007/979-8-8688-2891-1_5

5.1.1 Hash Puzzles: The Foundation of Proof of Work

Proof of Work turns kilowatt-hours and silicon into the right to publish the next block. The trick predates Bitcoin—Adam Back's Hashcash (1997) used the same asymmetry to fight spam. Satoshi repurposed it for consensus. Core idea: finding a hash under a threshold costs work; checking a candidate costs one hash. That verified cheap/work expensive split is what distributed systems people kill for.

In practice: you pack a candidate block—txs, parent hash, timestamp, and nonce field you can twiddle. Then you grind: bump nonce, hash header, compare to target, repeat until your eyes glaze over.

```
h = H(block_header)
```

H is whatever the chain fixed—Bitcoin uses double SHA-256; pre-merge Ethereum used Ethash. Validity means:

```
h < T
```

T is the target. Model the hash as a random oracle, and each try hits with p = T/2^256. Expected tries to success: 1/p = 2^256/T. No loyalty program for past failures—that's the progress-free bit coming next.

Table 5-1. *Hash Puzzle Properties*

Property	Description	Significance
Difficulty of finding	Expected 2^256 / T attempts	Controls block production rate
Ease of verification	Single hash computation	Any node can verify in microseconds
Progress-free	Each attempt is independent of previous	No advantage from partial work
Adjustable difficulty	T can be varied	Maintains target block interval
Non-parallelizable advantage	Linear speedup only	Proportional to hash rate, no shortcuts

Progress-free sounds fake until you sit with it. Jigsaw puzzles reward partial progress; hashes don't. Ten billion bad nonces buy you nothing—the next try is still a fresh coin flip. So inter-block times go memoryless; gaps follow an exponential with a rate tied to network hash / work per block:

```
P(next block found within time t) = 1 - e^(-λt)
```

with lambda roughly (network hashrate) / (expected hashes per valid block).

The Poisson Process Model

Treat block arrivals like a Poisson process. The network does R hashes/sec; a block needs expected D hashes on average; blocks show up at about lambda = R/D per second.

A few things fall out of that exponential picture:

Memorylessness: the expected wait for the next block stays 1/lambda—even if you've already waited twenty minutes on a ten-minute target. The chain isn't "due." Your gut hates this; the math doesn't care.

Variance: for exponential inter-arrival, std dev equals the mean. Bitcoin's ten-minute target still produces seconds-to-an-hour swings. Feature, not glitch.

Orphans: two miners find headers in the same propagation window—one wins, one dies. Faster block times and slower gossip both raise orphan pressure.

Table 5-2. *Block Interval Statistics for Selected Chains*

Chain	Target Interval	Actual Mean	Std Dev	Orphan Rate
Bitcoin	600s	~600s	~600s	~0.1%
Litecoin	150s	~150s	~150s	~0.5%
Dogecoin	60s	~60s	~60s	~1.5%
Pre-merge Ethereum	13s	~13s	~13s	~5-7%

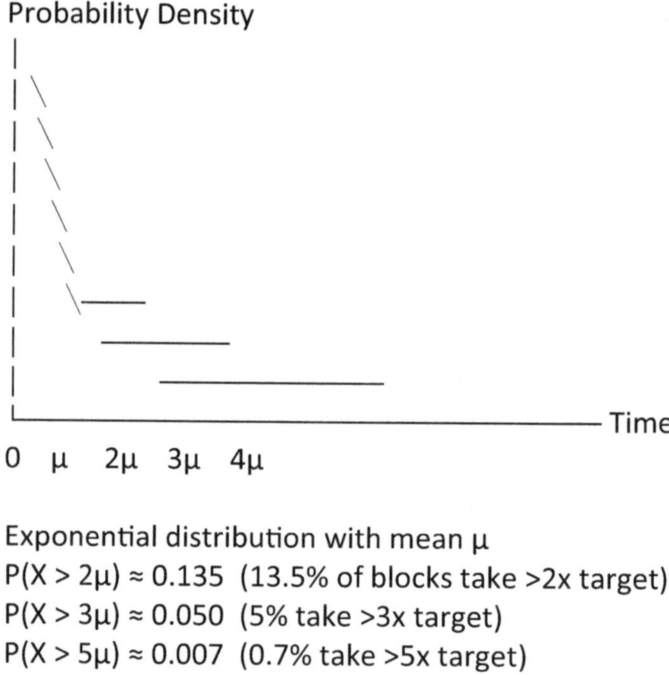

Figure 5-1. *Block Interval Distribution*

Code Example: Mining Simulation

```
import hashlib
import struct
import time
import random
from typing import Tuple, Optional

class BlockHeader:
    """Simplified block header for mining demonstration."""

    def __init__(self, prev_hash: bytes, merkle_root: bytes,
                 timestamp: int, difficulty_bits: int):
        self.prev_hash = prev_hash
        self.merkle_root = merkle_root
        self.timestamp = timestamp
        self.difficulty_bits = difficulty_bits
        self.nonce = 0
```

```
    def serialize(self) -> bytes:
        """Serialize header fields for hashing."""
        return (
            self.prev_hash +
            self.merkle_root +
            struct.pack('<I', self.timestamp) +
            struct.pack('<I', self.difficulty_bits) +
            struct.pack('<I', self.nonce)
        )

    def compute_hash(self) -> bytes:
        """Bitcoin-style double SHA-256."""
        first = hashlib.sha256(self.serialize()).digest()
        return hashlib.sha256(first).digest()

def bits_to_target(bits: int) -> int:
    """
    Convert compact difficulty representation to full target.

    Bitcoin encodes target as 4 bytes: 1 byte exponent, 3 bytes coefficient
    target = coefficient * 2^(8 * (exponent - 3))
    """
    exponent = bits >> 24
    coefficient = bits & 0x007fffff
    return coefficient * (1 << (8 * (exponent - 3)))

def target_to_difficulty(target: int) -> float:
    """
    Compute difficulty relative to genesis target.
    difficulty = max_target / current_target
    """
    max_target = bits_to_target(0x1d00ffff)  # Bitcoin genesis difficulty
    return max_target / target

def mine_block(header: BlockHeader, target: int,
               max_nonce: int = 2**32) -> Tuple[Optional[int], int, float]:
    """
    Mine a block by searching for valid nonce.
```

```
    Returns:
        Tuple of (nonce or None, attempts, elapsed_seconds)
    """
    start_time = time.time()
    attempts = 0

    for nonce in range(max_nonce):
        header.nonce = nonce
        block_hash = header.compute_hash()
        hash_int = int.from_bytes(block_hash, 'big')
        attempts += 1

        if hash_int < target:
            elapsed = time.time() - start_time
            return nonce, attempts, elapsed

    elapsed = time.time() - start_time
    return None, attempts, elapsed

def demonstrate_mining():
    """Run mining demonstration with different difficulties."""
    prev_hash = hashlib.sha256(b"previous block").digest()
    merkle_root = hashlib.sha256(b"transaction data").digest()
    timestamp = int(time.time())

    # Test with increasing difficulty levels
    difficulties = [
        (0x20ffffff, "Very Easy (testing)"),
        (0x1f00ffff, "Easy"),
        (0x1e0fffff, "Medium"),
    ]

    for bits, label in difficulties:
        header = BlockHeader(prev_hash, merkle_root, timestamp, bits)
        target = bits_to_target(bits)
        difficulty = target_to_difficulty(target)

        print(f"\nDifficulty: {label}")
        print(f"  Target (hex): {target:064x}")
```

```
    print(f"  Relative difficulty: {difficulty:.2f}")

    nonce, attempts, elapsed = mine_block(header, target)

    if nonce is not None:
        header.nonce = nonce
        block_hash = header.compute_hash()
        print(f"  Block found! Nonce: {nonce}")
        print(f"  Hash: {block_hash.hex()}")
        print(f"  Attempts: {attempts:,}")
        print(f"  Time: {elapsed:.3f}s")
        print(f"  Hash rate: {attempts/elapsed:,.0f} H/s")
    else:
        print(f"  No solution found in {attempts:,} attempts")

# Run demonstration
demonstrate_mining()
```

The toy miner loop above is the real loop, just smaller integers. Notice difficulty isn't linear: tighten the target a little and expected work explodes—each extra leading-zero nibble is a multiplicative hammer.

5.1.2 Difficulty Adjustment Algorithms

Double hashrate with fixed difficulty and blocks arrive twice as fast. Halve hashrate and everything crawls. Neither is acceptable, so chains retarget difficulty to keep mean block time in the ballpark.

Bitcoin's Difficulty Adjustment

Bitcoin retunes every 2,016 blocks (~two weeks at ten minutes). The update rule is almost embarrassingly simple:

```
new_target = old_target × (actual_time / expected_time)
```

actual_time is wall-clock time across those 2,016 blocks; expected_time is 2,016 * 600 seconds if the clock were perfect.

There's a clamp: difficulty can't jump more than 4x up or down in one step—buffers timestamp games and wild swings.

```
def bitcoin_difficulty_adjustment(old_target: int, actual_time:
int) -> int:
    """
    Bitcoin difficulty adjustment algorithm.

    Args:
        old_target: Previous target value
        actual_time: Actual time for last 2016 blocks (seconds)

    Returns:
        New target value
    """
    expected_time = 2016 * 600  # 2 weeks in seconds

    # Clamp adjustment factor to [0.25, 4.0]
    if actual_time < expected_time // 4:
        actual_time = expected_time // 4
    elif actual_time > expected_time * 4:
        actual_time = expected_time * 4

    new_target = old_target * actual_time // expected_time


    # Ensure target doesn't exceed maximum
    max_target = 0x00000000FFFF00000000000000000000000000000000000000
    00000000000000
    if new_target > max_target:
        new_target = max_target

    return new_target
```

It works, but slowly. ASIC waves in 2013–2014 cranked blocks fast for days before the next adjustment. China's 2021 crackdown nuked hashrate and blocks dragged until difficulty caught down. Two-week inertia cuts both ways.

Alternative Adjustment Algorithms

Other chains got impatient and tried fancier controllers:

EMA: tweak every block off a weighted recent window—snappier, but parameters can oscillate if you're sloppy.

```
def ema_difficulty(parent_difficulty: int, parent_timestamp: int,
                   current_timestamp: int, target_interval: int,
                   adjustment_factor: int = 2048) -> int:
    """
    EMA-style difficulty adjustment (similar to pre-merge Ethereum).

    Adjusts every block by a small fraction based on whether the
    previous block was faster or slower than target.
    """
    time_diff = current_timestamp - parent_timestamp

    if time_diff < target_interval:
        # Block was fast: increase difficulty
        adjustment = parent_difficulty // adjustment_factor
    elif time_diff > target_interval * 2:
        # Block was very slow: decrease difficulty
        multiplier = min((time_diff - target_interval) // target_
        interval, 99)
        adjustment = -(parent_difficulty // adjustment_factor) * multiplier
    else:
        adjustment = 0

    return max(parent_difficulty + adjustment, 1)
```

LWMA (Monero and friends): weight recent blocks more—tracks shift without fainting at every blip.

```
def lwma_difficulty (timestamps: list, cumulative_difficulties: list,
                     target_interval: int, window: int = 60) -> int:
    """
    LWMA difficulty algorithm.

    Linearly weights recent solve times, giving more influence
    to the most recent blocks. Resistant to timestamp manipulation.
    """
    n = min(len(timestamps) - 1, window)

    weighted_solvetimes = 0
    total_weight = 0
```

```
    for i in range(1, n + 1):
        solvetime = timestamps[i] - timestamps[i - 1]
        # Clamp solve time to prevent manipulation
        solvetime = max(solvetime, -6 * target_interval)
        solvetime = min(solvetime, 6 * target_interval)

        weight = i  # Linear weight: recent blocks weigh more
        weighted_solvetimes += solvetime * weight
        total_weight += weight

    # Average difficulty over the window
    avg_difficulty = (cumulative_difficulties[-1] -
                      cumulative_difficulties[-n - 1]) / n

    # Adjust based on weighted solve time
    target_sum = target_interval * total_weight
# Guard: if all timestamps are identical, avoid division by zero
 if weighted_solvetimes == 0:          return max(int(avg_difficulty), 1)
    new_difficulty = avg_difficulty * target_sum // weighted_solvetimes

    return max(int(new_difficulty), 1)
```

Table 5-3. *Difficulty Adjustment Algorithm Comparison*

Algorithm	Response Time	Manipulation Resistance	Stability	Used By
Bitcoin (2016-block)	~2 weeks	High (large window)	Excellent for stable hashrate	Bitcoin, Litecoin
Per-block EMA	1 block	Medium	Can oscillate with variable hashrate	Pre-merge Ethereum
LWMA	~60 blocks	High	Good balance of responsiveness	Monero, Zcash
ASERT (aserti3-412d)	Per block, exponential	High	Smooth, no oscillation	Bitcoin Cash

Difficulty and Security

Difficulty isn't separate from security—it's the knob that scales how much work honest miners pour in. Rough attack cost tracks:

```
Security = Difficulty × Hash_Cost_Per_Unit
```

Hash_Cost_Per_Unit lumps power, amortized rigs, cooling—higher difficulty means more hashes, which means a heavier bill for anyone trying to race the chain.

The math connecting difficulty to reorganization resistance looks like this:

```
P(reorg of depth k) ≈ (q/p)^k
```

q is the attacker's hashrate share; p = 1 - q honest. Example: q = 0.30:

```
P(reorg depth 1) ≈ 0.43
P(reorg depth 3) ≈ 0.08
P(reorg depth 6) ≈ 0.006
```

Watch it fall off geometrically—that's why merchants talk about six confirmations. Each block depth isn't cosmetic; it's exponential dampening on catch-up probability.

5.1.3 Mining Economics

Mining is capex and opex stacked on volatile revenue. Your rig efficiency, power price, and coin price decide if you eat or exit. For the protocol, aggregate miner spend is the security budget—so this isn't hobby trivia.

Hardware Evolution

Bitcoin hardware went through four rough generations; each one rewrote who could compete:

CPU days (2009–2010): Satoshi client on a laptop, single-digit to tens of MH/s. Democratic, slow, cute in retrospect.

GPU era: 10–100x jump, hundreds of MH/s per card. Suddenly gamers and custom farms mattered.

FPGA interlude: another 2–5x efficiency bump—short-lived but proof that specialized silicon wins this game.

ASICs (2013 onward): single-purpose SHA-256 machines, 100–400 TH/s class now, tens of J/TH. Without ASICs you're not playing Bitcoin; you're cosplaying.

Table 5-4. *Mining Hardware Generations*

Generation	Hash Rate	Power Efficiency	Capital Cost	Era
CPU	2–20 MH/s	~10,000 J/TH	~$500 (existing hardware)	2009–2010
GPU	200–800 MH/s	~500 J/TH	~$300–500 per GPU	2010–2013
FPGA	1–2 GH/s	~100 J/TH	~$500–2000 per board	2011–2013
ASIC (gen 1)	1–10 TH/s	~1000 J/TH	~$2000–5000	2013–2016
ASIC (current)	100–400 TH/s	~20–35 J/TH	~$2000–15000	2020–present

Profitability Analysis

Profitability fits in one line before depreciation:

```
Daily Revenue = (hash_rate / network_hash_rate) × daily_block_rewards
Daily Cost = hash_rate × energy_per_hash × electricity_price × 86400
Daily Profit = Daily Revenue - Daily Cost
```

Throw in hardware wearing out and the spreadsheet gets uglier fast:

```
Break-even Price = (Daily Cost + Daily Depreciation) / Daily BTC Mined
```

```
def mining_profitability(hash_rate_th: float, power_watts: float,
                         electricity_cost_kwh: float,
                         network_hash_rate_eh: float,
                         block_reward_btc: float,
                         btc_price_usd: float,
                         hardware_cost_usd: float,
                         hardware_lifespan_days: int = 730) -> dict:
    """
    Calculate mining profitability.

    Args:
        hash_rate_th: Miner hash rate in TH/s
        power_watts: Power consumption in watts
```

```
        electricity_cost_kwh: Electricity cost in USD per kWh
        network_hash_rate_eh: Total network hash rate in EH/s
        block_reward_btc: Current block reward in BTC
        btc_price_usd: Bitcoin price in USD
        hardware_cost_usd: Hardware purchase price
        hardware_lifespan_days: Expected hardware lifespan

    Returns:
        Dictionary with profitability metrics
    """
    # Convert units: 1 EH = 1,000,000 TH
    miner_share = hash_rate_th / (network_hash_rate_eh * 1e6)

    # Daily block rewards: 144 blocks per day (24 * 6)
    blocks_per_day = 144
    daily_btc = miner_share * blocks_per_day * block_reward_btc
    daily_revenue_usd = daily_btc * btc_price_usd

    # Daily electricity cost
    daily_kwh = power_watts * 24 / 1000
    daily_electricity_usd = daily_kwh * electricity_cost_kwh

    # Hardware depreciation
    daily_depreciation = hardware_cost_usd / hardware_lifespan_days

    # Profit calculation
    daily_profit = daily_revenue_usd - daily_electricity_usd - daily_
    depreciation

    # Break-even BTC price
    daily_btc_mined = daily_btc if daily_btc > 0 else 1e-18
    breakeven_price = (daily_electricity_usd + daily_depreciation) / daily_
    btc_mined

    # Energy efficiency
    joules_per_th = power_watts / hash_rate_th
```

```
    return {
        'daily_btc': daily_btc,
        'daily_revenue_usd': daily_revenue_usd,
        'daily_electricity_usd': daily_electricity_usd,
        'daily_depreciation_usd': daily_depreciation,
        'daily_profit_usd': daily_profit,
        'monthly_profit_usd': daily_profit * 30,
        'breakeven_btc_price': breakeven_price,
        'energy_efficiency_j_per_th': joules_per_th,
        'roi_days': hardware_cost_usd / daily_profit if daily_profit > 0
        else float('inf'),
    }

# Example: Modern ASIC miner
result = mining_profitability(
    hash_rate_th=140,           # Antminer S19 XP
    power_watts=3010,           # Watts
    electricity_cost_kwh=0.05, # $0.05/kWh (competitive rate)
    network_hash_rate_eh=550,  # ~550 EH/s network
    block_reward_btc=3.125,    # Post-2024 halving
    btc_price_usd=60000,       # Assumed price
    hardware_cost_usd=5000,    # Purchase price
)

print("Mining Profitability Analysis")
print(f"  Daily BTC mined:      {result['daily_btc']:.8f}")
print(f"  Daily revenue:        ${result['daily_revenue_usd']:.2f}")
print(f"  Daily electricity:    ${result['daily_electricity_usd']:.2f}")
print(f"  Daily depreciation:   ${result['daily_depreciation_usd']:.2f}")
print(f"  Daily profit:         ${result['daily_profit_usd']:.2f}")
print(f"  Monthly profit:       ${result['monthly_profit_usd']:.2f}")
print(f"  Break-even BTC:       ${result['breakeven_btc_price']:,.0f}")
print(f"  ROI (days):           {result['roi_days']:.0f}")
print(f"  Efficiency:           {result['energy_efficiency_j_per_
th']:.1f} J/TH")
```

ASIC Resistance

Some chains tried to blunt ASIC advantage with algorithms that favor big RAM or weird programs—make the bottleneck memory or flexibility, not raw SHA gates.

Memory-hard means you need fast, fat RAM wired close—expensive on a custom chip:

Ethash (pre-merge ETH): multi-GB DAG; GPUs bound by VRAM bandwidth more than ALU count.

RandomX (Monero): randomly generated programs per block—great on CPUs, annoying to freeze into fixed silicon.

Equihash (Zcash family): birthday problem structure; sorting step wants bandwidth.

Table 5-5. *ASIC Resistance Approaches*

Algorithm	Memory Requirement	ASIC Status	Primary Hardware	Resistance Mechanism
SHA-256	Minimal	Fully ASIC-dominated	ASIC	None (compute-bound)
Ethash	4+ GB	Some ASICs, GPU-competitive	GPU/ASIC	Large DAG dataset
RandomX	2+ GB L3 cache	No viable ASICs	CPU	Random program execution
Equihash	1-3 GB	Some ASICs	GPU/ASIC	Memory-bound sorting
ProgPoW	4+ GB	No production ASICs	GPU	Programmatic access patterns

Nobody wins the ASIC-resistance debate permanently. One side: ASICs centralize around fabs and bulk buyers. Other side: “GPU-only” often just recentralizes on NVIDIA clouds, and specialized hardware usually buys more security per dollar, which matters for the chain.

5.1.4 The 51% Attack

Classic PoW nightmare: control enough hashrate and you can outrun everyone else's chain—people say "51%" but any $q > 0.5$ does the job given time. The longest-accumulated work wins, so the majority hash eventually writes history.

Attack Mechanics

The exchange-deposit double-spend script:

1. Deposit coins, sell for something withdrawable.
2. Wait for their confirmation policy to clear.
3. Privately mine a fork that never included the deposit.
4. When your hidden chain passes public work, broadcast it.
5. Longest chain rule adopts your fork—deposit tx never existed on the winning tip.

You walk away with fiat (or whatever) and still hold the coins. Textbook double-spend.

Nakamoto's Analysis

Satoshi modeled catch-up as Gambler's Ruin: attacker fraction q, honest $p = 1-q$. Starting z blocks back, the probability of ever catching up:

```
If q < p:  P(catch up) = (q/p)^z
If q >= p: P(catch up) = 1
```

Random walk intuition: attacker gains a step with prob q, loses ground with p. When $q < p$, gaps usually widen and catch-up odds crater exponentially in z.

For burying a payment z deep, success probability scales like:

```
P(success) = 1 - Σ(k=0 to z-1) [λ^k × e^(-λ) / k!] × (1 - (q/p)^(z-k))
```

"with λ_attack = z × (q/p)—this means the attacker is expected to catch up with these many blocks (using Poisson approximation).

Note: this λ_attack is different from the λ used in §5.1.

They use the same symbol, but meanings are different:
λ_attack → number of blocks attacker may catch up
λ (in §5.1) → how fast the network finds blocks per second"

```
import math
from typing import List, Tuple

def attack_probability_exact(q: float, z: int) -> float:
    """
    Compute exact probability of successful double-spend attack.

    Based on Nakamoto's analysis, Poisson approximation is used.

    Args:
        q: Attacker's fraction of total hash rate (0 < q < 0.5)
        p: Honest fraction = 1 - q
        z: Number of confirmations

    Returns:
        Probability of successful attack
    """
    if q >= 0.5:
        return 1.0

    p = 1.0 - q
    lam = z * (q / p)

    total = 0.0
    for k in range(z):
        poisson = math.exp(-lam) * (lam ** k) / math.factorial(k)
        total += poisson * (1 - (q / p) ** (z - k))

    return 1.0 - total

def gamblers_ruin_probability(q: float, z: int) -> float:
    """
    Simplified Gambler's Ruin model.

    Probability attacker catches up from z blocks behind.
    """
```

```
    if q >= 0.5:
        return 1.0
    p = 1.0 - q
    return (q / p) ** z

def required_confirmations(q: float, target_security: float) -> int:
    """
    Find minimum confirmations for desired security level.

    Args:
        q: Attacker hash rate fraction
        target_security: Maximum acceptable attack probability

    Returns:
        Minimum number of confirmations
    """
    for z in range(1, 200):
        prob = attack_probability_exact(q, z)
        if prob < target_security:
            return z
    return 200  # Very high attacker power

# Print attack probability table
print("Attack Success Probability by Confirmations and Attacker Hash Rate")
print("-" * 72)
print(f"{'Confirmations':>14}", end="")
for q in [0.10, 0.20, 0.25, 0.30, 0.35, 0.40, 0.45]:
    print(f"  q={q:.2f}", end="")
print()
print("-" * 72)

for z in [1, 2, 3, 4, 5, 6, 10, 15, 20, 30]:
    print(f"{z:>14}", end="")
    for q in [0.10, 0.20, 0.25, 0.30, 0.35, 0.40, 0.45]:
        prob = attack_probability_exact(q, z)
        print(f"  {prob:.4f}", end="")
    print()
```

```
print()

# Required confirmations for different security levels
print("Required Confirmations for 99.9% Security (attack prob < 0.001)")
print("-" * 50)
for q in [0.05, 0.10, 0.15, 0.20, 0.25, 0.30, 0.35, 0.40]:
    confs = required_confirmations(q, 0.001)
    print(f"  Attacker has {q*100:4.1f}% hash rate: {confs:3d}
    confirmations")
```

Table 5-6. *Confirmation Requirements by Attacker Hash Rate*

Attacker Hash Rate	1 Confirmation	6 Confirmations	For 99.9% Security
10%	20.5%	0.024%	5 confirmations
20%	37.8%	2.4%	10 confirmations
30%	54.0%	17.7%	24 confirmations
40%	69.9%	52.3%	89 confirmations
45%	77.4%	72.0%	340 confirmations

Glance at the confirmation table: as q approaches half, needed depth explodes. PoW safety is “honest majority with margin,” not vibes.

5.1.5 Selfish Mining

Eyal & Sirer (2013) ruined everyone’s lunch: under ~50% hashrate, you can still earn extra by withholding blocks and releasing them strategically. They called it selfish mining.

The Strategy

Honest miners broadcast immediately; selfish miners sit on blocks and race the public tip selectively:

1. Mine a block? Don’t announce—extend privately first.
2. Honest network ties you? Broadcast withheld block; fraction gamma of peers may build on you.

3. Get two ahead before they match one? Drop both—your chain wins; their work orphans.

4. Fall two behind? Abandon the private fork and crawl back to consensus before you bleed more.

Profitability Threshold

Profitable when reward share beats hashrate share—threshold moves with gamma (propagation advantage):

```
Threshold hash rate = (1 - γ) / (3 - 2γ)
```

gamma = 0 needs ~33% to start the game; gamma = 0.5 pulls the threshold toward 25%; gamma -> 1 is the absurd full-spy case where even a tiny hashrate prints—unrealistic, but shows the lever.

```
from enum import Enum

class MiningState(Enum):
    EVEN = 0        # Selfish miner has no private blocks
    AHEAD_1 = 1     # Selfish miner is 1 block ahead
    AHEAD_2 = 2     # Selfish miner is 2+ blocks ahead
    RACE = 3        # Competing chains of equal length

def selfish_mining_simulation(alpha: float, gamma: float,
                              num_rounds: int = 100000) -> dict:
    """
    Simulate selfish mining to determine profitability.

    Args:
        alpha: Selfish miner's fraction of hash rate
        gamma: Fraction of honest miners that adopt selfish block in race
        num_rounds: Number of simulation rounds

    Returns:
        Statistics on mining rewards
    """
    import random
```

```
state = MiningState.EVEN
selfish_lead = 0

selfish_blocks = 0
honest_blocks = 0
total_blocks_mined = 0

for _ in range(num_rounds):
    # Determine who finds the next block
    selfish_finds = random.random() < alpha
    total_blocks_mined += 1

    if state == MiningState.EVEN:
        if selfish_finds:
            selfish_lead = 1
            state = MiningState.AHEAD_1
        else:
            honest_blocks += 1

    elif state == MiningState.AHEAD_1:
        if selfish_finds:
            selfish_lead = 2
            state = MiningState.AHEAD_2
        else:
            # Race condition: both chains length 1
            state = MiningState.RACE

    elif state == MiningState.AHEAD_2:
        if selfish_finds:
            selfish_lead += 1
        else:
            # Release entire private chain
            selfish_blocks += selfish_lead
            selfish_lead -= 1
            if selfish_lead <= 1:
                if selfish_lead == 1:
                    state = MiningState.AHEAD_1
```

```
                else:
                    selfish_blocks += selfish_lead
                    selfish_lead = 0
                    state = MiningState.EVEN

        elif state == MiningState.RACE:
            if selfish_finds:
                # Selfish miner wins the race
                selfish_blocks += 2  # Both the withheld block and new one
                selfish_lead = 0
                state = MiningState.EVEN
            else:
                if random.random() < gamma:
                    # Honest miner builds on selfish block
                    selfish_blocks += 1
                    honest_blocks += 1
                else:
                    # Honest miner wins: selfish block orphaned
                    honest_blocks += 2
                selfish_lead = 0
                state = MiningState.EVEN

    total_valid = selfish_blocks + honest_blocks
    selfish_share = selfish_blocks / total_valid if total_valid > 0 else 0

    return {
        'alpha': alpha,
        'gamma': gamma,
        'selfish_blocks': selfish_blocks,
        'honest_blocks': honest_blocks,
        'selfish_share': selfish_share,
        'relative_gain': selfish_share / alpha if alpha > 0 else 0,
        'profitable': selfish_share > alpha,
    }

# Test profitability at various hash rates
print("Selfish Mining Profitability Analysis")
print("=" * 65)
```

```
for gamma in [0.0, 0.25, 0.5, 0.75]:
    print(f"\nNetwork advantage gamma = {gamma}")
    print(f"{'Alpha':>7} {'Selfish Share':>14} {'Relative Gain':>14}
    {'Profitable':>11}")
    print("-" * 50)

    for alpha_pct in range(5, 50, 5):
        alpha = alpha_pct / 100
        result = selfish_mining_simulation(alpha, gamma, num_rounds=200000)
        print(f"  {alpha:.2f}   {result['selfish_share']:.4f}"
              f"         {result['relative_gain']:.4f}"
              f"         {'Yes' if result['profitable'] else 'No'}")
```

Defenses Against Selfish Mining

Mitigations people argue about:

Random tie-break instead of first-seen—mixes gamma toward 0.5, raises selfish entry cost.

Timestamp heuristics for weird delays—helpful signal, not gospel (timestamps are soft).

Uncle rewards (Ethereum/GHOST family): pay something for uncles so honest losers aren't zeroed—trims selfish edge.

Freshness rules: prefer blocks wired to recent activity so stale withheld stuff loses ties.

5.1.6 Energy Consumption and Sustainability

Yes, PoW burns serious electricity—that's literally where the cost anchor comes from. Rough equilibrium story: miners spend up toward block value, so joules track price times issuance (plus fees) in the long run.

Quantifying Energy Use

Back-of-envelope network power:

```
Power = Network_Hash_Rate × Energy_Per_Hash
```

Plug ~550 EH/s and ~30 J/TH fleet average—you land in small-country grid territory.

```
Power ≈ 550 × 10^18 × 30 / 10^12 W = 16.5 GW
Annual Energy ≈ 16.5 × 8760 = ~145 TWh/year
```

Big number, real wires. Whether that's "waste" depends on what you think the security is worth—not on the headline alone.

```
def estimate_network_energy(hash_rate_eh: float, efficiency_j_per_th:
float) -> dict:
    """
    Estimate network energy consumption.

    Args:
        hash_rate_eh: Network hash rate in EH/s
        efficiency_j_per_th: Average hardware efficiency (joules per
        terahash)

    Returns:
        Energy consumption metrics
    """
    hash_rate_th = hash_rate_eh * 1e6  # Convert to TH/s
    power_watts = hash_rate_th * efficiency_j_per_th
    power_gw = power_watts / 1e9

    annual_twh = power_gw * 8760 / 1000

    # Comparison data (approximate)
    country_comparisons = [
        ("Netherlands", 110),
        ("Argentina", 130),
        ("Norway", 140),
        ("Egypt", 160),
    ]

    nearest = min(country_comparisons,
                  key=lambda x: abs(x[1] - annual_twh))
```

```
    return {
        'power_gw': power_gw,
        'annual_twh': annual_twh,
        'comparable_country': nearest[0],
        'co2_mt': annual_twh * 0.5,  # Rough: 500g CO2/kWh global average
    }

result = estimate_network_energy(550, 30)
print(f"Estimated Power Draw: {result['power_gw']:.1f} GW")
print(f"Annual Consumption: {result['annual_twh']:.0f} TWh")
print(f"Comparable to: {result['comparable_country']}")
print(f"Estimated CO2 (global avg mix): {result['co2_mt']:.0f} Mt/year")
```

The Energy-Security Relationship

Critics quote kilowatt-hours; defenders quote security budgets—both are talking past each other if they skip the model. Roughly: PoW security scales with what honest miners spend; a sustained majority attack has to outbid that burn. Annualized security spend follows:

```
Annual Security = Annual Block Rewards × Cryptocurrency Price
```

Plug the headline numbers: 3.125 BTC per block, 144 blocks per day, and whatever spot USD/BTC you believe for a back-of-envelope—the product is the order of magnitude to rent the hash rate.

```
Annual Security ≈ 3.125 × 144 × 365 × 60,000 ≈ $9.86 billion
```

That's the scale of economic weight you'd need to shoulder to keep a majority going—messy in practice (hardware isn't liquid hash), but the point stands: big spend, big deterrent.

Efficiency Improvements

The curve isn't static, though:

ASICs keep shaving J/TH—roughly an order of magnitude per decade of aggressive engineering.

Miners chase the cheapest electrons—stranded hydro, geothermal pockets, and flare gas that would vent anyway.

Waste heat reuse stops being a meme: greenhouses, district heat, and industrial drying—rigs as fancy radiators.

Table 5-7. *Bitcoin Mining Energy Efficiency Timeline*

Year	Dominant Hardware	Efficiency (J/TH)	Network Hash Rate	Estimated Power
2009	CPU	~10,000,000	~0.001 GH/s	~10 kW
2013	Early ASIC	~1,000	~10 TH/s	~10 MW
2016	16nm ASIC	~100	~2 EH/s	~200 MW
2019	7nm ASIC	~40	~60 EH/s	~2.4 GW
2023	5nm ASIC	~25	~450 EH/s	~11 GW

5.1.7 Mining Pools and Centralization

Solo mining today is lottery math with a painful tail. A tiny hashrate share means years between blocks while power bills arrive monthly—pools merge variance so humans can budget.

Pool Mechanics

Pools track work via "shares"—partial solutions above an easier pool target. Proves you're hashing; when someone hits network difficulty, rewards split by contributed shares.

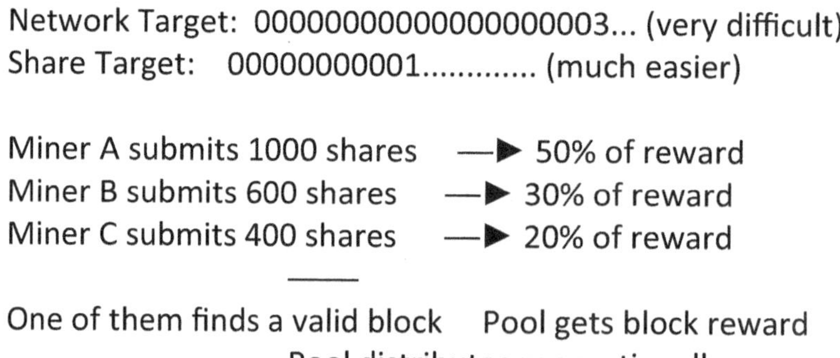

Figure 5-2. *Mining Pool Share Distribution*

Reward Distribution Schemes

```
class PoolRewardScheme:
    """Implement common mining pool reward schemes."""

    @staticmethod
    def proportional(shares: dict, block_reward: float) -> dict:
        """
        Proportional (PROP): Divide reward by share count.

        Simple but vulnerable to pool hopping: miners join only
        at the start of rounds (when expected payout is highest).
        """
        total_shares = sum(shares.values())
        if total_shares == 0:
            return {miner: 0 for miner in shares}
        return {
            miner: (count / total_shares) * block_reward
            for miner, count in shares.items()
        }

    @staticmethod
    def pay_per_share(shares: dict, block_reward: float,
                      difficulty: float, share_difficulty: float) -> dict:
        """
        Pay Per Share (PPS): Fixed payment per share.

        Pool absorbs variance risk. Miner gets predictable income.
        Payment = share_difficulty / network_difficulty * block_reward
        """
        pps_rate = (share_difficulty / difficulty) * block_reward
        return {
            miner: count * pps_rate
            for miner, count in shares.items()
        }

    @staticmethod
    def pay_per_last_n_shares(shares_history: list, block_reward: float,
```

```
                                    n: int) -> dict:
        """
        PPLNS: Pay based on last N shares before block found.

        Resistant to pool hopping because only recent shares count.
        Miners must maintain consistent participation to earn.
        """
        # Take last N shares from history
        recent = shares_history[-n:] if len(shares_history) >= n else
        shares_history

        # Count shares per miner
        miner_shares = {}
        for miner in recent:
            miner_shares[miner] = miner_shares.get(miner, 0) + 1

        total = len(recent)
        return {
            miner: (count / total) * block_reward
            for miner, count in miner_shares.items()
        }

# Demonstrate reward schemes
shares = {'Alice': 500, 'Bob': 300, 'Carol': 200}
block_reward = 3.125

prop_rewards = PoolRewardScheme.proportional(shares, block_reward)
pps_rewards = PoolRewardScheme.pay_per_share(
    shares, block_reward, difficulty=1e12, share_difficulty=1e6
)

print("Proportional Rewards:")
for miner, reward in prop_rewards.items():
    print(f"  {miner}: {reward:.6f} BTC")

print("\nPPS Rewards (per share):")
for miner, reward in pps_rewards.items():
    print(f"  {miner}: {reward:.10f} BTC")
```

Table 5-8. Pool Reward Scheme Comparison

Scheme	Variance for Miner	Pool Risk	Hopping Resistance	Complexity
Proportional	Medium	None	Low	Low
PPS	None	High (pool absorbs luck)	High	Medium
PPLNS	Medium-Low	Low	High	Medium
FPPS (Full PPS)	None (includes fees)	High	High	High
Score-based	Low	Low	High	High

Centralization Concerns

Pool dominance is policy power: transaction selection, block template quirks, and in worst-case scenarios, coordination leverage over consensus.

Table 5-9. Mining Pool Centralization Risks

Concentration Level	Risk	Example Scenario
Single pool > 25%	Transaction censorship feasible	Pool refuses to include specific transactions
Single pool > 33%	Selfish mining profitable	Pool earns disproportionate rewards
Single pool > 50%	Double-spend attacks possible	Pool can reverse confirmed transactions
Top 3 pools > 50%	Coordinated attack surface	Collusion or simultaneous compromise
Top 3 pools > 75%	Effective centralization	The mining cartel controls block production

Ghash.io cracked 50% in 2014—no exploit fired, but miners fled anyway. Lesson: pool economics can centralize what PoW tried to spread out.

Game-Theoretic Analysis of Pool Selection

Choosing a pool is a game: small pools—higher payout variance, healthier distribution; whales—smoother income, fatter operator influence.

In proportional schemes, expected BTC/day is about your hashrate share—pool size mostly moves variance, not mean (fees aside).

PPS smooths payouts for a fee because the house absorbs variance—the fee structure nudges people toward mid-size pools that can afford insurance math.

5.1.8 Summary

PoW is weirdly elegant: burn physics to buy ordering rights. Progress-free mining keeps the lottery honest; retargeting keeps tempo stable when the world throws ASICs at the problem.

Compressed takeaways:

- **Hashes**: expensive to mine, cheap to verify; interblock times exponential/poisson-flavored.
- Difficulty rules aren't decorative—Bitcoin's 2016-block cadence vs. per-block algos trade lag vs. twitchiness.
- Security budget ~= what miners spend; ASIC eras concentrated who could afford to play.
- 51% math is Gambler's Ruin—depth buys exponential safety until q gets scary-close to 0.5.
- **Selfish Mining**: honesty isn't always Nash—mid-20s–30% hashrate can game propagation if gamma helps.
- Energy is the price tag printed on that security—evaluate it with the threat model, not slogans.
- Pools trade variance smoothing for coordination risk—PROP/PPS/PPLNS split variance between miners and operators differently.

One breath of numbers: puzzles are memoryless; Bitcoin retargets every 2,016 blocks while others tweak each block; profitability is efficiency * power * price algebra; catch-up ~ (q/p)^z style decay; selfish threshold (1-gamma)/(3-2*gamma) can dip near 25% with friendly gamma; pool schemes shuffle variance; big pools centralize policy; PoW joules are the security budget line item, not a rounding error.

You need this mental model to judge when PoW fits—next chapter swaps work for stake and change the assumptions entirely.

5.1.9 Exercises

Problem 1 (Basic): 120s target, last 100 blocks average 95s—what multiplicative difficulty tweak does that imply?

Problem 2 (Calculation): q=25%—Gambler's Ruin probability after 3 and 6 confirmations. Show algebra.

Problem 3 (Implementation): Simulate 10k blocks; check mean/variance vs. exponential; histogram.

Problem 4 (Analysis): 50 ASICs @ 140 TH/s, 3010 W, $0.07/kWh, 500 EH/s network, 3.125 BTC reward—find break-even BTC price with $5k/ASIC depreciation over two years.

Problem 5 (Design): Faster retarget than 2,016 blocks without opening timestamp games—specify, analyze, and attack it.

Problem 6 (Theory): Derive the selfish-mining threshold (1-gamma)/(3-2*gamma) from the Markov steady-state story; state assumptions.

Problem 7 (Comparative): Hourly 51% rent for Bitcoin vs. Litecoin vs. a third chain—what drives the gap?

Problem 8 (Critical Thinking): 30-second PoW like Bitcoin—orphans, confirmations, propagation, and security-per-confirm tradeoffs.

Problem 9 (Advanced): Add censorship to your selfish-mining sim—how does optimal strategy shift?

Problem 10 (Research): Pick a real smaller-cap 51% incident—cost, duration, theft, patch response, lesson for low-hash networks.

(Solutions in Appendix D)

5.1.10 Further Reading

History: Hashcash (2002 writeup) for spam; Dwork-Naor (1992) even earlier on pricing abuse with puzzles.

Cambridge's mining map/energy trackers are the sober charts—use them instead of viral infographics.

Selfish mining: Eyal-Sirer first; Sapirshtein et al. for nastier optimal strategies.

51% mechanics: Rosenfeld for worked examples; Gervais et al. add propagation realism.

Pools: Lewenberg et al. on formation; Eyal's "Miner's Dilemma" for pool-on-pool sketch.

Skip: PoW is pure waste with no security model; also skip static TWh quotes that ignore chip efficiency gains and stranded power sitting.

CHAPTER 6

Proof of Stake

6.1 Security, Slashing, and Long-Range Attacks

This chapter covers Proof of Stake in full—how locked capital replaces burned electricity as the security mechanism, the nothing-at-stake problem and the fixes that make PoS shippable, Ethereum's Gasper consensus (LMD-GHOST fork choice and Casper FFG finality), slashing mechanics, long-range attacks and weak subjectivity, validator economics and MEV, and how PoS security compares to PoW. Roughly what you'll be able to defend in conversation:

- Skin in the game, literally: PoS is money locked up, not megawatts burned
- The nothing-at-stake headache and the pile of patches (slash, finality, delays, leaks) that make PoS shippable
- Gasper without the acronym soup: ghost picks the tip; Casper hammers epochs shut
- Slashing—the part that stops "rational" validators from signing every fork for fun
- Long-range weirdness + weak subjectivity (yeah, it's a philosophical bruise)
- Yield, MEV, and the ways staking recentralizes stuff that isn't a hydro dam
- Scribble attack economics: when PoS math looks cheaper or scarier than PoW, and why
- Day-to-day validator life (it's not just "run geth and chill")

N. Savant, *Blockchain Foundations*, https://doi.org/10.1007/979-8-8688-2891-1_6

6.1.1 From Computation to Capital

PoW writes the tab in kilowatt-hours. PoS writes it in locked coins you might never see again. Hashcash-style puzzles predate Bitcoin; the hard part was making the stake slashable without turning the chain into judge-jury-executioner by accident. Took years.

Miners pay utilities; that spend is gone whether the attack lands or not. Validators park collateral—security is "we will delete your money if you cheat," and it has to be believable. Months of honest work feel like passive income until someone misconfigures a client and the protocol disagrees.

The security deposit mental model still works. The landlord doesn't light your deposit on fire monthly; the *threat* shapes behavior. PoS just automates the fire if you break the lease in a provable way.

Table 6-1. *PoW vs. PoS Security Model*

Property	Proof of Work	Proof of Stake
Security source	Computational cost	Economic bond
Attack cost	Hardware + electricity	Staked capital at risk
Resource consumption	High (energy)	Low (standard computing)
Attack recovery	Attacker keeps hardware	Attacker's stake can be destroyed
Capital efficiency	Low (specialized hardware)	Higher (capital still exists)
Entry barrier	Hardware procurement	Capital acquisition
Exit cost	Hardware depreciation	Unbonding period only
Revenue model	Block rewards + fees	Staking rewards + fees + MEV

Failed PoW attacks still leave you hardware to sell. Aggressive PoS slashing can vaporize the principal—a different recovery curve for the attacker and a different deterrence shape.

PoW burns power even if nobody notices mischief in time. PoS often needs on-chain evidence—if your evil never surfaces in a slashable message, penalties don't trigger. So rule coverage and observation windows aren't footnotes; they're load-bearing.

The Validator Role

Validators = miner job title, new uniform. 32 ETH in, chores out (Ethereum-shaped example):

1. **Proposal Shifts:** you get picked, you package txs, you gossip a block.
2. **Attestations:** you stick your neck out on validity + which branch you think is real.
3. Finality machinery eats your votes to glue epochs shut.
4. If the sync committee drafts you, light clients lean on you—extra homework.

Leader election isn't one-size-fits-all across chains:

RANDAO-ish mix plus stake weight: not cosmic randomness, but messy enough to game expensively.

More stake, more lottery tickets—two minipools aren't magic, they're roughly double the draw rate vs. one.

Sharding attention via committees because full all-to-all attestation every 12s would melt gossip.

VRF worlds (Algorand-ish): you privately test "am I proposer?" so attackers can't camp your IP before the fact.

The code below shows how validator registration and selection work in practice—how stake is registered, how a proposer is chosen for each slot, and how committees are formed. The idea of why these rules are important—and what problems happen without slashing—is explained in 6.2. So first read the code here to understand how it works, then read 6.2 to understand why it must work this way.

```
import hashlib
import random
from typing import Dict, List, Optional, Tuple

class ValidatorRegistry:
    """Manage validator set with stake-weighted selection."""

    def __init__(self):
        self.validators: Dict[int, dict] = {}
```

```
        self.total_stake = 0
        self.next_id = 0

    def register(self, deposit: int, pubkey: str) -> int:
        """Register a new validator with deposit."""
        if deposit < 32:
            raise ValueError("Minimum deposit is 32 ETH")

        vid = self.next_id
        self.next_id += 1

        # Effective balance capped at 32 ETH
        effective = min(deposit, 32)

        self.validators[vid] = {
            'id': vid,
            'pubkey': pubkey,
            'balance': deposit,
            'effective_balance': effective,
            'active': True,
            'slashed': False,
            'exit_epoch': None,
            'activation_epoch': 0,
        }
        self.total_stake += effective
        return vid

    def select_proposer(self, slot: int, epoch_seed: bytes) -> int:
        """
        Select block proposer using RANDAO-like mechanism.

        Probability proportional to effective balance.
        """
        active = [(vid, v['effective_balance'])
                  for vid, v in self.validators.items()
                  if v['active'] and not v['slashed']]

        if not active:
            raise ValueError("No active validators")
```

```
        # Deterministic selection from slot + seed
        seed_data = epoch_seed + slot.to_bytes(8, 'big')
        h = hashlib.sha256(seed_data).digest()
        random_value = int.from_bytes(h[:8], 'big')

        total = sum(eb for _, eb in active)
        target = random_value % total

        cumulative = 0
        for vid, eb in active:
            cumulative += eb
            if target < cumulative:
                return vid

        return active[-1][0]

    def select_committee(self, slot: int, epoch_seed: bytes,
                         committee_size: int = 128) -> List[int]:
        """Select attestation committee for a slot."""
        active_ids = [vid for vid, v in self.validators.items()
                      if v['active'] and not v['slashed']]

        # Shuffle using Fisher-Yates with deterministic seed
        seed_data = epoch_seed + slot.to_bytes(8, 'big') + b"committee"
        rng = random.Random(int.from_bytes(
            hashlib.sha256(seed_data).digest()[:8], 'big'))

        shuffled = list(active_ids)
        rng.shuffle(shuffled)

        return shuffled[:min(committee_size, len(shuffled))]

# Demonstrate validator operations
registry = ValidatorRegistry()

# Register validators with different stakes
validators = [
    registry.register(32, f"pubkey_validator_{i}")
    for i in range(10)
]
```

```
# Large staker runs multiple validators
large_staker_validators = [
    registry.register(32, f"pubkey_large_staker_{i}")
    for i in range(5)
]

epoch_seed = hashlib.sha256(b"epoch_0_randomness").digest()

# Track proposer selection distribution over many slots
proposer_counts = {}
for slot in range(1000):
    proposer = registry.select_proposer(slot, epoch_seed)
    proposer_counts[proposer] = proposer_counts.get(proposer, 0) + 1

print("Validator Selection Demonstration")
print("=" * 55)
print(f"Total validators: {len(registry.validators)}")
print(f"Total effective stake: {registry.total_stake} ETH")
print(f"\nProposer distribution over 1000 slots:")

# Group by staker
regular_proposals = sum(proposer_counts.get(v, 0) for v in validators)
large_proposals = sum(proposer_counts.get(v, 0) for v in large_staker_
validators)
print(f"  Regular stakers (10 validators):  {regular_proposals} proposals "
      f"({regular_proposals/10:.1f} avg)")
print(f"  Large staker (5 validators):      {large_proposals} proposals "
      f"({large_proposals/5:.1f} avg)")
print(f"  Expected per validator: {1000/15:.1f}")

# Committee selection
committee = registry.select_committee(0, epoch_seed, 8)
print(f"\nSlot 0 committee ({len(committee)} members): {committee}")
```

6.1.2 The Nothing-at-Stake Problem

Nothing-at-stake was the decade-long migraine. You can't meaningfully double-hash PoW across two tips without paying twice; signing two PoS blocks is basically free. Scarcity of work forced commitment in PoW; PoS had to manufacture scarcity elsewhere.

Naive stake? You sign everything, hope something wins, and never leave money on the table. If that spreads, consensus signals evaporate.

```
PoW (Physical Constraint):

    Block N ── Fork A (miner allocates 100% hash power here)
           \
            ─ Fork B (no hash power = no chance of reward)

    Mining is a physical process. Each hash targets one chain.
    Splitting hash power reduces probability on each fork.

Naive PoS (No Constraint):

    Block N ── Fork A (validator signs ✓ - might win)
           \
            ─ Fork B (validator also signs ✓ - might also win)

    Signing is free. Rational validator signs BOTH forks.
    No lost revenue. Double the chance of earning rewards.

Consequence: If ALL validators follow this rational strategy,
forks never resolve. The chain splits permanently.
```

Figure 6-1. *Nothing-at-Stake Problem*

Not a seminar paradox—without fixes, fork choice collapses because votes cost nothing.

Formalizing the Problem

Toy model: fork at height N into A and B; you hold stake s. Three strategies people actually write down:

Pick one fork like a sport: payoff ties to whether your pick wins—real risk.

Vote for both forks: you harvest rewards either way; dominate honest single-fork betting if slash-free.

Tiny bribes: another signature costs epsilon CPU, so attackers can rent votes for pocket change unless rules punish conflicts.

```
def nothing_at_stake_payoffs(stake: float, reward_rate: float,
                              prob_fork_a: float) -> dict:
    """Compare payoffs for honest vs nothing-at-stake strategies."""
    prob_fork_b = 1 - prob_fork_a

    honest_a = stake * prob_fork_a * reward_rate
    honest_b = stake * prob_fork_b * reward_rate

    # Nothing-at-stake: vote on both forks
    noas = stake * reward_rate  # Always earn regardless of outcome

    # With slashing penalty for double-voting
    slash_rate = 0.5  # Lose 50% of stake if caught
    prob_caught = 0.95  # High detection rate
    noas_with_slashing = (
        stake * reward_rate -
        prob_caught * slash_rate * stake
    )

    return {
        'honest_fork_a': honest_a,
        'honest_fork_b': honest_b,
        'best_honest': max(honest_a, honest_b),
        'nothing_at_stake': noas,
        'noas_gain_pct': ((noas - max(honest_a, honest_b)) /
                          max(honest_a, honest_b) * 100),
        'noas_with_slashing': noas_with_slashing,
        'slashing_deters': noas_with_slashing < max(honest_a, honest_b),
    }

print("Nothing-at-Stake Payoff Analysis")
print("=" * 60)
for prob_a in [0.5, 0.7, 0.9]:
    result = nothing_at_stake_payoffs(32, 0.05, prob_a)
    print(f"\nP(Fork A wins) = {prob_a}")
```

```
    print(f"  Best honest payoff:     {result['best_honest']:.4f} ETH")
    print(f"  Nothing-at-stake:       {result['nothing_at_stake']:.4f} ETH "
          f"(+{result['noas_gain_pct']:.1f}%)")
    print(f"  With slashing:          {result['noas_with_
slashing']:.4f} ETH")
    print(f"  Slashing deters NaS:    {result['slashing_deters']}")
```

Solutions to Nothing-at-Stake

Production systems layer fixes; none alone is enough:

Slashing makes "free" votes expensive after the fact—fines must beat upside or it's a line item, not deterrence.

Finality layers mean unwinding deep history implies burning enormous stake chunks, not editing a row.

Exit queues/delays: you don't rage-quit the validator set mid-attack with the loot.

Leaks for going offline: ugly, but keeps the beast from finalizing when big chunks vanish.

6.1.3 Ethereum's Gasper Consensus

Gasper sounds like one brand; it's really fork-choice glue plus a finality overlay. LMD-GHOST: where's the tip today? Casper FFG: what epoch got buried for real? Break one subsystem, have a different disaster.

Time Structure

Clocks on the beacon chain are almost fussy:

Twelve-second slots, each with a proposer plus a committee's babysitting attestations.

Thirty-two slots stitch an epoch (~6.4 minutes)—bookkeeping for finality and committee roulette.

Across that window, active validators usually attest once; 32 committees, no double shifts.

```
# Ethereum PoS time structure constants
SECONDS_PER_SLOT = 12
SLOTS_PER_EPOCH = 32
```

```
SECONDS_PER_EPOCH = SECONDS_PER_SLOT * SLOTS_PER_EPOCH
# 384 seconds = 6.4 min
EPOCHS_PER_SYNC_COMMITTEE = 256  # ~27 hours
MIN_VALIDATOR_WITHDRAWABILITY_DELAY = 256  # epochs (~27 hours)
SHARD_COMMITTEE_PERIOD = 256  # epochs

def slot_to_epoch(slot: int) -> int:
    return slot // SLOTS_PER_EPOCH

def epoch_start_slot(epoch: int) -> int:
    return epoch * SLOTS_PER_EPOCH

def time_to_slot(genesis_time: int, current_time: int) -> int:
    elapsed = current_time - genesis_time
    if elapsed < 0:
        return 0
    return elapsed // SECONDS_PER_SLOT

def compute_shuffled_index(index: int, index_count: int, seed:
bytes) -> int:
    """
    Swap-or-not shuffle used in Ethereum beacon chain.

    Deterministic permutation based on seed. Each validator
    is assigned to exactly one slot per epoch.
    """
    for current_round in range(90):  # 90 rounds of swap-or-not
        pivot_data = seed + current_round.to_bytes(1, 'big')
        pivot_hash = hashlib.sha256(pivot_data).digest()
        pivot = int.from_bytes(pivot_hash[:8], 'big') % index_count

        flip = (pivot + index_count - index) % index_count
        position = max(index, flip)

        source_data = (seed + current_round.to_bytes(1, 'big') +
                       (position // 256).to_bytes(4, 'big'))
        source_hash = hashlib.sha256(source_data).digest()

        byte_val = source_hash[(position % 256) // 8]
```

```
        bit = (byte_val >> (position % 8)) & 1

        index = flip if bit else index

    return index

print("Ethereum PoS Time Structure")
print(f"  Slot duration: {SECONDS_PER_SLOT}s")
print(f"  Epoch duration: {SECONDS_PER_EPOCH}s ({SECONDS_PER_
EPOCH/60:.1f} min)")
print(f"  Slots per epoch: {SLOTS_PER_EPOCH}")
print(f"  Finality: 2 epochs = {2 * SECONDS_PER_EPOCH}s ({2 * SECONDS_PER_
EPOCH/60:.1f} min)")
```

LMD-GHOST Fork Choice

LMD-GHOST: silly name, concrete rule—chase the subtree with the most recent attestation weight behind it, not the tallest chain by block count.

Only your latest vote counts; you can't snowball reputation by repeating old attestations.

Algorithm sketch starting from the newest justified checkpoint:

1. Land on that checkpoint.
2. At a fork, follow the child subtree that currently carries more effective balance under the latest votes.
3. Stop at a leaf; that's your head.

```
from typing import Dict, List, Set, Optional from dataclasses import
dataclass, field
@dataclass class BeaconBlock: slot: int parent_hash: str block_hash: str
proposer_index: int state_root: str = ""
@dataclass class Attestation: slot: int block_hash: str validator_index:
int effective_balance: int source_epoch: int = 0 target_epoch: int = 0
class LMDGhost: """"Simplified LMD-GHOST fork choice implementation."""
 def __init__(self):
     self.blocks: Dict[str, BeaconBlock] = {}
     self.children: Dict[str, List[str]] = {}
```

```
        self.latest_messages: Dict[int, Attestation] = {}
        self.justified_checkpoint: str = "genesis"

    def add_block(self, block: BeaconBlock):
        """Add a block to the block tree."""
        self.blocks[block.block_hash] = block
        if block.parent_hash not in self.children:
            self.children[block.parent_hash] = []
        self.children[block.parent_hash].append(block.block_hash)

    def add_attestation(self, attestation: Attestation):
        """
        Store latest attestation per validator.
        Only the most recent message from each validator counts.
        This prevents validators from accumulating votes.
        """
        current = self.latest_messages.get(attestation.validator_index)
        if current is None or attestation.slot > current.slot:
            self.latest_messages[attestation.validator_index] = attestation

    def get_weight(self, block_hash: str) -> int:
        """
        Compute total weight of subtree rooted at block_hash.

        Weight = sum of effective balances of all validators whose
        latest attestation targets this block or any descendant.
        This is what makes it "heaviest observed subtree."
        """
        supported_blocks = self._get_subtree(block_hash)
        weight = 0
        for att in self.latest_messages.values():
            if att.block_hash in supported_blocks:
                weight += att.effective_balance
        return weight

    def _get_subtree(self, root_hash: str) -> Set[str]:
        """Get all blocks in subtree rooted at root_hash (BFS)."""
        subtree = {root_hash}
```

```
        queue = [root_hash]
        while queue:
            current = queue.pop(0)
            for child_hash in self.children.get(current, []):
                if child_hash not in subtree:
                    subtree.add(child_hash)
                    queue.append(child_hash)
        return subtree

    def find_head(self) -> str:
        """
        Execute LMD-GHOST fork choice rule.

        Start from justified checkpoint, greedily follow the child
        with the heaviest subtree at each fork point.
        """
        current = self.justified_checkpoint

        while current in self.children and self.children[current]:
            children = self.children[current]
            if len(children) == 1:
                current = children[0]
            else:
                # At a fork: choose child with greatest subtree weight
                best_child = max(children, key=lambda c: (
                    self.get_weight(c),
                    c  # Tiebreak by hash for determinism
                ))
                current = best_child

        return current

    def get_chain(self, head: str) -> List[str]:
        """Trace chain from head back to justified checkpoint."""
        chain = [head]
        current = head
        while current in self.blocks:
            parent = self.blocks[current].parent_hash
```

```
        if parent == self.justified_checkpoint or parent == "genesis":
            chain.append(parent)
            break
        chain.append(parent)
        current = parent
    return list(reversed(chain))
# Demonstration: fork scenario ghost = LMDGhost()
# Build a chain with a fork at block 1 blocks = [ BeaconBlock(1,
“genesis”, “block_1”, 0), BeaconBlock(2, “block_1”, “block_2a”, 1), #
Fork A BeaconBlock(2, “block_1”, “block_2b”, 2), # Fork B BeaconBlock(3,
“block_2a”, “block_3a”, 3), # Fork A continues BeaconBlock(3, “block_2b”,
“block_3b”, 4), # Fork B continues BeaconBlock(4, “block_3a”, “block_4a”,
5), # Fork A deeper ] for b in blocks: ghost.add_block(b)
# Simulate validator attestations (10 validators, 32 ETH each)
attestations = [ # 6 validators support Fork A (various blocks in subtree)
Attestation(4, “block_4a”, 0, 32), Attestation(3, “block_3a”, 1, 32),
Attestation(2, “block_2a”, 2, 32), Attestation(4, “block_4a”, 3, 32),
Attestation(3, “block_3a”, 4, 32), Attestation(4, “block_4a”, 5, 32), # 4
validators support Fork B Attestation(3, “block_3b”, 6, 32), Attestation(2,
“block_2b”, 7, 32), Attestation(3, “block_3b”, 8, 32), Attestation(2,
“block_2b”, 9, 32), ] for att in attestations: ghost.add_attestation(att)
head = ghost.find_head() chain = ghost.get_chain(head)
print(“LMD-GHOST Fork Choice Demonstration”) print(“=” * 55) print(f”Fork
A subtree weight: {ghost.get_weight(‘block_2a’)} ETH” f”(6 validators)“)
print(f”Fork B subtree weight: {ghost.get_weight(‘block_2b’)} ETH” f”(4
validators)“) print(f”Selected chain head: {head}“) print(f”Canonical
chain: {’ -> ’.join(chain)}“)
# Now demonstrate validator switching print(“– Validator 9 switches from
Fork B to Fork A –”) ghost.add_attestation(Attestation(5, “block_4a”,
9, 32)) new_head = ghost.find_head() print(f”Fork A weight: {ghost.
get_weight(‘block_2a’)} ETH”) print(f”Fork B weight: {ghost.get_
weight(‘block_2b’)} ETH”) print(f”New chain head: {new_head}“)
```

Casper FFG (Friendly Finality Gadget)

Ghost handles liveness-ish fork choice; Casper slaps finality on top. Neither replaces the other.

Checkpoints: basically epoch seams, the first slot of each epoch tied to a block hash.

Justified vs. finalized (you will mix them up once):

Justified = fat supermajority link saying "we're converging here"—serious, but not carved in marble.

Finalized = that two-step dance where the next epoch also justifies through—undoing it means slashing on the order of a third of stake, i.e., not your casual 1-deep reorg.

Two epochs of agreement on purpose so one lucky attestation burst can't "finalize" by accident.

```
@dataclass
class Checkpoint:
    epoch: int
    block_hash: str
    justified: bool = False
    finalized: bool = False

@dataclass
class CasperVote:
    validator_index: int
    source_epoch: int
    target_epoch: int
    source_root: str
    target_root: str
    stake: int

class CasperFFG:
    """Simplified Casper FFG finality gadget."""

    def __init__(self, total_stake: int):
        self.total_stake = total_stake
        self.checkpoints: Dict[int, Checkpoint] = {}
        self.supermajority_threshold = (total_stake * 2) // 3 + 1
```

```
        # Track votes for each (source, target) link
        self.link_votes: Dict[Tuple[int, int], int] = {}
        self.link_voters: Dict[Tuple[int, int], Set[int]] = {}

    def add_checkpoint(self, epoch: int, block_hash: str):
        self.checkpoints[epoch] = Checkpoint(epoch, block_hash)

    def cast_vote(self, vote: CasperVote) -> dict:
        """
        Validator casts a Casper FFG vote (supermajority link).

        A vote (s, t) says: "I attest that checkpoint at epoch s
        is justified and checkpoint at epoch t descends from it."
        """
        key = (vote.source_epoch, vote.target_epoch)

        # Prevent double-voting (same validator, same key)
        if key not in self.link_voters:
            self.link_voters[key] = set()

        if vote.validator_index in self.link_voters[key]:
            return {'accepted': False, 'reason': 'Already voted for
            this link'}

        self.link_voters[key].add(vote.validator_index)
        self.link_votes[key] = self.link_votes.get(key, 0) + vote.stake

        result = {'accepted': True, 'new_justification': False,
                  'new_finalization': False}

        # Check if this creates a supermajority link
        if self.link_votes[key] >= self.supermajority_threshold:
            result.update(self._process_supermajority_link(
                vote.source_epoch, vote.target_epoch))

        return result

    def _process_supermajority_link(self, source: int, target: int)
    -> dict:
        """Process a newly formed supermajority link."""
```

```
        result = {'new_justification': False, 'new_finalization': False}

        if target not in self.checkpoints:
            return result

        # Source must be justified for the link to justify the target
        if source in self.checkpoints and self.checkpoints[source].
        justified:
            if not self.checkpoints[target].justified:
                self.checkpoints[target].justified = True
                result['new_justification'] = True

            # Finalization: if source is justified and target = source + 1
            if target == source + 1 and not self.checkpoints[source].
            finalized:
                self.checkpoints[source].finalized = True
                result['new_finalization'] = True

        return result

    def get_status(self) -> str:
        lines = []
        for epoch in sorted(self.checkpoints.keys()):
            cp = self.checkpoints[epoch]
            status = "FINALIZED" if cp.finalized else (
                "JUSTIFIED" if cp.justified else "pending")

            # Show vote progress for links from this epoch
            vote_info = ""
            for (s, t), votes in self.link_votes.items():
                if s == epoch:
                    pct = votes / self.total_stake * 100
                    vote_info += f" [->epoch {t}: {pct:.0f}%]"

            lines.append(f"  Epoch {epoch}: [{status:>10}] {cp.block_hash}
            {vote_info}")
        return "\n".join(lines)

# Demonstration: Casper FFG finality
NUM_VALIDATORS = 100
```

```
STAKE_PER = 32
total_stake = NUM_VALIDATORS * STAKE_PER

casper = CasperFFG(total_stake=total_stake)


# Genesis is justified by definition
casper.add_checkpoint(0, "genesis_root")
casper.checkpoints[0].justified = True

casper.add_checkpoint(1, "epoch_1_root")
casper.add_checkpoint(2, "epoch_2_root")
casper.add_checkpoint(3, "epoch_3_root")

print("Casper FFG Finality Demonstration")
print("=" * 60)
print(f"Total stake: {total_stake} ETH ({NUM_VALIDATORS} validators)")
print(f"Supermajority threshold: {casper.supermajority_threshold} ETH "
      f"(>{total_stake * 2 / 3:.0f})")

# Epoch 0 -> 1: validators vote
print("\n--- Voting epoch 0 -> epoch 1 ---")
for i in range(70):  # 70 of 100 validators vote (70%)
    casper.cast_vote(CasperVote(i, 0, 1, "genesis_root", "epoch_1_root",
STAKE_PER))
print(casper.get_status())

# Epoch 1 -> 2: validators vote
print("\n--- Voting epoch 1 -> epoch 2 ---")
for i in range(68):  # 68 of 100 (68%)
    casper.cast_vote(CasperVote(i, 1, 2, "epoch_1_root", "epoch_2_root",
STAKE_PER))
print(casper.get_status())

# Epoch 2 -> 3: validators vote
print("\n--- Voting epoch 2 -> epoch 3 ---")
for i in range(75):
    casper.cast_vote(CasperVote(i, 2, 3, "epoch_2_root", "epoch_3_root",
STAKE_PER))
print(casper.get_status())
```

The Accountable Safety Guarantee

Accountable safety: if two conflicting checkpoints both finalize, someone with ≥1/3 stake was provably naughty—that's the theorem flavor.

Double-vote evidence: two incompatible attestations in the same target epoch—usually obvious side-by-side.

Surround votes: nesting epoch intervals—takes a minute to detect, still on-chain provable.

```
def check_slashing_conditions(votes: List[CasperVote]) -> List[dict]:
    """
    Check for Casper FFG slashing violations.

    Two conditions:
    1. Double vote: same target epoch, different source
    2. Surround vote: one vote's range contains another's
    """
    violations = []

    # Group votes by validator
    by_validator: Dict[int, List[CasperVote]] = {}
    for vote in votes:
        if vote.validator_index not in by_validator:
            by_validator[vote.validator_index] = []
        by_validator[vote.validator_index].append(vote)

    for vid, validator_votes in by_validator.items():
        for i in range(len(validator_votes)):
            for j in range(i + 1, len(validator_votes)):
                v1 = validator_votes[i]
                v2 = validator_votes[j]

                # Check double vote
                if (v1.target_epoch == v2.target_epoch and
                    v1.source_epoch != v2.source_epoch):
                    violations.append({
                        'validator': vid,
                        'type': 'double_vote',
```

```
                    'vote_1': (v1.source_epoch, v1.target_epoch),
                    'vote_2': (v2.source_epoch, v2.target_epoch),
                })

            # Check surround vote
            if (v1.source_epoch < v2.source_epoch and
                v2.target_epoch < v1.target_epoch):
                violations.append({
                    'validator': vid,
                    'type': 'surround_vote',
                    'outer': (v1.source_epoch, v1.target_epoch),
                    'inner': (v2.source_epoch, v2.target_epoch),
                })
            elif (v2.source_epoch < v1.source_epoch and
                  v1.target_epoch < v2.target_epoch):
                violations.append({
                    'validator': vid,
                    'type': 'surround_vote',
                    'outer': (v2.source_epoch, v2.target_epoch),
                    'inner': (v1.source_epoch, v1.target_epoch),
                })

    return violations

# Demonstrate slashing detection
honest_votes = [
    CasperVote(0, 0, 1, "r0", "r1", 32),
    CasperVote(0, 1, 2, "r1", "r2", 32),
    CasperVote(1, 0, 1, "r0", "r1", 32),
]

# Add a malicious double vote from validator 2
malicious_votes = honest_votes + [
    CasperVote(2, 0, 1, "r0", "r1", 32),        # First vote
    CasperVote(2, 0, 1, "r0_alt", "r1_alt", 32), # Same target,
different source!
]
```

```
# Add a surround vote from validator 3
surround_votes = malicious_votes + [
    CasperVote(3, 0, 3, "r0", "r3", 32),  # Outer vote: epoch 0->3
    CasperVote(3, 1, 2, "r1", "r2", 32),  # Inner vote: epoch 1->2
(surrounded)
]

violations = check_slashing_conditions(surround_votes)
print("\nSlashing Condition Detection")
print("=" * 55)
if violations:
    for v in violations:
        print(f"  VIOLATION: Validator {v['validator']} - {v['type']}")
        if v['type'] == 'double_vote':
            print(f"     Vote 1: epoch {v['vote_1'][0]} ->
{v['vote_1'][1]}")
            print(f"     Vote 2: epoch {v['vote_2'][0]} ->
{v['vote_2'][1]}")
        else:
            print(f"     Outer: epoch {v['outer'][0]} -> {v['outer'][1]}")
            print(f"     Inner: epoch {v['inner'][0]} -> {v['inner'][1]}")
else:
    print("  No violations detected")
```

6.1.4 Slashing Mechanisms

Missed rewards hurt feelings; slashing deletes money. Different incentive gradient than PoW's "burned electricity."

Parameters are thankless: soft penalties become line items for attackers; brutal penalties nuke unlucky engineers on buggy releases. Correlation scoring tries to tell solo oops from mob action.

Slashable Offenses in Ethereum

Same-slot double propose: two headers, one slot—hard to plead innocence.

Attester slash: double-vote or surround—the chain stores the receipts.

Penalty Calculation

```
def calculate_slashing_penalty(validator_balance_gwei: int,
                               total_slashed_balance_gwei: int,
                               total_active_balance_gwei: int,
                               is_proposer_of_slashing: bool = False)
-> dict:
    """
    Calculate Ethereum slashing penalty with all three components.

    The penalty has three parts:
    1. Initial penalty: 1/32 of effective balance (immediate)
    2. Correlation penalty: proportional to total slashed in window
       (applied at midpoint of exit period, ~18 days after slash)
    3. Attestation penalties: missed rewards during forced exit period
       (~36 days of missed attestations)

    The correlation penalty is the key innovation. It ensures:
    - Isolated mistakes (software bugs): minimal penalty (~3%)
    - Coordinated attacks: catastrophic penalty (up to 100%)
    """
    effective_balance = min(validator_balance_gwei, 32 * 10**9)

    # Component 1: Initial penalty (1/32 of effective balance)
    initial_penalty = effective_balance // 32

    # Component 2: Correlation penalty
    # penalty = effective_balance * (3 * total_slashed / total_active)
    # Capped at effective_balance
    if total_active_balance_gwei > 0:
        correlation_numerator = 3 * total_slashed_balance_gwei
        correlation_penalty = min(
            effective_balance * correlation_numerator // total_active_
            balance_gwei,
            effective_balance
        )
    else:
        correlation_penalty = 0
```

```
    # Component 3: Missed attestation penalties during exit period
    # Approximately 36 days (~8192 epochs) of missed attestations
    # Simplified: estimate as proportion of annual reward missed
    exit_period_days = 36
    annual_reward_estimate = effective_balance * 4 // 100  # ~4% yield
    daily_reward = annual_reward_estimate // 365
    missed_attestation_loss = daily_reward * exit_period_days

    # Whistleblower reward (for the validator that reported the offense)
    whistleblower_reward = effective_balance // 512

    total_penalty = initial_penalty + correlation_penalty + missed_
    attestation_loss
    total_penalty = min(total_penalty, validator_balance_gwei)

    remaining = validator_balance_gwei - total_penalty

    return {
        'initial_penalty_gwei': initial_penalty,
        'initial_penalty_eth': initial_penalty / 10**9,
        'correlation_penalty_gwei': correlation_penalty,
        'correlation_penalty_eth': correlation_penalty / 10**9,
        'missed_attestation_gwei': missed_attestation_loss,
        'missed_attestation_eth': missed_attestation_loss / 10**9,
        'total_penalty_gwei': total_penalty,
        'total_penalty_eth': total_penalty / 10**9,
        'remaining_eth': remaining / 10**9,
        'penalty_percentage': (total_penalty / validator_balance_
        gwei) * 100,
        'whistleblower_reward_eth': whistleblower_reward / 10**9,
    }

total_active = 20_000_000 * 10**9  # 20M ETH in Gwei

# Scenario 1: Single validator slashed (honest mistake / bug)
single = calculate_slashing_penalty(
    validator_balance_gwei=32 * 10**9,
    total_slashed_balance_gwei=32 * 10**9,
```

```
    total_active_balance_gwei=total_active,
)

# Scenario 2: 100 validators slashed (small coordinated incident)
small_group = calculate_slashing_penalty(
    validator_balance_gwei=32 * 10**9,
    total_slashed_balance_gwei=3200 * 10**9,
    total_active_balance_gwei=total_active,
)

# Scenario 3: 1/3 of validators slashed (finality attack)
attack = calculate_slashing_penalty(
    validator_balance_gwei=32 * 10**9,
    total_slashed_balance_gwei=int(total_active / 3),
    total_active_balance_gwei=total_active,
)

print("Slashing Penalty Analysis")
print("=" * 65)
scenarios = [
    ("Isolated mistake (1 validator)", single),
    ("Small group (100 validators)", small_group),
    ("Finality attack (1/3 of stake)", attack),
]
for name, result in scenarios:
    print(f"\n{name}:")
    print(f"  Initial:       {result['initial_penalty_eth']:.4f} ETH")
    print(f"  Correlation:   {result['correlation_penalty_eth']:.4f} ETH")
    print(f"  Missed attest: {result['missed_attestation_eth']:.4f} ETH")
    print(f"  Total penalty: {result['total_penalty_eth']:.4f} ETH "
          f"({result['penalty_percentage']:.1f}%)")
    print(f"  Remaining:     {result['remaining_eth']:.4f} ETH")
```

Table 6-2. *Slashing Penalty Scaling*

Validators Slashed	Correlation Factor	Approximate Penalty	Total Cost (20M ETH staked)
1 (accident)	~0.0000048	~3.2%	~1 ETH
10	~0.000048	~3.2%	~10 ETH
100	~0.00048	~3.3%	~106 ETH
1,000	~0.0048	~4.6%	~1,470 ETH
10,000 (~1.6%)	~0.048	~17.6%	~56,300 ETH
62,500 (~10%)	~0.30	~33%	~660,000 ETH
208,333 (~33%)	~1.00	~100%	~6.67M ETH

Correlation is the twist: one validator getting slashed stings; a third of the set in the same window triggers the nuclear tier. PoW doesn't automatically punish co-conspirators harder per head that way.

6.1.5 Long-Range Attacks

Long-range hurts PoS's marketing vs. PoW: redoing work is expensive; resurrecting old keys after exit is cheap cryptographically even if socially weird.

Attack Variants

Boot-from-history attack: ex-stakers mint an alt timeline that still verifies—brand-new nodes can't smell which timeline is "real" without context.

Buy old keys from people who already banked withdrawals—they sold the car and still had a spare key in a drawer.

Stake-bleed fork: mine your private branch forever, stack rewards, confuse late syncers—slow, weird, not purely academic.

```
Epoch:  0    100   200   300   400   500   ...   2000

Real:   [=====|=====|=====|=====|=====|=====|.....|=====]
                                                  ↑ current

Attacker obtains old keys from validators who exited at epoch 200.
Those validators no longer have stake to slash.

Fake:                 [=====|=====|=====|=====|.....|=====]
                      ↑ fork point

A new node joining at epoch 2000 sees TWO valid-looking chains.
Both have valid signatures. Both follow protocol rules.
The protocol alone cannot distinguish them.
```

Figure 6-2. *Long-Range Attack Timeline*

Weak Subjectivity

Weak subjectivity = you import a recent trusted hash from meatspace when you've been gone too long. Not pure code-from-genesis purity. Deal with it or argue in the forums.

Bitcoin full node wakes up from a coma, downloads headers, longest work wins—no friend required. PoS long offline? You might need a checkpoint tweet you trust. Whether that bugs you probably tracks how much you already trust Binance's website.

```
def calculate_weak_subjectivity_period(
        total_active_validators: int,
        churn_limit_per_epoch: int,
        min_per_epoch_churn: int = 4,
        safety_decay: int = 100) -> dict:
    """
    Calculate the weak subjectivity period.

    This is the maximum time a node can be offline and still
    safely determine the canonical chain without an external checkpoint.

    The period depends on how quickly validators can exit.
    If enough validators withdraw before being detected,
    they could construct a long-range attack.
```

```
    Args:
        total_active_validators: Number of active validators
        churn_limit_per_epoch: Max validators entering/exiting per epoch
        min_per_epoch_churn: Minimum churn rate
        safety_decay: Safety decay parameter (100 = default)
    """
    # Effective churn per epoch
    churn = max(churn_limit_per_epoch, min_per_epoch_churn)

    # Validators that need to exit for attack (1/3 of total)
    validators_to_exit = total_active_validators // 3

    # Time for 1/3 to exit through normal churn
    epochs_to_exit = validators_to_exit // churn

    # Apply safety margin
    ws_period_epochs = int(epochs_to_exit * safety_decay / 100)

    ws_seconds = ws_period_epochs * SLOTS_PER_EPOCH * SECONDS_PER_SLOT
    ws_days = ws_seconds / 86400

    return {
        'total_validators': total_active_validators,
        'validators_to_exit': validators_to_exit,
        'churn_per_epoch': churn,
        'ws_period_epochs': ws_period_epochs,
        'ws_period_days': ws_days,
        'recommendation': (
            f"Nodes offline > {ws_days:.0f} days need an external
checkpoint"
        ),
    }

# Current Ethereum parameters (approximate)
ws = calculate_weak_subjectivity_period(
    total_active_validators=625_000,  # ~625K validators
    churn_limit_per_epoch=9,          # ~9 per epoch
)
```

```
print("Weak Subjectivity Analysis")
print("=" * 55)
print(f"  Active validators:     {ws['total_validators']:,}")
print(f"  Need 1/3 to exit:      {ws['validators_to_exit']:,} validators")
print(f"  Churn rate:            {ws['churn_per_epoch']} per epoch")
print(f"  WS period:             {ws['ws_period_epochs']:,} epochs")
print(f"  WS period:             {ws['ws_period_days']:.0f} days")
print(f"  {ws['recommendation']}")
```

Table 6-3. *Long-Range Attack Defenses*

Defense	Mechanism	Limitation
Weak subjectivity checkpoints	Nodes verify against a trusted recent state	Requires social infrastructure for checkpoint distribution
Long unbonding periods	Delay stake withdrawal	Capital inefficiency; doesn't prevent attacks from very old validators
Key deletion commitment	Validators destroy old signing keys after exit	Cannot be verified or enforced by the protocol
Slashing window extension	Extend the period during which misbehavior is slashable	Must balance against capital lockup burden
Social consensus	Community agrees on canonical chain during disputes	Centralizing; relies on coordination
Checkpoint sync	New nodes bootstrap from a recent finalized checkpoint	Requires trust in checkpoint source

6.1.6 Validator Economics

Yields move stake; stake backs security—mispriced yield either starves validators or overpays defense.

Staking Yield

Revenue isn't monolithic: issuance vs. fees vs. MEV has different variance and politics:

```
import math

def ethereum_staking_economics(total_staked_eth: float,
                                eth_price_usd: float,
                                avg_base_fee_gwei: float = 20,
                                avg_priority_fee_gwei: float = 2,
                                avg_gas_per_block: int = 15_000_000,
                                avg_mev_per_block_eth: float = 0.05
                                ) -> dict:
    """
    Comprehensive Ethereum validator economics model.

    Sources of revenue:
    1. Consensus rewards (attestation + proposer + sync committee)
    2. Priority fees (tips from users)
    3. MEV rewards (from MEV-boost)

    Note: Base fees are burned (EIP-1559), not paid to validators.
    """
    validators = total_staked_eth / 32

    # 1. Consensus layer rewards
    # Base reward per validator per epoch
    base_reward_factor = 64
    total_staked_gwei = total_staked_eth * 10**9
    sqrt_total = math.isqrt(int(total_staked_gwei))

    base_reward_per_epoch = (32 * 10**9 * base_reward_factor //
                             sqrt_total // 4)

    epochs_per_year = 365.25 * 24 * 3600 / (SLOTS_PER_EPOCH * SECONDS_
    PER_SLOT)

    # Attestation rewards (source, target, head): ~84% of base reward
    annual_attestation_eth = (base_reward_per_epoch * 0.84 *
                              epochs_per_year * 4 / 10**9)

    # Proposer rewards: earned only when selected (~1/validators chance
    per slot)
```

```
slots_per_year = 365.25 * 24 * 3600 / SECONDS_PER_SLOT
proposals_per_year = slots_per_year / validators
proposer_reward_per_proposal = base_reward_per_epoch * 8 / 10**9  #
Simplified
annual_proposer_eth = proposals_per_year * proposer_reward_per_proposal

# 2. Execution layer rewards (priority fees)
blocks_per_day = 24 * 3600 / SECONDS_PER_SLOT
annual_priority_fees_eth = (avg_priority_fee_gwei * 10**-9 *
                            avg_gas_per_block * blocks_per_day * 365.25)
annual_priority_per_validator = annual_priority_fees_eth / validators

# 3. MEV rewards
annual_mev_eth = avg_mev_per_block_eth * blocks_per_day * 365.25
annual_mev_per_validator = annual_mev_eth / validators

# Total per validator
total_annual_per_validator = (annual_attestation_eth + annual_
proposer_eth +
                              annual_priority_per_validator +
                              annual_mev_per_validator)

annual_yield_pct = (total_annual_per_validator / 32) * 100


# Network issuance and burn
total_issuance_eth = (annual_attestation_eth + annual_proposer_eth) *
validators
total_burned_eth = (avg_base_fee_gwei * 10**-9 * avg_gas_per_block *
                    blocks_per_day * 365.25)
net_issuance = total_issuance_eth - total_burned_eth

return {
    'validators': int(validators),
    'annual_attestation_eth': annual_attestation_eth,
    'annual_proposer_eth': annual_proposer_eth,
    'annual_priority_eth': annual_priority_per_validator,
    'annual_mev_eth': annual_mev_per_validator,
```

```
        'total_annual_eth': total_annual_per_validator,
        'annual_yield_pct': annual_yield_pct,
        'total_issuance_eth': total_issuance_eth,
        'total_burned_eth': total_burned_eth,
        'net_issuance_eth': net_issuance,
        'net_inflation_pct': (net_issuance / 120_000_000) * 100,
    }

print("Ethereum Validator Economics")
print("=" * 60)

for staked_m in [10, 20, 30, 40]:
    result = ethereum_staking_economics(staked_m * 1e6, 3000)
    print(f"\n{staked_m}M ETH staked ({result['validators']:,}
    validators):")
    print(f"  Attestation:   {result['annual_attestation_eth']:.4f}
    ETH/yr")
    print(f"  Proposer:      {result['annual_proposer_eth']:.4f} ETH/yr")
    print(f"  Priority fees: {result['annual_priority_eth']:.4f} ETH/yr")
    print(f"  MEV:           {result['annual_mev_eth']:.4f} ETH/yr")
    print(f"  Total yield:   {result['annual_yield_pct']:.2f}% APR")
    print(f"  Net issuance:  {result['net_issuance_eth']:,.0f} ETH/yr "
          f"({result['net_inflation_pct']:.3f}%)")
```

Table 6-4. *Validator Revenue Sources and Characteristics*

Source	Typical Share	Variability	Requires	Notes
Attestation rewards	55–65%	Low (predictable)	Online presence	Earned every epoch for correct votes
Proposer rewards	5–10%	High (lottery)	Block proposal slot	Selected ~once per 2 months per validator
Sync committee	2–5%	Very high (lottery)	Sync committee selection	512 of ~625K validators per period
Priority fees	10–15%	Medium	Block proposal	Varies with network demand
MEV rewards	15–25%	Very high	MEV-boost relay	Varies with DeFi activity

Centralization Dynamics

The centralization story here isn't "who has cheap rivers":

Liquid staking routes capital through governance—stETH holders aren't the ones swapping NVMe drives at 3 a.m.

Ops overhead is mostly flat per rack—big shops amortize monitoring across hundreds of keys.

MEV pipeline: if you don't speak builder market, you leave money on the table.

Retail loves exchange staking; the chain maybe doesn't love the concentration.

6.1.7 PoS Security Analysis

Threat modeling shifts: stake Gini, slash magnitudes, token liquidity for sneaky buys, not terahash maps.

```
def comprehensive_attack_cost(total_staked_eth: float,
                              eth_price_usd: float) -> dict:
    """
    Comprehensive PoS attack cost analysis.

    Considers multiple attack vectors and their costs.
    """
    total_staked_usd = total_staked_eth * eth_price_usd

    # Attack 1: Finality reversion (need 1/3 of stake)
    finality_attack_stake = total_staked_eth / 3

    # Market impact: acquiring 1/3 of staked ETH is not possible
    # at current price. Price would rise dramatically.
    # Simple model: price impact = base_price * (1 + amount/liquidity)
    daily_trading_volume_eth = 10_000_000  # ~$30B daily volume
    acquisition_days = finality_attack_stake / (daily_trading_volume_
    eth * 0.1)
    avg_slippage = 1.5 + (acquisition_days * 0.01)  # Increasing slippage

    acquisition_cost = finality_attack_stake * eth_price_usd * avg_slippage

    # If caught (which is certain for finality violation):
    # Correlation penalty = 100% of stake
```

```
    slashing_loss = finality_attack_stake * eth_price_usd

    # Token value crash: successful attack would likely crash ETH ~80%
    # Attacker's remaining portfolio loses value too
    value_destruction = total_staked_usd * 0.8

    # Attack 2: Censorship (need 1/2 of stake)
    censorship_stake = total_staked_eth / 2
    censorship_cost = censorship_stake * eth_price_usd * 2.0  # Higher
    slippage

    # Attack 3: Liveness (need 1/3 of stake offline)
    # Inactivity leak gradually drains inactive validators
    # After ~4 days, inactive validators lose ~1% of stake per day

    return {
        'finality_attack': {
            'required_eth': finality_attack_stake,
            'acquisition_cost_usd': acquisition_cost,
            'slashing_loss_usd': slashing_loss,
            'total_cost_usd': acquisition_cost + slashing_loss,
        },
        'censorship_attack': {
            'required_eth': censorship_stake,
            'acquisition_cost_usd': censorship_cost,
        },
        'value_destruction_usd': value_destruction,
    }

result = comprehensive_attack_cost(20_000_000, 3000)
print("\nComprehensive PoS Attack Cost Analysis")
print("=" * 60)
fa = result['finality_attack']
print(f"\nFinality Attack (revert finalized blocks):")
print(f"  Required stake:     {fa['required_eth']:,.0f} ETH")
print(f"  Acquisition cost:   ${fa['acquisition_cost_usd']:,.0f}")
print(f"  Slashing loss:      ${fa['slashing_loss_usd']:,.0f}")
print(f"  Total economic cost: ${fa['total_cost_usd']:,.0f}")
```

```
ca = result['censorship_attack']
print(f"\nCensorship Attack (exclude transactions):")
print(f"  Required stake:     {ca['required_eth']:,.0f} ETH")
print(f"  Acquisition cost:   ${ca['acquisition_cost_usd']:,.0f}")

print(f"\nEcosystem value destruction: ${result['value_destruction_
usd']:,.0f}")
```

Table 6-5. *PoW vs. PoS Security Comparison*

Factor	PoW (Bitcoin)	PoS (Ethereum)
Finality attack threshold	>50% hash rate	>2/3 stake
Capital required	~$10B in hardware	~$40B+ in ETH
Ongoing attack cost	~$15M/day electricity	Opportunity cost of locked capital
Post-attack state	Attacker keeps hardware	Attacker's stake destroyed by slashing
Recovery	Attacker can attack again immediately	Attacker must re-acquire stake
Market impact	Moderate (hardware is off-market)	Severe (must buy 1/3 of circulating staked supply)
Detection	Visible (hash rate spike)	Visible (abnormal attestation patterns)
Social response	Change PoW algorithm	Emergency hard fork to slash attacker

6.1.8 Summary

PoS is "security as accounting with teeth." Nothing-at-stake gets wrestled down with economic penalties, finality gadgets, and occasional social scaffolding.

TL;DR if you're cramming:

- Joules out, collateral in—audits talk in ETH burned, not kWh.
- Free double-signing dies once conflicts cost real stakes and finals need huge quorums.
- Gasper = tip-follower + epoch finalizer; say it that way at dinner.

- Correlation curve: solo fault ≠ mob fault, by design.
- Ancient keys + fresh nodes = long-range headache; weak subjectivity is the messy patch.
- More stake usually drags baseline yield; MEV randomizes who gets rich on Tuesdays.
- New choke points: Lido votes, MEV shops, exchanges—not shovels in Sichuan.

Staking supplants mining: capital gatekeeps blocks. Nothing-at-stake loses to slashing + 2/3 finality games. Gasper mashes LMD-GHOST (weighted fork choice) with Casper FFG (checkpoint finality). Tiny isolated fault ~few-percent haircut; mob slash up to total loss. Conflicting finals ⇒ ≥1/3 stake must have been slashable (that's the safety story). Long-range needs social checkpoints because exited keys still sign. Yield slides as more ETH locks (think ~4% ballpark near ~20M ETH—parameters drift). Attacking finality for real still runs into stupid money once you price stake acquisition, slashing, and markets dumping on you—think on the order of tens of billions USD, in the same ballpark people quote for a full assault, not a grocery receipt.

Next chapter: BFT classics—the stuff FFG is riffing on.

6.1.9 Exercises

Problem 1 (Basic): In your own words: nothing-at-stake; why PoW dodges it; what fixes PoS actually ships.

Problem 2 (Calculation): 500*32 ETH validators, 50 simultaneous slashes, 16M ETH active stake—correlation factor, per-validator pain, percent obliterated. Show work.

Problem 3 (Implementation): Three-fork LMD-GHOST toy; flip the head by moving one validator's vote.

Problem 4 (Analysis): ~625k validators, churn cap 9 exits/epoch—how cold can you go before weak subjectivity forces a checkpoint? Math out epochs/days.

Problem 5 (Design): 1,000-validator pretend chain: define slashable sins, how penalties scale with simultaneous faults, defend the curve.

Problem 6 (Theory): Show two finals ⇒ ≥1/3 slashable stake (pigeonhole supermajorities).

Problem 7 (Comparative): Mining pools vs. liquid staking—who actually picks block builders, what's Nakamoto coefficient-ish?

Problem 8 (Critical Thinking): Weak subjectivity vs. objective PoW fork choice—strongest case for each side; compare to trust you already place in wallets/explorers/CeFi.

Problem 9 (Advanced): Posterior corruption napkin model: cheap keys + churn—fake history budget vs. renting half of Bitcoin hashrate for a week.

Problem 10 (Research): Merge postmortem: timeline, feared failures, what happened live, stake/energy/centralization after.

(Solutions in Appendix D)

6.1.10 Further Reading

FFG Paper (Buterin/Griffith) for Proofs: execution nitpicks live in consensus specs, not Medium.

GHOST Family Tree Starts with Sompolinsky/Zohar: the beacon spec is where Ethereum-specific glue lives.

Vitalik's Early PoS Rants Age Well: EthResearch threads for people who like pain.

Exact Slash Constants: consensus repo. Monnot if you want intuition on the curve shapes.

MEV: read Flashbots; yields: stare at rated.network until it matches your node.

Mute podcasts that "prove" PoS centralized with zero stake distribution plots.

CHAPTER 7

Byzantine Fault Tolerance

7.1 PBFT, HotStuff, and Tendermint

This chapter covers BFT consensus: the 3f + 1 bound, FLP impossibility, PBFT's three-phase protocol, HotStuff's linear communication, Tendermint's ABCI architecture, and how synchrony assumptions shape partition behavior. By the time you finish, you should be comfortable with:

- How classical BFT protocols manage to reach agreement even when some nodes are actively lying or malfunctioning
- PBFT's three-phase protocol and why its communication costs become a problem once you scale past a handful of nodes
- The FLP impossibility result, which every consensus designer has to either work around or pretend doesn't apply to them
- How HotStuff gets communication complexity down to linear by funneling everything through a leader and using threshold signatures
- Tendermint Core and its Application Blockchain Interface, which is the reason the Cosmos ecosystem exists
- What synchrony assumptions actually mean in practice and how different protocols behave when the network partitions
- Practical performance numbers and the tradeoffs that show up in real deployments
- How all this classical distributed systems theory connects to modern blockchain consensus

N. Savant, *Blockchain Foundations*, https://doi.org/10.1007/979-8-8688-2891-1_7

7.1.1 Byzantine Agreement Fundamentals

BFT protocols are older than blockchain by a wide margin. Decades older. They tackle the same core problem: getting a group of distributed machines to agree on something when some of those machines might be broken, lying, confused, or outright malicious. The term "Byzantine" traces back to the Byzantine Generals Problem from Chapter 1. The label stuck because it captures the worst-case scenario: failures that don't announce themselves.

Crash-fault-tolerant systems only worry about nodes that stop responding. Dead is dead. BFT is harder because Byzantine nodes can do anything. Send contradictory messages to different peers. Pretend to be offline. Produce messages that look perfectly valid but are designed to cause harm. Coordinate with other compromised nodes. When your adversary model says "the bad guys can do literally anything," the protocol design space gets very constrained very quickly.

What BFT consensus actually guarantees comes down to two things:

Safety. Every honest node agrees on the same sequence of decisions. Two honest nodes never finalize conflicting values. This has to hold even during network partitions, even when Byzantine nodes are actively trying to create disagreement. No exceptions.

Liveness. The system keeps making forward progress. Honest nodes eventually decide on new values even when some participants have failed. Liveness is the trickier guarantee and often comes with an asterisk: it may depend on the network eventually behaving well enough to deliver messages in a timely fashion.

Lamport, Shostak, and Pease nailed down the lower bound in 1982: you need at least $n = 3f + 1$ nodes to tolerate f Byzantine faults. With anything less, a Byzantine adversary can create situations where honest nodes end up with irreconcilable views of reality. No protocol, no matter how clever, can fix that.

Why 3f + 1? The Quorum Intersection Argument

The $3f + 1$ bound isn't arbitrary. It falls out of a quorum intersection argument, and it's worth walking through because this same logic appears again and again in blockchain consensus design.

For safety, any two quorums need to overlap in at least one honest node. A quorum Q is a set of nodes large enough that the protocol treats their collective agreement as decisive. If two quorums could proceed independently without sharing any honest participant, they could finalize conflicting decisions. That's the scenario you have to prevent.

With n total nodes, f of which might be Byzantine:

1. A quorum has to be larger than (n + f) / 2 to guarantee it overlaps with any other quorum of the same size. Two sets that each contain more than half of n + f elements must share at least f + 1 members between them. Basic counting.

2. But those shared members might include Byzantine nodes. Up to f of the overlapping nodes could be compromised. So the overlap has to exceed f to guarantee at least one honest node sits in the intersection. That gives you the constraint: $2Q - n > f$, meaning $Q > (n + f) / 2$.

3. There also has to be enough honest nodes to actually form a quorum. If n – f (the honest count) can't even reach the quorum size, the whole thing collapses. So: $n - f \geq Q$.

4. Put it together: $n - f > (n + f) / 2$. Multiply both sides by 2 and simplify, and you get $n > 3f$.

Therefore, $n \geq 3f + 1$.

```
def bft_parameters(n: int) -> dict:
    """Calculate BFT consensus parameters for n nodes."""
    f = (n - 1) // 3  # Maximum tolerated faults
    quorum = 2 * f + 1  # Minimum quorum size for safety

    # Verify the three conditions
    assert n >= 3 * f + 1, "Need n >= 3f+1"
    assert 2 * quorum > n + f, "Quorum overlap must exceed f"
    assert n - f >= quorum, "Honest nodes must form a quorum"

    return {
        'total_nodes': n,
        'max_faults': f,
        'min_honest': n - f,
        'quorum_size': quorum,
        'fault_tolerance_pct': (f / n) * 100,
        'quorum_overlap_min': 2 * quorum - n,
        'honest_surplus': (n - f) - quorum,
    }
```

```
print("BFT Parameters by Network Size")
print("=" * 70)
print(f"{'n':>4} {'f':>4} {'Quorum':>8} {'Honest':>8} {'Tolerance':>11}
{'Overlap':>9}")
print("-" * 70)
for n in [4, 7, 10, 13, 16, 19, 25, 50, 100, 200]:
    p = bft_parameters(n)
    print(f"  {n:3d}  {p['max_faults']:3d}  {p['quorum_size']:6d}  "
          f"{p['min_honest']:6d}  {p['fault_tolerance_pct']:9.1f}%  "
          f"{p['quorum_overlap_min']:7d}")
```

Table 7-1. *BFT Capacity and Communication Costs*

Total Nodes (n)	Max Byzantine (f)	Quorum Size	Messages/Round (PBFT)	Messages/Round (HotStuff)
4	1	3	~48	~8
7	2	5	~147	~14
10	3	7	~300	~20
25	8	17	~1,875	~50
100	33	67	~30,000	~200
1,000	333	667	~3,000,000	~2,000

The FLP Impossibility Result

In 1985, Fischer, Lynch, and Paterson proved something that sent a shockwave through the distributed systems community. No deterministic consensus protocol can guarantee both safety and liveness in a fully asynchronous network with even a single faulty process. One fault. That's all it takes. This is the FLP impossibility result, and it's one of those theorems that fundamentally shapes what's possible.

The proof itself is beautiful in its construction. You start by showing that there exists an initial configuration where both decision values (0 and 1) are still reachable. Then you demonstrate that no matter what step the protocol takes next, the adversary can schedule message deliveries in a way that keeps both outcomes alive. And the adversary doesn't even need to corrupt a node. Just delaying messages is enough. Indefinitely preventing consensus, without any actual malice.

The core intuition: in an asynchronous system, there's no way to tell the difference between a process that's slow and one that's crashed. If the protocol waits for the slow process (to make sure its vote counts), it might wait forever. Liveness gone. If the protocol pushes ahead without that vote (to maintain liveness), it risks making a decision that the "slow" process would have vetoed. Safety compromised. You can't have both. That's the trap.

Every practical BFT protocol has to find a way around FLP. There are several escape routes:

Partial synchrony. Assume the network will eventually start behaving, delivering messages within some bound Δ after a Global Stabilization Time (GST). Before GST, messages can be delayed however the adversary wants. After GST, liveness kicks back in. Safety holds throughout. This is what PBFT, Tendermint, and HotStuff all rely on, and it's probably the most practical assumption for real networks.

Randomization. Use cryptographic coin flips to break symmetry so the adversary can't keep the protocol stuck. Ben-Or figured this out in 1983. Modern protocols like Algorand use VRFs for randomized committee selection, which is a descendant of the same idea.

Economic incentives. Instead of assuming nodes are arbitrarily malicious, assume they respond to incentives. They might be greedy, but they're not irrational. Nakamoto consensus is the poster child for this approach. Miners follow the protocol because it pays them to, not because they're forced to.

Timeouts. When the leader doesn't produce a result fast enough, move on to a new leader. This technically sacrifices pure liveness (you're stalling while the timeout runs), but in practice it provides strong enough progress guarantees for most applications.

7.1.2 PBFT: Practical Byzantine Fault Tolerance

Miguel Castro and Barbara Liskov published PBFT in 1999, and it was a breakthrough. Previous BFT protocols had exponential message complexity. Nobody was going to run those in production. PBFT brought it down to $O(n^2)$ messages per round. Still quadratic, but suddenly feasible for small networks. That was a dramatic improvement over what existed before.

Protocol Overview

PBFT runs in a series of numbered views, each with a designated primary (the leader). Who is primary is determined by a simple formula: primary = view_number mod n. Deterministic rotation. Every replica eventually gets a turn leading, which keeps any single node from monopolizing the role.

Each consensus round has three phases:

Pre-prepare. The primary takes a client request, assigns it a sequence number within the current view, and broadcasts a PRE-PREPARE message to every replica. The message basically says, "in view v, the request with digest d gets sequence number n." That's the primary's proposal.

Prepare. When a backup replica gets a valid pre-prepare, it broadcasts a PREPARE message to all other replicas. A replica considers itself "prepared" once it has the matching pre-prepare from the primary plus 2f matching prepares from different replicas. At that point, at least f+1 honest replicas have agreed on the assignment. That's the threshold where the decision starts to crystallize.

Commit. Once prepared, a replica broadcasts COMMIT to everyone. When it collects 2f + 1 matching commits, it executes the request and replies to the client. Done. The request is committed with finality.

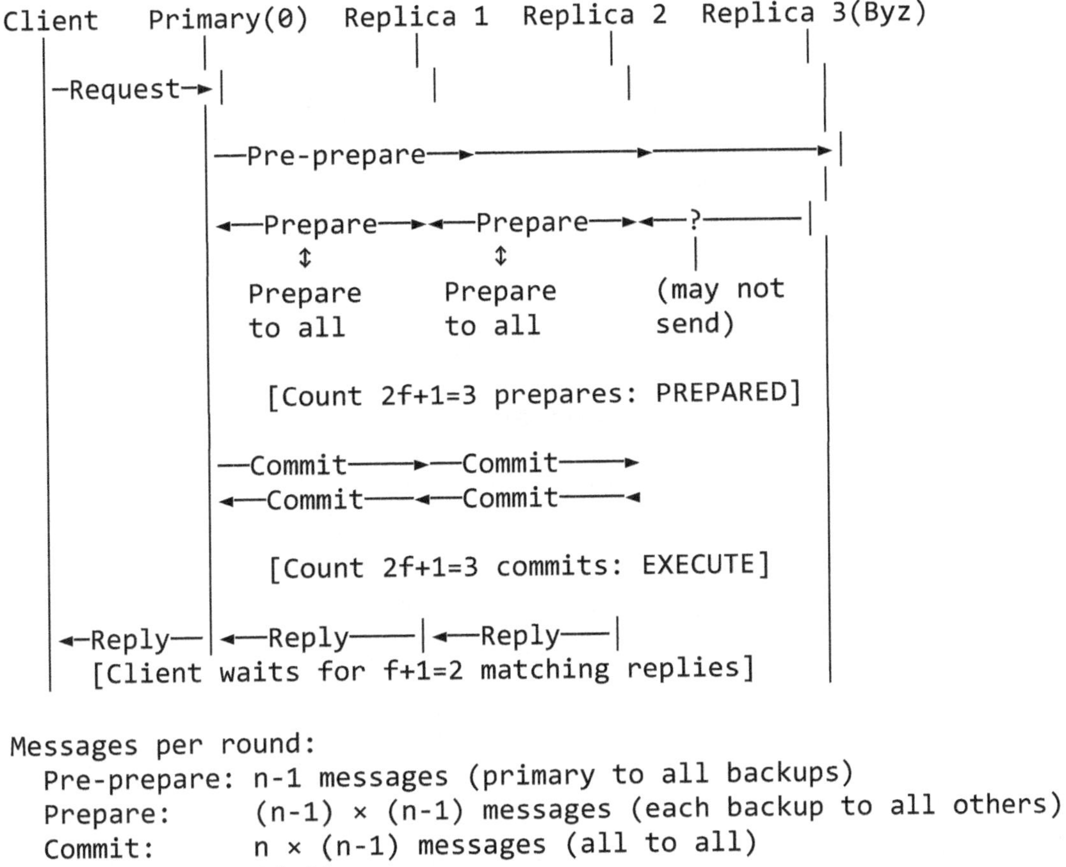


```
Messages per round:
  Pre-prepare: n-1 messages (primary to all backups)
  Prepare:     (n-1) × (n-1) messages (each backup to all others)
  Commit:      n × (n-1) messages (all to all)
  Total:       O(n²)
```

Figure 7-1. *PBFT Message Flow (n=4, f=1)*

Complete PBFT Implementation

```
from dataclasses import dataclass, field
from enum import Enum
from typing import Dict, List, Optional, Set, Tuple
import hashlib
import time

class Phase(Enum):
    IDLE = "idle"
    PRE_PREPARED = "pre-prepared"
    PREPARED = "prepared"
    COMMITTED = "committed"
```

```
@dataclass
class PBFTMessage:
    msg_type: str  # "pre-prepare", "prepare", "commit"
    view: int
    sequence: int
    digest: str
    sender: int
    request: Optional[bytes] = None

class PBFTNode:
    """Complete PBFT replica implementation."""

    def __init__(self, node_id: int, total_nodes: int):
        self.id = node_id
        self.n = total_nodes
        self.f = (total_nodes - 1) // 3
        self.quorum = 2 * self.f + 1  # 2f+1 including self

        self.view = 0
        self.next_sequence = 0
        self.is_byzantine = False

        # Message log: (view, sequence) -> data
        self.pre_prepare_log: Dict[Tuple[int,int], PBFTMessage] = {}
        self.prepare_log: Dict[Tuple[int,int], Dict[int, PBFTMessage]] = {}
        self.commit_log: Dict[Tuple[int,int], Dict[int, PBFTMessage]] = {}

        self.phase: Dict[Tuple[int,int], Phase] = {}
        self.executed: List[Tuple[int, bytes]] = []  # (seq, request)

        # View change state
        self.view_change_timeout = 5.0  # seconds
        self.last_activity = time.time()

    @property
    def primary_id(self) -> int:
        return self.view % self.n
```

```
@property
def is_primary(self) -> bool:
    return self.primary_id == self.id

def digest(self, data: bytes) -> str:
    return hashlib.sha256(data).hexdigest()[:16]

def handle_client_request(self, request: bytes) -> List[PBFTMessage]:
    """Primary assigns sequence number and broadcasts pre-prepare."""
    if not self.is_primary:
        return []

    self.next_sequence += 1
    seq = self.next_sequence
    d = self.digest(request)
    key = (self.view, seq)

    msg = PBFTMessage("pre-prepare", self.view, seq, d, self.id,
    request)
    self.pre_prepare_log[key] = msg
    self.phase[key] = Phase.PRE_PREPARED

    # Also generate own prepare
    my_prepare = PBFTMessage("prepare", self.view, seq, d, self.id)
    if key not in self.prepare_log:
        self.prepare_log[key] = {}
    self.prepare_log[key][self.id] = my_prepare

    return [msg]  # Broadcast pre-prepare to all backups

def handle_pre_prepare(self, msg: PBFTMessage) ->
Optional[PBFTMessage]:
    """Backup validates and responds with prepare."""
    key = (msg.view, msg.sequence)

    # Validate: sender must be primary for this view
    if msg.sender != msg.view % self.n:
        return None
```

```
        # No conflicting pre-prepare for same view+sequence
        if key in self.pre_prepare_log:
            existing = self.pre_prepare_log[key]
            if existing.digest != msg.digest:
                return None  # Byzantine primary: conflicting pre-prepares

        # Accept pre-prepare
        self.pre_prepare_log[key] = msg
        self.phase[key] = Phase.PRE_PREPARED
        self.last_activity = time.time()

        # Generate and broadcast prepare
        prepare = PBFTMessage("prepare", msg.view, msg.sequence,
                              msg.digest, self.id)

        # Log own prepare
        if key not in self.prepare_log:
            self.prepare_log[key] = {}
        self.prepare_log[key][self.id] = prepare

        return prepare

    def handle_prepare(self, msg: PBFTMessage) -> Optional[PBFTMessage]:
        """Collect prepares. When 2f+1 reached, enter prepared state."""
        key = (msg.view, msg.sequence)

        # Validate: must match a pre-prepare we accepted
        if key not in self.pre_prepare_log:
            return None  # No matching pre-prepare
        if msg.digest != self.pre_prepare_log[key].digest:
            return None  # Digest mismatch

        # Log this prepare
        if key not in self.prepare_log:
            self.prepare_log[key] = {}
        self.prepare_log[key][msg.sender] = msg

        # Check if we have 2f+1 prepares (including our own)
        prepare_count = len(self.prepare_log[key])
```

```
        if (prepare_count >= self.quorum and
            self.phase.get(key) == Phase.PRE_PREPARED):

            self.phase[key] = Phase.PREPARED

            # Generate commit message
            commit = PBFTMessage("commit", msg.view, msg.sequence,
                                 msg.digest, self.id)

            # Log own commit
            if key not in self.commit_log:
                self.commit_log[key] = {}
            self.commit_log[key][self.id] = commit

            return commit

        return None

    def handle_commit(self, msg: PBFTMessage) -> bool:
        """Collect commits. When 2f+1 reached, execute the request."""
        key = (msg.view, msg.sequence)

        if key not in self.commit_log:
            self.commit_log[key] = {}
        self.commit_log[key][msg.sender] = msg

        commit_count = len(self.commit_log[key])

        if (commit_count >= self.quorum and
            self.phase.get(key) == Phase.PREPARED):

            self.phase[key] = Phase.COMMITTED

            # Execute the request
            pre_prepare = self.pre_prepare_log.get(key)
            if pre_prepare and pre_prepare.request:
                self.executed.append((msg.sequence, pre_prepare.request))

            self.last_activity = time.time()
            return True  # Committed!

        return False
```

```
    def get_stats(self) -> dict:
        return {
            'id': self.id,
            'view': self.view,
            'executed': len(self.executed),
            'is_primary': self.is_primary,
            'is_byzantine': self.is_byzantine,
        }

class PBFTNetwork:
    """Simulate a PBFT network with message passing."""

    def __init__(self, n: int, num_byzantine: int = 0):
        self.n = n
        self.nodes = [PBFTNode(i, n) for i in range(n)]
        self.total_messages = 0

        # Mark last num_byzantine nodes as Byzantine
        for i in range(n - num_byzantine, n):
            self.nodes[i].is_byzantine = True

    def _broadcast(self, msg: PBFTMessage, exclude: Optional[Set[int]] =
    None) -> int:
        """
        Count how many nodes would receive this message.

        NOTE: This does NOT actually deliver messages to nodes.
        It is a message counter for simulation purposes only.
        Real PBFT would serialize and send msg to each recipient
        over the network. Here we handle delivery manually in
        process_request() by calling each node's handler directly.
        """
        if exclude is None:
            exclude = set() # Fix mutable default argument bug
        count = 0
        for node in self.nodes:
            if node.id != msg.sender and node.id not in exclude:
```

```
        if not node.is_byzantine:
            count += 1
return count

 def process_request(self, request: bytes) -> dict:
     """Run full PBFT consensus for one request.""" # Primary is
     determined by current view, not fixed at node 0
     primary = self.nodes[0]  # View 0
     messages_this_round = 0

     # Phase 1: Primary creates pre-prepare
     pre_prepares = primary.handle_client_request(request)
     if not pre_prepares:
         return {'success': False, 'reason': 'Not primary'}

     pp = pre_prepares[0]
     messages_this_round += self.n - 1  # Broadcast to all

     # Phase 2: Backups send prepares
     prepares = []
     for node in self.nodes[1:]:
         if node.is_byzantine:
             continue
         prepare = node.handle_pre_prepare(pp)
         if prepare:
             prepares.append(prepare)

     # Deliver prepares to all nodes
     commits = []
     for prepare_msg in prepares:
         messages_this_round += self.n - 1  # Each prepare broadcast
         for node in self.nodes:
             if node.is_byzantine:
                 continue
             commit = node.handle_prepare(prepare_msg)
             if commit and commit not in commits:
                 commits.append(commit)
```

```
        # Phase 3: Deliver commits to all nodes
        committed_nodes = []
        for commit_msg in commits:
            messages_this_round += self.n - 1
            for node in self.nodes:
                if node.is_byzantine:
                    continue
                if node.handle_commit(commit_msg):
                    if node.id not in committed_nodes:
                        committed_nodes.append(node.id)

        self.total_messages += messages_this_round

        # Verify safety: all committed nodes have same execution
        executions = {}
        for node in self.nodes:
            if not node.is_byzantine and node.executed:
                last = node.executed[-1]
                executions[node.id] = last

        values = set(str(v) for v in executions.values())
        safety = len(values) <= 1

        return {
            'success': len(committed_nodes) > 0,
            'committed_nodes': committed_nodes,
            'messages': messages_this_round,
            'safety_maintained': safety,
        }

# Run PBFT with different configurations
print("PBFT Consensus Simulation")
print("=" * 65)

for n, f_actual in [(4, 0), (4, 1), (7, 2), (10, 3)]:
    net = PBFTNetwork(n, f_actual)

    results = []
    for i in range(5):
```

```
        result = net.process_request(f"tx_{i}".encode())
        results.append(result)

    committed = sum(1 for r in results if r['success'])
    safe = all(r['safety_maintained'] for r in results)
    avg_msgs = sum(r['messages'] for r in results) / len(results)

    print(f"\nn={n}, f_actual={f_actual} (max_f={(n-1)//3}):")
    print(f"  Committed:          {committed}/5 requests")
    print(f"  Safety maintained: {safe}")
    print(f"  Avg messages/req: {avg_msgs:.0f}")
    print(f"  Theoretical O(n²): ~{n*n*3}")

    # Show execution consistency
    for node in net.nodes:
        stats = node.get_stats()
        if not node.is_byzantine:
            print(f"  Node {stats['id']}: {stats['executed']} executed"
                  f" {'(primary)' if stats['is_primary'] else ''}")
```

PBFT View Change

When the primary looks like it's failed, or worse, gone Byzantine, the replicas trigger a view change. This part of PBFT is notoriously complex. It has historically been a major source of implementation bugs, and for good reason. Coordinating the handoff while preserving everything that was already decided is genuinely hard.

A replica starts a timer when it receives a client request. If the timer runs out without the request reaching commitment, the replica decides the primary is either dead or malicious, and it broadcasts a VIEW-CHANGE message that includes:

1. The new view number (just the old view plus one)
2. The sequence number of the last stable checkpoint
3. Prepared certificates for any requests that made it through the prepare phase but didn't get committed before the primary went down

Once the new primary (determined by new_view mod n) gathers 2f + 1 valid VIEW-CHANGE messages, it broadcasts NEW-VIEW. That message bundles:

1. The 2f + 1 view-change messages as proof that the transition is legitimate
2. Pre-prepare messages for anything that was prepared in the old view but never committed so those requests don't get lost in the shuffle

The NEW-VIEW message lets every replica resynchronize. They pick up where they left off, with all committed and prepared states intact. It works. But the machinery to make it work is substantial, and getting it right is one of those things that separates a correct PBFT implementation from one that subtly breaks under edge cases.

Table 7-2. *PBFT View Change Complexity*

Phase	Messages	Purpose
View-Change (each replica -> new primary)	n - 1	Signal primary failure
New-View (new primary -> all)	n - 1	Resynchronize with proof
Re-prepare (for pending requests)	(n-1) per request	Re-run prepare phase
Total view change	$O(n^2)$ to $O(n^3)$	Depends on pending requests

PBFT Scalability Limitations

PBFT's quadratic message complexity is its Achilles' heel. $O(n^2)$ per round means doubling the number of nodes doesn't just double the cost. It quadruples it. For four nodes, you're looking at maybe 48 messages per round. Manageable. At 100 nodes, it's roughly 30,000. At 1,000 nodes? Nearly 3 million. The protocol just doesn't scale to large validator sets. Period.

```
def pbft_scalability_analysis(max_n: int = 200) -> None:
    """Analyze PBFT communication costs at various network sizes."""
    print("\nPBFT Scalability Analysis")
    print(f"{'Nodes':>7} {'Messages/Round':>16} {'Bandwidth (1KB msgs)':>22}
    {'Latency (1ms/msg)':>20}")
    print("-" * 70)
```

```
    for n in [4, 10, 20, 50, 100, 200, 500, 1000]:
        # Pre-prepare: n-1, Prepare: (n-1)², Commit: n(n-1)
        pp = n - 1
        prep = (n - 1) * (n - 1)
        commit = n * (n - 1)
        total = pp + prep + commit

        bandwidth_mb = total * 1 / 1024  # 1KB per message
        latency_ms = (3 * n)  # 3 sequential phases, each ~n parallel msgs

        practical = "OK" if n <= 20 else ("Marginal" if n <= 50 else
        "Impractical")

        print(f"  {n:5d}  {total:14,d}  {bandwidth_mb:18.1f} MB  {latency_
        ms:16d} ms  [{practical}]")

pbft_scalability_analysis()
```

7.1.3 HotStuff: Linear Complexity BFT

HotStuff came out of work by Abraham, Gueta, Malkhi, and Dolev in 2018, and it solved the big problem. O(n) communication per round instead of O(n^2). Two ideas made that possible: threshold signatures that let you compress many votes into a single compact proof and a pipelined three-phase commit structure that avoids the all-to-all messaging pattern entirely.

Threshold Signatures Enable Linear Communication

In PBFT, the quadratic blowup happens because every replica sends its prepare and commit messages to every other replica. All-to-all. HotStuff changes the topology by funneling all communication through the leader and using threshold signatures (BLS, specifically) to aggregate votes:

1. Replicas send their vote (a signature share) to the leader. Not to each other. Just the leader.

2. The leader takes those signature shares and combines them into a single Quorum Certificate. One compact object proves 2f+1 replicas agreed.

3. The leader broadcasts the QC to everyone. One message to all replicas, done.

A QC is a self-contained proof of agreement. Any replica can verify it independently, without needing to see the individual votes. That compression is what takes each communication round from $O(n^2)$ (everyone talking to everyone) down to $O(n)$ (everyone talks to the leader, leader talks to everyone).

Three-Phase Commit with Pipelining

HotStuff commits through three phases: PREPARE, PRE-COMMIT, and COMMIT. Each phase produces a QC. The rule for commitment: a block is final when it has three consecutive QCs chained together. That's called a "three-chain," and it's the structure that guarantees safety while keeping communication linear.

```
from dataclasses import dataclass
from typing import Dict, List, Optional, Set
import hashlib

@dataclass
class QuorumCertificate:
    """Aggregated signature proof from 2f+1 validators."""
    block_hash: str
    view: int
    signers: frozenset  # Set of validator IDs who signed

    @property
    def voter_count(self) -> int:
        return len(self.signers)

@dataclass
class HotStuffBlock:
    parent_hash: str
    block_hash: str
    view: int
    justify: Optional[QuorumCertificate]  # QC that justifies this proposal
    payload: bytes
    height: int = 0
```

```
class HotStuffNode:
    """HotStuff consensus node with pipelined three-chain commit."""

    def __init__(self, node_id: int, total_nodes: int):
        self.id = node_id
        self.n = total_nodes
        self.f = (total_nodes - 1) // 3
        self.quorum = 2 * self.f + 1

        self.current_view = 0
        self.voted_view = -1  # Last view we voted in

        # QC tracking
        self.locked_qc: Optional[QuorumCertificate] = None
        self.prepare_qc: Optional[QuorumCertificate] = None
        self.highest_qc: Optional[QuorumCertificate] = None

        # Block storage
        self.blocks: Dict[str, HotStuffBlock] = {}
        self.committed: List[HotStuffBlock] = []

        # Vote collection (leader only)
        self.votes: Dict[int, Dict[int, bool]] = {}

    def propose(self, payload: bytes, parent_hash: str) -> HotStuffBlock:
        """Leader creates a new proposal."""
        block_data = f"{parent_hash}:{self.current_view}:{payload.hex()}"
        block_hash = hashlib.sha256(block_data.encode()).hexdigest()[:16]

        block = HotStuffBlock(
            parent_hash=parent_hash,
            block_hash=block_hash,
            view=self.current_view,
            justify=self.highest_qc,
            payload=payload,
            height=len(self.committed) + len(self.blocks)
        )
        self.blocks[block_hash] = block
        return block
```

```
    def vote_for(self, block: HotStuffBlock) -> bool:
        """
        Decide whether to vote for a block.

        SAFETY RULE: Only vote if the block extends from our
        locked QC or higher. This prevents voting for chains
        that conflict with previously locked decisions.

        LIVENESS RULE: Always vote if the block's justify QC
        has a higher view than our locked QC.
        """
        # Don't vote twice in the same view
        if block.view <= self.voted_view:
            return False

        # Safety check
        if self.locked_qc is not None:
            if block.justify is None:
                return False
            if block.justify.view < self.locked_qc.view:
                # Block's justification is older than our lock
                # Only vote if the justify is strictly higher (liveness)
                return False

        # Cast vote
        self.voted_view = block.view
        self.blocks[block.block_hash] = block

        # Update highest QC
        if block.justify is not None:
            if (self.highest_qc is None or
                block.justify.view > self.highest_qc.view):
                self.highest_qc = block.justify

        return True

    def collect_vote(self, view: int, voter_id: int) ->
    Optional[QuorumCertificate]:
        """Leader collects votes and forms QC when quorum reached."""
```

```
    if view not in self.votes:
        self.votes[view] = {}

    self.votes[view][voter_id] = True

    if len(self.votes[view]) >= self.quorum:
        # Form QC by aggregating signatures
        block_hash = None
        for bh, block in self.blocks.items():
            if block.view == view:
                block_hash = bh
                break

        if block_hash:
            qc = QuorumCertificate(
                block_hash=block_hash,
                view=view,
                signers=frozenset(self.votes[view].keys())
            )
            return qc

    return None

def update_on_qc(self, qc: QuorumCertificate):
    """
    Process a new QC. Check for three-chain commit.

    Three-chain rule:
    b* <- b'' <- b' <- b (each with QC)
    If b*, b'', b' form a direct three-chain, b* is committed.
    """
    # Update prepare QC
    if (self.prepare_qc is None or
        qc.view > self.prepare_qc.view):

        old_prepare = self.prepare_qc
        self.prepare_qc = qc
```

```
            # Update locked QC (two-chain: prepare of prepare)
            if old_prepare is not None:
                if (self.locked_qc is None or
                    old_prepare.view > self.locked_qc.view):
                    self.locked_qc = old_prepare

        # Update highest QC
        if self.highest_qc is None or qc.view > self.highest_qc.view:
            self.highest_qc = qc

def simulate_hotstuff(n: int, num_rounds: int, f_byzantine: int = 0)
-> dict:
    """Simulate HotStuff consensus."""
    nodes = [HotStuffNode(i, n) for i in range(n)]
    byzantine_ids = set(range(n - f_byzantine, n))

    leader = nodes[0]
    parent = "genesis"
    total_messages = 0
    committed_blocks = 0

    for round_num in range(num_rounds):
        # Leader proposes
        payload = f"batch_{round_num}".encode()
        block = leader.propose(payload, parent)
        total_messages += n - 1  # Broadcast proposal

        # Replicas vote
        vote_count = 0
        for node in nodes:
            if node.id in byzantine_ids:
                continue
            if node.vote_for(block):
                vote_count += 1
                total_messages += 1  # Vote to leader
```

```
        # Leader forms QC
        for node in nodes:
            if node.id in byzantine_ids:
                continue
            qc = leader.collect_vote(leader.current_view, node.id)
            if qc:
                total_messages += n - 1  # Broadcast QC
                # All honest nodes process QC
                for other in nodes:
                    if other.id not in byzantine_ids:
                        other.update_on_qc(qc)
                break

        parent = block.block_hash
        for node in nodes:
            node.current_view += 1

    return {
        'rounds': num_rounds,
        'total_messages': total_messages,
        'messages_per_round': total_messages / num_rounds,
        'theoretical_per_round': 3 * n,  # 3 phases × n messages each
    }

print("\nHotStuff Simulation")
print("=" * 60)
for n in [4, 10, 25, 100]:
    result = simulate_hotstuff(n, 10)
    f = (n - 1) // 3
    print(f"\nn={n} (f={f}):")
    print(f"  Messages per round: {result['messages_per_round']:.0f}")
    print(f"  Theoretical O(n):   ~{result['theoretical_per_round']}")
    print(f"  Compare PBFT O(n²): ~{n*n*3}")
    print(f"  Improvement:        ~{(n*n*3) / max(result['messages_per_
    round'],1):.0f}x")
```

View Change in HotStuff

One of HotStuff's most underappreciated advantages: its view change mechanism is almost comically simple compared to PBFT's. When a view times out:

1. Each replica sends its highest QC to the incoming leader. That's O(n) messages.

2. The new leader looks at what it received and picks the highest QC among them.

3. That QC becomes the justification for the leader's first proposal. And that's it.

Why is it so simple? Because QCs are self-certifying. A QC carries within it an aggregated signature from 2f+1 validators. Anyone who sees it can verify it independently. The new leader doesn't have to jump through hoops to prove the transition is valid. It just includes the best QC it knows about, proposes a block that extends from it, and everyone can confirm for themselves.

Compare that to PBFT, where a view change means collecting and rebroadcasting complex prepared certificates. $O(n^3)$ in the worst case. The difference is night and day.

7.1.4 Tendermint Core

Tendermint was put together by Jae Kwon and Ethan Buchman starting in 2014, and its contribution wasn't just the consensus protocol itself. It was the architecture. Tendermint separates consensus from application logic through something called the Application Blockchain Interface, or ABCI. That separation is what makes the entire Cosmos ecosystem possible.

Consensus Protocol

The consensus protocol itself borrows heavily from PBFT. Three phases per block height:

Propose. A designated proposer (rotated based on voting power) broadcasts a block proposal to the network.

Prevote. Every validator looks at the proposal and casts a prevote. If the proposal looks valid and the validator isn't locked onto a different value from a previous round, they prevote for it. Otherwise, they pre-vote nil. Locking is the mechanism that prevents validators from flip-flopping between conflicting values across rounds.

Precommit. Once a validator sees 2f+1 prevotes for a value (or nil), it casts a precommit. Collect 2f+1 precommits for a block, and that block is committed. Immediate finality. No probabilistic waiting, no confirmation depth. Just done.

When a round fails because not enough prevotes or precommits materialize, validators increment the round number, select a new proposer, and try again. Same block height, different round, fresh attempt.

```
from enum import Enum
from typing import Dict, Set, Optional
from dataclasses import dataclass

class TendermintStep(Enum):
    PROPOSE = "propose"
    PREVOTE = "prevote"
    PRECOMMIT = "precommit"
    COMMIT = "commit"

class TendermintValidator:
    """Complete Tendermint consensus validator."""

    def __init__(self, validator_id: int, num_validators: int,
                 voting_power: int = 1):
        self.id = validator_id
        self.n = num_validators
        self.voting_power = voting_power
        self.f = (num_validators - 1) // 3

        self.height = 0
        self.round = 0
        self.step = TendermintStep.PROPOSE

        # Locking mechanism
        self.locked_round = -1
        self.locked_value: Optional[str] = None
        self.valid_round = -1
        self.valid_value: Optional[str] = None
```

```
        # Vote tracking for current height
        self.prevotes: Dict[int, Dict[Optional[str], Set[int]]] = {}
        self.precommits: Dict[int, Dict[Optional[str], Set[int]]] = {}

        self.committed_blocks: List[dict] = []

    def get_proposer(self, height: int, round: int) -> int:
        """Weighted round-robin proposer selection."""
        return (height + round) % self.n

    def propose(self, block_data: str) -> Optional[dict]:
        """Generate proposal if this validator is the proposer."""
        if self.get_proposer(self.height, self.round) != self.id:
            return None

        # If locked, must propose locked value
        value = self.locked_value if self.locked_value else block_data

        return {
            'type': 'proposal',
            'height': self.height,
            'round': self.round,
            'value': value,
            'valid_round': self.valid_round if self.locked_value else -1,
            'proposer': self.id,
        }

    def prevote(self, proposal: Optional[dict]) -> dict:
        """
        Cast prevote based on proposal and lock state.

        Prevote rules (Tendermint spec):
        1. If locked on value V and proposal = V: prevote V
        2. If locked on value V and proposal != V: prevote nil
        3. If not locked and proposal is valid: prevote proposal
        4. If proposal has valid_round >= 0 and we saw 2f+1 prevotes
           for that value in valid_round: can unlock and prevote it
        5. If no valid proposal: prevote nil
        """
```

```
        vote_value = None

        if proposal is not None:
            proposed_value = proposal['value']

            if self.locked_value is None:
                # Not locked: accept any valid proposal
                vote_value = proposed_value
            elif self.locked_value == proposed_value:
                # Locked on this value: vote for it
                vote_value = proposed_value
            elif proposal.get('valid_round', -1) >= 0:
                # Check if we can unlock (POL - Proof of Lock)
                vr = proposal['valid_round']
                if (vr in self.prevotes and
                    proposed_value in self.prevotes[vr] and
                    len(self.prevotes[vr][proposed_value]) >= 2 *
                    self.f + 1):
                    # Unlock and vote for new value
                    vote_value = proposed_value
            # else: locked on different value, vote nil

        return {
            'type': 'prevote',
            'height': self.height,
            'round': self.round,
            'value': vote_value,
            'voter': self.id,
        }

    def receive_prevote(self, vote: dict):
        """Record a prevote."""
        r = vote['round']
        v = vote['value']

        if r not in self.prevotes:
            self.prevotes[r] = {}
```

```
        if v not in self.prevotes[r]:
            self.prevotes[r][v] = set()
        self.prevotes[r][v].add(vote['voter'])

    def has_prevote_quorum(self, round: int, value: Optional[str]) -> bool:
        """Check for 2f+1 prevotes for a value."""
        if round not in self.prevotes:
            return False
        return len(self.prevotes[round].get(value, set())) >= 2 * self.f + 1

    def precommit(self) -> dict:
        """
        Cast precommit based on prevote results.

        If 2f+1 prevotes for block B: precommit B and LOCK on B
        If 2f+1 prevotes for nil: precommit nil (unlock)
        Otherwise: precommit nil
        """
        vote_value = None

        if self.round in self.prevotes:
            for value, voters in self.prevotes[self.round].items():
                if value is not None and len(voters) >= 2 * self.f + 1:
                    vote_value = value
                    # LOCK on this value
                    self.locked_round = self.round
                    self.locked_value = value
                    self.valid_round = self.round
                    self.valid_value = value
                    break

        return {
            'type': 'precommit',
            'height': self.height,
            'round': self.round,
            'value': vote_value,
            'voter': self.id,
        }
```

```
    def receive_precommit(self, vote: dict):
        """Record a precommit."""
        r = vote['round']
        v = vote['value']

        if r not in self.precommits:
            self.precommits[r] = {}
        if v not in self.precommits[r]:
            self.precommits[r][v] = set()
        self.precommits[r][v].add(vote['voter'])

    def try_commit(self) -> Optional[str]:
        """Check for 2f+1 precommits for any value -> COMMIT."""
        for r in self.precommits:
            for value, voters in self.precommits[r].items():
                if value is not None and len(voters) >= 2 * self.f + 1:
                    self.committed_blocks.append({
                        'height': self.height,
                        'round': r,
                        'value': value,
                    })
                    # Advance to next height
                    self.height += 1
                    self.round = 0
                    self.locked_round = -1
                    self.locked_value = None
                    self.valid_round = -1
                    self.valid_value = None
                    self.prevotes = {}
                    self.precommits = {}
                    return value
        return None

def simulate_tendermint(n: int, heights: int, f_byzantine: int = 0):
    """Simulate Tendermint consensus over multiple heights."""
    validators = [TendermintValidator(i, n) for i in range(n)]
    byzantine = set(range(n - f_byzantine, n))
```

```
    committed = 0
    total_rounds = 0

    for h in range(heights):
        # Current height consensus
        max_rounds = 5
        for round_num in range(max_rounds):
            proposer_id = validators[0].get_proposer(h, round_num)
            block = f"block_h{h}_r{round_num}"

            # Propose
            proposal = None
            if proposer_id not in byzantine:
                proposal = validators[proposer_id].propose(block)

            # Prevote phase
            for v in validators:
                if v.id in byzantine:
                    continue
                vote = v.prevote(proposal)
                for other in validators:
                    if other.id not in byzantine:
                        other.receive_prevote(vote)

            # Precommit phase
            for v in validators:
                if v.id in byzantine:
                    continue
                vote = v.precommit()
                for other in validators:
                    if other.id not in byzantine:
                        other.receive_precommit(vote)

            # Try commit
            commit_value = None
            for v in validators:
                if v.id not in byzantine:
                    result = v.try_commit()
```

```
                if result:
                    commit_value = result

            total_rounds += 1

            if commit_value:
                committed += 1
                # Sync all honest validators
                for v in validators:
                    if v.id not in byzantine and v.height <= h:
                        v.try_commit()
                break
            else:
                # Move to next round
                for v in validators:
                    if v.id not in byzantine:
                        v.round += 1

    return {
        'committed': committed,
        'total_rounds': total_rounds,
        'avg_rounds_per_height': total_rounds / max(heights, 1),
    }

print("\nTendermint Consensus Simulation")
print("=" * 55)
for n, f in [(4, 0), (4, 1), (7, 2), (10, 3)]:
    result = simulate_tendermint(n, 5, f)
    print(f"\nn={n}, f={f}:")
    print(f"  Committed blocks: {result['committed']}/5")
    print(f"  Total rounds: {result['total_rounds']}")
    print(f"  Avg rounds/height: {result['avg_rounds_per_height']:.1f}")
```

The Application Blockchain Interface (ABCI)

Tendermint's ABCI is a socket-based protocol that creates a clean boundary between the consensus engine and whatever application you want to run on top of it. The application is a separate process entirely. It talks to Tendermint Core through a defined set of method calls.

That architecture means you can build any application on top of Tendermint without reimplementing consensus from scratch. The Cosmos ecosystem runs on this idea. Hundreds of application-specific blockchains (appchains, in Cosmos parlance) are all sharing the same consensus layer underneath but running completely different application logic on top.

The ABCI methods that matter:

CheckTx. Gets called when a transaction first arrives in the mempool. The application checks if it's valid (signature, format, business rules, whatever) and returns accept or reject. This is the gatekeeper. Invalid transactions get filtered out before they waste anyone's time.

BeginBlock, DeliverTx, EndBlock. These get called during block execution, in sequence. BeginBlock gives the application metadata about the block being processed. DeliverTx fires for each individual transaction (this is where the application actually processes state transitions). EndBlock runs at the end and handles things like validator set updates.

Commit. Called after every transaction in the block has been delivered. The application computes its state root (a Merkle hash over its current state) and hands it back. That hash goes into the next block header, chaining the application state to the consensus layer.

Table 7-3. *BFT Protocol Comparison*

Property	**PBFT**	**HotStuff**	**Tendermint**
Message complexity	$O(n^2)$	$O(n)$	$O(n^2)$
Phases per decision	3	3 (pipelined)	3 per round
View change cost	$O(n^3)$	$O(n)$	$O(n^2)$
Finality	Immediate	Immediate	Immediate
Responsiveness	Yes	Optimistic	No (fixed timeouts)
Threshold signatures	Not required	Required (BLS)	Not required
Application separation	No	No	Yes (ABCI)
Max practical validators	~20	~500	~150
Production deployments	Hyperledger Fabric	Diem/Aptos lineage	Cosmos ecosystem

7.1.5 Synchrony Assumptions and Network Partitions

How a BFT protocol behaves during a network partition comes down to its synchrony assumptions. This choice has real consequences, and it's one of the most important design decisions in any consensus system.

Synchronous model. Messages arrive within a known time bound Δ. Always. This is the strongest assumption you can make about the network, and it almost never holds in reality. Routers crash. Cables get cut. DNS gets poisoned. Assuming synchrony is convenient for proofs but dangerous for production.

Partially synchronous model. Somewhere in the future, there's a moment called GST (Global Stabilization Time) after which messages start getting delivered within bound Δ. Before GST, the adversary can delay messages as long as it wants. Safety holds the whole time. Liveness only kicks in after GST. PBFT, HotStuff, and Tendermint all live in this model. It's a reasonable bet for real networks: things might go wrong for a while, but eventually they recover.

Asynchronous model. No timing guarantees at all. Messages arrive whenever they feel like it, if ever. FLP says deterministic consensus is impossible here. Protocols like HoneyBadger BFT use randomization to make progress anyway, but the throughput costs are real.

When the network actually does partition, partially synchronous BFT protocols stop producing blocks. They halt. Deliberately. Rather than risk two halves of the network making conflicting decisions, the protocol chooses to do nothing until connectivity is restored. For permissioned systems and application-specific chains where inconsistency would be catastrophic, that's the right call.

Framed in CAP theorem terms: BFT protocols pick CP (consistency plus partition tolerance). They sacrifice availability to preserve consistency. Nakamoto consensus goes the other direction, choosing AP. Bitcoin keeps producing blocks on both sides of a partition, accepting that forks will happen and will need to be resolved later. Different philosophy, different tradeoffs.

Table 7-4. Partition Behavior by Protocol

Protocol Family	During Partition	After Partition	Trade-off
BFT (Tendermint, PBFT)	Halts (no new blocks)	Resumes from the last finalized state	Consistency over availability
Nakamoto (Bitcoin, Ethereum PoW)	Continues on both sides	Longer chain wins; shorter chain reorged	Availability over consistency
Gasper (Ethereum PoS)	Continues with inactivity leak	Inactivity leak penalizes offline validators	Hybrid: eventual consistency with penalties

7.1.6 Summary

BFT consensus delivers strong finality guarantees, but the price is limited scalability. PBFT cracked the problem open in 1999 by making BFT feasible for small networks. HotStuff brought communication costs down to linear, opening the door to larger validator sets. And Tendermint took the whole thing and wrapped it in a clean application interface that spawned hundreds of blockchains.

What you should take away:

- The $3f + 1$ bound is fundamental. BFT consensus requires at least $3f + 1$ nodes to survive f Byzantine faults. That comes from the quorum intersection argument: two quorums of $2f + 1$ must overlap in at least one honest node. Not a design choice. A mathematical requirement.
- FLP impossibility puts a hard ceiling on what deterministic protocols can do in asynchronous networks. Even one fault is enough to make consensus impossible. Every practical protocol works around it: partial synchrony, randomization, economic incentives, and timeouts. Pick your poison.
- PBFT runs three phases (pre-prepare, prepare, commit) at $O(n^2)$ messages per round. Fine for maybe 20 nodes. Beyond that, the quadratic scaling eats you alive. And the view change protocol, at $O(n^3)$ worst case, is where most implementation bugs have historically lived.

- HotStuff collapses message complexity to O(n) by routing everything through the leader and using threshold signature aggregation to compress votes into compact Quorum Certificates. The view change becomes trivially simple because QCs carry their own proof of validity.
- Tendermint took BFT consensus and made it modular. The ABCI separation lets any application bolt onto a production-quality consensus engine. The Cosmos ecosystem is living proof that the idea works. Hundreds of chains, one underlying consensus layer.
- BFT protocols sacrifice liveness for safety during partitions. They stop. No new blocks until connectivity returns. In CAP terms, that's a CP system. Whether that tradeoff is acceptable depends entirely on the application.
- Which protocol fits depends on context. PBFT still works for small permissioned networks where the validator set is tiny. HotStuff is the choice when you need more validators without drowning in messages. Tendermint is what you use when you want a standalone chain with its own application logic and don't want to rebuild consensus yourself.

BFT consensus tolerates f = (n-1)/3 Byzantine nodes; requires a quorum of 2f+1 for safety—FLP impossibility: no deterministic asynchronous protocol solves consensus with even one fault—PBFT: three-phase (pre-prepare, prepare, commit); O(n^2) messages; practical for n <= 20—HotStuff: leader-based with threshold signatures; O(n) messages; practical for n <= 500—Tendermint: ABCI separates consensus from application logic; powers Cosmos ecosystem—View change: PBFT O(n^3) complex; HotStuff O(n) simple (QCs are self-certifying)—Partial synchrony: safety always holds; liveness only after GST—During partitions: BFT halts (CP); Nakamoto continues on both sides (AP)

Next chapter: novel consensus mechanisms that move beyond the classical BFT playbook. Avalanche's probabilistic finality approach and Ouroboros's provably secure Proof of Stake, among others.

7.1.7 Exercises

Problem 1 (Basic): A BFT system has 13 nodes. What is the maximum number of Byzantine nodes it can tolerate? What is the minimum quorum size? Verify the three conditions (quorum overlap, honest quorum existence, n >= 3f+1).

Problem 2 (Calculation): Compute the exact message count for one round of PBFT consensus with 25 nodes (pre-prepare + prepare + commit phases). Compare with HotStuff for the same network. What is the improvement factor?

Problem 3 (Implementation): Extend the PBFT implementation to handle view changes when the primary fails (stops responding). Demonstrate that committed state from the old view survives the transition to the new primary.

Problem 4 (Analysis): Walk through the quorum intersection argument for n=6, f=2. Show that two quorums of 2f+1=5 nodes each must overlap in at least 4 nodes. Why is this insufficient (since up to 2 of those 4 could be Byzantine)?

Problem 5 (Design): Design a BFT protocol that achieves O(n) message complexity without requiring threshold signatures (HotStuff requires BLS aggregate signatures). What trade-offs are necessary? Can you achieve it with a leader-based protocol using standard signatures?

Problem 6 (Theory): Explain the FLP impossibility result in your own words. How does each of the following circumvent it: (a) PBFT's timeout-based view change, (b) Nakamoto's probabilistic consensus, (c) randomized BFT protocols like Ben-Or?

Problem 7 (Comparative): Compare Tendermint's round-based protocol (with fixed timeouts) and HotStuff's pipelined protocol (with responsive leader). Under what network conditions does each perform better? Consider varying message delays and leader failure rates.

Problem 8 (Critical Thinking): BFT protocols provide immediate finality while Nakamoto consensus requires multiple confirmations. Is immediate finality always desirable? Consider: user experience, exchange deposit policies, smart contract composability, and the risk of halting during partitions.

Problem 9 (Advanced): Implement a simplified version of HotStuff with threshold signatures (using a mock aggregate signature scheme that concatenates validator IDs). Verify that the three-chain commit rule correctly identifies committed blocks. Test with f Byzantine nodes sending conflicting votes.

Problem 10 (Research): Study one production BFT deployment: Cosmos Hub (Tendermint), Aptos (HotStuff derivative), or Hyperledger Fabric (PBFT-inspired). Document: the validator set size, observed block times, any downtime incidents, and how the theoretical BFT properties held in practice.

(Solutions in Appendix D)

7.1.8 Further Reading

Start with Castro and Liskov's 1999 paper, "Practical Byzantine Fault Tolerance." It's the foundational work. Their safety and liveness proofs under partial synchrony are worth reading carefully, not just for the results but for how they structure the arguments.

For HotStuff: Abraham et al.'s 2018 paper has the full protocol with proofs. If you want to see how theory translates to practice, look at the Diem (originally Libra) documentation, which covers what they ran into when they actually deployed a HotStuff variant.

Tendermint's formal treatment is in Buchman, Kwon, and Milosevic's "The Latest Gossip on BFT Consensus" (2018). For the current production reality, check the CometBFT documentation, which reflects what's actually running.

On FLP: the original Fischer, Lynch, and Paterson paper from 1985 is one of those landmark results that every distributed systems person should read at least once. Nancy Lynch's textbook "Distributed Algorithms" puts it in context alongside related impossibility results.

One Common Mistake Worth Flagging: don't confuse the number of consensus participants (n) with total network node count. A blockchain might have 10,000 full nodes but only 100 validators. The BFT parameters are based on n=100. The other 9,900 nodes are verifying, not voting.

CHAPTER 8

Novel Consensus Mechanisms

8.1 Avalanche, GHOST, and Ouroboros

This chapter covers consensus mechanisms beyond the classical BFT and Nakamoto families—Avalanche's subsampled voting, DAG-based ledgers, the GHOST fork-choice rule, Ouroboros's provably secure PoS, Nakamoto variants like Bitcoin-NG and PHANTOM, and how probabilistic, deterministic, and economic finality compare in practice. By the end you should at least be able to sniff-test a deck that waves the word "consensus" around.

- How Avalanche-ish protocols get agreement by polling random handfuls of peers instead of electing a boss or shouting at the whole network.
- Why DAG-shaped ledgers (not a single spine of blocks) can squeeze out more throughput when the workload isn't one long serial story.
- GHOST, i.e., what you bolt when the longest chain starts lying to you once blocks arrive faster than gossip can carry them.
- The Ouroboros line (Cardano's backbone) and why the nerdy bit matters: real proof for PoS, not a medium post with hand-waving.
- A grab bag of Nakamoto descendants (Bitcoin-NG, PHANTOM/SPECTRE, Prism...) that still feel "anyone can show up."

N. Savant, *Blockchain Foundations*, https://doi.org/10.1007/979-8-8688-2891-1_8

- Probabilistic versus deterministic finality, and the boring-sounding detail that becomes expensive when bridges are involved.
- A side-by-side read on finality tradeoffs so you stop ranking chains by headline TPS alone.

8.1.1 Beyond Classical BFT and Nakamoto Consensus

We already spent serious time on two big families. Classical BFT (PBFT, HotStuff, Tendermint) gives you fast, crisp finality if you keep the validator set small enough that quadratic chatter doesn't eat the planet. Plain Nakamoto (PoW, naive longest-chain PoS) scales participation but leaves you babysitting confirmations because finality stays stubbornly probabilistic. For a long while that felt like the whole menu.

This chapter wanders the shelf labeled "neither of the above, exactly." You get subsampled voting where nobody is the permanent coordinator, fork-choice rules that weigh whole subtrees instead of counting links like a yardstick, and PoS designs that dragged in the kind of theorem statements distributed systems people actually respect. Some of these ideas stack; some fight; all of them redraw what you can plausibly claim about throughput and safety.

Treat the protocols as data points on a map. The individual blueprints are useful, sure, but the shape of the design space (what pairs nicely, what trades off brutally) is what sticks once you're picking a stack for real.

8.1.2 Avalanche Consensus Family

Avalanche (Team Rocket, later Ava Labs, 2018) quietly drops two habits older protocols treated as mandatory: you do not need a rotating leader, and you do not need every node to hear from every other node every round. Instead, each participant samples a handful of random peers, tilts their vote toward whatever that sample said, and repeats. After enough rounds the mesh locks in. No conductor waving a baton, and no all-pairs traffic storm.

The engine is metastable. Imagine the network leaning 52% toward option A on day one. Each sampling round widens that tilt the way a ferromagnet snaps near its critical temperature; physicists reach for the same intuition, only here the spins are gossiped preferences instead of atoms lining up.

The Protocol Family

The Avalanche family stacks four ideas on top of each other. Think of it as adding memory until the thing stops wobbling.

Slush is the toy version. Everyone paints themselves a color, asks k strangers each round, and if at least α of them agree on some color, you hop to it. Run that for m rounds and call it a day. It is deliberately memoryless, which keeps the math clean and also means one weird batch of answers can jerk you around forever if luck hates you.

Snowflake remembers a little. You keep a confidence counter: supermajority agrees with you, the counter ticks up; supermajority disagrees, the counter resets, and you switch. You only lock in after β consecutive happy rounds, so a single lucky draw cannot rewrite your mind.

Snowball remembers more. Besides the streak counter, you keep running totals of how often each color has looked convincing across the whole run. Preference tracks whichever color has banked the most evidence. An attacker who briefly poisons the network now has to erase an entire ledger of past polls, not win twice in a row.

The full protocol lifts Snowball onto a transaction DAG. Vertices reference parents, unrelated spends can ride separate Snowball instances in parallel, and when two spends collide, you walk confidence through ancestry: a transaction only graduates if it and every ancestor it drags along look preferred.

```
import random
from typing import List, Dict, Optional
from collections import Counter
from enum import Enum

class Color(Enum):
    RED = "red"
    BLUE = "blue"
    NONE = "none"

class SnowballNode:
    """
    Snowball protocol: adds persistent preference counters to Snowflake.

    Each node maintains:
    - Current color (what it would respond to queries)
    - Persistent counters per color (total successful queries)
```

```
    - Confidence counter (consecutive successes for current color)
    - Decision state and threshold
    """

    def __init__(self, node_id: int, initial_color: Color = Color.NONE):
        self.id = node_id
        self.color = initial_color

        # Persistent counters: total successful queries per color
        self.counters: Dict[Color, int] = {Color.RED: 0, Color.BLUE: 0}

        # Confidence counter: consecutive successes for current color
        self.confidence = 0
        self.last_result = Color.NONE

        # Decision state
        self.decided = False
        self.decision: Optional[Color] = None

    def query_response(self) -> Color:
        """Respond to a query with current color."""
        return self.color

    def process_query_result(self, responses: List[Color],
                              alpha: int, beta: int):
        """
        Process responses from a random sample of k peers.

        1. Count responses per color
        2. If any color has >= alpha responses (supermajority):
           a. Increment that color's persistent counter
           b. If same color as last round: increment confidence
           c. If different: reset confidence, switch
           d. Update preference to color with highest counter
           e. If confidence >= beta: DECIDE
        """
        if self.decided:
            return

        counts = Counter(responses)
```

```
        for color in [Color.RED, Color.BLUE]:
            if counts[color] >= alpha:
                # Supermajority found for this color
                self.counters[color] += 1

                # Update confidence
                if color == self.last_result:
                    self.confidence += 1
                else:
                    self.confidence = 1
                    self.last_result = color

                # Switch to color with highest persistent counter
                if self.counters[color] > self.counters[
                        Color.RED if color == Color.BLUE else Color.BLUE]:
                    self.color = color

                # Check for decision
                if self.confidence >= beta:
                    self.decided = True
                    self.decision = color

                return  # Only process first supermajority found

def simulate_snowball(num_nodes: int, k: int, alpha: int,
                      beta: int, max_rounds: int,
                      initial_red_fraction: float = 0.6,
                      byzantine_fraction: float = 0.0,
                      byzantine_strategy: str = "constant") -> dict:
    """
    Simulate Snowball consensus with configurable parameters.

    Args:
        num_nodes: Total network size
        k: Sample size per query
        alpha: Quorum threshold within sample
        beta: Consecutive success threshold for decision
        max_rounds: Maximum rounds before giving up
```

```
        initial_red_fraction: Fraction of honest nodes starting red
        byzantine_fraction: Fraction of adversarial nodes
        byzantine_strategy: "constant" (always blue) or "random"
    """
    num_byzantine = int(num_nodes * byzantine_fraction)
    num_honest = num_nodes - num_byzantine
    num_red = int(num_honest * initial_red_fraction)

    # Create nodes
    nodes = []
    for i in range(num_nodes):
   if i < num_byzantine:
       # Apply byzantine_strategy – was always BLUE before, now respects
       parameter
       if byzantine_strategy == "random":
           color = random.choice([Color.RED, Color.BLUE])
       else:
           # "constant" strategy – always vote against majority (Blue)
           color = Color.BLUE
       node = SnowballNode(i, color)
       node.decided = True
       node.decision = color
       nodes.append(node)
   elif i < num_byzantine + num_red:
       nodes.append(SnowballNode(i, Color.RED))
   else:
       nodes.append(SnowballNode(i, Color.BLUE))

    # Run consensus rounds
    convergence_round = max_rounds
    history = []

    for round_num in range(max_rounds):
        red_count = sum(1 for n in nodes if n.color == Color.RED)
        decided_count = sum(1 for n in nodes if n.decided)
```

```
    history.append({
        'round': round_num,
        'red': red_count,
        'blue': num_nodes - red_count,
        'decided': decided_count,
        'red_pct': red_count / num_nodes * 100,
    })

    # Check if all honest nodes decided
    honest_decided = sum(1 for n in nodes
                        if n.decided and n.id >= num_byzantine)
    if honest_decided >= num_honest:
        convergence_round = round_num
        break

    # Each undecided node queries
    for node in nodes:
        if node.decided:
            continue

        # Sample k random peers (excluding self)
        peers = random.sample(
            [n for n in nodes if n.id != node.id],
            min(k, len(nodes) - 1)
        )
        responses = [p.query_response() for p in peers]
        node.process_query_result(responses, alpha, beta)

# Analyze final state
red_decided = sum(1 for n in nodes if n.decision == Color.RED and n.id
>= num_byzantine)
blue_decided = sum(1 for n in nodes if n.decision == Color.BLUE and
n.id >= num_byzantine)
undecided = sum(1 for n in nodes if not n.decided and n.id >= num_
byzantine)
```

```
    consensus = (red_decided == num_honest) or (blue_decided == num_honest)

    return {
        'rounds': convergence_round,
        'red_decided': red_decided,
        'blue_decided': blue_decided,
        'undecided': undecided,
        'consensus': consensus,
        'winning_color': Color.RED if red_decided > blue_decided else
        Color.BLUE,
        'history': history,
    }

# Run comprehensive simulations
print("Snowball Consensus Simulation")
print("=" * 70)

# Test 1: Standard parameters with clear majority
result = simulate_snowball(
    num_nodes=500, k=20, alpha=14, beta=20,
    max_rounds=200, initial_red_fraction=0.6
)
print(f"\nTest 1: Standard (500 nodes, 60% initial red)")
print(f"  Converged in {result['rounds']} rounds")
print(f"  Result: {result['winning_color'].value} "
      f"(red={result['red_decided']}, blue={result['blue_decided']})")
print(f"  Consensus: {result['consensus']}")

# Test 2: Tight split
result = simulate_snowball(
    num_nodes=500, k=20, alpha=14, beta=20,
    max_rounds=300, initial_red_fraction=0.52
)
print(f"\nTest 2: Tight split (52% initial red)")
print(f"  Converged in {result['rounds']} rounds")
print(f"  Result: {result['winning_color'].value}")
print(f"  Consensus: {result['consensus']}")
```

```
# Test 3: With Byzantine adversary
result = simulate_snowball(
    num_nodes=500, k=20, alpha=14, beta=20,
    max_rounds=300, initial_red_fraction=0.6,
    byzantine_fraction=0.15
)
print(f"\nTest 3: With 15% Byzantine nodes (always blue)")
print(f"  Converged in {result['rounds']} rounds")
print(f"  Result: {result['winning_color'].value}")
print(f"  Consensus: {result['consensus']}")

# Test 4: Different k values
print(f"\nTest 4: Effect of sample size k (500 nodes, 60% red)")
for k in [5, 10, 20, 40]:
    alpha = int(k * 0.7)  # 70% supermajority
    result = simulate_snowball(
        num_nodes=500, k=k, alpha=alpha, beta=15,
        max_rounds=200, initial_red_fraction=0.6
    )
    print(f"  k={k:2d} (α={alpha:2d}): {result['rounds']:3d} rounds, "
          f"consensus={result['consensus']}")
```

Table 8-1. *Avalanche Protocol Family Comparison*

Protocol	Memory	Persistence	Structure	Byzantine Resilience
Slush	None (memoryless)	No counters	Single decision	Weak: can oscillate
Snowflake	Consecutive counter	Single counter	Single decision	Moderate: needs sustained disruption
Snowball	All-time counters	Per-color counters	Single decision	Strong: needs sustained majority override
Avalanche	DAG + counters	Per-vertex confidence	Transaction DAG	Strong: conflict resolution via DAG ancestry

Avalanche DAG Structure

Where Snowball answers one binary question, the shipping Avalanche design answers many by laying transactions out as a DAG. Each vertex hangs off one or more parents instead of pointing at a single global tail block.

So what does buying a DAG buy you in practice?

Honest concurrency shows up for free-ish. Two transfers that never touch the same coin should not wait in one serial line just because a linear chain only exposes a single next slot. Independent Snowball runs chew through them in parallel.

When spends actually collide, the DAG forces you to respect ancestry. Confidence walks upward; you cannot adore a descendant while still side-eyeing its parent. That transitive rule is what keeps double-spend games from sneaking in sideways.

You also stop pretending block time is the only throttle. On a classic chain, how fast you ingest and how fast you finalize tend to be welded together. Here those worries peel apart enough that tuning one does not automatically strangle the other.

```
Conflicting transactions T3 and T3' (spend same UTXO):
```

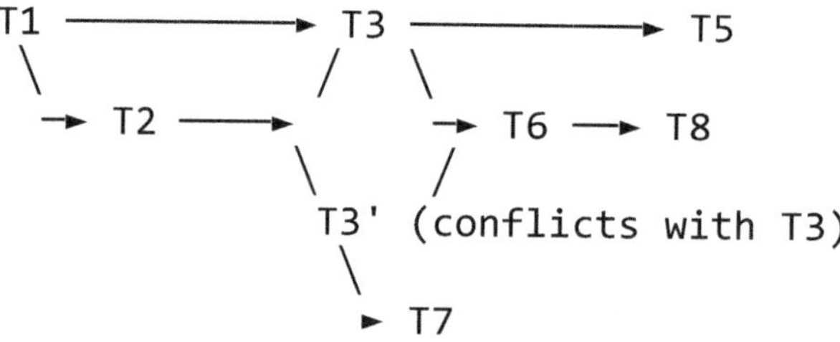


```
Snowball voting determines winner:
If T3 gains confidence → T3, T5, T6, T8 accepted; T3', T7 rejected
If T3' gains confidence → T3', T7 accepted; T3, T5, T6, T8 rejected

Note: T5, T6, T8 depend on T3's acceptance (transitive confidence)
```

Figure 8-1. *Avalanche Transaction DAG with Conflict*

Performance and Security Characteristics

If you only ever stared at PBFT graphs or Bitcoin graphs, Avalanche's performance story looks like it came from another planet. Same words on the slide, different scaling curves hiding underneath.

Each node only ships O(k) messages per round, and k is a knob you hold constant. Pick twenty peers whether the network has a thousand nodes or a hundred thousand; the per-node load does not balloon with n. That alone is weird if you are used to protocols whose gossip work explodes as membership grows.

Round count tends toward O(log n) in the usual analyses because every poll shoves the mass further from the 50/50 knife edge. After a dozen rounds in a big deployment you are usually arguing about engineering noise, not about whether the network still disagrees.

Once messages are cheap, throughput stops being a pure consensus theorem and starts being "how fast can your NIC and your mempool implementation go." Public C-Chain benchmarks in the multi-thousand TPS range had consensus headroom left over, which is not something you can say about every classical BFT deployment.

Finality is still probabilistic: after you cross the β threshold, the chance of undo drops roughly like (1−α/k) raised to the β power, i.e., stupidly fast toward zero for sane parameters. You still do not get a stone tablet.

That last sentence annoys some people. Mathematically there is always a nonzero reversal probability, even if it is 10^-40 after a couple of seconds. For buying coffee, nobody cares. For wiring a bridge to another chain, the difference between "effectively never" and "never" occasionally shows up in a risk memo.

8.1.3 GHOST Protocol

Sompolinsky and Zohar published GHOST in 2015 for a painfully concrete reason: the longest-chain rule starts cheating honest miners once blocks arrive faster than they can propagate. Honest hash ends up raising orphans; an attacker grinding a private fork raises almost none. That asymmetry is not academic trivia.

The Problem with Longest Chain at High Block Rates

Bitcoin's ten-minute target is basically a safety margin for gossip. Orphans sit near a tenth of a percent. The moment you shrink the block interval to chase throughput, the orphan math stops being polite.

Stylized example that shows up in talks: one-second blocks with about a one-second propagation lag. Roughly half of the blocks mined honestly never make the main view. Half the electricity, half the silicon, straight into the void, while an attacker on a single private chain barely discards anything.

Write honest chain growth as (1−orphan_rate) times honest hash rate, but the attacker's private branch pays no orphan tax at all. Once orphan rates climb, an adversary with well under half the hash power can still outrun the public chain long enough to break the bedtime story about "50% security."

```
from typing import Dict, List, Set
from dataclasses import dataclass, field
import hashlib

@dataclass
class BlockNode:
    block_hash: str
    parent_hash: str
    miner: str
    height: int
    timestamp: float = 0.0

class ForkChoiceComparison:
    """Compare GHOST and Longest Chain fork choice rules."""

    def __init__(self):
        self.blocks: Dict[str, BlockNode] = {}
        self.children: Dict[str, List[str]] = {}
        self.genesis = "genesis"

    def add_block(self, block: BlockNode):
        self.blocks[block.block_hash] = block
        parent = block.parent_hash
        if parent not in self.children:
            self.children[parent] = []
        self.children[parent].append(block.block_hash)

    def subtree_weight(self, block_hash: str) -> int:
        """Total blocks in subtree including root."""
        weight = 1
        for child in self.children.get(block_hash, []):
            weight += self.subtree_weight(child)
        return weight
```

```
def chain_length(self, block_hash: str) -> int:
    """Length of longest chain from this block."""
    children = self.children.get(block_hash, [])
    if not children:
        return 1
    return 1 + max(self.chain_length(c) for c in children)

def longest_chain_head(self) -> str:
    """Longest chain rule: follow longest path."""
    current = self.genesis
    while current in self.children and self.children[current]:
        current = max(self.children[current],
                      key=lambda c: self.chain_length(c))
    return current

def ghost_head(self) -> str:
    """GHOST: follow heaviest subtree at each fork."""
    current = self.genesis
    while current in self.children and self.children[current]:
        current = max(self.children[current],
                      key=lambda c: self.subtree_weight(c))
    return current

def count_by_miner(self, subtree_root: str) -> Dict[str, int]:
    """Count blocks by miner in a subtree."""
    counts: Dict[str, int] = {}

    def traverse(bh: str):
        if bh in self.blocks:
            miner = self.blocks[bh].miner
            counts[miner] = counts.get(miner, 0) + 1
        for child in self.children.get(bh, []):
            traverse(child)

    traverse(subtree_root)
    return counts
```

```
# Build a scenario where GHOST and Longest Chain disagree
fc = ForkChoiceComparison()

# Honest miners produce blocks with high orphan rate
# (simulating fast block times with network delay)
honest_chain = [
    BlockNode("H1", "genesis", "honest", 1),
    BlockNode("H2", "H1", "honest", 2),
    BlockNode("H3", "H2", "honest", 3),
    BlockNode("H4", "H3", "honest", 4),
    BlockNode("H5", "H4", "honest", 5),
]

# Orphaned honest blocks (would be uncles in Ethereum)
orphans = [
    BlockNode("O1", "H1", "honest", 2),
    BlockNode("O2", "H1", "honest", 2),
    BlockNode("O3", "H2", "honest", 3),
    BlockNode("O4", "H3", "honest", 4),
    BlockNode("O5", "H3", "honest", 4),
    BlockNode("O6", "H4", "honest", 5),
]

# Attacker chain: no orphans (mines on single chain)
attacker_chain = [
    BlockNode("A1", "genesis", "attacker", 1),
    BlockNode("A2", "A1", "attacker", 2),
    BlockNode("A3", "A2", "attacker", 3),
    BlockNode("A4", "A3", "attacker", 4),
    BlockNode("A5", "A4", "attacker", 5),
    BlockNode("A6", "A5", "attacker", 6),
]

for b in honest_chain + orphans + attacker_chain:
    fc.add_block(b)

longest = fc.longest_chain_head()
ghost = fc.ghost_head()
```

```
print("GHOST vs Longest Chain Fork Choice")
print("=" * 60)
print(f"Honest: 5 chain blocks + 6 orphans = 11 total blocks")
print(f"Attacker: 6 chain blocks, 0 orphans")

print(f"\nLongest Chain:")
print(f"  Head: {longest}")
print(f"  Honest chain length: {fc.chain_length('H1')}")
print(f"  Attacker chain length: {fc.chain_length('A1')}")
print(f"  Winner: {'Attacker' if 'A' in longest else 'Honest'}")

print(f"\nGHOST:")
print(f"  Head: {ghost}")
print(f"  Honest subtree weight: {fc.subtree_weight('H1')}")
print(f"  Attacker subtree weight: {fc.subtree_weight('A1')}")
print(f"  Winner: {'Attacker' if 'A' in ghost else 'Honest'}")

print(f"\nConclusion: Attacker with 6 blocks beats honest 5-block chain")
print(f"  under Longest Chain, but honest 11-block subtree wins under GHOST.")

# Security threshold analysis
print(f"\nSecurity Threshold Analysis:")
for orphan_rate in [0.0, 0.1, 0.3, 0.5, 0.7]:
    honest_effective_lc = 1.0 * (1 - orphan_rate)
    ghost_effective = 1.0  # GHOST counts all honest blocks
    lc_threshold = honest_effective_lc / (1 + honest_effective_lc)
    ghost_threshold = 0.5  # Always 50% for GHOST

    print(f"  Orphan rate {orphan_rate:.0%}: "
          f"Longest Chain safe below {lc_threshold:.1%} attacker, "
          f"GHOST safe below {ghost_threshold:.0%}")
```

Uncle Rewards: Ethereum's GHOST Adaptation

Ethereum before the merge borrowed GHOST-adjacent ideas and sweetened them with uncle rewards. If your block got orphaned, you could still catch a partial payout when a later block referenced you inside the uncle window, which beat losing everything.

Uncles were doing several jobs at the same time, which is why the mechanism stuck around as long as it did.

1. They kept variance from absolutely brutalizing small miners: partial credit beats a hard zero when your block lost the race by milliseconds.
2. They let fork choice see honest work that would otherwise vanish from the heaviest-tree accounting, which matters when you are trying not to hand attackers a free boost.
3. They also trimmed the upside of selfish mining games, because withholding a block is less tasty when orphans still pay something to the people you screwed over.

8.1.4 Ouroboros: Provably Secure Proof of Stake

Ouroboros landed in 2017 from Kiayias, Russell, Bernardo David, and Oliynykov; Cardano is the headline deployment. The part that actually shifted the field's mood was the bundle of proofs: not "we think this is safe," but definitions, explicit assumptions, and theorems in the same tone classical distributed systems people use.

Plenty of earlier PoS chains (Peercoin, NXT, others) shipped on intuition and blog-grade arguments. Ouroboros went the other way, which sounds slower on paper but ages better when someone asks you to justify the design in court.

Ouroboros Classic: Epoch-Based PoS with Formal Security

The original protocol slices time into epochs, slices epochs into slots, and enforces at most one block per slot with a single leader drawn per slot from the stake distribution.

Leader selection hinges on fresh randomness each epoch: multiparty coin tossing so nobody can pencil themselves in for every slot and so stake proportion actually maps to probability without backstage rigging.

Inside an epoch, the story unfolds in three beats that the code walkthrough below mirrors.

1. Stakeholders first run a verifiable secret sharing ceremony: commit randomness, reveal, and XOR the reveals into epoch entropy. Even a chunk of malicious participants cannot fully bias the outcome if the VSS math does its job.

2. That randomness then feeds follow-the-satoshi: imagine total stake as a line segment, hash the epoch seed with the slot index, see where it lands, and whichever stakeholder owns that slice gets to speak for the slot. More stake, wider slice, more microphone time in expectation.

3. Finally, when the schedule calls your name, you publish a block. Fork choice inside the epoch is still longest-chain flavored, which keeps the engineering story familiar even if the cryptography underneath got heavier.

```
import hashlib from typing import List, Dict, Tuple
class OuroborosProtocol: """ Simplified Ouroboros Classic implementation.
 In production:
 - Randomness uses verifiable secret sharing, not simple hashing
 - Leader selection uses follow-the-satoshi with the full UTXO set
 - Security proof requires honest majority of stake and synchronous network
 """

 def __init__(self, stakeholders: Dict[str, int],
              slots_per_epoch: int = 20):
     self.stakeholders = stakeholders
     self.total_stake = sum(stakeholders.values())
     self.slots_per_epoch = slots_per_epoch
     self.epoch = 0
     self.chain: List[dict] = []

 def generate_epoch_randomness(self, epoch: int,
                               commitments: Dict[str, bytes]) -> bytes:
     """
     Generate epoch randomness from stakeholder commitments.

     In real Ouroboros, this uses a VSS-based coin tossing protocol
     that is secure even if some stakeholders are adversarial.
     Simplified here as hash of all commitments.
     """
     combined = b""
```

```
        for name in sorted(commitments.keys()):
            combined += commitments[name]
        combined += epoch.to_bytes(8, 'big')

        return hashlib.sha256(combined).digest()

    def follow_the_satoshi(self, randomness: bytes, slot: int) -> str:
        """
        Select slot leader using follow-the-satoshi.

        Imagine all stake units laid out in a line:
        [Alice: 0-999] [Bob: 1000-1749] [Carol: 1750-2249]

        Hash randomness + slot to get a position on this line.
        Whoever "owns" that position is the slot leader.
        """
        slot_seed = hashlib.sha256(
            randomness + slot.to_bytes(8, 'big')
        ).digest()

        position = int.from_bytes(slot_seed[:8], 'big') % self.total_stake

        cumulative = 0
        for name, stake in self.stakeholders.items():
            cumulative += stake
            if position < cumulative:
                return name

        return list(self.stakeholders.keys())[-1]

    def run_epoch(self, epoch: int) -> dict:
        """Run one epoch of Ouroboros consensus."""
        # Phase 1: Generate randomness
        commitments = {}
        for name in self.stakeholders:
            secret = hashlib.sha256(
                f"{name}:{epoch}:secret".encode()
            ).digest()
            commitments[name] = secret

        randomness = self.generate_epoch_randomness(epoch, commitments)
```

```
    # Phase 2: Generate slot leader schedule
    schedule = []
    for slot in range(self.slots_per_epoch):
        leader = self.follow_the_satoshi(randomness, slot)
        schedule.append(leader)

    # Phase 3: Block production
    blocks_produced = 0
    leader_blocks = {}
    for slot, leader in enumerate(schedule):
        blocks_produced += 1
        leader_blocks[leader] = leader_blocks.get(leader, 0) + 1
        self.chain.append({
            'epoch': epoch,
            'slot': slot,
            'leader': leader,
            'randomness_seed': randomness.hex()[:8],
        })

    return {
        'epoch': epoch,
        'blocks': blocks_produced,
        'leader_distribution': leader_blocks,
        'schedule': schedule,
    }
```

Demonstrate Ouroboros stakeholders = { "Alice": 4000, # 40% stake "Bob": 3000, # 30% stake "Carol": 2000, # 20% stake "Dave": 1000, # 10% stake } protocol = OuroborosProtocol(stakeholders, slots_per_epoch=100) print("Ouroboros Protocol Demonstration") print("=" * 60) print(f"Stakeholders: {stakeholders}") print(f"Total stake: {protocol.total_stake}")
Run 3 epochs all_leader_counts = {name: 0 for name in stakeholders} for epoch in range(3): result = protocol.run_epoch(epoch) print(f": {result['blocks']} blocks") for name, count in sorted(result['leader_distribution'].items()): expected = stakeholders[name] / protocol.total_stake * 100 actual = count / result['blocks'] * 100 all_leader_counts[name] += count print(f" {name}: {count} blocks ({actual:.1f}%, expected ~{expected:.0f}%)")

```
print(f"over 3 epochs (300 slots):") for name in stakeholders: expected_pct = stakeholders[name] / protocol.total_stake * 100 actual_pct = all_leader_counts[name] / 300 * 100 print(f" {name}: {all_leader_counts[name]} blocks " f"({actual_pct:.1f}%, expected {expected_pct:.0f}%)")
```

Ouroboros Protocol Family

Ouroboros did not freeze in 2017. Each follow-on paper attacked a specific bruise: synchrony assumptions that felt too crisp for the real internet, public leader schedules that invited DDoS, cold-start trust, wall-clock fetishes, or throughput ceilings that researchers wanted to push without throwing away the proof style.

Classic (2017) assumed a synchronous enough network, demanded an honest majority of stakes, and leaned on VSS for randomness. The proofs were the draw; the assumptions were the argument starter at conferences.

Praos (2018) swapped the billboard leader schedule for VRFs so each stakeholder privately learns whether it owns a slot. You cannot DDoS tomorrow's proposer if the network itself does not yet know who that is.

Genesis (2018) tackled the awkward bootstrap question: how a new node tells the real chain from a lovingly crafted fake without speed-dialing a trusted checkpoint. Density statistics across recent epochs give the hint honest activity looks denser than theater.

Chronos (2019) tried to stop the protocol from quietly trusting GPS or NTP. Timing cues get inferred from observed block spacing instead, which removes one external dependency that loves to fail at 3 a.m.

Leios (2024) chases throughput by decoupling who leads from who endorses data, adding parallelism while keeping the security narrative in the same family as the earlier proofs.

***Table 8-2.** Ouroboros Protocol Variants*

Variant	Network Model	Leader Privacy	Bootstrap	Clock	Key Innovation
Classic	Synchronous	Public schedule	Needs checkpoint	External	First provably secure PoS
Praos	Semi-synchronous	VRF (private)	Needs checkpoint	External	Targeted attack resistance
Genesis	Semi-synchronous	VRF	From genesis	External	Secure bootstrapping
Chronos	Semi-synchronous	VRF	From genesis	Self-derived	Clock independence
Leios	Semi-synchronous	VRF	From genesis	Self-derived	Input endorsers for throughput

8.1.5 Nakamoto Consensus Variants

Avalanche, GHOST, and Ouroboros are not the entire zoo. A pile of other designs keeps Nakamoto's permissionless spirit but stretches block production, DAG-ifies the graph, or splits responsibilities so single-threaded bottlenecks loosen.

Bitcoin-NG (Eyal et al., 2016) split the problem in two: a heavy proof-of-work "key block" elects a temporary leader, and then that leader streams lightweight microblocks full of transactions until the next key block arrives. Throughput jumps because you are not re-solving a puzzle for every handful of transfers.

PHANTOM and SPECTRE (Sompolinsky's group, 2016–2018) replace the lonely spine with a block DAG so miners can produce in parallel, then apply graph algorithms to decide which cluster of blocks looks honest and how to order them. Honest parallel work stops getting deleted just because it was not on the longest path.

Prism (Bagaria et al., 2019) goes maximalist: parallel proposer chains, voter chains, and a transaction chain, all wired together so throughput hugs physical bandwidth while the paper argues Bitcoin-grade security. Nobody calls it easy to implement, but the headline numbers are loud on purpose.

Table 8-3. *Nakamoto Consensus Variants*

Protocol	Structure	Throughput vs. Bitcoin	Finality	Key Trade-off
Bitcoin (original)	Linear chain	1x (~7 TPS)	~60 min	Simple, proven, slow
Bitcoin-NG	Key + microblocks	~100x	~10 min	Leader can censor during tenure
GHOST	Heaviest subtree	Same base rate	Better per-confirmation	More complex fork choice
PHANTOM	Block-DAG	~10-50x	~1-5 min	Complex ordering algorithm
SPECTRE	Block-DAG	~10-50x	~10s per-tx	Weak total ordering
Prism	Parallel chains	~1000x	~10s	Complex multi-chain architecture

8.1.6 Finality Models: Probabilistic, Deterministic, and Economic

Whenever you pick a consensus mechanism, you are also picking a finality model, even if the marketing page never uses that phrase. The boring question underneath is simply: at what moment may a merchant treat a payment as settled?

Deterministic finality is the BFT story. Once the protocol is finalized, the ledger does not rewrite itself unless your fault assumptions are broken. The trade is liveness: if the network partitions badly enough, honest nodes may prefer to stall rather than finalize two incompatible histories.

Probabilistic finality is the Bitcoin and Avalanche story. Every extra confirmation multiplies down the odds of a reorg, but the probability never literally hits zero, so pedants always have a footnote. The upside is the chain keeps producing blocks through messy network weather instead of freezing for cleanliness.

Economic finality sits in the middle on paper but feels different in practice. Ethereum after the merge layers Casper FFG with slashing, so reverting a finalized checkpoint means destroying a huge chunk of staked ETH. The attack stays theoretically possible in the same way storming Fort Knox is theoretically possible; the bill is measured in billions of dollars at realistic stake prices, and nobody should treat that napkin math as a trading signal.

```
import math

def finality_comparison(attacker_fraction: float = 0.3) -> None:
    """Compare finality models across protocols."""

    print(f"Finality Comparison (attacker fraction = {attacker_fraction})")
    print("=" * 65)

    q = attacker_fraction
p = 1 - q
print(f"\nNakamoto (Bitcoin, q={q}):")
if q >= p:
   # Formula (q/p)^z only valid when q < p.
   # When q >= p, attacker always wins eventually – no safe
   confirmation depth.
   print(f" Attacker controls >= 50% hash rate.")
   print(f" Reversal probability = 1.0 for all confirmation depths.")
   print(f" No number of confirmations provides safety.")
else:
   print(f" {'Confirmations':>14} {'Reversal Prob':>15} {'Wait Time':>12}")
   for z in [1, 3, 6, 12, 24, 50]:
       prob = (q / p) ** z
       if prob > 1.0:
           # Defensive check – should not happen when q < p but
           guard anyway
           print(f" {z:14d} {'> 1.0 (invalid)':>15} {z*10:10d} min")
       else:
           wait = z * 10 # minutes (Bitcoin ~10 min blocks)
           print(f" {z:14d} {prob:15.2e} {wait:10d} min")

    # Avalanche: P(reversal after decision) exponentially small
    print(f"\nAvalanche (k=20, α=14, β=20):")
    k, alpha, beta = 20, 14, 20
```

```
    p_honest_query = sum(
        math.comb(k, i) * ((1-q)**i) * (q**(k-i))
        for i in range(alpha, k+1)
    )
    p_reversal = (1 - p_honest_query) ** beta
    print(f"  After β={beta} queries: P(reversal) ≈ {p_reversal:.2e}")
    print(f"  Time: ~{beta * 0.1:.1f} seconds")

    # BFT (Tendermint): deterministic
    print(f"\nTendermint (BFT, n=100):")
    print(f"  Finality: DETERMINISTIC (immediate after commit)")
    print(f"  P(reversal) = 0 if f < n/3 = 33 nodes honest")
    print(f"  Time: ~6 seconds (1 block)")

    # Economic (Ethereum Casper)
    eth_staked = 20_000_000  # ETH
    eth_price = 3000
    attack_cost = eth_staked / 3 * eth_price
    print(f"\nEthereum Casper (economic finality):")
    print(f"  Finality: ~12.8 minutes (2 epochs)")
    print(f"  Reversal cost: ≥ ${attack_cost:,.0f}")
    print(f"  P(reversal) = 0 unless attacker spends >{attack_
    cost/1e9:.0f}B USD")

finality_comparison(0.3)
```

8.1.7 Summary

Stepping back, these third-generation ideas refuse the old binary. Avalanche shows subsampled gossip can land you in sub-second probabilistic territory without quadratic chatter. GHOST reminds fork choice that subtree weight matters when orphans spike. Ouroboros drags PoS into the same proof culture PBFT lived in for decades. None of them is a silver bullet, but together they redraw what you can honestly promise users.

If your brain is full, park these few anchors:

- Avalanche keeps per-node load at O(k) by polling random micro-samples, layers Snowball's memory on top, and extends the idea to a DAG so unrelated transactions do not wait on each other. That is the elevator pitch engineers repeat.
- GHOST (and Ethereum's uncle tweaks) weighs entire subtrees so honest orphan hash still counts toward security. When block times shrink, the naive longest-chain rule quietly hands gifts to private attackers; GHOST tries to take the ribbon back.
- Ouroboros was the early PoS family that showed up with real proofs, then Praos hid leaders behind VRFs, Genesis taught cold nodes how to orient, Chronos relaxed global-clock worship, and Leios chased throughput. Each version patched a hole the previous release admitted in the assumptions section.
- The Nakamoto-flavored variants (NG, PHANTOM/SPECTRE, Prism, friends) mostly explore the same trick: decouple leader election from transaction plumbing, or let the graph be a DAG, so you stop pretending one block every ten seconds is the only way to stay open to participation.
- Finality is not one flavor with different marketing. Deterministic BFT gives you stone-tablet irreversibility but may pause under partitions. Probabilistic chains never quite promise zero reorg risk but keep limping forward. Economic finality makes reorgs a balance-sheet suicide mission. Those are genuinely different failure modes, not shades of gray on the same axis.
- Nobody gets every axis simultaneously. Push throughput and you stress bandwidth or state growth. Push validator count, and you stress messaging. Push instant finality and you tighten assumptions. The honest exercise is matching the protocol to the application instead of chasing leaderboard screenshots.

Avalanche: subsampled voting, Snowball counters, DAG execution for non-conflicting traffic, O(k) chatter per node. GHOST: heaviest subtree fork choice so orphan work still counts when block times shrink. Ouroboros Classic: epochs, VSS randomness, follow-the-Satoshi leaders, and early rigorous PoS proofs; Praos hides leaders with VRFs. Bitcoin-NG: PoW key blocks plus microblock streams. PHANTOM/SPECTRE: block DAGs with parallel production and ordering tricks. Finality splits three ways: probabilistic chains keep a vanishing reorg tail, deterministic BFT freezes rather than lies under bad partitions, and economic finality makes reorgs a balance-sheet fire drill.

The next chapter turns this intuition into something you can score systematically: tools for comparing protocols without relying on whoever bought the biggest booth at the conference.

8.1.8 Exercises

Problem 1 (Basic). Explain metastability in Snowball: why does a small initial lean in one direction get amplified across the whole network, and what do Snowball's persistent tallies buy you over Snowflake's single confidence counter?

Problem 2 (Calculation). In Avalanche with k=20 and α=15, what is the smallest adversarial stake fraction (roughly) that can stall consensus? Also compute the probability that one random query returns 15 honest answers if the adversary controls 25% of the nodes. Show the combinatorics.

Problem 3 (Implementation). Extend the Snowball simulator so you sweep network size (100, 500, 1000, 5000, 10000 nodes) with k fixed at 20, plot time-to-convergence, and argue whether the curve looks like the promised O(log n) behavior or if constant factors dominate at small n.

Problem 4 (Analysis). Compare longest-chain versus GHOST when the network mints one block per second and propagation takes about two seconds. Estimate orphan rates and sketch at which attacker hash share longest-chain becomes shaky while GHOST still keeps the 50% story honest.

Problem 5 (Design). Sketch a two-layer stack where Avalanche gives fast pre-confirmations and a Tendermint-like BFT layer supplies deterministic finality. Spell out how the layers talk, what latency users feel at each tier, when they can disagree, and how you resolve fights without losing money.

Problem 6 (Theory). Ouroboros Praos uses VRFs for private leader selection. Explain why publishing the whole leader schedule early is dangerous, how a VRF fixes that, what formal property you actually get, and what breaks if the VRF implementation is biased or leaky.

Problem 7 (Comparative). Build a serious comparison table for Avalanche, Tendermint, and Nakamoto consensus: messages per round per node, total messages to a practical finality depth, wall-clock finality, throughput headroom, fault threshold, network model, and finality type.

Problem 8 (Critical Thinking). Avalanche advertises sub-second finality while Bitcoin wants an hour for comparable reorg odds. Is Avalanche strictly better? Discuss Sybil resistance, validator sets, adversary models, and real outages where you might still pick Bitcoin's slower grind.

Problem 9 (Advanced). Implement a toy DAG Avalanche that processes non-conflicting transactions in parallel, generate a workload that is half double-spends and half independent spends, and benchmark throughput against a sequential chain eating the same traffic.

Problem 10 (Research). Pick one production deployment (Avalanche C-Chain, Cardano's Ouroboros stack, Solana's Tower BFT, your call). Document observed throughput, finality times, validator geography, any consensus incidents, and whether the live behavior matched the whitepaper promises.

Full worked solutions for these exercises sit in Appendix D if you want to cheat-check your algebra.

8.1.9 Further Reading

For Avalanche, read the Team Rocket metastability whitepaper (2020) for the Slush-to-Avalanche pipeline, then chase Amores-Sesar-style analyses if you want explicit Byzantine bounds instead of vibes.

For GHOST, start with Sompolinsky and Zohar's 2015 paper on high-rate Bitcoin processing, then follow the PHANTOM and SPECTRE work if you want the full DAG rabbit hole.

For Ouroboros, the 2017 Kiayias et al. paper is the spine; each later variant (Praos, Genesis, Chronos, Leios) ships its own write-up with proofs tucked into the IOHK research library.

For Nakamoto remixes, grab Eyal et al. on Bitcoin-NG (2016), Bagaria et al. on Prism (2019), and Sompolinsky et al. on SPECTRE (2016); the earlier chapters already gave you the vocabulary to read them without drowning.

Skip anything that claims a single protocol "solved" consensus forever, and treat vendor TPS charts as guilty until they document transaction complexity, finality depth, network conditions, and the hardware they hid behind the curtain.

CHAPTER 9

Consensus Comparison Framework

9.1 Systematic Methodology for Evaluating Consensus Mechanisms

This chapter builds a proper framework for comparing consensus mechanisms—adversary models, normalized throughput and latency metrics, decentralization measures, energy numbers, and cost-of-attack calculations—and shows how to apply it when picking a protocol for something real. Here's what it covers:

- A real framework for sizing up consensus protocols. Not a feature checklist—an actual methodology that looks at security, performance, and decentralization together, because looking at them in isolation is how bad decisions get made
- Adversary models and attack taxonomies, sorted by protocol family. You need to know what a protocol is actually built to withstand before you can call it secure or insecure
- Throughput and latency measurement done right. Most published comparisons skip the normalization steps that make numbers comparable, so we cover those explicitly
- Tools for quantifying decentralization—Nakamoto coefficient, Gini index, Shannon entropy, geographic distribution. Each metric catches something the others miss, which is exactly why you need more than one

N. Savant, *Blockchain Foundations*, https://doi.org/10.1007/979-8-8688-2891-1_9

- Hard energy consumption numbers across consensus families. Not estimates, not projections. Actual data
- Cost-of-attack calculations that tell you, in real dollar amounts, how expensive it is to compromise each kind of system
- Practical guidance on applying all of this when you're sitting in a room trying to pick a consensus mechanism for something real

9.1.1 Why a Framework Matters

Your choice of consensus mechanism shapes almost everything about a blockchain. Security guarantees, transaction capacity, how long people wait for confirmations, how distributed the power actually is, the electricity bill. All of it flows from that one decision. You'd think, given the stakes, that protocol comparisons would be done carefully. They're not. Most of what gets published is somewhere between sloppy and actively misleading—cherry-picked metrics, benchmarks run under conditions that favor one protocol, marketing copy dressed up as analysis.

You've probably seen the classic example. "Solana processes 65,000 TPS, Bitcoin handles 7." That comparison gets repeated constantly, and it's close to meaningless. Bitcoin's 7 TPS is finalized simple transfers on adversarial mainnet with hundreds of thousands of miners. Solana's 65,000 includes different transaction types, counted at a different point in the finality pipeline, on a network where validators need expensive hardware. One number comes from a war zone, the other from a controlled lab. Putting them next to each other without context is like timing a marathon runner and a sprinter over different distances and declaring the sprinter faster.

So a useful comparison framework has to juggle multiple dimensions simultaneously. Improve one thing, and something else gets worse. The scalability trilemma (pick two of decentralization, security, scalability) captures the intuition, but crudely. The real tradeoff space has more axes than three, and the boundaries are blurrier than a neat triangle suggests.

What this chapter provides is the analytical machinery to cut through that noise. Structural analysis, not headline metrics.

9.1.2 Security Analysis Framework

Any consensus protocol starts from assumptions about who might try to attack it and what they're capable of. That's the adversary model. And here's the thing: if two protocols assume different adversaries, comparing their security guarantees head-to-head doesn't make sense. You're measuring them against different yardsticks.

Adversarial Models

Table 9-1. *Adversary Model Dimensions*

Dimension	Options	Impact on Protocol Design
Corruption threshold	f < n/3 (BFT), f < n/2 (Nakamoto), parameterized	Maximum adversarial power the protocol tolerates
Adversary timing	Static (fixed before execution), Adaptive (corrupts during execution), Mildly adaptive (with delay)	Dynamic corruption is harder to defend; requires key rotation
Network model	Synchronous (bounded delay), Partially synchronous (eventual bound), Asynchronous (no bound)	Determines liveness guarantees; asynchronous is strongest adversary
Fault type	Crash (stop responding), Byzantine (arbitrary behavior), Rational (self-interested)	Byzantine is strongest; rational allows game-theoretic analysis
Computational bound	Polynomially bounded, Computationally unbounded	Affects cryptographic assumption validity
Knowledge	Rushing (sees honest messages before acting), Non-rushing	Rushing adversary can adapt messages based on honest behavior

```
from dataclasses import dataclass, field
from typing import List, Dict, Optional, Tuple
from enum import Enum
import math
```

```
class NetworkModel(Enum):
    SYNCHRONOUS = "synchronous"
    PARTIAL_SYNC = "partially_synchronous"
    ASYNCHRONOUS = "asynchronous"

class AdversaryType(Enum):
    CRASH = "crash_only"
    BYZANTINE = "byzantine"
    RATIONAL = "rational"

class FinalityType(Enum):
    DETERMINISTIC = "deterministic"
    PROBABILISTIC = "probabilistic"
    ECONOMIC = "economic"

class CorruptionModel(Enum):
    STATIC = "static"
    ADAPTIVE = "adaptive"
    MILDLY_ADAPTIVE = "mildly_adaptive"

@dataclass
class AdversaryProfile:
    """Complete adversary model specification."""
    corruption_threshold: float
    adversary_type: AdversaryType
    network_model: NetworkModel
    corruption_model: CorruptionModel
    computational_bound: str  # "polynomial", "unbounded"
    rushing: bool

    def strength_score(self) -> int:
        """Score adversary strength (higher = stronger adversary
        tolerated)."""
        score = 0
        score += {0.5: 3, 0.33: 2, 0.25: 1}.get(self.corruption_
        threshold, 0)
        score += {AdversaryType.BYZANTINE: 3, AdversaryType.RATIONAL: 2,
                  AdversaryType.CRASH: 1}[self.adversary_type]
```

```
        score += {NetworkModel.ASYNCHRONOUS: 3, NetworkModel.PARTIAL_
        SYNC: 2,
                  NetworkModel.SYNCHRONOUS: 1}[self.network_model]
        score += {CorruptionModel.ADAPTIVE: 3, CorruptionModel.MILDLY_
        ADAPTIVE: 2,
                  CorruptionModel.STATIC: 1}[self.corruption_model]
        score += 1 if self.rushing else 0
        return score

@dataclass
class ConsensusProfile:
    """Complete profile of a consensus mechanism for comparison."""
    name: str
    family: str

    # Security model
    adversary: AdversaryProfile
    finality_type: FinalityType
    safety_proven: bool
    liveness_proven: bool

    # Performance
    throughput_tps: float
    latency_to_inclusion_s: float
    latency_to_finality_s: float
    message_complexity: str

    # Decentralization
    max_validators: int
    permissionless: bool
    min_hardware: str  # "consumer", "datacenter", "specialized"

    # Economics
    energy_per_tx_kwh: float
    annual_security_budget_usd: float

    # Metadata
    production_since: int  # Year
    market_cap_usd: float
```

```
def create_comprehensive_profiles() -> List[ConsensusProfile]:
    """Create detailed profiles for major protocols."""
    return [
        ConsensusProfile(
            name="Bitcoin (Nakamoto PoW)",
            family="nakamoto_pow",
            adversary=AdversaryProfile(
                0.5, AdversaryType.BYZANTINE, NetworkModel.PARTIAL_SYNC,
                CorruptionModel.STATIC, "polynomial", False
            ),
            finality_type=FinalityType.PROBABILISTIC,
            safety_proven=True, liveness_proven=True,
            throughput_tps=7, latency_to_inclusion_s=600,
            latency_to_finality_s=3600,
            message_complexity="O(n) gossip",
            max_validators=1000000, permissionless=True,
            min_hardware="specialized",
            energy_per_tx_kwh=700.0,
            annual_security_budget_usd=9_800_000_000,
            production_since=2009, market_cap_usd=1_200_000_000_000,
        ),
        ConsensusProfile(
            name="Ethereum (Gasper PoS)",
            family="hybrid_pos_bft",
            adversary=AdversaryProfile(
                0.33, AdversaryType.BYZANTINE, NetworkModel.PARTIAL_SYNC,
                CorruptionModel.ADAPTIVE, "polynomial", True
            ),
            finality_type=FinalityType.ECONOMIC,
            safety_proven=True, liveness_proven=True,
            throughput_tps=15, latency_to_inclusion_s=12,
            latency_to_finality_s=768,
            message_complexity="O(n) with aggregation",
            max_validators=1000000, permissionless=True,
            min_hardware="consumer",
```

```
        energy_per_tx_kwh=0.03,
        annual_security_budget_usd=2_400_000_000,
        production_since=2022, market_cap_usd=400_000_000_000,
    ),
    ConsensusProfile(
        name="Tendermint (BFT)",
        family="classical_bft",
        adversary=AdversaryProfile(
            0.33, AdversaryType.BYZANTINE, NetworkModel.PARTIAL_SYNC,
            CorruptionModel.STATIC, "polynomial", False
        ),
        finality_type=FinalityType.DETERMINISTIC,
        safety_proven=True, liveness_proven=True,
        throughput_tps=1000, latency_to_inclusion_s=6,
        latency_to_finality_s=6,
        message_complexity="O(n^2)",
        max_validators=150, permissionless=False,
        min_hardware="datacenter",
        energy_per_tx_kwh=0.001,
        annual_security_budget_usd=500_000_000,
        production_since=2019, market_cap_usd=3_000_000_000,
    ),
    ConsensusProfile(
        name="Avalanche (Snowball)",
        family="metastable",
        adversary=AdversaryProfile(
            0.5, AdversaryType.BYZANTINE, NetworkModel.PARTIAL_SYNC,
            CorruptionModel.STATIC, "polynomial", False
        ),
        finality_type=FinalityType.PROBABILISTIC,
        safety_proven=True, liveness_proven=True,
        throughput_tps=4500, latency_to_inclusion_s=2,
        latency_to_finality_s=2,
        message_complexity="O(k) per node",
        max_validators=10000, permissionless=True,
```

```
        min_hardware="datacenter",
        energy_per_tx_kwh=0.0005,
        annual_security_budget_usd=300_000_000,
        production_since=2020, market_cap_usd=15_000_000_000,
    ),
    ConsensusProfile(
        name="HotStuff (Linear BFT)",
        family="classical_bft",
        adversary=AdversaryProfile(
            0.33, AdversaryType.BYZANTINE, NetworkModel.PARTIAL_SYNC,
            CorruptionModel.STATIC, "polynomial", True
        ),
        finality_type=FinalityType.DETERMINISTIC,
        safety_proven=True, liveness_proven=True,
        throughput_tps=3000, latency_to_inclusion_s=3,
        latency_to_finality_s=3,
        message_complexity="O(n)",
        max_validators=500, permissionless=False,
        min_hardware="datacenter",
        energy_per_tx_kwh=0.001,
        annual_security_budget_usd=200_000_000,
        production_since=2022, market_cap_usd=5_000_000_000,
    ),
    ConsensusProfile(
        name="Ouroboros Praos (PoS)",
        family="nakamoto_pos",
        adversary=AdversaryProfile(
            0.5, AdversaryType.BYZANTINE, NetworkModel.PARTIAL_SYNC,
            CorruptionModel.MILDLY_ADAPTIVE, "polynomial", False
        ),
        finality_type=FinalityType.PROBABILISTIC,
        safety_proven=True, liveness_proven=True,
        throughput_tps=250, latency_to_inclusion_s=20,
        latency_to_finality_s=600,
        message_complexity="O(n) gossip",
```

```
            max_validators=50000, permissionless=True,
            min_hardware="consumer",
            energy_per_tx_kwh=0.005,
            annual_security_budget_usd=800_000_000,
            production_since=2020, market_cap_usd=20_000_000_000,
        ),
    ]

profiles = create_comprehensive_profiles()
print("Consensus Protocol Security Profiles")
print("=" * 75)
for p in profiles:
    adv = p.adversary
    print(f"\n{p.name}")
    print(f"  Fault tolerance: {adv.corruption_threshold:.0%} "
          f"{adv.adversary_type.value}")
    print(f"  Network: {adv.network_model.value}, "
          f"Corruption: {adv.corruption_model.value}")
    print(f"  Finality: {p.finality_type.value} "
          f"({p.latency_to_finality_s}s)")
    print(f"  Safety proven: {p.safety_proven}, "
          f"Liveness proven: {p.liveness_proven}")
    print(f"  Adversary strength score: {adv.strength_score()}/13")
```

Attack Vector Taxonomy

You also need to look at specific attacks. Every protocol family has blind spots—types of attacks it handles well and types it's exposed to. Slapping a generic "secure" label on something without specifying what it's secure against is the kind of hand-waving that leads to expensive surprises.

```
@dataclass
class AttackVector:
    name: str
    category: str  # "consensus", "network", "economic", "governance"
    affected_property: str  # "safety", "liveness", "fairness"
    required_power: str
```

```
    applicable_families: List[str]
    description: str
    estimated_cost_usd: Optional[float] = None

def build_attack_taxonomy() -> List[AttackVector]:
    """Comprehensive attack vector taxonomy across protocol families."""
    return [
        AttackVector(
            "51% / Majority Hash Rate Attack", "consensus", "safety",
            ">50% of network hash rate",
            ["nakamoto_pow"],
            "Attacker produces a longer chain, enabling double-spending. "
            "Cost proportional to network hash rate and duration."
        ),
        AttackVector(
            "34% Finality Attack", "consensus", "safety",
            ">33% of staked value",
            ["hybrid_pos_bft", "classical_bft"],
            "Attacker controls enough stake to prevent finalization or "
            "finalize conflicting checkpoints. Detected and slashed."
        ),
        AttackVector(
            "Selfish Mining", "consensus", "fairness",
            ">25-33% hash rate (depends on connectivity)",
            ["nakamoto_pow"],
            "Strategic block withholding earns disproportionate rewards. "
            "Threshold depends on network connectivity parameter gamma."
        ),
        AttackVector(
            "Long-Range Attack", "consensus", "safety",
            "Old validator keys (exited validators)",
            ["hybrid_pos_bft", "nakamoto_pos"],
            "Create alternative history using keys from validators who "
            "have already withdrawn. Mitigated by weak subjectivity."
        ),
```

```
AttackVector(
    "Nothing-at-Stake", "consensus", "safety",
    "Any PoS validator",
    ["nakamoto_pos", "hybrid_pos_bft"],
    "Vote on multiple forks at zero marginal cost. "
    "Mitigated by slashing and finality gadgets."
),
AttackVector(
    "Eclipse Attack", "network", "safety",
    "Network control over target node",
    ["nakamoto_pow", "hybrid_pos_bft", "classical_bft",
    "metastable"],
    "Isolate a node from honest network, feeding it only "
    "attacker-controlled information."
),
AttackVector(
    "Transaction Censorship", "consensus", "liveness",
    ">50% consensus power (sustained)",
    ["nakamoto_pow", "hybrid_pos_bft", "classical_bft"],
    "Block producer refuses to include specific transactions. "
    "Effective if attacker produces majority of blocks."
),
AttackVector(
    "MEV Extraction / Sandwiching", "economic", "fairness",
    "Block proposer role",
    ["nakamoto_pow", "hybrid_pos_bft", "classical_bft"],
    "Reorder, insert, or censor transactions within a block "
    "for profit. Harms users through worse execution prices."
),
AttackVector(
    "Grinding Attack", "consensus", "fairness",
    "Block proposer role",
    ["nakamoto_pos", "hybrid_pos_bft"],
    "Manipulate on-chain randomness by selectively producing "
    "or withholding blocks. Mitigated by VRF-based randomness."
),
```

```
        AttackVector(
            "Liveness Attack (Partition)", "network", "liveness",
            "Network infrastructure control",
            ["classical_bft"],
            "BFT protocols halt during partitions. Attacker who can "
            "partition the network prevents block production."
        ),
        AttackVector(
            "Validator Bribery", "economic", "safety",
            "Sufficient capital to bribe >33% of validators",
            ["classical_bft", "hybrid_pos_bft"],
            "Bribe validators to sign conflicting messages. Cost "
            "must exceed slashing penalties for each bribed validator."
        ),
    ]

attacks = build_attack_taxonomy()
print("\nAttack Vector Taxonomy")
print("=" * 75)
for a in attacks:
    print(f"\n{a.name}")
    print(f"  Category: {a.category} | Affects: {a.affected_property}")
    print(f"  Requires: {a.required_power}")
    print(f"  Applies to: {', '.join(a.applicable_families)}")

# Cross-reference: which protocols are vulnerable to which attacks
print("\n\nVulnerability Matrix")
print("=" * 75)
families = ["nakamoto_pow", "hybrid_pos_bft", "classical_bft",
            "nakamoto_pos", "metastable"]
family_labels = ["Nakamoto PoW", "Hybrid PoS", "Classical BFT",
                 "Nakamoto PoS", "Metastable"]

print(f"{'Attack':<30}", end="")
for label in family_labels:
    print(f" {label:>12}", end="")
```

```
print()
print("-" * 90)

for attack in attacks:
    print(f"{attack.name[:29]:<30}", end="")
    for fam in families:
        vulnerable = "●" if fam in attack.applicable_families else "○"
        print(f" {vulnerable:>12}", end="")
    print()
```

9.1.3 Performance Metrics

Throughput: Beyond Raw TPS

TPS. The metric everyone loves, the metric that lies the most. To get a throughput comparison that isn't garbage, you have to control for a list of variables that most people skip:

Start with transaction complexity. A simple Bitcoin transfer is one operation. An Ethereum Uniswap swap touches multiple storage locations, runs cryptographic verification, fires off events—it's an order of magnitude more work. Calling both a "transaction" and comparing counts is like comparing the number of meals a food truck serves versus a five-star restaurant and concluding the food truck is more productive.

Then there's the finality level. When exactly are you counting a transaction as "processed"? At mempool acceptance? Block inclusion? Actual finality? The gap between these is enormous for some protocols. A transaction sitting in an unfinalized block isn't really done yet—it could **still** vanish. Counting it inflates the numbers in a way that flatters the protocol without reflecting reality.

Network conditions. Nobody wants to talk about this one. Testnet throughput with cooperative validators and low-latency links is a fantasy number. Mainnet throughput with real geographic distribution, variable bandwidth, and occasionally hostile participants is the number that matters. The gap between the two can be 10x.

Hardware. Some protocols post impressive TPS figures that quietly require every validator to run data-center equipment costing thousands per month. That's not free performance. You're trading decentralization for speed, and the comparison should reflect that.

```
@dataclass
class ThroughputMeasurement:
    protocol: str
    raw_tps: float
    tx_type: str  # "simple_transfer", "token_transfer", "swap", "complex_
    contract"
    finality_level: str  # "mempool", "included", "finalized"
    node_count: int
    node_hardware: str  # "consumer", "datacenter", "specialized"
    conditions: str  # "testnet", "mainnet", "adversarial"

def normalize_throughput(measurements: List[ThroughputMeasurement]) ->
List[dict]:
    """
    Normalize throughput measurements for fair cross-protocol comparison.

    Adjustments:
    1. Complexity multiplier: normalize to "simple transfer equivalent"
    2. Finality discount: penalize unfinalized throughput
    3. Conditions discount: penalize controlled/testnet measurements
    4. Hardware penalty: penalize datacenter-required throughput
    """
    complexity_multipliers = {
        "simple_transfer": 1.0,
        "token_transfer": 1.3,
        "swap": 3.5,
        "complex_contract": 6.0,
        "nft_mint": 2.0,
    }

    finality_multipliers = {
        "finalized": 1.0,
        "included": 0.6,      # Included but not finalized
        "soft_confirmed": 0.4, # Optimistic confirmation
        "mempool": 0.1,        # Only accepted to mempool
    }
```

```
condition_multipliers = {
    "mainnet": 1.0,
    "testnet": 0.7,
    "benchmark": 0.5,
}

hardware_multipliers = {
    "consumer": 1.0,
    "datacenter": 0.8,
    "specialized": 0.6,
}

results = []
for m in measurements:
    complexity = complexity_multipliers.get(m.tx_type, 1.0)
    finality = finality_multipliers.get(m.finality_level, 1.0)
    conditions = condition_multipliers.get(m.conditions, 1.0)
    hardware = hardware_multipliers.get(m.node_hardware, 1.0)

    normalized = m.raw_tps * finality * conditions * hardware /
    complexity

    results.append({
        'protocol': m.protocol,
        'raw_tps': m.raw_tps,
        'normalized_tps': normalized,
        'tx_type': m.tx_type,
        'finality': m.finality_level,
        'conditions': m.conditions,
        'hardware': m.node_hardware,
        'discount_factor': normalized / m.raw_tps,
    })

return results
```

```
measurements = [
    ThroughputMeasurement("Bitcoin", 7, "simple_transfer", "finalized",
                          15000, "specialized", "mainnet"),
    ThroughputMeasurement("Ethereum L1", 15, "token_transfer", "finalized",
                          6000, "consumer", "mainnet"),
    ThroughputMeasurement("Solana", 4000, "simple_transfer", "included",
                          2000, "datacenter", "mainnet"),
    ThroughputMeasurement("Avalanche", 4500, "simple_transfer", "finalized",
                          1200, "datacenter", "mainnet"),
    ThroughputMeasurement("Tendermint (Cosmos)", 1000, "simple_transfer",
    "finalized",
                          150, "datacenter", "mainnet"),
    ThroughputMeasurement("Aptos", 10000, "simple_transfer", "included",
                          100, "datacenter", "benchmark"),
    ThroughputMeasurement("Arbitrum (L2)", 2000, "swap", "included",
                          1, "datacenter", "mainnet"),
]

results = normalize_throughput(measurements)
print("Throughput Comparison (Normalized to Finalized Simple Transfers)")
print("=" * 80)
print(f"{'Protocol':<22} {'Raw TPS':>9} {'Normalized':>11} {'Discount':>9}
{'Notes'}")
print("-" * 80)

for r in sorted(results, key=lambda x: x['normalized_tps'], reverse=True):
    notes = f"{r['tx_type']}, {r['finality']}, {r['conditions']}"
    print(f"  {r['protocol']:<20} {r['raw_tps']:>7.0f}    {r['normalized_
    tps']:>9.1f}    "
          f"{r['discount_factor']:>7.1%}    {notes}")
```

Latency and Finality Time

Latency is another metric that gets oversimplified. It's not a single number. A payment app cares about how fast the user sees confirmation. A bridge protocol cares about when reversal becomes cryptographically or economically impossible. Those are different questions with very different answers:

```
def comprehensive_latency_analysis() -> None:
    """Analyze latency at multiple finality levels for each protocol."""

    protocols = {
        "Bitcoin": {
   "submission_to_mempool": 1,
   "mempool_to_1st_confirmation": 600,  # First block = 1 confirmation
   # Note: removed "inclusion_to_1_conf" – it was the same 600s wait,
   # double-counting the first block and inflating total by 600 seconds.
   "1_conf_to_6_conf": 3000,            # 5 more blocks at ~600s each
   "6_conf_to_final": 0,                # 6 confirmations IS the finality
                                          threshold
   "finality_type": "probabilistic",
   "finality_security": "99.9% at 6 conf (vs 30% attacker)",
},
        "Ethereum": {
            "submission_to_mempool": 1,
            "mempool_to_inclusion": 12,         # 1 slot
            "inclusion_to_justified": 384,      # 1 epoch
            "justified_to_finalized": 384,      # 1 more epoch
            "finality_type": "economic",
            "finality_security": "Reversal costs >$20B (1/3 stake
            slashed)",
        },
        "Tendermint": {
            "submission_to_mempool": 0.5,
            "mempool_to_inclusion": 6,
            "inclusion_to_final": 0,            # Inclusion IS finality
            "finality_type": "deterministic",
            "finality_security": "Absolute if f < n/3",
        },
        "Avalanche": {
            "submission_to_mempool": 0.5,
            "mempool_to_inclusion": 1,
            "inclusion_to_final": 1,            # ~20 Snowball rounds
```

```
            "finality_type": "probabilistic",
            "finality_security": "~10^-9 reversal probability",
        },
    }

    print("Comprehensive Latency Analysis")
    print("=" * 65)

    for name, data in protocols.items():
        total_to_finality = sum(v for k, v in data.items()
                                if isinstance(v, (int, float)))
        print(f"\n{name} ({data['finality_type']} finality):")
        for key, value in data.items():
            if isinstance(value, (int, float)):
                if value >= 60:
                    display = f"{value/60:.1f} min"
                else:
                    display = f"{value}s"
                print(f"  {key:>30}: {display}")
        print(f"  {'Total to finality':>30}: "
              f"{total_to_finality/60:.1f} min ({total_to_finality}s)")
        print(f"  {'Security guarantee':>30}: {data['finality_security']}")

comprehensive_latency_analysis()
```

9.1.4 Decentralization Measurement

Of all the dimensions in this framework, decentralization is the one that fights back hardest when you try to measure it. The problem is that "decentralized" describes several independent things at once, and they don't always move in the same direction. You can have nicely distributed hash power, but everyone runs the same client software. Or a thousand validators, sure, but two thirds of them are on AWS. No single metric captures all of that. You need a dashboard, not a dial.

Nakamoto Coefficient

The Nakamoto coefficient, an idea Balaji Srinivasan put forward, asks a pointed question: what's the smallest group of entities that could collude to take over? For a PoW chain, count the fewest mining pools that add up to half the hash rate. For BFT-based PoS, count the fewest validators holding a third of the stake. It gives you one clean number. Useful. But incomplete—it says nothing about client diversity, geographic concentration, or infrastructure dependencies.

```
def nakamoto_coefficient(entity_shares: List[float],
                         threshold: float = 0.5) -> int:
    """
    Calculate Nakamoto coefficient.

    The minimum number of entities whose combined share exceeds
    the threshold. Higher is better (more entities must collude).
    """
    sorted_shares = sorted(entity_shares, reverse=True)
    cumulative = 0.0
    for i, share in enumerate(sorted_shares):
        cumulative += share
        if cumulative > threshold:
            return i + 1
    return len(sorted_shares)

def _normalize_shares(shares: List[float]) -> List[float]:
    """
    Normalize shares to sum to 1.0.
    Always call this before computing any distribution metric.
    Raw share lists (e.g. from on-chain data) may not sum exactly to 1.0.
    """
    total = sum(shares)
    if total == 0:
        return shares
    return [s / total for s in shares]
```

```
def gini_coefficient(shares: List[float]) -> float:
    """
    Gini coefficient (inequality measure).
    0 = perfect equality, 1 = maximum inequality.
    """
    shares = _normalize_shares(shares)
    n = len(shares)
    if n == 0:
        return 0
    sorted_shares = sorted(shares)
    cumulative = sum((i + 1) * s for i, s in enumerate(sorted_shares))
    # With normalized shares, total = 1.0
    return (2 * cumulative) / n - (n + 1) / n
def shannon_entropy (shares: List[float]) -> Tuple[float, float]:
    """
    Shannon entropy and normalized entropy.
    Higher = more uniform distribution.
    """
    shares = _normalize_shares(shares)
    entropy = -sum (s * math.log2(s) for s in shares if s > 0)
    max_entropy = math.log2(len(shares)) if len(shares) > 1 else 1
    normalized = entropy / max_entropy if max_entropy > 0 else 0
    return entropy, normalized
def herfindahl_hirschman_index (shares: List[float]) -> float:
    """
    HHI: sum of squared market shares.
    0 = perfect competition, 1 = monopoly.
    """
    shares = _normalize_shares(shares)
    return sum(s ** 2 for s in shares)

def comprehensive_decentralization(name: str,
                                   consensus_shares: List[float],
                                   consensus_threshold: float,
                                   geographic_regions: int,
                                   client_implementations: int,
```

```
                                  hosting_providers: int,
                                  governance_token_gini: float = 0.0
                                  ) -> dict:
    """Multi-dimensional decentralization assessment."""
    nc = nakamoto_coefficient(consensus_shares, consensus_threshold)
    gini = gini_coefficient(consensus_shares)
    entropy, norm_entropy = shannon_entropy(consensus_shares)
    hhi = herfindahl_hirschman_index(consensus_shares)

    # Composite score (weighted average, 0-100)
    # Higher = more decentralized
    score = (
        min(nc / 10, 1.0) * 25 +                    # Nakamoto coefficient
                                                      (up to 10)
        (1 - gini) * 20 +                            # Equality
        norm_entropy * 15 +                          # Distribution uniformity
        min(geographic_regions / 20, 1) * 15 +       # Geographic diversity
        min(client_implementations / 5, 1) * 15 +   # Client diversity
        min(hosting_providers / 10, 1) * 10          # Infrastructure diversity
    )

    return {
        'name': name,
        'nakamoto_coefficient': nc,
        'gini': gini,
        'entropy': entropy,
        'normalized_entropy': norm_entropy,
        'hhi': hhi,
        'geographic_regions': geographic_regions,
        'client_implementations': client_implementations,
        'hosting_providers': hosting_providers,
        'composite_score': score,
        'num_entities': len(consensus_shares),
    }

# Analyze real-world decentralization (approximate data)
bitcoin = comprehensive_decentralization(
```

```
    "Bitcoin",
    [0.28, 0.16, 0.13, 0.10, 0.08, 0.07, 0.05, 0.04, 0.03, 0.06],
    0.50,
    geographic_regions=15, client_implementations=3, hosting_providers=8
)

ethereum = comprehensive_decentralization(
    "Ethereum",
    [0.29, 0.13, 0.08, 0.06, 0.05, 0.04, 0.04, 0.03, 0.03, 0.25],
    0.33,
    geographic_regions=18, client_implementations=5, hosting_providers=12
)

cosmos_hub = comprehensive decentralization (
   "Cosmos Hub",
   # Top 10 validators: 0.39 total
   # 30 mid validators: 0.02 each = 0.60 – too high, corrected to 0.013
     each = 0.39
   # 60 small validators: 0.005 each = 0.30 – corrected to 0.0037
     each = 0.22
   # Total must sum to 1.0
   [0.07, 0.06, 0.05, 0.05, 0.04, 0.04, 0.04, 0.03, 0.03, 0.03] + # 0.44
   [0.013] * 30 +  # 0.39
   [0.0028] * 60,  # 0.168 → total ≈ 1.0
   ...
)
geographic_regions=10, client_implementations=1, hosting_providers=6
)

Solana",
   # Approximate stake distribution across ~156 validators
   # Raw shares sum to ~1.20 – _normalize_shares() corrects this
   # Or corrected values that sum to 1.0:
   [0.042] * 6 +   # Top 6: 0.252
   [0.025] * 10 +  # Mid 10: 0.250
   [0.008] * 40 +  # Small: 0.320
```

```
        [0.0018] * 100, # Tail:  0.180 → total ≈ 1.002 ≈ 1.0
        0.33,
        ...
    )
        geographic_regions=12, client_implementations=2, hosting_providers=5
    )

results = [bitcoin, ethereum, cosmos_hub, solana]

print("\nComprehensive Decentralization Analysis")
print("=" * 75)
print(f"{'Metric':<28}", end="")
for r in results:
    print(f" {r['name']:>12}", end="")
print()
print("-" * 75)

metrics = [
    ('Entities', 'num_entities'),
    ('Nakamoto Coefficient', 'nakamoto_coefficient'),
    ('Gini Coefficient', 'gini'),
    ('Normalized Entropy', 'normalized_entropy'),
    ('HHI', 'hhi'),
    ('Geographic Regions', 'geographic_regions'),
    ('Client Implementations', 'client_implementations'),
    ('Hosting Providers', 'hosting_providers'),
    ('Composite Score (/100)', 'composite_score'),
]

for label, key in metrics:
    print(f"  {label:<26}", end="")
    for r in results:
        val = r[key]
        if isinstance(val, float):
            print(f" {val:>12.3f}", end="")
        else:
            print(f" {val:>12}", end="")
    print()
```

9.1.5 Energy Efficiency Comparison

```
def energy_comparison() -> None:
    """Compare energy efficiency across consensus families."""

    protocols = [
        {"name": "Bitcoin (PoW)", "kwh_per_tx": 700, "annual_twh": 145,
         "security_budget_b": 9.8, "family": "PoW"},
        {"name": "Litecoin (PoW)", "kwh_per_tx": 19, "annual_twh": 1.5,
         "security_budget_b": 0.3, "family": "PoW"},
        {"name": "Ethereum (PoS)", "kwh_per_tx": 0.03, "annual_twh": 0.01,
         "security_budget_b": 2.4, "family": "PoS"},
        {"name": "Cardano (PoS)", "kwh_per_tx": 0.005, "annual_twh": 0.002,
         "security_budget_b": 0.8, "family": "PoS"},
        {"name": "Solana (PoH+PoS)", "kwh_per_tx": 0.0005, "annual_
        twh": 0.002,
         "security_budget_b": 0.5, "family": "PoS"},
        {"name": "Cosmos (Tendermint)", "kwh_per_tx": 0.001, "annual_
        twh": 0.0001,
         "security_budget_b": 0.5, "family": "BFT"},
        {"name": "Avalanche", "kwh_per_tx": 0.0005, "annual_twh": 0.001,
         "security_budget_b": 0.3, "family": "Metastable"},
        {"name": "Visa (reference)", "kwh_per_tx": 0.001, "annual_
        twh": 0.7,
         "security_budget_b": 0, "family": "Centralized"},
    ]

    print("Energy Efficiency by Consensus Family")
    print("=" * 80)
    print(f"{'Protocol':<24} {'kWh/tx':>10} {'Annual TWh':>12} "
          f"{'Security $B':>12} {'Energy/Security':>16}")
    print("-" * 80)

    for p in protocols:
        ratio = (p['annual_twh'] / p['security_budget_b']
                 if p['security_budget_b'] > 0 else 0)
        print(f"  {p['name']:<22} {p['kwh_per_tx']:>10.4f} "
```

```
            f"{p['annual_twh']:>12.3f} {p['security_budget_b']:>12.1f} "
            f"{ratio:>14.2f} TWh/$B")

    print("\nKey Insight: PoW converts energy into security (high TWh/$B
    ratio)")
    print("  PoS achieves security through capital risk, not energy (low
    TWh/$B ratio)")

energy_comparison()
```

9.1.6 Economic Security: Cost of Attack Analysis

```
def comprehensive_attack_cost() -> None:
    """Compare the economic cost of attacking different protocols."""

    print("\nEconomic Cost of Attack Analysis")
    print("=" * 70)

    # Bitcoin: 51% hash rate attack
    btc_network_hashrate_eh = 550
    btc_hardware_cost_per_eh = 15_000_000  # $15M per EH/s
    btc_electricity_per_eh_hour = 15_000  # $15K per EH/s per hour

    btc_attack_hardware = btc_network_hashrate_eh * 1.01 * btc_hardware_
    cost_per_eh
    btc_hourly_electricity = btc_network_hashrate_eh * 1.01 * btc_
    electricity_per_eh_hour
    btc_total_1h = btc_attack_hardware + btc_hourly_electricity
    btc_recoverable = btc_attack_hardware * 0.5  # Can resell hardware

    print(f"\nBitcoin (51% Hash Rate Attack):")
    print(f"  Hardware acquisition: ${btc_attack_hardware:,.0f}")
    print(f"  Hourly electricity:   ${btc_hourly_electricity:,.0f}")
    print(f"  Total 1-hour cost:    ${btc_total_1h:,.0f}")
    print(f"  Recoverable (resell): ${btc_recoverable:,.0f}")
    print(f"  Net irreversible cost: ${btc_total_1h - btc_
    recoverable:,.0f}")

    # Ethereum: 1/3 stake attack (finality)
```

```
    eth_staked = 20_000_000  # ETH
    eth_price = 3000
    eth_attack_fraction = 0.34
    eth_required = eth_staked * eth_attack_fraction
    eth_slippage = 2.5  # Market impact multiplier
    eth_acquisition = eth_required * eth_price * eth_slippage
    eth_slashing = eth_required * eth_price  # 100% slashed (correlation
    penalty)

    print(f"\nEthereum (1/3 Stake Finality Attack):")
    print(f"  Required stake:       {eth_required:,.0f} ETH")
    print(f"  Acquisition cost:     ${eth_acquisition:,.0f}")
    print(f"  Slashing loss:        ${eth_slashing:,.0f}")
    print(f"  Total cost:           ${eth_acquisition + eth_
                                    slashing:,.0f}")
    print(f"  Recoverable:          $0 (stake destroyed)")

    # Tendermint: 1/3 validator bribery
    tendermint_validators = 150
    tendermint_avg_stake = 500_000  # USD per validator
    tendermint_bribe_per = tendermint_avg_stake * 1.5  # Must exceed slashing
    tendermint_total = int(tendermint_validators * 0.34) * tendermint_bribe_per

    print(f"\nTendermint/Cosmos (1/3 Validator Bribery):")
    print(f"  Validators to bribe:  {int(tendermint_validators * 0.34)}")
    print(f"  Cost per validator:   ${tendermint_bribe_per:,.0f}")
    print(f"  Total bribery cost:   ${tendermint_total:,.0f}")

    # Avalanche: sampling manipulation
    print(f"\nAvalanche (Consensus Manipulation):")
    print(f"  Requires >50% of stake to reliably influence sampling")
    print(f"  With ~$15B market cap, cost exceeds $5B+ for stake
    acquisition")

comprehensive_attack_cost()
```

9.1.7 Applying the Framework: Decision Methodology

Putting this framework to work on a real decision follows a sequence. None of these steps are complicated individually. What matters is not skipping any:

Figure out what's non-negotiable. Does the application need sub-second finality? A DeFi protocol probably does. Does it need maximum decentralization for credible neutrality? A base layer probably does. Do regulators need to identify every validator? Some jurisdictions require that. The requirements have to be specific—vague goals like "fast and secure" are useless for protocol selection.

Map the hard constraints. Permissionless or permissioned? There's a ceiling on finality time—what is it? Below what security threshold does the whole effort become pointless? How much can validator operators realistically spend on hardware? These constraints eliminate candidates before you even start scoring.

Run every remaining candidate through the framework dimensions. Adversary model, normalized throughput, latency at the finality levels that matter, decentralization metrics, energy footprint, attack cost. Use the tools from this chapter. Don't eyeball it.

Look at the tradeoffs honestly. Every protocol gives something up. The question isn't "which one is best"—it's "which sacrifices are acceptable for this particular application." A supply chain platform and a global settlement network have completely different answers to that question.

Test under adversarial assumptions. Cooperative-condition performance numbers are ceiling estimates. The protocol that handles 10,000 TPS when everyone's behaving might handle 2,000 when a third of validators go offline. You want the second number.

Table 9-2. *Consensus Selection Guide by Use Case*

Requirement	Recommended Family	Primary Rationale	Key Sacrifice
Maximum censorship resistance	Nakamoto PoW (Bitcoin)	15+ years proven, permissionless, no minimum stake	Throughput, energy
Fast deterministic finality	BFT (Tendermint, HotStuff)	Instant finality, well-proven	Validator set size, liveness during partitions
High throughput + permissionless	Metastable (Avalanche)	Sub-sampled voting scales well	Probabilistic finality
Base layer with smart contracts	Hybrid PoS (Ethereum Gasper)	Large validator set, economic finality	Throughput limited on L1
Application-specific chain	BFT + ABCI (Tendermint)	Customizable execution, instant finality	Must recruit validator set
Regulatory compliance	Permissioned BFT	Known validators, auditable, accountable	Decentralization
Maximum energy efficiency	PoS or BFT	Orders of magnitude less than PoW	Different security model than PoW
Provably secure PoS	Ouroboros (Cardano)	Formal security proofs	Lower throughput than some alternatives

9.1.8 Summary

If there's one message from this chapter, it's that serious protocol comparison means looking at security, performance, decentralization, and economics together, not in isolation. The moment you focus on one axis and ignore the rest, you're going to miss something important. That's not a bug in the analysis—it's the nature of the design space.

The pieces worth remembering:

- Security comparisons are only valid when the adversary models match. Corruption threshold, adversary capabilities, network timing assumptions, how corruption happens. All of that has to line up.

Declaring one protocol "more secure" based on a comparison where the adversary models are different is meaningless—you're measuring against different rulers.

- Published throughput numbers mislead more often than they inform. What kind of transactions? Counted at what point in the finality pipeline? Measured on what kind of network? Running on what hardware? Without answers to all four questions, a TPS number is decoration, not data.
- No single decentralization metric tells the full story. Nakamoto coefficient captures collusion resistance. Gini and entropy capture distribution uniformity. Geographic spread, client diversity, and infrastructure diversity capture fault correlation. A protocol can ace one of these and fail another.
- PoW and PoS differ on energy by five or six orders of magnitude. Around 700 kWh per transaction for PoW versus fractions of a kWh for PoS and BFT. But there's a subtlety that gets lost in the outrage: PoW's electricity bill is literally the price of its security. That energy expenditure is what makes permissionless Sybil resistance expensive to attack. It's a cost, not a defect.
- Attack cost analysis needs to look past the sticker price. What happens to the attacker's capital afterward matters. A PoS attacker who gets slashed loses everything—the stake is burned. A PoW attacker retains the mining hardware and can sell it. The upfront dollar amount might be similar, but the finality of the loss is completely different, and that changes the incentive calculation.
- No protocol dominates. Bitcoin gives you censorship resistance nobody else can match. Tendermint gives you finality the instant a block commits. Avalanche gives you high throughput with sub-second probabilistic finality. Ethereum hedges across multiple dimensions via its rollup-centric roadmap. Each protocol is the right tool for a different job. Asking which one is "best" without specifying the job is asking the wrong question.

- What matters most from this chapter is the framework itself—not any specific ranking it produces. Rankings change as protocols evolve and as application requirements shift. The methodology for making principled comparisons is what stays useful.

Security comparison requires matching adversary models: fault threshold, corruption type, network assumptions—Throughput must be normalized for tx complexity, finality level, test conditions, and hardware requirements—Nakamoto coefficient: minimum entities to compromise consensus; higher = more decentralized—Multiple decentralization metrics needed: Gini, entropy, HHI, geographic/client/infrastructure diversity—PoW energy ~700 kWh/tx vs. PoS ~0.03 kWh/tx (orders of magnitude difference)—Bitcoin 51% attack: ~$8.5B hardware + electricity; Ethereum 1/3 attack: >$70B including slashing—No consensus protocol dominates all dimensions; selection depends on application requirements—The framework provides a structured methodology: define requirements, identify constraints, evaluate, and compare trade-offs

9.1.9 Exercises

Problem 1 (Basic): Calculate the Nakamoto coefficient for a PoS network where three validators each control 12% of the stake and the remaining 64% is distributed equally among 100 validators. Use a 33% threshold.

Problem 2 (Calculation): Compare the cost of a 1-hour 51% attack on two PoW chains: Chain A with a 100 EH/s hash rate ($15M per EH/s hardware, $15K per EH/s electricity/hour) and Chain B with 1 EH/s. What ratio of attack costs do you get? What does this imply about the security of smaller PoW chains?

Problem 3 (Implementation): Build a consensus evaluation tool that accepts protocol parameters (fault tolerance, TPS, finality, validator count, energy per tx) and produces a normalized scorecard across all framework dimensions. Test with at least five protocols.

Problem 4 (Analysis): A company needs to select a consensus mechanism for a supply chain tracking application requiring 500 TPS, 30-second finality, a known validator set of 20 organizations, and regulatory auditability. Evaluate Tendermint, HotStuff, and Raft using the framework.

Problem 5 (Design): Propose a new decentralization metric that captures the diversity of infrastructure providers (cloud providers, ISPs, hardware manufacturers) running validator nodes. How would you measure this? What data sources would you need?

Problem 6 (Theory): Why does the Nakamoto coefficient understate centralization risk? What additional factors beyond stake/hashrate concentration affect protocol capture? Consider: governance influence, development team composition, and infrastructure dependencies.

Problem 7 (Comparative): Create a radar chart (or equivalent table) comparing Bitcoin, Ethereum, Tendermint, Avalanche, and Cardano across these dimensions: decentralization (Nakamoto coefficient), throughput, finality speed, energy efficiency, censorship resistance, and proven security years. Justify your numerical scoring.

Problem 8 (Critical Thinking): Is the scalability trilemma a fundamental physical law, an empirical observation, or an engineering challenge? Present rigorous arguments for each position, citing specific protocols that appear to violate or confirm the trilemma.

Problem 9 (Advanced): Develop a formal model for consensus mechanism selection that incorporates changing requirements over time. For example, a protocol that starts permissioned (for regulatory compliance) and transitions to permissionless (for decentralization). What properties must be preserved during transition? Design the transition mechanism.

Problem 10 (Research): Select a live blockchain and apply the complete comparison framework. Gather real data on throughput, finality time, decentralization metrics (use on-chain data for stake distribution), and energy consumption. Compare measured values to the protocol's claims. Document any significant discrepancies.

(Solutions in Appendix D)

9.1.10 Further Reading

Bano et al. published "SoK: Consensus in the Age of Blockchains" in 2019. It remains the most comprehensive academic survey of the field. Gramoli's 2020 paper, "From blockchain consensus back to Byzantine consensus protocols," takes a more formal approach and is worth the effort if you want the mathematical side.

Srinivasan's Nakamoto coefficient paper introduced the idea. Trail of Bits followed up in 2022 with "Are Blockchains Decentralized?"—an empirical study whose findings are, to put it mildly, not flattering. Read it, especially if you build in this space.

Budish's "The Economic Limits of Bitcoin and the Blockchain" (2018) does uncomfortable but rigorous economic analysis of PoW security. Gervais et al. built a security framework that incorporates network-level dynamics Budish's model leaves out.

The Cambridge Centre for Alternative Finance maintains the best longitudinal data on Bitcoin's energy use. For PoW versus PoS comparisons, De Vries and Ethereum Foundation researchers have published well-controlled comparative studies.

PART III

Blockchain Architecture and Execution

CHAPTER 10

Data Structures

10.1 UTXO vs. Accounts and State Management

This chapter covers the two models for tracking blockchain state—UTXO and accounts—with Merkle proofs, state growth, and state rent proposals in between. What you'll walk away knowing:

- The UTXO model. Bitcoin uses it, so do Cardano and Ergo. Instead of account balances, value lives in unspent outputs. People tend to gloss over the formal semantics, which is a mistake, they matter quite a bit
- Ethereum's account model, and that state transition function Wood put down in the Yellow Paper
- A proper side-by-side of both approaches covering privacy, parallelism, smart contracts, state management. You won't see the tradeoffs compounding until you're actually building something
- Merkle proofs and state commitments, all the plumbing underneath that lets a phone verify somebody's balance without pulling down hundreds of gigs
- State growth. Quietly turning into one of the hardest unsolved problems in the space, and it doesn't get enough airtime
- State rent and expiry proposals. Years of arguing, nobody's settled it
- Working code for both models, at a level you could actually ship

N. Savant, *Blockchain Foundations*, https://doi.org/10.1007/979-8-8688-2891-1_10

10.1.1 Two Models of Blockchain State

Here's the thing about blockchain architecture that nobody warns you about early enough. Before you even think about consensus algorithms or networking layers, you've got to answer a question that sounds almost embarrassingly simple: how do you keep track of who owns what?

I know. Sounds like a weekend project. It is not.

That one call—just that one—cascades into everything. Your transaction format looks completely different depending on which way you go. Validation logic, privacy guarantees, whether parallelism is even possible, the shape smart contracts end up taking. All of it traces back to this single fork in the road. And the two designs that actually survived? They produce systems that barely resemble each other.

Bitcoin went with UTXOs. Unspent Transaction Outputs. There's no account with Alice's name on it anywhere in the protocol. What exists on-chain is a collection of outputs, each one carrying an amount and a spending condition. I usually explain it with sealed envelopes because that analogy actually holds up pretty well. Picture each envelope stuffed with some coins, sealed so only one specific key can open it. You want to pay somebody? Tear your envelope open, put the right amount into a new one for the recipient, stuff the leftovers into another envelope addressed back to yourself. Throw the old one away. Done. That's—and I'm not exaggerating—the entire mechanism. Cardano does the same thing. Ergo too. If you've spent your whole life thinking of money as a number in a bank account, this approach feels wrong. Backwards, even. I felt the same way at first. But once you understand what properties you get out of it, the weirdness starts looking like a feature.

Ethereum went the other direction entirely. Persistent accounts. Much closer to what a traditional database looks like. Every address gets an account object—balance, a transaction counter called a nonce, and if it's a contract, some code and storage tacked on. Sending ETH is just subtraction on one end and addition on the other. Solana did something similar. Aptos too. And yeah, on the surface it's clearly simpler. Then you actually start building production software, and the two models drag you into engineering worlds that have almost nothing in common.

The downstream effects go further than you'd think. Way further.

10.1.2 The UTXO Model in Depth

No such thing as a "balance" in a UTXO system. Not at the protocol level. That concept simply does not exist there. What the chain actually tracks is outputs—each one tagged with an amount and a script dictating who's allowed to spend it. On Bitcoin, that script is almost always just "prove you hold the private key matching this public key hash." When your wallet shows you a number and calls it your balance? That's a white lie. A helpful one, sure. But behind the curtain, all your wallet did was scan through the entire UTXO set, pull out every output your keys can unlock, and add up the amounts. The protocol itself couldn't care less what your total holdings are.

Transactions in this model consume existing UTXOs (those become your inputs) and mint fresh ones (those are your outputs). Outputs can never add up to more than the inputs—the difference is what the miner pockets as a fee. And here's a detail that trips up almost everyone who's new to this: there is no fee field in a Bitcoin transaction. I mean that literally. There is no data field anywhere in the structure where you declare the fee amount. The fee is implicit. It's just the gap—whatever value you didn't bother assigning to an output, the miner takes. Kind of elegant when you think about it. Also kind of terrifying. Screw up your output math, and congratulations, you just handed some miner a ridiculously generous tip by accident.

```
Coinbase TX (Block 1):
    Inputs:  [None - coinbase]
    Outputs: [UTXO_A: 50 BTC → Alice's pubkey hash]

TX_1 (Alice pays Bob 30 BTC):
    Inputs:  [UTXO_A (50 BTC) + Alice's signature]
    Outputs: [UTXO_B: 30 BTC → Bob's pubkey hash,
              UTXO_C: 19.99 BTC → Alice's NEW pubkey hash (change)]
    Fee: 0.01 BTC (implicit: inputs - outputs)

TX_2 (Bob pays Carol 10 BTC):
    Inputs:  [UTXO_B (30 BTC) + Bob's signature]
    Outputs: [UTXO_D: 10 BTC → Carol,
              UTXO_E: 19.99 BTC → Bob (change)]

UTXO Set after TX_2: {UTXO_C (Alice: 19.99), UTXO_D (Carol: 10), UTXO_E (Bob:
19.99)}
```

Figure 10-1. *UTXO Transaction Chain*

```
import hashlib
from dataclasses import dataclass, field
from typing import Dict, List, Optional, Set, Tuple

@dataclass
class TxOutput:
    """An unspent transaction output (UTXO)."""
    amount: int             # In satoshis (1 BTC = 100,000,000 satoshis)
    script_pubkey: str      # Spending condition (simplified: address/
                            pubkey hash)
    tx_hash: str = ""       # Transaction that created this output
    index: int = 0          # Output index within the creating transaction
    block_height: int = 0 # Block that included the creating transaction

    @property
    def outpoint(self) -> str:
        """Unique identifier: transaction hash + output index."""
        return f"{self.tx_hash}:{self.index}"

    @property
    def size_bytes(self) -> int:
        """Approximate serialized size of this output."""
        return 8 + len(self.script_pubkey) + 4  # amount + script +
        overhead

@dataclass
class TxInput:
    """Reference to a UTXO being spent."""
    prev_tx_hash: str
    prev_index: int
    signature: str      # Proof of authorization (simplified)
    sequence: int = 0xffffffff

    @property
    def outpoint(self) -> str:
        return f"{self.prev_tx_hash}:{self.prev_index}"

@dataclass
```

```
class Transaction:
    """A complete transaction consuming and creating UTXOs."""
    inputs: List[TxInput]
    outputs: List[TxOutput]
    version: int = 1
    locktime: int = 0

    def __post_init__(self):
        self.tx_hash = self._compute_hash()
        # Assign output metadata
        for i, out in enumerate(self.outputs):
            out.tx_hash = self.tx_hash
            out.index = i

    def _compute_hash(self) -> str:
        """Compute transaction identifier."""
        data = f"v{self.version}:"
        for inp in self.inputs:
            data += f"in({inp.outpoint}):"
        for out in self.outputs:
            data += f"out({out.amount},{out.script_pubkey}):"
        data += f"lt{self.locktime}"
        return hashlib.sha256(data.encode()).hexdigest()[:16]

    @property
    def is_coinbase(self) -> bool:
        return len(self.inputs) == 0

class UTXOSet:
    """
    The global UTXO set: all currently unspent transaction outputs.

    This is the fundamental state of a UTXO-based blockchain.
    Bitcoin's UTXO set is approximately 5-7 GB, containing
    roughly 80-90 million individual UTXOs.
    """

    def __init__(self):
```

```
        self.utxos: Dict[str, TxOutput] = {}  # outpoint -> TxOutput
        self._total_value = 0
        self._address_index: Dict[str, Set[str]] = {}  # address ->
        outpoints

    def add_utxo(self, utxo: TxOutput):
        """Add a new UTXO to the set."""
        outpoint = utxo.outpoint
        self.utxos[outpoint] = utxo
        self._total_value += utxo.amount

        # Maintain address index for balance lookups
        if utxo.script_pubkey not in self._address_index:
            self._address_index[utxo.script_pubkey] = set()
        self._address_index[utxo.script_pubkey].add(outpoint)

    def remove_utxo(self, outpoint: str) -> Optional[TxOutput]:
        """Remove (spend) a UTXO from the set."""
        utxo = self.utxos.pop(outpoint, None)
        if utxo:
            self._total_value -= utxo.amount
            if utxo.script_pubkey in self._address_index:
                self._address_index[utxo.script_pubkey].discard(outpoint)
        return utxo

    def get_utxo(self, outpoint: str) -> Optional[TxOutput]:
        """Look up a UTXO by its outpoint."""
        return self.utxos.get(outpoint)

    def get_balance(self, address: str) -> int:
        """Calculate total balance for an address."""
        outpoints = self._address_index.get(address, set())
        return sum(self.utxos[op].amount for op in outpoints if op in
        self.utxos)

    def get_utxos_for_address(self, address: str) -> List[TxOutput]:
        """Get all UTXOs spendable by an address."""
        outpoints = self._address_index.get(address, set())
```

```
        return [self.utxos[op] for op in outpoints if op in self.utxos]

    def select_utxos(self, address: str, target_amount: int,
                     strategy: str = "largest_first") -> Optional
                     [List[TxOutput]]:
        """
        Coin selection: choose UTXOs to fund a transaction.

        Strategies:
        - largest_first: Use largest UTXOs first (minimizes input count)
        - smallest_first: Use smallest first (consolidates dust)
        - exact_match: Try to find exact match (no change output)
        """
        available = sorted(
            self.get_utxos_for_address(address),
            key=lambda u: u.amount,
            reverse=(strategy == "largest_first")
        )

        if strategy == "exact_match":
            # Try to find a single UTXO matching the target
            for utxo in available:
                if utxo.amount == target_amount:
                    return [utxo]

        selected = []
        total = 0
        for utxo in available:
            selected.append(utxo)
            total += utxo.amount
            if total >= target_amount:
                return selected

        return None  # Insufficient funds

    def validate_transaction(self, tx: Transaction) -> Tuple[bool, str]:
        """
        Validate a transaction against the UTXO set.
```

```
    Checks:
    1. All inputs reference existing UTXOs
    2. Signatures authorize spending (simplified)
    3. Total outputs <= total inputs (fee must be non-negative)
    4. No output has negative or zero amount
    5. No duplicate inputs (no double-spend within transaction)
    """
    if tx.is_coinbase:
        return True, "Coinbase transaction"

    # Check for duplicate inputs
    input_outpoints = [inp.outpoint for inp in tx.inputs]
    if len(input_outpoints) != len(set(input_outpoints)):
        return False, "Duplicate input detected"

    total_input = 0
    for inp in tx.inputs:
        utxo = self.get_utxo(inp.outpoint)
        if utxo is None:
            return False, f"UTXO {inp.outpoint} not found (spent or
            invalid)"

        # Verify spending authorization (simplified: signature
        matches script)
        if inp.signature != utxo.script_pubkey:
            return False, f"Invalid signature for {inp.outpoint}"

        total_input += utxo.amount

    total_output = 0
    for out in tx.outputs:
        if out.amount <= 0:
            return False, "Output amount must be positive"
        total_output += out.amount

    if total_output > total_input:
        return False, f"Outputs ({total_output}) exceed inputs
        ({total_input})"
```

```
        fee = total_input - total_output
        return True, f"Valid. Fee: {fee} satoshis ({fee/1e8:.8f} BTC)"

    def apply_transaction(self, tx: Transaction) -> bool:
        """Apply a validated transaction: spend inputs, create outputs."""
        valid, reason = self.validate_transaction(tx)
        if not valid:
            return False

        # Atomically: remove all spent UTXOs, then add all new UTXOs
        for inp in tx.inputs:
            self.remove_utxo(inp.outpoint)

        for out in tx.outputs:
            self.add_utxo(out)

        return True

    @property
    def size(self) -> int:
        return len(self.utxos)

    @property
    def total_value(self) -> int:
        return self._total_value

    def statistics(self) -> dict:
        """Compute UTXO set statistics."""
        if not self.utxos:
            return {'count': 0, 'total_value': 0}

        amounts = [u.amount for u in self.utxos.values()]
        sizes = [u.size_bytes for u in self.utxos.values()]

        return {
            'count': len(amounts),
            'total_value_btc': sum(amounts) / 1e8,
            'avg_value_btc': (sum(amounts) / len(amounts)) / 1e8,
            'median_value_btc': sorted(amounts)[len(amounts)//2] / 1e8,
```

```
            'dust_count': sum(1 for a in amounts if a < 1000),  # < 10 sat/
            byte cost
            'total_size_bytes': sum(sizes),
            'unique_addresses': len(self._address_index),
        }

# Complete UTXO demonstration
utxo_set = UTXOSet()

# Genesis: coinbase creates initial UTXOs
coinbase = Transaction(
    inputs=[],
    outputs=[
        TxOutput(amount=5_000_000_000, script_pubkey="alice"),  # 50 BTC
    ]
)
for out in coinbase.outputs:
    utxo_set.add_utxo(out)

print("UTXO Model Complete Demonstration")
print("=" * 60)
print(f"After coinbase: Alice = {utxo_set.get_
balance('alice')/1e8:.2f} BTC")
print(f"UTXO set size: {utxo_set.size}")

# Alice sends 30 BTC to Bob, gets 19.99 BTC change
tx1 = Transaction(
    inputs=[TxInput(coinbase.tx_hash, 0, "alice")],
    outputs=[
        TxOutput(amount=3_000_000_000, script_pubkey="bob"),
        TxOutput(amount=1_999_000_000, script_pubkey="alice_change"),
    ]
)
valid, reason = utxo_set.validate_transaction(tx1)
print(f"\nTX1 (Alice->Bob 30 BTC): {reason}")
utxo_set.apply_transaction(tx1)

# Bob sends 10 BTC to Carol
```

```
tx2 = Transaction(
    inputs=[TxInput(tx1.tx_hash, 0, "bob")],
    outputs=[
        TxOutput(amount=1_000_000_000, script_pubkey="carol"),
        TxOutput(amount=1_999_000_000, script_pubkey="bob_change"),
    ]
)
utxo_set.apply_transaction(tx2)

# Coin selection: Alice wants to send 15 BTC (needs her change UTXO)
selected = utxo_set.select_utxos("alice_change", 1_500_000_000)
print(f"\nCoin selection for 15 BTC from alice_change:")
if selected:
    for u in selected:
        print(f"  {u.outpoint}: {u.amount/1e8:.4f} BTC")
else:
    print("  Insufficient funds")

# Attempt double-spend
double_spend = Transaction(
    inputs=[TxInput(coinbase.tx_hash, 0, "alice")],
    outputs=[TxOutput(amount=5_000_000_000, script_pubkey="eve")]
)
valid, reason = utxo_set.validate_transaction(double_spend)
print(f"\nDouble-spend attempt: {reason}")

# Statistics
stats = utxo_set.statistics()
print(f"\nUTXO Set Statistics:")
print(f"  UTXOs: {stats['count']}")
print(f"  Total value: {stats['total_value_btc']:.4f} BTC")
print(f"  Unique addresses: {stats['unique_addresses']}")
print(f"  Set size: {stats['total_size_bytes']} bytes")
```

UTXO Advantages and Disadvantages

Table 10-1. UTXO Model Properties

Property	Assessment	Details
Parallel validation	Strong advantage	Independent UTXOs have no shared state; transactions touching different UTXOs can be validated concurrently
Privacy	Moderate advantage	Change addresses create new identifiers per transaction; harder to link all transactions to one user
Deterministic verification	Strong advantage	Transaction validity depends only on referenced UTXOs, not on execution order
SPV proofs	Strong advantage	Light clients verify inclusion with compact Merkle proofs
Smart contracts	Disadvantage	Limited scripting (Bitcoin Script is intentionally restricted); eUTXO (Cardano) partially addresses this
State bloat	Moderate disadvantage	UTXO set grows with outputs; dust outputs may never be economically spendable
User experience	Moderate disadvantage	Coin selection, change addresses, and UTXO management add complexity
Multi-party transactions	Disadvantage	Combining inputs from multiple parties requires coordination

10.1.3 The Account Model in Depth

Flip everything you just read on its head. That's the account model. No outputs floating around. No envelopes. Each address just has a persistent entry in the ledger, like a row in a database—because that's basically what it is. Ethereum splits these into two flavors:

EOAs. Externally Owned Accounts. Fancy name for a wallet. You've got a private key, a balance, and a nonce that ticks up by one every time you broadcast a transaction. The nonce is there to kill replay attacks. And that's it. Seriously, that is the complete data structure. Nothing else hiding under the hood.

Contract accounts are a different animal altogether. They store bytecode—gets set once at deployment, then it's frozen forever. They've also got a key-value storage map that only the contract's own logic can touch. Nobody holds a private key for a contract account; there isn't one. What happens when someone interacts with it is dictated entirely by the code. You fire a transaction at a contract address, the EVM pulls up the bytecode, and executes it. End result is this little autonomous program just sitting on-chain, humming along for as long as the network keeps producing blocks.

So at any given block height, the world state is really just one big lookup table: feed in an address, get back account data. When a transaction hits, the state transition function kicks in. Balances shift. Nonces increment. Contract storage gets rewritten. Then all of that—every account, every storage slot—gets hashed into a Merkle-Patricia trie structure. The root of that trie goes into the block header, and that single hash is what anybody needs to verify the entire state is legit and untampered.

```
@dataclass
class Account:
    """Ethereum-style account."""
    address: str
    balance: int = 0             # In Wei (1 ETH = 10^18 Wei)
    nonce: int = 0               # Transaction count (EOA) or contract
                                 creation count
    code: bytes = b""            # Empty for EOA, bytecode for contract
    storage: Dict[str, str] = field(default_factory=dict)
    # Contract storage

    @property
    def is_contract(self) -> bool:
        return len(self.code) > 0

    @property
    def is_empty(self) -> bool:
        """EIP-161: empty account has zero balance, zero nonce, no code."""
        return self.balance == 0 and self.nonce == 0 and not self.code

class WorldState:
    """
    The global account state of an account-based blockchain.

    In Ethereum, this is stored as a Merkle-Patricia Trie where:
    - Keys: account addresses (Keccak-256 hashed)
    - Values: RLP-encoded (nonce, balance, storageRoot, codeHash)
```

```
    - Root hash: committed in each block header
    """

    def __init__(self):
        self.accounts: Dict[str, Account] = {}
        self.block_number = 0
        self.state_root = self._compute_root()

    def get_account(self, address: str) -> Account:
        """Get or create account (accounts are implicitly created)."""
        if address not in self.accounts:
            self.accounts[address] = Account(address=address)
        return self.accounts[address]

    def get_balance(self, address: str) -> int:
        return self.get_account(address).balance

    def get_nonce(self, address: str) -> int:
        return self.get_account(address).nonce

    def _compute_root(self) -> str:
        """Simplified state root computation."""
        data = ""
        for addr in sorted(self.accounts):
            acc = self.accounts[addr]
            data += f"{addr}:{acc.balance}:{acc.nonce}:{acc.code.hex()}:"
            for k in sorted(acc.storage):
                data += f"{k}={acc.storage[k]};"
        return hashlib.sha256(data.encode()).hexdigest()[:16]

    def apply_transfer(self, sender: str, recipient: str,
                       value: int, gas_price: int, gas_limit: int,
                       nonce: int,          # Required - prevents replay
                                            attacks
                       data: bytes = b"") -> Tuple[bool, str, dict]:
  sender_acc = self.get_account(sender)

  # Step 1: Validate nonce - this IS the replay protection
  # If nonce doesn't match, transaction is rejected entirely
```

```
    if nonce != sender_acc.nonce:
        return False, (
            f"Nonce mismatch: expected {sender_acc.nonce}, got {nonce}. "
            f"Replayed or out-of-order transaction rejected."
        ), {}

    # Upfront cost check
    upfront = value + gas_limit * gas_price
    if sender_acc.balance < upfront:
        return False, f"Insufficient balance: {sender_acc.balance}
        < {upfront}", {}
```

Also update the demo call:

```
# First transaction — nonce must be 0 (Alice's starting nonce)
success, msg, details = world.apply_transfer(
    "alice", "bob",
    30 * 10**18,
    gas_price=20 * 10**9,
    gas_limit=21000,
    nonce=0             # Must match alice's current nonce
)

# Show replay protection working
print("\nReplay attack attempt (same nonce=0 again):")
success2, msg2, _ = world.apply_transfer(
    "alice", "bob",
    30 * 10**18,
    gas_price=20 * 10**9,
    gas_limit=21000,
    nonce=0             # Alice's nonce is now 1 — this should be rejected
)
print(f" Result: {msg2}") # Should print nonce mismatch
```

```
        # Gas accounting
        intrinsic_gas = 21000  # Base transaction gas
        if data:
            intrinsic_gas += len(data) * 16  # 16 gas per non-zero byte
```

```
        if gas_limit < intrinsic_gas:
            return False, f"Gas limit {gas_limit} below intrinsic
            {intrinsic_gas}", {}

        gas_used = intrinsic_gas
        gas_refund = (gas_limit - gas_used) * gas_price
        actual_fee = gas_used * gas_price

        # Execute transfer
        sender_acc.balance -= (value + actual_fee)
        sender_acc.nonce += 1

        recipient_acc = self.get_account(recipient)
        recipient_acc.balance += value

        # Update state root
        self.state_root = self._compute_root()

        return True, "Success", {
            'gas_used': gas_used,
            'fee_paid': actual_fee,
            'new_sender_balance': sender_acc.balance,
            'new_recipient_balance': recipient_acc.balance,
            'state_root': self.state_root,
        }

    def apply_contract_storage(self, contract_addr: str,
                               key: str, value: str) -> int:
        """
        Write to contract storage. Returns gas cost.

        EIP-2200 gas costs:
        - Cold access (first touch): 2,100 gas for read
        - Zero to nonzero: 20,000 gas (new storage slot)
        - Nonzero to nonzero: 2,900 gas (update)
        - Nonzero to zero: 2,900 gas + 4,800 refund
        """
        acc = self.get_account(contract_addr)
        old_value = acc.storage.get(key, "0x0")
```

```
        if old_value == "0x0" and value != "0x0":
            gas = 20000  # New storage slot
        elif old_value != "0x0" and value != "0x0":
            gas = 2900   # Update existing
        elif old_value != "0x0" and value == "0x0":
            gas = 2900   # Delete (with refund)
        else:
            gas = 100    # Zero to zero (no-op)

        acc.storage[key] = value
        return gas

    def statistics(self) -> dict:
        """Compute world state statistics."""
        total_balance = sum(a.balance for a in self.accounts.values())
        contracts = sum(1 for a in self.accounts.values() if a.is_contract)
        storage_slots = sum(len(a.storage) for a in self.accounts.values())
        empty = sum(1 for a in self.accounts.values() if a.is_empty)

        return {
            'total_accounts': len(self.accounts),
            'eoa_accounts': len(self.accounts) - contracts,
            'contract_accounts': contracts,
            'empty_accounts': empty,
            'total_balance_eth': total_balance / 1e18,
            'total_storage_slots': storage_slots,
            'state_root': self.state_root,
        }

# Complete account model demonstration
world = WorldState()

# Set initial balances (from block rewards)
world.get_account("alice").balance = 100 * 10**18  # 100 ETH
world.get_account("bob").balance = 50 * 10**18

print("\nAccount Model Complete Demonstration")
print("=" * 60)
```

```
print(f"Alice: {world.get_balance('alice')/1e18:.2f} ETH")
print(f"Bob: {world.get_balance('bob')/1e18:.2f} ETH")

# Transfer
success, msg, details = world.apply_transfer(
    "alice", "bob", 30 * 10**18,
    gas_price=20 * 10**9,  # 20 Gwei
    gas_limit=21000
)
print(f"\nTransfer 30 ETH Alice->Bob: {msg}")
if success:
    print(f"  Gas used: {details['gas_used']}")
    print(f"  Fee: {details['fee_paid']/1e18:.6f} ETH")
    print(f"  Alice: {details['new_sender_balance']/1e18:.6f} ETH")
    print(f"  Bob: {details['new_recipient_balance']/1e18:.2f} ETH")
    print(f"  Nonce: {world.get_nonce('alice')}")

# Demonstrate nonce replay protection
print(f"\nAlice nonce after tx: {world.get_nonce('alice')}")
print("  (Next transaction must use nonce = 1)")

# Contract storage costs
gas = world.apply_contract_storage("contract_A", "slot_0", "0x42")
print(f"\nStorage write (new slot): {gas} gas")
gas = world.apply_contract_storage("contract_A", "slot_0", "0x43")
print(f"Storage write (update):   {gas} gas")

# Statistics
stats = world.statistics()
print(f"\nWorld State Statistics:")
for k, v in stats.items():
    print(f"  {k}: {v}")
```

Table 10-2. *UTXO vs. Account Model Detailed Comparison*

Dimension	UTXO	Account
State representation	Set of unspent outputs	Mapping of address to account state
Transaction format	Explicit inputs (UTXOs consumed) + outputs (UTXOs created)	Sender, recipient, value, data, nonce
Parallel validation	Natural: independent UTXOs, no shared state	Requires dependency analysis on accounts
Privacy	Better: change addresses, no persistent identity	Worse: persistent address links all transactions
Smart contracts	Limited: Bitcoin Script, eUTXO for Cardano	Natural: arbitrary code execution with state
Replay protection	Inherent: UTXOs are consumed (one-time use)	Nonce-based: each tx increments the account nonce
Light client proofs	Simple: Merkle proof of UTXO existence	Complex: state proof requires trie traversal
Fungibility	Each UTXO has a distinct history (taint analysis possible)	Balance is a single number (more fungible)
State size	UTXO set: ~7 GB for Bitcoin	State trie: ~150+ GB for Ethereum
State growth	Grows with outputs; dust problem	Grows with accounts; empty account problem

10.1.4 State Management with Merkle Proofs

Doesn't matter if you picked UTXOs or accounts. The state layer still has to nail two things, and these two things are non-negotiable regardless of which camp you're in.

First: compress the entire state into a single hash that fits in the block header. That's your state commitment. Second: give someone a way to prove that a specific piece of data lives in the state without making them download the whole thing. Hundreds of gigs of state data—you can't just ship that to a phone.

Merkle trees solve both problems. And they solve them shockingly well, actually. The math is old, the concept is straightforward, and the efficiency is hard to beat.

Merkle Trees for UTXO Commitments

```
class MerkleStateTree:
    """
    Merkle tree for state commitments and proofs.

    Enables light clients to verify state inclusion without
    downloading the full state. Proof size is O(log n) where
    n is the number of state entries.
    """

    def __init__(self):
        self.entries: Dict[str, str] = {}  # key -> value

    def update(self, key: str, value: str):
        self.entries[key] = value

    def delete(self, key: str):
        self.entries.pop(key, None)

    def compute_root(self) -> str:
        """Compute Merkle root of all entries."""
        if not self.entries:
            return hashlib.sha256(b"empty_tree").hexdigest()

        # Create leaf hashes from sorted entries
        leaves = []
        for key in sorted(self.entries):
            leaf_data = f"{key}:{self.entries[key]}"
            leaf_hash = hashlib.sha256(leaf_data.encode()).hexdigest()
            leaves.append(leaf_hash)

        return self._build_root(leaves)

    def _build_root(self, hashes: List[str]) -> str:
        """Build Merkle tree from leaf hashes."""
        if len(hashes) == 1:
            return hashes[0]

        # Pad to even number
```

```
        if len(hashes) % 2 != 0:
            hashes.append(hashes[-1])

        next_level = []
        for i in range(0, len(hashes), 2):
            combined = hashes[i] + hashes[i + 1]
            parent = hashlib.sha256(combined.encode()).hexdigest()
            next_level.append(parent)

        return self._build_root(next_level)

    def generate_proof(self, key: str) -> Optional[dict]:
        """
        Generate a Merkle inclusion proof for a key.

        Returns the sibling hashes along the path from leaf to root,
        enabling independent verification with just the proof + root.
        """
        if key not in self.entries:
            return None

        sorted_keys = sorted(self.entries)
        target_idx = sorted_keys.index(key)

        leaves = []
        for k in sorted_keys:
            leaf_data = f"{k}:{self.entries[k]}"
            leaves.append(hashlib.sha256(leaf_data.encode()).hexdigest())

        proof_path = []
        current_hashes = list(leaves)
        idx = target_idx
       while len(current_hashes) > 1:
    if len(current_hashes) % 2 != 0:
        current_hashes.append(current_hashes[-1])

    next_level = []
    for i in range(0, len(current_hashes), 2):
        if i == idx or i + 1 == idx:
```

```
            sibling = i + 1 if i == idx else i
            side = "right" if i == idx else "left"
            proof_path.append({
                'hash': current_hashes[sibling],
                'side': side,
            })

        combined = current_hashes[i] + current_hashes[i + 1]
        next_level.append(hashlib.sha256(combined.encode()).hexdigest())

    idx = idx // 2
    current_hashes = next_level
```

With this:

```
while len(current_hashes) > 1:
    # Pad BEFORE recording sibling so idx always has a valid partner
    if len(current_hashes) % 2 != 0:
        current_hashes.append(current_hashes[-1])
        # If idx pointed to last real leaf, it now has a sibling (the
        duplicate)
        # This is correct - the duplicate IS the sibling in this padded tree

    next_level = []
    for i in range(0, len(current_hashes), 2):
        left_idx = i
        right_idx = i + 1

        # Determine which side our target node is on
        if left_idx == idx:
            # Target is left child - sibling is on the right
            proof_path.append({
                'hash': current_hashes[right_idx],
                'side': 'right',  # sibling is to the RIGHT of target
            })
        elif right_idx == idx:
            # Target is right child - sibling is on the left
            proof_path.append({
```

```
                'hash': current_hashes[left_idx],
                'side': 'left',   # sibling is to the LEFT of target
            })
        combined = current_hashes[left_idx] + current_hashes[right_idx]
        next_level.append(hashlib.sha256(combined.encode()).hexdigest())

    idx = idx // 2
    current_hashes = next_level
```

Also add a test to the demo to confirm odd-leaf trees verify correctly:

```
# Test proof works for all entries including last (odd-position) leaf
print("\nVerification check for all entries:")
all_pass = True
for key in tree.entries:
    p = tree.generate_proof(key)
    result = MerkleStateTree.verify_proof(
        key, p['value'], p['proof'], p['root']
    )
    if not result:
        print(f" FAIL: {key}")
        all_pass = False
print(f" All proofs valid: {all_pass}")
```

```
        return {
            'key': key,
            'value': self.entries[key],
            'leaf_hash': leaves[target_idx],
            'proof': proof_path,
            'root': self.compute_root(),
            'proof_size_hashes': len(proof_path),
        }

    @staticmethod
    def verify_proof(key: str, value: str, proof: List[dict],
                     root: str) -> bool:
        """Verify a Merkle inclusion proof against a known root."""
```

```
        leaf_data = f"{key}:{value}"
        current = hashlib.sha256(leaf_data.encode()).hexdigest()

        for step in proof:
            if step['side'] == 'right':
                combined = current + step['hash']
            else:
                combined = step['hash'] + current
            current = hashlib.sha256(combined.encode()).hexdigest()

        return current == root

# Demonstrate state proofs
tree = MerkleStateTree()

# Add account states
accounts_data = {
    "alice": "balance:50000000000,nonce:5",
    "bob": "balance:30000000000,nonce:2",
    "carol": "balance:10000000000,nonce:1",
    "dave": "balance:8000000000,nonce:0",
    "eve": "balance:5000000000,nonce:3",
    "frank": "balance:2000000000,nonce:1",
    "grace": "balance:1000000000,nonce:0",
    "heidi": "balance:500000000,nonce:0",
}

for addr, data in accounts_data.items():
    tree.update(addr, data)

root = tree.compute_root()
print("\nMerkle State Proof Demonstration")
print("=" * 55)
print(f"State root: {root[:32]}...")
print(f"Total entries: {len(tree.entries)}")

# Generate and verify proof for Bob's account
proof_result = tree.generate_proof("bob")
if proof_result:
```

```
    print(f"\nProof for Bob's account:")
    print(f"  Value: {proof_result['value']}")
    print(f"  Proof nodes: {proof_result['proof_size_hashes']}")
    print(f"  Proof size: ~{proof_result['proof_size_hashes'] * 32} bytes")
    print(f"  Tree depth: {proof_result['proof_size_hashes']}")

    # Light client verification
    verified = MerkleStateTree.verify_proof(
        "bob", proof_result['value'],
        proof_result['proof'], proof_result['root']
    )
    print(f"  Verification: {'PASS' if verified else 'FAIL'}")

    # Tampered value verification
    tampered = MerkleStateTree.verify_proof(
        "bob", "balance:99999999999,nonce:0",
        proof_result['proof'], proof_result['root']
    )
    print(f"  Tampered verification: {'PASS' if tampered else 'FAIL
    (correct)'}")

# Show proof size scaling
print(f"\nProof Size Scaling:")
for n in [10, 100, 1000, 10000, 100000, 1000000]:
    depth = math.ceil(math.log2(max(n, 2)))
    proof_bytes = depth * 32  # Each node is 32 bytes (SHA-256)
    print(f"  {n:>10,} entries: depth={depth:2d}, "
          f"proof={proof_bytes:5d} bytes ({proof_bytes/1024:.1f} KB)")
```

10.1.5 State Growth and Sustainability

Nobody escapes this one. I don't care which model you chose—the state only ever gets bigger. It never shrinks. Not on its own, anyway. Every year dumps more onto the pile. More accounts showing up, more UTXOs accumulating, more contract storage writes stacking up block after block after block. And full nodes? They carry all of it. Every byte.

What happens over time is kind of insidious. Sync times creep up. Hardware requirements get a little stiffer each year. And at some point—there's no dramatic moment or anything—running a node just costs enough that individual operators start shutting theirs down. Quietly. One by one. The network gets a little more centralized, a little more dependent on well-funded operators, and nobody really talks about it until the trend's been going on long enough to be embarrassing.

Table 10-3. *State Growth Across Major Chains*

Chain	State Type	Approximate Size	Growth Rate	Primary Component
Bitcoin UTXO set	UTXO	~5-7 GB	~0.5-1 GB/year	Unspent outputs
Ethereum state	Merkle-Patricia Trie	~150+ GB	~30+ GB/year	Contract storage
Ethereum full archive	All historical states	~15+ TB	~2+ TB/year	State snapshots
Solana accounts	Account data	~50+ GB	Variable	Program accounts and data

Pruning Strategies

```
def model_state_growth(initial_gb: float, annual_growth_gb: float,
                       years: int, strategy: str) -> List[dict]:
    """Model state growth under different management strategies."""
    history = []

    for year in range(years + 1):
        if strategy == "archive":
            # Keep everything: linear growth forever
            size = initial_gb + annual_growth_gb * year

        elif strategy == "full_pruned":
            # Keep recent state (last 128 blocks) + current state
            # State itself still grows, but old state versions are
            discarded
            current_state = initial_gb + annual_growth_gb * year * 0.3
            recent_history = min(annual_growth_gb * 0.1, 10)  # Cap
            at 10 GB
            size = current_state + recent_history
```

```
        elif strategy == "state_expiry":
    # Expire state not accessed in last epoch (~1 year)
    # Active state stabilizes; dormant state archived
    active_fraction = 0.4 # ~40% of state is actively used
    size = initial_gb * active_fraction + annual_growth_gb * active_fraction
```

With this:

```
elif strategy == "state_expiry":
    # Expire state not accessed in last epoch (~1 year).
    # Only the active fraction of state is retained each year.
    # Dormant state is archived off-chain and can be restored with a proof.
    # State still grows - just at a reduced rate (active_fraction of full
    growth).
    active_fraction = 0.4 # ~40% of state is actively touched per year
    size = (initial_gb + annual_growth_gb * year) * active_fraction
    # Before fix: 'year' was missing - every year showed the same size.
    # After fix: state grows at 40% of the archive rate (slower, not flat).

        elif strategy == "stateless":
            # Stateless clients: no persistent state, receive proofs with
            each block
            size = 0.1  # Just client software

        else:
            size = initial_gb + annual_growth_gb * year

        history.append({
            'year': year,
            'size_gb': size,
            'strategy': strategy,
        })

    return history

print("\nState Growth Projections (Ethereum-like, 10 years)")
print("=" * 60)
print(f"{'Year':>5}", end="")
strategies = ["archive", "full_pruned", "state_expiry", "stateless"]
```

```
for s in strategies:
    print(f"  {s:>14}", end="")
print(" (GB)")
print("-" * 70)

all_histories = {s: model_state_growth(150, 30, 10, s) for s in strategies}

for year in range(0, 11, 2):
    print(f"  {2024+year}", end="")
    for s in strategies:
        size = all_histories[s][year]['size_gb']
        print(f"  {size:>12.0f}", end="")
    print()
```

State Rent and Expiry Proposals

State rent. This idea has been floating around for years, and it absolutely will not die. The pitch is simple enough: make users pay recurring fees to keep their data sitting on-chain. And honestly? The reasoning holds up if you just look at the economics. Every single byte in the state trie costs every full node operator money. Forever. The person who wrote that data originally? They paid once. A one-time fee for permanent storage—that's a subsidy, and it doesn't scale.

The pro-rent crowd has a defensible argument here. You're occupying shared resources, so pay for them. Ongoing charges give people a real reason to clean up after themselves and delete data they no longer need. And it puts a natural ceiling on state growth before the problem gets completely out of hand. But here's the thing—state growth is one of those slow-burn problems. The kind that everybody acknowledges and nobody prioritizes. It'll be urgent eventually, just not today. So it sits there.

And the anti-rent crowd isn't wrong either. The eviction part is what makes everyone nervous. Think about this scenario: somebody buys a bunch of tokens, locks them into a smart contract, and then drops off the grid for three years. Maybe they lost interest, maybe they just forgot. They come back, and—surprise—the contract got evicted because nobody was around to pay the rent. Those tokens? Stuck. Gone into some kind of limbo. Now multiply that across millions of users and you've got a nightmare on your hands. Beyond that, the engineering work is enormous. You need machinery to track who owes what, mechanisms to evict gracefully without corrupting neighboring states, and restoration paths for data that got kicked out. And then there's this really uncomfortable question about fairness: how do you justify charging contracts retroactively when the rules at the time they were deployed said nothing about ongoing fees?

10.1.6 Summary

There is no winner here. I want to be clear about that. These two models excel at different things, and the right choice depends entirely on what you're trying to build and what tradeoffs you're willing to eat.

Here's what matters:

- UTXO keeps value locked in self-contained outputs. Two transactions that reference different outputs? They can be validated at the same time with zero coordination between them. You don't have to design for that—it's baked into how the model works from the ground up.
- Account-based systems keep state around between blocks. Balances, nonces, contract storage—it all persists. Most developers find it more intuitive when they're writing smart contract logic. The catch is that transactions from a single sender must execute in strict order because the nonce needs to go up by exactly one each time. You can't parallelize those, period.
- UTXO wallets automatically generate new addresses for change outputs, which means a user's on-chain activity ends up scattered across many different identifiers. Account wallets tie everything to one address. Privacy defaults are basically opposites.
- Light clients use Merkle proofs to check specific entries against the block header without downloading everything. Proof size? It grows logarithmically. For a million accounts, you're looking at roughly a kilobyte. That's why mobile wallets are even feasible.
- State growth is an open problem and nobody has a definitive answer yet. Bitcoin's UTXO set grows maybe a gig a year. Manageable. Ethereum's state trie puts on thirty-plus gigs annually. That's a very different conversation. There are proposals on the table—pruning, state expiry, stateless clients—but nothing has been adopted as the solution.

- Both models have operational headaches that'll bite you in production. With UTXOs you get coin selection puzzles: which outputs should you spend, how do you handle change, and what do you do about dust accumulating in tiny fragments that cost more to spend than they're worth? With accounts you get nonce management problems: send transactions out of sequence, and they just sit in the mempool doing nothing until the gap fills in.
- Cardano's eUTXO is an interesting attempt to get the best of both worlds—UTXO parallelism combined with account-style smart contract capability. It works reasonably well when transactions aren't fighting over the same contract. But throw a popular DeFi contract with hundreds of concurrent users at it? Contention is still very much an unsolved problem there.

UTXO treats value as discrete outputs. Each transaction destroys old ones and creates new ones. Since outputs are independent, parallel validation just works. Change addresses mean user activity gets spread across many identities by default.—Accounts keep persistent state per address. Most developers find smart contract work more natural with this model. Nonces stop replays but they also force strict ordering on same-sender transactions.—With UTXO, transaction order doesn't affect validation. With accounts, it does. Nonces have to line up or the transaction gets rejected.—Merkle proof size is logarithmic. Roughly a kilobyte can cover millions of entries.—Bitcoin UTXO set: about 7 GB. Ethereum state trie: past 150 GB, growing at 30+ GB a year.—Coin selection is about tradeoffs. Largest-first keeps input count down. Smallest-first consolidates dust. Exact-match skips the change output.—State rent sounds reasonable until you think about eviction risk, protocol complexity, and retroactive cost on deployed contracts.—Neither model is better in all cases. What you care about most (privacy, parallelism, contract ergonomics, sustainable state management) should drive the choice.

10.1.7 Exercises

Problem 1 (Basic): How does the UTXO model catch a double-spend? Walk through validation step by step for a case where someone tries spending an output that's already been consumed.

Problem 2 (Calculation): Alice has four UTXOs: 0.3, 0.5, 1.2, and 2.0 BTC. She wants to send 1.5 BTC to Bob with a 0.0001 BTC fee. With largest-first selection, which UTXOs get used? What does the change output look like?

Problem 3 (Implementation): Take the UTXO code from the chapter and add P2SH support. Build a 2-of-3 multisig and show a transaction where two of the three keyholders sign.

Problem 4 (Analysis): Run the storage numbers for 10 million users. UTXO: 3 outputs per user, 50 bytes each. Accounts: 1 per user, 100 bytes. Include index overhead. Which model is smaller?

Problem 5 (Design): Design state rent for Ethereum. Cover the rate formula, what happens at zero balance, how an evicted state gets restored, and how you deal with contracts deployed before rent existed.

Problem 6 (Theory): Prove that UTXO transactions on disjoint output sets give the same result in any order. Then build a counterexample where reordering account transactions on one account changes the outcome.

Problem 7 (Comparative): Look into Cardano's eUTXO model. How does it handle smart contract state, concurrent access, contention? Where does it still lag behind Ethereum's account model?

Problem 8 (Critical Thinking): Ethereum keeps every account ever created, including zero-balance ones. EIP-161 introduced pruning for empty accounts. Is that enough? What would more aggressive cleanup get you, and what would you lose?

Problem 9 (Advanced): Build a Merkle-Patricia trie from scratch. Insert, update, delete, root computation, proof generation and verification. Benchmark proof size from 100 accounts to 1,000,000.

Problem 10 (Research): Read EIP-6800. How do Verkle trees compare to Merkle-Patricia tries on structure, proof size, and update cost? What changes for stateless clients? Estimate proof-size reduction for a realistic access pattern.

(Solutions in Appendix D)

10.1.8 Further Reading

Bitcoin Developer Guide is where you want to start for UTXO mechanics. If you want actual empirical data on UTXO set growth over time—hard numbers, not estimates—Delgado-Segura et al. published a paper with exactly that.

Wood's Yellow Paper remains the formal reference for Ethereum's account model. You'll find the Merkle-Patricia trie specification there as well, buried somewhere in the appendices.

EIP-6800 is the proposal to swap in Verkle trees and compress proof sizes dramatically. Separately, there's a whole thread of research asking whether full nodes even need to persist in state at all—a radical idea if it ever pans out.

IOHK's academic papers lay out the eUTXO formal semantics if you want the theory. Cardano's developer docs cover the practical engineering side of actually building on that model.

CHAPTER 11

Virtual Machines

11.1 EVM, WASM, and Execution Environments

This chapter covers EVM architecture and gas mechanics, EIP-1559's dynamic base fee, WASM as an alternative execution environment, parallel transaction processing, and the deterministic execution constraints that shape all VM design. By the end, you will understand:

- The Ethereum Virtual Machine architecture, its stack-based design, and complete opcode categories
- Gas mechanics, including the fee market, EIP-1559 dynamic base fee adjustment, and access lists
- WebAssembly (WASM) as an alternative execution environment with performance characteristics
- Execution sharding and parallel transaction processing with conflict detection
- Deterministic execution requirements and why they constrain VM design
- Security implications of virtual machine design including reentrancy and stack depth

11.1.1 Why Blockchain Needs a Virtual Machine

A blockchain VM occupies a peculiar niche in computing. Unlike a desktop application that can read files, call APIs, and adapt to its hardware, a blockchain program must produce bit-identical results on every machine that runs it—from a Raspberry Pi in

N. Savant, *Blockchain Foundations*, https://doi.org/10.1007/979-8-8688-2891-1_11

Nairobi to a datacenter rack in Frankfurt. If two nodes disagree on even a single bit of output, the chain forks and consensus breaks. This constraint eliminates entire categories of normal programming: no floating-point arithmetic (different CPUs round differently), no system clock access (clocks drift), no filesystem or network calls (different nodes have different environments), and no hardware random numbers (by definition non-reproducible). What remains must be bounded in execution time and memory. The result is an environment that feels deliberately crippled compared to conventional VMs, but every restriction exists to preserve the property that matters most: agreement.

This requirement imposes severe constraints on VM design. The VM cannot access external state: no network calls, no filesystem access, no system clock reads (beyond block-provided timestamps), no hardware random number generators. Floating-point arithmetic is forbidden because different CPUs round differently (e.g., x87 vs. SSE). Execution must be bounded to prevent infinite loops—hence gas metering. Memory access must be bounded to prevent a single contract from consuming all available RAM.

These constraints explain many design decisions that seem unusual compared to traditional programming environments. The EVM uses 256-bit integers natively (not 32-bit or 64-bit) because cryptographic operations dominate blockchain computation. WASM-based chains must inject metering code at compile time because WASM itself has no built-in gas concept.

11.1.2 The Ethereum Virtual Machine

The EVM is a stack-based virtual machine that executes bytecode compiled from high-level languages (primarily Solidity and Vyper). Its design prioritizes simplicity, determinism, and crypto-native operation over raw performance.

Architecture Components

The stack holds intermediate computation values. It operates on 256-bit words—a size chosen not for CPU efficiency (modern processors use 64-bit registers) but because the dominant operations in blockchain are cryptographic: hash outputs, curve coordinates, and Ethereum addresses are all 256-bit or smaller values that fit in a single stack word without splitting. The stack holds at most 1,024 entries, a limit that prevents unbounded recursion and keeps memory requirements predictable.

Working memory provides scratch space that exists only for the duration of a single transaction. It starts at zero size and expands on demand, with costs that rise more steeply the more memory you claim. The first few kilobytes are cheap. Claiming a megabyte is prohibitively expensive. This graduated pricing discourages contracts from treating on-chain execution like a general-purpose computing environment.

```
memory_cost = 3 * num_words + (num_words^2 / 512)
```

This quadratic term discourages contracts from allocating large memory regions, preventing memory-based denial of service.

Persistent storage is the expensive tier—and deliberately so. Every byte written to storage must be maintained by every full node that will ever sync the chain, from now until the chain ceases to exist. A single 32-byte write to a new storage slot costs roughly 7,000 times more gas than an arithmetic addition. This ratio reflects the reality that computation is transient (done once and forgotten) while storage is permanent (replicated across thousands of machines indefinitely).

Program counter: Points to the current bytecode instruction. Increments by 1 for single-byte opcodes, by 1 + N for PUSH instructions that embed N bytes of data.

Gas counter: Tracks remaining gas. Each operation deducts its gas cost. If gas reaches zero during execution, the transaction reverts (all state changes are undone), but the gas is still consumed (paid to the block producer).

Call data: Read-only input data provided with the transaction. Contains the function selector (first 4 bytes of keccak256 of function signature) and ABI-encoded arguments.

Return data: Output data from the most recent external call. Available via RETURNDATASIZE and RETURNDATACOPY.

```
from typing import List, Dict, Optional, Tuple
from dataclasses import dataclass, field
import hashlib

class EVMStack:
    """EVM stack: 256-bit words, max depth 1024."""
    MAX_DEPTH = 1024
    MAX_UINT256 = (1 << 256) - 1

    def __init__(self):
        self.items: List[int] = []
```

```
    def push(self, value: int):
        if len(self.items) >= self.MAX_DEPTH:
            raise Exception("Stack overflow (depth 1024)")
        self.items.append(value & self.MAX_UINT256)

    def pop(self) -> int:
        if not self.items:
            raise Exception("Stack underflow")
        return self.items.pop()

    def peek(self, depth: int = 0) -> int:
        if depth >= len(self.items):
            raise Exception(f"Stack peek at depth {depth} (size {len(self.
            items)})")
        return self.items[-(depth + 1)]

    def dup(self, position: int):
        """DUP1-DUP16: duplicate Nth stack item to top."""
        if position > len(self.items) or position < 1:
            raise Exception(f"Invalid DUP position {position}")
        self.push(self.items[-position])

    def swap(self, position: int):
        """SWAP1-SWAP16: swap top with (N+1)th item."""
        if position + 1 > len(self.items):
            raise Exception(f"Invalid SWAP position {position}")
        self.items[-1], self.items[-(position + 1)] = (
            self.items[-(position + 1)], self.items[-1])

    @property
    def depth(self) -> int:
        return len(self.items)

class EVMMemory:
    """EVM memory: byte-addressable, expandable, gas-metered."""

    def __init__(self):
        self.data = bytearray()
        self._highest_accessed = 0
```

```
    def _expand_to(self, offset: int, size: int = 32) -> int:
        """Expand memory and return gas cost for expansion."""
        required = offset + size
        if required <= len(self.data):
            return 0

        old_words = (len(self.data) + 31) // 32
        new_words = (required + 31) // 32

        # Gas formula: 3 * words + words^2 / 512
        old_cost = 3 * old_words + (old_words * old_words) // 512
        new_cost = 3 * new_words + (new_words * new_words) // 512
        expansion_gas = new_cost - old_cost

        self.data.extend(bytes(required - len(self.data)))
        return expansion_gas

    def store(self, offset: int, value: int, size: int = 32) -> int:
        """Store value at offset. Returns expansion gas cost."""
        gas = self._expand_to(offset, size)
        data = value.to_bytes(size, 'big')
        self.data[offset:offset + size] = data
        return gas

    def load(self, offset: int, size: int = 32) -> Tuple[int, int]:
        """Load value from offset. Returns (value, expansion_gas)."""
        gas = self._expand_to(offset, size)
        value = int.from_bytes(self.data[offset:offset + size], 'big')
        return value, gas

    @property
    def size_bytes(self) -> int:
        return len(self.data)

class SimpleEVM:
    """
    Simplified but functional EVM implementation.

    Supports core opcodes for arithmetic, comparison, memory,
```

```
    storage, stack manipulation, and control flow.
    """

    # Opcode definitions
    STOP = 0x00; ADD = 0x01; MUL = 0x02; SUB = 0x03
    DIV = 0x04; SDIV = 0x05; MOD = 0x06; SMOD = 0x07
    ADDMOD = 0x08; MULMOD = 0x09; EXP = 0x0a
    LT = 0x10; GT = 0x11; SLT = 0x12; SGT = 0x13
    EQ = 0x14; ISZERO = 0x15
    AND = 0x16; OR = 0x17; XOR = 0x18; NOT = 0x19
    BYTE = 0x1a; SHL = 0x1b; SHR = 0x1c; SAR = 0x1d
    SHA3 = 0x20
    POP = 0x50; MLOAD = 0x51; MSTORE = 0x52; MSTORE8 = 0x53
    SLOAD = 0x54; SSTORE = 0x55
    JUMP = 0x56; JUMPI = 0x57; PC = 0x58; MSIZE = 0x59
    GAS = 0x5a; JUMPDEST = 0x5b
    PUSH1 = 0x60; PUSH32 = 0x7f
    DUP1 = 0x80; DUP16 = 0x8f
    SWAP1 = 0x90; SWAP16 = 0x9f
    RETURN = 0xf3; REVERT = 0xfd; INVALID = 0xfe

    # Gas cost table
    GAS_COSTS = {
        0x00: 0,    # STOP
        0x01: 3, 0x02: 5, 0x03: 3, 0x04: 5, 0x05: 5,  # Arithmetic
        0x06: 5, 0x07: 5, 0x08: 8, 0x09: 8,
        0x10: 3, 0x11: 3, 0x12: 3, 0x13: 3, 0x14: 3, 0x15: 3, # Comparison
        0x16: 3, 0x17: 3, 0x18: 3, 0x19: 3, # Bitwise
        0x1a: 3, 0x1b: 3, 0x1c: 3, 0x1d: 3,
        0x50: 2,    # POP
        0x51: 3, 0x52: 3, 0x53: 3,  # Memory (base cost, expansion extra)
        0x56: 8, 0x57: 10, 0x58: 2, 0x59: 2, 0x5a: 2, 0x5b: 1,
        0xf3: 0, 0xfd: 0, 0xfe: 0,
    }
```

```
# Storage costs (EIP-2929/3529)
SLOAD_COLD = 2100
SLOAD_WARM = 100
SSTORE_SET = 20000    # Zero to nonzero
SSTORE_RESET = 2900   # Nonzero to nonzero
SSTORE_CLEAR_REFUND = 4800

MOD_256 = 1 << 256

def __init__(self, gas_limit: int = 300000):
    self.stack = EVMStack()
    self.memory = EVMMemory()
    self.storage: Dict[int, int] = {}
    self.warm_storage: set = set()  # EIP-2929 access list
    self.gas_remaining = gas_limit
    self.gas_used = 0
    self.pc = 0
    self.stopped = False
    self.reverted = False
    self.return_data = b""

def _use_gas(self, amount: int):
    if amount > self.gas_remaining:
        raise Exception(f"Out of gas: need {amount}, have {self.gas_
        remaining}")
    self.gas_remaining -= amount
    self.gas_used += amount

def execute(self, bytecode: bytes) -> dict:
    """Execute EVM bytecode and return execution result."""
    try:
        while self.pc < len(bytecode) and not self.stopped:
            opcode = bytecode[self.pc]
            self._execute_opcode(opcode, bytecode)

        return {
            'success': not self.reverted,
            'gas_used': self.gas_used,
```

```
                'gas_remaining': self.gas_remaining,
                'return_data': self.return_data.hex() if self.return_data
                else "",
                'storage': dict(self.storage),
                'stack': list(self.stack.items),
                'memory_size': self.memory.size_bytes,
            }
        except Exception as e:
            return {
                'success': False,
                'gas_used': self.gas_used,
                'error': str(e),
                'storage': dict(self.storage),
                'stack': list(self.stack.items),
            }

    def _execute_opcode(self, opcode: int, bytecode: bytes):
        """Execute a single opcode."""

        # PUSH1-PUSH32: push N bytes as single value
        if 0x60 <= opcode <= 0x7f:
            num_bytes = opcode - 0x5f
            self._use_gas(3)  # VeryLow
            value = int.from_bytes(
                bytecode[self.pc + 1:self.pc + 1 + num_bytes], 'big')
            self.stack.push(value)
            self.pc += 1 + num_bytes
            return

        # DUP1-DUP16
        if 0x80 <= opcode <= 0x8f:
            self._use_gas(3)
            position = opcode - 0x7f
            self.stack.dup(position)
            self.pc += 1
            return
```

```
# SWAP1-SWAP16
if 0x90 <= opcode <= 0x9f:
    self._use_gas(3)
    position = opcode - 0x8f
    self.stack.swap(position)
    self.pc += 1
    return

# Standard opcodes
base_gas = self.GAS_COSTS.get(opcode, 0)
if base_gas > 0:
    self._use_gas(base_gas)

if opcode == self.STOP:
    self.stopped = True
elif opcode == self.ADD:
    a, b = self.stack.pop(), self.stack.pop()
    self.stack.push((a + b) % self.MOD_256)
elif opcode == self.MUL:
    a, b = self.stack.pop(), self.stack.pop()
    self.stack.push((a * b) % self.MOD_256)
elif opcode == self.SUB:
    a, b = self.stack.pop(), self.stack.pop()
    self.stack.push((a - b) % self.MOD_256)
elif opcode == self.DIV:
    a, b = self.stack.pop(), self.stack.pop()
    self.stack.push(a // b if b != 0 else 0)
elif opcode == self.MOD:
    a, b = self.stack.pop(), self.stack.pop()
    self.stack.push(a % b if b != 0 else 0)
elif opcode == self.EXP:
    base, exp = self.stack.pop(), self.stack.pop()
    # EXP gas: 10 + 50 * byte_size(exponent)
    exp_bytes = (exp.bit_length() + 7) // 8
    self._use_gas(10 + 50 * exp_bytes)
    self.stack.push(pow(base, exp, self.MOD_256))
```

```
        elif opcode == self.LT:
            a, b = self.stack.pop(), self.stack.pop()
            self.stack.push(1 if a < b else 0)
        elif opcode == self.GT:
            a, b = self.stack.pop(), self.stack.pop()
            self.stack.push(1 if a > b else 0)
        elif opcode == self.EQ:
            a, b = self.stack.pop(), self.stack.pop()
            self.stack.push(1 if a == b else 0)
        elif opcode == self.ISZERO:
            a = self.stack.pop()
            self.stack.push(1 if a == 0 else 0)
        elif opcode == self.AND:
            a, b = self.stack.pop(), self.stack.pop()
            self.stack.push(a & b)
        elif opcode == self.OR:
            a, b = self.stack.pop(), self.stack.pop()
            self.stack.push(a | b)
        elif opcode == self.XOR:
            a, b = self.stack.pop(), self.stack.pop()
            self.stack.push(a ^ b)
        elif opcode == self.NOT:
            a = self.stack.pop()
            self.stack.push(self.MAX_UINT256 ^ a)
        elif opcode == self.SHL:
            shift, val = self.stack.pop(), self.stack.pop()
            self.stack.push((val << shift) % self.MOD_256 if shift <
            256 else 0)
        elif opcode == self.SHR:
            shift, val = self.stack.pop(), self.stack.pop()
            self.stack.push(val >> shift if shift < 256 else 0)
        elif opcode == self.SHA3:
            offset, length = self.stack.pop(), self.stack.pop()
            # Dynamic gas: 6 * ceil(length/32) + memory expansion
            word_gas = 6 * ((length + 31) // 32)
```

```
        self._use_gas(30 + word_gas)
        mem_gas = self.memory._expand_to(offset, length)
        self._use_gas(mem_gas)
        data = bytes(self.memory.data[offset:offset + length])
        h = hashlib.sha256(data).digest()  # Using SHA-256 as stand-in
        for Keccak
        self.stack.push(int.from_bytes(h, 'big'))
    elif opcode == self.POP:
        self.stack.pop()
    elif opcode == self.MLOAD:
        offset = self.stack.pop()
        value, gas = self.memory.load(offset)
        self._use_gas(gas)
        self.stack.push(value)
    elif opcode == self.MSTORE:
        offset = self.stack.pop()
        value = self.stack.pop()
        gas = self.memory.store(offset, value)
        self._use_gas(gas)
    elif opcode == self.MSTORE8:
        offset = self.stack.pop()
        value = self.stack.pop() & 0xff
        gas = self.memory.store(offset, value, 1)
        self._use_gas(gas)
    elif opcode == self.SLOAD:
        key = self.stack.pop()
        # EIP-2929: cold/warm access
        if key in self.warm_storage:
            self._use_gas(self.SLOAD_WARM)
        else:
            self._use_gas(self.SLOAD_COLD)
            self.warm_storage.add(key)
        self.stack.push(self.storage.get(key, 0))
```

```
        elif opcode == self.SSTORE:
            key = self.stack.pop()
            value = self.stack.pop()
            old_value = self.storage.get(key, 0)
            # Calculate SSTORE gas cost
            if old_value == 0 and value != 0:
                self._use_gas(self.SSTORE_SET)
            elif old_value != 0 and value != 0:
                self._use_gas(self.SSTORE_RESET)
            elif old_value != 0 and value == 0:
                self._use_gas(self.SSTORE_RESET)
            else:
                self._use_gas(self.SLOAD_WARM)
            self.storage[key] = value
            self.warm_storage.add(key)
        elif opcode == self.JUMP:
            dest = self.stack.pop()
            if dest >= len(bytecode) or bytecode[dest] != self.JUMPDEST:
                raise Exception(f"Invalid jump to {dest}")
            self.pc = dest
            return  # Don't increment PC
        elif opcode == self.JUMPI:
            dest = self.stack.pop()
            condition = self.stack.pop()
            if condition != 0:
                if dest >= len(bytecode) or bytecode[dest] != self.
                JUMPDEST:
                    raise Exception(f"Invalid jump to {dest}")
                self.pc = dest
                return
        elif opcode == self.PC:
            self.stack.push(self.pc)
        elif opcode == self.MSIZE:
            self.stack.push(self.memory.size_bytes)
```

```
        elif opcode == self.GAS:
            self.stack.push(self.gas_remaining)
        elif opcode == self.JUMPDEST:
            pass  # Marker only, no operation
        elif opcode == self.RETURN:
            offset = self.stack.pop()
            length = self.stack.pop()
            mem_gas = self.memory._expand_to(offset, length)
            self._use_gas(mem_gas)
            self.return_data = bytes(self.memory.data[offset:offset +
            length])
            self.stopped = True
        elif opcode == self.REVERT:
            offset = self.stack.pop()
            length = self.stack.pop()
            self.return_data = bytes(self.memory.data[offset:offset +
            length])
            self.reverted = True
            self.stopped = True
        elif opcode == self.INVALID:
            raise Exception("INVALID opcode")
        else:
            raise Exception(f"Unimplemented opcode: 0x{opcode:02x}")

        self.pc += 1

# Demonstration programs
print("EVM Execution Demonstrations")
print("=" * 60)

# Program 1: Compute (3 + 5) * 2 = 16
# PUSH1 2, PUSH1 5, PUSH1 3, ADD, MUL, STOP
prog1 = bytes([0x60, 0x02, 0x60, 0x05, 0x60, 0x03, 0x01, 0x02, 0x00])
evm1 = SimpleEVM()
r1 = evm1.execute(prog1)
print(f"Program 1: (3 + 5) * 2")
```

```
print(f"  Result: {r1['stack'][-1] if r1['stack'] else 'empty'}
(expected: 16)")
print(f"  Gas used: {r1['gas_used']}")

# Program 2: Store value 42 at slot 0, load it, double it, store at slot 1
# PUSH1 42, PUSH1 0, SSTORE, PUSH1 0, SLOAD, DUP1, ADD, PUSH1 1,
SSTORE, STOP
prog2 = bytes([
    0x60, 42,      # PUSH1 42
    0x60, 0x00,    # PUSH1 0
    0x55,          # SSTORE (slot 0 = 42)
    0x60, 0x00,    # PUSH1 0
    0x54,          # SLOAD (load slot 0)
    0x80,          # DUP1 (duplicate value)
    0x01,          # ADD (42 + 42 = 84)
    0x60, 0x01,    # PUSH1 1
    0x55,          # SSTORE (slot 1 = 84)
    0x00,          # STOP
])
evm2 = SimpleEVM()
r2 = evm2.execute(prog2)
print(f"\nProgram 2: Store 42, load, double, store 84")
print(f"  Storage: {r2['storage']}")
print(f"  Gas used: {r2['gas_used']} (note: storage writes are expensive)")

# Program 3: Simple loop - sum 1 to 5
# We'll construct this manually using JUMP/JUMPI
prog3 = bytes([
    0x60, 0x00,    # PC 0-1:  PUSH1 0  (sum = 0)
    0x60, 0x01,    # PC 2-3:  PUSH1 1  (counter = 1)
    # Loop start
    0x5b,          # PC 4:    JUMPDEST (loop target)
    0x80,          # PC 5:    DUP1     (copy counter)
    0x60, 0x05,    # PC 6-7:  PUSH1 5  (limit) ← FIXED: was 6, gives
                              sum=21; 5 gives sum=15
                   #          EVM LT: pops top(5) then second(counter)
```

```
                #         result=1 when top < second, i.e. 5 < counter
                #         JUMPI exits when counter > 5 → processes
                          1,2,3,4,5 ✓
    0x10,       # PC 8:   LT
    0x60, 0x16, # PC 9-10: PUSH1 22 (exit JUMPDEST) ← FIXED: was 21
                          (JUMP opcode)
    0x57,       # PC 11:  JUMPI    (exit loop when counter > 5)
    # Loop body
    0x90,       # PC 12:  SWAP1    (bring sum to top)
    0x81,       # PC 13:  DUP2     (copy counter)
    0x01,       # PC 14:  ADD      (sum + counter)
    0x90,       # PC 15:  SWAP1    (put sum back, counter on top)
    0x60, 0x01, # PC 16-17: PUSH1 1
    0x01,       # PC 18:  ADD      (counter + 1)
    0x60, 0x04, # PC 19-20: PUSH1 4 (loop start)
    0x56,       # PC 21:  JUMP     (back to loop)
    # Exit
    0x5b,       # PC 22:  JUMPDEST (exit) ← correct target now
    0x50,       # PC 23:  POP      (remove counter, sum stays on stack)
    0x00,       # PC 24:  STOP
])
evm3 = SimpleEVM()
r3 = evm3.execute(prog3)
print(f"\nProgram 3: Sum of 1 to 5")
print(f"  Result: {r3['stack'][-1] if r3['stack'] else 'empty'}
(expected: 15)")
print(f"  Gas used: {r3['gas_used']}")

evm3 = SimpleEVM()
r3 = evm3.execute(prog3)
print(f"\nProgram 3: Sum of 1 to 5")
print(f"  Result: {r3['stack'][-1] if r3['stack'] else 'empty'}
(expected: 15)")
print(f"  Gas used: {r3['gas_used']}")
```

11.1.3 Gas Mechanics and EIP-1559

Every EVM instruction consumes gas, a unit of account that translates computational effort into economic cost. Without gas, a contract containing an infinite loop would consume every node's CPU forever, halting the entire network. Gas caps each transaction's resource consumption, making denial-of-service attacks expensive rather than free. Before the August 2021 fee market reform, users competed for block space through a sealed-bid auction: each transaction specified a gas price, and miners cherry-picked the highest bidders. This created volatile, unpredictable pricing—users routinely overpaid during congestion because they could not observe competing bids.

EIP-1559, activated in August 2021, introduced a base fee that adjusts algorithmically based on block utilization, plus an optional priority fee (tip) to incentivize faster inclusion.

Table 11-1. *EIP-1559 Fee Structure*

Component	Who Pays	Who Receives	Determined By
Base fee	Transaction sender	Burned (destroyed)	Protocol algorithm based on block fullness
Priority fee (tip)	Transaction sender	Block proposer	User choice (incentivizes inclusion)
Max fee	User's maximum willingness to pay	N/A	Set by user as ceiling

The effective fee per gas is: min(max_fee, base_fee + priority_fee). The base fee adjusts each block:

```
def eip1559_simulation(blocks: int, demand_pattern: list) -> list:
    """
    Simulate EIP-1559 base fee dynamics.

    The base fee adjusts up/down by at most 12.5% per block,
    targeting 50% block utilization (15M gas of 30M limit).
    """
    GAS_TARGET = 15_000_000       # Target: 50% of limit
    GAS_LIMIT = 30_000_000        # Maximum block size
    MAX_CHANGE_DENOM = 8          # 1/8 = 12.5% max change per block
```

```
base_fee = 30_000_000_000   # Starting: 30 Gwei
history = []

for block in range(blocks):
    # Simulate demand (gas used this block)
    demand_idx = block % len(demand_pattern)
    gas_used = min(int(demand_pattern[demand_idx] * GAS_LIMIT),
    GAS_LIMIT)

    # Calculate fees
    total_base_fees = base_fee * gas_used  # Total burned
    utilization = gas_used / GAS_LIMIT

    history.append({
        'block': block,
        'base_fee_gwei': base_fee / 1e9,
        'gas_used': gas_used,
        'utilization': utilization,
        'burned_eth': total_base_fees / 1e18,
    })

    # Adjust base fee for next block
    if gas_used > GAS_TARGET:
        # Block was more than half full: increase
        gas_delta = gas_used - GAS_TARGET
        fee_delta = max(
            base_fee * gas_delta // GAS_TARGET // MAX_CHANGE_DENOM,
            1
        )
        base_fee += fee_delta
    elif gas_used < GAS_TARGET:
        # Block was less than half full: decrease
        gas_delta = GAS_TARGET - gas_used
        fee_delta = base_fee * gas_delta // GAS_TARGET // MAX_
        CHANGE_DENOM
        base_fee = max(base_fee - fee_delta, 1)

return history
```

```
# Simulate demand spike and recovery
demand = (
    [0.5] * 5 +   # Normal load
    [0.95] * 10 + # Spike (near-full blocks)
    [0.5] * 5 +   # Recovery
    [0.2] * 5 +   # Low demand
    [0.5] * 5     # Return to normal
)

history = eip1559_simulation(30, demand)
print("\nEIP-1559 Base Fee Simulation")
print("=" * 65)
print(f"{'Block':>6} {'Base Fee (Gwei)':>16} {'Utilization':>13} {'Burned
ETH':>12}")
print("-" * 50)
for h in history:
    bar = "█" * int(h['utilization'] * 20)
    print(f"  {h['block']:4d}  {h['base_fee_gwei']:14.2f}  "
          f"{h['utilization']:11.1%}  {h['burned_eth']:10.6f}  {bar}")
```

Table 11-2. *Gas Costs for Common EVM Operations*

Operation	Opcode	Gas Cost	Category
ADD, SUB	0x01, 0x03	3	Arithmetic (VeryLow)
MUL, DIV	0x02, 0x04	5	Arithmetic (Low)
EXP	0x0a	10 + 50/byte	Arithmetic (dynamic)
SHA3/Keccak	0x20	30 + 6/word	Cryptographic
SLOAD (warm)	0x54	100	Storage read (cached)
SLOAD (cold)	0x54	2,100	Storage read (first access)
SSTORE (new slot)	0x55	20,000	Storage write (create)
SSTORE (update)	0x55	2,900	Storage write (modify)
CALL (warm)	0xf1	100	External call

(*continued*)

Table 11-2. (*continued*)

Operation	Opcode	Gas Cost	Category
CALL (cold)	0xf1	2,600	External call (first)
CREATE	0xf0	32,000	Deploy contract
BALANCE (cold)	0x31	2,600	Account access
Simple transfer	-	21,000	Base transaction

11.1.4 WebAssembly for Blockchain

The EVM was purpose-built in 2014 for a world that did not yet exist. Its design choices—256-bit words, a stack-only architecture, no native support for common data structures—made sense for a platform whose primary operations were cryptographic. But as smart contract applications expanded beyond simple token transfers into compute-heavy territory (gaming, machine learning, complex financial simulations), the EVM's performance limitations became apparent. WebAssembly offers an alternative execution target. Born from a collaboration between browser vendors who needed a portable, high-performance compilation target for the web, WASM provides a register-based instruction set with native 32-bit and 64-bit integer operations, structured control flow, and a memory model that maps efficiently to modern hardware. Compilers for Rust, C++, Go, and dozens of other languages can target WASM, opening smart contract development to a vastly larger developer base than Solidity alone serves.

WASM was designed by a W3C working group including engineers from Apple, Google, Microsoft, and Mozilla. It has been tested across billions of browser installations and has a mature specification, toolchain, and formal semantics.

Table 11-3. EVM vs. WASM Comparison

Property	EVM	WASM
Word size	256-bit	32/64-bit native
Architecture	Stack-based (untyped)	Stack-based (typed)
Source languages	Solidity, Vyper (specialized)	Rust, C/C++, AssemblyScript, Go (general)
Performance	~100-1000x slower than native	~1.2-2x slower than native
Crypto operations	Native 256-bit math	Requires library (slower for crypto)
Formal verification	Growing tooling	Established tooling
Gas metering	Built into opcodes	Injected at compile time
Adoption	Ethereum and EVM-compatible chains	Polkadot, NEAR, Cosmos (CosmWasm), Dfinity

The performance gap is significant. Benchmarks consistently show WASM executing 10-100x faster than the EVM for compute-intensive operations. The EVM's 256-bit word size, while convenient for cryptographic operations, introduces substantial overhead for operations that would naturally use 32-bit or 64-bit integers (loop counters, array indices, conditional logic).

However, the EVM has advantages for blockchain-specific operations. Its native 256-bit arithmetic aligns with hash outputs and Ethereum addresses. The EVM's ecosystem (Solidity, development tools, auditing expertise, deployed contracts) represents substantial network effects that WASM-based platforms must overcome.

11.1.5 Parallel Transaction Processing

Sequential execution is the default in both the EVM and WASM runtimes. Each transaction modifies state, and the next transaction operates on the modified state. This creates a throughput bottleneck: even with a fast VM, processing is limited to one transaction at a time.

Parallel execution allows multiple transactions to execute simultaneously on different processor cores but requires detecting and handling state conflicts.

```
from dataclasses import dataclass
```

```
from typing import Set, List, Optional

@dataclass
class ParallelTransaction:
    tx_id: int
    read_set: Set[str]    # State keys this transaction reads
    write_set: Set[str]   # State keys this transaction writes
    gas_limit: int = 21000

def detect_conflict(tx_a: ParallelTransaction,
                    tx_b: ParallelTransaction) -> Tuple[bool, str]:
    """
    Detect state conflicts between two transactions.

    Conflicts occur when:
    - Write-Write: both transactions write to the same key
    - Read-Write: one reads a key the other writes

    Read-Read is safe: multiple transactions can read the same state.
    """
    ww = tx_a.write_set & tx_b.write_set
    if ww:
        return True, f"Write-Write conflict on {ww}"

    rw_a = tx_a.read_set & tx_b.write_set
    if rw_a:
        return True, f"Read-Write conflict: A reads, B writes {rw_a}"

    rw_b = tx_b.read_set & tx_a.write_set
    if rw_b:
        return True, f"Read-Write conflict: B reads, A writes {rw_b}"

    return False, "No conflict"

def schedule_parallel(transactions: List[ParallelTransaction]) ->
List[List[int]]:
    """
    Greedy parallel scheduling: batch non-conflicting transactions.

    Each batch can execute in parallel. Batches execute sequentially.
```

```
    Optimal scheduling is NP-hard; this greedy approach is practical.
    """
    batches = []
    remaining = list(range(len(transactions)))

    while remaining:
        batch = []
        batch_reads: Set[str] = set()
        batch_writes: Set[str] = set()
        next_remaining = []

        for idx in remaining:
            tx = transactions[idx]

            # Check conflict with current batch
            has_conflict = (
                bool(tx.write_set & batch_writes) or   # WW
                bool(tx.write_set & batch_reads) or    # WR
                bool(tx.read_set & batch_writes)       # RW
            )

            if has_conflict:
                next_remaining.append(idx)
            else:
                batch.append(idx)
                batch_reads |= tx.read_set
                batch_writes |= tx.write_set

        if batch:
            batches.append(batch)
        remaining = next_remaining

    return batches

# Demonstrate parallel scheduling
transactions = [
    ParallelTransaction(0, {"bal_A"}, {"bal_A", "bal_B"}),
    # A sends to B
```

```
    ParallelTransaction(1, {"bal_C"}, {"bal_C", "bal_D"}),
    # C sends to D
    ParallelTransaction(2, {"bal_E"}, {"bal_E", "bal_F"}),
    # E sends to F
    ParallelTransaction(3, {"bal_A"}, {"bal_A", "bal_G"}),
    # A sends to G (conflicts with 0)
    ParallelTransaction(4, {"bal_B"}, {"bal_B", "bal_H"}),
    # B sends to H (conflicts with 0)
    ParallelTransaction(5, {"bal_I"}, {"bal_I", "bal_J"}),
    # I sends to J (independent)
    ParallelTransaction(6, {"bal_C", "bal_D"}, {"bal_K"}),
    # Read C,D, write K (conflicts with 1)
]

batches = schedule_parallel(transactions)
print("\nParallel Transaction Scheduling")
print("=" * 55)
for i, batch in enumerate(batches):
    tx_ids = [transactions[idx].tx_id for idx in batch]
    writes = set()
    for idx in batch:
        writes |= transactions[idx].write_set
    print(f"  Batch {i}: TX {tx_ids} (writes: {writes})")

sequential_time = len(transactions)
parallel_time = len(batches)
speedup = sequential_time / parallel_time
print(f"\n  Sequential: {sequential_time} steps")
print(f"  Parallel:   {parallel_time} batches")
print(f"  Speedup:    {speedup:.1f}x")
print(f"  Utilization: {sequential_time / (parallel_time * max(len(b) for b
in batches)):.0%}")
```

11.1.6 Summary

Blockchain virtual machines enable deterministic, sandboxed program execution across all network nodes. The EVM's 256-bit stack architecture serves the blockchain domain well despite performance limitations. WASM offers dramatically better performance and broader language support. Gas metering, whether built-in (EVM) or injected (WASM), is the mechanism that prevents resource abuse.

Key takeaways:

- **The EVM** is a stack-based VM with 256-bit words, a 1024-depth stack, expandable memory, and persistent storage. Its design prioritizes determinism and crypto-native operations over raw performance.
- Gas caps resource consumption per transaction, making DoS attacks expensive. The EIP-1559 reform replaced first-price auctions with an algorithmic base fee that adjusts ±12.5% per block, targeting 50% utilization. The base fee is burned; only tips go to proposers.
- **Storage is expensive by design**: 20,000 gas for a new slot vs. 3 gas for an addition. This reflects the permanent burden storage imposes on all full nodes.
- **WASM** offers 10-100x performance improvement with broader language support. The trade-off is loss of native 256-bit arithmetic and the EVM's extensive ecosystem.
- **EIP-2929 access lists** distinguish cold (first-touch, 2100 gas) from warm (subsequent, 100 gas) storage access. This better reflects the actual cost of state access patterns.
- **Parallel execution** requires conflict detection on read/write sets. Greedy scheduling groups non-conflicting transactions into parallel batches. Real-world speedup depends on workload conflict density.
- Determinism is absolute: any execution divergence between nodes causes consensus failure. This forbids floating-point arithmetic, external I/O, and non-deterministic system calls.

EVM: 256-bit stack machine; max depth 1024; bytecode execution; native big-integer arithmetic—Gas costs: ADD 3, MUL 5, SLOAD cold 2100, SLOAD warm 100, SSTORE new 20000, SSTORE update 2900—EIP-1559: base fee adjusts ±12.5% per block targeting

50% utilization; base fee burned, tip to proposer—Memory cost: 3 gas per word + quadratic expansion penalty (prevents memory DoS)—WASM: 10-100x faster than EVM; supports Rust/C++; adopted by Polkadot, NEAR, Cosmos—EIP-2929: cold/warm storage access distinguishes first touch from subsequent access—Parallel execution: conflict detection via read/write sets; greedy batch scheduling; speedup depends on conflict rate—Determinism constraint: no floating point, no external I/O, no randomness, bounded execution

11.1.7 Exercises

Problem 1 (Basic): Explain why the EVM uses 256-bit words instead of standard 64-bit integers. What computational advantages does this provide for blockchain operations? What is the performance cost?

Problem 2 (Calculation): A smart contract function executes: 500 ADDs, 100 MULs, reads 20 storage slots (10 cold, 10 warm), writes 5 slots (3 new, 2 updates), and hashes 64 bytes. Calculate the total gas cost. What percentage comes from storage operations?

Problem 3 (Implementation): Extend the SimpleEVM to support the CALLDATALOAD and CALLDATASIZE opcodes. Write a bytecode program that reads a 32-byte argument from calldata and stores it.

Problem 4 (Analysis): Simulate EIP-1559 base fee behavior during a 100-block demand spike (100% utilization). How many blocks does it take for the base fee to: (a) double, (b) 10x, (c) reach the maximum practical level? Plot the progression.

Problem 5 (Design): Design a gas pricing scheme for a WASM-based blockchain. How would you meter WASM instructions? What should memory allocation, table access, and host function calls cost? Justify your pricing.

Problem 6 (Theory): Why must blockchain VMs be deterministic? Construct a specific scenario where non-deterministic execution (e.g., floating-point rounding differences) would cause a consensus failure.

Problem 7 (Comparative): Compare the developer experience of Solidity (EVM) versus Rust (CosmWasm) for smart contract development. Consider: safety guarantees, tooling maturity, audit ecosystem, testing frameworks, and learning curve.

Problem 8 (Critical Thinking): Should the Ethereum ecosystem migrate from EVM to WASM, maintain both, or stay with EVM? Consider backwards compatibility, ecosystem investment, performance needs, and migration costs.

Problem 9 (Advanced): Implement an optimistic parallel execution engine: execute all transactions in parallel, detect conflicts by comparing read/write sets with actual state modifications, and re-execute conflicting transactions sequentially. Measure speedup vs. the greedy scheduling approach.

Problem 10 (Research): Study Solana's Sealevel parallel runtime. How does it declare transaction dependencies? What performance improvement does it achieve over sequential execution? How does the account-locking mechanism handle conflicts?

(Solutions in Appendix D)

11.1.8 Further Reading

On the EVM: The Ethereum Yellow Paper provides the definitive formal specification. The evm.codes website offers an interactive opcode reference with gas costs.

On EIP-1559: Tim Roughgarden's "Transaction Fee Mechanism Design for the Ethereum Blockchain" (2021) provides game-theoretic analysis of the fee market.

On WASM for Blockchain: The CosmWasm documentation covers WASM smart contract development. The NEAR Protocol documentation describes their WASM runtime.

On Parallel Execution: Solana's Sealevel documentation describes their parallel runtime. The Aptos Block-STM paper formalizes optimistic parallel execution.

CHAPTER 12

Transaction Models and MEV

12.1 Transaction Lifecycle and Maximal Extractable Value

This chapter traces a transaction from construction to finality, covers mempool dynamics, MEV strategies (arbitrage, sandwiching, liquidations), the Flashbots and MEV-boost supply chain, mitigation approaches from encrypted mempools to batch auctions, and how MEV is measured in practice. After this chapter, you'll have a handle on:

- How a transaction moves through the system, from the moment it's built on someone's machine all the way to finality
- What goes on inside the mempool. Ordering, replacement, and eviction. The stuff that matters when transactions are sitting there waiting
- MEV (Maximal Extractable Value), including real numbers on how much is being pulled out and through what strategies
- The big MEV plays: DEX arbitrage, sandwich attacks, liquidations, JIT liquidity
- Flashbots, MEV-boost, and how the private transaction pipeline works these days
- The various attempts to deal with MEV: fair ordering, encrypted mempools, threshold encryption, batch auctions

N. Savant, *Blockchain Foundations*, https://doi.org/10.1007/979-8-8688-2891-1_12

- Proposer-Builder Separation and what it does to market structure
- How people measure MEV, what the numbers look like, and why they matter economically

12.1.1 Transaction Lifecycle

A transaction goes through a pretty specific set of stages between the moment you create it and the moment it's permanently baked into the chain. Worth understanding each one, because MEV extraction happens at very particular points in this pipeline, and the various mitigation strategies each target different stages.

Stage 1: Construction and Signing

The user puts together a transaction: recipient address, how much to send, calldata if it's a contract interaction, gas limit, and fee parameters. With EIP-1559, that means setting a max fee per gas and a priority fee (the tip). Then they sign it with their private key using ECDSA on secp256k1. You get a 65-byte signature (r, s, v) that authorizes the state change without giving away the key itself.

At this point the transaction only exists on the user's device. Nothing has gone to the network yet. The wallet software estimates gas by simulating the transaction against the current state and checking fee oracles for the base fee and a reasonable priority fee.

Stage 2: Submission and Propagation

The signed transaction goes to a node via JSON-RPC (usually eth_sendRawTransaction). That node checks the basics: is the signature valid, does the sender have enough balance to cover value plus gas_limit times max_fee_per_gas, does the nonce line up with what's expected.

If it passes, the node drops it into its local mempool and forwards it to peers through gossip. Within a couple seconds it's typically reached most of the network. And this is where MEV exposure starts. Once a transaction hits the public mempool, anyone watching can see exactly what it does.

Stage 3: Mempool Residence

The mempool is just a per-node data structure holding valid transactions that haven't made it into a block yet. Every node runs its own mempool independently. There's no single global one. A transaction sits there until it gets included in a block, evicted because the pool is full, replaced by a higher-fee transaction with the same nonce, or invalidated because the sender's state changed (like their balance dropping below what the transaction needs).

While transactions sit in the mempool, they're completely visible. MEV searchers run monitoring infrastructure specifically to watch this. They're looking at pending transactions for profitable opportunities: arbitrage paths opened up by big swaps, positions about to get liquidated, and transactions ripe for sandwiching.

Stage 4: Block Construction and Inclusion

A block producer (validator under PoS, miner under PoW) picks transactions out of their mempool, decides on an order, and proposes the block. With MEV-boost in the picture, the process gets more layered:

1. Searchers spot MEV opportunities and build bundles, which are ordered sets of transactions meant to capture value atomically
2. Builders take those bundles from searchers, mix them with regular mempool transactions, and assemble full blocks
3. Builders bid for the right to construct the block, paying the proposer for the privilege
4. The proposer picks whichever builder's block pays the most, routing through a relay

Transaction ordering inside the block is entirely up to the builder (or the proposer directly, if MEV-boost isn't being used). That ordering power is where all of MEV comes from.

```
import hashlib
import time
from dataclasses import dataclass, field
from typing import Dict, List, Optional, Tuple, Set
from collections import defaultdict
```

```
@dataclass
class Transaction:
    tx_hash: str
    sender: str
    recipient: str
    value: int                      # In Wei
    gas_limit: int = 21000
    max_fee_per_gas: int = 0        # EIP-1559
    max_priority_fee: int = 0       # EIP-1559 tip
    nonce: int = 0
    data: bytes = b""
    timestamp: float = field(default_factory=time.time)

    def effective_tip(self, base_fee: int) -> int:
        """EIP-1559 effective priority fee."""
        if self.max_fee_per_gas < base_fee:
            return 0
        return min(self.max_priority_fee, self.max_fee_per_gas - base_fee)

    def max_cost(self) -> int:
        """Maximum possible cost of this transaction."""
        return self.value + self.gas_limit * self.max_fee_per_gas

class Mempool:
    """
    Transaction mempool with EIP-1559 ordering, replacement,
    nonce tracking, and eviction policies.
    """

    MAX_POOL_SIZE = 5000
    MAX_PER_SENDER = 16
    REPLACEMENT_BUMP_PCT = 10  # Minimum 10% fee increase for replacement

    def __init__(self):
        self.transactions: Dict[str, Transaction] = {}
        self.by_sender: Dict[str, Dict[int, Transaction]] =
        defaultdict(dict)
        self.pending_nonce: Dict[str, int] = {}
```

```
def add(self, tx: Transaction) -> Tuple[bool, str]:
    """
    Add transaction to mempool with full validation.

    Checks:
    1. Gas limit minimum (21000 for simple transfer)
    2. Per-sender transaction limit
    3. Nonce replacement with fee bump requirement
    4. Pool size eviction if full
    """
    if tx.gas_limit < 21000:
        return False, "Gas limit below minimum"

    sender_txs = self.by_sender[tx.sender]

    # Check for nonce replacement
    if tx.nonce in sender_txs:
        existing = sender_txs[tx.nonce]
        min_new_fee = existing.max_priority_fee * (100 + self.
        REPLACEMENT_BUMP_PCT) // 100
        if tx.max_priority_fee < min_new_fee:
            return False, (f"Replacement fee {tx.max_priority_
            fee} below "
                          f"minimum {min_new_fee} (need +{self.
                          REPLACEMENT_BUMP_PCT}%)")
        # Remove old transaction
        self.transactions.pop(existing.tx_hash, None)
        del sender_txs[tx.nonce]

    # Per-sender limit
    if len(sender_txs) >= self.MAX_PER_SENDER and tx.nonce not in
    sender_txs:
        return False, f"Sender limit reached ({self.MAX_PER_SENDER})"

    # Pool full: evict lowest priority
    while len(self.transactions) >= self.MAX_POOL_SIZE:
        self._evict_lowest()
```

```
        # Accept
        self.transactions[tx.tx_hash] = tx
        sender_txs[tx.nonce] = tx
        return True, "Accepted"

    def remove(self, tx_hash: str):
        """Remove a transaction (e.g., after block inclusion)."""
        tx = self.transactions.pop(tx_hash, None)
        if tx and tx.nonce in self.by_sender.get(tx.sender, {}):
            del self.by_sender[tx.sender][tx.nonce]

    def _evict_lowest(self):
        if not self.transactions:
            return
        worst = min(self.transactions.values(), key=lambda t: t.max_
        priority_fee)
        self.remove(worst.tx_hash)

    def get_pending(self, sender: str) -> List[Transaction]:
        """Get all pending transactions for a sender, sorted by nonce."""
        txs = list(self.by_sender.get(sender, {}).values())
        return sorted(txs, key=lambda t: t.nonce)

    def build_block(self, gas_limit: int, base_fee: int,
                on_chain_nonces: Optional[Dict[str, int]] = None
                ) -> Tuple[List[Transaction], dict]:
    """
    Greedy block construction algorithm.
    Selects highest-tip transactions while respecting:
    - Block gas limit
    - Nonce ordering per sender (both on-chain and within block)
    - Base fee minimum
    Args:
        gas_limit:        Maximum gas this block can consume
        base_fee:         Current EIP-1559 base fee in Wei
        on_chain_nonces:  Dict of sender -> current on-chain nonce.
                          If None, first-tx nonce validation is skipped
```

```
                        (with a warning). Production must always
                        pass this.
        """
        if on_chain_nonces is None:
            print("WARNING: on_chain_nonces not provided - "
                  "first transaction per sender will NOT be validated "
                  "against chain state. Invalid nonces may be included.")
            on_chain_nonces = {}
        eligible = [tx for tx in self.transactions.values()
                    if tx.effective_tip(base_fee) > 0]
        eligible.sort(key=lambda t: t.effective_tip(base_fee), reverse=True)
        selected = []
        gas_used = 0
        total_tips = 0
        total_base_fees = 0
        sender_next_nonce: Dict[str, int] = {}
        for tx in eligible:
            if gas_used + tx.gas_limit > gas_limit:
                continue
            if tx.sender in sender_next_nonce:
                # Enforce ordering relative to earlier txs in this block
                if tx.nonce != sender_next_nonce[tx.sender]:
                    continue
            else:
                # First transaction for this sender in this block:
                # validate nonce against on-chain state
                expected = on_chain_nonces.get(tx.sender, None)
                if expected is not None and tx.nonce != expected:
                    # Nonce mismatch vs chain state - skip this tx
                    # (e.g. mempool has stale tx from a previous block)
                    continue
            selected.append(tx)
            gas_used += tx.gas_limit
            tip = tx.effective_tip(base_fee)
            total_tips += tip * tx.gas_limit
```

```
        total_base_fees += base_fee * tx.gas_limit
        sender_next_nonce[tx.sender] = tx.nonce + 1
    stats = {
        'tx_count': len(selected),
        'gas_used': gas_used,
        'gas_utilization': gas_used / gas_limit,
        'total_tips_gwei': total_tips,
        'total_base_fees_gwei': total_base_fees,
        'burned_eth': total_base_fees / 1e18,
        'proposer_revenue_eth': total_tips / 1e18,
    }
    return selected, stats
Also update the demo call:
# Build a block – pass on-chain nonces so first-tx validation works
# In this demo all senders start at nonce 0
on_chain_nonces = {sender: 0 for sender in senders}
block_txs, stats = pool.build_block(block_gas, base_fee,
                                    on_chain_nonces=on_chain_nonces)
# Demonstration
pool = Mempool()

# Simulate realistic transaction mix
import random
random.seed(42)

senders = [f"user_{i}" for i in range(50)]
tx_count = 0
for sender in senders:
    num_txs = random.randint(1, 4)
    for nonce in range(num_txs):
        tx = Transaction(
            tx_hash=f"tx_{tx_count}",
            sender=sender,
            recipient=f"recipient_{random.randint(0, 99)}",
            value=random.randint(0, 10**18),
```

```
            gas_limit=random.choice([21000, 50000, 100000, 200000]),
            max_fee_per_gas=random.randint(20, 200) * 10**9,
            max_priority_fee=random.randint(1, 30) * 10**9,
            nonce=nonce,
        )
        pool.add(tx)
        tx_count += 1

print("Mempool Simulation")
print("=" * 60)
print(f"Transactions in mempool: {len(pool.transactions)}")
print(f"Unique senders: {len(pool.by_sender)}")

# Build a block
base_fee = 30 * 10**9  # 30 Gwei
block_gas = 30_000_000  # 30M gas limit
block_txs, stats = pool.build_block(block_gas, base_fee)

print(f"\nBlock Construction (base_fee=30 Gwei, limit=30M gas):")
print(f"  Transactions included: {stats['tx_count']}")
print(f"  Gas used: {stats['gas_used']:,} ({stats['gas_
utilization']:.1%})")
print(f"  Proposer revenue (tips): {stats['proposer_revenue_
eth']:.6f} ETH")
print(f"  Burned (base fees): {stats['burned_eth']:.6f} ETH")

# Show top 5 transactions by tip
print(f"\nTop 5 transactions by effective tip:")
sorted_block = sorted(block_txs, key=lambda t: t.effective_tip(base_fee),
reverse=True)
for tx in sorted_block[:5]:
    tip = tx.effective_tip(base_fee)
    print(f"  {tx.tx_hash}: tip={tip/10**9:.1f} Gwei, gas={tx.gas_
    limit:,}")
```

12.1.2 Maximal Extractable Value (MEV)

MEV is the maximum value you can squeeze out of block production on top of normal block rewards and gas fees, by including, excluding, or reordering transactions. The term started as "Miner Extractable Value" in Daian et al.'s "Flash Boys 2.0" paper back in 2019. Got renamed to "Maximal Extractable Value" after Ethereum moved to PoS.

MEV isn't a bug. It's not an exploit either, not in the usual sense. It's a structural property of any system where the person building blocks gets to choose the transaction order, and those transactions have state-dependent outcomes. As long as ordering affects who gets what, whoever controls the order can extract surplus. That's just how it works.

MEV Taxonomy

DEX arbitrage is the bread and butter, roughly 40-50% of all extracted MEV. Same token pair, different prices on two exchanges. Buy on the cheap one, sell on the expensive one, single atomic transaction. This type of MEV is actually useful. It pushes prices into alignment across markets, better price discovery for everyone.

Sandwich attacks are the nasty ones, about 20-30% of total MEV, and they're the most damaging to regular users. The attacker sees a big pending swap in the mempool, shoves a buy order in front of it to move the price, lets the victim execute at that worse price, and then drops a sell order right after to pocket the difference. The victim ends up paying more than they should have.

Liquidations make up maybe 10-20% of MEV. Lending protocols like Aave and Compound require borrowers to keep collateral above a certain ratio. Collateral drops below threshold; anyone can liquidate and claim a bonus, usually 5-10% of the collateral. Searchers race to be first.

Just-in-Time liquidity, or JIT, is newer. A searcher drops concentrated liquidity into a Uniswap V3 pool right before a big swap goes through (earning fees from that swap), then pulls the liquidity right back out. They collect trading fees without sitting there exposed to price risk.

Backrunning is simpler. You place your transaction immediately after someone else's to catch whatever opportunity their trade created, like an arbitrage that opens up after a big price-moving swap.

```
import math
from dataclasses import dataclass

@dataclass
class ConstantProductPool:
    """
    Constant-product AMM (Uniswap V2 style).

    Invariant: reserve_x * reserve_y = k (constant)
    Price of X in terms of Y: reserve_y / reserve_x
    """
    reserve_x: float
    reserve_y: float
    fee_rate: float = 0.003  # 0.3% swap fee (Uniswap V2 default)

    @property
    def price(self) -> float:
        """Spot price of X in terms of Y."""
        return self.reserve_y / self.reserve_x

    @property
    def k(self) -> float:
        return self.reserve_x * self.reserve_y

    def quote_x_to_y(self, amount_x: float) -> float:
        """Quote: how much Y for selling amount_x of X (no state
        change)."""
        effective = amount_x * (1 - self.fee_rate)
        new_rx = self.reserve_x + effective
        new_ry = self.k / new_rx
        return self.reserve_y - new_ry

    def quote_y_to_x(self, amount_y: float) -> float:
        """Quote: how much X for selling amount_y of Y."""
        effective = amount_y * (1 - self.fee_rate)
        new_ry = self.reserve_y + effective
        new_rx = self.k / new_ry
        return self.reserve_x - new_rx
```

```
    def swap_x_to_y(self, amount_x: float) -> float:
        """
        Execute swap: sell X, receive Y. Modifies pool state.
        How AMM fees work:
        - Output (out_y) is computed on reduced effective input: amount_x *
          (1 - fee)
        - But the FULL amount_x enters reserve_x – the fee stays in the pool
        - This grows k slightly on every swap (fee accumulates for LPs)
        - Previous code added only amount_x*(1-fee) to reserve_x – fee
          disappeared
        """
        out_y = self.quote_x_to_y(amount_x)
        self.reserve_x += amount_x   # Full amount enters pool – fee captured
        implicitly
        self.reserve_y -= out_y
        return out_y
def swap_y_to_x(self, amount_y: float) -> float:
        """
        Execute swap: sell Y, receive X. Modifies pool state.
        Same fee logic as swap_x_to_y – full input enters pool,
        fee is captured implicitly through reduced output calculation.
        """
        out_x = self.quote_y_to_x(amount_y)
        self.reserve_y += amount_y   # Full amount enters pool – fee captured
        implicitly
        self.reserve_x -= out_x
        return out_x

        def price_impact_pct(self, amount_x: float) -> float:
            """Price impact of selling amount_x as percentage."""
            spot = self.price
            output = self.quote_x_to_y(amount_x)
            effective_price = output / amount_x if amount_x > 0 else spot
            return ((spot - effective_price) / spot) * 100
```

```
    def clone(self) -> 'ConstantProductPool':
        """Create an independent copy of this pool."""
        return ConstantProductPool(self.reserve_x, self.reserve_y, self.
        fee_rate)

def find_optimal_sandwich(pool_rx: float, pool_ry: float,
                          victim_amount: float,
                          fee_rate: float = 0.003) -> dict:
    """
    Find the optimal sandwich attack parameters using ternary search.

    The attacker's profit function is concave in frontrun size:
    - Too small frontrun: insufficient price movement to profit
    - Too large frontrun: excessive slippage on attacker's own trades
    - Optimal: maximizes (backrun_revenue - frontrun_cost)

    Returns detailed attack analysis.
    """
    def compute_profit(frontrun_x: float) -> Tuple[float, dict]:
        pool = ConstantProductPool(pool_rx, pool_ry, fee_rate)

        # Step 1: Attacker frontruns (buys Y with X)
        attacker_y = pool.swap_x_to_y(frontrun_x)
        price_after_front = pool.price

        # Step 2: Victim swaps (buys Y with X at worse price)
        victim_y = pool.swap_x_to_y(victim_amount)
        price_after_victim = pool.price

        # Step 3: Attacker backruns (sells Y for X)
        attacker_x_back = pool.swap_y_to_x(attacker_y)

        profit = attacker_x_back - frontrun_x

        return profit, {
            'frontrun': frontrun_x,
            'attacker_y': attacker_y,
            'victim_y': victim_y,
            'attacker_x_back': attacker_x_back,
```

```
            'profit': profit,
            'price_after_front': price_after_front,
            'price_after_victim': price_after_victim,
            'final_price': pool.price,
        }

    # Ternary search for optimal frontrun amount
    lo = 0.0
    hi = victim_amount * 5  # Search up to 5x victim size

    for _ in range(100):  # Sufficient precision
        m1 = lo + (hi - lo) / 3
        m2 = hi - (hi - lo) / 3
        p1, _ = compute_profit(m1)
        p2, _ = compute_profit(m2)
        if p1 < p2:
            lo = m1
        else:
            hi = m2

    optimal_frontrun = (lo + hi) / 2
    best_profit, details = compute_profit(optimal_frontrun)

    # Compute victim's loss
    clean_pool = ConstantProductPool(pool_rx, pool_ry, fee_rate)
    victim_expected = clean_pool.swap_x_to_y(victim_amount)
    victim_loss = victim_expected - details['victim_y']

    return {
        'optimal_frontrun': optimal_frontrun,
        'attacker_profit': best_profit,
        'victim_expected_output': victim_expected,
        'victim_actual_output': details['victim_y'],
        'victim_loss': victim_loss,
        'victim_loss_pct': (victim_loss / victim_expected) * 100 if victim_
        expected > 0 else 0,
        'attacker_roi_pct': (best_profit / optimal_frontrun) * 100 if
        optimal_frontrun > 0 else 0,
```

```
        'price_impact_from_front': details['price_after_front'],
        'initial_price': pool_ry / pool_rx,
    }

def simulate_arbitrage(pool_a_rx: float, pool_a_ry: float,
                       pool_b_rx: float, pool_b_ry: float,
                       fee_rate: float = 0.003) -> dict:
    """
    Find optimal arbitrage between two constant-product pools.

    If price_A < price_B: buy on A, sell on B.
    Profit = amount received on B - amount spent on A.
    """
    pool_a = ConstantProductPool(pool_a_rx, pool_a_ry, fee_rate)
    pool_b = ConstantProductPool(pool_b_rx, pool_b_ry, fee_rate)

    price_a = pool_a.price
    price_b = pool_b.price

    if abs(price_a - price_b) / max(price_a, price_b) < 0.001:
        return {'profitable': False, 'reason': 'Prices too close'}

    # Determine direction
    if price_a < price_b:
        # Buy X on A (sell Y), sell X on B (buy Y)
        # This means: swap Y->X on pool_a, then swap X->Y on pool_b
        direction = "Buy on A, sell on B"
        buy_pool, sell_pool = pool_a, pool_b
    else:
        direction = "Buy on B, sell on A"
        buy_pool, sell_pool = pool_b, pool_a

    # Binary search for optimal trade size
    best_profit = 0
    best_amount = 0

    lo, hi = 0.0, min(buy_pool.reserve_y, sell_pool.reserve_x) * 0.5
    for _ in range(100):
        mid = (lo + hi) / 2
```

```
        # Test with mid amount of Y spent on buying pool
        test_buy = buy_pool.clone()
        test_sell = sell_pool.clone()

        x_received = test_buy.swap_y_to_x(mid)
        y_received = test_sell.swap_x_to_y(x_received)
        profit = y_received - mid

        if profit > best_profit:
            best_profit = profit
            best_amount = mid

        # Check gradient
        test_buy2 = buy_pool.clone()
        test_sell2 = sell_pool.clone()
        x2 = test_buy2.swap_y_to_x(mid + 1)
        y2 = test_sell2.swap_x_to_y(x2)
        profit2 = y2 - (mid + 1)

        if profit2 > profit:
            lo = mid
        else:
            hi = mid

    return {
        'profitable': best_profit > 0,
        'direction': direction,
        'optimal_input_y': best_amount,
        'profit_y': best_profit,
        'price_a': price_a,
        'price_b': price_b,
        'price_spread_pct': abs(price_a - price_b) / min(price_a,
        price_b) * 100,
    }

# === Sandwich Attack Analysis ===
print("MEV Analysis: Sandwich Attacks")
print("=" * 65)
```

```
# Pool: 10M USDC / 5000 ETH (ETH = $2000)
pool_rx = 5000.0   # ETH
pool_ry = 10_000_000.0  # USDC

print(f"Pool: {pool_rx:.0f} ETH / {pool_ry:,.0f} USDC (price: ${pool_ry/
pool_rx:,.0f}/ETH)")

# Different victim swap sizes
print(f"\n{'Victim Swap':>14} {'Optimal Front':>14} {'Profit':>12} "
      f"{'Victim Loss':>12} {'Loss %':>8} {'ROI %':>8}")
print("-" * 75)

for victim_eth in [10, 25, 50, 100, 200, 500]:
    result = find_optimal_sandwich(pool_rx, pool_ry, victim_eth)
    print(f"  {victim_eth:>10} ETH  {result['optimal_
    frontrun']:>10.2f} ETH"
          f"  ${result['attacker_profit'] * (pool_ry/pool_rx):>9,.0f}"
          f"  ${result['victim_loss'] * (pool_ry/pool_rx):>9,.0f}"
          f"  {result['victim_loss_pct']:>6.2f}%"
          f"  {result['attacker_roi_pct']:>6.2f}%")

# === Arbitrage Analysis ===
print(f"\n\nMEV Analysis: DEX Arbitrage")
print("=" * 65)

# Two pools with price discrepancy
arb_result = simulate_arbitrage(
    5000, 10_000_000,    # Pool A: ETH=$2000
    5000, 10_500_000,    # Pool B: ETH=$2100 (5% premium)
)
print(f"Pool A price: ${arb_result['price_a']:,.0f}/ETH")
print(f"Pool B price: ${arb_result['price_b']:,.0f}/ETH")
print(f"Spread: {arb_result['price_spread_pct']:.2f}%")
print(f"Profitable: {arb_result['profitable']}")
if arb_result['profitable']:
    print(f"Direction: {arb_result['direction']}")
    print(f"Optimal input: {arb_result['optimal_input_y']:,.2f} USDC")
    print(f"Profit: ${arb_result['profit_y']:,.2f} USDC")
```

12.1.3 The MEV Supply Chain: From Searcher to Proposer

Ethereum's MEV ecosystem has turned into a proper supply chain at this point. Distinct roles, specialized players at each level. If you're designing protocols or trying to capture MEV yourself, you need to understand how this pipeline fits together.

Searchers

Searchers are the ones out there finding MEV. They run infrastructure to watch the public mempool, simulate what transactions will do, and build bundles that capture value. Some are solo developers running simple arb bots. Others are well-funded firms with custom low-latency setups.

What gives a searcher an edge? Speed, mainly. Detecting opportunities faster than everyone else. Also simulation accuracy, getting the outcome prediction right. And strategy depth, finding complex multi-step extraction paths that simpler bots miss. Competition among searchers is fierce. Over time it drives most of the profit toward zero, and what's left flows up to builders and proposers.

Builders

Builders assemble complete blocks. They take searcher bundles, combine them with regular mempool transactions, and try to maximize total block value: tips from users plus MEV from bundles. They compete by offering the highest payment to the proposer.

The builder market is concentrated. Seriously concentrated. Top three builders consistently produce over 90% of MEV-boost blocks. It's an economies-of-scale thing: builders who have more searcher connections get better bundles and can build more valuable blocks, which attracts more searchers. Feedback loop.

```
@dataclass
class MEVBundle:
    """A searcher's MEV bundle: ordered transactions for atomic
    execution."""
    bundle_id: str
    transactions: List[str]  # Ordered transaction hashes
    searcher: str
    target_block: int
```

```
    mev_value: float          # Total MEV captured
    searcher_payment: float  # Payment to builder for inclusion

    @property
    def builder_revenue(self) -> float:
        """Revenue builder keeps from including this bundle."""
        return self.searcher_payment

@dataclass
class BlockBid:
    """A builder's bid for block construction rights."""
    builder: str
    block_number: int
    bid_value: float           # Payment to proposer (ETH)
    bundles_included: int
    regular_txs: int
    total_gas: int
    total_mev: float

class MEVBoostRelay:
    """
    Simplified MEV-boost relay connecting builders and proposers.

    The relay:
    1. Receives block bids from builders
    2. Validates bid blocks (correct state transitions)
    3. Forwards the highest bid to the proposer
    4. Ensures the proposer cannot see block contents before committing
    """

    def __init__(self):
        self.bids: Dict[int, List[BlockBid]] = defaultdict(list)
        self.stats = {
            'total_blocks': 0,
            'total_mev': 0,
            'total_proposer_payments': 0,
            'builder_wins': defaultdict(int),
        }
```

```
    def submit_bid(self, bid: BlockBid):
        """Builder submits a block bid."""
        self.bids[bid.block_number].append(bid)

    def get_winning_bid(self, block_number: int) -> Optional[BlockBid]:
        """Proposer requests the highest bid for their slot."""
        block_bids = self.bids.get(block_number, [])
        if not block_bids:
            return None

        winner = max(block_bids, key=lambda b: b.bid_value)

        self.stats['total_blocks'] += 1
        self.stats['total_mev'] += winner.total_mev
        self.stats['total_proposer_payments'] += winner.bid_value
        self.stats['builder_wins'][winner.builder] += 1

        return winner

# Simulate MEV-boost market
relay = MEVBoostRelay()

builders = ["Builder_A", "Builder_B", "Builder_C", "Builder_D"]

import random
random.seed(123)

for block in range(100):
    # Each builder constructs a block and bids
    for builder in builders:
        mev = random.uniform(0.01, 0.5)  # ETH
        regular_tips = random.uniform(0.05, 0.2)

        # Builder keeps some margin, passes rest to proposer
        margin = random.uniform(0.1, 0.3)  # Builder's cut
        proposer_payment = (mev + regular_tips) * (1 - margin)

        # Top builders have access to more searcher bundles
        if builder == "Builder_A":
            mev *= 1.3  # 30% more MEV from better searcher connections
            proposer_payment = (mev + regular_tips) * (1 - margin)
```

```
        bid = BlockBid(
            builder=builder,
            block_number=block,
            bid_value=proposer_payment,
            bundles_included=random.randint(1, 10),
            regular_txs=random.randint(50, 200),
            total_gas=random.randint(15_000_000, 30_000_000),
            total_mev=mev,
        )
        relay.submit_bid(bid)

    relay.get_winning_bid(block)

print("\n\nMEV-Boost Market Simulation (100 blocks)")
print("=" * 60)
print(f"Total MEV captured: {relay.stats['total_mev']:.2f} ETH")
print(f"Total proposer payments: {relay.stats['total_proposer_
payments']:.2f} ETH")
print(f"\nBuilder market share:")
for builder, wins in sorted(relay.stats['builder_wins'].items(),
                            key=lambda x: x[1], reverse=True):
    share = wins / relay.stats['total_blocks'] * 100
    bar = "█" * int(share / 2)
    print(f"  {builder:<12}: {wins:3d} blocks ({share:5.1f}%) {bar}")

# Check concentration
shares = [w / relay.stats['total_blocks']
          for w in relay.stats['builder_wins'].values()]
hhi = sum(s**2 for s in shares)
top2 = sum(sorted(shares, reverse=True)[:2])
print(f"\nConcentration metrics:")
print(f"  HHI: {hhi:.4f} ({'concentrated' if hhi > 0.25 else
'competitive'})")
print(f"  Top-2 share: {top2:.1%}")
```

12.1.4 MEV Mitigation Approaches

People have come up with several approaches to deal with MEV, and each one involves a different set of tradeoffs:

Flashbots and MEV-boost: Takes the messy, chaotic mempool competition and turns it into an organized auction. Searchers compete for MEV, builders compete to build the best block, and proposers capture the surplus through bidding. MEV doesn't disappear. But it flows more predictably and you get fewer of the ugly side effects like failed transactions and gas price spikes.

Fair ordering, like Chainlink's FSS: Transactions get ordered by arrival time instead of by fee. If nobody can reorder, content-based MEV (sandwiching, frontrunning) can't happen. The hard part is defining "arrival time" in a distributed system where different nodes see transactions at different moments.

Encrypted mempools: Encrypt transactions before they enter the pool. Block producers just see encrypted blobs, they can't extract content-based MEV. Decryption happens only after the ordering is locked in. You can do this with threshold encryption (a committee cooperates to decrypt) or timelock encryption (decryption becomes possible after a set time period).

Batch auctions, like CoW Protocol: Instead of executing swaps one at a time, you collect all swaps in a time window and run them at one uniform clearing price. Everything in the batch trades at the same price, so there's no "before" and "after." Sandwiching becomes impossible.

Order flow auctions (MEV Share): Users route their transactions through a private channel. Searchers bid for the right to backrun them. Part of the MEV goes back to the user. What used to be pure extraction becomes a revenue share.

Proposer-Builder Separation (PBS): Put it in the protocol itself, not as an external bolt-on like MEV-boost. Split the right to propose blocks from the right to build them. Proposers can't extract MEV directly anymore, and you get a competitive builder market instead.

Table 12-1. MEV Mitigation Comparison

Approach	MEV Impact	Frontrunning	Sandwich	Arbitrage	Centralization Risk	Latency Impact
MEV-Boost	Redistributed	Reduced (private bundles)	Persists	Persists	Builder concentration	Minimal
Fair ordering	Eliminated (content-based)	Eliminated	Eliminated	Persists	Sequencer trust	~1 block
Encrypted mempool	Eliminated (content-based)	Eliminated	Eliminated	Delayed	Committee trust	+encryption time
Batch auctions	Partially eliminated	N/A (uniform price)	Eliminated	Captured in clearing	Solver concentration	Batch window
Order flow auctions	Shared with users	Reduced	Reduced	Persists	Router centralization	Minimal
PBS (enshrined)	Redistributed	Reduced	Persists	Persists	Builder market	Minimal

12.1.5 Quantitative MEV Measurement

To measure MEV, you first have to pin down what "extractable" actually means, then build the tools to spot extraction events on-chain.

```
def estimate_daily_mev(blocks_per_day: int = 7200,
                       avg_mev_per_block_eth: float = 0.1,
                       eth_price_usd: float = 3000) -> dict:
    """
    Estimate daily MEV on Ethereum.

    Data sources: mev-inspect, Flashbots, EigenPhi.
    These track on-chain MEV by detecting known patterns
    (arbitrage, sandwich, liquidation).
    """
    daily_mev_eth = blocks_per_day * avg_mev_per_block_eth
```

```
    daily_mev_usd = daily_mev_eth * eth_price_usd
    annual_mev_usd = daily_mev_usd * 365

    # Breakdown by type (approximate from Flashbots data)
    breakdown = {
        'arbitrage': 0.45,
        'sandwich': 0.25,
        'liquidation': 0.15,
        'jit_liquidity': 0.05,
        'other': 0.10,
    }

    results = {
        'daily_mev_eth': daily_mev_eth,
        'daily_mev_usd': daily_mev_usd,
        'annual_mev_usd': annual_mev_usd,
        'breakdown': {},
    }

    for mev_type, fraction in breakdown.items():
        results['breakdown'][mev_type] = {
            'daily_eth': daily_mev_eth * fraction,
            'daily_usd': daily_mev_usd * fraction,
            'annual_usd': annual_mev_usd * fraction,
        }

    return results

mev = estimate_daily_mev()
print("\n\nEstimated MEV on Ethereum")
print("=" * 55)
print(f"Daily MEV: {mev['daily_mev_eth']:.0f} ETH (${mev['daily_mev_
usd']:,.0f})")
print(f"Annual MEV: ${mev['annual_mev_usd']:,.0f}")
print(f"\nBreakdown by type:")
for mev_type, data in mev['breakdown'].items():
    print(f"  {mev_type:<20}: {data['daily_eth']:>6.0f} ETH/day "
          f"(${data['annual_usd']:>12,.0f}/year)")
```

12.1.6 Summary

The transaction lifecycle is a sequence of stages, and at several of those stages value can be extracted or lost. MEV is baked into any blockchain where block producers choose transaction order and outcomes depend on state. The ecosystem around it (searchers, builders, relays, proposers) has grown into its own specialized industry.

Key takeaways:

- Transaction ordering inside blocks is up to the block producer. That one fact is the root of the entire MEV phenomenon. Every mitigation strategy, when you boil it down, is about who controls ordering and what information they have when they do it.
- Sandwich attacks are the worst kind of MEV from the user's perspective. Value gets taken directly from them. Profit for the attacker scales roughly quadratically with how big the victim's trade is relative to pool reserves. Big trades in thin pools get hit the hardest.
- DEX arbitrage, on the other hand, is helpful MEV. It aligns prices across pools and improves price discovery. If you wiped out all MEV without thinking about it, you'd kill this beneficial activity along with the harmful stuff.
- The MEV supply chain (searchers, builders, relays, proposers) creates a market for block construction. Competition makes it more efficient but also pushes toward centralization, particularly on the builder side.
- Builder concentration is a real worry. The top builders produce north of 90% of MEV-boost blocks. A handful of entities with outsized control over which transactions get included and in what order.
- There's no silver bullet. Fair ordering kills frontrunning but needs trusted infrastructure. Encrypted mempools prevent content-based MEV but add latency. Batch auctions stop sandwiching but change how trading feels. Every approach has costs.
- PBS is becoming the standard architecture, separating who proposes blocks from who builds them. Whether it's enshrined in the protocol or running externally through MEV-boost, it shapes how MEV moves through the system.

Transaction lifecycle: construction, mempool, block inclusion, execution, and finality.—The public mempool exposes pending transactions to anyone watching. That's where MEV exposure starts.—MEV = value from controlling transaction order. Inherent in any system with ordering flexibility and state-dependent outcomes.—Sandwich attacks: frontrun, victim trade, backrun. Profit goes up roughly with trade size and down with pool depth.—DEX arbitrage is good MEV (price alignment). Sandwich attacks are bad MEV (takes from users).—Supply chain: searchers find it, builders package it, relays mediate, and proposers choose the winning block.—Builder concentration: top three produce over 90% of MEV-boost blocks. Market is tight.—'Mitigation options: fair ordering, encrypted mempools, batch auctions, order flow auctions, enshrined PBS. All have tradeoffs.—Estimated Ethereum MEV: around 720 ETH per day, roughly $2.2M daily at $3K ETH, about $790M a year.

12.1.7 Exercises

Problem 1 (Basic): Walk through the five stages of a transaction's life, from signing to finality. At which points can MEV be extracted, and who does the extracting?

Problem 2 (Calculation): A Uniswap V2 pool holds 10M USDC and 5,000 ETH. Someone submits a swap of 100 ETH for USDC. Calculate: (a) expected USDC out without MEV, (b) price impact, (c) optimal sandwich frontrun size, (d) attacker profit, (e) how much the victim loses in USDC.

Problem 3 (Implementation): Build an MEV searcher simulator. It should watch a mock mempool, spot arbitrage between two AMM pools, construct atomic arb transactions, and figure out profit after gas.

Problem 4 (Analysis): Use the builder market simulation to explain why MEV-boost leads to builder concentration. What are the economies of scale? How does searcher connectivity create a feedback loop for dominant builders?

Problem 5 (Design): Design an encrypted mempool using threshold encryption with n validators where t must cooperate to decrypt. Specify the encryption scheme, commit-reveal timing, committee selection, and what happens when t validators go offline.

Problem 6 (Theory): Can you prove (or disprove) that in any blockchain with state-dependent outcomes and discretionary ordering, some form of MEV extraction is always possible? What's the minimum constraint on ordering that would kill all content-based MEV?

Problem 7 (Comparative): Compare MEV across three setups: Ethereum L1 with MEV-boost, Arbitrum with a centralized sequencer, and dYdX v4 as an app-specific Cosmos chain. Where does extraction happen in each, who captures it, and which design hurts users least?

Problem 8 (Critical Thinking): Should MEV be eliminated, given back to users, or just accepted as a cost of decentralized markets? For each position, lay out specific mechanisms, check whether they're actually feasible, and think about what unintended consequences they'd create.

Problem 9 (Advanced): Implement a batch auction clearing algorithm, CoW Protocol style. Takes swap intents, finds a uniform clearing price. Show that sandwiching can't work inside a batch. Analyze the latency cost compared to continuous execution.

Problem 10 (Research): Pull real MEV-boost relay data for one week (public APIs, relay.flashbots.net). Report: total blocks through MEV-boost, builder concentration (HHI and Nakamoto coefficient), average proposer payment, most common MEV types. Compare what you find to the simulation results from the chapter.

(Solutions in Appendix D)

12.1.8 Further Reading

For MEV Origins: Daian et al.'s "Flash Boys 2.0" paper from 2019 is the foundational work. Documented how prevalent MEV was and gave the concept a formal framework.

For MEV-Boost and PBS: Flashbots docs cover the architecture. Vitalik's Ethereum research posts and others discuss enshrined PBS design.

For Fair Ordering: Kelkar et al.'s "Order-Fairness for Byzantine Consensus" (2020) has the formal definitions. Chainlink's Fair Sequencing Services documents a practical implementation.

For Measurement: mev-inspect-py is open source and detects MEV on-chain. EigenPhi and Flashbots both run dashboards with real-time data.

Watch out for anyone claiming one mechanism "solves" MEV. MEV comes from ordering flexibility. It's structural, not a bug. Anything that claims to eliminate it entirely is either redefining what MEV means or just moving it somewhere else.

CHAPTER 13

Cryptoeconomic Security

13.1 Game Theory, Incentive Mechanisms, and Economic Attack Analysis

This chapter covers blockchain cryptoeconomics: game theory and Nash equilibria in protocol design, tokenomics and issuance schedules, PoW and PoS attack cost modeling, slashing and penalty design, fee market dynamics, and economic stress testing when markets crash. What this chapter will give you:

- Game theory applies to blockchains. When is honest behavior actually a Nash equilibrium? When does it break down? The math matters here more than most people think
- Tokenomics, meaning issuance schedules, halvings, and burn mechanics. All the economic plumbing underneath
- Attack costs for PoW and PoS, modeled with actual numbers
- Slashing. Penalty design. What real deterrence looks like when you can't send anyone to jail
- Validator incentives and what keeps them aligned over time
- The link between token price, security budget, and whether the whole thing is sustainable. These three interact in ways that surprise people
- How fee markets work and why the issuance-vs-fees split shapes what security you end up with
- Economic stress-testing: what happens to security when markets crash

N. Savant, *Blockchain Foundations*, https://doi.org/10.1007/979-8-8688-2891-1_13

13.1.1 Game Theory in Blockchain Protocols

Blockchains run in adversarial environments. Every participant is assumed to be self-interested; that's baked right into the model. Traditional distributed systems get to assume nodes are either honest or they fail. Clean. Simple. Blockchains can't make that assumption. You're building for a world where people will cheat if it pays, and your job is to make sure it never pays. That's what game theory is for here; it gives you tools to reason about whether the incentives hold or fall apart once a sufficiently motivated adversary shows up.

A blockchain protocol is, formally speaking, a game:

Players are anyone making strategic decisions. Miners on a PoW chain, mostly, decide how to mine, which transactions make it into a block, and when to release blocks to the network. On PoS it gets more crowded. Validators choosing attestation and proposal strategies, pulling MEV when they see the chance. Delegators deciding which validators deserve their stake. Even regular users matter here, choosing fee levels and transaction timing.

Then there's the strategy space, which is really just a catalog of everything a player could possibly do. For a miner that includes honest behavior (follow the longest chain, include all valid transactions) but also selfish mining, block withholding, censorship, double-spend attempts, and MEV extraction. Mix and match across every player in the system, and each unique combination produces a different result.

The payoff function tells you what everyone earns (or loses) given the full picture of choices. Rewards, fees, and MEV on one side. Slashing opportunity costs, on the other. The important thing is it's not just about what you do. A selfish miner's expected profit depends a lot on how the honest miners react when they see a fork.

Incentive compatibility is the goal: make honest behavior a Nash equilibrium so that no individual player gains anything by deviating while everyone else plays straight. That's the floor. You can aim higher. A dominant strategy means honest play is optimal no matter what anyone else does, which is stronger. Coalition-proof means even groups working together can't find a profitable deviation. Most real protocols settle for Nash and cross their fingers a bit beyond that.

Formal Analysis: Mining as a Game

To keep it tractable, reduce it to two players. Honest miner controls fraction p of total hash. Attacker controls $q = 1 - p$. Both choose mine honestly, or attack.

```
from dataclasses import dataclass
from typing import Dict, List, Tuple
import math

@dataclass
class StrategyProfile:
    honest_payoff: float
    attack_payoff: float
    is_nash: bool
    deterrence_gap: float  # How much better honest is than attack

class ConsensusGame:
    """
    Model blockchain consensus as a two-player game between
    an honest coalition and a potential attacker.
    """

    def __init__(self, protocol_name: str):
        self.name = protocol_name

    def analyze_pow(self, attacker_hash_fraction: float,
                    block_reward_usd: float,
                    blocks_per_day: int,
                    daily_fees_usd: float,
                    electricity_cost_per_hash_usd: float,
                    network_hashrate: float,
                    double_spend_value: float,
                    confirmations: int = 6) -> StrategyProfile:
        """
        Analyze PoW mining game.

        Honest strategy: Mine on longest chain, include all valid txs
        Revenue = fraction × (block_rewards + fees)
        Cost = fraction × electricity

        Attack strategy: Attempt double-spend
        Revenue = P(success) × double_spend_value
        Cost = electricity during attack + opportunity cost
```

```
    """
    q = attacker_hash_fraction
    p = 1 - q

    # Honest payoff (annual)
    annual_rewards = blocks_per_day * 365 * block_reward_usd
    annual_fees = daily_fees_usd * 365
    honest_revenue = q * (annual_rewards + annual_fees)
    honest_cost = q * network_hashrate * electricity_cost_per_hash_usd
    * 3600 * 24 * 365
    honest_payoff = honest_revenue - honest_cost

    # Attack payoff
    # Success probability using Nakamoto's formula
    if q >= 0.5:
        success_prob = 1.0
    else:
        lam = confirmations * (q / p)
        success_prob = 1.0
        total = 0.0
        for k in range(confirmations):
            poisson = math.exp(-lam) * (lam ** k) / math.factorial(k)
            total += poisson * (1 - (q / p) ** (confirmations - k))
        success_prob = 1.0 - total

    attack_revenue = success_prob * double_spend_value

    # Attack cost: electricity for attack duration
    # Expected attack duration: confirmations × block_time / (p - q)
    if q < p
    block_time_seconds = 86400 / blocks_per_day
    if q < p:
# Attacker is behind — needs multiple attempts on average
# Expected blocks until success = confirmations / (p - q)
# This is the mean of a geometric distribution on catching up
expected_duration_s = confirmations * block_time_seconds / max(p - q, 0.01)
```

```
else:
    # Attacker has majority — always catches up, takes roughly
    # confirmations block-times to build the competing chain
    expected_duration_s = confirmations * block_time_seconds

        attack_electricity = q * network_hashrate * electricity_cost_per_
        hash_usd * expected_duration_s

        # Opportunity cost: forgoing honest mining during attack
# If honest mining is already unprofitable (high electricity costs),
# there is no opportunity being given up — floor at 0.
# Without this floor, a negative honest_payoff makes opportunity_cost
# negative, which adds to attack_payoff — completely backwards.
honest_per_second = max(honest_payoff, 0) / (365 * 86400)
opportunity_cost = honest_per_second * expected_duration_s
attack_payoff = attack_revenue - attack_electricity - opportunity_cost
        is_nash = honest_payoff > attack_payoff
        gap = honest_payoff - attack_payoff

        return StrategyProfile(honest_payoff, attack_payoff, is_nash, gap)

    def analyze_pos(self, attacker_stake_fraction: float,
                    total_staked_usd: float,
                    annual_yield_pct: float,
                    double_spend_value: float,
                    operational_cost_pct: float = 0.5) -> StrategyProfile:
        """
        Analyze PoS validation game.

        Honest: earn staking rewards
        Attack: attempt finality violation (requires >1/3 stake)
        Penalty: correlation slashing (up to 100% of stake)
        """
        stake_value = attacker_stake_fraction * total_staked_usd

        # Honest payoff (annual)
        gross_yield = stake_value * annual_yield_pct / 100
        operational_cost = stake_value * operational_cost_pct / 100
        honest_payoff = gross_yield - operational_cost
```

```
        # Attack payoff
        can_attack = attacker_stake_fraction > 1/3

        if not can_attack:
            attack_payoff = -stake_value * 0.031  # Attempted equivocation:
            ~3.1% slash
        else:
            # Correlation penalty when >1/3 slashed
            correlation_factor = min(3 * attacker_stake_fraction, 1.0)
            slashing_loss = stake_value * correlation_factor

            # Token price crash from successful attack
            price_crash_loss = stake_value * 0.5  # Remaining stake loses
            50% value

            # Detection probability is ~1.0 (on-chain evidence)
            detection_prob = 0.99

            attack_payoff = (double_spend_value -
                             detection_prob * (slashing_loss + price_
                             crash_loss))

        is_nash = honest_payoff > attack_payoff
        gap = honest_payoff - attack_payoff

        return StrategyProfile(honest_payoff, attack_payoff, is_nash, gap)

# === PoW Analysis ===
pow_game = ConsensusGame("Bitcoin PoW")

print("Cryptoeconomic Security: Game-Theoretic Analysis")
print("=" * 70)

print("\n1. Bitcoin PoW - Mining Game Analysis")
print(f"{'Hash Rate':>11} {'Honest $/yr':>14} {'Attack $/yr':>14}
{'Nash?':>7} {'Gap':>14}")
print("-" * 65)
```

```
for q in [0.05, 0.10, 0.20, 0.30, 0.40, 0.49]:
    result = pow_game.analyze_pow(
        attacker_hash_fraction=q,
        block_reward_usd=3.125 * 60000,
        blocks_per_day=144,
        daily_fees_usd=500_000,
        electricity_cost_per_hash_usd=1e-20,  # Tiny per hash
        network_hashrate=5.5e20,  # 550 EH/s
        double_spend_value=10_000_000,  # $10M double-spend attempt
        confirmations=6,
    )
    print(f"  {q:>8.0%}   ${result.honest_payoff:>11,.0f}   "
          f"${result.attack_payoff:>11,.0f}   {'Yes' if result.is_nash else
          'NO':>5}   "
          f"${result.deterrence_gap:>11,.0f}")

# === PoS Analysis ===
pos_game = ConsensusGame("Ethereum PoS")

print("\n2. Ethereum PoS - Validation Game Analysis")
print(f"{'Stake':>11} {'Honest $/yr':>14} {'Attack $':>14} {'Nash?':>7}
{'Gap':>14}")
print("-" * 65)

for q in [0.05, 0.10, 0.20, 0.34, 0.40, 0.50]:
    result = pos_game.analyze_pos(
        attacker_stake_fraction=q,
        total_staked_usd=60_000_000_000,
        annual_yield_pct=4.0,
        double_spend_value=5_000_000_000,  # $5B double-spend
    )
    print(f"  {q:>8.0%}   ${result.honest_payoff:>11,.0f}   "
          f"${result.attack_payoff:>11,.0f}   {'Yes' if result.is_nash else
          'NO':>5}   "
          f"${result.deterrence_gap:>11,.0f}")
```

13.1.2 Tokenomics and Monetary Policy

Tokenomics is the economic rule set of a cryptocurrency. Supply dynamics, value distribution, and incentive structures. Get these wrong and the security budget collapses, or the protocol slowly becomes unviable economically. Get them right, and consensus participants have enough to work with for the foreseeable future.

Bitcoin's Disinflationary Model

Bitcoin's monetary policy is the simplest in the entire space and by far the most analyzed. Fifty BTC per block at the start. Halves every 210,000 blocks, roughly a four-year cycle. Supply caps at 21 million and approaches it asymptotically. Inflation drops with each halving but technically never reaches zero. The last coin gets mined somewhere around the year 2140, if you trust the math that far out.

Each halving is really a security event dressed up as a monetary policy. Mining revenue from issuance drops 50% overnight. Unless the price has doubled since the last halving or fee revenue has grown enough to cover the gap, security gets weaker. This is the existential question for Bitcoin: are transaction fees ever going to be enough? We don't know. Nobody does.

```
def bitcoin_economics(years: int = 40) -> List[dict]:
    """
    Model Bitcoin's complete economic trajectory.

    Tracks: issuance, supply, inflation rate, and security budget
    under different price and fee assumptions.
    """
    blocks_per_year = 52560
    halving_interval = 210_000
    results = []
    total_mined = 0

    for year in range(years):
        calendar_year = 2009 + year
        block_number = blocks_per_year * year
        halvings = block_number // halving_interval
        reward = 50.0 / (2 ** halvings)
```

```
annual_issuance = reward * blocks_per_year
total_mined = min(total_mined + annual_issuance, 21_000_000)
inflation = (annual_issuance / total_mined * 100) if total_mined >
0 else 100
remaining = 21_000_000 - total_mined

# Price scenarios
# Conservative: 10% annual growth from 2024 baseline
years_from_2024 = max(0, calendar_year - 2024)
price_conservative = 60000 * (1.10 ** years_from_2024)

# Moderate: 15% annual growth
price_moderate = 60000 * (1.15 ** years_from_2024)

# Fee scenarios
# Growing: fees grow 8% annually from $500K/day baseline
fees_growing = 500000 * (1.08 ** years_from_2024) * 365

# Stagnant: fees stay at $500K/day
fees_stagnant = 500000 * 365

# Security budgets
budget_best = annual_issuance * price_moderate + fees_growing
budget_moderate = annual_issuance * price_conservative +
fees_growing
budget_worst = annual_issuance * price_conservative + fees_stagnant

# Fee percentage of total budget
fee_pct_best = fees_growing / budget_best * 100 if budget_best >
0 else 0
fee_pct_worst = fees_stagnant / budget_worst * 100 if budget_worst
> 0 else 0

results.append({
    'year': calendar_year,
    'reward_btc': reward,
    'annual_issuance': annual_issuance,
    'total_supply': total_mined,
    'remaining': remaining,
```

```
            'inflation_pct': inflation,
            'budget_best_usd': budget_best,
            'budget_moderate_usd': budget_moderate,
            'budget_worst_usd': budget_worst,
            'fee_pct_best': fee_pct_best,
            'fee_pct_worst': fee_pct_worst,
        })

    return results

btc = bitcoin_economics(36)
print("\nBitcoin Economic Trajectory")
print("=" * 85)
print(f"{'Year':>6} {'Reward':>8} {'Supply (M)':>11} {'Inflation':>10} "
      f"{'Budget(best)':>14} {'Budget(worst)':>14} {'Fee%(worst)':>11}")
print("-" * 85)

for entry in btc:
    if entry['year'] >= 2024 and entry['year'] % 4 == 0:
        print(f"  {entry['year']} {entry['reward_btc']:>8.4f} "
              f"{entry['total_supply']/1e6:>9.2f}M {entry['inflation_
              pct']:>9.2f}% "
              f"${entry['budget_best_usd']/1e9:>11.1f}B "
              f"${entry['budget_worst_usd']/1e9:>11.1f}B "
              f"{entry['fee_pct_worst']:>10.1f}%")
```

Ethereum's Dynamic Equilibrium Model

Ethereum post-merge is a completely different economic creature. Issuance depends on the square root of total staked ETH, which creates this natural feedback. Too much staking and yield drops, discouraging more. Staking falls and yield climbs, pulling people back in. Self-balancing, no intervention required.

On top of that, you've got the EIP-1559 burn. Busy network? More ETH burned than minted. Supply shrinks. Quiet network? Issuance outpaces burn, and supply grows. The end result is monetary policy that actually reacts to how much people use the chain. Very different philosophy from Bitcoin's "set the rules once, never touch them" approach.

```
def ethereum_economics(staking_levels: list, base_fee_levels: list) -> None:
    """
    Analyze Ethereum's economic equilibrium across staking
    and usage scenarios.
    """
    TOTAL_SUPPLY = 120_000_000

    print(f"\nEthereum PoS Economic Equilibrium Analysis")
    print("=" * 80)

    for base_fee_gwei in base_fee_levels:
        # Annual burn from EIP-1559
        # burn = base_fee × gas_per_block × blocks_per_day × 365
        annual_burn = base_fee_gwei * 1e-9 * 15_000_000 * 7200 * 365

        print(f"\n  Base fee = {base_fee_gwei} Gwei (annual burn = {annual_
        burn:,.0f} ETH)")
        print(f"  {'Staked (M)':>11} {'Yield %':>8} {'Issuance':>12}
        {'Burn':>12} "
              f"{'Net':>12} {'Inflation':>10} {'Status':>12}")
        print("  " + "-" * 80)

        for staked_m in staking_levels:
            staked = staked_m * 1e6

            # Issuance formula (simplified)
            annual_issuance = 166 * math.sqrt(staked)

            # Staking yield
            yield_pct = (annual_issuance / staked) * 100

            # Net supply change
            net = annual_issuance - annual_burn
            inflation = (net / TOTAL_SUPPLY) * 100

            status = "DEFLATIONARY" if net < 0 else "inflationary"

            print(f"  {staked_m:>9}M {yield_pct:>7.2f}% {annual_
            issuance:>10,.0f} "
                  f"{annual_burn:>10,.0f} {net:>10,.0f} {inflation:>9.3f}%
                  {status:>12}")
```

```
ethereum_economics(
    staking_levels=[5, 10, 15, 20, 25, 30, 40],
    base_fee_levels=[10, 20, 40, 80]
)
```

13.1.3 Security Budget: The Price of Consensus

The security budget is just the total value consensus participants receive in a year. It sets the floor for what an attacker needs to spend. You want to know if a chain can survive a serious, well-funded attack? Look at the security budget first. Everything else is secondary.

PoW makes it straightforward. Miner revenue is the budget. Rewards plus fees. All of it goes to hardware and power bills. Attack the chain? You need to outspend the miners or somehow grab over half the hash power.

PoS reframes it entirely. Not about spending, about exposure. How much total value is staked, and what happens to that stake if the owner tries something. The attacker's capital doesn't vanish into electricity. It stays locked up, and if they cheat, the protocol seizes it.

```
# Note: staked amounts and prices are approximate as of 2024.
# Verify against current on-chain data before publishing.
# Staking ratios: Bitcoin N/A, Ethereum ~26%, Cardano ~62%, Solana ~65-70%
protocols = {

def comprehensive_security_comparison() -> None:
    """Compare security budgets across major protocols."""

    protocols = {
        "Bitcoin": {
            'type': 'pow',
            'blocks_per_day': 144,
            'block_reward': 3.125,
            'token_price': 60000,
            'daily_fees_usd': 500_000,
            'market_cap': 1_200_000_000_000,
            'daily_txs': 350_000,
```

```
        'attack_description': 'Acquire >50% hash rate',
        'attack_cost_est': 8_500_000_000,  # Hardware
        'attack_reversible': True,  # Attacker keeps hardware
    },
    "Ethereum": {
        'type': 'pos',
        'total_staked': 20_000_000,
        'token_price': 3000,
        'annual_yield_pct': 4.0,
        'market_cap': 400_000_000_000,
        'daily_txs': 1_200_000,
        'attack_description': 'Acquire >33% of staked ETH',
        'attack_cost_est': 60_000_000_000,  # Stake value × slippage
        'attack_reversible': False,  # Slashed
    },
    "Cardano": {
        'type': 'pos',
        'total_staked': 22_000_000_000,
        'token_price': 0.50,
        'annual_yield_pct': 3.5,
        'market_cap': 18_000_000_000,
        'daily_txs': 80_000,
        'attack_description': 'Acquire >50% of staked ADA',
        'attack_cost_est': 5_500_000_000,
        'attack_reversible': False,
    },
    "Solana": {
'type': 'pos',
'total_staked': 280_000_000,    # ~65-70% of circulating supply staked
                                # was 380M – implied 87% staking ratio
                                # which is unrealistically high
'token_price': 150,
'annual_yield_pct': 6.5,
'market_cap': 65_000_000_000,
'daily_txs': 30_000_000,
```

```
        'attack_description': 'Acquire >33% of staked SOL',
        'attack_cost_est': 14_000_000_000,  # Updated: 280M × $150 × 0.33
        = $13.9B
        'attack_reversible': False,
},
    }

    print("\nComprehensive Security Budget Analysis")
    print("=" * 80)

    for name, p in protocols.items():
        if p['type'] == 'pow':
            daily_budget = (p['blocks_per_day'] * p['block_reward'] *
                           p['token_price'] + p['daily_fees_usd'])
            annual_budget = daily_budget * 365
        else:
            staked_value = p['total_staked'] * p['token_price']
            annual_budget = staked_value * p['annual_yield_pct'] / 100
            daily_budget = annual_budget / 365

        security_ratio = annual_budget / p['market_cap']
        cost_per_tx = daily_budget / p['daily_txs']

        print(f"\n{name}:")
        print(f"  Market cap:             ${p['market_cap']:>15,.0f}")
        print(f"  Annual security budget: ${annual_budget:>13,.0f}")
        print(f"  Daily security budget:  ${daily_budget:>13,.0f}")
        print(f"  Security ratio:          {security_ratio:>13.4f}
        (budget/mcap)")
        print(f"  Cost per transaction:   ${cost_per_tx:>13.2f}")
        print(f"  Attack vector:           {p['attack_description']}")
        print(f"  Estimated attack cost:  ${p['attack_cost_est']:>13,.0f}")
        print(f"  Attack reversible:       {'Yes (hardware retained)' if
        p['attack_reversible'] else 'No (stake destroyed)'}")

comprehensive_security_comparison()
```

13.1.4 Optimal Deterrence and Penalty Design

Getting penalties right is genuinely hard. Too soft, and attacks are a rounding error. Too aggressive and you wipe out honest operators over minor glitches. Same problem criminal justice systems deal with, come to think of it. Lenient sentencing invites repeat offenders. Disproportionate sentencing punishes people who made honest mistakes.

Four ideas matter here:

Proportionality. Big offense, big penalty. Small offense, small penalty. Double-voting can break consensus entirely, so Ethereum slashes you hard for that, a minimum of 1/32 of your stake gone permanently. Missing a few attestations because your node went down? That just triggers a slow inactivity leak. The distinction matters a lot in practice because one is an accident waiting to happen and the other looks like an attack.

Correlation is probably the most elegant part of the design. A single validator getting slashed could be anything, software bug, bad configuration, key compromised. The penalty is about 3% of the stake. You survive that. But a third of all validators tripping the slash condition in the same window? That pattern doesn't look like bad luck. It looks like coordination. And the penalty reflects that: everyone caught loses 100%. This one mechanism alone makes large-scale coordinated attacks absurdly expensive.

Attribution means you only punish what's provable on-chain. Was the double-vote deliberate, or did the key get stolen? Protocol doesn't know and can't know. What it can see: two conflicting messages, the same validator key, both signed. That's enough. The evidence is the evidence. Intent is irrelevant to the slashing logic.

And finally, honest participants need bounded risk. Internet dies for an hour? Predictable small loss. One accidental equivocation from a race condition in your client software? Roughly 1/32 of the stake—that's the cap. The really devastating penalties are reserved for behavior that only makes sense as a coordinated, intentional attack.

```
def penalty_analysis(total_staked_eth: float, num_validators: int,
                     eth_price: float) -> None:
    """
    Comprehensive penalty analysis across attack scales.

    Demonstrates how the correlation penalty creates exponentially
    increasing cost for coordinated attacks while keeping isolated
    mistakes affordable.
    """
    effective_balance = 32  # ETH per validator
```

```
effective_balance_gwei = 32 * 10**9
total_active_gwei = int(total_staked_eth * 10**9)

print(f"\nPenalty Scaling Analysis")
print(f"Total staked: {total_staked_eth/1e6:.0f}M ETH "
      f"({num_validators:,} validators)")
print("=" * 75)

print(f"\n{'Validators Slashed':>20} {'Fraction':>10} {'Penalty
%':>10} "
      f"{'Per-Validator $':>16} {'Total Attack $':>16}")
print("-" * 75)

scenarios = [
    (1, "Bug/accident"),
    (10, "Small incident"),
    (100, "Infrastructure failure"),
    (1000, "Cloud provider outage"),
    (int(num_validators * 0.01), "1% of validators"),
    (int(num_validators * 0.05), "5% of validators"),
    (int(num_validators * 0.10), "10% of validators"),
    (int(num_validators * 0.20), "20% of validators"),
    (int(num_validators * 0.33), "33% (finality attack)"),
]

for num_slashed, description in scenarios:
    slashed_balance_gwei = num_slashed * effective_balance_gwei

    # Initial penalty: 1/32
    initial = effective_balance_gwei // 32

    # Correlation penalty: EB × 3 × slashed_total / active_total
    correlation_factor = min(3 * slashed_balance_gwei / total_active_
    gwei, 1.0)
    correlation = int(effective_balance_gwei * correlation_factor)

    # Missed attestation during ~36 day exit
    missed_attest = int(effective_balance_gwei * 36 / 365 * 0.04)
    # ~4% annual yield missed
```

```
        total_penalty_gwei = min(initial + correlation + missed_attest,
        effective_balance_gwei)
        penalty_pct = total_penalty_gwei / effective_balance_gwei * 100

        penalty_usd = (total_penalty_gwei / 10**9) * eth_price
        total_attack_cost = penalty_usd * num_slashed

        print(f"  {num_slashed:>8} ({description:>20}) {num_slashed/num_
        validators:>9.2%} "
              f"{penalty_pct:>9.1f}% ${penalty_usd:>14,.0f} ${total_attack_
              cost:>14,.0f}")

penalty_analysis(20_000_000, 625_000, 3000)
```

13.1.5 Fee Market Dynamics and Security Budget Composition

Where security money comes from shapes everything. If it's mostly issuance, you get stable, predictable security, but token holders get diluted steadily. If it's mostly fees, you're gambling on sustained demand for block space. Demand dips and suddenly security dips too. The balance between the two is, I think, underappreciated. It determines whether a protocol stays viable over decades.

```
def fee_dependency_analysis() -> None:
    """
    Analyze how security budget composition changes over time.

    Bitcoin: halvings force increasing fee dependency
    Ethereum: EIP-1559 burn means fees reduce supply rather than fund
    security
    """
    print("\nFee Dependency Over Time")
    print("=" * 70)

    # Bitcoin fee dependency at each halving
    print("\nBitcoin: Fee Revenue as % of Security Budget")
    print(f"{'Year':>6} {'Reward BTC':>12} {'Reward $(60K)':>14} "
          f"{'Fee $/day':>12} {'Fee % Budget':>13}")
    print("-" * 60)
```

```
    for year, reward, era in [
        (2012, 50, "Pre-halving"),
        (2016, 25, "1st halving"),
        (2020, 12.5, "2nd halving"),
        (2024, 6.25, "3rd halving"),
        (2028, 3.125, "4th halving"),
        (2032, 1.5625, "5th halving"),
        (2036, 0.78125, "6th halving"),
        (2040, 0.390625, "7th halving"),
    ]:
        daily_reward_usd = reward * 144 * 60000  # Assume constant $60K
        daily_fees = 500_000  # Assume constant $500K/day fees
        daily_total = daily_reward_usd + daily_fees
        fee_pct = daily_fees / daily_total * 100

        print(f"  {year} {reward:>12.6f} ${daily_reward_usd:>12,.0f} "
              f"${daily_fees:>10,.0f} {fee_pct:>12.1f}%")

    print(f"\n  Observation: At constant price and fees, Bitcoin becomes")
    print(f"  majority fee-funded by ~2036 (6th halving).")
    print(f"  If fees don't grow, security budget shrinks with each
    halving.")

fee_dependency_analysis()
```

13.1.6 Economic Attacks Beyond Double-Spending

Double-spending gets most of the attention, but it's only one category:

Bribing. Skip buying the stake yourself. Pay existing validators to misbehave on your behalf. Often cheaper than direct acquisition because you only need to cover the expected slashing cost for each validator, which can be a fraction of their total stake. And good luck detecting it when the payments happen off-chain.

Short-selling. Take out a huge short position on derivatives, then attack the chain and crash the token price. Your profit comes from the short, not from anything on-chain. Completely external revenue source for the attacker.

Governance capture. Voting power proportional to token holdings means someone with enough money can buy enough tokens to dictate outcomes. Change the parameters. Drain the treasury. Rewrite the consensus rules themselves if the governance surface is broad enough.

Table 13-1. *Economic Attack Vector Comparison*

Attack Type	Required Resource	Cost Basis	Detection	Recovery
PoW double-spend	>50% hash rate	Hardware + electricity	Visible on-chain	Attacker keeps hardware
PoS finality attack	>33% stake	Token acquisition + slashing	Provable on-chain	Stake destroyed
Bribery	Cash to pay validators	Below full stake cost	Hard to detect off-chain	Depends on detection
Short + attack	Derivatives position + attack capacity	Derivatives margin + attack cost	Off-chain + on-chain	Market losses
Governance capture	Governance tokens	Token acquisition	Visible in votes	Protocol fork
Censorship	>50% block production	Sustained hash/ stake majority	Observable (missing txs)	Social consensus / fork

13.1.7 Summary

All of cryptoeconomic security comes back to one thing: making honest behavior the obviously rational choice. Game theory provides the framework. Mechanism design provides the tools. Monetary economics provides the fuel. But the real question is whether the security budget, the penalties, and the tokenomics actually line up. Get any one of them wrong and the rational choice for participants might not be honesty anymore.

What matters most from this chapter:

- Use Nash equilibrium to check if honesty pays. PoW: it does when the attacker has less than half the hash and selfish mining doesn't beat honest returns. PoS: it does when slashing costs more than cheating gains.

- Bitcoin's PoW security budget is roughly $10B per year today. Halvings cut the issuance portion in half each cycle. Fees need to pick up the slack, and they haven't yet. Not at the scale that matters.
- Ethereum's security rests on $60B+ in staked ETH. The correlation penalty does the heavy lifting: lone mistake, about 3% lost. Coordinated attack, 100% lost. Makes the cost of a real attack catastrophic.
- Bitcoin's halvings give you a declining security trajectory with predictable timing. Ethereum's sqrt issuance plus the 1559 burn tries for self-correcting equilibrium. Two very different philosophies are betting on different futures.
- Four rules for penalty design: match the severity of the offense, ramp up penalties when multiple validators fail simultaneously, only punish what you can prove cryptographically, and don't bankrupt honest operators over one bad day.
- The big unresolved question is sustainability. Bitcoin's clock is ticking with each halving. Ethereum's approach is more adaptive on paper but still depends on the network staying busy enough to matter.
- Don't stop at double-spending when you think about threats. Bribery. Short-selling. Governance takeovers. Censorship. The 51% attack is the one everyone knows, but the attack surface goes well past it.

Protocols are games. Honest play needs to be Nash equilibrium, or the security argument collapses.—Bitcoin PoW: roughly $10B/yr. 3.125 BTC per block times 144 blocks per day at $60K, plus around $500K in daily fees.—Ethereum PoS: $60B+ staked. Correlation penalty makes individual failures cost ~3% and coordinated attacks cost everything.—A double-spend is only rational when (success probability × stolen value) exceeds (electricity + opportunity cost).—Each Bitcoin halving shifts more security burden onto fees. By 2036 that transition needs to be mostly complete.—Penalty design: proportional, correlated, attributable, bounded.—The attack menu is bigger than most people assume: bribery, derivatives-funded attacks, governance capture, sustained censorship.—Whether fee revenue can permanently sustain chain security is the question that hangs over everything. Nobody has proven it can.

13.1.8 Exercises

Problem 1 (Basic): What does Nash equilibrium mean for mining, and what goes wrong if honest behavior doesn't sit at equilibrium?

Problem 2 (Calculation): Next halving drops the reward to 1.5625 BTC. What BTC price holds the annual security budget at $10B with daily fee revenue of $500K?

Problem 3 (Implementation): Build a simulator. Payoff matrix, honest mining versus selfish mining, attacker hash rate ranging from 10% to 49%. Find where Nash equilibrium sits at each level. Plot the threshold.

Problem 4 (Analysis): Bitcoin halving model versus Ethereum's sqrt-plus-burn model. If the token price falls 80%, which degrades more gracefully? Run the numbers.

Problem 5 (Design): New PoS chain, 1000 validators, $100K each staked. Design the penalty system: slashable offenses, base penalties, correlation scaling formula, inactivity leak, and whistleblower cut. Justify each parameter.

Problem 6 (Theory): PoW with proportional reward distribution. Prove honest mining is Nash equilibrium when no miner exceeds 50% hash rate. State assumptions explicitly.

Problem 7 (Comparative): Cost a 1-hour sustained attack on Bitcoin, Ethereum, and a Cosmos appchain ($1B staked). Cheapest per dollar of market cap? What minimum market cap keeps a chain safe?

Problem 8 (Critical Thinking): Could any mechanism produce a security budget that's stable in USD terms without requiring perpetual token appreciation? Design one. Check if incentive compatibility survives.

Problem 9 (Advanced): Say MEV is 30% of validator income. What does that do to minimum viable yield? To revenue variance? Is a security budget that leans on MEV this heavily actually sustainable?

Problem 10 (Research): Five years of Bitcoin fee data. Annual fee revenue, fees as a share of miner income, per-transaction average, trendline. Extrapolate: when do fees match today's block reward revenue? Before or after the next halving?

(Solutions in Appendix D)

13.1.9 Further Reading

Roughgarden, "Transaction Fee Mechanism Design for the Ethereum Blockchain" (2021). Auction theory meets fee markets. Rigorous, but you can follow it.

Budish, "The Economic Limits of Bitcoin and the Blockchain" (2018). The core argument: PoW security comes from flow (current spending), not stock (accumulated work). Reframes how you should think about halvings.

Chitra and Kulkarni on staking derivatives. If you care about how liquid staking changes PoS security dynamics, start here.

Daian et al. cover MEV as an attack vector. Bonneau's "Hostile Blockchain Takeovers" covers the short-selling angle.

CHAPTER 14

Formal Verification and Security Analysis

14.1 Applying Formal Methods to Blockchain Protocol Verification

This chapter covers formal verification applied to blockchain protocols—temporal logic specs, model checking, proof assistants (Coq, Isabelle, Lean), symbolic execution, security audit methodology, and where the gap between verified and actually secure still bites. What this chapter will give you:

- Why formal verification matters when the code you ship controls billions of dollars and can't be patched after the fact
- How to write formal specs for blockchain protocols using temporal logic (LTL, CTL)
- Model checking. Exhaustive state-space exploration of consensus protocols, what it can do and where it hits walls
- Proof assistants like Coq, Isabelle, and Lean, and how they're used for machine-checked proofs of protocol and cryptographic properties
- Symbolic execution applied to protocol-level smart contract security
- How to actually run a security audit across consensus, cryptography, networking, and economics
- Common vulnerability patterns and how to find them systematically
- The uncomfortable gap between "formally verified" and "actually secure"

N. Savant, *Blockchain Foundations*, https://doi.org/10.1007/979-8-8688-2891-1_14

14.1.1 Why Formal Methods Matter for Blockchain

Blockchain protocols handle billions in value with code that, once deployed, you can't easily patch or roll back. A consensus bug leads to chain splits where nodes disagree on what's real. A smart contract vulnerability can drain a liquidity pool in seconds. We've seen it happen: the $60M DAO hack in 2016, Poly Network losing $600M in 2021, the $325M Wormhole bridge exploit in 2022. The stakes are not theoretical.

Testing finds bugs, but it can't prove they're all gone. A test suite checks that certain inputs produce expected outputs. Fine. But a blockchain protocol has to be correct for every possible input, every message ordering, every adversary strategy, and every network condition. That space is enormous, and adversaries are actively hunting for the inputs your tests didn't cover.

Formal verification closes that gap. Instead of checking specific scenarios, you prove mathematically that properties hold across all reachable states. If the proof is right and the spec captures what you intended, the property is guaranteed. Not probably true. Guaranteed.

It's expensive. You need specialized people, a serious time investment, and very careful specification of what you're trying to prove. But when the system holds billions and there's no undo button, the cost is justified. A number of major protocols have invested in it:

- Casper FFG's finality proof was mechanized in Isabelle. It proves conflicting finalized checkpoints require at least 1/3 of the stake to be slashable
- Tendermint's safety and liveness properties were formalized and verified in TLA+ and Coq both
- Tezos had parts of its system verified in Coq, specifically the Michelson smart contract language
- Algorand's consensus went through the UPPAAL model checker

14.1.2 Formal Specification with Temporal Logic

Blockchain protocols have properties that have to hold over time, not just at a single instant. Temporal logic gives you a way to express this. It extends regular propositional logic with operators that talk about how truth values change across time steps. Natural fit for specifying distributed protocol behavior.

Linear Temporal Logic (LTL)

LTL works on a single execution path, a linear sequence of states. The temporal operators:

G (Globally): φ holds at every future state. "The chain never includes an invalid transaction" becomes G(¬invalid_tx_included).

F (Finally): φ holds at some future state. "Every submitted transaction eventually gets included or rejected" is F(included ∨ rejected).

X (neXt): φ holds in the next state. "Block number always increases" is G(block_number(next) > block_number(current)).

U (Until): φ holds until ψ becomes true. "The chain stays live until a partition happens" is live U partition.

Safety and Liveness Properties

Consensus properties split into two categories, the same as the classic distinction in distributed systems:

Safety says "nothing bad ever happens." A safety violation shows up in finite time. If it's ever false, you can point to the exact moment. The key safety properties for blockchains:

Agreement: Two honest nodes can't finalize different blocks at the same height. Formally: $G(\forall i,j \in honest, \forall h: finalized(i,h,b_1) \wedge finalized(j,h,b_2) \rightarrow b_1 = b_2)$.

Validity: Only valid transactions end up in finalized blocks. What "valid" means depends on the protocol, but usually: correct signatures, sufficient balances, non-negative outputs, and no double-spending.

Consistency: Honest nodes agree on the finalized transaction order. If A is finalized before B on any honest node, that same order holds on every honest node.

Liveness says "something good eventually happens." Liveness violations are trickier. You can only prove one by observing that the desired event never occurs across an unbounded execution. The key liveness properties:

Termination: Every submitted transaction eventually gets included in a finalized block or gets definitively rejected. G(submitted(tx) → F(finalized(tx) ∀ rejected(tx))).

Progress: Chain height increases without bound. G(F(height > current_height)). The chain never permanently stalls.

Finality liveness: For systems with explicit finality gadgets, new checkpoints eventually get finalized. G(F(new_finalized_checkpoint)).

```
from dataclasses import dataclass
from typing import List, Optional, Callable
from enum import Enum

class TemporalOp(Enum):
    GLOBALLY = "G"      # Always true
    FINALLY = "F"       # Eventually true
    NEXT = "X"          # True at next state
    UNTIL = "U"         # True until

@dataclass
class ProtocolProperty:
    """Formal specification of a blockchain protocol property."""
    name: str
    category: str           # "safety" or "liveness"
    description: str
    ltl_formula: str        # LTL specification
    violation_example: str  # How this property can be violated
    verified_in: List[str]  # Tools where this was verified

def define_complete_properties() -> List[ProtocolProperty]:
    """Define the complete set of formal properties for BFT consensus."""
    return [
        ProtocolProperty(
            "Agreement (Safety)",
            "safety",
            "No two honest nodes finalize conflicting values at the same
            height",
            "G(∀i,j∈Honest, ∀h: finalized(i,h,b1) ∧ finalized(j,h,b2) →
            b1=b2)",
            "Chain split: two groups finalize different blocks at
            height 100",
            ["Isabelle (Casper FFG)", "Coq (Tendermint)", "TLA+ (Cosmos)"],
        ),
        ProtocolProperty(
            "Validity",
            "safety",
```

```
        "Only valid state transitions are finalized",
        "G(finalized(block) → valid_state_transition(block))",
        "Invalid transaction included in finalized block (e.g.,
        spending nonexistent UTXO)",
        ["K Framework (KEVM)", "Coq (Tezos Michelson)"],
    ),
    ProtocolProperty(
        "Accountable Safety",
        "safety",
        "Conflicting finalized checkpoints imply ≥1/3 stake is
        slashable",
        "G(finalized(b1,h) ∧ finalized(b2,h) ∧ b1≠b2 → slashable_
        stake ≥ total/3)",
        "Two checkpoints finalized without detectable misbehavior",
        ["Isabelle (Casper FFG proof by Palmskog et al.)"],
    ),
    ProtocolProperty(
        "Liveness (Progress)",
        "liveness",
        "The chain eventually produces new finalized blocks",
        "G(F(new_finalized_block))",
        "Chain stalls permanently and never produces another block",
        ["TLA+ (partial, requires synchrony assumptions)"],
    ),
    ProtocolProperty(
        "Transaction Liveness",
        "liveness",
        "Every valid submitted transaction is eventually finalized or
        rejected",
        "G(submitted(tx) ∧ valid(tx) → F(finalized(tx) ∨
        rejected(tx)))",
        "Valid transaction remains pending indefinitely (censorship)",
        ["Difficult to verify formally due to censorship resistance
        complexity"],
    ),
```

```
        ProtocolProperty(
            "Finality Irreversibility",
            "safety",
            "Once finalized, a block is never reverted",
            "G(finalized(node,h,b) → G(finalized(node,h,b)))",
            "Finalized block is reverted (chain reorganization past
            finality)",
            ["Isabelle (Casper FFG)", "TLA+ (Tendermint)"],
        ),
    ]

properties = define_complete_properties()
print("Formal Protocol Properties")
print("=" * 75)
for p in properties:
    print(f"\n{p.name} [{p.category}]")
    print(f"  Description: {p.description}")
    print(f"  LTL: {p.ltl_formula}")
    print(f"  Violation: {p.violation_example}")
    print(f"  Verified: {', '.join(p.verified_in)}")
```

14.1.3 Model Checking

Model checking is automated. It exhaustively explores every reachable state of a finite-state model and checks that your properties hold in all of them. Either it confirms the property or hands you a counterexample, a specific execution trace that breaks it.

For consensus, the model is a state machine. Each state captures what every node sees (their chain view, pending messages, committed values) and what the network looks like (messages in transit, partitions). Transitions are protocol steps: receive a message, cast a vote, commit a block, and time out.

The problem is state explosion. Reachable states grow exponentially with nodes, messages, and rounds. Four nodes, five states each, messages arriving in arbitrary order. That's millions of configurations even for a handful of rounds.

Some techniques help manage the explosion:

Bounded model checking. Verify properties up to a fixed number of rounds. Can't prove things for unbounded runs but catches bugs within the bound.

Symmetry reduction. Consensus nodes are interchangeable, so states that only differ in which specific node holds which role get collapsed into equivalence classes.

Abstraction. Replace concrete values with abstract ones. Don't track exact message contents; just track whether messages have been sent, received, or lost.

Partial order reduction. If two messages arriving at the same node in either order produce the same result, only explore one ordering.

```
from collections import deque
from typing import Dict, Set, FrozenSet, Tuple

@dataclass(frozen=True)
class ProtocolState:
    """Immutable state for model checking (hashable for set membership)."""
    round_number: int
    node_phases: tuple        # (node_id, phase) pairs
    node_decisions: tuple     # (node_id, decision) pairs
    messages_pending: frozenset  # Messages not yet delivered

class ConsensusModelChecker:
    """
    Exhaustive state-space explorer for consensus protocol verification.

    This simplified model checker demonstrates the approach used by
    tools like TLA+/TLC, SPIN, and Alloy for consensus verification.
    Production model checkers handle much larger state spaces through
    sophisticated state compression, symmetry reduction, and
    distributed exploration.
    """

    def __init__(self, num_nodes: int, max_rounds: int,
                 max_byzantine: int):
        self.n = num_nodes
        self.max_rounds = max_rounds
        self.f = max_byzantine
        self.explored: Set[ProtocolState] = set()
        self.violations: List[dict] = []
        self.max_states = 50000  # Exploration budget
```

```
    def initial_state(self) -> ProtocolState:
        """Create the initial protocol state."""
        return ProtocolState(
            round_number=0,
            node_phases=tuple((i, "idle") for i in range(self.n)),
            node_decisions=tuple(),
            messages_pending=frozenset(),
        )

    def successors(self, state: ProtocolState) -> List[ProtocolState]:
        """
        Generate all possible successor states.

        In a real model checker, this would encode the full protocol
        semantics including all possible message deliveries, Byzantine
        behaviors, and timeout triggers.
        """
        succs = []

        if state.round_number >= self.max_rounds:
            return succs

        # Simplified: generate states for different decision combinations
        # Each honest node can decide 0, decide 1, or not decide
        honest_count = self.n - self.f

        # Generate a subset of possible next states
        decisions = dict(state.node_decisions)

        for node_id in range(honest_count):
            for value in [0, 1, None]:
                new_decisions = dict(decisions)
                if value is not None:
                    new_decisions[node_id] = value

                new_state = ProtocolState(
                    round_number=state.round_number + 1,
                    node_phases=tuple((i, "decided" if i in new_decisions
                    else "idle")
```

```
                        for i in range(self.n)),
                node_decisions=tuple(sorted(new_decisions.items())),
                messages_pending=frozenset(),
            )

            if new_state not in self.explored:
                succs.append(new_state)

        return succs[:10]  # Limit branching for demonstration

    def check_agreement(self, state: ProtocolState) -> bool:
        """
        SAFETY CHECK: Do all decided honest nodes agree?

        Agreement: ∀i,j ∈ honest: decided(i) ∧ decided(j) → value(i) =
        value(j)
        """
        decisions = dict(state.node_decisions)
        honest_values = set()

        for node_id in range(self.n - self.f):
            if node_id in decisions:
                honest_values.add(decisions[node_id])

        return len(honest_values) <= 1  # All agree or none decided

    def check_validity(self, state: ProtocolState) -> bool:
        """
        SAFETY CHECK: Are all decisions valid values?

        Validity: decided values must come from proposed values.
        """
        decisions = dict(state.node_decisions)
        valid_values = {0, 1}  # The set of valid proposals

        for value in decisions.values():
            if value not in valid_values:
                return False
        return True
```

```
    def verify(self) -> dict:
        """
        Run BFS model checking over all reachable states.

        For each state, check all safety properties.
        Report violations as counterexamples.
        """
        initial = self.initial_state()
        queue = deque([initial])
        self.explored.add(initial)

        states_checked = 0
        agreement_violations = 0
        validity_violations = 0

        while queue and len(self.explored) < self.max_states:
            state = queue.popleft()
            states_checked += 1

            # Check safety properties
            if not self.check_agreement(state):
                agreement_violations += 1
                if len(self.violations) < 5:  # Store first few violations
                    self.violations.append({
                        'property': 'agreement',
                        'state': state,
                        'decisions': dict(state.node_decisions),
                    })

            if not self.check_validity(state):
                validity_violations += 1

            # Explore successors
            for succ in self.successors(state):
                if succ not in self.explored:
                    self.explored.add(succ)
                    queue.append(succ)
```

```
        hit_state_limit = len(self.explored) >= self.max_states

        return {
            'states_explored': len(self.explored),
            'states_checked': states_checked,
            'agreement_violations': agreement_violations,
            'validity_violations': validity_violations,
            # WARNING: if hit_state_limit is True, all_safe may be a FALSE
            NEGATIVE.
            # Violations could exist in the unexplored portion of the
            state space.
            # Do NOT conclude the protocol is safe if exploration was
            incomplete.
            'all_safe': agreement_violations == 0 and validity_
            violations == 0,
            'exploration_complete': len(queue) == 0 and not hit_
            state_limit,
            'hit_state_limit': hit_state_limit,
            'counterexamples': self.violations[:3],
        }

# Run model checking for different configurations
print("\nModel Checking Results")
print("=" * 60)

for n, f, rounds in [(3, 0, 2), (4, 1, 2), (4, 0, 3), (7, 2, 2)]:
    checker = ConsensusModelChecker(n, rounds, f)
    result = checker.verify()

    status = "SAFE" if result['all_safe'] else f"VIOLATIONS:
    {result['agreement_violations']}"
    complete = "complete" if result['exploration_complete'] else "partial
    (hit state limit)"

    print(f"\n  n={n}, f={f}, rounds={rounds}:")
    print(f"    States explored: {result['states_explored']:,}
    ({complete})")
    print(f"    Agreement: {status}")
```

```
    # Warn explicitly if results may be incomplete
    if result['hit_state_limit']:
        print(f"    WARNING: State limit hit - 'SAFE' result is not
        guaranteed.")
        print(f"                Increase max_states or reduce n/rounds for
        full exploration.")

    if result['counterexamples']:
        ce = result['counterexamples'][0]
        print(f"    Counterexample: {ce['decisions']}")
```

14.1.4 Proof Assistants for Protocol Verification

Model checking covers finite state spaces. Proof assistants go further: they let you build mathematical proofs that properties hold for all configurations, unbounded rounds, arbitrary network sizes. Strictly more powerful. Also requires a lot more human effort.

A proof assistant checks formal proofs step by step. You supply the strategy and the key insights. The tool verifies every logical step follows correctly. If it type-checks, the proof is valid. No shortcuts.

Coq is built on the Calculus of Inductive Constructions. Programs and proofs are the same thing via Curry-Howard. You can extract verified executable code directly from Coq proofs. Used for Tezos's Michelson verification and various cryptographic proofs.

Isabelle/HOL uses higher-order logic. It's what was used to mechanize the Casper FFG accountable safety proof. That verification proved that conflicting finalized checkpoints require slashing at least 1/3 of the total stake. Big deal, because it puts a hard floor on attack cost.

Lean is the newer entrant, gaining traction in the blockchain space. Better performance characteristics than Coq in some areas, and its programming language features make it more approachable for developers.

TLA+ is Leslie Lamport's specification language for distributed systems. Not a proof assistant in the traditional sense, but the TLC model checker lets you verify bounded instances. Amazon used TLA+ extensively for internal distributed systems. Tendermint and Cosmos IBC both have TLA+ specs.

Table 14-1. *Formal Verification Tools for Blockchain*

Tool	Type	Strength	Blockchain Applications
TLA+/TLC	Spec language + model checker	Protocol design, distributed systems	Tendermint, Cosmos IBC, Amazon internal systems
Coq	Proof assistant (type theory)	Cryptographic proofs, verified compilers	Tezos Michelson, DeepSEA, CertiKOS
Isabelle/ HOL	Proof assistant (HOL)	Mechanized mathematics, large libraries	Casper FFG safety proof
Lean	Proof assistant (type theory)	Performance, modern language features	Emerging blockchain applications
SPIN	Model checker (Promela)	Exhaustive exploration, LTL properties	Early consensus protocol analysis
K Framework	Formal semantics framework	Language semantics, symbolic execution	KEVM (formal EVM semantics)
Alloy	Relational model finder	Structural properties, small-scope verification	Protocol design exploration

14.1.5 Symbolic Execution for Protocol-Level Security

Symbolic execution treats inputs as symbolic variables instead of concrete values and explores all possible execution paths simultaneously. When a branch depends on input, it forks: one path where the condition is true, one where it's false. Each path accumulates constraints that describe what inputs would reach it.

At the protocol level, symbolic execution can find:

State inconsistencies. Inputs that cause different nodes to land in different states despite running the same protocol code. That's a determinism bug or an underspecified step.

Invariant violations. Execution paths where something like "total supply never exceeds 21 million BTC" breaks. The executor gives you the exact input conditions that trigger it.

Unreachable code. Protocol branches that can never execute, which might signal spec errors or dead code that makes auditing harder.

Integer overflow and underflow. Arithmetic that wraps around, potentially letting an attacker mint tokens from nothing or produce negative balances.

14.1.6 Security Audit Methodology

A proper security audit covers five domains. Each one needs different people and different tools.

```
@dataclass
class AuditCategory:
    name: str
    description: str
    checklist: List[str]
    tools: List[str]
    severity_if_failed: str

def comprehensive_audit_checklist() -> List[AuditCategory]:
    """Complete security audit framework for blockchain protocols."""
    return [
        AuditCategory(
            "Consensus Safety",
            "Verify that the consensus mechanism maintains agreement "
            "under all specified adversary conditions",
            [
                "Verify agreement property holds with maximum Byzantine
                faults (f = floor((n-1)/3))",
                "Test for chain splits under network partitions with
                message delays exceeding assumed bounds",
                "Simulate concurrent block proposals from multiple
                validators in the same slot",
                "Verify finality guarantee: finalized blocks are never
                reverted under fault tolerance assumptions",
                "Test view change / leader rotation for state preservation
                across transitions",
```

```
            "Verify liveness: chain progresses after partition heals
            and GST is reached",
            "Check for equivocation detection completeness: all double-
            voting is caught",
            "Verify fork choice rule selects the correct chain under
            all fork scenarios",
            "Test behavior when exactly f nodes are Byzantine (boundary
            condition)",
            "Verify that honest nodes converge on the same chain within
            bounded time",
        ],
        ["TLA+", "SPIN", "Custom simulation", "Jepsen-style testing"],
        "Critical: consensus failure can cause double-spending",
    ),
    AuditCategory(
        "Cryptographic Implementation",
        "Verify correct implementation of all cryptographic
        primitives "
        "including signatures, hashes, and random number generation",
        [
            "Verify ECDSA/EdDSA nonce generation uses CSPRNG with no
            reuse possibility",
            "Check signature verification handles all malformed inputs
            without crashing",
            "Verify hash function implementations pass NIST test
            vectors",
            "Test for timing side-channels in signature verification
            and comparison operations",
            "Verify key derivation follows BIP-32/39/44 standards (for
            HD wallets)",
            "Check that private key material is zeroed from memory
            after use",
            "Verify Merkle proof generation and verification for all
            tree types",
```

```
            "Test hash collision handling in data structures (Merkle
            trees, tries)",
            "Verify random beacon / VRF implementations produce
            unpredictable outputs",
            "Check for weak randomness in any protocol component
            (leader selection, etc.)",
        ],
        ["Cryptographic test vectors", "Side-channel analyzers",
        "Fuzzing tools"],
        "Critical: cryptographic failure compromises all security",
    ),
    AuditCategory(
        "Network Layer Security",
        "Verify resistance to network-level attacks including "
        "eclipse attacks, Sybil attacks, and message manipulation",
        [
            "Test behavior under network partition: safety maintained,
            liveness degrades gracefully",
            "Verify eclipse attack resistance: peer diversity
            requirements enforced",
            "Check message authentication: spoofed messages are
            rejected",
            "Test DoS resistance of message handlers: malformed
            messages don't crash nodes",
            "Verify gossip protocol convergence under adverse network
            conditions",
            "Test peer scoring and banning for misbehaving peers",
            "Verify TLS/Noise protocol for node-to-node encryption",
            "Check for amplification attacks via gossip protocol",
            "Verify that time-based protocol steps tolerate reasonable
            clock skew",
            "Test discovery mechanism for Sybil resistance",
        ],
        ["Network simulation", "Chaos engineering", "Traffic
        analysis"],
```

```
        "High: network attacks can enable consensus attacks",
    ),
    AuditCategory(
        "Economic Security",
        "Verify that the incentive mechanism makes honest behavior "
        "the rational strategy under all plausible adversary budgets",
        [
            "Model attack profitability for adversaries with 10%, 25%,
            33%, 50% of consensus power",
            "Verify slashing conditions are complete: no equivocation
            escapes penalty",
            "Check for MEV extraction vectors in default transaction
            ordering",
            "Analyze fee market mechanism under extreme demand (10x,
            100x normal)",
            "Verify that block rewards + fees provide adequate security
            budget",
            "Model validator incentives under various token price
            scenarios (bull/bear/crash)",
            "Check for nothing-at-stake vulnerabilities in fork
            scenarios",
            "Verify that the inactivity leak restores finality within
            expected timeframe",
            "Analyze long-range attack feasibility given unbonding
            period length",
            "Check for governance attack vectors via token
            accumulation",
        ],
        ["Game-theoretic modeling", "Agent-based simulation", "Economic
        analysis"],
        "High: economic attacks can be more practical than protocol
        attacks",
    ),
```

```
        AuditCategory(
            "State Management and Data Integrity",
            "Verify correct state transition execution, storage, "
            "and proof generation across all protocol components",
            [
                "Verify state transition determinism: identical inputs
                always produce identical outputs",
                "Test state proof generation and verification for
                correctness and completeness",
                "Verify state recovery after node crash at various protocol
                stages",
                "Check that pruning preserves all consensus-
                critical state",
                "Test for state growth DoS: cheap creation of persistent
                state entries",
                "Verify database consistency under concurrent access
                patterns",
                "Check state migration correctness during protocol upgrades
                (hard forks)",
                "Verify that genesis state initialization produces
                identical state roots across implementations",
                "Test checkpoint sync for correctness: does checkpoint-
                synced node match full-synced node?",
                "Verify that archive node state queries return correct
                historical data",
            ],
            ["Differential testing", "Fuzzing", "Property-based testing"],
            "Medium-High: state bugs cause consensus failures or
            data loss",
        ),
    ]

checklist = comprehensive_audit_checklist()
print("\nBlockchain Protocol Security Audit Framework")
print("=" * 70)
```

```
total_items = 0
for category in checklist:
    print(f"\n{category.name} [{category.severity_if_failed}]")
    print(f"  {category.description}")
    print(f"  Tools: {', '.join(category.tools)}")
    print(f"  Checklist ({len(category.checklist)} items):")
    for i, item in enumerate(category.checklist, 1):
        print(f"    {i:2d}. {item}")
        total_items += 1

print(f"\n  Total audit items: {total_items}")
print(f"  Estimated audit duration: {total_items * 2}-{total_items * 4}
person-days")
```

14.1.7 The Gap Between Verification and Security

Formal verification proves that a model satisfies a spec. That's valuable. But real-world security has three additional dimensions that formal methods can't fully cover:

Specification completeness. Your spec has to capture every security-relevant property. Miss one (say, censorship resistance or MEV fairness) and verification tells you nothing about it. Writing a complete spec is itself a hard problem that requires deep domain knowledge.

Model fidelity. The formal model has to match the real implementation. Abstraction is necessary to make verification tractable, but every abstraction potentially hides a bug. A verified TLA+ model of Tendermint doesn't guarantee the Go implementation is correct. It guarantees the abstract design is correct. Those are different things.

Environmental assumptions. Proofs assume things about the world: message delivery bounds, what the adversary can do, and that cryptographic primitives hold up. If those assumptions fail in practice (a primitive gets broken, or partitions last longer than expected), the guarantees may not hold.

Despite all that, formal verification is still far more valuable than testing alone. It forces you to be precise about what properties you care about. It finds edge cases testing would never hit. And for the properties it does verify, the assurance level is as high as it gets.

Table 14-2. What Formal Verification Can and Cannot Guarantee

Can Verify	Cannot Verify
Protocol safety (agreement, validity) given fault tolerance assumptions	Implementation correctness (unless implementation itself is verified)
Protocol liveness under synchrony assumptions	Behavior under assumption violations (broken crypto, permanent partition)
Cryptographic proof correctness (reduction proofs)	Side-channel resistance in hardware
State machine determinism	Economic incentive alignment (requires game-theoretic analysis)
Specific vulnerability absence	Unknown vulnerability classes
Specification consistency	Specification completeness

14.1.8 Summary

Formal verification changes the security claim from "we tested it and found no bugs" to "we proved these specific properties hold for all inputs." It's not a complete security solution. But for the properties it covers, nothing else comes close.

Key takeaways:

- Temporal logic (LTL, CTL) is how you formally express blockchain properties. Safety is "nothing bad happens" (agreement, validity). Liveness is "something good eventually happens" (progress, termination).
- Model checking explores finite-state models exhaustively. State explosion keeps it limited to small configurations, but bounded checking and abstraction extend its reach. The counterexamples it produces are incredibly useful for debugging.
- Proof assistants like Coq, Isabelle, Lean produce machine-checked proofs valid for all configurations, not just bounded ones. Casper FFG and Tendermint both went through this process.

- TLA+ sits between specification and verification. The language itself eliminates ambiguity in protocol descriptions. The TLC model checker handles automated verification for bounded instances.
- Security audits need to cover five domains: consensus safety, cryptographic implementation, network security, economic incentives, state management. Different expertise for each.
- There's always a gap between the formal model and reality. Spec completeness, model fidelity, environmental assumptions. Three places where verification can be right and the system can still break.
- Formal verification complements testing, fuzzing, auditing, bug bounties, operational monitoring. None of these alone is enough. Together they get you closer.

Safety: G(nothing bad). Violated by finite traces (chain split, invalid finalization).—Liveness: G(F(something good)). Only violated by infinite traces (permanent stall).—Model checking: exhaustive but bounded. State explosion limits it to small n. Great for finding counterexamples.—Proof assistants (Coq, Isabelle): unbounded proofs. Require human effort. Highest assurance available.—Casper FFG accountable safety was proven in Isabelle. Tendermint safety was proven in Coq and TLA+.—Security audits span 5 domains: consensus, crypto, network, economics, state. 50+ checklist items.—The verification gap: spec completeness, model fidelity, environmental assumptions. All three can cause a verified system to still fail.—Formal methods and testing/auditing complement each other. Neither alone is sufficient.

14.1.9 Exercises

Problem 1 (Basic): What's the difference between safety and liveness? Two blockchain-specific examples of each. Which kind can testing over finite executions actually verify?

Problem 2 (Calculation): BFT protocol, 7 nodes, 5 possible states each, 10 possible messages in flight. Estimate the state space. Why does this make exhaustive model checking impractical at scale?

Problem 3 (Implementation): Write a TLA+ spec (or pseudocode equivalent) for a simplified 3-node consensus protocol. Define the state machine, a safety invariant (agreement), and at least one liveness property.

Problem 4 (Analysis): FLP impossibility says no deterministic asynchronous protocol solves consensus with even one fault. How do these get around it: (a) PBFT's timeout-based view change, (b) Nakamoto's probabilistic consensus, (c) randomized BFT (Ben-Or)?

Problem 5 (Design): Build a security audit checklist for a ZK-rollup. What properties are rollup-specific that don't show up in L1 consensus? Think: data availability, proof soundness, escape hatch, sequencer behavior.

Problem 6 (Theory): Can formal verification eliminate all security risks? Name three categories of vulnerabilities it fundamentally cannot catch. Explain why for each.

Problem 7 (Comparative): Casper FFG verified in Isabelle. Tendermint in TLA+ and Coq. Algorand in UPPAAL. What got verified in each case? What didn't? Why those tools?

Problem 8 (Critical Thinking): Someone claims their consensus is "formally verified." What should you ask? Consider: what exactly was verified, in which tool, against which spec, under what assumptions.

Problem 9 (Advanced): Use KEVM, Mythril, or Manticore to verify a simple smart contract. Document what properties you specified, the verification process, and what came up.

Problem 10 (Research): Find a real protocol bug that formal verification could have caught. Candidates: the 2020 Ethereum Medalla testnet incident, any BFT consensus split, a smart contract exploit. Describe the bug, the impact, the formal property it violated, and how verification would have found it.

(Solutions in Appendix D)

14.1.10 Further Reading

Lamport's "Specifying Systems" is the TLA+ reference. Amazon's paper on TLA+ at AWS shows it works in industrial settings.

Palmskog et al.'s Isabelle proof of Casper FFG accountable safety is the biggest formal verification result in blockchain so far. Tendermint's TLA+ spec lives in the Cosmos GitHub repo.

The K Framework's formal EVM semantics (KEVM) is the foundation for symbolic execution-based contract verification. Runtime Verification, Inc. maintains it.

Trail of Bits publishes audit methodologies and open-source tools. OpenZeppelin's audit reports are good examples of thorough blockchain security analysis in practice.

Be careful with claims of "formally verified." Verification is only as good as the spec and the model. A verified protocol with an incomplete spec or an inaccurate model can still have critical vulnerabilities. Don't treat it as a stamp of total security.

PART IV

Scalability and Advanced Topics

CHAPTER 15

Layer-2 Scaling

15.1 Rollups, State Channels, and Plasma

L1 throughput is capped by design. Layer-2 is how you work around that without giving up L1 security. This chapter covers optimistic rollups and their fraud proof challenge games, ZK rollups and what validity proofs cost to generate, state channels and Lightning, Plasma's exit game and why it lost to rollups, validiums, and the cross-L2 composability mess nobody has cleanly solved yet. Here's what it covers:

- Why Layer-2 exists in the first place and how it borrows security from Layer-1 without reinventing it
- **Optimistic Rollups**: fraud proofs, interactive verification games, the challenge window, and why seven days feels like forever
- **ZK Rollups**: validity proofs, circuit constraints, proving costs, and data availability
- **State Channels**: Bidirectional payments, HTLC routing, generalized state, the whole Lightning story
- Plasma's exit game, the mass exit nightmare, and why rollups ended up winning
- Cross-L2 composability headaches, liquidity fragmentation, and the shared sequencing ideas trying to fix it
- A real comparison of L2 approaches on security, cost, latency, and trust assumptions

N. Savant, *Blockchain Foundations*, https://doi.org/10.1007/979-8-8688-2891-1_15

15.1.1 The Layer-2 Thesis

Layer-1 blockchains have a throughput ceiling, and it's there by design. Every full node validates every transaction. That gives you the strongest possible verification guarantee—any node can independently check the entire chain from genesis—but it means throughput is capped by whatever the weakest node you want to support can handle.

Bitcoin does about 7 transactions per second. Ethereum manages 15–30 on L1. Those aren't engineering failures. They're deliberate choices. Want higher throughput? Bigger blocks push out hobbyist validators and hurt decentralization. Faster blocks increase orphan rates and favor validators clustered in one geography. Pick your poison.

Layer-2 takes a different route. Move execution off-chain but keep L1's security guarantees through cryptographic or economic mechanisms. The insight: L1 doesn't need to process every transaction. It just needs to be the dispute resolution layer and the data availability backstop. Most transactions settle off-chain, and L1 only steps in when someone disagrees about the state.

Think of it like the court system. Most business deals happen without a courtroom in sight. But the fact that courts exist and contracts are enforceable—that's what lets strangers trust each other. Courts handle the tiny fraction of deals that go sideways. L1 works the same way. It's the security foundation that makes L2 safe, but it only processes the transactions that need on-chain verification: fraud proofs, validity proofs, and dispute resolution.

Economics are hard to argue with. A simple L1 Ethereum transfer runs $0.50 to $5.00 depending on congestion. Same thing on an L2 rollup? $0.01 to $0.10. For complex DeFi operations—swaps, lending, derivatives—the savings hit 50–100x. It works because the L1 costs of posting data and verifying proofs get split across thousands of L2 transactions per batch.

Table 15-1. Layer-2 Architecture Taxonomy

Approach	Data On-Chain	Proof Mechanism	Withdrawal Delay	Throughput	Security Assumption
Optimistic Rollup	Full tx data (calldata/blobs)	Fraud proof (reactive, on dispute)	~7 days challenge period	~2,000–4,000 TPS	At least 1 honest verifier
ZK Rollup	Full tx data or state diffs	Validity proof (proactive, every batch)	Minutes to hours (proof time)	~2,000–10,000 TPS	Cryptographic proof soundness
State Channel	None (except open/close/dispute)	Signed state updates	Instant (cooperative)/hours (dispute)	Unlimited between participants	Both parties online and responsive
Plasma	Merkle roots only	Fraud proof + exit game	~7–14 days (about 2 weeks)	~1,000 TPS	Operator publishes data; users monitor
Validium	Off chain (DA committee)	Validity proof	Minutes to hours	~10,000+ TPS	DA committee honest majority

15.1.2 Optimistic Rollups

Optimistic rollups are the most widely deployed L2 technology right now. Arbitrum, Optimism (OP Stack), Base—all optimistic. The name tells you the philosophy: state transitions posted by the sequencer are assumed valid unless someone challenges them. No need to verify every transition on L1. Gas costs drop dramatically for the common case where the sequencer is honest.

Architecture Components

The Sequencer takes user transactions, orders them, executes them off-chain to compute the new state, and posts results to L1. Right now, the sequencer is typically a single centralized operator (Offchain Labs for Arbitrum, OP Labs for Optimism). Decentralizing it is an active research problem. Users get soft confirmations within seconds, much faster than L1 finality, but those confirmations carry an implicit asterisk: they depend on the sequencer being honest.

The Rollup Contract sits on L1 and stores state roots. The sequencer posts batches periodically—compressed transaction data plus the resulting state root. Each posted route enters a pending state, and the challenge clock starts ticking. During that window, anyone watching the rollup can re-execute the transactions and check if the posted root matches.

Data availability is what separates rollups from plasma and sidechains. The rollup posts complete transaction data to L1 (calldata or EIP-4844 blobs). That means anyone can reconstruct the rollup's state from L1 data alone, no dependence on the sequencer or any third party. If the sequencer vanishes tomorrow, users can still figure out their balances and withdraw.

The Fraud Proof System is the teeth. If the sequencer posts a wrong state root—a bug, deliberate manipulation, a compromised key, whatever—any observer who catches it submits a fraud proof to L1. Successful proof reverts the bad root and everything built on it. The sequencer's bond gets slashed. The challenger gets rewarded.

Interactive Fraud Proofs

The design challenge is efficiency. Re-executing 10,000 transactions on L1 to check a batch would cost a fortune. Two approaches deal with this:

Non-interactive fraud proofs (Optimism's Cannon): The challenger provides a single proof identifying the exact execution step that went wrong. Pinpointing that step takes real off-chain computation, but the on-chain verification is minimal.

Interactive fraud proofs (Arbitrum's BOLD): A multi-round bisection game. Challenger and defender agree on the starting state but disagree on the ending state. They keep cutting the execution trace in half—"I say the state after 5,000 steps is X"—until they isolate one single step where they diverge. Only that step gets executed on L1. Gas cost becomes constant no matter how big the batch.

```
import hashlib
from dataclasses import dataclass, field
from typing import Dict, List, Optional, Tuple

@dataclass
class ExecutionStep:
    """A single step in the rollup execution trace."""
    step_number: int
    state_hash: str
```

```
    instruction: str
    gas_used: int

@dataclass
class RollupBatch:
    """A batch of transactions posted to L1."""
    batch_id: int
    transactions: List[dict]
    pre_state_root: str
    post_state_root: str
    execution_trace: List[ExecutionStep]
    sequencer: str
    l1_block: int
    challenge_deadline: int

class OptimisticRollupWithBisection:
    """
    Optimistic rollup with interactive fraud proof bisection.

    The bisection game:
    1. Challenger claims the sequencer's post_state_root is wrong
    2. Both parties bisect execution trace until they disagree on a
       single step
    3. That single step is executed on L1
    4. L1 determines who is correct

    This reduces L1 verification cost from O(n) to O(log n) rounds,
    with each round requiring only a constant amount of on-chain work.
    """

    CHALLENGE_PERIOD_BLOCKS = 50400  # ~7 days at 12s/block
    SEQUENCER_BOND = 100_000  # USD equivalent

    def __init__(self, initial_state: Dict[str, int]):
        self.state = dict(initial_state)
        self.batches: List[RollupBatch] = []
        self.finalized_roots: List[str] = []
        self.batch_counter = 0
```

```
    def _compute_root(self, state: Dict[str, int]) -> str:
        data = str(sorted(state.items()))
        return hashlib.sha256(data.encode()).hexdigest()[:16]

    def _execute_batch(self, state: Dict[str, int],
                       transactions: List[dict]) -> Tuple[Dict[str, int],
                       List[ExecutionStep]]:
        """Execute transactions and record execution trace."""
        working_state = dict(state)
        trace = []

        for i, tx in enumerate(transactions):
            step_state_before = self._compute_root(working_state)

            sender_bal = working_state.get(tx['sender'], 0)
            if sender_bal >= tx['amount']:
                working_state[tx['sender']] = sender_bal - tx['amount']
                working_state[tx['recipient']] = (
                    working_state.get(tx['recipient'], 0) + tx['amount'])
                instruction = f"transfer({tx['sender']},{tx['recipient']},{
                tx['amount']})"
            else:
                instruction = f"skip(insufficient_balance)"

            trace.append(ExecutionStep(
                step_number=i,
                state_hash=self._compute_root(working_state),
                instruction=instruction,
                gas_used=21000,
            ))

        return working_state, trace

    def submit_batch(self, transactions: List[dict],
                     l1_block: int) -> RollupBatch:
        """Sequencer posts a new batch."""
        pre_root = self._compute_root(self.state)
        new_state, trace = self._execute_batch(self.state, transactions)
```

```
        post_root = self._compute_root(new_state)

        self.batch_counter += 1
        batch = RollupBatch(
            batch_id=self.batch_counter,
            transactions=transactions,
            pre_state_root=pre_root,
            post_state_root=post_root,
            execution_trace=trace,
            sequencer="sequencer_0",
            l1_block=l1_block,
            challenge_deadline=l1_block + self.CHALLENGE_PERIOD_BLOCKS,
        )

        self.state = new_state
        self.batches.append(batch)
        return batch

    def bisection_game(self, batch: RollupBatch,
                       challenger_trace: List[ExecutionStep]) -> dict:
        """
        Simulate the interactive bisection fraud proof game.

        The challenger has independently executed the batch and produced
        a different trace. The game narrows the disagreement to one step.

        Each round:
        1. Find the midpoint of the disagreement range
        2. Both parties reveal their state at the midpoint
        3. If they agree at midpoint, disagreement is in second half
        4. If they disagree at midpoint, disagreement is in first half
        5. Repeat until range is a single step
        """
        sequencer_trace = batch.execution_trace
        n = len(sequencer_trace)

        if n == 0:
```

```
            return {'dispute': False, 'reason': 'Empty batch'}

        lo = 0
        hi = n - 1
        rounds = 0

        while lo < hi:
            mid = (lo + hi) // 2
            rounds += 1

            # Compare state at midpoint
            seq_state = sequencer_trace[mid].state_hash
            chal_state = challenger_trace[mid].state_hash

            if seq_state == chal_state:
                # Agree at midpoint: disagreement is after midpoint
                lo = mid + 1
            else:
                # Disagree at midpoint: disagreement is at or before
                  midpoint
                hi = mid

        # lo == hi: single disputed step
        disputed_step = lo

        return {
            'disputed_step': disputed_step,
            'bisection_rounds': rounds,
            'total_steps': n,
            'sequencer_state': sequencer_trace[disputed_step].state_hash,
            'challenger_state': challenger_trace[disputed_step].state_hash,
            'instruction': sequencer_trace[disputed_step].instruction,
            'on_chain_verification': 'Execute single instruction on L1',
            'gas_savings': f"Verified 1 of {n} steps on-chain ({n}x
            reduction)",
        }

    def verify_fraud(self, batch: RollupBatch,
```

```
                   correct_pre_state: Dict[str, int]) -> dict:
        """
        Independent verifier checks batch correctness.
        If incorrect, initiates bisection game.
        """
        # Re-execute independently
        _, challenger_trace = self._execute_batch(correct_pre_state, batch.
        transactions)

        if not challenger_trace:
            return {'fraud': False}

        # Compare final state
        challenger_final = challenger_trace[-1].state_hash
        sequencer_final = batch.post_state_root

        if challenger_final == sequencer_final:
            return {'fraud': False, 'message': 'Batch is correct'}

        # State mismatch: run bisection
        bisection = self.bisection_game(batch, challenger_trace)

        return {
            'fraud': True,
            'message': 'Fraud detected via bisection',
            'bisection_result': bisection,
        }

# === Demonstration ===
rollup = OptimisticRollupWithBisection({
    'alice': 100000, 'bob': 50000, 'carol': 30000, 'dave': 20000
})

print("Optimistic Rollup with Interactive Fraud Proofs")
print("=" * 65)

# Submit a legitimate batch
batch1 = rollup.submit_batch([
    {'sender': 'alice', 'recipient': 'bob', 'amount': 5000},
```

```
    {'sender': 'bob', 'recipient': 'carol', 'amount': 3000},
    {'sender': 'carol', 'recipient': 'dave', 'amount': 1000},
    {'sender': 'alice', 'recipient': 'dave', 'amount': 2000},
    {'sender': 'dave', 'recipient': 'bob', 'amount': 500},
], l1_block=100)

print(f"Batch 1: {len(batch1.transactions)} transactions")
print(f"  Pre-state:  {batch1.pre_state_root}")
print(f"  Post-state: {batch1.post_state_root}")
print(f"  Trace steps: {len(batch1.execution_trace)}")

# Verify (honest case: should find no fraud)
pre_state = {'alice': 100000, 'bob': 50000, 'carol': 30000, 'dave': 20000}
result = rollup.verify_fraud(batch1, pre_state)
print(f"  Verification: {result['message']}")

# Simulate fraud: create a batch with wrong post_state_root
print(f"\n--- Simulating Fraudulent Batch ---")
fraudulent_batch = RollupBatch(
    batch_id=99,
    transactions=[
        {'sender': 'alice', 'recipient': 'bob', 'amount': 5000},
        {'sender': 'bob', 'recipient': 'carol', 'amount': 3000},
        {'sender': 'carol', 'recipient': 'dave', 'amount': 1000},
    ],
    pre_state_root=rollup._compute_root(pre_state),
    post_state_root="FRAUDULENT_ROOT",
    execution_trace=[
        ExecutionStep(0, "state_0_correct",
        "transfer(alice,bob,5000)", 21000),
        ExecutionStep(1, "state_1_correct",
        "transfer(bob,carol,3000)", 21000),
        ExecutionStep(2, "FRAUDULENT_ROOT",
        "transfer(carol,dave,1000)", 21000),
    ],
    sequencer="malicious_seq",
    l1_block=200,
```

```
    challenge_deadline=200 + 50400,
)

# Challenger re-executes honestly
_, honest_trace = rollup._execute_batch(pre_state, fraudulent_batch.
transactions)

bisection = rollup.bisection_game(fraudulent_batch, honest_trace)
print(f"  Bisection result:")
print(f"    Disputed step: {bisection['disputed_step']} of
{bisection['total_steps']}")
print(f"    Bisection rounds: {bisection['bisection_rounds']}")
print(f"    {bisection['gas_savings']}")
print(f"    On-chain: {bisection['on_chain_verification']}")

# Show scaling of bisection
print(f"\n  Bisection Scaling (rounds = log2(steps)):")
for n_txs in [100, 1000, 10000, 100000, 1000000]:
    import math
    rounds = math.ceil(math.log2(max(n_txs, 2)))
    print(f"    {n_txs:>10,} transactions: {rounds:3d} bisection rounds")
```

15.1.3 ZK Rollups

ZK rollups swap the optimistic assumption for a mathematical one. No more "assume it's correct until someone complains." The sequencer generates a zero-knowledge proof (validity proof) that cryptographically certifies every state transition in the batch. The L1 contract checks the proof and only accepts the new state root if it passes.

How ZK Rollup Proofs Work

Here's how it works. The sequencer collects transactions, executes them off-chain, and computes the new state. Then it generates a succinct proof that the computation was done correctly. This proof is a compact cryptographic object—typically 200–500 bytes for a SNARK, a few KB for a STARK—that says, "Starting from state root S_1, applying transactions $T_1...T_n$ produces state root S_2." The L1 contract verifies it in constant time (a few hundred thousand gas, independent of n) and accepts the new root.

The big advantages over optimistic rollups:

No challenge period. State transitions are final the moment the proof verifies. Withdrawals from L2 to L1 take minutes or hours (proof generation and verification time), not seven days.

Cryptographic security. Soundness guarantees that no computationally bounded adversary can fake a valid proof for an incorrect state transition. That's strictly stronger than the optimistic model, which needs at least one honest watcher to spot and challenge fraud.

Constant verification cost. Verifying the proof on L1 costs the same whether the batch has 100 transactions or 100,000. Amortization gets better the bigger the batch.

The downside is proof generation cost. Producing a ZK proof for general computation is orders of magnitude more expensive than running the code directly. Current ZK-EVM implementations need roughly 1,000–1,000,000x more computation. That means: (a) higher operational costs for whoever runs the prover, (b) latency between execution and proof availability, (c) specialized hardware like GPUs, FPGAs, or eventually ASICs.

ZK-EVM Compatibility Levels

Vitalik Buterin classified ZK-EVM compatibility into types:

Type 1 (Ethereum-equivalent). Proves the exact Ethereum execution spec. Any Ethereum contract runs unmodified. The catch: Ethereum wasn't designed to be ZK-friendly, so proving is expensive. No production Type 1 exists yet, though the Ethereum Foundation's ZK-EVM effort is working toward it.

Type 2 (EVM-equivalent). Same bytecode as Ethereum, minor internal differences (slightly different gas costs for some operations, different state representation). Most existing contracts work without changes. Scroll and Polygon zkEVM fall here.

Type 2.5 (EVM-equivalent except gas). Like Type 2 but with altered gas costs that reflect ZK-proof generation reality. Operations cheap on the EVM but expensive to prove (non-ZK-friendly hash functions, for instance) get repriced.

Type 3 (almost EVM-equivalent). Compatible with most EVM features but not all. Some precompiles or opcodes might be missing or behave differently. Faster proving, but you give up some compatibility.

Type 4 (high-level language compatible). Compiles Solidity or other languages to a ZK-friendly VM instead of the EVM. Different bytecode, so existing deployed contracts need recompilation. zkSync Era (custom VM) and Starknet (Cairo language) are examples.

Table 15-2. Optimistic vs. ZK Rollup Detailed Comparison

Dimension	Optimistic Rollup	ZK Rollup
Proof mechanism	Fraud proof (only if challenged)	Validity proof (every batch)
Finality to L1	~7 days (challenge period)	Minutes-hours (proof generation)
L1 verification cost per batch	Zero (happy path) / high (fraud proof)	~300K-500K gas (constant per batch)
Proof generation cost	Zero	1,000-1,000,000× execution overhead
EVM compatibility	Full (can run unmodified bytecode)	Varies by type (1-4)
Data requirement	Full transaction data on L1	Full data or state diffs on L1
Security assumption	≥1 honest verifier in 7-day window	Cryptographic soundness of proof system
Withdrawal to L1	7 days (or via liquidity bridge ~minutes)	Minutes-hours (after proof)
Production maturity	Mature (Arbitrum since 2021)	Newer (zkSync Era 2023, Scroll 2024)
Hardware for prover	Standard servers	Specialized (GPU/FPGA clusters)
Recursive proofs	Not applicable	Enables proof aggregation across batches

```
def rollup_cost_comparison(num_transactions: int,
                           l1_calldata_cost_per_byte: float = 0.0001,
                           l1_execution_gas_cost: float = 0.00000005,
                           avg_tx_calldata_bytes: int = 100,
                           zk_proof_verification_gas: int = 400000,
                           optimistic_fraud_proof_gas: int = 5000000,
                           fraud_proof_probability: float = 0.001)
                           -> dict:
    """
    Compare costs of optimistic vs ZK rollup per transaction.
```

```
    Costs include:
    - L1 data posting (shared by both: must post tx data for DA)
    - L1 verification (ZK: proof per batch; Optimistic: fraud proof rarely)
    - Off-chain execution (both: execute transactions)
    - Proof generation (ZK only: significant compute cost)
    """
    # L1 data cost (same for both)
    total_data_bytes = num_transactions * avg_tx_calldata_bytes
    l1_data_cost = total_data_bytes * l1_calldata_cost_per_byte
    per_tx_data_cost = l1_data_cost / num_transactions

    # Optimistic: no proof cost normally; rare fraud proof
    opt_verification_cost = (fraud_proof_probability *
                             optimistic_fraud_proof_gas * l1_execution_
                             gas_cost)
    opt_per_tx_cost = per_tx_data_cost + opt_verification_cost / num_
    transactions

    # ZK: proof verification per batch (amortized)
    zk_verification_cost = zk_proof_verification_gas * l1_execution_
    gas_cost
    zk_prover_cost = num_transactions * 0.001  # ~$0.001 per tx prover cost
    zk_per_tx_cost = (per_tx_data_cost +
                      zk_verification_cost / num_transactions +
                      zk_prover_cost / num_transactions)

    # L1 baseline
    l1_per_tx_cost = 21000 * l1_execution_gas_cost + avg_tx_calldata_bytes
    * l1_calldata_cost_per_byte

    return {
        'num_transactions': num_transactions,
        'l1_cost_per_tx': l1_per_tx_cost,
        'optimistic_cost_per_tx': opt_per_tx_cost,
        'zk_cost_per_tx': zk_per_tx_cost,
        'optimistic_savings_vs_l1': (1 - opt_per_tx_cost / l1_per_tx_
        cost) * 100,
```

```
        'zk_savings_vs_l1': (1 - zk_per_tx_cost / l1_per_tx_cost) * 100,
    }

print("\nRollup Cost Comparison (per transaction)")
print("=" * 70)
print(f"{'Batch Size':>12} {'L1 Cost':>10} {'Optimistic':>12} {'ZK':>12} "
      f"{'Opt Savings':>12} {'ZK Savings':>11}")
print("-" * 70)

for batch_size in [100, 500, 1000, 5000, 10000, 50000]:
    r = rollup_cost_comparison(batch_size)
    print(f"  {batch_size:>10,} ${r['l1_cost_per_tx']:>8.4f} "
          f"${r['optimistic_cost_per_tx']:>10.4f} "
          f"${r['zk_cost_per_tx']:>10.4f} "
          f"{r['optimistic_savings_vs_l1']:>10.1f}% "
          f"{r['zk_savings_vs_l1']:>9.1f}%")
```

15.1.4 State Channels

State channels take a different approach entirely. Interactions happen completely off-chain between a fixed group of participants. They lock funds in an on-chain contract, exchange signed state updates off-chain, and only submit the final state to L1 when they want to close up. Thousands or millions of state transitions for the cost of two on-chain transactions: open and close.

The Lightning Network is the most prominent example. Two parties open a payment channel by creating a multisig funding transaction that locks funds on-chain. From there, they send payments back and forth by exchanging signed commitment transactions that update who owns what. When either party wants to settle, they broadcast the latest commitment to the blockchain.

Payment Channel Mechanics

The critical piece is revocation. Neither party can be allowed to broadcast an old state that favors them. In Lightning, each state update creates a new commitment transaction and hands the other party a revocation key for the old one. Try to broadcast a revoked state? The counterparty uses that key to claim all the channel funds. That's the penalty.

```
from dataclasses import dataclass
from typing import Dict, List, Optional
import hashlib

@dataclass
class ChannelState:
    nonce: int
    balances: Dict[str, int]
    channel_id: str

    @property
    def state_hash(self) -> str:
        data = f"{self.channel_id}:{self.nonce}:{sorted(self.balances.
        items())}"
        return hashlib.sha256(data.encode()).hexdigest()[:16]

class BidirectionalChannel:
    """
    Bidirectional payment channel with revocation-based cheating
    prevention.

    Lifecycle:
    1. Open: both parties deposit funds into on-chain contract
    2. Operate: exchange signed state updates off-chain
    3. Close: submit final state to L1
       - Cooperative: both sign final state, instant settlement
       - Uncooperative: one party submits state, challenge period begins
       - Cheating: party submits old state, counterparty uses
         revocation key
    """

    CHALLENGE_PERIOD_BLOCKS = 144  # ~24 hours for Bitcoin

    def __init__(self, party_a: str, party_b: str,
                 deposit_a: int, deposit_b: int):
        self.party_a = party_a
        self.party_b = party_b
        self.channel_id = hashlib.sha256(
```

```
            f"{party_a}:{party_b}:{deposit_a}:{deposit_b}".encode()
        ).hexdigest()[:12]

        self.capacity = deposit_a + deposit_b
        self.current = ChannelState(
            nonce=0,
            balances={party_a: deposit_a, party_b: deposit_b},
            channel_id=self.channel_id,
        )

        # Revocation secret storage
        self.revocation_secrets: Dict[int, str] = {}
        self.history: List[ChannelState] = [self.current]
        self.on_chain_txs = 1  # Opening transaction
        self.closed = False

def pay(self, sender: str, recipient: str,
        amount: int) -> Optional[ChannelState]:
    if self.closed:
        return None
    if sender not in self.current.balances:
        return None
    if recipient not in self.current.balances:
        # Payment channels only exist between two fixed parties.
        # Paying a third party creates a new balance key,
        # corrupting the channel state silently.
        return None
    if self.current.balances[sender] < amount:
        return None
    new_balances = dict(self.current.balances)
    new_balances[sender] -= amount
    new_balances[recipient] += amount
# One line added – the recipient not in self.current.balances check.

        # Store revocation for old state
        old_nonce = self.current.nonce
        self.revocation_secrets[old_nonce] = hashlib.sha256(
```

```
            f"revoke:{self.channel_id}:{old_nonce}".encode()
        ).hexdigest()[:16]

        self.current = ChannelState(
            nonce=old_nonce + 1,
            balances=new_balances,
            channel_id=self.channel_id,
        )
        self.history.append(self.current)
        return self.current

    def cooperative_close(self) -> dict:
        """Both parties agree on final state. Instant settlement."""
        self.closed = True
        self.on_chain_txs += 1
        return {
            'type': 'cooperative_close',
            'final_state': self.current.balances,
            'total_updates': self.current.nonce,
            'on_chain_txs': self.on_chain_txs,
            'gas_saved': self.current.nonce * 21000,
            'efficiency': f"{self.current.nonce} payments in {self.on_
            chain_txs} on-chain txs",
        }

    def unilateral_close(self, submitter: str,
                         submitted_state: ChannelState) -> dict:
        """One party closes unilaterally. Challenge period begins."""
        self.on_chain_txs += 1

        # Check if submitted state is outdated (cheating attempt)
        is_outdated = submitted_state.nonce < self.current.nonce

        if is_outdated and submitted_state.nonce in self.revocation_
        secrets:
            return {
                'type': 'cheating_detected',
                'submitted_nonce': submitted_state.nonce,
```

```
                'current_nonce': self.current.nonce,
                'penalty': f"All funds awarded to counterparty",
                'revocation_key': self.revocation_secrets[submitted_
                state.nonce],
            }

        return {
            'type': 'unilateral_close',
            'submitted_state': submitted_state.balances,
            'challenge_period': self.CHALLENGE_PERIOD_BLOCKS,
            'counterparty_can_dispute': is_outdated,
        }

# Demonstrate payment channel
channel = BidirectionalChannel("alice", "bob", 50000, 30000)

print("\nPayment Channel Demonstration")
print("=" * 60)
print(f"Channel: {channel.channel_id}")
print(f"Capacity: {channel.capacity} (Alice: 50000, Bob: 30000)")

# Execute many off-chain payments
payments = [
    ("alice", "bob", 1000), ("alice", "bob", 500), ("bob", "alice", 300),
    ("alice", "bob", 2000), ("bob", "alice", 1500), ("alice", "bob", 800),
    ("bob", "alice", 400), ("alice", "bob", 600), ("bob", "alice", 200),
    ("alice", "bob", 1100),
] * 10  # 100 total payments

for sender, recipient, amount in payments:
    channel.pay(sender, recipient, amount)

print(f"\nAfter {channel.current.nonce} off-chain payments:")
print(f"  Current balances: {channel.current.balances}")

# Cooperative close
close = channel.cooperative_close()
print(f"\n  Close type: {close['type']}")
```

```
print(f"  {close['efficiency']}")
print(f"  Gas saved: ~{close['gas_saved']:,} gas")

# Demonstrate cheating detection
channel2 = BidirectionalChannel("carol", "dave", 10000, 10000)
channel2.pay("carol", "dave", 5000)  # State 1: Carol 5000, Dave 15000
old_state = channel2.history[0]  # State 0: Carol 10000, Dave 10000
channel2.pay("carol", "dave", 2000)  # State 2: Carol 3000, Dave 17000

print(f"\n--- Cheating Detection ---")
print(f"  Current state (nonce {channel2.current.nonce}): {channel2.
current.balances}")
print(f"  Carol tries to submit old state (nonce {old_state.nonce}): {old_
state.balances}")

cheat_result = channel2.unilateral_close("carol", old_state)
print(f"  Result: {cheat_result['type']}")
if 'penalty' in cheat_result:
    print(f"  Penalty: {cheat_result['penalty']}")
```

Multi-Hop Payments and the Lightning Network

A single channel connects two people. The Lightning Network lets you pay someone you don't share a channel with by routing through intermediaries. Alice has a channel with Bob; Bob has one with Carol. Alice pays Carol through Bob.

Routing uses Hash Time-Locked Contracts (HTLCs). Each hop locks funds that can only be claimed by revealing a secret (a hash preimage). The recipient generates the secret, and knowledge of it propagates backward along the route, unlocking each hop in sequence. If any hop fails, everything reverts after a timeout.

Table 15-3. *State Channel Properties*

Property	Payment Channels	Generalized State Channels
Participants	Exactly 2 per channel	2+ per channel
Operations	Balance transfers only	Any state transition (games, contracts)
Routing	Multi-hop via HTLCs	Not standardized
Capital efficiency	Funds locked per channel	Funds locked per channel
Liveness requirement	Both parties must be online periodically	All participants must monitor
Use case	Micropayments, streaming payments	Turn-based games, off-chain contracts
Production examples	Lightning Network (Bitcoin), Raiden (Ethereum)	Counterfactual, StateChannels.org

15.1.5 Plasma: Child Chains with Exit Games

Plasma was proposed by Poon and Buterin in 2017. The idea: child chains that commit only Merkle roots to L1. No full transaction data on L1 like rollups do. That makes L1 costs tiny—just a 32-byte root per Plasma block versus hundreds of kilobytes for rollups—but it creates the data availability problem. If the operator withholds the data behind a Merkle root, users can't verify their balances or build the proofs they need to exit.

The Exit Game Mechanism

The exit game is Plasma's central security mechanism. It's how users withdraw to L1 even when the operator is acting maliciously. Three stages:

Exit initiation. A user submits an exit request to the L1 Plasma contract with a Merkle proof showing they own a specific output (UTXO-based) or have a certain balance (account-based) in a committed block. They also post a bond that gets forfeited if the exit turns out to be fraudulent.

Challenge period. A window opens, typically 7–14 days. Anyone can challenge by proving the claimed output was already spent—a signed transaction plus a Merkle proof of inclusion in a later block. A successful challenge cancels the exit, and the challenger takes the bond.

Finalization. If nobody successfully challenges within the window, the exit goes through and the user gets their funds from the L1 contract.

```
import hashlib
import time
from dataclasses import dataclass, field
from typing import Dict, List, Optional, Tuple
from enum import Enum

class ExitStatus(Enum):
    PENDING = "pending"
    CHALLENGED = "challenged"
    FINALIZED = "finalized"
    CANCELLED = "cancelled"

@dataclass
class PlasmaBlock:
    block_number: int
    merkle_root: str
    transactions: List[dict]
    timestamp: float

@dataclass
class ExitRequest:
    exit_id: int
    user: str
    amount: int
    plasma_block: int
    merkle_proof: str
    bond: int
    status: ExitStatus
    initiated_at: float
    challenge_deadline: float
```

```
class PlasmaChain:
    """
    Simplified Plasma chain with exit game mechanics.

    Demonstrates:
    1. Operator commits Merkle roots to L1
    2. Users can exit by proving ownership
    3. Challenges prevent double-exit fraud
    4. Mass exit problem when operator withholds data
    """

    CHALLENGE_PERIOD = 7 * 24 * 3600  # 7 days in seconds
    EXIT_BOND = 100  # Bond amount for exit request

    def __init__(self):
        self.blocks: List[PlasmaBlock] = []
        self.balances: Dict[str, int] = {}
        self.spent_outputs: Dict[str, bool] = {}  # Track spent UTXOs
        self.exit_queue: List[ExitRequest] = []
        self.exit_counter = 0
        self.l1_contract_balance = 0

    def deposit(self, user: str, amount: int):
        """User deposits funds from L1 into Plasma chain."""
        self.balances[user] = self.balances.get(user, 0) + amount
        self.l1_contract_balance += amount

    def submit_block(self, transactions: List[dict]) -> PlasmaBlock:
        """Operator creates a block and commits Merkle root to L1."""
        # Execute transactions
        for tx in transactions:
            sender_bal = self.balances.get(tx['sender'], 0)
            if sender_bal >= tx['amount']:
                self.balances[tx['sender']] = sender_bal - tx['amount']
                self.balances[tx['recipient']] = (
                    self.balances.get(tx['recipient'], 0) + tx['amount'])
                # Record output as unspent
```

```
                output_id = f"{len(self.blocks)}:{tx['recipient']}:{tx['
                amount']}"
                self.spent_outputs[output_id] = False

        # Create Merkle root (simplified)
        data = str(sorted(self.balances.items()))
        root = hashlib.sha256(data.encode()).hexdigest()[:16]

        block = PlasmaBlock(
            block_number=len(self.blocks),
            merkle_root=root,
            transactions=transactions,
            timestamp=time.time(),
        )
        self.blocks.append(block)
        return block

    def initiate_exit(self, user: str, amount: int,
                      plasma_block: int) -> ExitRequest:
        """User initiates exit from Plasma to L1."""
        self.exit_counter += 1
        now = time.time()

        # Create Merkle proof (simplified as hash)
        proof = hashlib.sha256(
            f"{user}:{amount}:{plasma_block}".encode()
        ).hexdigest()[:16]

        exit_req = ExitRequest(
            exit_id=self.exit_counter,
            user=user,
            amount=amount,
            plasma_block=plasma_block,
            merkle_proof=proof,
            bond=self.EXIT_BOND,
            status=ExitStatus.PENDING,
```

```
            initiated_at=now,
            challenge_deadline=now + self.CHALLENGE_PERIOD,
        )

        self.exit_queue.append(exit_req)
        return exit_req

    def challenge_exit(self, exit_id: int,
                       spending_tx: dict,
                       spending_block: int) -> Tuple[bool, str]:
        """
        Challenge an exit by proving the output was already spent.

        The challenger must provide:
        1. A transaction signed by the exiting user that spends the output
        2. Proof that this transaction was included in a later Plasma block
        """
        exit_req = None
        for e in self.exit_queue:
            if e.exit_id == exit_id:
                exit_req = e
                break

        if exit_req is None:
            return False, "Exit not found"

        if exit_req.status != ExitStatus.PENDING:
            return False, f"Exit already {exit_req.status.value}"

        # Verify the spending transaction is valid
        if (spending_tx.get('sender') == exit_req.user and
            spending_block > exit_req.plasma_block):
            exit_req.status = ExitStatus.CANCELLED
            return True, (f"Challenge successful: user spent funds in "
                          f"block {spending_block} after exit block {exit_
                          req.plasma_block}")

        return False, "Invalid challenge: spending tx does not match"
```

```
    def finalize_exits(self, current_time: float) -> List[ExitRequest]:
        """Finalize exits whose challenge period has expired."""
        finalized = []
        for exit_req in self.exit_queue:
            if (exit_req.status == ExitStatus.PENDING and
                current_time >= exit_req.challenge_deadline):
                exit_req.status = ExitStatus.FINALIZED
                self.l1_contract_balance -= exit_req.amount
                finalized.append(exit_req)
        return finalized

    def simulate_mass_exit(self, num_users: int,
                           l1_capacity_per_day: int) -> dict:
        """
        Simulate the mass exit problem.

        If operator withholds data, all users must exit simultaneously.
        L1 has limited block space, so not all exits can process in time.
        """
        # Each exit requires ~200 bytes on L1 (Merkle proof + metadata)
        exit_size_bytes = 200
        exits_per_day = l1_capacity_per_day // exit_size_bytes

        days_to_process_all = num_users / exits_per_day
        challenge_period_days = self.CHALLENGE_PERIOD / 86400

        users_processed_in_time = min(
            num_users,
            int(exits_per_day * challenge_period_days)
        )
        users_stuck = num_users - users_processed_in_time

        return {
            'total_users': num_users,
            'exits_per_day': exits_per_day,
            'days_to_clear': days_to_process_all,
            'challenge_period_days': challenge_period_days,
            'users_processed_in_time': users_processed_in_time,
```

```
            'users_at_risk': users_stuck,
            'risk_percentage': (users_stuck / num_users) * 100,
        }

# Demonstrate Plasma mechanics
plasma = PlasmaChain()

# Deposits
for user in ['alice', 'bob', 'carol']:
    plasma.deposit(user, 10000)

# Normal operation
plasma.submit_block([
    {'sender': 'alice', 'recipient': 'bob', 'amount': 3000},
    {'sender': 'bob', 'recipient': 'carol', 'amount': 1000},
])

print("Plasma Exit Game Demonstration")
print("=" * 60)

# Alice initiates exit
exit1 = plasma.initiate_exit('alice', 7000, 0)
print(f"Exit initiated: {exit1.user} for {exit1.amount}")
print(f"  Challenge deadline: {exit1.challenge_deadline - exit1.initiated_
at:.0f}s from now")

# Bob challenges (Alice spent some funds in block 0)
success, msg = plasma.challenge_exit(
    exit1.exit_id,
    {'sender': 'alice', 'recipient': 'bob', 'amount': 3000},
    spending_block=0
)
print(f"  Challenge result: {msg}")

# Mass exit simulation
print(f"\nMass Exit Problem Analysis:")
# Realistic Ethereum calldata capacity:
# ~150KB calldata per block (not 1MB – that is total block size,
# most of which is taken by execution, not calldata)
```

```
# 150,000 bytes × 7200 blocks/day = ~1.08 GB/day
# Using 1MB × 7200 = 7.2 GB/day overstates capacity 7x
# and makes the mass exit problem look far less severe than it is.
for num_users in [10000, 100000, 1000000]:
    result = plasma.simulate_mass_exit(
        num_users,
        l1_capacity_per_day=150_000 * 7200  # ~150KB calldata × 7200
        blocks/day
    )

    print(f"  {num_users:>10,} users: {result['days_to_clear']:.1f} days to
    clear, "
          f"{result['users_at_risk']:,} users at risk ({result['risk_
          percentage']:.1f}%)")
```

Plasma Variants

Several plasma variants tried to solve the mass exit problem:

Plasma Cash (2018). Each deposited token gets a unique serial number instead of tracking balances. Users only need to watch their own tokens, not the whole chain. Simplifies exits (each token exits independently) but makes fungible transfers awkward.

Plasma Debit. Tried to combine Plasma Cash with payment channel mechanics for fungible payments. Got complicated. Largely abandoned.

Plasma MVP (Minimum Viable Plasma). The simplest version, UTXO-based. Each exit requires a confirmation signature from the operator, which adds a trust dependency that defeats part of the purpose.

None of these fixed the fundamental data availability problem. Rollups did, by posting everything to L1. If the rollup operator disappears, anyone can reconstruct the full state from L1 data. That architectural advantage is why the industry moved from Plasma to rollups around 2020–2021.

Why Rollups Won Over Plasma

The plasma-to-rollup transition is worth studying because it shows a broader principle: stronger data availability guarantees make for simpler, more secure protocol designs, even when they cost more on L1.

Table 15-4. Plasma vs. Rollup Architecture Comparison

Property	Plasma	Optimistic Rollup	ZK Rollup
Data on L1	Merkle roots only (32 bytes/block)	Full tx data (~100 KB/ batch)	Full data or state diffs
Mass exit risk	Critical vulnerability	No risk (data always on L1)	No risk
Exit mechanism	Merkle proof + challenge period	Standard withdrawal after challenge	Standard withdrawal after proof
State reconstruction	Requires operator cooperation	Anyone can reconstruct from L1	Anyone can reconstruct from L1
Complexity	High (exit games, priority queues)	Moderate (fraud proofs)	High (ZK circuits)
Security model	Operator must publish data; user must monitor	At least 1 honest verifier	Cryptographic soundness
EVM support	None (too complex for exit games)	Full	Varies by type
Production status	Abandoned	Mature (Arbitrum, Optimism)	Growing (zkSync, Scroll)

15.1.6 Validiums and the Data Availability Spectrum

Between rollups (all data on L1) and Plasma (no data on L1), there's a whole spectrum. Validiums sit in the middle: they use validity proofs like ZK rollups for correctness but store data off-chain with a Data Availability Committee (DAC).

The upside is much lower L1 cost. A validium's L1 footprint is just the validity proof (~200–500 bytes) plus the state root, regardless of transaction count. That can push throughput past 10,000 TPS for simple transfers—way beyond rollups, which are bottlenecked by L1 data capacity.

The trade-off: weaker data availability. If the DAC withholds data, users can't reconstruct their state. The validity proof guarantees the transition was correct, but without the data, users may not be able to prove what they own. They know their funds weren't stolen (the proof prevents that), but they might not be able to prove ownership for withdrawal.

Volitions (StarkWare's proposal) let each transaction choose its own data availability: L1 (rollup mode, higher cost, strongest guarantee) or off-chain (validium mode, cheaper, DAC trust assumption). High-value transactions pick rollup mode. Low-value ones pick validium. Flexible.

Table 15-5. *Data Availability Spectrum*

Approach	Data Location	DA Guarantee	L1 Cost	Security	Examples
Rollup	L1 calldata/blobs	L1 consensus guarantees DA	High	Strongest	Arbitrum, zkSync
Volition	User choice per-tx	L1 or DAC (per transaction)	Variable	Hybrid	StarkEx (future)
Validium	Off-chain DAC	DAC majority honest	Low	Medium	StarkEx (current), Immutable X
Plasma	Off-chain (operator)	Operator publishes	Very Low	Weakest	OMG Network (deprecated)

15.1.7 Cross-L2 Composability and the Fragmentation Problem

In a world with multiple L2s, composability breaks. On L1 Ethereum, a single transaction can interact with multiple protocols atomically. Across L2s? That's gone. And it creates real problems.

The fragmentation shows up in several ways:

Liquidity fragmentation. A token exists on multiple L2s, but its liquidity is scattered. A DEX on Arbitrum might have $50M in ETH-USDC liquidity while the same pair on zkSync has $10M. Neither pool has the combined depth. Slippage is worse for everyone.

Broken DeFi composability. Flash loans can't cross L2 boundaries because borrow-and-repay has to be atomic. A flash loan on Arbitrum can't arbitrage a price discrepancy on Optimism. The multi-protocol strategies that drove L1 DeFi innovation? Impossible across L2s.

User experience mess. Users juggle assets across multiple L2s, deal with different bridges (each with different trust assumptions, fees, delays), and have to decide which L2 to use for what. Newcomers get confused. Mistakes happen. Bridging to the wrong L2, losing funds in a bridge exploit.

Emerging Solutions

Shared sequencing. Multiple L2s use the same entity to order their transactions. If rollups A and B share a sequencer, it can coordinate cross-rollup transactions by including matching transactions in both batches. Espresso Systems and Astria are building this. The risk: the shared sequencer becomes a centralization bottleneck.

Based rollups (Justin Drake's proposal) use L1 validators as the sequencer. Since L1 already determines block ordering, based rollups inherit those guarantees. Cross-based-rollup transactions can be atomic because they're ordered by the same L1 block. The trade-off is latency: inclusion depends on L1 block time (12 seconds for Ethereum) instead of faster sequencer confirmations (~2 seconds).

Intent-based protocols hide the cross-L2 complexity. Users declare what they want ("swap 10 ETH on Arbitrum for 10,000 USDC on my zkSync address") without specifying how. Solvers compete to fulfill it, handling all the bridging and routing behind the scenes. The user sees one operation. The solver deals with multi-chain headaches.

Superchain / L2 ecosystems. The Optimism Superchain and Polygon 2.0 group multiple rollups under shared governance and interoperability. Rollups in the same ecosystem share message passing, sequencing infrastructure, and potentially a common bridge to L1. Fast, cheap cross-rollup communication within the ecosystem. The cost: ecosystem lock-in.

```
def analyze_fragmentation_cost(liquidity_per_l2: List[float],
                                trade_size: float,
                                num_l2s: int) -> dict:
    """
    Analyze the cost of liquidity fragmentation across L2s.

    Compare: executing a trade against fragmented liquidity (worst L2)
    versus hypothetical unified liquidity (all L2s combined).
    """
    total_liquidity = sum(liquidity_per_l2)
best_l2_liquidity = max(liquidity_per_l2)
worst_l2_liquidity = min(liquidity_per_l2)
# Correct constant-product AMM price impact formula:
# price_impact = trade_size / (liquidity + trade_size)
#
```

```
# The old formula trade/(2*liq) is a linear approximation
# valid only for tiny trades (trade << liquidity).
# For large trades it seriously understates the impact:
#
# Example: $5M trade vs $50M pool
#   Old formula: 5M / (2 * 50M) = 5.0%
#   Correct:     5M / (50M + 5M) = 9.1%  ← nearly 2x worse
#
# This matters most where fragmentation is most damaging – large trades.
slippage_best_l2 = trade_size / (best_l2_liquidity + trade_size) * 100
slippage_unified = trade_size / (total_liquidity + trade_size) * 100
slippage_worst_l2 = trade_size / (worst_l2_liquidity + trade_size) * 100

    # Bridge cost to access best L2 if user is on worst L2
    bridge_cost_pct = 0.1  # 0.1% typical bridge fee
    bridge_time_minutes = 10  # Typical liquidity bridge

    # Effective cost: slippage + bridge cost
    effective_cost_fragmented = slippage_best_l2 + bridge_cost_pct
    effective_cost_unified = slippage_unified

    fragmentation_tax = effective_cost_fragmented - effective_cost_unified

    return {
        'num_l2s': num_l2s,
        'total_liquidity': total_liquidity,
        'best_l2_liquidity': best_l2_liquidity,
        'slippage_best_l2': slippage_best_l2,
        'slippage_unified': slippage_unified,
        'slippage_worst_l2': slippage_worst_l2,
        'bridge_cost_pct': bridge_cost_pct,
        'fragmentation_tax_pct': fragmentation_tax,
        'trade_size': trade_size,
    }

print("\nLiquidity Fragmentation Cost Analysis")
print("=" * 65)
```

```
# Simulate ETH-USDC liquidity across 5 L2s
l2_liquidity = [50_000_000, 30_000_000, 15_000_000, 10_000_000, 5_000_000]
l2_names = ["Arbitrum", "Optimism", "Base", "zkSync", "Scroll"]

print(f"Liquidity distribution:")
for name, liq in zip(l2_names, l2_liquidity):
    print(f"  {name:>10}: ${liq/1e6:.0f}M")

print(f"\nTrade size impact (slippage comparison):")
print(f"{'Trade Size':>12} {'Best L2':>10} {'Unified':>10} {'Fragmentation
Tax':>18}")
print("-" * 55)

for trade_size in [100_000, 500_000, 1_000_000, 5_000_000]:
    r = analyze_fragmentation_cost(l2_liquidity, trade_size, 5)
    print(f"  ${trade_size/1e6:.1f}M    {r['slippage_best_l2']:>8.3f}%  "
          f"{r['slippage_unified']:>8.3f}%  {r['fragmentation_tax_
          pct']:>16.3f}%")
```

15.1.8 Summary

Layer-2 moves execution off-chain while keeping L1 as the security backstop. Which approach you pick depends on where you want to land on the trade-offs between finality speed, cost, security assumptions, and composability.

Key takeaways:

- Optimistic rollups assume transitions are valid and use fraud proofs to catch problems. Interactive bisection narrows disputes to a single step (O(log n) rounds). The seven-day challenge window is the main UX pain point.
- ZK rollups prove correctness upfront with zero-knowledge proofs. No challenge period, so withdrawals are faster. Proof generation is expensive (1,000–1,000,000x overhead). ZK-EVM compatibility varies across types 1 through 4.

- State channels give you instant off-chain payments between fixed participants. Revocation stops cheating. Multi-hop routing with HTLCs makes network-wide payments possible. Main drawbacks: capital lockup and the need to stay online.
- Plasma posts only Merkle roots to L1, keeping data costs minimal. But if the operator withholds data, you get the mass exit problem—simultaneous withdrawals that can overwhelm L1. That's why rollups replaced it.
- On cost: both rollup types cut per-transaction costs 10–100x through batch amortization. ZK rollups have higher fixed costs (proof generation) but lower marginal costs, so they get more efficient as batches grow.
- Cross-L2 composability is the big unsolved problem. Liquidity fragmentation and broken atomic composability make the multi-rollup ecosystem harder to use than it should be. Shared sequencing and based rollups are the most promising emerging fixes.

L1 is the dispute resolution court. L2 handles execution. Most transactions never touch L1.—Optimistic rollups: post data to L1, assume valid, bisection narrows fraud to 1 step in O(log n) rounds.—ZK rollups: validity proof per batch. No challenge period. ZK-EVM types 1–4 offer different compatibility.—Interactive fraud proofs: bisection reduces a million-tx batch to one on-chain verification step.—State channels: unlimited off-chain payments. Revocation prevents cheating. HTLCs enable routing.—Lightning Network: multi-hop payments. Each hop is secured by hash time-lock.—Plasma: Merkle roots on L1. Mass exit problem when operator withholds data. Superseded by rollups.—Cost: rollups cut per-tx cost 10–100x by amortizing L1 data and proof costs across a batch.—Cross-L2: liquidity fragmentation is the major unsolved problem. Shared sequencing is emerging.

15.1.9 Exercises

Problem 1 (Basic): What's the difference between fraud proofs and validity proofs? Which one uses more L1 computation in the normal case? Which gives you faster finality?

Problem 2 (Calculation): An optimistic rollup posts batches of 10,000 transactions. Each uses 100 bytes of calldata at $0.0001/byte. L1 fraud proof verification costs $50 and happens 0.1% of the time. What's the amortized L1 cost per transaction?

Problem 3 (Implementation): Extend the bisection fraud proof to handle 1,000,000 transactions. Verify the number of bisection rounds is ceil(log2(1,000,000)) = 20. Measure actual on-chain gas savings versus full re-execution.

Problem 4 (Analysis): Compare withdrawal experiences: (a) optimistic rollup with 7-day delay, (b) ZK rollup with 2-hour proof time, (c) optimistic rollup via liquidity bridge with 10-minute delivery and 0.1% fee. For a $100K withdrawal, work out the cost and opportunity cost for each.

Problem 5 (Design): Design a state channel network for pay-per-second video streaming. Specify: channel capacity requirements, payment granularity, what happens if the viewer disconnects, how to handle the provider going offline.

Problem 6 (Theory): Why does Plasma's mass exit problem make it impractical while rollups avoid it completely? Define the data availability requirement formally and show how rollups satisfy it and Plasma doesn't.

Problem 7 (Comparative): Build a decision matrix for choosing between optimistic rollups, ZK rollups, state channels, and validiums. Five criteria: finality speed, data privacy, throughput, trust assumptions, EVM compatibility. Apply to three use cases: DeFi, gaming, and enterprise supply chain.

Problem 8 (Critical Thinking): Do rollups actually solve the scalability trilemma or just push trade-offs somewhere else? Look at: sequencer centralization, data posting as a bottleneck, and composability loss across L2s.

Problem 9 (Advanced): Implement a simplified HTLC routing algorithm for a 10-node payment channel network. Given a payment from node A to node J, find a route, lock funds at each hop, and show the atomic settlement when the secret is revealed.

Problem 10 (Research): Compare real per-transaction costs (L1 data, proof verification, user fees) on Arbitrum and zkSync Era using current on-chain data. How do actual costs compare to the theoretical minimums from this chapter? What explains the gap?

(Solutions in Appendix D)

15.1.10 Further Reading

Arbitrum's docs describe BOLD interactive fraud proofs. The Optimism spec covers the OP Stack and Cannon faultproof system.

Vitalik's "The different types of ZK-EVMs" blog post lays out the compatibility levels. zkSync, Scroll, and Polygon zkEVM docs describe their respective approaches.

Poon and Dryja's Lightning Network paper (2016) is foundational reading. The BOLT spec documents the Lightning protocol. Counterfactual's work covers generalized state channels.

Poon and Buterin's Plasma paper (2017) describes the original architecture. Follow-up research on Plasma Cash and the mass exit problem explains the shift toward rollups.

L2Beat (l2beat.com) has real-time data on rollup TVL, risk assessments, and technology classification.

CHAPTER 16

Sharding and Parallel Execution

16.1 Data Availability Sharding, Cross-Shard Communication, and Danksharding

Sharding is how you scale horizontally without blowing up node requirements. Split the state, split the processing, and keep shared security. It sounds clean. The single-shard takeover problem is why it isn't. This chapter works through that problem and its solutions—committee rotation, erasure coding, and data availability sampling—then covers execution vs. DA sharding, cross-shard communication trade-offs, how Ethereum's sharding story went from Eth 2.0 to EIP-4844 to full danksharding, and what Zilliqa, NEAR, and Polkadot each chose differently. Here's what it covers:

- Why sharding matters for horizontal blockchain scaling and what it means to partition state and processing
- The single-shard takeover problem. It's the fundamental vulnerability, and committee rotation is how you fight it
- Execution sharding versus data availability sharding and why the whole industry changed its mind
- The math behind erasure coding and how Data Availability Sampling lets light clients verify data without downloading it all
- Cross-shard communication and the painful trade-off between atomicity and latency

N. Savant, *Blockchain Foundations*, https://doi.org/10.1007/979-8-8688-2891-1_16

- How Ethereum's sharding story evolved from the Eth 2.0 vision through proto-danksharding (EIP-4844) to full danksharding
- Real sharding implementations: Zilliqa, NEAR, and Polkadot, and how each made different design bets

16.1.1 The Sharding Thesis

Sharding splits blockchain state and processing across multiple parallel chains, called shards. Each shard handles a slice of the total transactions independently. In theory, aggregate throughput scales linearly with shard count while shared security covers the whole system.

The idea comes from databases. A billion-row database gets split across 100 shards of 10 million rows each. Queries route to the right shard based on a partition key; each shard runs on its own hardware, and total throughput scales with the number of shards. Straightforward.

Blockchains make this much harder. Databases have a trusted operator who has no reason to corrupt their own data. Blockchains don't have that luxury. Any participant could be an adversary trying to forge transactions, double-spend, or manipulate state. That adversarial setting is what creates the central challenge of blockchain sharding: the single-shard takeover problem.

The Single-Shard Takeover Problem

On an unsharded chain, an adversary has to control a majority (or supermajority, depending on the consensus mechanism) of the entire network. With 1,000 validators staking $100K each, you need to compromise more than 333 (for BFT) or 500+ (for Nakamoto consensus). That's $33M–$50M at stake.

Split that into 100 shards, and each shard has 10 validators. Now an adversary only needs 4 of those 10 to take over one shard. Cost: $400,000. The whole system's security collapses to whatever its weakest shard can withstand.

The defense is random committee rotation. Validators get assigned to shards randomly via an unpredictable beacon, and assignments shuffle periodically. If an adversary controls 10% of total validators, the probability they end up controlling a majority in any one shard follows the hypergeometric distribution (or binomial, for large populations). With decent committee sizes, that probability drops fast.

```
import math
from typing import Dict, List, Tuple
from dataclasses import dataclass

def shard_takeover_probability(total_validators: int,
                               committee_size: int,
                               adversary_fraction: float,
                               threshold_fraction: float = 1/3) -> float:
    """
    Calculate probability that adversary controls more than threshold
    fraction in a randomly selected committee.

    Uses binomial approximation (valid when total_validators >>
    committee_size).
    P(X >= k) where X ~ Binomial(committee_size, adversary_fraction)
    and k = ceil(committee_size * threshold_fraction) + 1
    """
    n = committee_size
    p = adversary_fraction
    k = int(math.ceil(n * threshold_fraction)) + 1

    # P(X >= k) = sum_{i=k}^{n} C(n,i) * p^i * (1-p)^(n-i)
    prob = 0.0
    for i in range(k, n + 1):
        prob += math.comb(n, i) * (p ** i) * ((1 - p) ** (n - i))

    return prob

def system_security(total_validators: int,
                    committee_size: int,
                    num_shards: int,
                    adversary_fraction: float) -> dict:
    """
    Calculate system-wide shard security.

    P(any shard compromised) = 1 - (1 - P(single shard))^num_shards

    This uses the union bound, which slightly overestimates
    the probability for non-independent shard assignments.
```

```
    """
    p_single = shard_takeover_probability(
        total_validators, committee_size, adversary_fraction)

    p_any = 1.0 - (1.0 - p_single) ** num_shards

    # Expected number of compromised shards
    expected_compromised = num_shards * p_single

    # Security margin: how much adversary power before probability
      exceeds target
    # Binary search for threshold
    target_prob = 1e-9  # 1 in a billion
    lo, hi = 0.0, 0.49
    for _ in range(50):
        mid = (lo + hi) / 2
        p = shard_takeover_probability(total_validators, committee_
        size, mid)
        if 1 - (1 - p) ** num_shards > target_prob:
            hi = mid
        else:
            lo = mid

    return {
        'p_single_shard': p_single,
        'p_any_shard': p_any,
        'expected_compromised': expected_compromised,
        'max_safe_adversary': lo,
        'safe_adversary_pct': lo * 100,
    }

print("Shard Security Analysis")
print("=" * 80)

# Impact of committee size on security
print(f"\n1. Committee Size vs Security (10% adversary, 64 shards)")
print(f"{'Committee':>10} {'P(single shard)':>18} {'P(any shard)':>15}
{'Max safe adv%':>15}")
```

```
print("-" * 60)
for committee in [16, 32, 64, 128, 256, 512]:
    r = system_security(10000, committee, 64, 0.10)
    print(f"  {committee:>8}  {r['p_single_shard']:>16.2e}  "
          f"{r['p_any_shard']:>13.2e}  {r['safe_adversary_pct']:>13.1f}%")

# Impact of adversary fraction
print(f"\n2. Adversary Fraction vs Security (committee=128, 64 shards)")
print(f"{'Adversary':>10} {'P(single shard)':>18} {'P(any shard)':>15}")
print("-" * 45)
for adv_pct in [5, 10, 15, 20, 25, 30]:
    r = system_security(10000, 128, 64, adv_pct / 100)
    print(f"  {adv_pct:>7}%  {r['p_single_shard']:>16.2e}  {r['p_any_
    shard']:>13.2e}")
```

16.1.2 Execution Sharding vs. Data Availability Sharding

The industry went through a real shift on this. The original Ethereum 2.0 plan (phases 0–2) called for execution sharding: 64 shard chains, each a full blockchain with its own state, execution environment, validators, and block production. Cross-shard transactions would use receipt-based asynchronous messaging.

Three problems killed that vision:

Cross-shard composability is brutal. DeFi runs on composability—chaining multiple protocol calls into one atomic transaction. Execution sharding breaks that. A DEX swap on shard A followed by a lending deposit on shard B needs cross-shard messages, destroys atomicity, adds multi-block latency, and if the second step fails, you need yet another cross-shard message to unwind the first.

Per-shard security is limited by committee size. With 1,000 validators spread across 64 shards, each shard gets about 16 validators. That's not enough for robust BFT consensus. Make committees bigger and you get fewer shards, which defeats the purpose.

Rollups turned out to solve execution scaling better. This was the insight that rewrote Ethereum's roadmap. Rollups give you full composability within each rollup, stronger security (inherited from L1 through proofs), and simpler architecture. What rollups need from L1 isn't more execution capacity. It's cheap data availability.

Hence the "rollup-centric roadmap." Instead of sharding execution, shard data availability. L1 becomes a large, cheap data layer for rollups to post transaction data. The consensus layer ensures that data stays available through erasure coding and data availability sampling. Rollups handle execution and provide their own proofs.

The Composability Crisis: A Concrete Example

A concrete example makes the composability problem visceral. Take a common DeFi operation: one transaction on L1, but multiple cross-shard hops on an execution-sharded chain.

On L1 Ethereum, one atomic transaction can: (1) take a flash loan from Aave, (2) swap the borrowed tokens on Uniswap, (3) deposit the swapped tokens into Compound, (4) borrow against that Compound position, (5) repay the flash loan with profit. All five steps—either everything succeeds or everything reverts.

On an execution-sharded chain with Aave on shard A, Uniswap on shard B, Compound on shard C:

- **Block 1**: Initiate a flash loan on shard A, send a receipt to shard B
- **Block 2**: Receive receipt on shard B, execute swap, send receipt to shard C
- **Block 3**: Receive receipt on shard C, deposit and borrow, send receipt to shard A
- **Block 4**: Receive receipt on shard A, repay flash loan

Four blocks instead of one transaction. But atomicity is the real killer: what if step 3 fails (say Compound rejects the deposit because the collateral ratio moved)? Now you have to unwind across shards:

- **Block 5**: Send failure receipt from shard C to shard B
- **Block 6**: Reverse swap on shard B, send reverse receipt to shard A
- **Block 7**: Cancel flash loan repayment on shard A

Seven blocks for a failed transaction that on L1 would simply revert in one step. The complexity, the latency, the failure modes—execution sharding is fundamentally hostile to the composability patterns that drive DeFi.

That's why Ethereum pivoted to data availability sharding. In the rollup model, Aave, Uniswap, and Compound all deploy on the same rollup. The flash loan operation executes atomically, exactly like L1. L1 just needs to make sure the rollup's data is available and its state transitions check out.

```
def composability_latency_comparison(operation_steps: int,
                                     cross_shard_pct: float,
                                     block_time_seconds: int) -> dict:
    """
    Compare latency for multi-step DeFi operations:
    L1 (atomic) vs execution sharding (multi-block) vs rollup (atomic).
    """
    # L1: all steps in one block
    l1_latency = block_time_seconds

    # Execution sharding: each cross-shard step adds a block of latency
    cross_shard_steps = int(operation_steps * cross_shard_pct)
    sharded_latency = (operation_steps + cross_shard_steps) * block_
    time_seconds

    # With failure: add rollback latency
    sharded_failure_latency = sharded_latency + cross_shard_steps * block_
    time_seconds

    # Rollup: atomic within rollup (like L1)
    rollup_latency = 2  # Sequencer soft-confirmation ~2 seconds
    rollup_finality = 768  # L1 finality for the rollup batch

    return {
        'l1_latency_s': l1_latency,
        'sharded_latency_s': sharded_latency,
        'sharded_failure_latency_s': sharded_failure_latency,
        'rollup_soft_latency_s': rollup_latency,
        'rollup_final_latency_s': rollup_finality,
        'sharding_slowdown': sharded_latency / l1_latency,
    }
```

```
print("\nComposability Latency: Sharding vs Rollup")
print("=" * 60)
for steps in [2, 3, 5, 8]:
    r = composability_latency_comparison(steps, 0.6, 12)
    print(f"  {steps}-step DeFi operation:")
    print(f"    L1 (atomic):         {r['l1_latency_s']:>5}s")
    print(f"    Execution sharding: {r['sharded_latency_s']:>5}s
({r['sharding_slowdown']:.0f}× slower)")
    print(f"    Sharding (failure): {r['sharded_failure_latency_s']:>5}s")
    print(f"    Rollup (soft-conf): {r['rollup_soft_latency_s']:>5}s")
```

Table 16-1. *Execution Sharding vs. DA Sharding*

Property	Execution Sharding (original Eth 2.0)	DA Sharding (danksharding)
What is sharded	State + execution + consensus	Data availability only
Execution model	Each shard executes independently	Rollups execute; L1 verifies proofs
Cross-shard transactions	Complex cross-shard protocols	Handled within rollups
Composability	Limited across shards	Full within each rollup
Per-shard security	Depends on committee size	Not applicable (no shard-specific execution)
Data verification	Shard validators download all shard data	DAS: sample random cells
Current status	Abandoned	Active development (EIP-4844 → danksharding)

16.1.3 Erasure Coding and Data Availability Sampling

Data Availability Sampling is the technology that makes data sharding work. It lets light clients verify data is available without downloading the whole thing. Just random sampling of a small number of cells.

Erasure Coding Foundation

Erasure coding takes k data chunks and encodes them into n > k chunks so that any k of the n are enough to reconstruct the original. Simplest example: given chunks A and B, create C = A XOR B. Any two of {A, B, C} reconstruct all three.

For blockchain data availability, 2D Reed-Solomon erasure coding is the approach. Arrange data in a square matrix (say, 256×256 cells). Extend each row and column with parity data, doubling the size in both dimensions. Result: a 512×512 matrix where any 256 cells in any row or column reconstruct the full row or column. Reconstruct all rows and columns, and you get back the entire original data.

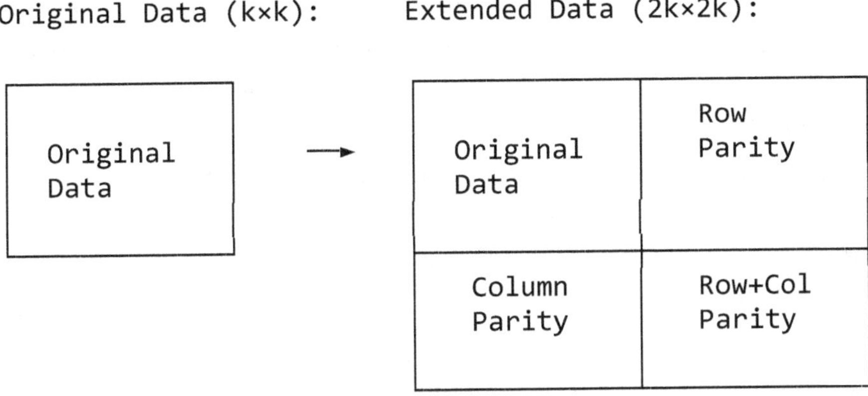


```
Any 50% of the extended data suffices to reconstruct everything.
Light clients sample random cells to verify availability.
```

Figure 16-1. *2D Erasure Coding*

KZG Polynomial Commitments for DAS

There's a critical piece here: the commitment scheme. When a light client samples a cell, it needs to know that cell is consistent with the actual committed data. Otherwise a malicious producer could hand out fake cells that pass availability checks but don't match the real block.

KZG polynomial commitments (Kate-Zaverucha-Goldberg, 2010) solve this. Here's how:

Setup. A trusted setup ceremony generates a structured reference string—powers of a secret value τ in an elliptic curve group: $[\tau^0 G, \tau^1 G, \tau^2 G, \ldots, \tau^d G]$. The secret τ gets destroyed afterward. That's the "toxic waste" that absolutely must not survive.

Commit. To commit to a polynomial $p(x) = a_0 + a_1x + a_2x^2 + ... + a_nx^n$, compute $C = a_0(\tau^0G) + a_1(\tau^1G) + ... + a_n(\tau^nG) = p(\tau)G$. One elliptic curve point. 48 bytes on BLS12-381. Binds the polynomial without revealing its coefficients.

Open/Prove. To show that $p(z) = y$ for some specific z, compute the quotient polynomial $q(x) = (p(x) - y) / (x - z)$ and its commitment $Q = q(\tau)G$. The proof is that single point Q. 48 bytes.

Verify. Given commitment C, point z, claimed value y, and proof Q, check the pairing equation: $e(C - yG, H) = e(Q, \tau G - zG)$. Constant time regardless of polynomial degree. Very fast.

For DAS, each row of the erasure-coded matrix gets treated as a polynomial. The block header holds KZG commitments for every row and column. When a light client samples cell (row_i, col_j), it gets the value plus a KZG opening proof. Valid proof? The cell matches the committed row. Invalid? The data's been tampered with.

Properties that make KZG ideal for this:

Succinctness. Each commitment and proof is one elliptic curve point (48 bytes). Header overhead scales with rows and columns, not total data size.

Homomorphic. KZG commitments are additively homomorphic. That lets you efficiently verify erasure coding correctness: a parity row's commitment should equal the sum of the data row commitments it covers.

Constant-time verification. Two pairing operations per proof, regardless of data size. Per-sample cost is fixed for every light client.

The downside is the trusted setup. Ethereum's KZG ceremony (2023) had over 140,000 participants contributing randomness. The guarantee: as long as even one participant honestly destroyed their contribution, the setup is secure. With that many people, it's a reasonable bet.

```
def kzg_commitment_simulation() -> None:
    """
    Simulate KZG commitment and verification for DAS.

    In production, these operations use BLS12-381 elliptic curve
    pairings. This simplified version demonstrates the concept
    using modular arithmetic as a stand-in.
    """

    # Simplified modular arithmetic version (not cryptographically secure)
    # In production: use py_ecc or blst library for BLS12-381
```

```
PRIME = 2**31 - 1  # Mersenne prime (simplified)

def poly_eval(coeffs, x, mod):
    """Evaluate polynomial at point x."""
    result = 0
    for i, c in enumerate(coeffs):
        result = (result + c * pow(x, i, mod)) % mod
    return result

def commit(coeffs, srs, mod):
    """Compute commitment: sum(coeff_i * srs_i) mod prime."""
    c = 0
    for i, coeff in enumerate(coeffs):
        c = (c + coeff * srs[i]) % mod
    return c

# Setup: generate SRS (in production: from trusted setup)
tau = 12345  # Secret (would be destroyed in real setup)
max_degree = 16
srs = [pow(tau, i, PRIME) for i in range(max_degree)]

# Data row as polynomial coefficients
# Row data: [10, 20, 30, 40] representing 4 data cells
data_row = [10, 20, 30, 40]

# Commit to the row polynomial
commitment = commit(data_row, srs, PRIME)

# Evaluate at specific points (cell values in extended row)
evaluation_points = list(range(1, 9))  # 8 points (4 data + 4 parity)
cell_values = [poly_eval(data_row, x, PRIME) for x in
evaluation_points]

print(f"  Polynomial coefficients (data): {data_row}")
print(f"  Commitment: {commitment}")
print(f"  Cell values at points 1-8: {cell_values}")

# Verify a cell: check that cell value is consistent with commitment
# (In production: uses pairing-based proof)
```

```
    test_point = 3
    test_value = poly_eval(data_row, test_point, PRIME)
    expected = cell_values[test_point - 1]
    print(f"\n  Verify cell at point {test_point}:")
    print(f"    Claimed value: {expected}")
    print(f"    Recomputed: {test_value}")
    print(f"    Match: {test_value == expected}")

    # Tampered cell: wrong value
    tampered_value = test_value + 1
    print(f"\n  Tampered cell at point {test_point}:")
    print(f"    Claimed value: {tampered_value}")
    print(f"    Correct value: {test_value}")
    print(f"    Fraud detectable: {tampered_value != test_value}")

print("\nKZG Commitment Simulation for DAS")
print("=" * 55)
kzg_commitment_simulation()
```

DAS Protocol

A light client doing DAS follows these steps:

1. Receive the block header with commitments to each row and column of the extended matrix (KZG commitments)
2. Pick s random cells from the 2k×2k matrix
3. Request those cells from the network, from different peers
4. Verify each cell against the row/column commitment
5. If all s cells check out, conclude the data is available

The math is clean. If a fraction f of the data is withheld, the chance that all s samples miss it is (1-f)^s. For s=75 and f=0.50, that's (0.5)^75 ≈ 2.6 × 10^-23. Astronomically unlikely to miss.

```
def das_analysis(data_size_kb: int, cell_size_bytes: int = 512) -> dict:
    """
    Analyze DAS parameters and detection probabilities.
```

```
For a given data size, compute:
- Number of cells in extended matrix
- Required samples for target detection probability
- Bandwidth overhead for light clients
"""
data_bytes = data_size_kb * 1024
k = int(math.ceil(math.sqrt(data_bytes / cell_size_bytes)))
total_cells = (2 * k) ** 2  # Extended 2D matrix
original_cells = k * k

# Detection probability for various sample counts and withholding
  fractions
results = {}
for withheld_pct in [1, 5, 10, 25, 50]:
    f = withheld_pct / 100
    for num_samples in [30, 50, 75, 100]:
        p_miss = (1 - f) ** num_samples
        p_detect = 1 - p_miss
        results[(withheld_pct, num_samples)] = p_detect

# Bandwidth for light client
samples_needed_99_99 = {}
for withheld_pct in [1, 5, 10, 25, 50]:
    f = withheld_pct / 100
    # Solve (1-f)^s < 0.0001 for s
    if f > 0:
        s = math.ceil(math.log(0.0001) / math.log(1 - f))
    else:
        s = float('inf')
    samples_needed_99_99[withheld_pct] = s

return {
    'data_size_kb': data_size_kb,
    'grid_dimension': k,
    'extended_dimension': 2 * k,
    'total_cells': total_cells,
    'original_cells': original_cells,
```

```
        'cell_size_bytes': cell_size_bytes,
        'detection_probs': results,
        'samples_for_99_99': samples_needed_99_99,
    }

analysis = das_analysis(128)  # 128 KB data (like EIP-4844 blob)
print("\nData Availability Sampling Analysis")
print("=" * 70)
print(f"Data size: {analysis['data_size_kb']} KB")
print(f"Grid: {analysis['grid_dimension']}×{analysis['grid_dimension']} "
      f"(extended to {analysis['extended_dimension']}×{analysis['extende
      d_dimension']})")
print(f"Total cells: {analysis['total_cells']}")
print(f"Cell size: {analysis['cell_size_bytes']} bytes")

print(f"\nDetection Probability by Withheld Fraction and Sample Count:")
print(f"{'Withheld':>10}", end="")
for s in [30, 50, 75, 100]:
    print(f"  {s} samples", end="")
print()
print("-" * 60)

for w in [1, 5, 10, 25, 50]:
    print(f"  {w:>6}%  ", end="")
    for s in [30, 50, 75, 100]:
        p = analysis['detection_probs'][(w, s)]
        if p > 0.9999:
            print(f"  {'~100%':>9}", end="")
        else:
            print(f"  {p:>9.4%}", end="")
    print()

print(f"\nSamples needed for 99.99% detection:")
for w, s in analysis['samples_for_99_99'].items():
    bandwidth = s * analysis['cell_size_bytes']
    print(f"  {w}% withheld: {s:3d} samples ({bandwidth/1024:.1f} KB
    bandwidth)")
```

16.1.4 Cross-Shard Communication

Cross-shard transactions are where execution sharding gets messy. Sender on shard A, recipient on shard B, and the transaction has to update both shards' state atomically. Several approaches exist, each trading latency for atomicity:

Asynchronous receipts (Ethereum's original plan, NEAR Nightshade). The source shard runs the first half (deducts from the sender) and generates a receipt. The receipt gets picked up by the destination shard in the next block, which credits the recipient. Minimum latency: 2 blocks. Atomicity is eventual—if the second half fails, a rollback receipt has to go back to the source.

Relay chain coordination (Polkadot XCMP/HRMP). A central relay chain mediates all cross-shard messages. Relay chain validators verify both sides, providing ordering and guaranteed delivery. Latency: 2–3 relay chain blocks. The relay chain can bottleneck if cross-shard traffic gets heavy.

Synchronous cross-shard committees. A committee that spans both shards validates the transaction simultaneously, giving the strongest atomicity guarantee. But it requires overlapping memberships, which is complex and limits how many cross-shard transactions can run at once.

Yanking (contract migration). When a contract on shard A needs to talk to a contract on shard B, one contract gets temporarily "yanked" to the other shard. The interaction happens locally, then the contract moves back. Turns a cross-shard call into a local one, but you pay migration latency.

```
@dataclass
class CrossShardMessage:
    source_shard: int
    dest_shard: int
    sender: str
    recipient: str
    amount: int
    msg_hash: str
    status: str = "pending"  # pending, delivered, failed, rolled_back
    created_block: int = 0
    delivered_block: int = 0
```

```
class ShardedNetwork:
    """Simulate cross-shard communication with receipt-based approach."""

    def __init__(self, num_shards: int, validators_per_shard: int):
        self.num_shards = num_shards
        self.shard_states: Dict[int, Dict[str, int]] = {
            i: {} for i in range(num_shards)
        }
        self.pending_receipts: List[CrossShardMessage] = []
        self.completed_messages: List[CrossShardMessage] = []
        self.current_block = 0

    def address_to_shard(self, address: str) -> int:
        """Deterministic shard assignment by address hash."""
        h = int(hashlib.sha256(address.encode()).hexdigest()[:8], 16)
        return h % self.num_shards

    def submit_transaction(self, sender: str, recipient: str,
                           amount: int) -> dict:
        """Process a transaction, handling cross-shard if needed."""
        import hashlib

        src_shard = self.address_to_shard(sender)
        dst_shard = self.address_to_shard(recipient)

        # Check sender balance
        balance = self.shard_states[src_shard].get(sender, 0)
        if balance < amount:
            return {'success': False, 'reason': 'Insufficient balance'}

        if src_shard == dst_shard:
            # Intra-shard: process immediately
            self.shard_states[src_shard][sender] = balance - amount
            self.shard_states[dst_shard][recipient] = (
                self.shard_states[dst_shard].get(recipient, 0) + amount)
            return {
                'success': True, 'type': 'intra-shard',
                'shard': src_shard, 'latency_blocks': 1,
            }
```

```
        else:
            # Cross-shard: deduct from source, create receipt
            self.shard_states[src_shard][sender] = balance - amount

            msg_hash = hashlib.sha256(
                f"{sender}:{recipient}:{amount}:{self.current_block}".
                encode()
            ).hexdigest()[:12]

            msg = CrossShardMessage(
                source_shard=src_shard,
                dest_shard=dst_shard,
                sender=sender,
                recipient=recipient,
                amount=amount,
                msg_hash=msg_hash,
                status="pending",
                created_block=self.current_block,
            )
            self.pending_receipts.append(msg)

            return {
                'success': True, 'type': 'cross-shard',
                'source_shard': src_shard, 'dest_shard': dst_shard,
                'receipt': msg_hash, 'latency_blocks': '2+ (async)',
            }

    def process_receipts(self):
        """Process pending cross-shard receipts (next block)."""
        self.current_block += 1
        still_pending = []

        for msg in self.pending_receipts:
            if msg.status == "pending":
                # Deliver to destination shard
                self.shard_states[msg.dest_shard][msg.recipient] = (
                    self.shard_states[msg.dest_shard].get(msg.recipient, 0)
                    + msg.amount)
```

```
                msg.status = "delivered"
                msg.delivered_block = self.current_block
                self.completed_messages.append(msg)
            else:
                still_pending.append(msg)

        self.pending_receipts = still_pending

# Demonstrate cross-shard communication
import hashlib

network = ShardedNetwork(4, 25)

# Initialize balances
accounts = {f"user_{i}": 10000 for i in range(20)}
for addr, bal in accounts.items():
    shard = network.address_to_shard(addr)
    network.shard_states[shard][addr] = bal

print("\nCross-Shard Communication Demonstration (4 shards)")
print("=" * 60)

# Show address-to-shard mapping
shard_counts = {}
for addr in accounts:
    s = network.address_to_shard(addr)
    shard_counts[s] = shard_counts.get(s, 0) + 1
print(f"Accounts per shard: {dict(sorted(shard_counts.items()))}")

# Submit transactions (mix of intra and cross-shard)
intra = 0
cross = 0
for i in range(0, 20, 2):
    result = network.submit_transaction(f"user_{i}", f"user_{i+1}", 500)
    if result['success']:
        if result['type'] == 'intra-shard':
            intra += 1
```

```
        else:
            cross += 1

print(f"\nTransactions: {intra} intra-shard, {cross} cross-shard")
print(f"Pending receipts: {len(network.pending_receipts)}")

# Process next block (delivers receipts)
network.process_receipts()
print(f"After receipt processing: {len(network.completed_messages)}
delivered")

# Cross-shard latency analysis
for msg in network.completed_messages[:3]:
    latency = msg.delivered_block - msg.created_block
    print(f"  {msg.sender} -> {msg.recipient}: "
          f"shard {msg.source_shard} -> {msg.dest_shard}, "
          f"latency={latency} blocks")
```

Table 16-2. *Cross-Shard Communication Approaches*

Approach	Latency	Atomicity	Complexity	Example
Receipt-based (async)	2+ blocks	Eventual (with rollback)	Low	NEAR Nightshade, original Eth 2.0
Relay chain	2-3 relay blocks	Guaranteed delivery	Medium	Polkadot XCMP
Synchronous committee	1 block	Atomic	High	Research proposals
Yanking (contract migration)	2+ blocks	Atomic (after migration)	Medium	Ethereum research
Shared sequencer	1 block	Atomic (within batch)	Medium	Espresso, Astria

16.1.5 Ethereum's Sharding Evolution

Ethereum's sharding roadmap has changed dramatically. Each pivot came from practical experience and recognizing that simpler designs with stronger guarantees beat complex designs with weaker ones.

Phase 0 (December 2020). The Beacon Chain went live with Proof of Stake consensus, but no sharding yet. It established the infrastructure: validator registration, epoch processing, and fork choice. Critically, it proved Ethereum could run a parallel consensus layer safely.

The Merge (September 2022). Ethereum's execution layer moved from PoW to PoS, unifying with the Beacon Chain. Still no sharding. But the consensus infrastructure was live and battle-tested. Energy consumption dropped ~99.95%. Mining hardware became irrelevant.

Proto-Danksharding/EIP-4844 (March 2024). The pivotal step. It introduced "blob-carrying transactions"—a new transaction type that carries large data blobs (~128 KB each, up to 6 per block, targeting 3 on average). Blobs are temporary (pruned after ~18 days, roughly 4,096 epochs), not permanent like calldata.

Blobs get their own fee market, separate from execution gas. The blob base fee adjusts dynamically based on demand versus the target (3 per block). Demand above target? Fees rise up to 12.5% per block. Below? It drops. Blob demand can't spike execution gas prices and vice versa.

```
def eip4844_blob_market_simulation(blocks: int = 50) -> None:
    """
    Simulate the EIP-4844 blob fee market.

    The blob fee market operates independently from execution gas:
    - Target: 3 blobs per block
    - Maximum: 6 blobs per block
    - Base fee adjusts ±12.5% per block based on demand vs target
    - Minimum base fee: 1 Wei
    """
    BLOB_TARGET = 3
    BLOB_MAX = 6
    MIN_BLOB_BASE_FEE = 1  # 1 Wei
    BLOB_BASE_FEE_UPDATE_FRACTION = 3338477  # Controls adjustment speed
```

```
import math

blob_base_fee = 20_000_000_000  # Start at 20 Gwei

# Simulate varying blob demand
import random
random.seed(42)

print(f"EIP-4844 Blob Fee Market Simulation")
print(f"=" * 70)
print(f"{'Block':>6} {'Blobs':>7} {'Blob Fee (Gwei)':>16} {'Total Blob
Cost':>16} {'Status':>10}")
print("-" * 58)

total_blobs = 0
total_fees = 0

for block in range(blocks):
    # Simulate demand: rollups submit blobs based on their activity
    # Higher demand when fee is low, lower when fee is high
    max_willing_blobs = max(1, int(6 * (50_000_000_000 / (blob_base_
    fee + 1))))
    actual_blobs = min(max_willing_blobs, BLOB_MAX)
    actual_blobs = max(actual_blobs, 0)

    # Cost per blob
    blob_cost_gwei = blob_base_fee / 1e9
    total_block_blob_cost = actual_blobs * blob_base_fee /
    1e18  # In ETH

    total_blobs += actual_blobs
    total_fees += total_block_blob_cost

    status = "HIGH" if actual_blobs > BLOB_TARGET else ("LOW" if
    actual_blobs < BLOB_TARGET else "TARGET")


    if block % 5 == 0:  # Print every 5th block
        print(f"  {block:>4}  {actual_blobs:>5}  {blob_cost_
        gwei:>14.4f}  "
              f"{total_block_blob_cost:>14.8f} ETH  {status:>8}")
```

```
        # Update blob base fee for next block
# Real EIP-4844 formula from the spec:
# new_fee = old_fee * e^(excess / BLOB_BASE_FEE_UPDATE_FRACTION)
#
# BLOB_BASE_FEE_UPDATE_FRACTION = 3338477 (spec constant).
# Previous code used BLOB_TARGET * 2 = 6 instead – making fees
# adjust ~556,000× too fast, causing wild oscillation each block.
#
# With the correct constant, fee adjusts gradually:
# - At excess=+3 (6 blobs vs target 3): multiplier = e^(3/3338477) ≈
1.0000009
# - At excess=-3 (0 blobs vs target 3): multiplier = e^(-3/3338477) ≈
0.9999991
# This mirrors the real EIP-1559 execution fee market behavior.
#
# The if/elif split was also unnecessary – math.exp handles both
# positive excess (fee increase) and negative excess (fee decrease)
# with the same formula.
excess = actual_blobs - BLOB_TARGET
blob_base_fee = max(
    int(blob_base_fee * math.exp(excess / BLOB_BASE_FEE_UPDATE_FRACTION)),
    MIN_BLOB_BASE_FEE
)
    print(f"\n  Summary over {blocks} blocks:")
    print(f"    Total blobs: {total_blobs}")
    print(f"    Avg blobs/block: {total_blobs/blocks:.1f} (target: {BLOB_
    TARGET})")
    print(f"    Total blob fees: {total_fees:.6f} ETH")
    print(f"    Avg fee per blob: {total_fees/max(total_
    blobs,1)*1e9:.4f} Gwei")

eip4844_blob_market_simulation()
```

Full Danksharding (still ahead). Extends EIP-4844 with full data availability sampling. Target: around 64 blobs per block (up from 6), giving roughly 16 MB of data per block. Light clients verify availability through random sampling of erasure-coded blob data. No need for full nodes to download every blob.

The name honors Dankrad Feist, the Ethereum researcher behind the design. It differs from traditional sharding in one critical way: there's still a single block proposer for all blob data, not separate per-shard proposers. Blobs aren't independent shard chains. They're data attached to the main Ethereum block. DAS ensures availability without requiring every node to download everything.

The progression is designed to be incremental. EIP-4844 sets up the blob format, the separate fee market, and rollup integration patterns. Full danksharding adds DAS and bumps the blob count. Ship it in stages and reduce the risk.

16.1.6 Practical Sharding Implementations

Zilliqa: Pioneer of Transaction Sharding

Zilliqa, launched in 2019, was one of the first production chains to implement sharding. Its approach: transaction sharding (route transactions to shards based on sender address) combined with network sharding (nodes partitioned into shard committees).

Three-layer architecture. A directory service committee (DS committee) handles shard assignments and cross-shard transactions. Shard committees process intra-shard transactions in parallel. A lookup service routes clients to the right shard.

Each shard runs PBFT internally—instant finality, but committee sizes cap at a few hundred nodes. Cross-shard transactions use a two-phase commit-and-confirm: source shard deducts, DS committee validates the receipt, and destination shard credits.

Benchmarks show around 2,800 TPS with 6 shards and 3,600 nodes. But the DS committee bottlenecks cross-shard transactions, and PBFT consensus limits how often committees can rotate.

NEAR Protocol: Nightshade Sharding

NEAR uses Nightshade, where the chain has multiple logical shards but produces a single physical block. Each block contains "chunks" from every shard. A chunk is that shard's slice of the block: the transactions its validators processed.

The single-block design has a nice property: since all chunks live in one block, cross-shard communication is simple. A receipt from shard A's chunk is available to shard B in the very next block. Cross-shard latency: exactly one block time.

Validators get assigned to shards by stake weight, rotating each epoch. A validator on shard 2 validates all of shard 2's chunks and produces chunks when selected as the chunk producer.

NEAR runs 4 shards today and plans for 100+ via stateless validation. Validators don't keep the full shard state. Each transaction comes with a state witness—a proof of every state value it reads. The validator checks the witness and execution without persistent state. Hardware requirements per shard drop significantly.

```
def near_nightshade_simulation(num_shards: int, txs_per_shard: int,
                               cross_shard_fraction: float) -> dict:
    """
    Simulate NEAR's Nightshade sharding model.

    Key property: all shard chunks are part of a single block,
    so cross-shard receipts are available in the next block.
    """
    total_txs = num_shards * txs_per_shard
    cross_shard_txs = int(total_txs * cross_shard_fraction)
    intra_shard_txs = total_txs - cross_shard_txs

    # Intra-shard: processed in 1 block
    # Cross-shard: processed in 2 blocks (source + receipt delivery)
    avg_latency_blocks = (intra_shard_txs * 1 + cross_shard_txs * 2) /
    total_txs

    # Throughput scales linearly with shards (for intra-shard)
    # Cross-shard creates overhead proportional to cross_shard_fraction
    effective_throughput_multiplier = num_shards * (1 - cross_shard_
    fraction * 0.5)

    return {
        'num_shards': num_shards,
        'total_txs_per_block': total_txs,
        'cross_shard_txs': cross_shard_txs,
        'avg_latency_blocks': avg_latency_blocks,
        'throughput_multiplier': effective_throughput_multiplier,
    }
```

```
print("\nNEAR Nightshade Scaling Analysis")
print("=" * 60)
print(f"{'Shards':>8} {'TXs/block':>12} {'Cross-shard %':>14} {'Avg
latency':>12} {'Throughput ×':>13}")
print("-" * 62)
for shards in [4, 8, 16, 32, 64, 100]:
    for cross_pct in [0.1, 0.3]:
        r = near_nightshade_simulation(shards, 200, cross_pct)
        print(f"  {shards:>6} {r['total_txs_per_block']:>10,} "
              f"{cross_pct:>12.0%} {r['avg_latency_blocks']:>10.2f} blocks"
              f" {r['throughput_multiplier']:>11.1f}×")
```

Polkadot: Heterogeneous Sharding via Relay Chain

Polkadot takes a fundamentally different path: heterogeneous sharding via a relay chain. Instead of identical shards running the same environment, Polkadot's parachains are independent blockchains. Each can have its own consensus, state transition function, token economics, and governance. What they share: security and interoperability through the relay chain.

The relay chain does three things. First, shared security. Relay chain validators verify parachain blocks (called Proofs of Validity). A parachain with $1M staked inherits security from Polkadot's multi-billion-dollar validator set.

Second, message ordering. Cross-parachain messages (XCMP) are ordered by the relay chain. Canonical sequence for inter-chain communication. Messages arrive in order, exactly once.

Third, validator assignment. Validators rotate randomly across parachains each session. No single parachain can be permanently captured by a colluding group.

Parachain slots are allocated by auction. Projects bid for 96-week leases. That creates a market for blockspace—more valuable applications pay more for dedicated slots. There's also an "on-demand" model: pay per block without a full lease.

Table 16-3. *Sharding Implementations Compared*

Property	Zilliqa	NEAR (Nightshade)	Polkadot	Ethereum (Danksharding)
Sharding type	Transaction + network	State + single-block chunks	Heterogeneous parachains	Data availability
Number of shards	6 (current)	4 (current, scaling to 100+)	~100 parachains	64 blobs (target)
Cross-shard mechanism	DS committee 2-phase commit	Same-block receipts (1 block)	XCMP via relay chain (2-3 blocks)	N/A (rollups handle execution)
Execution model	Identical shards (Scilla)	Identical shards (WASM)	Heterogeneous (any runtime)	Rollups execute independently
Stateless validation	No	Planned (state witnesses)	Yes (PoV includes state proof)	Yes (DAS for data, proofs for execution)
Consensus per shard	PBFT (instant finality)	Nightshade + PoS	BABE (production) + GRANDPA (finality)	N/A (Gasper for DA layer)
Smart contracts	Scilla language	Rust (WASM)	Substrate framework (per-chain choice)	EVM/WASM (via rollups)
Unique feature	First production sharding	Single-block multi-shard	Heterogeneous chains, shared security	Pure DA sharding for rollups

State Witnesses and Stateless Validation

Stateless validation is the innovation that makes practical sharding work. The idea: validators don't need the full state of their assigned shard. Each block comes with a state witness—a proof containing every state value the block's transactions touch, plus Merkle proofs back to the state root.

The validator gets the block, the transactions, and the witness. It checks the Merkle proofs against the previous state root (confirming the witness has correct pre-state values), re-executes the transactions against the witnessed state, and verifies the resulting root matches the claimed post-state root. At no point does it need the full shard state in memory or on disk.

The implications for sharding scalability are significant:

Hardware requirements drop. Without stateless validation, each validator stores the entire shard state—potentially tens or hundreds of gigabytes. With it, they need only enough memory for one block's state witness (megabytes). Validators can participate in multiple shards simultaneously or switch shards fast.

Committee rotation gets cheaper. Traditionally, moving a validator to a new shard means downloading that shard's full state—hours or days for large shards. With stateless validation, rotation is instant. Just start processing the new shard's blocks using the included witnesses.

Shard count can grow. No persistent per-shard state means adding more shards doesn't proportionally increase individual validator burden. The bottleneck shifts from storage to bandwidth (downloading witnesses) and computation (verifying proofs, re-executing transactions).

The trade-off is witness size. A witness has to include every state value the block accesses, plus Merkle proofs from each value to the root. For blocks touching many state locations (common in smart contract execution), witnesses can hit several megabytes. That becomes the new bandwidth bottleneck.

Verkle trees (proposed as a replacement for Ethereum's Merkle-Patricia trie) directly tackle witness size. Verkle proofs run about 150 bytes per state element, versus roughly 1 KB for Merkle-Patricia proofs. That 6–7× reduction makes stateless validation realistic under real bandwidth constraints.

```
def stateless_validation_analysis(state_accesses_per_block: int,
                                  proof_size_bytes: int,
                                  block_time_seconds: int) -> dict:
```

```
    """
    Analyze bandwidth requirements for stateless validation.

    Each state access requires a proof linking the accessed value
    to the state root. The total witness size determines bandwidth.
    """
    # Each access: value (32 bytes) + proof
    per_access = 32 + proof_size_bytes
    witness_bytes = state_accesses_per_block * per_access
    witness_kb = witness_bytes / 1024
    witness_mb = witness_bytes / (1024 * 1024)

    # Bandwidth requirement: witness per block_time
    bandwidth_kbps = witness_kb / block_time_seconds * 8  # kbits/s
    bandwidth_mbps = bandwidth_kbps / 1024

    return {
        'accesses': state_accesses_per_block,
        'proof_size': proof_size_bytes,
        'witness_kb': witness_kb,
        'witness_mb': witness_mb,
        'bandwidth_mbps': bandwidth_mbps,
    }

print("\nStateless Validation Bandwidth Analysis")
print("=" * 65)
print(f"{'State Accesses':>16} {'Proof Type':>14} {'Witness Size':>14}
{'Bandwidth':>12}")
print("-" * 58)

for accesses in [500, 1000, 5000, 10000]:
    for proof_type, proof_bytes in [("Merkle-Patricia", 1024),
    ("Verkle", 150)]:
        r = stateless_validation_analysis(accesses, proof_bytes, 12)
        print(f"  {accesses:>14,}  {proof_type:>12}  {r['witness_
        kb']:>10.0f} KB  "
               f"{r['bandwidth_mbps']:>9.2f} Mbps")
```

16.1.7 Summary

Sharding multiplies throughput by parallelizing across multiple chains. The shift from execution sharding to data availability sharding reflects a hard-won understanding of where the real bottleneck sits: not computation (rollups handle that) but data availability (which L1 has to provide).

Key takeaways:

- Single-shard takeover is the core security challenge. An adversary needs only a fraction of total resources to compromise one shard. Random committee rotation makes that exponentially harder as committee sizes grow.
- Execution sharding was the original vision, but the complexity was prohibitive. Cross-shard composability is fundamentally limited. Per-shard security depends on committee size. The throughput-security trade-off doesn't resolve cleanly.
- DA sharding (danksharding) scales what rollups need most: cheap data space. Execution stays on rollups, sidestepping the composability nightmare.
- 2D Reed-Solomon erasure coding transforms k×k data into 2k×2k extended data. Any 50%+ of the encoded data reconstructs the original. DAS exploits this: light clients sample random cells and detect withholding with exponentially high probability.
- 75 random samples detect 50% data withholding with probability greater than 1-10^$^{-22}$. Even 1% withholding gets caught more than half the time per sampling round.
- EIP-4844 (proto-danksharding) is the first step: 6 blobs per block (~768 KB) with a separate fee market. Full danksharding will scale that to ~64 blobs with DAS verification.
- Cross-shard communication is inherently latency-limited. Async receipts are the simplest approach but add multi-block delays. Shared sequencing might eventually enable atomic cross-L2 transactions. Maybe.

Sharding splits processing across parallel chains. Throughput scales linearly with shard count.—Single-shard takeover: adversary needs only 1/N resources for N shards. Committee rotation is the fix.—P(shard compromised) drops exponentially with committee size. 128-validator committees are practical.—Execution sharding gave way to DA sharding: rollups handle execution, L1 handles data availability.—2D Reed-Solomon erasure coding: k×k data → 2k×2k extended. Any 50%+ reconstructs original.—DAS: s random samples catch f-fraction withholding with probability 1-(1-f)^s.—EIP-4844: 6 blobs per block (~768 KB). Separate fee market. First step toward full danksharding.—Cross-shard: async receipts (2+ block latency), relay chain (Polkadot), shared sequencer (emerging).

16.1.8 Exercises

Problem 1 (Basic): Why does sharding create a single-shard takeover vulnerability? How does random committee rotation help? What determines whether a takeover succeeds?

Problem 2 (Calculation): 10,000 validators, 64 shards (156 per shard), BFT consensus needing >1/3 to attack. Adversary controls 15% of validators. What's the probability a single shard is compromised? What about at least one of 64 shards?

Problem 3 (Implementation): Build a complete 2D erasure coding scheme. 4×4 data grid, compute row and column parities for an 8×8 extended matrix. Remove 50% of cells at random and reconstruct. Show that 51% removal breaks reconstruction.

Problem 4 (Analysis): Execution sharding versus DA sharding. Compare on: cross-shard composability, per-shard security, implementation complexity, and DeFi suitability. Why did Ethereum switch?

Problem 5 (Design): Design a cross-shard DEX swap for an execution-sharded chain. Token A on shard 1, token B on shard 2. Specify message flow, commit-reveal mechanism, failure handling, and minimum cross-shard blocks needed.

Problem 6 (Theory): Prove that 2× erasure coding extension allows reconstruction from any 50%+ of the encoded data. What happens at exactly 50%? Below? Derive the information-theoretic lower bound.

Problem 7 (Comparative): Zilliqa's transaction sharding, NEAR's Nightshade, Polkadot's parachains. For each: what gets sharded, how validators are assigned, how cross-shard transactions work, and performance characteristics.

Problem 8 (Critical Thinking): Is sharding even necessary if rollups scale execution well enough? What happens when rollup data demand exceeds L1 capacity? How does danksharding address that bottleneck?

Problem 9 (Advanced): Build a DAS simulator. Erasure-code a 64 KB block. Simulate an adversary withholding 1%–75%. Have 100 light clients each sample 75 cells. Measure detection rate versus withholding fraction.

Problem 10 (Research): Study EIP-4844 blob transactions since deployment. Report: average blobs per block, blob fee market dynamics, impact on rollup L1 costs, whether blob demand has approached the target and limit.

(Solutions in Appendix D)

CHAPTER 17

Data Availability and Modular Blockchains

17.1 The Data Availability Problem and Modular Architecture

A valid block header proves nothing about whether the data behind it was actually published. That gap—the data availability problem—breaks fraud proofs, light clients, and rollup security in ways that aren't obvious until something goes wrong. This chapter covers DAS, the erasure coding math underneath it, Celestia's purpose-built DA architecture, the modular blockchain paradigm, EigenLayer restaking and its correlation risks, and when monolithic still beats modular. Here's what it covers:

- The data availability problem and why it's a real threat to light clients, fraud proofs, and rollup security
- How data availability Sampling lets you verify data without downloading the whole thing
- The math underneath—erasure coding for DA and its roots in coding theory
- Celestia's architecture: the first blockchain built specifically to be a data availability layer
- The modular blockchain idea and what it means to separate execution, consensus, DA, and settlement into independent pieces
- Restaking and shared security through Eigen Layer, including the correlation risks nobody wants to talk about

N. Savant, *Blockchain Foundations*, https://doi.org/10.1007/979-8-8688-2891-1_17

- When monolithic designs beat modular ones and when they don't
- How "fat protocols" are giving way to thin, specialized layers

17.1.1 The Data Availability Problem

Data availability sounds simple. Block data has been published and everyone who needs it can get it. Turns out, enforcing that in a trustless setting is surprisingly hard, and the consequences of getting it wrong touch every layer of the stack.

The problem comes from an asymmetry. A block header commits to the block's data—usually a Merkle root or polynomial commitment—but that commitment is just a few dozen bytes regardless of the data size. A malicious producer could build a perfectly valid-looking header (correct proofs, valid signatures, well-formed structure) while withholding some or all of the actual data behind it.

Full nodes catch this. They request block data and if it never shows up, they know. Light nodes don't have that luxury. They only check headers for efficiency, and a header with withheld data looks identical to one with available data. The cryptographic commitment is valid either way.

This matters for several things that really can't break:

Fraud proofs for optimistic rollups. The whole security model depends on verifiers catching invalid state transitions. To build a fraud proof, you need to re-execute the transactions. But if the sequencer posts a state root to L1 while hiding the transaction data, nobody can construct the proof. The bad state root just gets accepted after the challenge window closes. The sequencer walks away with the funds.

Light client verification. Mobile wallets, browser extensions, resource-constrained devices—they all rely on light clients that check headers but skip execution. If data is unavailable, a light client might accept a block that full nodes would reject. Divergent views of the chain state, exploitable for fake payments.

State reconstruction. A new node joining the network has to rebuild the current state, either by replaying transactions or verifying a state snapshot. If the historical block data is gone, the node has to trust whatever state it receives. No independent verification.

Chain recovery. If a big chunk of nodes go offline at once (network partition, infrastructure failure, coordinated attack), the survivors need to reconstruct from what's available. Missing data during one of those events can mean permanent state loss.

Demonstrating the Data Withholding Attack

The data withholding attack is subtle. A valid Merkle root proves the data existed when the root was computed. It does not prove the data was published. That gap is the whole DA problem in one sentence.

```
import hashlib
from typing import Dict, List, Optional, Tuple
from dataclasses import dataclass
@dataclass
class RollupBlock:
    block_number: int
    state_root: str
    data_root: str  # Merkle root of transaction data
    data: Optional[List[dict]]  # The actual data (None if withheld)

class DataWithholdingDemo:
    """
    Demonstrate the data withholding attack on a rollup.
    The malicious sequencer:
    1. Executes transactions honestly (computing correct state root)
    2. Computes valid Merkle root of transaction data
    3. Posts state_root and data_root to L1
    4. WITHHOLDS the actual transaction data
    Result: L1 contract accepts the block (valid roots),
    but no verifier can construct a fraud proof because the
    data needed for re-execution is unavailable.
    """
    def __init__(self, initial_state: Dict[str, int]):
        self.state = dict(initial_state)
        self.blocks: List[RollupBlock] = []
    def _compute_state_root(self, state: Dict[str, int]) -> str:
        return hashlib.sha256(str(sorted(state.items())).encode()).
        hexdigest()[:16]

    def _compute_data_root(self, transactions: List[dict]) -> str:
        return hashlib.sha256(str(transactions).encode()).hexdigest()[:16]
```

```
    def honest_block(self, transactions: List[dict]) -> RollupBlock:
        """Honest sequencer: publishes both roots AND data."""
        for tx in transactions:
            if self.state.get(tx['sender'], 0) >= tx['amount']:
                self.state[tx['sender']] -= tx['amount']
                self.state[tx['recipient']] = self.state.
                get(tx['recipient'], 0) + tx['amount']

        block = RollupBlock(
            block_number=len(self.blocks),
            state_root=self._compute_state_root(self.state),
            data_root=self._compute_data_root(transactions),
            data=transactions,  # DATA PUBLISHED
        )
        self.blocks.append(block)
        return block

    def malicious_block(self, transactions: List[dict],
                        fake_state: Dict[str, int]) -> RollupBlock:
        """
        Malicious sequencer: publishes roots but WITHHOLDS data.
        The state root may be fraudulent (stealing funds),
        but no one can prove it without the transaction data.
        """
        block = RollupBlock(
            block_number=len(self.blocks),
            state_root=self._compute_state_root(fake_state),
            data_root=self._compute_data_root(transactions),
            data=None,  # DATA WITHHELD!
        )
        self.blocks.append(block)
        return block

    def attempt_fraud_proof(self, block: RollupBlock,
                            pre_state: Dict[str, int]) -> dict:
        """
        Verifier attempts to construct a fraud proof.
```

```
        Requires the transaction data to re-execute and compare
        the resulting state root against the posted one.
        """
        if block.data is None:
            return {
                'can_prove_fraud': False,
                'reason': 'DATA UNAVAILABLE: Cannot re-execute
                transactions. '
                          'Fraud proof construction is impossible. '
                          'The potentially fraudulent state root will be '
                          'accepted after the challenge period expires.',
            }

        # Re-execute transactions
        test_state = dict(pre_state)
        for tx in block.data:
            if test_state.get(tx['sender'], 0) >= tx['amount']:
                test_state[tx['sender']] -= tx['amount']
                test_state[tx['recipient']] = test_state.
                get(tx['recipient'], 0) + tx['amount']

        correct_root = self._compute_state_root(test_state)

        if correct_root != block.state_root:
            return {
                'can_prove_fraud': True,
                'correct_root': correct_root,
                'posted_root': block.state_root,
                'reason': 'Fraud detected: state root mismatch',
            }

        return {
            'can_prove_fraud': False,
            'reason': 'Block is valid (roots match)',
        }

# Demonstrate the attack
demo = DataWithholdingDemo({'alice': 100000, 'bob': 50000})
```

```
print("Data Withholding Attack Demonstration")
print("=" * 65)

# Honest block: verifier can check
txs = [{'sender': 'alice', 'recipient': 'bob', 'amount': 5000}]
honest = demo.honest_block(txs)
result = demo.attempt_fraud_proof(honest, {'alice': 100000, 'bob': 50000})
print(f"Honest block: data={'AVAILABLE' if honest.data else 'WITHHELD'}")
print(f"  Fraud proof: {result['reason']}")

# Malicious block: sequencer steals ALL funds by posting fake state root.
# Pre-state after honest block: alice=95000, bob=55000 (total=150000)
# Fake state claims attacker received everything — total must still
be 150000.
# Previous code had attacker=145000, losing 5000 ETH with no explanation.
pre_state = {'alice': 95000, 'bob': 55000}  # State after honest block
(total=150000)
fake_state = {'alice': 0, 'bob': 0, 'attacker': 150000}  # Stole ALL
150000 ← FIXED
# The malicious txs show what the sequencer CLAIMS happened.
# They are used only to compute data_root — the actual state posted
# is the fraudulent fake_state above.
malicious_txs = [
    {'sender': 'alice', 'recipient': 'attacker', 'amount': 95000},
    {'sender': 'bob',   'recipient': 'attacker', 'amount': 55000},
    # Also stole Bob's funds
]
malicious = demo.malicious_block(malicious_txs, fake_state)
result = demo.attempt_fraud_proof(malicious, pre_state)
print(f"\nMalicious block: data={'AVAILABLE' if malicious.data else
'WITHHELD'}")
print(f"  Pre-state:   alice={pre_state['alice']}, bob={pre_state['bob']} "
      f"(total={sum(pre_state.values())})")
print(f"  Fake state:  alice=0, bob=0, attacker=150000 "
      f"(total={sum(fake_state.values())})")
print(f"  State root posted: {malicious.state_root}")
print(f"  Fraud proof: {result['reason']}")
```

```
print(f"\n  CONSEQUENCE: After 7-day challenge period, the malicious")
print(f"  state root is accepted. Attacker withdraws 150,000 in stolen
funds.")
print(f"  THIS is why data availability is critical for rollup security.")
```

The Subtlety of Detection

Here's the really tricky part: the DA problem isn't just about data being missing. It's about the inability to prove it's missing. A node that can't download a block has two possibilities: the data exists but its connection is bad, or the data was never published. It can't tell the difference, and it can't prove either case to a third party. That's fundamentally different from data validity, which you can prove or disprove with cryptography.

Classic thought experiment: a block producer publishes a header but sends the data to only 1% of the network. The 99% suspect it's unavailable. The 1% can reconstruct the full block. Is the data "available"? Depends who you ask and what their connectivity looks like. Which is exactly why DA requires careful protocol design, not simple checks.

17.1.2 Data Availability Sampling: The Solution

DAS solves the problem for light clients by combining erasure coding (adds redundancy to data) with random sampling (probabilistically catches withholding). Together, a light client can verify availability by downloading just a small number of random samples. Verification cost doesn't scale with data size.

Erasure Coding for DA

Standard erasure coding takes k data symbols and encodes them into n > k symbols so that any k of the n reconstruct the original. For blockchain DA, the specific tool is polynomial evaluation over finite fields—Reed-Solomon codes.

The block's transaction data gets interpreted as a polynomial of degree k-1 over a finite field. Evaluate it at n > k points and you get n encoded values. Any k of those values pin down the polynomial (and therefore the original data) through interpolation. The extra n - k values are redundant parity.

For 2D DAS (Ethereum's danksharding approach), arrange the data in a k×k matrix. Treat each row as a polynomial and extend it to 2k points. Then treat each column of the extended matrix as a polynomial and extend to 2k points. Result: a 2k×2k matrix with the original data in one quadrant.

The key property: any k cells from any row or column reconstruct that entire row or column. Reconstruct all rows and you've got the complete data. An adversary has to withhold at least 50% of the extended data to prevent reconstruction. And withholding 50% is extremely easy to detect by random sampling.

The Sampling Protocol

A light client doing DAS:

1. Gets the block header with polynomial commitments (KZG) to each row and column of the extended matrix
2. Picks s cells uniformly at random from the 2k × 2k matrix
3. Requests each cell from network peers, along with a proof that it matches the row/column commitment
4. Checks each cell-proof pair against the header commitments
5. If all s cells check out, accepts the block as data-available

The detection math. An adversary hiding fraction f from a client sampling s cells gets away with it with probability (1-f)^s. For 75 samples:

- 50% withheld: (0.5)^75 ≈ 2.6 × 10^$^{-23}$. Effectively zero
- 25% withheld: (0.75)^75 ≈ 1.8 × 10^$^{-9}$. Still negligible
- 10% withheld: (0.9)^75 ≈ 0.0003. Very unlikely to miss
- 1% withheld: (0.99)^75 ≈ 0.47. About a coin flip

That last case is interesting. 1% withholding is hard to detect with moderate samples. But 1% withholding can't prevent reconstruction (any 50% is enough), so it's not a security threat. It just signals unreliable data propagation.

```
import math

def das_security_analysis(extended_size: int = 512,
                          cell_size_bytes: int = 512) -> None:
    """
    Comprehensive DAS security and performance analysis.

    Analyzes detection probability, bandwidth requirements,
    and the relationship between sampling and security guarantees.
```

```
"""
total_cells = extended_size * extended_size
data_cells = (extended_size // 2) * (extended_size // 2)
total_data_kb = data_cells * cell_size_bytes / 1024

print(f"DAS Security Analysis")
print(f"=" * 70)
print(f"Extended matrix: {extended_size}×{extended_size} = {total_
cells:,} cells")
print(f"Original data: {extended_size//2}×{extended_size//2} = {data_
cells:,} cells")
print(f"Total data size: {total_data_kb:.0f} KB")
print(f"Cell size: {cell_size_bytes} bytes")

# Detection probability curves
print(f"\n1. Detection Probability by Withholding Fraction")
print(f"{'Withheld':>10}", end="")
for s in [16, 32, 64, 75, 100, 150]:
    print(f"  s={s:>3}", end="")
print()
print("-" * 70)

for f_pct in [1, 2, 5, 10, 25, 50, 75]:
    f = f_pct / 100
    print(f"  {f_pct:>6}%  ", end="")
    for s in [16, 32, 64, 75, 100, 150]:
        p_detect = 1 - (1 - f) ** s
        if p_detect > 0.99999:
            print(f"  ~100%", end="")
        elif p_detect > 0.999:
            print(f" {p_detect:.3%}", end="")
        else:
            print(f" {p_detect:.1%}", end="")
    print()

# Bandwidth requirements per light client
print(f"\n2. Light Client Bandwidth per Block")
for s in [30, 50, 75, 100]:
```

```
        bandwidth = s * cell_size_bytes
        # Include proof overhead (~48 bytes per KZG proof)
        with_proofs = s * (cell_size_bytes + 48)
        print(f"  {s} samples: {bandwidth/1024:.1f} KB data + "
              f"{s * 48 / 1024:.1f} KB proofs = {with_proofs/1024:.1f}
              KB total")

    # Minimum withholding to prevent reconstruction
print(f"\n3. Reconstruction Threshold")
print(f"  Extended matrix:  {extended_size}×{extended_size} = {total_
cells:,} total cells")
print(f"  Original data:    {extended_size//2}×{extended_size//2} = {data_
cells:,} cells "
      f"({data_cells/total_cells*100:.0f}% of extended matrix)")
print()
print(f"  IMPORTANT: Reconstruction does NOT require any 25% of total
cells.")
print(f"  2D Reed-Solomon works row-by-row and column-by-column:")
print(f"    - Need ≥{extended_size//2} cells from any single row to
reconstruct that row")
print(f"    - That means ≥50% of each row (or column) must be available")
print(f"    - Reconstructing all rows gives all original data")
print()
print(f"  Adversary strategy: must withhold >50% of at least one row/
column")
print(f"  to prevent reconstruction of that row/column.")
print(f"  Withholding any random 25% of total cells is NOT sufficient to")
print(f"  block reconstruction – those cells are spread across all rows.")
print()
print(f"  DAS detects this because: withholding >50% per row means")
print(f"  >50% of total cells are withheld, which 75 samples detect")
print(f"  with probability > 1 - (0.5)^75 ≈ 1 - 2.6×10^-23")

    # Network-wide detection with multiple light clients
    print(f"\n4. Network-Wide Detection (each client samples 75 cells)")
    for f_pct in [10, 25, 50]:
```

```
        f = f_pct / 100
        p_single_miss = (1 - f) ** 75
        for num_clients in [10, 100, 1000]:
            p_all_miss = p_single_miss ** num_clients
            print(f"  {f_pct}% withheld, {num_clients:>4} clients: "
                  f"P(all miss) = {p_all_miss:.2e}")

das_security_analysis()
```

17.1.3 Celestia: Purpose-Built Data Availability

Celestia is the first blockchain built purely as a DA layer. No transaction execution. No application state. No smart contracts. The entire point: order data blobs and guarantee their availability through DAS.

The philosophy is radical specialization. Strip execution from the consensus layer's job and you can optimize entirely for data throughput and availability verification. Validators just agree on ordering and availability of opaque blobs. They don't need to understand what's in them.

Architecture

Consensus layer. Tendermint-based BFT with roughly 100 validators. They determine blob ordering and produce headers with commitments to the blob data.

Data availability layer. Each block's data is erasure-coded into a 2D matrix with KZG commitments for every row and column. Light clients sample random cells. Bridge nodes download full blocks and serve sample requests.

Namespace Merkle Trees (NMTs). This is Celestia's key innovation. Each blob gets tagged with a namespace identifier (29 bytes, chosen by the posting rollup). Blobs within a block are sorted by namespace and organized into a modified Merkle tree where internal nodes track the min and max namespace of their children.

NMTs enable namespace proofs. A rollup requests its own namespace's blobs from a Celestia block, plus a compact proof that the returned set is complete. Download only your data, not the whole block. The proof guarantees nothing was left out.

```
import hashlib
from dataclasses import dataclass
from typing import List
```

```
@dataclass
class CelestiaBlob:
    """A data blob posted to Celestia with a namespace tag."""
    namespace: str      # Rollup identifier
    data: bytes         # Opaque transaction data

    @property
    def size_bytes(self) -> int:
        return len(self.data) + len(self.namespace.encode())

@dataclass
class NMTNode:
    """Namespace Merkle Tree node with namespace range tracking."""
    min_ns: str
    max_ns: str
    digest: str

class NamespaceMerkleTree:
    """
    Namespace Merkle Tree: Celestia's core data structure.

    Properties:
    1. Blobs sorted by namespace within each block
    2. Internal nodes track min/max namespace of their subtree
    3. Namespace inclusion proofs: prove all blobs for a namespace
    4. Namespace absence proofs: prove no blobs exist for a namespace
    """

    def __init__(self, blobs: List[CelestiaBlob]):
        self.blobs = sorted(blobs, key=lambda b: b.namespace)
        self.root = self._build(
            [self._leaf(b) for b in self.blobs]
        )

    def _leaf(self, blob: CelestiaBlob) -> NMTNode:
        h = hashlib.sha256(blob.namespace.encode() + blob.data).
        hexdigest()[:16]
        return NMTNode(blob.namespace, blob.namespace, h)
```

```
    def _build(self, nodes: List[NMTNode]) -> NMTNode:
        if not nodes:
            return NMTNode("", "", hashlib.sha256(b"empty").
            hexdigest()[:16])
        if len(nodes) == 1:
            return nodes[0]
        if len(nodes) % 2:
            nodes.append(nodes[-1])
        parents = []
        for i in range(0, len(nodes), 2):
            l, r = nodes[i], nodes[i+1]
            h = hashlib.sha256((l.digest + r.digest).encode()).
            hexdigest()[:16]
            parents.append(NMTNode(
                min(l.min_ns, r.min_ns), max(l.max_ns, r.max_ns), h
            ))
        return self._build(parents)

    def get_namespace_data(self, namespace: str) -> dict:
        ns_blobs = [b for b in self.blobs if b.namespace == namespace]
        return {
            'namespace': namespace,
            'blob_count': len(ns_blobs),
            'total_bytes': sum(b.size_bytes for b in ns_blobs),
            'root': self.root.digest,
            'complete': True,  # NMT guarantees completeness
        }

# Demonstrate Celestia Namespace Merkle Tree
blobs = [
    CelestiaBlob("arbitrum", b"arb_batch_001" * 500),
    CelestiaBlob("arbitrum", b"arb_batch_002" * 400),
    CelestiaBlob("optimism", b"op_batch_001" * 600),
    CelestiaBlob("starknet", b"stark_da_001" * 300),
    CelestiaBlob("starknet", b"stark_da_002" * 450),
    CelestiaBlob("zksync", b"zk_batch" * 550),
]
```

```
nmt = NamespaceMerkleTree(blobs)
print("\nCelestia Namespace Merkle Tree")
print("=" * 55)
print(f"Block: {len(blobs)} blobs, {len(set(b.namespace for b in blobs))}
namespaces")
print(f"Root: {nmt.root.digest} [{nmt.root.min_ns}..{nmt.root.max_ns}]")

for ns in sorted(set(b.namespace for b in blobs)):
    info = nmt.get_namespace_data(ns)
    print(f"  {ns:<12}: {info['blob_count']} blobs, {info['total_
    bytes']:,}B")
```

How Rollups Use Celestia

A rollup on Celestia follows this lifecycle:

1. **Transaction Collection**: The sequencer collects user transactions
2. **Execution**: The sequencer runs them off-chain and computes the new state root
3. **Blob Posting**: The sequencer submits transaction data as a blob to Celestia under its namespace. Celestia orders and commits it, producing a DA attestation
4. **Settlement**: The sequencer posts the state root and DA attestation to the settlement layer (Ethereum L1). ZK rollups include a validity proof. Optimistic rollups enter a challenge period
5. **Verification**: Any verifier pulls the namespace's blobs from Celestia (not the whole block) and re-executes to check correctness

The security model splits cleanly. Settlement (Ethereum) handles proofs and disputes. DA (Celestia) guarantees publication. Execution (the rollup) handles computation. Each piece optimizes independently.

Alternative DA Layers

Celestia isn't the only option. The DA market has spread out:

EigenDA. Built on Ethereum restaking through EigenLayer. Validators who opt in store and serve data blobs. Security comes from staked ETH at risk—fail to serve data, get slashed. Throughput around 10 MB/s, cheaper than L1 calldata.

Avail (Polygon's project). Standalone DA chain, own validators, own token. Similar to Celestia in concept but different under the hood: GRANDPA/BABE consensus from Substrate, Kate commitments for data verification.

Ethereum blobs (EIP-4844). Not a separate chain—integrated into Ethereum itself. Each blob transaction carries ~128 KB, separate fee market. Inherits Ethereum's full validator set and consensus security. Downside: limited to 6 blobs per block, about 768 KB total.

Table 17-1. *DA Layer Comparison*

Property	Celestia	EigenDA	Avail	Ethereum Blobs
Architecture	Standalone chain	Restaked from Ethereum	Standalone chain	Integrated in Ethereum
Consensus	CometBFT (~100 validators)	Ethereum restakers	GRANDPA/BABE	Gasper (600K+ validators)
Throughput	~2 MB/s (current)	~10 MB/s	~1 MB/s	~100 KB/s (6 blobs/12s)
DAS support	Yes (production)	Planned	Yes	Planned (full danksharding)
Security source	Celestia token staking	Ethereum ETH restaking	Avail token staking	Ethereum ETH staking
Cost per MB	~$0.01-0.10	~$0.01-0.05	~$0.01-0.10	~$1-10 (varies with demand)
Trust assumption	Celestia consensus honest	EigenLayer slashing conditions	Avail consensus honest	Ethereum consensus (strongest)

17.1.4 The Modular Blockchain Paradigm

The modular thesis breaks a blockchain into four specialized layers, each independently optimizable:

Execution. Where transactions get processed and state transitions happen. Smart contracts run here. Token transfers execute here. The execution layer determines the programming model (EVM, WASM, Move, Cairo), transaction format, and state structure. Think rollups like Arbitrum, zkSync, Starknet.

Consensus. Orders transactions and agrees on block contents. Provides the canonical sequence everything else depends on. Different mechanisms, different trade-offs: finality speed, decentralization, throughput. Ethereum Gasper, Tendermint, Solana Tower BFT.

Data Availability. Ensures transaction data is published and accessible. Guarantees anyone can reconstruct execution state from what's been published. This is the piece that makes fraud proofs work and prevents sequencer fraud. Celestia, Ethereum blobs, EigenDA, Avail.

Settlement. Verifies proofs and serves as the final arbiter of truth. Resolves disputes for optimistic rollups, verifies validity proofs for ZK rollups. The ultimate source of truth for rollup state. Ethereum L1 for most, or any L1 that can verify proofs.

A monolithic chain like Solana (or original Ethereum) does all four in one system. Simpler architecture—one codebase, one validator set, one token. But everything's tightly coupled. Throughput is capped by whichever layer is the bottleneck. Faster execution doesn't help if DA is the constraint. And upgrading any layer means changing the whole thing.

Modular: each layer is its own system, separately optimized. A compute-heavy game might run a custom WASM VM for execution, post data to Celestia, settle on Ethereum. A privacy-focused financial app might use ZK-based execution with encrypted state, its own DA solution, and a custom settlement layer with compliance features. Mix and match.

***Table 17-2.** Monolithic vs. Modular Architecture*

Property	Monolithic (e.g., Solana)	Modular (e.g., Celestia + Rollup + Ethereum)
Architecture	Single chain handles all functions	Specialized layers with clean interfaces
Scaling model	Vertical (faster hardware for one system)	Horizontal (add execution layers independently)
Customization	Limited by L1 design constraints	Full flexibility per execution layer
Security model	Single chain's security budget	Shared/inherited security across layers
Complexity	Lower (single system)	Higher (multiple systems + interfaces)
Upgradeability	Requires hard fork for any change	Each layer upgrades independently
Throughput ceiling	One node's processing capacity	Sum of all execution layers × DA capacity
Failure domains	One system: total outage if consensus fails	Isolated: execution layer fails, DA layer continues

Designing a Modular Stack: Worked Examples

Modularity gets concrete when you see specific stack designs. Different applications pick different layer combinations based on what they need:

```
from dataclasses import dataclass
from typing import List

@dataclass
class LayerChoice:
    function: str
    provider: str
    cost_per_tx_usd: float
    latency_s: float
    trust: str

def design_modular_stack(name: str, use_case: str,
                         layers: List[LayerChoice]) -> dict:
    total_cost = sum(l.cost_per_tx_usd for l in layers)
```

```
    bottleneck_latency = max(l.latency_s for l in layers)
    return {
        'name': name,
        'use_case': use_case,
        'total_cost_per_tx': total_cost,
        'finality_latency_s': bottleneck_latency,
        'layers': layers,
    }

stacks = [
    design_modular_stack("DeFi Rollup", "High-value financial ops", [
        LayerChoice("Execution", "Arbitrum (EVM)", 0.01, 2, "Sequencer"),
        LayerChoice("DA", "Ethereum blobs", 0.005, 12, "ETH consensus"),
        LayerChoice("Settlement", "Ethereum L1", 0.002, 768, "ETH
        consensus"),
    ]),
    design_modular_stack("Gaming Chain", "High-throughput game state", [
        LayerChoice("Execution", "Custom WASM", 0.0001, 0.5, "Sequencer"),
        LayerChoice("DA", "Celestia", 0.0005, 12, "Celestia BFT"),
        LayerChoice("Settlement", "Ethereum L1", 0.002, 768, "ETH
        consensus"),
    ]),
    design_modular_stack("Privacy L2", "Confidential transactions", [
        LayerChoice("Execution", "ZK-encrypted VM", 0.05, 60, "ZK
        soundness"),
        LayerChoice("DA", "Validium (DAC)", 0.0001, 5, "DAC honest"),
        LayerChoice("Settlement", "Ethereum L1", 0.002, 768, "ETH
        consensus"),
    ]),
    design_modular_stack("Enterprise", "Supply chain tracking", [
        LayerChoice("Execution", "Hyperledger", 0.001, 1, "Consortium"),
        LayerChoice("DA", "EigenDA", 0.0003, 12, "ETH restaking"),
        LayerChoice("Settlement", "Ethereum L1", 0.002, 768, "ETH
        consensus"),
    ]),
]
```

```
print("Modular Stack Designs by Use Case")
print("=" * 75)
for s in stacks:
    print(f"\n  {s['name']} ({s['use_case']}):")
    for l in s['layers']:
        print(f"    {l.function:<12}: {l.provider:<18} ${l.cost_per_tx_
        usd:.4f}/tx  [{l.trust}]")
    print(f"    {'TOTAL':<12}: {'':18} ${s['total_cost_per_tx']:.4f}/tx  "
          f"finality: {s['finality_latency_s']}s")

# Compare with monolithic chains
print(f"\n  Monolithic comparison:")
for name, cost, finality in [
    ("Ethereum L1 (monolithic)", 0.50, "768s"),
    ("Solana (monolithic)", 0.0005, "0.4s"),
]:
    print(f"    {name:<30} ${cost:.4f}/tx  finality: {finality}")
```

The numbers tell the story. Modular stacks hit costs comparable to monolithic high-throughput chains (Solana's $0.0005/tx) while inheriting settlement security from Ethereum ($60B+ staked). A gaming chain at $0.0026/tx is 5× more than Solana but gets Ethereum-grade settlement finality. For DeFi, $0.017/tx is 30× cheaper than Ethereum L1's $0.50/tx with the same security guarantees.

17.1.5 Restaking and Shared Security

Modular architectures create a new problem: every layer needs economic security. A new DA layer or oracle or bridge has to attract validators and staked capital. Bootstrapping a validator set from scratch is slow and expensive. Restaking shortcuts this by letting existing validators (especially Ethereum's large set) extend their security to additional services.

EigenLayer

EigenLayer launched on Ethereum in 2023-2024 as the first restaking protocol. Ethereum validators opt in by granting extra slashing rights to "Actively Validated Services" (AVSs). Each AVS defines its own slashing conditions—rules that, if broken, cost the validator a portion of their restaked ETH.

The economics are symmetric. Validators earn extra rewards beyond their base Ethereum staking yield. AVSs get Ethereum's multi-billion-dollar security budget without building a validator set from zero. The market sets the price: AVSs compete for validator attention with higher rewards, validators pick AVSs based on risk versus return.

Security analysis. EigenLayer's security for each AVS depends on total value restaked to it. If an AVS needs $100M in security but only $50M is restaked, an attacker controlling those validators could profit if the attack's value exceeds the slashing penalty. The system is secure when restaked value exceeds max attack profit.

Correlation risk. This is the big concern. A validator restaked across 10 AVSs could face simultaneous slashing if a common failure hits multiple services at once—network partition, software bug, infrastructure outage. If total penalties exceed the validator's stake, it's forced to exit. Widespread enough, that could trigger mass exits threatening Ethereum's own consensus security.

EigenLayer mitigates this with attribution limits (each AVS can only claim a fraction of a validator's stake) and pushes AVSs toward independent slashing conditions unlikely to trigger simultaneously. But truly correlated failures (a major cloud provider going down) can't be fully designed away.

```
def restaking_correlation_risk(num_validators: int,
                               num_avs: int,
                               avg_avs_per_validator: int,
                               slash_fraction_per_avs: float,
                               correlation_probability: float) -> dict:
    """
    Model cascading slashing risk in a restaking system.

    When multiple AVSs experience simultaneous failures (correlated event),
    validators restaked across those AVSs face combined slashing.
    If total slashing exceeds their stake, they are force-exited.
    """
```

```
import random
random.seed(42)

# Assign validators to random AVSs
validator_avs = {}
for v in range(num_validators):
    assigned = random.sample(range(num_avs),
                             min(avg_avs_per_validator, num_avs))
    validator_avs[v] = set(assigned)

# Simulate correlated failure: a cloud provider outage
# triggers slashing across a correlated subset of AVSs
num_correlated_avs = max(1, int(num_avs * correlation_probability))
affected_avs = set(random.sample(range(num_avs), num_correlated_avs))

# Calculate per-validator slashing
force_exited = 0
total_slashed_pct = 0

for v, avs_set in validator_avs.items():
    affected = avs_set & affected_avs
    slash_pct = len(affected) * slash_fraction_per_avs * 100
    total_slashed_pct += min(slash_pct, 100)

    if slash_pct >= 100:  # Force exit: slashing exceeds stake
        force_exited += 1

avg_slash = total_slashed_pct / num_validators

return {
    'num_validators': num_validators,
    'num_avs': num_avs,
    'correlated_avs': num_correlated_avs,
    'force_exited': force_exited,
    'force_exit_pct': force_exited / num_validators * 100,
    'avg_slash_pct': avg_slash,
    'ethereum_security_impact': (
        'CRITICAL' if force_exited > num_validators * 0.1 else
        'Moderate' if force_exited > num_validators * 0.01 else
```

```
            'Minimal'
        ),
    }

print("\nRestaking Correlation Risk Analysis")
print("=" * 70)
print(f"{'Correlation':>12} {'Affected AVSs':>14} {'Force Exits':>13} "
      f"{'Exit %':>8} {'Avg Slash':>10} {'Impact':>10}")
print("-" * 70)

for corr_prob in [0.05, 0.10, 0.20, 0.30, 0.50]:
    r = restaking_correlation_risk(
        num_validators=1000, num_avs=20,
        avg_avs_per_validator=5, slash_fraction_per_avs=0.15,
        correlation_probability=corr_prob,
    )
    print(f"  {corr_prob:>10.0%} {r['correlated_avs']:>12}  "
          f"{r['force_exited']:>11} {r['force_exit_pct']:>6.1f}%  "
          f"{r['avg_slash_pct']:>8.1f}% {r['ethereum_security_
          impact']:>10}")
```

Table 17-3. *Shared Security Approaches*

Approach	Mechanism	Examples	Advantages	Risks
Restaking	Reuse L1 stake for additional services	EigenLayer, Symbiotic	Capital efficiency, immediate security	Cascading slashing, correlation
Relay chain	Shared validators secure child chains	Polkadot	Unified security, guaranteed availability	Relay bottleneck, limited parachain slots
Mesh security	Cross-chain stake delegation	Cosmos (proposed)	Flexible, chain-to-chain	Coordination complexity
Proof verification	L1 verifies L2 proofs	Ethereum rollups	Strongest guarantee	L1 capacity limits
Committee attestation	Bridge validators attest cross-chain	Wormhole, LayerZero	Simple, fast	Committee trust assumption

17.1.6 The Future of Modular Design

The modular paradigm is still early. Several trends are shaping where it goes:

Deeper specialization. DA layers optimize purely for throughput, sampling efficiency, cost per byte. Execution layers optimize for specific domains—DeFi with MEV-aware ordering, gaming with sub-second updates, social media with content-addressable storage. Settlement layers optimize for proof verification speed and security budget depth. Same pattern as internet infrastructure evolving from general servers to specialized CDNs, DNS resolvers, load balancers, compute platforms.

Interoperability standards. For the modular stack to work as a coherent system, layers need well-defined interfaces. DA attestation formats consistent across providers so rollups can switch without redesigning proofs. Settlement interfaces that accept different proof systems (Groth16, PLONK, STARKs). Standardized sequencer APIs. These standards are emerging through multi-team collaboration. Not settled yet.

Proof aggregation. More rollups mean more individual proofs posted to L1, and aggregate cost grows linearly. Aggregation combines multiple proofs into one that verifies all of them. L1 checks one proof instead of N. Settlement costs drop by a factor of N. NEBRA and Aligned Layer are building this.

Shared sequencing. Multiple rollups using one sequencer can get atomic cross-rollup transactions. The shared sequencer sees all participating rollups' transactions and can match them across batches. Espresso Systems and Astria are working on it. Goal: atomic cross-L2 DeFi.

Based rollups. Skip the centralized sequencer entirely—let L1 proposers handle ordering. You inherit L1's decentralization, censorship resistance, and liveness for free. Trade-off: latency tied to L1 block times (12 seconds for Ethereum) instead of the 1–2 second soft confirmations centralized sequencers give. Maximum decentralization on the sequencing spectrum.

Sovereign rollups. No separate settlement layers. The rollup's own full nodes verify state transitions directly (re-execute or check proofs). The DA layer just provides ordering and data availability. Own fork-choice rules, own governance—functionally independent chains that share a DA layer. Maximum sovereignty. Cost: you give up shared security from settling on a major L1.

17.1.7 Summary

Data availability is fundamental. Without it, fraud proofs fail, light clients are exposed, and rollup security collapses. Modular architectures address this by letting each layer specialize.

Key takeaways:

- Data availability means block data is published and accessible. Lose it and fraud proofs can't be built (optimistic rollup security breaks), light clients can't verify state (wallet security breaks), new nodes can't sync (network resilience breaks).
- DAS lets light clients verify availability probabilistically with minimal bandwidth. 75 random samples catch 50% withholding with probability exceeding $1 - 10^{-22}$.
- Erasure coding is the mathematical foundation. 2D Reed-Solomon transforms k×k data into a 2k×2k matrix where any 50%+ is enough to reconstruct. Turns withholding detection into a sampling problem with exponentially strong guarantees.
- Celestia is the first dedicated DA layer. Orders blobs, verifies availability, doesn't execute. Rollups post data there and handle execution on their own.
- Modular blockchains split execution, consensus, DA, and settlement into separate layers. Each one gets independently optimized and upgraded. Contrast with monolithic designs where all functions share one system.
- Restaking through EigenLayer extends L1 security to additional services without bootstrapping new validator sets. The correlation risk of cascading slashing across AVSs is the primary concern.
- The paradigm shift: from "fat protocols" (one chain does everything) to "thin specialized layers" (each does one thing well). Same pattern as internet infra going from monolithic servers to microservices.

DA problem: producer publishes header but withholds data. Light clients can't detect it.—Without DA: fraud proofs break, light clients are exposed, new nodes can't sync, rollup security collapses.—DAS: random sampling of erasure-coded data. P(detect f withholding) = 1-(1-f)^s.—75 samples catch 50% withholding with probability > 1-10^-22. Bandwidth cost ~40 KB per block.—Erasure coding: 2D Reed-Solomon.k×k data → 2k×2k extended; reconstruction from ≥50% of any row/column—Celestia: dedicated DA layer. Orders blobs, provides DAS, doesn't execute. Rollups post data blobs.—Modular architecture: execution + consensus + DA + settlement as separate specialized layers.—Monolithic vs. modular: simplicity and tight coupling vs. flexibility and independent optimization.—EigenLayer restaking: extends ETH security to AVSs. Correlation risk from cascading slashing.—Shared sequencing and based rollups tackle cross-L2 composability in modular setups.

17.1.8 Exercises

Problem 1 (Basic): Why is data availability necessary for optimistic rollup security? What attack does a data-withholding sequencer enable?

Problem 2 (Calculation): DAS system with 256×256 = 65,536 cells (2D erasure-coded from 128×128 original). Light client samples 75 random cells. Calculate detection probability for 5%, 25%, and 50% withholding. How many samples for 99.99% detection of 10% withholding?

Problem 3 (Implementation): Build a simplified DAS protocol. Create a 4×4 data grid, extend to 8×8 with row/column XOR parity. Simulate an adversary withholding 50% of cells. Show that 10 random samples detect it reliably. Run 1,000 trials and report the detection rate.

Problem 4 (Analysis): Compare three DA approaches: Ethereum blobs (EIP-4844), Celestia, and EigenDA. For each: trust assumptions, throughput capacity, cost per byte, and impact on rollup security.

Problem 5 (Design): Design a modular stack for decentralized social media. Requirements: 10,000 TPS, sub-second confirmation, content storage, user privacy. Specify each layer (execution, consensus, DA, settlement) and justify the choices.

Problem 6 (Theory): Prove that 2D Reed-Solomon erasure coding with 2× extension allows reconstruction from any 25% of the extended matrix. What's the relationship between extension factor and reconstruction threshold?

Problem 7 (Comparative): Monolithic (Solana) versus modular (Celestia + rollup + Ethereum) under three scenarios: (a) 10× demand spike, (b) execution layer critical bug, (c) DA layer temporary outage. Which handles each better and why?

Problem 8 (Critical Thinking): EigenLayer systemic risk. 60% of Ethereum's validators restake across 10 AVSs. A correlated failure slashes 30% of restaked validators. What happens to Ethereum's consensus security? Is restaking net positive or net negative for the ecosystem?

Problem 9 (Advanced): Build a complete DAS system with simplified KZG-style polynomial commitments. Generate commitments for a data matrix, create opening proofs per cell, verify proofs against commitments. Measure proof generation and verification time.

Problem 10 (Research): Study Celestia's mainnet since launch. Report: average blob size, blob throughput, number of rollups posting data, DAS light client adoption, cost comparison to Ethereum L1 calldata for equivalent data sizes.

(Solutions in Appendix D)

17.1.9 Further Reading

Al-Bassam, Sonnino, and Buterin's "Fraud and Data Availability Proofs" is the theoretical foundation. Formally defines the DA problem and proves DAS security.

Celestia's docs cover architecture, namespace Merkle trees, and DAS implementation. The original LazyLedger paper describes the design rationale.

The Celestia team's writing on "The Modular Blockchain Thesis" is the most accessible introduction. Ethereum research posts on the rollup-centric roadmap cover the Ethereum-specific vision.

The EigenLayer whitepaper describes the restaking mechanism. Risk analyses from Gauntlet and others evaluate correlation risks and economic security.

Berlekamp's "Algebraic Coding Theory" gives the mathematical foundations of the Reed-Solomon codes used in DAS. The polynomial interpolation over finite fields is directly applicable.

CHAPTER 18

Post-Quantum Cryptography

18.1 Preparing Blockchain for the Quantum Computing Era

Every blockchain in production today relies on ECDSA or EdDSA. Shor's algorithm breaks both. This chapter covers the quantum threat model, how Shor's and Grover's algorithms hit different layers of the stack, the three NIST post-quantum signature standards (ML-DSA, FN-DSA, SLH-DSA), migration challenges, and why the harvest-now-decrypt-later threat means planning can't wait. By the end, you'll understand:

- The quantum computing threat model and why it is relevant to blockchain security today
- **Shor's Algorithm**: how it breaks ECDSA, EdDSA, RSA, and Diffie-Hellman key exchange
- **Grover's Algorithm**: how it weakens hash functions and symmetric cryptography
- The NIST post-quantum cryptography standardization process and its three signature schemes
- **ML-DSA (Dilithium)**: lattice-based signatures with balanced performance characteristics
- **FN-DSA (Falcon)**: NTRU-based signatures with the smallest post-quantum signature sizes

N. Savant, *Blockchain Foundations*, https://doi.org/10.1007/979-8-8688-2891-1_18

- **SLH-DSA (SPHINCS+)**: hash-based signatures with the most conservative security assumptions
- **Migration Challenges**: signature size impact, address format changes, and backwards compatibility
- Quantum-resistant blockchain design strategies and timeline considerations
- The "harvest now, decrypt later" threat and why planning must begin before quantum computers arrive

18.1.1 The Quantum Threat to Blockchain

The cryptographic assumptions that underpin every production blockchain—the hardness of factoring large numbers, the intractability of discrete logarithms on elliptic curves—are artifacts of the computational model we happen to inhabit. Classical computers manipulate bits one at a time (or a few at a time, with parallelism). Quantum computers manipulate quantum states that can represent exponentially many possibilities simultaneously. For most problems, this does not help much. But for the specific number-theoretic problems that protect digital signatures and key exchange, quantum computation offers a devastating shortcut. This is not speculative. The relevant quantum algorithms have been known since the 1990s, have been experimentally verified on small-scale quantum hardware, and their resource requirements scale predictably with key size. What remains uncertain is the engineering timeline: how many years until quantum hardware reaches sufficient scale, qubit quality, and error correction capability to attack real cryptographic keys.

The threat is asymmetric across different types of cryptography:

Public key cryptography faces an existential threat. Peter Shor's 1994 discovery demonstrated that a quantum computer can find the period of modular exponentiation in polynomial time. Period-finding is the mathematical core of both integer factoring (which breaks RSA) and discrete logarithm computation (which breaks ECDSA, EdDSA, Schnorr, and Diffie-Hellman). For blockchain: ECDSA on secp256k1 hides the private key d behind the assumption that recovering d from $Q = d \times G$ is computationally intractable. Shor's algorithm transforms this from a 2^128-operation problem into one requiring roughly n^3 quantum gate operations—a few billion rather than a few hundred undecillion. Current resource estimates put this at approximately 2,330 error-free logical qubits for secp256k1.

Symmetric cryptography and hash functions face a milder but still significant threat. Lov Grover's 1996 algorithm searches an unstructured space of N possibilities using only about $\sqrt{N}$ quantum evaluations, compared to the N/2 evaluations a classical computer needs on average. Applied to the SHA-256 preimage search: a classical attacker must try roughly 2^256 inputs; a quantum attacker using Grover needs roughly 2^128—still enormous, but the security margin has been cut in half. A critical nuance often overlooked: Grover's speedup does not distribute across multiple quantum machines the way classical parallelism does. Running the algorithm on M quantum computers provides only an M^(1/4) factor improvement because the amplitude amplification process requires sequential iterations that cannot be split across independent machines.

The practical implications for blockchain are severe. Bitcoin, Ethereum, and every other major blockchain use ECDSA or EdDSA for transaction authorization. A quantum attacker could:

1. Derive private keys from public keys exposed on-chain (from any address that has previously sent a transaction)
2. Forge signatures on arbitrary transactions, transferring funds from any exposed address to the attacker's address
3. Break the Diffie-Hellman key exchange used for peer-to-peer communication, enabling network-level attacks
4. Potentially manipulate consensus mechanisms that rely on public key cryptography (validator signatures, VRFs for leader selection)

Table 18-1. *Quantum Impact on Blockchain Cryptographic Primitives*

Primitive	Blockchain Usage	Quantum Algorithm	Classical Security	Post-Quantum Security	Impact
ECDSA (secp256k1)	Bitcoin/Ethereum tx signing	Shor	128-bit	0-bit (broken)	Complete compromise
EdDSA (Ed25519)	Solana, Cosmos, Polkadot	Shor	128-bit	0-bit (broken)	Complete compromise
RSA-2048	Rarely used in blockchain	Shor	112-bit	0-bit (broken)	Complete compromise
ECDH (Curve25519)	TLS/Noise key exchange	Shor	128-bit	0-bit (broken)	Network layer compromise
SHA-256	PoW mining, Merkle trees, addresses	Grover	128-bit	64-bit (weakened)	Manageable (double output)
Keccak-256	Ethereum state, addresses	Grover	128-bit	64-bit (weakened)	Manageable
AES-128	Symmetric encryption	Grover	128-bit	64-bit (weakened)	Use AES-256 instead
AES-256	Symmetric encryption	Grover	256-bit	128-bit (adequate)	No change needed

18.1.2 Shor's Algorithm: Breaking Public Key Cryptography

Peter Shor's 1994 algorithm efficiently solves two computational problems that are believed to be hard for classical computers:

Integer factoring: Given a composite number n = p × q (the product of two large primes), find the factors p and q. The best classical algorithm (General Number Field Sieve) runs in sub-exponential time: approximately L(n) = exp(c × n^(1/3) × (ln n)^(2/3)). Shor's algorithm runs in polynomial time: $O(n^3)$ using O(n) logical qubits.

Discrete logarithm in any finite group: Given group elements g and h = g^x, find the integer x. This includes the Elliptic Curve Discrete Logarithm Problem (ECDLP) that secures ECDSA and EdDSA, and the classical DLP in multiplicative groups of integers mod p that secures Diffie-Hellman.

For secp256k1 (Bitcoin's elliptic curve), the private key is a 256-bit scalar d, and the public key is the point Q = d × G on the curve. Shor's algorithm on a quantum computer can recover d from Q in polynomial time. Current estimates suggest this requires approximately 2,330 *logical* qubits for secp256k1.

The qubit counts in Shor's algorithm analyses refer to logical qubits—idealized, error-free computational units. Actual quantum hardware is noisy: gate operations fail at rates between 0.1% and 1%, and qubit states decay on timescales of microseconds to milliseconds. Quantum error correction bridges this gap by encoding each logical qubit across a surface code that spreads information across many physical qubits, using redundancy to detect and correct errors as they occur. The overhead is steep. Depending on the physical error rate and the target logical error rate, each logical qubit may require between one thousand and ten thousand physical qubits. For secp256k1, where roughly 2,330 logical qubits are needed, this translates to a total machine size of two to twenty-five million physical qubits. The largest quantum processors demonstrated by early 2025 contain approximately one thousand physical qubits. Whether industry roadmaps projecting tens of thousands of qubits by the early 2030s will hold—and whether error rates improve commensurately—will determine when blockchain's current cryptographic foundations become genuinely vulnerable.

As of 2025, the largest quantum computers have approximately 1,000-1,500 physical qubits with high error rates and limited coherence times. The quantum computing industry projects reaching millions of physical qubits within 10-20 years, though timelines are uncertain. Most cryptographers estimate a 15-30 year window before Cryptographically Relevant Quantum Computers (CRQCs) exist, with significant variance in both directions.

The "Harvest Now, Decrypt Later" Threat

Even before CRQCs exist, there is an immediate concern: adversaries can record encrypted communications and signed transactions today, storing them for future decryption when quantum computers become available. For blockchain, this means:

- All blockchain transactions are permanently recorded on public ledgers

- Every transaction that reveals a public key creates a future target
- Once quantum computers arrive, attackers can retroactively derive private keys for any address whose public key was exposed
- Funds remaining in those addresses at that future date can be stolen

This "harvest now, decrypt later" scenario means the migration timeline is not "when will quantum computers exist?" but rather "how long do we expect funds to remain in currently-exposed addresses?" If an address is used once in 2025 and still holds funds in 2045, it is vulnerable even though no CRQC exists in 2025.

Quantum Resource Estimation

Understanding the quantum threat requires quantifying the resources needed. The following analysis estimates the physical qubit requirements for breaking different cryptographic primitives:

```
import math
from dataclasses import dataclass
from typing import Dict, List

@dataclass
class QuantumAttack:
    """Resource estimates for quantum attacks on cryptographic
    primitives."""
    primitive: str
    key_bits: int
    logical_qubits: int
    t_gate_count: float     # In billions
    physical_per_logical: int  # Depends on error rate
    total_physical_qubits: int
    estimated_runtime_hours: float

    @property
    def millions_physical(self) -> float:
        return self.total_physical_qubits / 1e6

def quantum_resource_estimates() -> List[QuantumAttack]:
    """

    Estimates based on published research:
```

```
    - Roetteler et al. (2017) for ECDSA
    - Gidney & Ekera (2021) for RSA
    - Grassl et al. (2016) for AES
    """
    return [
        QuantumAttack("ECDSA secp256k1", 256, 2330, 126,
                      3000, 2330 * 3000, 0.5),
        QuantumAttack("ECDSA P-256", 256, 2330, 126,
                      3000, 2330 * 3000, 0.5),
        QuantumAttack("EdDSA Ed25519", 256, 2330, 126,
                      3000, 2330 * 3000, 0.5),
        QuantumAttack("RSA-2048", 2048, 4096, 177,
                      5000, 4096 * 5000, 8.0),
        QuantumAttack("RSA-4096", 4096, 8192, 1400,
                      5000, 8192 * 5000, 24.0),
        QuantumAttack("AES-128 (Grover)", 128, 2953, 2.1e6,
                      3000, 2953 * 3000, 1e10),  # Impractical
        QuantumAttack("AES-256 (Grover)", 256, 6681, 1.5e12,
                      3000, 6681 * 3000, 1e20),  # Completely impractical
        QuantumAttack("SHA-256 preimage", 256, 2953, 2.1e6,
                      3000, 2953 * 3000, 1e10),  # Impractical
    ]

attacks = quantum_resource_estimates()
print("Quantum Attack Resource Estimates")
print("=" * 85)
print(f"{'Primitive':<22} {'Logical Q':>10} {'Physical Q':>12} "
      f"{'Physical (M)':>13} {'Runtime':>12} {'Feasible?':>10}")
print("-" * 82)

for a in attacks:
    if a.estimated_runtime_hours > 1e6:
        runtime = "Impractical"
        feasible = "No"
    elif a.estimated_runtime_hours > 100:
        runtime = f"{a.estimated_runtime_hours:.0f}h"
```

```
            feasible = "Eventually"
        else:
            runtime = f"{a.estimated_runtime_hours:.1f}h"
            feasible = "Yes (future)"

        print(f"  {a.primitive:<20} {a.logical_qubits:>8,} {a.total_physical_
        qubits:>10,} "
              f"{a.millions_physical:>11.1f}M {runtime:>12} {feasible:>10}")

# Current vs required quantum capability
print(f"\nQuantum Computing Progress:")
milestones = [
    (2019, "Google Sycamore", 53, "Quantum supremacy claim"),
    (2021, "IBM Eagle", 127, "Largest transmon processor"),
    (2022, "IBM Osprey", 433, "Error mitigation advances"),
    (2023, "IBM Condor", 1121, "Largest superconducting"),
    (2024, "Atom Computing", 1180, "Neutral atom platform"),
]

target = 7_000_000  # ~7M physical qubits for ECDSA
print(f"  Target for ECDSA break: ~{target/1e6:.0f}M physical qubits")
print(f"  Current largest: ~{milestones[-1][2]:,} qubits")
print(f"  Gap: {target / milestones[-1][2]:,.0f}× improvement needed")
print(f"  At 2× per year doubling: ~{math.log2(target / milestones[-1]
[2]):.0f} years")
print(f"  At 2× per 2 years: ~{2 * math.log2(target / milestones[-1]
[2]):.0f} years")
```

18.1.3 Grover's Algorithm: Weakening Symmetric Cryptography

Grover's algorithm provides a generic quadratic speedup for searching unstructured databases. Applied to cryptography, it effectively halves the security level of any brute-force-vulnerable primitive:

Hash function preimage search: Finding an input that produces a specific SHA-256 output requires 2^256 classical operations. With Grover, this drops to 2^128 quantum operations. For blockchain PoW mining, this means a quantum miner could find valid blocks in approximately the square root of the time a classical miner requires.

Symmetric key recovery: Breaking AES-128 requires 2^128 classical operations but only 2^64 quantum operations. Since 2^64 operations are feasible, AES-128 is not quantum-safe. AES-256, reduced to 2^128 quantum operations, remains secure.

Hash collision search: Finding two inputs with the same SHA-256 hash requires 2^128 classical operations (birthday attack). Grover provides no additional speedup beyond the birthday bound for collision finding, but BHT (Brassard-Hoyer-Tapp) gives a modest improvement to 2^(n/3) for n-bit hashes.

A critical limitation of Grover's algorithm prevents it from being parallelized efficiently. Unlike classical brute force (where doubling the machines halves the time), Grover's speedup comes from quantum interference effects that do not parallelize. Running Grover on two quantum computers does not halve the search time—it provides only a sqrt(2) ≈ 1.4× improvement. This means the effective speedup remains quadratic regardless of available hardware, and SHA-256 with its 128-bit quantum security level is considered adequate for most applications.

Impact on Proof of Work Mining

The quantum threat to PoW mining is often overstated. Grover's algorithm provides a quadratic speedup for finding hash preimages, which means a quantum miner could find valid blocks in approximately the square root of the time required classically. However, several factors limit the practical impact:

Difficulty adjustment compensates: If quantum miners enter the network and find blocks faster, the difficulty adjusts upward to maintain the target block time. The quantum miner gains an advantage over classical miners during the adjustment period, but the network eventually stabilizes. The threat is to the *fairness* of mining (quantum miners earn disproportionate rewards) rather than to the *security* of the chain.

Grover does not parallelize: A quantum miner with one quantum computer gets a sqrt speedup. To double that advantage, they need four quantum computers (not two), because the speedup is quadratic, not linear. This severely limits the economic advantage compared to simply buying more classical hardware.

ASIC efficiency gap: Current Bitcoin ASICs are extraordinarily optimized for SHA-256. The energy efficiency of a quantum computer performing Grover's search must be compared not to general-purpose CPUs but to purpose-built ASICs. Current quantum computers are far less energy-efficient per hash than ASICs.

```
def quantum_mining_impact(classical_hashrate_eh: float,
                          quantum_speedup: float = 2**64) -> dict:
    """
    Analyze the impact of quantum miners on a PoW network.

    Grover gives sqrt speedup: a quantum miner with hash rate H_q
    can find blocks as if they had H_q^2 classical hash rate.

    But: difficulty adjusts, limiting sustained advantage.
    """
    import math

    # Effective hash rate of quantum miner
    # If quantum miner has 1 TH/s quantum, effective is sqrt(2^256) /
    sqrt(difficulty)
    # Simplified: quantum miner is equivalent to classical_hashrate *
    sqrt_speedup

    # Scenario: quantum miner enters with 1% of network's effective
    hash rate
    quantum_fraction = 0.01
    quantum_effective = classical_hashrate_eh * quantum_fraction * math.
    sqrt(quantum_speedup)

    # But Grover's sqrt speedup on 256-bit hash = 2^128 operations
    # vs classical 2^256 operations. If classical network does 550 EH/s,
    # each hash already represents targeted work.

    # More realistic: quantum miner gets sqrt speedup per query
    # Effective hash rate multiplier: sqrt(classical_queries)

    # Time to find a block vs classical miner of same cost
    classical_time_per_block = 600  # seconds (Bitcoin, 10 min average)
    quantum_time_per_block = classical_time_per_block / 2  # sqrt speedup
    per query

    # After difficulty adjustment
    post_adjustment_advantage = 1.0  # Difficulty catches up
```

```
    return {
        'classical_network_hashrate': f"{classical_hashrate_eh} EH/s",
        'quantum_speedup_per_query': 'sqrt (quadratic)',
        'pre_adjustment_advantage': '2× block finding speed',
        'post_adjustment': 'Network adjusts, advantage neutralized',
        'real_threat': 'Fairness (quantum miner earns more), not security',
        'timeline': 'PoW quantum threat < signature quantum threat',
    }

result = quantum_mining_impact(550)
print("\nQuantum Impact on PoW Mining")
print("=" * 55)
for key, value in result.items():
    print(f"  {key}: {value}")
```

Lamport One-Time Signatures: The Simplest Hash-Based Scheme

To understand how hash-based signatures work (the foundation of SLH-DSA), we implement the Lamport one-time signature, the simplest construction. It is quantum-resistant because its security depends only on the hash function's preimage resistance—which Grover only halves, leaving adequate security with doubled output sizes.

```
import hashlib
import os

class LamportSignature:
    """
    Lamport one-time signature scheme.

    Security: based solely on hash function preimage resistance.
    Quantum-safe: Grover only halves hash security (128→64 bits for
    SHA-256).
    Using SHA-256 with 256-bit outputs provides 128-bit post-quantum
    security.

    Key sizes:
    - Private key: 2 × 256 × 32 bytes = 16,384 bytes (16 KB)
    - Public key: 2 × 256 × 32 bytes = 16,384 bytes (16 KB)
```

```
    - Signature: 256 × 32 bytes = 8,192 bytes (8 KB)

    Limitation: each key pair can sign exactly ONE message.
    Reuse reveals private key material.
    """

    def __init__(self):
        self.private_key = None
        self.public_key = None
        self.used = False

    def keygen(self):
        """Generate a Lamport key pair."""
        # Private key: 256 pairs of random 256-bit values
        # private_key[i][0] = random value for bit i = 0
        # private_key[i][1] = random value for bit i = 1
        self.private_key = [
            (os.urandom(32), os.urandom(32))
            for _ in range(256)
        ]

        # Public key: hash of each private key value
        self.public_key = [
            (hashlib.sha256(pair[0]).digest(),
             hashlib.sha256(pair[1]).digest())
            for pair in self.private_key
        ]
        self.used = False

    def sign(self, message: bytes) -> list:
        """
        Sign a message (can only be done ONCE per key pair).

        1. Hash the message to get 256 bits
        2. For each bit i of the hash:
           - If bit i = 0: reveal private_key[i][0]
           - If bit i = 1: reveal private_key[i][1]
        """
```

```
        if self.used:
            raise Exception("Lamport key already used! One-time only.")
        if self.private_key is None:
            raise Exception("No key generated")

        self.used = True
        msg_hash = hashlib.sha256(message).digest()

        signature = []
        for i in range(256):
            byte_idx = i // 8
            bit_idx = 7 - (i % 8)
            bit = (msg_hash[byte_idx] >> bit_idx) & 1
            signature.append(self.private_key[i][bit])

        return signature

    @staticmethod
    def verify(message: bytes, signature: list, public_key: list) -> bool:
        """
        Verify a Lamport signature.

        For each bit i of H(message):
        - If bit i = 0: check H(signature[i]) == public_key[i][0]
        - If bit i = 1: check H(signature[i]) == public_key[i][1]
        """
        msg_hash = hashlib.sha256(message).digest()

        for i in range(256):
            byte_idx = i // 8
            bit_idx = 7 - (i % 8)
            bit = (msg_hash[byte_idx] >> bit_idx) & 1

            sig_hash = hashlib.sha256(signature[i]).digest()
            if sig_hash != public_key[i][bit]:
                return False

        return True
```

```
    def key_sizes(self) -> dict:
        """Report key and signature sizes."""
        return {
            'private_key_bytes': 256 * 2 * 32,  # 16,384
            'public_key_bytes': 256 * 2 * 32,    # 16,384
            'signature_bytes': 256 * 32,          # 8,192
            'total_overhead_bytes': 256 * 2 * 32 + 256 * 32,
        }

# Demonstrate Lamport signatures
lamport = LamportSignature()
lamport.keygen()

message = b"Transfer 1.5 BTC to addr_xyz"
sig = lamport.sign(message)
valid = LamportSignature.verify(message, sig, lamport.public_key)

sizes = lamport.key_sizes()
print("\nLamport One-Time Signature Demonstration")
print("=" * 55)
print(f"Message: {message}")
print(f"Signature valid: {valid}")
print(f"Private key: {sizes['private_key_bytes']:,} bytes ({sizes['private_
key_bytes']/1024:.0f} KB)")
print(f"Public key: {sizes['public_key_bytes']:,} bytes ({sizes['public_
key_bytes']/1024:.0f} KB)")
print(f"Signature: {sizes['signature_bytes']:,} bytes ({sizes['signature_
bytes']/1024:.0f} KB)")

# Tampered message
tampered = b"Transfer 100 BTC to addr_evil"
valid_tampered = LamportSignature.verify(tampered, sig, lamport.public_key)
print(f"\nTampered message valid: {valid_tampered} (correct: forgery
rejected)")

# Size comparison
print(f"\nSignature Size Comparison:")
print(f"  ECDSA:       {72:>8} bytes (quantum BROKEN)")
```

```
print(f"  ML-DSA-44:   {2420:>8} bytes (quantum SAFE)")
print(f"  FN-DSA-512:  {666:>8} bytes (quantum SAFE)")
print(f"  Lamport:     {8192:>8} bytes (quantum SAFE, one-time only)")
print(f"  SLH-DSA-128s: {7856:>8} bytes (quantum SAFE, reusable,
hash-only)")
```

18.1.4 NIST Post-Quantum Cryptography Standards

The U.S. National Institute of Standards and Technology launched its search for quantum-resistant algorithms in 2016, soliciting proposals from the global research community. The response was substantial: dozens of teams submitted candidate schemes based on diverse mathematical foundations (lattices, codes, multivariate polynomials, hash trees, isogenies). Over several years, NIST narrowed the field through iterative evaluation rounds, each accompanied by intensive public cryptanalysis—researchers worldwide attempted to break the surviving candidates, and those that withstood scrutiny advanced. By 2024, NIST had finalized standards for three digital signature schemes, each built on different mathematical assumptions and offering different performance trade-offs. This diversity is deliberate: if a breakthrough attack compromises one family of assumptions (as happened spectacularly with the isogeny-based scheme SIKE in 2022, broken by a classical attack after years of analysis), the others remain available.

ML-DSA (Module Learning with Errors Digital Signature Algorithm, Formerly Dilithium)

ML-DSA is based on the hardness of the Module Learning With Errors (MLWE) problem, a lattice-based computational problem believed to be hard for both classical and quantum computers. The signature scheme produces moderately sized signatures with good all-around performance, making it the recommended default choice for most applications.

The MLWE problem asks: given a matrix A and a vector b = As + e (where s is a secret vector and e is a small "error" vector), find s. The error term e makes this problem fundamentally different from (and harder than) solving a system of linear equations. The module structure (working with matrices of polynomials rather than integers) provides efficiency advantages over basic LWE.

ML-DSA comes in three security levels: **ML-DSA-44** (NIST Level 2): 1,312-byte public key, 2,420-byte signature—**ML-DSA-65** (NIST Level 3): 1,952-byte public key, 3,293-byte signature—**ML-DSA-87** (NIST Level 5): 2,592-byte public key, 4,595-byte signature

FN-DSA (FFT over NTRU Lattice Digital Signature Algorithm, Formerly Falcon)

FN-DSA achieves the smallest post-quantum signatures among the standardized schemes by using NTRU lattices with a Gaussian sampling-based signing procedure. The mathematical foundation is a lattice problem related to finding short vectors in NTRU lattices, which has been studied for over 25 years.

The trade-off: Falcon's signing procedure requires floating-point arithmetic with specific precision requirements for the Gaussian sampler. This creates implementation challenges and potential side-channel vulnerabilities if the sampler is not implemented correctly. Constant-time floating-point operations are notoriously difficult to guarantee across different hardware platforms.

- **FN-DSA-512 (NIST Level 1)**: 897-byte public key, 666-byte signature
- **FN-DSA-1024 (NIST Level 5)**: 1,793-byte public key, 1,280-byte signature

SLH-DSA (Stateless Hash-Based Digital Signature Algorithm, Formerly SPHINCS+)

SLH-DSA's security depends solely on the security of its underlying hash function (SHA-256 or SHAKE-256). This is the most conservative assumption possible: if SHA-256 is secure, SLH-DSA is secure. No additional mathematical assumptions (lattice problems, code problems, isogeny problems) are required.

The trade-off is signature size: SLH-DSA signatures are 10-100× larger than lattice-based schemes. This makes SLH-DSA impractical for high-volume transaction signing but suitable for scenarios where signatures are rare and verification is frequent (code signing, firmware updates, root CA certificates).

- **SLH-DSA-128s (NIST Level 1)**: 32-byte public key, 7,856-byte signature (small, slow)

- **SLH-DSA-128f (NIST Level 1)**: 32-byte public key, 17,088-byte signature (fast, larger)
- **SLH-DSA-256s (NIST Level 5)**: 64-byte public key, 29,792-byte signature

```
from dataclasses import dataclass
@dataclass class SignatureScheme: name: str nist_standard: str
security_level: int pubkey_bytes: int signature_bytes: int
keygen_ms: float sign_ms: float verify_ms: float assumption:
str blockchain_suitability: str
def comprehensive_pq_comparison() -> None: """Compare all NIST
PQ signature standards with classical baseline."""
```

```
schemes = [
    SignatureScheme("ECDSA (secp256k1)", "N/A (BROKEN)", 1,
                    33, 72, 0.01, 0.02, 0.03,
                    "ECDLP (broken by Shor)", "Current standard
                    (vulnerable)"),
    SignatureScheme("ML-DSA-44", "FIPS 204", 2,
                    1312, 2420, 0.15, 0.49, 0.17,
                    "Module-LWE", "Good: balanced size/speed"),
    SignatureScheme("ML-DSA-65", "FIPS 204", 3,
                    1952, 3293, 0.25, 0.78, 0.26,
                    "Module-LWE", "Good: higher security"),
    SignatureScheme("ML-DSA-87", "FIPS 204", 5,
                    2592, 4595, 0.40, 1.20, 0.40,
                    "Module-LWE", "Marginal: large sigs"),
    SignatureScheme("FN-DSA-512", "FIPS 206", 1,
                    897, 666, 8.0, 0.50, 0.10,
                    "NTRU Lattice", "Best: smallest PQ sigs"),
    SignatureScheme("FN-DSA-1024", "FIPS 206", 5,
                    1793, 1280, 15.0, 0.80, 0.15,
                    "NTRU Lattice", "Good: compact high-security"),
    SignatureScheme("SLH-DSA-128s", "FIPS 205", 1,
                    32, 7856, 3.0, 50.0, 1.0,
```

```
                    "Hash functions only", "Poor: 8 KB signatures"),
    SignatureScheme("SLH-DSA-256s", "FIPS 205", 5,
                    64, 29792, 5.0, 80.0, 1.5,
                    "Hash functions only", "Impractical: 30 KB sigs"),
]

print("NIST Post-Quantum Signature Standards Comparison")
print("=" * 100)
print(f"{'Scheme':<17} {'Standard':<10} {'PubKey':>8} {'Sig':>8} "
      f"{'Sign ms':>9} {'Verify ms':>11} {'Assumption':<18}
      {'Suitability'}")
print("-" * 100)

for s in schemes:
    print(f"  {s.name:<15} {s.nist_standard:<10} "
          f"{s.pubkey_bytes:>6}B {s.signature_bytes:>6}B "
          f"{s.sign_ms:>8.2f} {s.verify_ms:>10.2f} "
          f"{s.assumption:<18} {s.blockchain_suitability}")

# Size impact analysis
print(f"\n\nBlockchain Capacity Impact Analysis")
print("=" * 70)

ecdsa_overhead = 33 + 72  # pubkey + sig = 105 bytes
avg_btc_tx = 250  # bytes
btc_block = 1_000_000  # 1 MB
btc_txs_per_block = btc_block // avg_btc_tx

print(f"Baseline: ECDSA overhead = {ecdsa_overhead} bytes, "
      f"avg tx = {avg_btc_tx} bytes, {btc_txs_per_block} txs/block")
print(f"\n{'Scheme':<17} {'Overhead':>10} {'New Tx Size':>12} "
      f"{'Txs/Block':>11} {'Capacity Loss':>14} {'Block for Same':>14}")
print("-" * 80)

for s in schemes:
    pq_overhead = s.pubkey_bytes + s.signature_bytes
    new_tx_size = avg_btc_tx - ecdsa_overhead + pq_overhead
    new_txs = btc_block // new_tx_size
```

```
        capacity_loss = (1 - new_txs / btc_txs_per_block) * 100
        required_block = new_tx_size * btc_txs_per_block

        print(f"  {s.name:<15} {pq_overhead:>8}B {new_tx_size:>10}B "
              f"{new_txs:>9} {capacity_loss:>12.1f}% "
              f"{required_block/1e6:>12.1f} MB")
comprehensive_pq_comparison()
```

Post-Quantum Key Exchange for the Network Layer

Beyond transaction signatures, blockchain nodes rely on key exchange protocols for secure peer-to-peer communication. Ethereum uses the Noise protocol framework (based on Curve25519 Diffie-Hellman) for encrypted node-to-node communication. Bitcoin uses unencrypted communication for most messages but relies on TLS for some RPC connections. Both Diffie-Hellman and ECDH key exchanges are broken by Shor's algorithm.

NIST also standardized a post-quantum Key Encapsulation Mechanism (KEM) alongside the signature schemes:

ML-KEM (formerly CRYSTALS-Kyber): A lattice-based key encapsulation mechanism standardized as FIPS 203. ML-KEM provides post-quantum key exchange with modest overhead:

- **ML-KEM-512 (NIST Level 1)**: 800-byte public key, 768-byte ciphertext, 32-byte shared secret
- **ML-KEM-768 (NIST Level 3)**: 1,184-byte public key, 1,088-byte ciphertext, 32-byte shared secret
- **ML-KEM-1024 (NIST Level 5)**: 1,568-byte public key, 1,568-byte ciphertext, 32-byte shared secret

Compared to X25519 (Curve25519 Diffie-Hellman), which uses 32-byte public keys and produces 32-byte shared secrets, ML-KEM public keys are 25-50× larger. However, key exchange happens once per connection (during the handshake), not per transaction. The per-message overhead after the handshake is unchanged, making the impact on sustained communication performance negligible.

For blockchain networks, the migration to PQ key exchange is less urgent than the migration to PQ signatures because key exchange protects the *confidentiality* of peer-to-peer messages, and most blockchain messages (transactions, blocks) are intended to be public anyway. The exception is pre-consensus message confidentiality: if an attacker can decrypt peer-to-peer communication, they can see proposed blocks and transactions before they are publicly announced, enabling frontrunning and MEV extraction. This makes PQ key exchange important for fairness even if it is not critical for security.

Table 18-2. *Network Layer Quantum Impact*

Protocol Component	Current Primitive	Quantum Vulnerability	PQ Replacement	Migration Urgency
Node-to-node encryption	X25519 (ECDH)	Broken by Shor	ML-KEM-768	Medium (confidentiality)
TLS for RPC	ECDHE + AES	ECDHE broken	ML-KEM + AES-256	Medium
VRF for leader selection	ECVRF	Broken by Shor	PQ-VRF (research)	High (consensus integrity)
Transaction signatures	ECDSA/ EdDSA	Broken by Shor	ML-DSA/FN-DSA	Critical (fund security)
Merkle tree hashes	SHA-256	Weakened (128→64 bit)	SHA-256 adequate or SHA-512	Low

18.1.5 Migration Strategies

Migrating a live blockchain from classical to post-quantum cryptography is among the most challenging engineering tasks in the field. The migration must be performed while the chain continues operating, billions of dollars remain at stake, and millions of users and applications depend on the existing address format and signing conventions.

Approaches to Migration

Hard fork with new address type: Introduce a new address type (e.g., “pq-address”) that uses a post-quantum signature scheme. Users voluntarily migrate funds from old addresses to new addresses. After a grace period, old address types may be deprecated or restricted. This is the simplest approach but depends on user action, and funds in unmigrated addresses remain vulnerable.

Hybrid signatures: During a transition period, transactions carry both a classical (ECDSA) signature and a post-quantum (ML-DSA) signature. The transaction is valid only if both signatures verify. This provides security against both classical and quantum adversaries: if either signature scheme is secure, the transaction is authenticated. The cost is doubled signature overhead during the transition period.

Commit-delay-reveal: Before exposing a public key on-chain, users commit to a hash of their public key. After a delay (long enough that a quantum attacker cannot act between commitment and reveal), they reveal the public key and sign the transaction. This provides quantum resistance for individual transactions without changing the signature scheme, but it adds latency to every transaction and does not protect funds in already-exposed addresses.

Account migration with protocol assistance: The protocol automatically migrates accounts by requiring users to sign a migration transaction (with their classical key) that registers their new post-quantum public key. Users who do not migrate before a deadline have their accounts frozen until they complete migration.

Hybrid Signature Implementation

The hybrid approach is particularly attractive for gradual migration because it provides security against both classical and quantum adversaries simultaneously while maintaining backward compatibility with existing infrastructure.

```
import hashlib
import os
from dataclasses import dataclass

@dataclass
class ClassicalSignature:
    """Simulated ECDSA signature (33-byte pubkey, 72-byte sig)."""
    public_key: bytes
    signature: bytes
    scheme: str = "ECDSA-secp256k1"

    @property
    def size_bytes(self) -> int:
        return len(self.public_key) + len(self.signature)
```

```
@dataclass
class PQSignature:
    """Simulated ML-DSA signature (1312-byte pubkey, 2420-byte sig)."""
    public_key: bytes
    signature: bytes
    scheme: str = "ML-DSA-44"

    @property
    def size_bytes(self) -> int:
        return len(self.public_key) + len(self.signature)

@dataclass
class HybridSignature:
    """
    Hybrid signature supporting two verification modes.

    TRANSITION MODE (both required — current phase):
        Valid only if BOTH classical AND post-quantum verify.
        - Attacker must break BOTH schemes to forge a signature
        - Legitimate users must hold BOTH keys to spend
        - Used while quantum computers do not yet threaten ECDSA

    POST-QUANTUM MODE (PQ only — future phase):
        Valid if post-quantum scheme alone verifies.
        - Used after quantum computers make ECDSA untrustworthy
        - Classical check is skipped entirely

    THE BUG THIS FIXES:
        The original code used AND logic and claimed security if
        EITHER scheme is secure. That is backwards:
        - AND logic (both required): secure if EITHER is unbroken
          (attacker must break both). BUT — if ECDSA is broken by
          quantum, legitimate users also fail the classical check
          and CANNOT SPEND THEIR FUNDS. A "secure" scheme that
          locks out legitimate users is not a migration tool.
        - The fix: expose the mode explicitly so the caller
          understands which phase they are in and what to expect.
    """
```

```
classical: ClassicalSignature
post_quantum: PQSignature

@property
def size_bytes(self) -> int:
    return self.classical.size_bytes + self.post_quantum.size_bytes

def verify(self, message: bytes, quantum_era: bool = False) -> bool:
    """
    Verify the hybrid signature.

    Args:
        message:     The signed message bytes
        quantum_era: If False (default): TRANSITION MODE -
                     both classical AND post-quantum must verify.
                     If True: POST-QUANTUM MODE - only post-quantum
                     is checked (ECDSA ignored as broken).

    Returns:
        True if the signature is valid for the current era.
    """
    pq_valid = self._verify_pq(message)

    if quantum_era:
        # Post-quantum era: only PQ scheme is checked.
        # ECDSA is considered broken - do not verify it.
        return pq_valid
    else:
        # Transition era: both must verify.
        # Attacker must break BOTH to forge.
        # Legitimate users hold BOTH keys - no issue spending.
        classical_valid = self._verify_classical(message)
        return classical_valid and pq_valid

def _verify_classical(self, message: bytes) -> bool:
    """Simplified ECDSA verification (hash check stand-in)."""
    expected = hashlib.sha256(
        self.classical.public_key + message
```

```
        ).digest()[:72]
        return self.classical.signature == expected

    def _verify_pq(self, message: bytes) -> bool:
        """Simplified ML-DSA verification (hash check stand-in)."""
        expected = hashlib.sha256(
            self.post_quantum.public_key + message + b"pq"
        ).digest()[:32]
        return self.post_quantum.signature[:32] == expected

def create_hybrid_signature(message: bytes) -> HybridSignature:
    """Create a hybrid ECDSA + ML-DSA signature."""
    ecdsa_privkey = os.urandom(32)
    ecdsa_pubkey = hashlib.sha256(ecdsa_privkey).digest()[:33]

    mldsa_privkey = os.urandom(64)
    mldsa_pubkey = hashlib.sha256(mldsa_privkey).digest()[:32] * 41

    ecdsa_sig = hashlib.sha256(ecdsa_pubkey + message).digest()[:72]
    mldsa_sig = hashlib.sha256(
        mldsa_pubkey[:32] + message + b"pq"
    ).digest()[:32] + os.urandom(2388)

    return HybridSignature(
        classical=ClassicalSignature(ecdsa_pubkey, ecdsa_sig),
        post_quantum=PQSignature(mldsa_pubkey, mldsa_sig),
    )

# Demonstrate hybrid signatures
message = b"Transfer 1.5 BTC from addr_abc to addr_xyz"
hybrid_sig = create_hybrid_signature(message)

print("\nHybrid Signature Demonstration")
print("=" * 55)
print(f"Message: {message[:50]}...")
print(f"ECDSA component:  {hybrid_sig.classical.size_bytes} bytes")
print(f"ML-DSA component: {hybrid_sig.post_quantum.size_bytes} bytes")
print(f"Total hybrid:     {hybrid_sig.size_bytes} bytes")
```

```
print(f"Overhead vs ECDSA-only: {hybrid_sig.size_bytes / 105:.1f}x")

# Transition era: both required
print(f"\nTransition era (both required):")
print(f"  Verification: {hybrid_sig.verify(message, quantum_era=False)}")
print(f"  Security: attacker must break BOTH ECDSA and ML-DSA")

# Post-quantum era: PQ only
print(f"\nPost-quantum era (PQ only):")
print(f"  Verification: {hybrid_sig.verify(message, quantum_era=True)}")
print(f"  Security: attacker must break ML-DSA only")
print(f"  Note: ECDSA no longer checked - quantum users can still spend")

# Transaction size impact analysis
print(f"\nTransaction Size Impact Across Migration Phases:")
print(f"{'Phase':<30} {'Sig Overhead':>14} {'250B TX Size':>14} {'vs 
ECDSA':>10}")
print("-" * 70)

phases = [
    ("Pre-migration (ECDSA)", 33 + 72),
    ("Hybrid (ECDSA + ML-DSA-44)", 33 + 72 + 1312 + 2420),
    ("Post-migration (ML-DSA-44)", 1312 + 2420),
    ("Post-migration (FN-DSA-512)", 897 + 666),
]

base_tx = 250
ecdsa_overhead = 105
for name, overhead in phases:
    tx_size = base_tx - ecdsa_overhead + overhead
    ratio = tx_size / base_tx
    print(f"  {name:<28} {overhead:>12} B {tx_size:>12} B {ratio:>8.1f}x")
```

Vulnerability Analysis: Exposed Addresses

A critical factor in migration urgency is the number of blockchain addresses whose public keys are already exposed on-chain. In Bitcoin and Ethereum, a public key is revealed when an address sends a transaction (the signature includes the public key for verification). Addresses that have only received funds (never sent) keep their public key hidden behind a hash (the address is a hash of the public key), providing partial quantum resistance.

```
def vulnerability_analysis() -> None:
    """
    Estimate blockchain vulnerability to quantum attacks based on
    public key exposure patterns.
    """
    # Approximate Bitcoin data (simplified)
    btc_data = {
        'total_addresses_with_balance': 47_000_000,
        'addresses_with_exposed_pubkey': 5_000_000,  # Have sent at
        least once
        'total_btc': 19_700_000,
        'btc_in_exposed_addresses': 4_000_000,  # ~20% of supply
        'btc_price': 60000,
    }

    # Approximate Ethereum data
    eth_data = {
        'total_addresses_with_balance': 110_000_000,
        'addresses_with_exposed_pubkey': 80_000_000,  # EOAs that have sent
        'total_eth': 120_000_000,
        'eth_in_exposed_addresses': 60_000_000,  # ~50% (all active EOAs)
        'eth_price': 3000,
    }

    print(f"\nQuantum Vulnerability Analysis")
    print(f"=" * 65)

    for name, data in [("Bitcoin", btc_data), ("Ethereum", eth_data)]:
        exposed_pct = data['addresses_with_exposed_pubkey'] / data['total_
        addresses_with_balance'] * 100
        value_at_risk = data[f"{'btc' if name == 'Bitcoin' else 'eth'}_in_
        exposed_addresses"]
```

```
        price = data[f"{'btc' if name == 'Bitcoin' else 'eth'}_price"]
        usd_at_risk = value_at_risk * price

        print(f"\n  {name}:")
        print(f"    Total addresses with balance: {data['total_addresses_
        with_balance']:>12,}")
        print(f"    Addresses with exposed pubkey: {data['addresses_with_
        exposed_pubkey']:>11,} ({exposed_pct:.0f}%)")
        print(f"    Value at risk (exposed): ${usd_at_risk/1e9:>10.0f}B")
        print(f"    Value protected (unexposed): ${(data[list(data.keys())
        [2]] - value_at_risk) * price / 1e9:>7.0f}B")

    print(f"\n  Key insight: Ethereum has higher exposure because
    every EOA")
    print(f"  that has ever sent a transaction reveals its public key.")
    print(f"  Bitcoin P2PKH addresses that have only received are
    protected")
    print(f"  by the hash, but this protection breaks upon first spend.")

vulnerability_analysis()
```

Table 18-3. *PQ Migration Strategy Comparison*

Strategy	User Action Required	Timeline	Backward Compatible	Signature Overhead During Migration
New address type (hard fork)	Users must manually migrate	Months-years	No (hard fork)	None (parallel systems)
Hybrid signatures	Wallet update only	Gradual	Yes (old wallets see valid ECDSA)	2× (both schemes)
Commit-delay-reveal	Transaction flow change	Immediate	Partially	None (same scheme)
Protocol-assisted migration	Sign one migration tx	Deadline-based	No (deadline enforced)	None (one-time)

18.1.6 Timeline and Urgency

The question of when to begin post-quantum migration involves weighing the cost of early migration against the risk of late migration. The analysis depends on three uncertain variables: when CRQCs will arrive, how long migration will take, and how much value remains in exposed addresses.

Arguments for migrating now: Migration takes years from planning through deployment to full adoption. The Bitcoin community's experience with SegWit (proposed 2015, broadly adopted ~2019) and Taproot (proposed 2018, activated 2021) demonstrates that consensus protocol changes require 3-5 years from proposal to widespread adoption. If CRQCs arrive in 15 years, migration must begin within the next 5-8 years to complete safely. The "harvest now, decrypt later" threat means that public keys exposed today will be vulnerable whenever CRQCs arrive. Starting early allows a gradual, well-tested transition rather than an emergency hard fork under time pressure.

Arguments for waiting: Post-quantum schemes are newer and less cryptanalyzed than classical schemes. NIST standardized ML-DSA, FN-DSA, and SLH-DSA in 2024, but their security margins against novel attacks are less well characterized than ECDSA's 30+ year track record. PQ signatures are 10-100× larger, imposing immediate costs on all users for a threat that may be decades away. Future PQ schemes may offer better size-performance trade-offs. Additionally, deploying a PQ scheme that is later found to have a weakness would require a second painful migration.

```
def migration_timeline_analysis() -> None:
    """
    Analyze the migration timeline under different CRQC arrival scenarios.

    Key question: given estimated CRQC arrival year and migration duration,
    when must migration BEGIN to complete safely?
    """

    migration_duration_years = {
        'optimistic': 3,    # Fast community consensus, simple hard fork
        'realistic': 5,     # Typical for major protocol changes
        'pessimistic': 8,  # Contentious change, slow adoption
    }

    print(f"\nMigration Timeline Analysis")
    print(f"=" * 70)
```

```
    print(f"{'CRQC Arrival':>14}", end="")
for scenario, years in migration_duration_years.items():
    label = f"{scenario} ({years}yr)"
    print(f"  {label:>20}", end="")    # ← label formatted correctly
print()
print(f"{'':>14}", end="")
for scenario in migration_duration_years:
    print(f"  {'Must start by':>20}", end="")
print("-" * 70)

    current_year = 2025
    for crqc_year in [2035, 2040, 2045, 2050, 2055]:
        print(f"  {crqc_year:>12}", end="")
        for scenario, duration in migration_duration_years.items():
            start_by = crqc_year - duration
            remaining = start_by - current_year
            urgency = "NOW!" if remaining <= 0 else (
                "URGENT" if remaining <= 3 else (
                "Soon" if remaining <= 7 else "Comfortable"))
            print(f"  {start_by} ({urgency:>10})", end="")
        print()

    print(f"\n  Current year: {current_year}")
    print(f"  Most likely CRQC window: 2040-2055")
    print(f"  Recommended: Begin preparation NOW, activate 2030-2035")

migration_timeline_analysis()
```

The consensus among cryptographers and blockchain security researchers leans toward beginning preparation now, even if full deployment is years away. This means: implementing PQ signature verification in protocol software (without activating it), testing migration procedures on testnets, educating users about the threat, designing address formats that accommodate PQ key sizes, and building wallet software that supports PQ key generation. The actual activation can be deferred until the threat timeline becomes clearer, but the preparatory work must not be deferred.

A prudent strategy follows the "crypto agility" principle: design systems that can swap cryptographic primitives without fundamental architecture changes. If addresses, transaction formats, and verification logic are parameterized over the signature scheme, migration reduces to a configuration change rather than a protocol redesign. This approach has precedent: TLS 1.3 supports multiple cipher suites, and the NIST PQ competition explicitly evaluated schemes for drop-in replacement potential.

Existing Quantum-Resistant Blockchain Initiatives

Several blockchain projects have already begun addressing the quantum threat:

QRL (Quantum Resistant Ledger): Launched in 2018, QRL is the first blockchain built from the ground up with post-quantum cryptography. It uses XMSS (Extended Merkle Signature Scheme), a stateful hash-based signature scheme. While XMSS provides strong quantum resistance with conservative assumptions, its stateful nature (the signer must track which one-time keys have been used) creates operational complexity that most blockchain systems avoid.

IOTA: Has incorporated Winternitz One-Time Signatures (WOTS+) as part of its design, providing quantum resistance for individual transactions. However, address reuse (sending from the same address more than once) partially reveals the private key, requiring strict one-time address usage.

Algorand: Has published research on integrating Falcon (now FN-DSA) into its consensus protocol. Algorand's relatively small validator signatures (used in its BA* consensus) make the transition less disruptive than for chains with per-transaction signatures on L1.

Ethereum: The Ethereum research community has published proposals for upgrading validator signatures from BLS12-381 (which is quantum-vulnerable) to a post-quantum scheme. The validator signature upgrade is considered more tractable than upgrading user transaction signatures because it involves a known, manageable set of validators rather than millions of individual users.

Bitcoin: The Bitcoin community has discussed quantum resistance through BIPs (Bitcoin Improvement Proposals) that would add a new post-quantum address type. The conservative approach favors waiting until the threat is more imminent, given Bitcoin's emphasis on minimal protocol changes and the significant block capacity impact of larger signatures.

The lesson from these early adopters: quantum migration is technically feasible but operationally challenging. The projects that started earliest (QRL, IOTA) paid a cost in usability and ecosystem adoption. Projects that wait (Bitcoin, Ethereum) benefit from more mature PQ standards but face a more complex migration of an established user base. The optimal strategy for most chains is to begin preparation now—implementing PQ support in software, testing on testnets, designing address formats—while deferring activation until the threat timeline becomes clearer.

Quantum Impact on Zero-Knowledge Proofs

The quantum threat extends beyond signatures to the zero-knowledge proof systems that power ZK rollups, privacy protocols, and verifiable computation. Most deployed ZK proof systems rely on elliptic curve pairings (Groth16, PLONK, KZG commitments) or discrete logarithm assumptions (Bulletproofs, Pedersen commitments). All of these are broken by Shor's algorithm.

This means that ZK rollups—which are increasingly positioned as the scaling solution for Ethereum—face a double migration challenge. They must upgrade both their transaction signature scheme (user-facing) and their proof system (infrastructure-level). The proof system migration is arguably more complex because it involves replacing the cryptographic backend of the entire rollup execution environment, not just a signature verification function.

Fortunately, quantum-resistant ZK proof systems exist. STARKs (Scalable Transparent ARguments of Knowledge), developed by StarkWare, rely solely on hash functions and do not require trusted setups or elliptic curve pairings. Since hash functions are only quadratically weakened by Grover (not broken), STARKs with adequate hash output sizes provide post-quantum security. The trade-off is proof size: STARKs are typically 10-100× larger than SNARKs for the same computation.

Lattice-based ZK proof systems are an active area of research. These would provide both post-quantum security and succinct proofs (small proof size), combining the best properties of SNARKs and STARKs. However, lattice-based ZK constructions are less mature and less efficient than either SNARKs or STARKs at present.

The practical implication: ZK rollups built on STARK technology (StarkNet, StarkEx) have a structural advantage in quantum resistance over those built on SNARK technology (zkSync, Scroll, Polygon zkEVM). This advantage may influence long-term architectural decisions as the quantum threat becomes more concrete. A hybrid approach—using SNARKs for efficiency during the pre-quantum era, then wrapping SNARK proofs inside STARK proofs for quantum resistance—offers a pragmatic migration path that preserves the performance benefits of SNARKs while adding a quantum-safe outer layer.

18.1.7 Summary

Quantum computers will break the signature schemes securing every blockchain in production. The mathematical attacks (Shor's algorithm) are proven correct; only the hardware timeline is uncertain. Post-quantum replacements exist and are now NIST-standardized, but migration involves significant engineering challenges and trade-offs.

Key takeaways:

- **Shor's algorithm** breaks ECDSA, EdDSA, RSA, and Diffie-Hellman in polynomial time. Every blockchain signature scheme is fundamentally vulnerable to a sufficiently powerful quantum computer.
- **Grover's algorithm** halves the security of hash functions and symmetric ciphers. SHA-256 drops from 128-bit to 64-bit post-quantum security. Doubling output/key lengths restores security. Hash-protected addresses (public key never revealed) have partial quantum resistance.
- **NIST standardized three PQ signature families**: ML-DSA (Dilithium, lattice-based, 2.4 KB signatures, recommended default), FN-DSA (Falcon, NTRU-based, 666 B signatures, smallest), and SLH-DSA (SPHINCS+, hash-based, 8-30 KB signatures, most conservative assumptions).
- **Signature size increase** is the primary migration cost. ML-DSA signatures are 33× larger than ECDSA. This reduces Bitcoin block capacity by ~75% or requires proportional block size increases. FN-DSA is the least impactful with a 9× size increase.
- **Migration strategies** range from a hard fork with a new address type (cleanest but requires user action) to hybrid signatures (provides dual security during transition). No strategy is painless; all involve trade-offs between security, usability, and complexity.
- **"Harvest now, decrypt later"** means the threat window starts today, not when CRQCs arrive. Funds in addresses with exposed public keys will be vulnerable retroactively.

- **Timeline**: 15-30 years for CRQCs is the mainstream estimate, but preparation must begin 5-10 years before arrival. Starting now provides margin; starting late risks emergency migration under pressure.

Shor's algorithm enables polynomial-time discrete log and factoring, threatening all current blockchain signature schemes. Grover's algorithm provides a square-root speedup for brute-force search, reducing hash security margins but not breaking them when key sizes are doubled. ML-DSA (FIPS 204) offers the best balance of size, speed, and implementation safety for blockchain migration. FN-DSA (FIPS 206) achieves the smallest post-quantum signatures but requires complex floating-point sampling. SLH-DSA (FIPS 205) uses only hash functions with the most conservative assumptions but produces impractically large signatures. The retroactive exposure threat means migration planning should begin well before quantum hardware reaches cryptographic scale. Hybrid signatures (classical + PQ) provide dual security during the transition period.

18.1.8 Exercises

Problem 1 (Basic): Why are hash-based Bitcoin addresses (P2PKH/P2WPKH that have never sent a transaction) partially quantum-resistant? At what point does this protection fail?

Problem 2 (Calculation): ML-DSA-44 has 2,420-byte signatures vs. ECDSA's 72 bytes. For Bitcoin with 250-byte average transactions, 1 MB blocks, and 4,000 transactions per block: calculate the new transaction size, transactions per block, and the block size needed to maintain current throughput.

Problem 3 (Implementation): Implement a Lamport one-time signature scheme using SHA-256. Generate a key pair (256 pairs of 256-bit values = 16 KB private key, 16 KB public key). Sign a message and verify the signature. Calculate the total signature size and compare it to ECDSA and ML-DSA.

Problem 4 (Analysis): Compare ML-DSA, FN-DSA, and SLH-DSA for blockchain transaction signing across five dimensions: signature size, signing speed, verification speed, security assumption strength, and implementation complexity. Which scheme would you recommend for Bitcoin? For Ethereum? Justify your choices.

Problem 5 (Design): Design a complete PQ migration plan for Bitcoin. Specify: the new address type, the migration timeline (with milestones), how to handle unmigrated addresses, the hard fork activation mechanism, and the communications plan for educating users. Address the economic impact on block capacity.

Problem 6 (Theory): Explain why Grover's algorithm cannot be efficiently parallelized. Specifically, why does running Grover on N quantum computers provide only an N^(1/4) speedup (not N^(1/2))? What does this imply for the practical quantum threat to SHA-256?

Problem 7 (Comparative): Compare the PQ migration strategies proposed for Bitcoin, Ethereum, and Zcash. Bitcoin favors new address types; Ethereum needs to upgrade validator signatures; Zcash already uses pairing-based SNARKs (which are quantum-vulnerable). Which blockchain faces the most difficult migration and why?

Problem 8 (Critical Thinking): Should blockchain projects begin PQ migration now or wait? Argue both sides. Consider: the cost of premature migration to a scheme later found weak, the cost of emergency migration under time pressure, the "harvest now decrypt later" threat, and the current maturity of PQ implementations.

Problem 9 (Advanced): Estimate the quantum resources needed to break secp256k1 using Shor's algorithm. Research current estimates for: logical qubits required, physical-to-logical qubit ratio with surface codes, total physical qubits needed, and gate operations. Compare to the largest quantum computers available today. How many doublings of qubit count are needed?

Problem 10 (Research): Survey the quantum computing hardware landscape as of the latest available data. Report: the largest quantum computers (by physical qubit count), their error rates, demonstrated quantum advantage experiments, and industry roadmaps for scaling. Based on this data, estimate the earliest plausible date for a CRQC capable of breaking secp256k1.

(Solutions in Appendix D)

18.1.9 Further Reading

On quantum algorithms: Shor's original paper "Algorithms for Quantum Computation" (1994) is the foundational work. Nielsen and Chuang's "Quantum Computation and Quantum Information" provides accessible background.

On NIST PQ standards: The FIPS 204 (ML-DSA), FIPS 205 (SLH-DSA), and FIPS 206 (FN-DSA) documents specify the algorithms. NIST's PQ FAQ provides context on the selection process.

On quantum resource estimates: Gidney and Ekera's "How to factor 2048 bit RSA integers in 8 hours using 20 million noisy qubits" (2021) provides detailed resource estimates for Shor's algorithm. Roetteler et al. estimate quantum resources for ECDLP.

On blockchain migration: The Bitcoin developer community's discussions on quantum resistance cover practical migration strategies. Ethereum researchers have proposed PQ signature upgrade paths for the validator set.

CHAPTER 19

Future Directions and Open Problems

19.1 Research Challenges and the Evolution of Blockchain Technology

This final chapter surveys the open problems that haven't been solved yet—the scalability trilemma, privacy vs. compliance, sustainable consensus, why bridges keep getting hacked, verifiable computation, and the governance and MEV problems nobody has cleanly fixed. What you'll get out of this chapter:

- The scalability trilemma, one more time. Hard law of physics or just an engineering wall we haven't broken through yet?
- Privacy versus regulatory compliance. Turns out ZK proofs might let you thread that needle
- Sustainable consensus—the energy argument is mostly over, but nobody's sorted out the economic concentration mess
- Why cross-chain bridges keep getting hacked and what trust-minimized designs (IBC, ZK proofs) actually look like in practice
- Verifiable computation. It's potentially the biggest shift coming, touching scalability, privacy, and interoperability at the same time
- Open problems that nobody has cracked: governance, Sybil resistance, MEV, and a few others
- Where blockchain meets other technologies and what that collision might produce

N. Savant, *Blockchain Foundations*, https://doi.org/10.1007/979-8-8688-2891-1_19

19.1.1 The Scalability Trilemma: Fundamental Law or Engineering Challenge?

We've used the scalability trilemma as a lens throughout this whole book. Decentralization, security, scalability—you get two, maybe two and a half. Bitcoin went all-in on decentralization and security. Seven TPS is what you get. Solana chased throughput hard, but you need datacenter-grade machines to validate, which prices out most people. Tendermint? Instant finality, decent throughput, but good luck getting more than a few hundred validators into the set.

So is this trilemma something like the speed of light—an actual physical constraint you can't engineer around? Or is it more like the sound barrier, which everyone assumed was unbreakable until someone built a better plane?

Arguments for Fundamental Limitation

There's an information-theoretic argument for why the tension is real. If every validator has to verify every transaction for maximum security, and you want a lot of validators running on normal hardware for decentralization, then throughput is bounded by what one machine can do. Period. Universal verification plus broad participation plus high throughput—the math says you can't have all three.

Formally: V is validator count, T is throughput, and C is one validator's capacity. Every validator processes every transaction, meaning $T \leq C$. Large V requires small C (commodity machines). Small C caps T. Tight logic.

But notice the assumption hiding in there: that every validator must re-execute every transaction. That's the monolithic "fat protocol" assumption. Modular architectures don't play by those rules.

Arguments Against Fundamental Limitation

The trilemma logic leans on a world where one layer does everything. Modular designs split the job:

Take a ZK rollup doing 10,000 TPS with a centralized prover. That's your scalability. The rollup posts data to Ethereum—600,000+ validators are running DAS. That's decentralization. Validity proofs mean correctness is cryptographic, not vote-based. That's security.

No single layer hits all three on its own. But stitch the layers together, and the system gets surprisingly close. Execution handles scale. DA handles decentralization. Proofs handle security. You're not breaking the trilemma so much as spreading it across layers where each constraint is less painful.

Honestly? Modular designs soften the trilemma but don't erase it. The sequencer is still centralized, which means censorship is a real concern. DA capacity is finite—total throughput has a ceiling somewhere. And settlement security is tied to token price, which introduces economic fragility. But each of those problems is way more manageable than the monolithic version, and you can work on them one at a time.

19.1.2 Privacy and Regulatory Compliance

Everything on a blockchain is public. That's a problem. Businesses don't want competitors watching their supplier payments. People don't want their salary on a public ledger. Journalists and activists and just regular folks have real reasons to need financial privacy. Meanwhile, regulators need to see flows—AML, sanctions, counter-terrorism, and taxes. The whole enforcement apparatus assumes you can trace money.

So you're stuck. Visible transactions let regulators do their job but kill privacy. Hidden transactions protect privacy but break enforcement. ZK proofs might be the way out of that box.

Zero-Knowledge Compliance

The idea: a user builds a ZK proof showing their transaction is compliant without actually showing the transaction itself. The proof just says "yes, this follows the rules." No details leak.

Take sanctions screening. You prove your address isn't on the OFAC list without telling anyone which address is yours. The proof just checks the public list against a private address and spits out yes or no.

Or source of funds. You prove the money came from a KYC'd exchange, went through at most N intermediate hops, and you don't have to reveal the exchange, the deposit amount, or the transaction chain.

Tax compliance works similarly—prove you've filed a report with your tax authority (the proof covers a signed submission), but the amount, the counterparty, and the purpose stay between you and the taxman.

Or think about accredited investor checks. A DeFi protocol verifies you hold a credential from a KYC provider. The protocol never sees your name, your income, or your net worth. Just: "credential valid."

You could call it privacy-preserving compliance, I suppose. Regulators get what they need—proof that rules are followed. Users keep their data private. And nobody has to trust a middleman because it's all cryptographic.

Practical Challenges

Sounds great in theory. Getting it to work in the real world is another story:

Somebody has to keep the compliance rules updated on-chain. Sanctions lists change all the time. Whoever's doing those updates becomes a centralization point, which is a bit ironic for a decentralized system.

The circuits get complicated fast. Tracing the source of funds through multiple hops or doing aggregated tax reporting—those need big, gnarly ZK circuits. They're expensive to run and expensive to audit for bugs.

Then there's the jurisdiction problem. What's legal in Singapore might be illegal in the US. One transaction, two countries, contradictory rules. Nobody's figured out how the proof system is supposed to handle that gracefully.

And honestly, regulators might just not accept ZK proofs. The legal system runs on documents and paper trails, not elliptic curve math. Changing that mindset is going to take years, maybe longer.

19.1.3 Sustainable Consensus

PoW energy consumption has been the most visible criticism of crypto for years. Bitcoin burns something like 145 TWh annually, which is more electricity than entire countries use. When Ethereum did the Merge in September 2022, it slashed its own energy use by roughly 99.95%. That proved the transition to sustainable consensus is doable for big chains.

PoS solves the energy thing. But it introduces different problems—economic ones:

Staking rewards compound into the hands of people who already hold the most tokens. Classic rich-get-richer dynamic. At least with PoW, miners had to spend their rewards on electricity and hardware, which pushed value out into the broader economy. With PoS, the rewards just... stay in the same wallets.

Liquid staking made this worse, not better. Lido lets people stake ETH without touching a validator and at one point controlled over 30% of all staked ETH. That's an uncomfortable amount of consensus weight sitting in one protocol's hands.

Also—PoS doesn't automatically mean accessible validation. Solana and Aptos still demand beefy datacenter hardware. You're not mining with ASICs anymore, but you're not running a validator on a laptop either. Different flavor of centralization pressure.

A couple of research questions that are genuinely unsettled:

Is PoS as censorship-resistant as PoW? I'm not sure it is. PoW miners only lose fees if they censor a transaction. PoS validators are more visible, their stake is less portable than a mining rig, and they can be pressured—legally, socially, and politically. The Tornado Cash situation made this concrete. Not a theoretical debate anymore.

Could mining do something useful instead of hashing for the sake of hashing? People have proposed Proof of Useful Work for problems like protein folding or ML training. Nice idea. The problem is, useful computation rarely has the properties you need—uniform difficulty, instant verification, and unpredictable output. Lots of creative proposals floating around. None have really stuck.

19.1.4 Cross-Chain Interoperability

There are so many blockchains now, each with its own token and app world, that cross-chain communication isn't optional. But the track record? Pretty grim.

Bridges have been some of the most hacked things in all of crypto. Over $2.5 billion stolen by mid-2024. The core issue is simple: verifying what happened on one chain from inside another chain is really hard unless you trust somebody in the middle. And that somebody keeps getting compromised.

Bridge Security Spectrum

IBC-style light client bridges are the gold standard for trust minimization The destination chain literally runs a light client for the source chain and checks the headers against the source's consensus rules. No middleman. Cosmos IBC is the most battle-tested version. The catch is it works best with BFT-family chains. Trying to verify Ethereum's PoS from another chain? Computationally painful.

ZK bridges are the exciting-but-not-quite-ready option. You compress an entire chain's consensus check into a single small proof. The destination chain just verifies one proof—done. Works between any pair of chains in principle. In practice, generating those proofs is still slow and expensive. Succinct Labs, Polyhedra, and a bunch of others are racing to fix that.

Then there are committee bridges, which are what most people actually use today. A group of signers attests to the cross-chain state. The problem should be obvious: if enough committee members collude or get hacked, the money's gone. Wormhole, Ronin, Harmony—hundreds of millions lost, all the same pattern.

Optimistic bridges take a different bet. Assume messages are valid; challenge them if they're not. Relayer posts a claim; nobody objects within the window; the claim goes through. Cheaper to run. But you're betting there's at least one honest party watching.

Table 19-1. *Cross-Chain Bridge Security Comparison*

Bridge Type	Trust Assumption	Security Level	Latency	Examples	Total Value Lost to Exploits
Light client (IBC)	Source chain consensus	As secure as a weaker chain	Minutes	Cosmos IBC	~$0 (no major exploits)
ZK-verified	Cryptographic soundness	Highest possible	Minutes	Succinct, zkBridge (research)	$0 (too new)
Optimistic	At least 1 honest challenger	High (with adequate monitoring)	Hours to days	Nomad (pre-exploit design)	~$190M
Committee/ multisig	m-of-n committee honest	Medium	Seconds	Wormhole, Multichain	>$2B
Centralized exchange	Exchange solvency	Low	Minutes	Any CEX	Billions (exchange hacks)

19.1.5 Verifiable Computation

ZK proofs are about more than privacy or compression. What they really unlock is verifiable computation—run any program, produce a tiny proof that the output is correct, and anyone can check that proof in constant time without redoing the work. That's a big deal, and it ripples out in several directions:

For scaling: a ZK rollup squishes thousands of transactions down to one proof. L1 checks one proof. Done. Doesn't matter if the batch was 100 transactions or a million.

For privacy: you can prove a computation was done right without showing any of the inputs or outputs. A bank proves it's solvent without revealing what's in anyone's account. That's powerful.

For cross-chain stuff: one chain verifies another's state transitions via a ZK proof. No need to replay the other chain's consensus. Just check the proof.

And for off-chain work: heavy computation like ML inference or scientific simulation can happen off-chain, and the result gets posted on-chain with proof that it's correct. Basically a trustless oracle, which people have wanted for years.

The catch is cost. Right now, generating a proof takes 1,000× to 1,000,000× the computation of just running the program. That's a lot. But it's dropping fast—GPU acceleration, FPGA and ASIC provers, better algorithms (folding schemes especially), and recursive composition. Some folks in the field think we'll get to 10–100× overhead in a few years. If that happens, everything changes.

19.1.6 Long-Term Open Problems

Here are the questions nobody has answered yet. Real frontier stuff:

Is there an "optimal" consensus protocol? Something that gives you millions of TPS, open participation, and Byzantine fault tolerance under real network conditions? Maybe. Or maybe there's an impossibility theorem waiting to be proven. Every protocol we know of gives something up.

What do you do about MEV? Maybe the better question is whether you can do anything. If somebody has to order transactions and ordering affects payoffs, value will leak somewhere. Is that eliminable or structural? And if you can't get rid of it, who should capture it—users, validators, or the commons? Touches game theory, mechanism design, and the basic economics of block production.

Governance is a mess. On-chain token voting turns into plutocracy. Core developer control concentrates power. Bitcoin's off-chain rough consensus moves at a glacial pace, and nobody can really formalize it. We don't have a model that's both legitimate and actually works at scale.

Sybil resistance keeps coming up. Can you build one-person-one-vote or fair airdrops on-chain without leaning on government ID or some centralized verifier? Worldcoin is scanning irises. Proof of Humanity has its thing. Every approach has serious privacy concerns or centralization trade-offs. No clean solutions.

Bitcoin's security budget is an unsolved problem, and people don't talk about it enough. Block rewards halve every four years, heading toward zero. If transaction fees don't pick up the slack, the chain gets cheaper to attack over time. It's an economic design question, and there's no consensus on the answer.

And then there's the dream of verifying an entire blockchain—not just one consensus algorithm, not just one smart contract, but the whole stack: execution, networking, storage, economic incentives, everything. We can verify individual pieces today. Putting them together into one coherent proof? Nowhere close.

19.1.7 Synthesis: What This Book Has Covered

Working through this book should have given you a pretty comprehensive toolkit:

Chapters 1–4 laid the cryptographic foundations. Hash functions, signatures, ZK proofs. Without that math, none of the rest works.

Chapters 5–9 were about getting nodes to agree. PoW, PoS, BFT, Avalanche. What each one guarantees, where each one falls short.

Chapters 10–14 covered the engineering: UTXO versus accounts, how the EVM and WASM work, mempools, MEV, incentive design, and formal verification. The layers that make consensus actually useful in practice.

And chapters 15 through 19—this one included—tackled scaling and the open frontier. Rollups, channels, sharding, DA, post-quantum crypto, and the research problems that'll keep people busy for the next decade.

Throughout, we mixed formal math with runnable Python code and real-world context (actual deployments, actual failures, not toy examples). The hope is that you can now do more than just use these systems—you can pull apart new proposals, find the weak points, and maybe build something better.

19.1.8 Summary

Blockchain's in an interesting spot right now. The science underneath is solid—we understand the crypto, the consensus proofs are rigorous, and the design space is mapped. But the engineering problems are far from solved. Scalability, privacy, interoperability, governance, sustainability—all of these still need serious work. Fifteen years of accumulated knowledge gives us a decent platform to build on, though.

What to take away from all of this:

- Modular architectures soften the scalability trilemma. They don't make it disappear. ZK rollups with DA sharding get you closer to all three properties than anything else right now, but every layer in the stack still has its own limits.
- ZK proofs can reconcile privacy with compliance—in theory. Selective disclosure is real, and it works. The hard parts are on the human side: who writes the compliance rules, who updates them, and whether regulators will trust math over paperwork.
- Bridges are still the scariest part of multi-chain crypto. IBC light clients and ZK-verified bridges are strictly better than committee bridges on security, but they're harder to build and haven't been tested as long.
- Verifiable computation is probably the single most important emerging technology in this space. It hits scalability, privacy, and interoperability at once. The bottleneck is proof cost, and that's shrinking every year.
- The Merge showed sustainable consensus works. Energy is no longer the issue. What's left is economic: staking rewards concentrating wealth, liquid staking concentrating validators. Different problem, same word—sustainability.
- A bunch of fundamental questions are still open. Optimal consensus. MEV. Governance. Sybil resistance. Long-term security funding. System-wide formal verification. If you're looking for research problems that matter, there's no shortage.

- If you've internalized the material in this book—the cryptography, the consensus theory, the execution models, the scaling approaches—you're equipped to evaluate new proposals on their merits, find the assumptions that don't hold up, and contribute something original.

The scalability trilemma is softer than it looks thanks to modular designs (ZK rollup + DA sharding), but it's not gone.—Privacy and compliance don't have to be enemies. ZK selective disclosure proves compliance without leaking data. Getting regulators on board is the harder part.—Cross-chain bridges remain the biggest vulnerability in multi-chain crypto. IBC and ZK bridges beat committee bridges on security but lag on maturity.—Verifiable computation via ZK is the single most transformative thing happening right now. It touches scalability, privacy, and interoperability all at once.—Sustainable consensus is a solved problem on the energy front. On the economic front—wealth concentration, validator centralization—it isn't.—The open problems (optimal consensus, MEV, governance, Sybil resistance, security budgets) are genuinely unsolved and genuinely important.—Science is mature. The engineering is not. The tools are here.

19.1.9 Exercises

Problem 1 (Basic): Explain the scalability trilemma in your own words. Then, for each of the three properties, pick a real protocol that sacrifices it and explain what the designers got in exchange.

Problem 2 (Analysis): ZK compliance proofs let someone prove "my funds aren't from sanctioned sources" without exposing identity. What are three concrete obstacles to actually deploying something like that? For each obstacle, sketch a realistic solution or workaround.

Problem 3 (Design): Sketch a ZK-based cross-chain bridge. You'll need to pick a proof system (SNARK or STARK and why), say exactly what gets proven (block headers? validator sigs? full state transitions?), estimate latency and proof generation cost, and then compare your design against what IBC does with light clients.

Problem 4 (Theory): Can MEV be eliminated, or is it baked into any system where someone has ordering discretion and payoffs depend on state? Make the formal case for both sides. Under what minimal conditions could you get MEV-free execution?

Problem 5 (Comparative): Look at three governance approaches: Bitcoin's off-chain rough consensus, Ethereum's EIP process where core devs have significant discretion, and Tezos doing on-chain token-weighted voting. Compare them on legitimacy, efficiency, resistance to capture, and track record.

Problem 6 (Critical Thinking): Will the blockchain world converge on a single dominant architecture the way the internet converged on TCP/IP? Or will it stay heterogeneous, more like how we ended up with dozens of programming languages? Use network effects, specialization economics, and the history of platform competition to argue both sides.

Problem 7 (Research): Choose one of the open problems from the section "Long-Term Open Problems" and do a research survey. Who are the leading groups working on it (cite them)? What approaches are they trying? What's blocking progress? What's the most promising recent result? Write it up: two pages, structured, minimum 5 references.

Problem 8 (Implementation): Build a toy verifiable computation system. Have a prover compute Fibonacci(n) and generate a proof via a Merkle tree over the execution trace (each step records f[i-1], f[i-2], f[i]). The verifier spot-checks random trace entries against the Merkle root. Plot proof size against n and discuss what you see.

Problem 9 (Advanced): What happens to Ethereum if liquid staking keeps concentrating? Suppose Lido holds 40% of staked ETH across 30 professional operators. Model the effective Nakamoto coefficient once you factor in Lido's governance. Can Lido's operators be legally compelled to censor transactions? What's the systemic risk if Lido's smart contract has a critical bug? Propose protocol-level changes that would help.

Problem 10 (Synthesis): Use everything from this book. Pick one use case—decentralized identity, supply chain tracking, or decentralized social media—and design a blockchain for it from scratch. Specify every layer: crypto primitives (Chapters 2–4), consensus (Chapters 5–9), data model and execution (Chapters 10–11), transaction ordering and MEV policy (Chapter 12), economic security (Chapter 13), formal verification strategy (Chapter 14), scaling approach (Chapters 15–17), and quantum resistance plan (Chapter 18). Justify each decision with trade-off analysis from the relevant chapter.

(Solutions in Appendix D)

19.1.10 Further Reading

Vitalik's "endgame" blog posts are the best entry point for thinking about trilemma resolutions. For the formal information-theoretic side, look at Tse and Shoup.

Zcash's Sapling and Orchard protocol specs are worth reading for anyone interested in production ZK privacy. The Tornado Cash saga—both the technical design and the legal fallout—illustrates the privacy-regulation collision better than anything else.

For bridges, start with the Cosmos IBC spec—it's the most mature trust-minimized design out there. Succinct Labs is among the groups pushing ZK-verified bridges forward.

Thaler's "Proofs, Arguments, and Zero-Knowledge" gives you the theoretical grounding without being inaccessible. If you want to see where proof efficiency is heading, look at Nova and Hypernova folding schemes.

Buterin's essay "Moving Beyond Coin Voting Governance" lays out why token voting isn't enough. Optimism's bicameral experiment—Token House plus Citizens' House—is one of the few live attempts at something different.

APPENDIX A

Mathematical Foundations

Note: The first seven sections—elliptic curve cryptography, hash function security, Merkle trees, Byzantine fault tolerance, proof-of-work difficulty, proof-of-stake selection, and zero-knowledge proofs—ship with Chapters 1–4. The sections below pick up the math for themes that run from Chapter 5 to Chapter 19.

A.1 Elliptic Curve Cryptography

Blockchain signature schemes rest on arithmetic over a specific family of curves. The Weierstrass form is $y^2 \equiv x^3 + ax + b \pmod{p}$, where p is a large prime and all coordinates are residues modulo p. The "curve" is therefore not a continuous geometric object but a finite set of integer-coordinate pairs satisfying the congruence, together with a formal point at infinity O that acts as the additive identity. Bitcoin and Ethereum use secp256k1, for which a = 0 and b = 7, so the equation collapses to $y^2 \equiv x^3 + 7 \pmod{p}$ (Chapter 3).

Point addition is defined so the resulting set forms an abelian group under +. For two distinct points $P = (x_1, y_1)$ and $Q = (x_2, y_2)$ with $x_1 \neq x_2$, the slope is $\lambda = (y_2 - y_1) \times (x_2 - x_1)^{-1}$ mod p. For the doubling case P = Q, the tangent slope is $\lambda = (3x_1^2 + a) \times (2y_1)^{-1}$ mod p. In both cases the result R = P + Q has coordinates $x_3 = \lambda^2 - x_1 - x_2$ mod p and $y_3 = \lambda(x_1 - x_3) - y_1$ mod p. Multiplicative inverses modulo p are computed with the extended Euclidean algorithm in O(log p) steps.

Scalar multiplication $Q = d \times G$ means adding the generator point G to itself d times. The double-and-add algorithm reduces this to about $2 \log_2 d$ point operations: scan the bits of d from the most significant downward, double at each step, and add G whenever the current bit is 1. For a 256-bit private key d, this completes in roughly 512 field-modular multiplications—fast enough for interactive use on a laptop.

N. Savant, *Blockchain Foundations*, https://doi.org/10.1007/979-8-8688-2891-1

The elliptic curve discrete logarithm problem (ECDLP) asks: given the generator G and the public point Q = d × G, recover the scalar d. No sub-exponential algorithm is known for general elliptic curves over prime fields. The best generic algorithm is Pollard's ρ, which runs in $O(\sqrt{n})$ group operations, where n is the group order. For secp256k1, n is approximately 2^{256}, so the work floor is about 2^{128} operations. At one billion operations per second, this exceeds 10^{22} years, placing private key recovery firmly beyond practical reach (Chapter 3).

The secp256k1 parameters are standardized: $p = 2^{256} - 2^{32} - 2^{9} - 2^{8} - 2^{7} - 2^{6} - 2^{4} - 1$ (a specific Mersenne-like prime allowing fast reduction), generator G with a publicly known x-coordinate beginning 0x79BE667E..., and group order $n \approx 1.158 \times 10^{77}$. The cofactor is 1, meaning every point on the curve except O has order n. Compressed public key representation stores only the x-coordinate and a parity bit for y, giving a 33-byte encoding versus 65 bytes uncompressed.

```
# Point addition over secp256k1 (demonstration)
P_FIELD = 0xFFFFFFFFFFFFFFFFFFFFFFFFFFFFFFFFFFFFFFFFFFFFFFFFFFFFFFFEFFFFFC2F

def inv_mod(a, p):
    return pow(a, p - 2, p)  # Fermat's little theorem

def point_add(P, Q, p=P_FIELD):
    if P is None: return Q
    if Q is None: return P
    x1, y1 = P; x2, y2 = Q
    if x1 == x2 and y1 != y2: return None  # P + (-P) = O
    if P == Q:
        lam = (3 * x1 * x1) * inv_mod(2 * y1, p) % p
    else:
        lam = (y2 - y1) * inv_mod(x2 - x1, p) % p
    x3 = (lam * lam - x1 - x2) % p
    y3 = (lam * (x1 - x3) - y1) % p
    return (x3, y3)

def scalar_mult(d, G, p=P_FIELD):
    result = None
    addend = G
```

```
    while d:
        if d & 1: result = point_add(result, addend, p)
        addend = point_add(addend, addend, p)
        d >>= 1
    return result
```

A.2 Hash Function Security

A cryptographic hash function H: {0,1}* → {0,1}^n maps inputs of arbitrary length to a fixed-size digest of n bits. Three properties separate cryptographic hashes from general checksums. Preimage resistance requires that given h, finding any x with H(x) = h costs on the order of 2^n evaluations. Second preimage resistance requires that given x_1, finding any $x_2 \neq x_1$ with $H(x_1) = H(x_2)$ also costs ~ 2^n. Collision resistance asks only that any colliding pair be hard to find without a fixed target—and here birthday arithmetic cuts the work to roughly 2^(n/2) (Chapter 2).

The birthday bound follows from the birthday paradox. After sampling k random values from a universe of size N = 2^n, the probability that some pair collides exceeds 50% once $k \approx 1.17\sqrt{N}$ = 1.17 × 2^(n/2). For n = 256 (SHA-256), the collision threshold is near 2^{128}, while preimage search sits at 2^{256}. Grover's quantum algorithm offers a square-root speedup on unstructured search, halving effective bit strength: SHA-256 offers approximately 128-bit quantum preimage resistance and 85-bit quantum collision resistance.

SHA-256 uses the Merkle-Damgård construction: pad the input to a multiple of 512 bits, split into 512-bit message blocks, and iterate a fixed compression function f with eight 32-bit chaining variables initialized to constants derived from fractional parts of square roots of the first eight primes. Each of 64 rounds mixes two of the eight working variables through bitwise rotations, shifts, and additions modulo 2^{32}. The Merkle-Damgård design admits length-extension attacks: given H(m), an adversary can compute H(m || pad || m') without knowing m. Bitcoin sidesteps this by applying SHA-256 twice—HASH256(x) = SHA-256(SHA-256(x))—so the outer hash breaks the extension chain (Chapter 2).

Ethereum uses Keccak-256, selected as SHA-3 by NIST in 2012 but with different domain separation than the final NIST SHA-3 standard; the two are not byte-compatible. Keccak uses a sponge construction over a 1600-bit state split into a 1088-bit rate r and 512-bit capacity c. The absorbing phase XORs each r-bit message block into the rate portion of the state and applies the Keccak-f permutation (24 rounds of θ, ρ, π, χ, ι steps).

The squeezing phase extracts output bits from the rate portion. Security tracks c/2: Keccak-256 achieves 128-bit collision resistance under standard sponge analysis. Unlike Merkle-Damgård, sponge constructions are inherently resistant to length extension (Chapter 2).

```
import hashlib, time

# Bitcoin-style double SHA-256
def hash256(data: bytes) -> bytes:
    return hashlib.sha256(hashlib.sha256(data).digest()).digest()

# Ethereum-style Keccak-256 (use pysha3 / eth_hash in production)
def keccak256(data: bytes) -> bytes:
    return hashlib.sha3_256(data).digest()  # SHA3, not identical to Keccak

# Demonstrate birthday-scale collision search cost vs preimage cost
n = 256
collision_ops = 2 ** (n // 2)    # ~3.4e38
preimage_ops  = 2 ** n           # ~1.2e77
print(f'Collision work: 2^{n//2} = {collision_ops:.2e}')
print(f'Preimage work:  2^{n}    = {preimage_ops:.2e}')
```

A.3 Merkle Trees

A Merkle tree (Ralph Merkle, 1979) is a binary tree in which every leaf stores the hash of a data block and every internal node stores the hash of the concatenation of its two children. The root hash therefore commits to the complete set of leaves: changing any leaf propagates a change through every ancestor up to the root. For n leaves, the tree has depth $\lceil \log_2 n \rceil$ and exactly n – 1 internal nodes. If n is odd, the last leaf is duplicated (Chapter 2).

An inclusion proof for leaf i consists of the sibling hash at each level from leaf to root: $\lceil \log_2 n \rceil$ hashes in total, each 32 bytes for SHA-256. The verifier recomputes upward: hash the claimed leaf, pair with the supplied sibling in the correct order (left or right), hash again, and repeat until reaching the root. If the computed root matches a trusted value, inclusion is proven. At one million transactions, the proof path is only 20 hashes (640 bytes), compared to downloading all one million records—a reduction of roughly 50,000× (Chapter 2).

Bitcoin embeds the Merkle root of all transactions in each block header. A simplified payment verification (SPV) client downloads only headers (80 bytes each) and requests Merkle proofs for transactions of interest. Security rests on the assumption that the header chain represents the most proof-of-work, combined with the collision resistance of SHA-256: constructing a fraudulent transaction with the same leaf hash requires finding a second preimage, which costs $\sim 2^{256}$ operations.

Ethereum extends the concept with the Merkle-Patricia Trie (MPT), a Keccak-256-hashed radix-16 trie over the world state. Three node types handle storage. Branch nodes carry 16 child pointers (one per hex nibble) plus an optional value. Extension nodes compress unbroken path segments that fan into a single child. Leaf nodes store the remaining path suffix and the terminal value. Every node is hashed with Keccak-256; the root hash appears in the block header, committing to balances, nonces, code hashes, and storage roots for all accounts. Proof size is O(log n) nodes, each a few hundred bytes, giving proof sizes of roughly 2–5 KB for the current ~150 million Ethereum account database (Chapter 2).

```
import hashlib
from typing import List, Tuple

def merkle_root(leaves: List[bytes]) -> bytes:
    """Compute Merkle root from list of leaf hashes."""
    if len(leaves) == 1: return leaves[0]
    if len(leaves) % 2 == 1: leaves = leaves + [leaves[-1]]
    parents = [hashlib.sha256(leaves[i] + leaves[i+1]).digest()
               for i in range(0, len(leaves), 2)]
    return merkle_root(parents)

def merkle_proof(leaves: List[bytes], idx: int) -> List[Tuple[bytes, str]]:
    """Return sibling hashes with positions for inclusion proof."""
    proof = []
    level = leaves[:]
    pos = idx
    while len(level) > 1:
        if len(level) % 2 == 1: level.append(level[-1])
        sib = pos ^ 1  # XOR flips last bit to get sibling index
        proof.append((level[sib], 'left' if pos % 2 == 1 else 'right'))
        level = [hashlib.sha256(level[i]+level[i+1]).digest()
```

```
                for i in range(0, len(level), 2)]
        pos //= 2
    return proof
```

A.4 Byzantine Fault Tolerance

The Byzantine Generals Problem (Lamport, Shostak, and Pease, 1982) formalizes distributed agreement in the presence of malicious participants. A set of n processes (generals) must reach consensus on a binary value despite up to f of them behaving arbitrarily—sending conflicting messages, withholding messages, or lying. A correct protocol must satisfy three properties simultaneously: Agreement (all loyal processes decide the same value), Validity (if the commanding process is loyal, all loyal processes adopt its value), and Termination (every loyal process eventually decides). In the blockchain context, Agreement maps to consistency of the transaction ledger, Validity to honest-block acceptance, and Termination to liveness—the chain keeps growing (Chapter 1).

The fundamental bound is $n > 3f$: with n processes and up to f Byzantine faults, consensus is achievable if and only if $n > 3f$, equivalently $f < n/3$. The necessity proof considers three groups of roughly $n/3$ processes each: A (commanded by the Byzantine commander to attack), B (commanded to retreat), and C (Byzantine). Process B cannot distinguish the scenario where the commander is Byzantine and C is honest from the scenario where the commander is honest and C is Byzantine, because the messages look identical. Breaking symmetry requires a third group large enough that honest overlap is guaranteed, forcing $n > 3f$. The sufficiency direction is constructive: the Lamport-Shostak-Pease oral messages algorithm achieves agreement with $3f + 1$ nodes in $f + 1$ rounds at O(n^(f+1)) message complexity (Chapter 1).

Practical BFT protocols reduce message complexity by leveraging authenticators. PBFT (Castro and Liskov, 1999) achieves $O(n^2)$ messages per consensus round through a three-phase pre-prepare/prepare/commit protocol, tolerating $f \leq \lfloor n/3 \rfloor$ faults. HotStuff (Yin et al., 2019) reaches $O(n)$ messages by having a leader aggregate votes into a quorum certificate using threshold signatures; any $2f + 1$ of n signers suffice to form a certificate that a single verifier can check in $O(1)$ time (Chapter 1).

The FLP impossibility result (Fischer, Lynch, and Paterson, 1985) proves that no deterministic protocol can simultaneously guarantee safety and liveness in a fully asynchronous network with even one crash-faulty process. The proof constructs an adversarial message schedule that keeps the system in a bivalent state—one where both 0 and 1 are still reachable—indefinitely by delaying messages from the faulty process at critical decision points. Real blockchain systems escape FLP by adopting partial synchrony: messages may stall arbitrarily before some unknown global stabilization time (GST) but arrive within a known bound Δ afterward. Protocols designed for partial synchrony maintain safety in all executions and guarantee liveness once the network stabilizes (Chapter 1).

```
# Minimum nodes required for f Byzantine faults
def min_nodes(f: int) -> int:
    return 3 * f + 1

# Maximum faults tolerable with n nodes
def max_faults(n: int) -> int:
    return (n - 1) // 3

# Quorum size: smallest set guaranteed to overlap any other quorum
def quorum_size(n: int) -> int:
    f = max_faults(n)
    return 2 * f + 1  # |Q1 ∩ Q2| >= f + 1

for f in [1, 2, 3, 10, 33]:
    n = min_nodes(f)
    print(f'f={f}: need n={n}, quorum={quorum_size(n)}')
```

A.5 Proof-of-Work Difficulty

Proof-of-work requires the miner to find a nonce such that the block header hash falls below a target T: H(nonce || header) < T, where H is SHA-256 applied twice and the output is interpreted as a 256-bit unsigned integer. The difficulty D is defined as D = max_target / T, where max_target = $2^{22'} - 1$ is the genesis difficulty target. Because each hash attempt produces an output that is uniformly distributed over $[0, 2^{256})$ under the random oracle model, the probability of success per attempt is $p = T / 2^{256} = 1/D$. Expected attempts per valid block is therefore E[attempts] = D (Chapter 1).

The inter-block time follows an exponential distribution by the memoryless property of Bernoulli trials at high speed. If the network's total hash rate is H_total attempts per second, the block arrival rate is λ = H_total / D, and inter-block gaps are distributed as $\mathrm{Exp}(\lambda)$ with mean $1/\lambda$. Bitcoin adjusts D every 2016 blocks (nominally two weeks) so that the average inter-block time stays near 600 seconds: D_new = D_old × (actual_time / target_time). The memoryless property $P(T > s + t \mid T > s) = P(T > t)$ means the expected remaining time to the next block is always 600 seconds regardless of how long the current block has been in progress—no miner gains an advantage from "warming up" (Chapter 1).

The Nakamoto double-spend probability quantifies the cost of rewriting history. If an attacker controls fraction q of hash rate and the honest network controls $p = 1 - q$, and the attacker must overcome a deficit of z blocks, the probability that the attacker ever catches up is P = (q/p)^z for $q < p$. This is the gambler's ruin formula with success probability q and failure probability p. For $q = 0.1$ and $z = 6$ confirmations, P ≈ (0.1/0.9)^6 ≈ 1.5×10^{-5}, establishing six confirmations as sufficient for ordinary transactions. As q approaches 0.5 from below, P approaches 1, and the security guarantee evaporates (Chapter 1).

Block reward halvings constrain long-run supply. Bitcoin's subsidy halves every 210,000 blocks. Starting at 50 BTC, the total supply is 210,000 × 50 × Σ(1/2)^i = 210,000 × 50 × 2 = 21,000,000 BTC. As the subsidy decays geometrically, fee revenue must replace it, or the security budget S = block_reward + fees shrinks below the threshold that makes an attack unprofitable (Chapter 1).

```
from math import exp

MAX_TARGET = 2**224 - 1  # Bitcoin genesis target

def expected_hashes(difficulty: float) -> float:
    return difficulty  # E[attempts] = D per block

def double_spend_prob(q: float, z: int) -> float:
    """Nakamoto formula: prob attacker overcomes z-block deficit."""
    p = 1.0 - q
    if q >= p: return 1.0
    return (q / p) ** z

# Six-confirmation safety for various attacker fractions
for q in [0.1, 0.2, 0.3, 0.4, 0.49]:
    p6 = double_spend_prob(q, 6)
    print(f'q={q:.2f}: P(catch up after 6 blocks) = {p6:.2e}')
```

A.6 Proof-of-Stake Selection

Proof-of-stake leader and committee selection must be unpredictable, unbiasable, and publicly verifiable. Verifiable Random Functions (VRFs) supply all three properties. A VRF is a tuple of algorithms (KeyGen, Evaluate, Verify). KeyGen produces a keypair (sk, pk). Evaluate takes sk and input x and returns a pseudorandom output y together with a proof π: $(y, \pi) = \text{VRF}(sk, x)$. Verify takes pk, x, y, and π and accepts if and only if y was correctly derived from sk and x. Crucially, for fixed sk and x, there is exactly one valid (y, π) pair, so the evaluator cannot shop for a favorable output (Chapter 4).

In practice, Algorand and Ouroboros Praos use VRFs for slot leadership. Each epoch begins with a public seed derived from recent block hashes. Validator i computes $(y\_i, \pi\_i) = \text{VRF}(sk\_i, seed \,||\, slot)$ and tests whether $y\_i / 2^{256} < \varphi(s\_i)$, where s_i is validator i's stake fraction and φ is a threshold function chosen so that the expected number of leaders per slot is 1. The validator broadcasts (y_i, π_i) only when selected, revealing slot leadership only at proposal time. An adversary monitoring the network cannot predict who will propose a block in a future slot because doing so requires knowing sk_i, which is never published (Chapter 4).

The threshold function $\varphi(s\_i) = 1 - (1 - f)\text{^}(s\_i)$ is chosen to give each staker a probability approximately proportional to their stake while ensuring P(at least one leader per slot) is close to 1. Setting the target leader count to $f \approx 0.05$ means any given slot has roughly a 5% chance of producing a block proposer, yielding an expected inter-block time that can be tuned by adjusting f. The probability that the slot has no leader is $(1 - f)\text{^}1 = 0.95$ for a single validator controlling the entire stake, falling exponentially as stake is distributed across many validators (Chapter 4).

Epoch randomness must itself be unbiasable. If the seed is derived from block hashes alone, the last block proposer in an epoch can withhold their block to select a more favorable seed—a form of last-revealer bias. Ouroboros Praos chains VRF outputs across epochs so that influencing the seed requires grinding against the VRF uniqueness guarantee, which is computationally intractable. Ethereum's RANDAO mixes BLS signature contributions from all validators who propose during the epoch, reducing but not eliminating last-revealer bias to a bounded range of slots (Chapter 4).

```
import hashlib, secrets

def vrf_evaluate(sk: bytes, x: bytes):
    """Toy VRF (real: ECVRF per RFC 9381 using elliptic curve)."""
    # Output: pseudorandom bytes
```

```
    y = hashlib.sha256(sk + x).digest()
    # Proof: simplified; real proof is an elliptic-curve NIZK
    proof = hashlib.sha256(sk + x + y).digest()
    return y, proof

def vrf_verify(pk: bytes, x: bytes, y: bytes, proof: bytes) -> bool:
    """Toy verification (real: check NIZK against pk)."""
    return len(y) == 32 and len(proof) == 32

def is_selected(y: bytes, stake_fraction: float) -> bool:
    """Check if VRF output falls below stake-proportional threshold."""
    y_int = int.from_bytes(y, 'big')
    threshold = int(stake_fraction * 2**256)
    return y_int < threshold
```

A.7 Zero-Knowledge Proofs

A zero-knowledge proof is an interactive or non-interactive protocol between a prover P and a verifier V. Three properties must hold. Completeness: if the statement is true and P follows the protocol honestly, V accepts with probability $\geq 1 - \varepsilon$. Soundness: if the statement is false, no computationally bounded cheating prover P* can convince V to accept except with probability $\leq \varepsilon$ (the soundness error). Zero-knowledge: there exists a probabilistic polynomial-time simulator S that, without access to the witness, produces a transcript distribution computationally indistinguishable from real interactions between P and V. The existence of S formalizes the intuition that V learns nothing beyond the truth of the statement (Chapter 4).

Pedersen commitments underpin confidential transactions and many ZK constructions. Given two independent elliptic curve generators G and H (with no known discrete logarithm relationship between them), the commitment to value v with blinding factor r is $C = vG + rH$. Hiding holds because C is uniformly distributed over the curve for any fixed v when r is chosen uniformly. Binding holds computationally: opening C to two different values would require computing the discrete log of H in base G. The homomorphic property $C_1 + C_2 = (v_1 + v_2)G + (r_1 + r_2)H$ means a verifier can confirm that input commitments sum to output commitments without learning any individual amount (Chapter 4).

The Schnorr identification protocol is the canonical interactive ZK proof for knowledge of a discrete logarithm. Prover P knows d such that Q = dG. The three-move protocol: (1) P samples nonce $k \leftarrow Z\_n$ uniformly, computes R = kG, and sends R to V. (2) V sends a random challenge $e \leftarrow Z\_n$. (3) P responds s = k + ed mod n. V accepts if sG = R + eQ. Correctness: sG = (k + ed)G = kG + e(dG) = R + eQ. Soundness: two accepting transcripts with the same R but different challenges, $e \neq e'$ yield (s – s') = (e – e')d mod n, so $d = (s - s')(e - e')^{-1}$ mod n is extracted efficiently. The Fiat-Shamir transform makes this non-interactive by replacing V's random challenge with e = H(R || Q || m), binding the challenge to the message m and preventing the prover from replaying a favorable transcript (Chapter 4).

zk-SNARKs (Succinct Non-Interactive Arguments of Knowledge) reduce any NP statement to an arithmetic circuit satisfiability problem, then prove circuit satisfaction in constant-size proofs. The Groth16 construction (2016) represents the circuit as a rank-1 constraint system and encodes it as polynomial equations evaluated at a secret point τ in the exponent via elliptic curve pairings. The common reference string contains values of the form $[\tau^i]_1$ and $[\tau^i]_2$ in two curve groups. A valid proof (A, B, C) satisfies the pairing equation $e(A, B) = e(\alpha, \beta) \cdot e(C, \delta) \cdot \prod e(public\_i, \gamma\_i)$. Verification requires exactly three pairing evaluations regardless of circuit size, producing proofs of about 200 bytes and verification times of roughly 1 ms. The trusted setup must destroy the toxic waste τ; exposure allows forging arbitrary proofs (Chapter 4).

zk-STARKs (Scalable Transparent Arguments of Knowledge) replace elliptic curve pairings with collision-resistant hash functions, eliminating the trusted setup entirely. The prover encodes the computation trace as a polynomial over a finite field, commits to it using a Merkle tree of evaluations, and applies the FRI (Fast Reed-Solomon Interactive Oracle Proof) protocol to prove the committed polynomial has bounded degree. Security reduces to the collision resistance of the hash function, so STARKs are post-quantum secure. The cost is proof size: a STARK for a computation of size T produces a proof of $O(\log^2 T)$ hashes, typically 50–200 KB versus the 200-byte SNARK. Verification is $O(\log^2 T)$ hash evaluations, which is still fast in absolute terms (Chapter 4).

Bulletproofs provide range proofs without any setup. To prove that a Pedersen-committed value v lies in [0, 2^k), the prover decomposes v in binary, creates bit commitments, and uses the inner product argument to prove that the bits are valid (each in {0,1}) and sum correctly to v. The inner product argument is itself a recursive protocol reducing an n-dimensional inner product to a single scalar check in O(log n) rounds. For a 64-bit range, a Bulletproof is approximately 670 bytes with no trusted setup, versus roughly 5 KB for naive per-bit range proofs. Multiple range proofs can be aggregated: proving m values in [0, 2^k) costs O(log(mk)) rather than m × O(log k) independently (Chapter 4).

```
import hashlib, secrets

# Schnorr identification protocol (toy; real: use secp256k1)
N = 0xFFFFFFFFFFFFFFFFFFFFFFFFFFFFFFFEBAAEDCE6AF48A03BBFD25E8CD0364141

def schnorr_prove(d: int, Q_bytes: bytes, message: bytes):
    """Non-interactive Schnorr proof via Fiat-Shamir."""
    k = secrets.randbelow(N - 1) + 1
    # R = k*G (omitting curve arithmetic; placeholder as bytes)
    R_bytes = hashlib.sha256(k.to_bytes(32, 'big')).digest()
    # Challenge e = H(R || Q || m)
    e = int.from_bytes(
        hashlib.sha256(R_bytes + Q_bytes + message).digest(), 'big') % N
    s = (k + e * d) % N
    return R_bytes, s

def pedersen_commit(v: int, r: int, G: int, H: int, p: int) -> int:
    """C = v*G + r*H (mod p); toy field version."""
    return (v * G + r * H) % p

# Homomorphic addition: C1 + C2 = commit(v1+v2, r1+r2)
p = 2**61 - 1  # Mersenne prime stand-in
G, H = 3, 5
v1, r1, v2, r2 = 10, 7, 5, 3
C1 = pedersen_commit(v1, r1, G, H, p)
C2 = pedersen_commit(v2, r2, G, H, p)
Csum = (C1 + C2) % p
Cdirect = pedersen_commit(v1 + v2, r1 + r2, G, H, p)
print(f'Homomorphic: C1+C2 == C(v1+v2, r1+r2): {Csum == Cdirect}')
```

A.8 Probability Distributions for Consensus Analysis

Binomial distribution: count successes across n independent Bernoulli trials, each with success probability p. The probability mass is $P(X = k) = C(n,k)\ p^k (1-p)^{(n-k)}$. For shard committee analysis (Chapter 16), suppose an adversary controls a fraction f of validators, you draw a committee of n members at random, and adversarial seats follow Binomial(n, f).

Chernoff bound: let X be the sum of independent Bernoulli variables with mean μ. Then $P(X > (1+\delta)\mu) \le \exp(-\mu\delta^2/3)$. Analysts use it to cap adversary concentration in shard committees when exact binomial arithmetic is overkill.

Exponential distribution: $P(T > t) = \exp(-\lambda t)$, mean $1/\lambda$, variance $1/\lambda^2$. It models inter-block gaps in PoW (Chapter 5). The memoryless fact $P(T > s+t \mid T > s) = P(T > t)$ is what keeps the race honest—extra time already burned does not buy a head start.

Gambler's ruin: a walk where the gambler holds i and the opponent N−i; each round the gambler wins with probability q. When $q < 1/2$, the probability of ever reaching N is $(q/p)^i / ((q/p)^N)$. Bitcoin (Chapter 5) maps the same formula onto a minority miner trying to erase a deficit of z blocks: $P = (q/p)^z$.

Selfish mining: a miner deviates from honest publication (Chapter 5) by hiding found blocks to skew rewards. If the selfish miner's hash share is α, expected revenue share can beat α once α climbs past about a third—or lower when the network tilts races their way. The payoff hinges on γ, the fraction of honest miners who build on the selfish fork during a race.

Block reward halving: Bitcoin's disinflationary rule (Chapter 5) halves the subsidy every 210,000 blocks—about four years. Supply is capped by the geometric sum $210{,}000 \times 50 \times \Sigma(1/2)^i = 21{,}000{,}000$ BTC. As subsidies fall, transaction fees must carry more of the security budget if incentives are to stay honest.

```
from math import comb, exp, sqrt, log

def binomial_cdf_upper(n, k_min, p):
    """P(X >= k_min) for X ~ Binomial(n, p)."""
    return sum(comb(n, k) * p**k * (1-p)**(n-k) for k in range(k_min, n+1))

def chernoff_upper(mu, delta):
    """Upper bound on P(X > (1+delta)*mu)."""
    return exp(-mu * delta**2 / 3)
```

```
# Example: shard security (Chapter 16)
# 156 validators per shard, 15% adversary, need >52 for takeover
p_exact = binomial_cdf_upper(156, 53, 0.15)
mu = 156 * 0.15
delta = (53 - mu) / mu
p_chernoff = chernoff_upper(mu, delta)
print(f'Shard takeover probability:')
print(f'  Exact binomial: {p_exact:.2e}')
print(f'  Chernoff bound: {p_chernoff:.2e} (upper bound)')
```

Birthday problem (collision resistance): sample n random values from a universe of size N; collision odds cross 50% near $n \approx 1.2\sqrt{N}$. For a k-bit hash, that is roughly 2^(k/2) work. Bitcoin's SHA-256 (k = 256), therefore, sits near 2^128 collision cost—far outside what is feasible. The same back-of-the-envelope fixes how wide hashes must be for block IDs and Merkle nodes (Chapter 5).

A.9 Information Theory for Decentralization

Shannon entropy: $H(X) = -\Sigma\, p(x) \log_2 p(x)$. It measures how "surprising" a distribution is. Chapter 9 uses it to score decentralization: fatter, more spread-out stake or hash shares mean higher entropy.

Normalized entropy: $H(X) / \log_2(n)$ with n participants. The scale runs from 0—one actor owns everything—to 1—a perfectly even split. That normalization beats raw entropy when you compare chains with different headcounts.

Gini coefficient: $G = (\Sigma_i \Sigma_r |x_i - x_r|) / (2n^2\mu)$, from 0 (perfect equality) to 1 (maximal inequality). It pairs with entropy by spotlighting how lumpy stake is.

Finality latency: clock time from submit to an irreversible commit (Chapter 9). Probabilistic finality under PoW follows P(reversal) = (q/p)^z, so you pick z confirmations to hit your risk budget. Deterministic BFT finality lands after a fixed number of rounds—often O(1) once GST holds. Economic finality in PoS waits until enough stake attests—on Ethereum, about two epochs (~12.8 minutes).

Nakamoto coefficient: the smallest number of entities that together control more than half the relevant resource—hash rate, stake, or block production. Sort shares descending; the coefficient is the smallest k with Σ_{i=1}^{k} s_i > 0.5. Larger numbers read as more decentralization (Chapter 9). A coefficient of 1 is full centralization; Bitcoin's pools often sit in the 3–5 range.

A.10 Finite Field Arithmetic for Erasure Coding

Data Availability Sampling (Chapter 17) leans on Reed–Solomon erasure codes over finite fields.

Reed–Solomon encoding: symbols d_0, d_1, ..., d_{k−1} define a degree-(k−1) polynomial $p(x) = \Sigma\, d_i\, x^i$. Evaluate at n > k distinct points for n coded symbols. Any k of them fix the polynomial (Lagrange interpolation), so you can rebuild the data.

2D extension (Chapter 16): lay k^2 data symbols in a k×k grid, extend every row from k to 2k symbols, then extend every column the same way. You end with a 2k×2k matrix where any k symbols along a row or column still suffice to recover the plane.

Celestia and dedicated DA layers: Celestia (Chapter 17) is a DA-only chain that couples 2D Reed–Solomon with sampling. Light nodes draw random cells from the extended matrix and check KZG proofs, so accepting unavailable data happens with probability at most (1/2)^s after s draws—confidence ramps exponentially.

Modular blockchain architecture: the modular story (Chapter 17) slices work into DA (publish the data), consensus (order it), settlement (arbitrate and bridge), and execution (update state). Each layer can be tuned on its own. The stack is only as strong as its weakest layer, while throughput scales with how far each layer can be pushed.

Cross-shard communication: transactions that touch more than one shard (Chapter 16) need atomicity across separate consensus zones. The usual choreography is to lock on the source (freeze state, emit a receipt), relay (a relayer may carry the receipt), and then commit or abort on the destination depending on validity. Message load scales as O(s) across s shards, and latency stacks the consensus rounds of every participant.

A.11 Lattice Problems for Post-Quantum Cryptography

ML-DSA (Chapter 18) rests on the Module Learning With Errors (MLWE) problem:

MLWE: you see public matrix A and public vector b = As + e, with secret s and a small discrete-Gaussian error e. Recovering s is far harder than solving a clean linear system. Best classical and quantum attacks still scale exponentially in the lattice dimension.

Shortest vector problem (SVP): given a lattice basis, find a shortest nonzero lattice vector. It is believed hard classically (best ~2^(0.292n)) and quantumly (~2^(0.265n)) once the dimension n passes roughly 500.

Grover's algorithm: quantum search over an unstructured N-item database in $O(\sqrt{N})$ queries—a quadratic edge on brute force. For symmetric crypto (Chapter 18), treat that as halving the bit strength: a 256-bit hash offers approximately 128-bit quantum resistance, and AES-128 about 64. That is why post-quantum symmetric designs double key sizes.

Hash-based signatures: schemes whose security is essentially collision resistance, not number-theoretic hardness (Chapter 18). SPHINCS+ (now SLH-DSA) stacks many-time Merkle trees over one-time Winternitz signatures in a hypertree, staying stateless. Signatures bulk up (~17–49 KB) versus lattice options (~2.4 KB for ML-DSA), but the assumption set is ultra-conservative.

Harvest now, decrypt later: record ciphertext today, break it once a big quantum machine arrives (Chapter 18). That prospect pushes early migration to post-quantum tools on chains, especially for long-lived secrets and payloads. Your planning horizon is roughly "quantum risk minus deployment lag."

A.12 Game Theory for Cryptoeconomic Analysis

Nash equilibrium (Chapter 13): a profile s* where every player i gets u_i(s*_i, s*_{-i}) ≥ u_i(s'_i, s*_{-i}) for every deviation s'_i.

Mechanism design: start from the behavior you want—honest play—and engineer rewards, penalties, and slashing so that outcome sits at equilibrium. PoS slashing (Chapter 6) is exactly that puzzle: penalties must make equivocation lose money for every stake size.

Nothing-at-stake: in naive PoS (Chapter 6), voting on every fork costs nothing extra because stake is not a consumable resource. Formally, hedging across forks beats picking one, so honest single-chain voting is dominated. Slashing fixes the incentive by burning capital for conflicting votes, flipping double-signing to negative expected value.

Gasper consensus: Ethereum's Gasper (Chapter 6) pairs Casper FFG for finality with LMD-GHOST for fork choice. FFG notarizes checkpoints every two epochs once a two-thirds supermajority attests. Accountable safety needs at least a third of total stake slashable before two finalized checkpoints can disagree.

Subgame-perfect equilibrium: Nash refined for sequential play—each player optimizes at every decision node, not only at the outset. Interactive fraud proofs (Chapter 15) assume both sides play that tightly through the bisection game.

State channels: an off-chain scaling pattern (Chapter 15). Parties lock state on-chain, then pass signed updates peer-to-peer. The contract is the judge: broadcast a stale state, and your counterparty can answer with a newer signature inside the challenge window. Safety needs at least one honest watcher who will post the latest state before the window shuts.

Plasma exit games: Plasma (Chapter 15) runs child chains that anchor roots to a parent. Users leave by proving balance inclusion in a committed route with a Merkle witness. A challenge window lets anyone disprove exits that spend already-spent outputs. If the operator hides data, exits collapse toward a messy mass-withdrawal because proofs vanish.

ZK-EVM compatibility levels: ZK rollups proving EVM work (Chapter 15) trade compatibility for prover cost. Type 1 proves raw Ethereum blocks—faithful but heavy. Type 2 tweaks state layouts for speed. Types 3–4 push further on prover time versus fidelity. Type 1 cost is dominated by Keccak and Merkle-style storage walks.

Cost-of-attack analysis: the cheapest spend to break safety or liveness. PoW bills hardware and power; PoS bills acquisition plus the opportunity cost of getting slashed. The budget must beat the upside from any attack, or rational actors will bite.

Tokenomics and monetary policy: how the native asset is issued and burned (Chapter 13). Bitcoin fixes supply at 21M with halving rewards. Ethereum chases a moving target: EIP-1559 burn tracks usage against issuance, aiming for net-zero or deflation when demand runs hot. Security needs S = block_reward + fees to exceed max extractable MEV from an attack.

Long-range attacks: PoS-specific (Chapter 6): an ex-staker forks from deep history. Old validators may have unstaked, so signatures on the alternate chain dodge today's slashing. Defenses include weak-subjectivity checkpoints—nodes refuse to rewind past a recently agreed finalized block—and unbonding windows longer than the worst-case reorg you will tolerate.

A.13 Quorum Systems and Message Complexity

Chapter 7 leans on quorum systems and communication complexity all the way through its BFT treatment. This section pins down the math.

Quorum intersection: a quorum family Q over nodes N meets the intersection property if every $Q1, Q2 \in Q$ satisfies $|Q1 \cap Q2| \geq f + 1$ for up to f Byzantines. Then any two quorums share an honest member, so they cannot certify conflicting truths. With $n = 3f + 1$ nodes, the smallest quorums have size $2f + 1$ and overlap in at least $f + 1$ nodes.

3f + 1 lower bound: the smallest node count for BFT consensus. The argument stitches three facts: (1) two quorums must share more than f nodes so some honest node lies in the intersection, giving quorum size $Q > (n + f)/2$; (2) honest nodes must still muster a full quorum, so $n - f \geq Q$; and (3) combine to get $2(n - f) > n + f$, i.e., $n > 3f$.

Message complexity: messages per consensus round as a function of n. PBFT blows up to $O(n^2)$ because every replica shouts in prepare and commit—pre-prepare costs $n - 1$, prepare $(n - 1)^2$, and commit $n(n - 1)$. HotStuff drops to $O(n)$ by aggregating votes with threshold signatures at the leader, who then multicasts one quorum certificate.

Threshold signatures: in a (t, n)-threshold scheme, any t signers (but no smaller set) can forge the group signature. In HotStuff (Chapter 7), $t = 2f + 1$; the leader fuses shares into a QC anyone can check in constant time, which is how communication goes linear.

FLP impossibility: Fischer, Lynch, and Paterson (1985) showed no deterministic consensus can guarantee both safety and liveness in a fully asynchronous network with even one faulty process. The proof builds a nasty schedule that keeps execution bivalent forever. Real BFT sidesteps this by partial synchrony: messages may stall until some unknown GST, then deliver within a known Δ.

View change correctness: handoff from one leader to the next must not drop a decided value. The new leader gathers $2f + 1$ VIEW-CHANGE messages carrying prepared evidence from the old view. Their union still covers at least $f + 1$ honest states, so nothing committed disappears.

Tendermint consensus: Tendermint Core (Chapter 7) runs two voting rounds—prevote and precommit—under partial synchrony. If more than two-thirds precommit the same block in a round, that block is final. ABCI splits consensus from the application, so arbitrary state machines inherit the same BFT shell.

A.14 DAG Theory and Probabilistic Sampling

Chapter 8 introduces DAG-based consensus and probabilistic sampling. The tools below back analyses of Avalanche, GHOST, and Ouroboros.

Directed Acyclic Graph (DAG): a directed graph $G = (V, E)$ with no cycles. In Avalanche (Chapter 8), vertices are transactions and edges point to parents. A topological order respects all ancestry. The shape lets non-conflicting txs run in parallel.

Metastable consensus: in Avalanche's Snowball, each node polls k random peers per round and flips toward a supermajority when at least α of k agree. A tiny initial tilt amplifies fast. With n nodes, you expect O(log n) rounds w.h.p., because each round multiplicatively widens the lead.

Snowball confidence threshold: a node finalizes after β straight rounds where the same value holds a supermajority. Reversal probability after that is bounded by $(1 - \alpha/k)^\beta$, dying off exponentially in β. Snowball's persistent tallies beat Snowflake's single counter—an attacker must unwind accumulated margin, not one lucky flip.

Subtree weight (GHOST): GHOST picks the child whose subtree is heaviest at each fork, counting every descendant block. Longest-chain discards honest orphans; GHOST folds their work into the weight. High orphan rates still leave the 50% threshold intact because honest hash power stacks in the subtree either way.

Verifiable Random Functions (VRFs): Ouroboros Praos (Chapter 8) uses them for stealthy leader lottery. A VRF F_sk(x) outputs y with proof π; verifiers with the public key check y = F_sk(x) without learning the secret, yet y looks uniform without sk. Each stakeholder can test locally whether they own a slot before broadcasting a block.

Formal security under simulation: Ouroboros Classic (Chapter 8) argues via an ideal functionality—no PPT adversary with a <50% stake can tell real runs from ideal ones beyond negligible bias. That simulation yields safety (common prefix) and liveness (growth and quality) in the synchronous model.

A.15 Authenticated Data Structures

Chapter 10 covers UTXO versus accounts and the authenticated structures that back state. Here is the math for Merkle trees, tries, and proof systems that the chapter cites.

Merkle tree proof complexity: n leaves give depth $\lceil \log_2 n \rceil$. An inclusion proof ships one sibling hash per level, so size is O(log n). Near 200M Ethereum accounts, expect about 28 SHA-256 nodes (~896 bytes). Verification walks from leaf to root in O(log n) hashes.

Merkle-Patricia Trie: Ethereum's world state lives in a radix-16 Patricia trie—branches (16 kids plus optional value), extensions (compressed shared path), and leaves (tail path + value). Nodes hash with Keccak-256. The trie root in each header commits to the whole world state, so light clients check balances or storage with O(log n) proofs.

UTXO set model: global state is the set of unspent outputs (Chapter 10). A transaction is legal when (1) inputs exist in the UTXO set, (2) scripts authorize the spend, and (3) output sums do not exceed input sums—the gap is the fee. Disjoint input sets validate in parallel.

Account state transition: in the account model (Chapter 10), $\sigma' = \Upsilon(\sigma, T)$ maps world state σ and transaction T to the next σ', adjusting sender balance and nonce, recipient balance, and contract storage as needed. The nonce serializes transactions so replays fail.

State growth and pruning: full nodes must hold the live UTXO set or full world state. Bitcoin's UTXO holds on the order of 80–90 million entries (~5–7 GB); Ethereum's trie blows past ~150 GB. Pruning drops historical snapshots but keeps the frontier, shrinking storage from O(blocks × state) to O(state). Expiry ideas go further—cold-state drops until a witness revives it.

Verkle trees: Chapter 10's vector-commitment hybrid keeps logarithmic proofs but shrinks constants versus Merkle-Patricia. Internal nodes commit to children with polynomial or inner-product arguments instead of concatenated hashes. Ethereum's hoped-for migration cuts witnesses from ~3 KB per account touch to ~150 bytes, easing stateless validation.

A.16 Computational Metering and Fee Markets

Chapter 11 walks VMs, gas, and EIP-1559. These notes formalize metering and fee dynamics.

Gas metering: every EVM opcode carries a gas price tied to compute and state touch. Arithmetic lands around 3–5 gas; first-time storage writes jump to 20,000—a ~7,000× gap that mirrors how permanent state taxes every future node. Memory expansion charges $3w + w^2/512$ for w 32-byte words, punishing ballooning RAM.

EIP-1559 base fee adjustment: the base fee moves block to block to chase 50% gas usage. With current fee B, used gas G_used, and target G_target (half the cap), the next block uses $B' = B \times (1 + (G\_used - G\_target) / G\_target / 8)$. The 8 cap limits swings to 12.5% per block, so fees converge exponentially toward the clearing price at half-full blocks.

EIP-2929 access lists: the first touch of a storage slot in a tx costs 2,100 gas; later reads of the same slot cost 100—a 21:1 split that mirrors disk miss versus cache hit. Declared access lists pre-warm slots, turning cold paths warm and stabilizing estimates.

Parallel execution scheduling: optimal batching is NP-hard (think graph coloring). Greedy schedulers pack txs so no batch contains write-write or read-write clashes on the same key. Speedup tracks how sparse that conflict graph is: plain transfers parallelize nicely; DeFi hitting shared pools often serializes. Chapter 11 shows read/write set tracking makes the practical version workable.

WebAssembly (WASM) execution model: WASM (Chapter 11) is a compact binary ISA built for sandboxed, near-native speed. Unlike the EVM's 256-bit words, WASM leans on 32- and 64-bit ints, yielding order-of-magnitude gains on heavy math. WASM has no native gas counter, so chain runtimes inject metering at compile time, ticking a gas variable on basic-block edges.

Turing completeness and the halting problem: the EVM (Chapter 11) can simulate any Turing machine given enough resources—and halting is undecidable in general. Gas is the circuit breaker: each step burns gas, and execution stops when the meter hits zero. Undecidability becomes a bounded resource question, so termination is guaranteed within the limit.

A.17 Auction Theory and Transaction Ordering

Chapter 12 follows txs through mempools and MEV. This block spells out the auction and ordering vocabulary underneath.

First-price sealed-bid auction: the pre-1559 gas market where users name a price and builders pack the highest bids first. Strategic overlap inflates payments under congestion. EIP-1559 swaps that for a posted base fee plus a priority tip.

MEV as ordering profit: maximal extractable value (Chapter 12) is what you can skim by reordering, inserting, or censoring pending txs. Formally, for pending set T and state σ, MEV is the maximum over valid permutations π of profit(σ, π(T)). Familiar plays are arbitrage, sandwiching, and liquidations.

Proposer-builder separation (PBS): split ordering from inclusion. Builders fight in an auction for the richest block; the proposer takes the winning package. MEV becomes a competitive market instead of a centralizing freebie for one validator.

Commit-reveal ordering: an MEV brake where txs land encrypted, then decrypt only after the order is fixed. Builders cannot front-run what they cannot read. You need threshold decryption so no single party unlocks early.

A.18 Temporal Logic and Model Checking

Chapter 14 applies formal methods to protocols. Below: temporal logics, model checking, and symbolic execution in compact form.

Linear Temporal Logic (LTL): specifications over infinite traces. Beyond Boolean connectives you get G (always), F (eventually), X (next), U (until), and R (release). G(proposed → F committed) is liveness—every proposal finishes. G(¬(committed_A ∧ committed_B)) for conflicting A, B is safety—no double commit.

Safety and liveness: safety means "nothing bad ever happens"—any violation has a finite prefix that cannot be salvaged. Liveness means "something good eventually happens"—every prefix can extend to success. Alpern and Schneider (1987) split any linear-time property into a safety part and a liveness part. In BFT, agreement sits on the safety side; termination on the liveness side.

Kripke structures: $M = (S, S_0, R, L)$ with finite states S, initials $S_0 \subseteq S$, transitions $R \subseteq S \times S$, and labels L: S → 2^AP. Protocols become Kripke models: states capture views, queues, and chain heads; edges are sends, receives, and timeouts.

Model checking: given M and an LTL formula φ, decide if M ⊨ φ. Standard pipeline builds a Büchi automaton for ¬φ, forms the product M × A_{¬φ}, and hunts accepting cycles—witnesses are counterexamples. Complexity is O(|M| × 2^|φ|): linear in the model, exponential in the formula size.

State space explosion: the curse of distributed verification. n processes with s local states can blow up to s^n globals—PBFT at n=4, s=10 is 10,000 states; n=100 is north of 10^200. Chapter 14 leans on symmetry collapse, partial-order reduction, and bounded depth to cope.

Symbolic execution: run code on symbolic inputs, forking at branches and feeding path conditions to an SMT solver. For chains (Chapter 14), it can surface Byzantine message sequences that drive two honest nodes to different commits.

Proof assistants: Coq, Isabelle/HOL, and kin (Chapter 14) check proofs interactively. Unlike finite model checking, they can quantify over infinite families—but human effort jumps. Highlights include machine-checked Casper FFG and Tendermint safety arguments.

A.19 Advanced Cryptographic Primitives and Open Problems

Chapter 19 surveys open fronts—verifiable computation, private compliance, and bridges. These notes ground the heavier crypto primitives that chapter references.

Verifiable computation: a prover runs f(x), emits π, and verifiers accept the output without redoing f. You only win if verification is o(T) in the compute time T; otherwise, re-execution was cheaper. ZK-SNARKs hit O(1) verification and O(T × polylog T) proving.

Incrementally verifiable computation (IVC): after each step, publish a proof that covers the step and the prior proof. After n steps, one proof vouches for the whole chain of steps yet verifies in constant time. Chapter 19 uses IVC as the hinge for trust-minimized light clients that check history with a single proof.

Polynomial commitment schemes: commit to p(x), later open p(z) = y without dumping the whole polynomial. KZG (Chapter 19) gets O(1)-size proofs from pairings—one group element and two pairings to verify. That engine powers Danksharding DA and plenty of SNARK stacks.

Zero-knowledge compliance: Chapter 19 describes protocols that prove regulatory compliance without revealing private data. In ZK, a user shows a transaction satisfies predicate P—for example, sender not on a sanctions list and amount below a threshold—without revealing the sender's identity or the amount. You prove overcommitments, e.g., Pedersen C = g^v h^r with v below the threshold without revealing v.

Bridge security models: bridges (Chapter 19) move value across chains. Trust lives on a spectrum: multisig committees (security = honesty of signers) versus light-client or ZK proofs of source consensus (security tracks the source chain). Neither chain natively understands the other's fork choice without help.

The scalability trilemma: Chapter 19 asks whether decentralization, security, and scale can coexist. If each node only handles a 1/c slice of traffic, corrupting a 1/c slice of nodes might own a shard—security and decentralization tug. DA sampling plus validity proofs are the usual escape hatch: verify without reading every byte, so throughput rises without linearly cheapening the attack.

Sustainable consensus: Chapter 19 looks for security with less energy. Proof-of-useful-work tries to mine socially useful puzzles, but the puzzle must stay verifiable, tunable, and actually useful—hard to square. PoS erases the energy bill yet concentrates capital when staking rewards compound for whales.

Homomorphic encryption: schemes where E(a) ⊗ E(b) matches E(a • b) for some • (Chapter 19). Partial schemes handle one op (Paillier adds). FHE allows anything on ciphertexts but pays 10,000–1,000,000× overhead. Chapter 19 floats FHE for private contracts that run on encrypted state validators never see in the clear.

Secure multi-party computation (MPC): n parties compute $f(x_1,\ldots,x\_n)$ on private inputs without leaking beyond the output (Chapter 19). Ideal world: party i learns only what f implies. On-chain, MPC shows up in DKG for threshold keys, sealed-bid auctions, and shared analytics; generic protocols often cost $O(n^2)$ communication per multiplied gate.

APPENDIX B

Security Best Practices

This appendix is practical security guidance for developers, node operators, and anyone designing protocols—pulled together from incidents and patterns the main text cites across Chapters 1–19.

B.1 Trust and System Design (Chapter 1)

Name your trust assumptions out loud. Every distributed system still trusts something. Before you build on a chain or put capital in, spell out what that is: the consensus layer (>50% honest hash power? >2/3 honest stake?), the software stack (clients, contracts), the crypto (curve hardness, hash security), and the network (how messages are delivered). "Trustless" is a slogan, not a fact—know what trust is left and whether it fits your threat model.

Byzantine fault awareness for system design. The Byzantine Generals setup (Chapter 1) already shows three nodes and one traitor can deadlock consensus. You need at least 3f+1 nodes to survive f Byzantines. Use that when sizing multisigs, validator sets, and bridge committees: 3-of-5 tolerates one bad signer; 2-of-3 tolerates none.

Avoid single points of failure. Centralized pieces blow up no matter how strong the math is. Mt. Gox (~850K BTC), Equifax (~147M records), and a long list of bridge hacks all trace to trusting one party too far. Where you cannot avoid centralization—sequencers, oracles—ship escape hatches, forced inclusion, and a credible path toward real decentralization.

N. Savant, *Blockchain Foundations*, https://doi.org/10.1007/979-8-8688-2891-1

Merkle proof verification (Chapter 2). For light clients, state reads, or cross-chain payloads, check proofs against a root you actually trust—a finalized header. Length should match the expected depth (O(log n) hashes for n leaves); odd lengths are a red flag. Treat roots from random peers as untrusted until proven.

B.2 Cryptographic Implementation (Chapters 2, 3)

Do not roll your own cryptography. Lean on audited, battle-tested libraries—Python: cryptography, pynacl, py_ecc; production C/C++: libsodium, OpenSSL, and Bitcoin's secp256k1.

Constant-time comparisons. MACs, signatures, and hashes—compare them with a constant-time primitive or you invite timing leaks. In Python, hmac.compare_digest(). Plain equality checks on secrets are asking for trouble.

Secure random number generation (Chapter 2). Pull bytes from a CSPRNG: secrets.token_bytes() or os.urandom(). random.random() is the wrong tool for keys, nonces, or anything an adversary might guess. Consensus itself leans on unguessable randomness for leaders, nonces, and derivations.

Hash function selection (Chapter 2). Match the hash to the job. SHA-256 gives ~ 128-bit collision strength (birthday bound), not 256. Keccak-256 diversifies structure away from SHA-2—if SHA-2 ever wobbles, Keccak may not. Bitcoin doubles SHA-256 partly to blunt length-extension issues in plain Merkle-Damgård SHA-256.

Birthday attack awareness (Chapter 2). Collision work scales like 2^(n/2) for an n-bit hash, so SHA-256's collision floor is 2^128. That matters for Merkle trees, commitments, and any scheme that assumes collision resistance. When in doubt, pick hashes whose birthday margin clears ~2^100.

Nonce management (Chapter 3). Reusing an ECDSA nonce across two signatures leaks the secret key—the PlayStation 3 break-in in 2010 was the poster child. RFC 6979 deterministic nonces remove that footgun; EdDSA is deterministic by design. For greenfield signing, EdDSA often beats ECDSA on this axis alone.

Signature malleability (Chapter 3). ECDSA admits (r, s) and (r, −s mod n) for the same message, so an outsider can flip the signature and the txid. Anything that treats the pre-confirm tx hash as a unique ID breaks. SegWit moved witness data out of the txid; Schnorr drops the malleability class entirely.

Rogue key attacks in multisig (Chapter 3). Naive Schnorr aggregation lets a malicious peer publish $Q_2 = Q_2' - Q_1$ and sign for the "combined" key alone. MuSig/MuSig2 fix that by committing to the full key set before aggregation. Never ship a naive key addition for Schnorr multisig.

Key storage. Encrypt at rest, wipe secrets from memory after use, and keep keys out of logs, prints, and stack traces. Validators belong on HSMs; in dev, environment variables or encrypted key files beat hardcoded literals every time.

B.3 Zero-Knowledge Proof Security (Chapter 4)

Trusted setup ceremony safety. Groth16-style SNARKs need a setup whose toxic waste must vanish—keep it, and you can forge proofs, mint an infinite supply of privacy coins, or drain a rollup. Mitigations: MPC, where only one honest participant must show up; universal setups like PLONK or STARKs that skip trusted setup entirely.

ZK proof system selection. Groth16: tiny proofs (~200 B) but per-circuit setup. PLONK: universal setup, ~500 B proofs. STARKs: no trusted setup, post-quantum flavor, and ~100 KB proofs. Bulletproofs: strong range proofs, no setup, slower verification. Pick the stack that fits your threat model and latency budget.

Range proof requirement. Hide amounts behind commitments, and you must prove every output sits in range—otherwise a "negative" commitment mints coins from air. Bulletproofs are the usual answer. If a confidential tx design skips range proofs, it is not safe.

Commitment scheme best practices. Pedersen gives you perfect hiding and computational binding—but always add randomness; deterministic commitments on small domains get brute-forced. Remember binding falls to discrete log, hence quantum pressure; for PQ settings, prefer hash-based commitments.

VRF for on-chain randomness. For leaders or any lottery, a VRF beats raw block hashes—miners can always withhold blocks they dislike. VRFs give uniqueness, pseudorandomness without the secret key, and public verifiability. Used by Algorand, Cardano (Ouroboros), and Ethereum's RANDAO.

B.4 Smart Contract Security

Reentrancy (Chapters 11, 14). Still the classic smart-contract exploit: an external call bounces back into your contract before balances and flags settle. Prefer checks-effects-interactions, or a reentrancy mutex, so state is sane before you hand control outward.

Integer overflow/underflow (Chapter 11). Pre-0.8.0 Solidity wrapped arithmetic silently. Use SafeMath or move to 0.8+, where overflows revert by default.

Access control. Pause, upgrade, and admin—gate them to real owners. OpenZeppelin's Ownable/AccessControl beats one-off modifiers that sprawl and rot.

Oracle manipulation (Chapter 12). Spot DEX prices on-chain are flash-loan toys. For anything material, lean on TWAPs with sane windows or decentralized feeds like Chainlink.

Front-running and MEV protection (Chapter 12). Public mempools leak your trade before it lands. For size, auctions, or governance, use commit-reveal, private relays (e.g., Flashbots Protect), or routing that understands MEV.

Slippage tolerance (Chapter 12). Cap slippage on DEX swaps—unbounded slippage is a sandwich invitation. Ballpark 0.5–1% on stables and 1–3% on volatile pairs; never ship "infinite" slippage in production.

Gas optimization and DoS resistance (Chapter 11). Loops over user-grown arrays are gas bombs—an attacker pads the array until the tx cannot finish. Prefer pull payments; keep on-chain data lean; remember EVM memory cost grows quadratically, and cap accordingly.

Stack depth attacks (Chapter 11). The EVM stack stops at 1,024 slots; deep nesting can revert in surprising places. Flatten call graphs and stress-test worst-case depth.

B.5 Consensus and Node Operation

Client diversity (Chapter 6). Run a minority client. If 70% of stakes run one implementation and it bricks, the chain forks around you. On Ethereum, Lighthouse, Lodestar, Nimbus, or Teku break concentration versus a single dominant binary.

Key management for validators (Chapter 6). Split hot keys (daily attestations) from cold keys (withdrawals, big moves). Threshold schemes help when policy demands more than one human.

Slashing protection database (Chapters 6, 13). Log every attestation and proposal you sign; before a new signature, refuse anything that would equivocate or surround-vote. That database has to survive crashes, migrations, and reinstalls.

Weak subjectivity checkpoints (Chapter 6). After a long nap, sync from a checkpoint you actually trust—explorer hash, team publish, and close friend's node. Past the weak-subjectivity window (~2–4 weeks on Ethereum), pure protocol rules no longer tell you which history is real; long-range fraud becomes plausible.

Nothing-at-stake awareness (Chapter 6). Without slashing, PoS voters can back every fork for free. Before you bond stake, confirm the chain punishes double-signing for real.

Inactivity leak monitoring (Chapters 6, 13). When finality stalls, Ethereum bleeds offline validators. Watch network-wide finality health and keep uptime—penalties compound.

Monitoring (Chapters 6, 9). Track inclusion rates, proposal luck, and sync-committee duty—and alert on weird swings. Network-wide slashings are an early smoke alarm for consensus trouble.

Disaster recovery (Chapter 6). Practice failover, but never duplicate the same validator keys online—that is slashable equivocation. Pair drills with a slashing DB that outlives reboots.

MEV-boost configuration (Chapter 12). Run multiple relays, watch their health, and fall back to the local building when they all fail. Read relay filters against your ethics; benchmark rewards against the network so misconfiguration does not hide in plain sight.

B.6 Proof of Work Security

Double-spending awareness (Chapter 1). The attack consensus exists to stop: pay, let the counterparty ship, then publish a longer chain without the payment. Defense is depth—more confirmations mean exponentially smaller reversal odds. High-value handoffs on zero confs are reckless.

51% attack defenses (Chapter 5). Match confirmation count to the chain's security budget. Bitcoin often uses six confs for serious value; tiny-hash chains need more headroom. Remember P(reversal) = (q/p)^z with attacker share q, honest p = 1−q, and z confirmations.

Selfish mining awareness (Chapter 5). With ~25–33% hash power (γ-dependent), withholding blocks turns profitable. If one pool nears that band, assumptions weaken—protocols and communities should push pool fragmentation.

Difficulty manipulation risks (Chapter 5). Short retarget windows invite miners to game cadence—hash in easy epochs, vanish in hard ones. Prefer difficulty logic that resists that timing (EMA-style tuning over naive ratios).

B.7 BFT and Consensus Monitoring

Quorum safety monitoring (Chapter 7). On BFT chains, watch how many validators are actually live. You need 2f+1 for progress; if you are skating near that line, page someone—at exactly 2f+1, there is zero slack for the next fault.

View change frequency (Chapter 7). Spiky view churn usually means bad leaders, bad networks, or someone poking the protocol. Periodic blips smell like ops; correlated spikes smell like attacks—investigate both.

Probabilistic finality understanding (Chapters 5, 8). On Bitcoin, Avalanche, and GHOSTy forks, "final" is a probability, not a light switch. Set confirmation tiers by ticket size—big value needs more confs; one conf is never "done" for serious money.

Decentralization monitoring (Chapter 9). Watch the Nakamoto coefficient, Gini, HHI, geography, and client mix. Drifting concentration means coordinated takeover gets easier. Useful tripwires: Nakamoto < 10, HHI > 0.1, or any actor past ~20% of consensus power.

Attack cost-benefit analysis (Chapter 13). Occasionally ask whether the security budget still dominates the upside of an exploit. If token price craters while TVL stays fat, economics can flip long before the crypto does.

B.8 Protocol Design

Adversarial thinking. Treat every role—miners, validators, users, and outsiders—as potentially hostile. Shape incentives so honesty pays better than the best deviation, even for whales.

Formal specification (Chapter 14). Before you code, pin the protocol in something precise—TLA+, Alloy, or tight state-machine pseudocode. English alone breeds incompatible implementations and consensus bugs.

Security budget (Chapter 13). The value flowing to consensus actors has to exceed the profit of the nastiest attack; otherwise, economics overrules Merkle roots every time.

Upgrade mechanisms. Plan how parameters evolve. Hard forks need everyone marching; soft forks need a supermajority. Anything that will move—gas limits, fees, staking knobs—should have a governance path instead of folklore.

B.9 Development Process

Audit before deployment (Chapter 14). Serious money deserves at least two serious, independent audits. They catch plenty; they still cannot promise zero bugs.

Bug bounty programs (Chapter 14). Pay for severity. Immunefi-style programs have bailed out protocols by paying whitehats instead of griefers.

Formal verification (Chapter 14). For crown-jewel contracts or core logic, tools like Certora, Halmos, or K can prove properties for all inputs—stronger than tests alone and expensive in time and expertise.

Incremental deployment. Launch with training wheels—admin keys, caps, circuit breakers, and timelocks—then shed them only as production evidence piles up.

Monitoring and incident response (Chapter 14). Automate alerts for weird on-chain moves, TVL cliffs, and sneaky governance. Keep a war room list: core team, auditors, and bounty platform.

B.10 Layer-2 and Rollup Operation

Sequencer monitoring (Chapter 15). If you run the sequencer, watch L1 inclusion, batch compression, and fraud windows. Keep an ETH buffer on L1—think ~48 hours of headroom for data posts.

Escape hatch testing (Chapter 15). Exercise the L1 forced-inclusion path on a schedule so a censoring sequencer cannot strand users silently.

Fraud proof readiness (Chapter 15). On optimistic rollups, someone honest must watch state roots for the full challenge window—seven days is a long time to nap if a bad root slips through.

UTXO management (Chapter 10). Use real coin selection (largest-first for simplicity and branch-and-bound to save fees), merge dust when fees are cheap, and stop address reuse—one receive, one address.

B.11 Data Availability and Sharding

Shard committee monitoring (Chapter 16). Watch how randomness assigns validators; rotation should feel unpredictable, and stake should not pile into one shard. Flag bins that beat what binomial noise allows.

Data availability verification (Chapters 16, 17). Run DAS light clients instead of trusting hand-wavy attestations. If you operate a rollup, periodically reconstruct DA blobs from Ethereum, Celestia, EigenDA, or whatever sits underneath.

Blob posting monitoring (Chapter 17). Under EIP-4844, blob fees breathe with demand—budget spikes, and keep a calldata fallback if blobs go irrational. Blobs expire ~18 days; archive anything you must keep longer.

Restaking correlation risk (Chapter 17). Stacking EigenLayer AVSs stacks correlated slash risk—one cloud region can wipe several commitments at once. Diversify AVSs and infra; never restake more than you can eat in a correlated blow-up.

B.12 Post-Quantum Preparation

Crypto agility (Chapter 18). Make crypto swappable—addresses, verifiers, and KDFs should not be hardwired to ECDSA forever.

Key exposure audit (Chapter 18). Any address that has sent a transaction has exposed its public key. Consider consolidating to fresh addresses that have never been sent—hash-based derivation buys a little PQ headroom.

Harvest-now-decrypt-later awareness (Chapter 18). Public chains are write-once posterity—today's exposed keys may fall to tomorrow's quantum machines. Long holds should sit behind addresses whose pubkeys have never hit the chain. Planning starts now, not when CRQCs land.

PQ software readiness (Chapter 18). Prototype with liboqs / pqcrypto so you know the signature size and verify latency before a forced migration.

B.13 Privacy and Compliance

Privacy-preserving compliance (Chapter 19). Bake compliance into private features from day one—ZK can prove policy without broadcasting amounts and counterparties. Build selective disclosure paths for AML/KYC, sanctions, and tax realities.

Bridge security evaluation (Chapter 19). Before using or building on a bridge, read its trust model. Prefer trust-minimized designs—IBC light clients, ZK-verified bridges—over committee multisigs when you can. Practice has burned >$2.5B, almost entirely on committee setups. Still check committee size, key handling, slashing, and insurance.

Governance attack prevention (Chapter 19). Watch flash-loan votes, apathy exploits, and trojan parameter tweaks. Timelocks and multi-phase votes on big changes buy time to react.

APPENDIX C

Formal Security Definitions

This appendix pulls together the formal security definitions the book uses across Chapters 1–19. Each entry is stated tightly, with pointers to where it shows up.

C.1 Byzantine Consensus Properties (Chapters 1, 7)

Definition C.1 (Agreement): Every honest participant settles on the same value. On a chain, that reads as one canonical history for all honest nodes. Formally: for honest i, j, if i decides v and j decides v′, then v = v′. (Chapters 1, 7, 14)

Definition C.2 (Validity): When the commander (proposer) is honest, every honest party adopts that proposal. For blockchains, the agreed state should reflect real inputs from honest actors—a valid block only carries valid transactions from honest proposers. (Chapters 1, 7)

Definition C.3 (Termination/Liveness): Every honest participant eventually decides; the protocol cannot spin forever. Operationally, the chain keeps finalizing blocks. Formally, for each valid submitted transaction, some finite time later it sits in a finalized block. Liveness may need synchrony caveats. (Chapters 1, 7, 14)

Definition C.4 (Byzantine Fault Tolerance): The protocol keeps agreement, validity, and termination even if up to f of n nodes behave arbitrarily—conflicting messages, lies, collusion, or silence. The textbook bound is $n \geq 3f + 1$; with three nodes and one traitor, consensus is impossible. (Chapters 1, 7)

Definition C.5 (FLP Impossibility): In a fully asynchronous network, no deterministic protocol solves consensus with even one faulty process while guaranteeing both safety and liveness. Real chains dodge FLP via partial synchrony (PBFT, Tendermint), probabilistic work (Nakamoto), randomness (Ben-Or, Algorand), or economics. (Chapter 7)

N. Savant, *Blockchain Foundations*, https://doi.org/10.1007/979-8-8688-2891-1

Definition C.6 (Partial Synchrony): There is an unknown global stabilization time (GST); after GST, every message arrives within a known Δ, while before GST, delays are unbounded. PBFT, Tendermint, and HotStuff assume this: safety always and liveness once the network settles. (Chapter 7)

Definition C.7 (CAP Theorem): You cannot have all three—Consistency (everyone sees the same data), Availability (every query answers), and Partition tolerance (the network splits cleanly)—at once. Chains trade off differently: Bitcoin and Ethereum lean AP (stay live in partitions, converge later); Tendermint and PBFT lean CP (stay consistent, may halt). (Chapter 1)

C.2 Cryptographic Hash Function Properties (Chapter 2)

Definition C.8 (Preimage Resistance/One-Wayness): Given h = H(x), finding any preimage x should be infeasible. For SHA-256, think ~2^256 classical work or ~2^128 under Grover. Typical uses: addresses from hashed public keys, PoW hashing. (Chapters 2, 5, 18)

Definition C.9 (Second Preimage Resistance/Weak Collision Resistance): Given x_1, finding $x_2 \neq x_1$ with $H(x_1) = H(x_2)$ should be infeasible—about 2^256 work for SHA-256. That backs transaction integrity: you cannot swap payloads while keeping the same digest. (Chapter 2)

Definition C.10 (Collision Resistance/Strong Collision Resistance): Finding any distinct x_1, x_2 with $H(x_1) = H(x_2)$ should be infeasible—birthday bound ~2^128 for SHA-256. Merkle trees, block linking, and commitments lean on this. Grover barely helps with collision search. (Chapters 2, 5, 18)

C.3 Digital Signature Properties (Chapter 3)

Definition C.11 (Authentication): Only the secret-key holder could have produced the signature; anyone with the public key can check it. Every on-chain spend is exactly that claim—"I authorize this move." (Chapter 3)

Definition C.12 (Integrity): Flip a single bit of the signed message, and verification fails. Tampering with a signed transaction is supposed to stick out immediately. (Chapters 2, 3)

Definition C.13 (Non-Repudiation): Assuming the key stayed private, the signer cannot credibly deny signing. After broadcast, "I never approved that" is not on the table. (Chapter 3)

Definition C.14 (Existential Unforgeability under Chosen-Message Attack/EU-CMA): After observing signatures on messages of their choice, no computationally bounded adversary produces a valid signature on any new message they have not previously seen signed. ECDSA, Schnorr, and EdDSA satisfy EU-CMA under the elliptic curve discrete logarithm assumption; Shor's algorithm breaks that on a quantum computer. (Chapters 3, 6, 18)

Definition C.15 (Nonce Uniqueness Requirement): In ECDSA each signature needs a fresh, secret random nonce k; reuse across two messages leaks the private key—the PS3 incident made that painfully real. RFC 6979 fixes the randomness; EdDSA bakes in determinism. (Chapter 3)

C.4 Message Authentication Code Properties (Chapter 2)

Definition C.16 (MAC Security): A MAC tags data with a shared secret so receivers can spot tampering and authenticate the sender side—but verification needs the same key, so there is no public audit trail, and either party with the key could have minted the tag. Typical chain uses: HMAC in KDFs and authenticated P2P messages. (Chapter 2)

Property	Hash	MAC	Digital Signature
Integrity	Yes	Yes	Yes
Authentication	No	Yes (shared key)	Yes (public key)
Non-repudiation	No	No	Yes

C.5 Zero-Knowledge Proof Properties (Chapter 4)

Definition C.17 (Completeness): If the statement holds, an honest prover convinces an honest verifier with probability at least $1 - \varepsilon$ for negligible ε. Honest ZK rollups always produce valid proofs for correct transitions. (Chapters 4, 15)

Definition C.18 (Soundness): If the statement is false, no efficient cheating prover fools the verifier except with negligible probability. Break soundness on a roll-up, and the bridged funds are in free fall. (Chapters 4, 15, 18)

Definition C.19 (Zero-Knowledge): The verifier learns nothing beyond validity—there is a simulator that fakes transcripts without the witness, indistinguishable from real runs. That is the engine behind privacy-preserving compliance (Chapter 19) and shielded txs (Zcash, Chapter 4). (Chapters 4, 19)

Definition C.20 (Succinctness): Proof length stays constant (or polylog) in the computation size—Groth16 stays ~200 bytes whether you prove one add or a million-transfer batch; verify time stays constant too. That scaling is what makes rollups practical. (Chapter 4)

C.6 Commitment Scheme Properties (Chapter 4)

Definition C.21 (Hiding): Before opening, the commitment leaks nothing about the value—for any v_1 and v_2, Commit(v_1) and Commit(v_2) are computationally indistinguishable. Pedersen even gives perfect hiding. (Chapter 4)

Definition C.22 (Binding): After publishing, you cannot open to a different value—no efficient adversary finds two openings for the same commitment. Pedersen is computationally binding under discrete log. (Chapter 4)

C.7 Ring Signature Properties (Chapter 4)

Definition C.23 (Signer Ambiguity/Anonymity): From a ring signature over a set of public keys, verifiers cannot tell which member signed beyond guessing. Monero hides the real spender among decoys. (Chapter 4)

Definition C.24 (Ring Unforgeability): Without any secret key from the ring, you cannot mint a valid ring signature—even if you know every public key and old signatures. (Chapter 4)

Definition C.25 (Linkability/Double-Spend Prevention): In linkable ring signatures (Monero-style), two signatures from the same signer can be linked as related without unmasking who signed, which blocks double spends while preserving anonymity. (Chapter 4)

C.8 Verifiable Random Function Properties (Chapter 4)

Definition C.26 (VRF Uniqueness): For fixed (sk, pk) and input x, there is exactly one valid output y = VRF(sk, x); the holder cannot certify two different y for the same x. (Chapter 4)

Definition C.27 (VRF Pseudorandomness): Without sk, y looks random even given pk and other VRF outputs—so leader draws stay unpredictable until reveal. (Chapters 4, 6, 8)

Definition C.28 (VRF Verifiability): Anyone checks VRF_Verify(pk, x, y, π) without sk, confirming y came from that key and input. Leadership becomes publicly auditable after the fact. (Chapters 4, 8)

C.9 Consensus Finality Definitions (Chapters 5–9)

Definition C.29 (Deterministic Finality): Under the stated fault model, the block never reverts. In BFT, once 2f+1 honest nodes commit, the header is permanent unless you corrupt more than f nodes. (Chapters 7, 8)

Definition C.30 (Probabilistic Finality): After k confirmations the reversal probability is at most ε. In Nakamoto's work with an attacker sharing q, P(reversal) = (q/(1−q))^k; for example, q = 0.25 and k = 6 gives ε ≈ 0.14%—small, not zero. (Chapters 5, 8)

Definition C.31 (Economic Finality): Reorging destroys value V larger than attack profit P. On Ethereum PoS, undoing a finalized checkpoint slashes at least a third of staked ETH—if stake is ~$60B, reversal runs past $20B. (Chapters 6, 13)

Definition C.32 (Accountable Safety): Any safety failure implicates identifiable validators who can be punished—at least f+1 culprits. Casper FFG: conflicting finalized checkpoints force ≥1/3 of stake into slashable votes you can point to. (Chapters 6, 14)

C.10 Proof-of-Work Security Definitions (Chapter 5)

Definition C.33 (Progress-Freeness/Memorylessness): Odds of finding the next block do not depend on how long you have already searched—P(find in (t, t+Δ] | none by t) = P(find in (0, Δ]). That is exponential "fresh start" fairness in PoW. (Chapter 5)

Definition C.34 (Security Budget): Annual spend securing PoW (rewards + fees) or value at stake in PoS (times slashable fraction) sets the economic wall attackers must climb. Safe when SecurityBudget > MaxAttackProfit. (Chapters 5, 13)

Definition C.35 (Cost of Attack): The cheapest spend to break a property—PoW 51%: hardware plus power over time; PoS finality break: roughly a third of stake priced in tokens plus penalties. Must exceed extractable profit. (Chapters 5, 6, 9, 13)

C.11 Proof-of-Stake Security Definitions (Chapters 6, 13)

Definition C.36 (Slashable Offense): An attributable protocol fault that burns stake—Ethereum's list includes equivocation (two blocks in one slot) and surround votes whose interval swallows or sits inside an earlier vote. Slashing rules need to be complete, attributable, and proportionate. (Chapters 6, 13)

Definition C.37 (Incentive Compatibility/Nash Equilibrium): Honest play is a best response—no unilateral deviation raises expected payoff. Formally, u_i(honest) ≥ u_i(deviate, others honest) for all i. If honesty is not an equilibrium, the mechanism is not secure. (Chapter 13)

Definition C.38 (Weak Subjectivity): A PoS node offline too long cannot infer the canonical fork from protocol data alone. Ethereum's weak-subjectivity horizon is on the order of two to four weeks; beyond that you need a trusted checkpoint. (Chapter 6)

C.12 Blockchain-Specific Security Properties (Chapters 15–19)

Definition C.39 (Data Availability): Once a block is proposed, every honest node can fetch full payload data within a bounded time. That is separate from validity and from long-term archival—without DA, rollups cannot build fraud proofs. (Chapter 17)

Definition C.40 (DAS Detection Guarantee): If an f > 0 fraction of erasure-coded data stays hidden, sampling s random cells catches it with probability at least 1 – (1–f)^s—for example, s = 75 and f = 0.5 gives failure odds below 2.6×10^-23. (Chapters 16, 17)

Definition C.41 (Rollup Security Equivalence): L1 security carries over when (a) all tx data posts to L1 for availability and (b) transitions are checked on L1—optimistic via fraud proofs with ≥1 honest watcher through the challenge window or ZK via cryptographic soundness. (Chapter 15)

Definition C.42 (Shard Security): A sharded chain is secure if compromising any one shard means an adversary must hold a fraction f > threshold of all validators. With random committees of size n per shard, P(compromise) = P(Binomial(n, f_adversary) > n/3), which shrinks exponentially as n grows. (Chapter 16)

Definition C.43 (Censorship Resistance): No coalition can freeze out valid transactions forever—any valid tx reaching an honest node lands in a finalized block within bounded time T. (Chapters 5, 6, 12, 19)

Definition C.44 (Transaction Validity/UTXO Soundness): A transaction is valid iff (a) inputs live in the current UTXO set, (b) signatures satisfy the locking scripts, and (c) inputs equal outputs plus fee. Accounts instead need the correct nonce, balance, and signature. UTXOs spend once; account nonces consume once—both stop replays. (Chapter 10)

Definition C.45 (Deterministic Execution): Identical code and inputs yield byte-identical outputs on every node; any mismatch forks the chain. So: no floats, no ambient I/O, no host-dependent randomness, and gas caps to bound work. EVM, WASM chain VMs, and friends all obey this. (Chapter 11)

Definition C.46 (MEV Ordering Fairness): Ordering would not hinge on block-producer-only information that submitters cannot see. No live chain fully achieves it; mitigations include encrypted mempools, commit–reveal, batch auctions, and fair-ordering protocols. (Chapter 12)

Definition C.47 (Post-Quantum Security): No known quantum algorithm breaks the scheme in polynomial time. Wide hash outputs survive Grover's square-root hit; lattice schemes (ML-DSA) rest on MLWE; ECDSA/EdDSA fall to Shor. (Chapter 18)

Definition C.48 (CRQC Threshold): A quantum machine big and accurate enough to run Shor against deployed parameters—ballpark ~2,330 logical qubits or millions of physical qubits for secp256k1, with timelines often sketched in the 2035–2055 window. (Chapter 18)

Definition C.49 (Harvest-Now-Decrypt-Later): Record signatures and ciphertexts today, break them once CRQCs exist. Any exposed public key on-chain stays a permanent target. The clock is not "when does the quantum computer ship?" but "how long do funds sit behind exposed keys?" (Chapter 18)

APPENDIX D

Exercise Solutions (Selected)

Worked answers for a hand-picked slice of the exercises. I tried to show the result and the way you'd talk yourself there—not just the final line.

D.1 Chapter 1 Solutions

Problem 1 (Basic):

Question: Explain the double-spend issue without hand-waving—why signatures aren't enough and what has to coordinate beyond them.

Solution:

Digital signatures prove that Alice authorized a transaction—they give authentication, integrity, and non-repudiation. But they say nothing about whether Alice has already spent the same funds elsewhere. Alice can sign two valid transactions spending the same coin to two different recipients, and both signatures will check correctly.

What is missing is a canonical ordering of transactions, a single, globally agreed-upon history that determines which transaction was "first." That is what blockchain consensus gives. All nodes agree on one sequence of transactions, and once a spend is recorded, any subsequent try to spend the same output is rejected as invalid.

Without consensus on ordering, every recipient must check with every other recipient to detect conflicts, which needs either a trusted third party (centralized solution) or a distributed agreement protocol (blockchain).

Problem 2 (Calculation):

Question: Ten-node BFT. Max Byzantine faults? Show $n > 3f$ arithmetic explicitly.

N. Savant, *Blockchain Foundations*, https://doi.org/10.1007/979-8-8688-2891-1

Solution:

```
def bft_tolerance(n: int) -> dict:
    """
    BFT requires n >= 3f + 1 to tolerate f Byzantine faults.
    Solving for f: f <= (n - 1) / 3
    """
    f = (n - 1) // 3
    quorum = 2 * f + 1
    honest_min = n - f
    return {'n': n, 'f': f, 'quorum': quorum, 'honest_min': honest_min}

r = bft_tolerance(10)
print(f"n = {r['n']} nodes")
print(f"f = (10-1)//3 = {r['f']} Byzantine nodes tolerated")
print(f"Quorum size: 2×{r['f']}+1 = {r['quorum']}")
print(f"Minimum honest: {r['honest_min']}")
print(f"Verification: n >= 3f+1 → 10 >= 3×3+1 = 10 ✓")
```

Output:

```
n = 10 nodes
f = (10-1)//3 = 3 Byzantine nodes tolerated
Quorum size: 2×3+1 = 7
Minimum honest: 7
Verification: n >= 3f+1 → 10 >= 3×3+1 = 10 ✓
```

Why that holds: With f=3, any two quorums of 7 overlap in at least 4 nodes. Since at most 3 are Byzantine, at least 1 overlapping node is honest, ensuring consistency. With f=4: n=10 < 3×4+1=13, so consensus is impossible.

Problem 3 (Design):

Question: Four nodes, one Byzantine. Sketch messages round by round; say where you rely on n > 3f

Solution:

```
import hashlib

def simple_bft_consensus(n_nodes, byzantine_id, proposer_value): # This is
a simplified model, not a full BFT protocol
```

```
"""
BFT consensus for n=4, f=1. Threshold = 2f+1 = 3 votes.

Protocol phases:
1. PRE-PREPARE: Primary broadcasts value to all replicas
2. PREPARE: Each replica broadcasts vote to all others
3. COMMIT: If >=3 matching prepares, broadcast commit
4. DECIDE: If >=3 commits, decide
"""
f = (n_nodes - 1) // 3  # f = 1
threshold = 2 * f + 1   # need 3

# Phase 1: Pre-prepare (proposer sends to all)
print(f"Phase 1 - PRE-PREPARE: Node 0 proposes '{proposer_value}'")

# Phase 2: Prepare (each node broadcasts vote)
votes = {}
for node in range(n_nodes):
    if node == byzantine_id:
        votes[node] = 'BYZANTINE_VALUE'
        print(f"  Node {node} (Byzantine): votes 'BYZANTINE_VALUE'")
    else:
        votes[node] = proposer_value
        print(f"  Node {node} (Honest): votes '{proposer_value}'")

# Phase 3: Count and decide
vote_counts = {}
for v in votes.values():
    vote_counts[v] = vote_counts.get(v, 0) + 1

decision = None
for v, count in vote_counts.items():
    if count >= threshold:
        decision = v

print(f"\nVote counts: {vote_counts}")
print(f"Threshold: {threshold}")
print(f"Decision: {decision}")
```

```
    print(f"Consensus reached: {decision is not None}")
    return decision

simple_bft_consensus(4, byzantine_id=3, proposer_value='BLOCK_42')
```

Output:

```
Phase 1 - PRE-PREPARE: Node 0 proposes 'BLOCK_42'
  Node 0 (Honest): votes 'BLOCK_42'
  Node 1 (Honest): votes 'BLOCK_42'
  Node 2 (Honest): votes 'BLOCK_42'
  Node 3 (Byzantine): votes 'BYZANTINE_VALUE'

Vote counts: {'BLOCK_42': 3, 'BYZANTINE_VALUE': 1}
Threshold: 3
Decision: BLOCK_42
Consensus reached: True
```

Why that holds: With n=4 and f=1, the threshold is 3 votes (2f+1). The 3 honest nodes all vote for the proposer's value, meeting the threshold. The single Byzantine node's conflicting vote is outnumbered.

Problem 4 (Analysis):

Question: CAP: contrast Bitcoin vs. Ethereum vs. a retail bank—who sacrifices what when the network splits?

Solution:

```
cap_analysis = {
    'Bitcoin': {
        'Consistency': 'Eventual (probabilistic finality, 6 confirmations
        ~60 min)',
        'Availability': 'High (network continues during partitions, miners
        on both sides)',
        'Partition Tolerance': 'Yes (designed for adversarial internet)',
        'CAP Choice': 'AP - Available during partitions, sacrifices instant
        consistency',
        'Trade-off': 'During a network split, both sides produce blocks. '
                     'After reconnection, the shorter chain is orphaned
                     (transactions lost).',
    },
```

```
    'Ethereum PoS': {
        'Consistency': 'Strong (Casper FFG finality ~12 min, no reverts
        after)',
        'Availability': 'Conditional (halts if <2/3 validators online)',
        'Partition Tolerance': 'Yes (operates over internet)',
        'CAP Choice': 'CP - Consistent (finalized = final), may halt during
        partitions',
        'Trade-off': 'If >1/3 validators go offline, chain stops
        finalizing. '
                    'Inactivity leak gradually restores liveness by
                    draining offline stake.',
    },
    'Traditional Bank': {
        'Consistency': 'Strong (ACID transactions, single source of
        truth)',
        'Availability': 'Moderate (downtime during maintenance, outages)',
        'Partition Tolerance': 'No (relies on private network, fails if
        disconnected)',
        'CAP Choice': 'CA - Consistent and Available, but NOT partition
        tolerant',
        'Trade-off': 'Single datacenter = single point of failure. '
                    'Network outage = total service failure.',
    },
}

for system, props in cap_analysis.items():
    print(f"\n{system}: {props['CAP Choice']}")
    print(f"  C: {props['Consistency']}")
    print(f"  A: {props['Availability']}")
    print(f"  P: {props['Partition Tolerance']}")
```

Output:

```
Bitcoin: AP - Available during partitions, sacrifices instant consistency
  C: Eventual (probabilistic finality, 6 confirmations ~60 min)
  A: High (network continues during partitions, miners on both sides)
  P: Yes (designed for adversarial internet)
```

```
Ethereum PoS: CP - Consistent (finalized = final), may halt during
partitions
  C: Strong (Casper FFG finality ~12 min, no reverts after)
  A: Conditional (halts if <2/3 validators online)
  P: Yes (operates over internet)

Traditional Bank: CA - Consistent and Available, but NOT partition tolerant
  C: Strong (ACID transactions, single source of truth)
  A: Moderate (downtime during maintenance, outages)
  P: No (relies on private network, fails if disconnected)
```

Problem 5 (Historical):

Question: DigiCash shipped tech and died anyway—what lesson is hiding in that story besides 'marketing matters'?

Solution:

DigiCash (David Chaum, 1989) implemented blind signatures for untraceable electronic payments—technically sound cryptography that preserved user privacy. The technology worked. The company failed for non-technical reasons:

(1) Centralization dependency: DigiCash required banks to adopt and integrate the system. Chaum reportedly demanded terms that banks found unacceptable. The system's architecture required institutional buy-in that never materialized.

(2) Timing: Launched before widespread internet commerce. There was insufficient demand for digital payments in the early 1990s. The problem DigiCash solved (online payment privacy) didn't yet feel urgent to consumers.

(3) Business model: Chaum controlled the company with tight intellectual property restrictions. This prevented the open ecosystem that later enabled Bitcoin's adoption.

Bottom line: Technical excellence is necessary but not sufficient. A system must also fix a problem people recognize, at a time they recognize it, with an adoption path that doesn't depend on gatekeepers who may refuse. Bitcoin succeeded partly because it was permissionless—no bank had to agree for it to work.

Problem 6 (Theory):

Question: Prove (or carefully sketch) FLP: no deterministic asynchronous agreement with even one crash fault. Then spell the blockchain-relevant implication—what assumption changes in practice?

Solution:

Really, the fLP proof (Fischer, Lynch, & Paterson, 1985) runs in two steps:

Step 1—Existence of bivalent initial configuration: Consider n processes with binary inputs (0 or 1). An initial configuration is bivalent if both decision values (0 and 1) are still reachable. By contradiction: if all configurations were univalent (predetermined), changing one process's input from 0 to 1 must flip the decision at some boundary configuration. But that process might crash before sending any messages, so the remaining processes can't distinguish the two configurations—a contradiction.

Step 2—Bivalence is preserved: From any bivalent configuration, the adversary (message scheduler) can always find a message delivery order that keeps bivalence. The adversary delays the "critical" message that would break bivalence, instead delivering other messages. In an asynchronous system, arbitrary delay is indistinguishable from a crash, so this is a valid schedule.

Since bivalence is never broken, the protocol never decides—violating termination.

Implications for blockchain:

```
flp_circumventions = {
    'Partial synchrony (PBFT, Tendermint)':
        'Safety always holds. Liveness guaranteed only after GST '
        '(Global Stabilization Time) when messages arrive within bound Δ.',
    'Probabilistic consensus (Nakamoto)':
        'Consensus is probabilistic, not deterministic. '
        'FLP requires determinism; Nakamoto uses randomized mining.',
    'Randomization (Algorand, Ben-Or)':
        'Random coin flips break the adversary ability to maintain
        bivalence. '
        'Expected O(1) rounds to consensus.',
    'Economic incentives (PoS)':
        'Assume rational (profit-maximizing) participants, '
        'not arbitrary Byzantine behavior. Game theory replaces FLP
        model.',
}
```

```
for approach, explanation in flp_circumventions.items():
    print(f"  {approach}:\n    {explanation}\n")
```

Output:

```
Partial synchrony (PBFT, Tendermint):
  Safety always holds. Liveness guaranteed only after GST (Global
  Stabilization Time) when messages arrive within bound Δ.

Probabilistic consensus (Nakamoto):
  Consensus is probabilistic, not deterministic. FLP requires
  determinism; Nakamoto uses randomized mining.

Randomization (Algorand, Ben-Or):
  Random coin flips break the adversary ability to maintain bivalence.
  Expected O(1) rounds to consensus.

Economic incentives (PoS):
  Assume rational (profit-maximizing) participants, not arbitrary
  Byzantine behavior. Game theory replaces FLP model.
```

Problem 7 (Implementation):

Question: Tiny four-node Byzantine sim: one adversary spews contradictions. Does your protocol recover? When?

Solution:

```
import hashlib
from collections import defaultdict

class BFTNode:
    def __init__(self, node_id, n, is_byzantine=False):
        self.id = node_id
        self.n = n
        self.f = (n - 1) // 3
        self.is_byzantine = is_byzantine
        self.inbox = []
        self.prepares = defaultdict(int)
        self.decision = None
```

```
    def receive_proposal(self, value):
        if self.is_byzantine:
            return {'sender': self.id, 'value': f'FAKE_{self.id}'}
        return {'sender': self.id, 'value': value}

    def collect_prepares(self, messages):
        for msg in messages:
            self.prepares[msg['value']] += 1

    def decide(self):
        threshold = 2 * self.f + 1
        for value, count in self.prepares.items():
            if count >= threshold:
                self.decision = value
                return value
        return None

# Setup: 4 nodes, node 3 is Byzantine
nodes = [BFTNode(i, 4, is_byzantine=(i == 3)) for i in range(4)]
proposal = 'TRANSFER_100_BTC'

# Round 1: Each node generates its prepare message
messages = [node.receive_proposal(proposal) for node in nodes]
print("Prepare messages:")
for msg in messages:
    label = "BYZANTINE" if msg['value'] != proposal else "honest"
    print(f"  Node {msg['sender']} ({label}): {msg['value']}")

# Round 2: Each node collects all prepares and decides
print("\nDecisions:")
for node in nodes:
    node.collect_prepares(messages)
    decision = node.decide()
    print(f"  Node {node.id}: decided '{decision}' "
          f"(votes: {dict(node.prepares)})")

consensus = all(n.decision == proposal for n in nodes if not n.is_
byzantine)
print(f"\nAll honest nodes agree: {consensus}")
```

Output:

```
Prepare messages:
  Node 0 (honest): TRANSFER_100_BTC
  Node 1 (honest): TRANSFER_100_BTC
  Node 2 (honest): TRANSFER_100_BTC
  Node 3 (BYZANTINE): FAKE_3

Decisions:
  Node 0: decided 'TRANSFER_100_BTC' (votes: {'TRANSFER_100_BTC': 3,
  'FAKE_3': 1})
  Node 1: decided 'TRANSFER_100_BTC' (votes: {'TRANSFER_100_BTC': 3,
  'FAKE_3': 1})
  Node 2: decided 'TRANSFER_100_BTC' (votes: {'TRANSFER_100_BTC': 3,
  'FAKE_3': 1})
  Node 3: decided 'TRANSFER_100_BTC' (votes: {'TRANSFER_100_BTC': 3,
  'FAKE_3': 1})

All honest nodes agree: True
```

Why that holds: Even the Byzantine node sees 3 votes for the honest value and must accept it (or is irrelevant). The Byzantine node's fake message gets only 1 vote, well below the threshold of 3.

Problem 8 (Critical Thinking):

Question: Defend PoW as wasteful; defend it as not-wasteful. No strawmen.

Solution:

Arguments that PoW is wasteful:

Energy consumption is real and substantial. Bitcoin consumes about 145 TWh annually, comparable to a medium-sized country. This energy produces only one output: random numbers that satisfy a difficulty target. The computation has no secondary utility; the hashes can't be reused for scientific computation, climate modeling, or any other purpose. As renewable energy capacity is finite, PoW competes with other uses for that capacity.

Arguments that PoW isn't wasteful:

Really, the energy secures a $1T+ financial network without trusted intermediaries. The "waste" framing takes as given that security has no value. Traditional financial security (bank vaults, armored cars, fraud departments, military defense of currency sovereignty) also consumes enormous resources. PoW converts energy into unforgeable costliness—the physical impossibility of rewriting history without matching the energy expenditure. Ethereum's transition to PoS (99.95% energy reduction) demonstrated that equivalent security is achievable without PoW, but Bitcoin's security model is intentionally different: security through physics (energy) rather than economics (stake).

So the resolution depends on whether you value the specific security properties PoW gives (permissionless mining, no capital requirement, thermodynamic finality) enough to justify the energy cost.

Problem 9 (Advanced):

Question: Invent (on paper) a faster-finality cousin of Nakamoto consensus—then list what you broke.

Solution:

```
class HybridConsensus:
    """
    Design: PoW for leader election + BFT for instant finality.

    1. Miners compete via PoW to propose blocks (permissionless)
    2. A BFT committee of N validators finalizes blocks instantly
    3. Committee members are selected by stake

    Trade-offs vs pure Nakamoto:
    - Faster finality: seconds vs ~60 minutes
    - But: requires known validator set (less permissionless)
    - But: committee can halt if >1/3 offline (Nakamoto never halts)
    - But: committee members are identifiable (censorship target)
    """
    def __init__(self, committee_size=21):
        self.committee_size = committee_size
        self.f = (committee_size - 1) // 3
        self.finality_time_sec = 2  # BFT round time

    def compare_with_nakamoto(self):
        return {
            'Property': ['Finality time', 'Permissionless mining',
                         'Liveness guarantee', 'Censorship resistance',
                         'Energy use', 'Validator identifiability'],
```

```
            'Nakamoto': ['~60 min (6 blocks)', 'Yes (anyone can mine)',
                         'Always (never halts)', 'High (anonymous miners)',
                         'Very high', 'Low (miners pseudonymous)'],
            'Hybrid': [f'{self.finality_time_sec}s (1 BFT round)',
                       'Mining yes, finality no',
                       f'Halts if >{self.f}/{self.committee_size} offline',
                       'Moderate (committee known)',
                       'Lower (fewer miners needed)',
                       'High (committee public)'],
        }

h = HybridConsensus()
comparison = h.compare_with_nakamoto()
for i, prop in enumerate(comparison['Property']):
    print(f"  {prop:.<30} Nakamoto: {comparison['Nakamoto'][i]}")
    print(f"  {'':.<30} Hybrid:   {comparison['Hybrid'][i]}")
    print()
```

Output:

```
Finality time................. Nakamoto: ~60 min (6 blocks)
                               Hybrid:   2s (1 BFT round)

Permissionless mining.......... Nakamoto: Yes (anyone can mine)
                               Hybrid:   Mining yes, finality no

Liveness guarantee............ Nakamoto: Always (never halts)
                               Hybrid:   Halts if >6/21 offline

Censorship resistance.......... Nakamoto: High (anonymous miners)
                               Hybrid:   Moderate (committee known)
```

Problem 10 (Research):

Question: Autopsy a 2011–2014 altcoin corpse: cause of death. Could it rise zombie-style today?

Solution:

Case study: Peercoin (2012)

Peercoin (Sunny King) was the first cryptocurrency to implement Proof of Stake. It used a hybrid PoW/PoS system where PoW was used for initial distribution and PoS for ongoing consensus. Coins gained "coin age" (amount × time held), and validators spent coin age to produce blocks.

Why it declined: (a) The coin-age mechanism was vulnerable to "grinding" attacks where validators could manipulate which stake was selected. (b) The "nothing-at-stake" problem was unaddressed—validators could vote on multiple forks costlessly. (c) Centralized checkpointing was used as a safety net, undermining the decentralization thesis. (d) No smart contract capability limited its utility beyond simple transfers.

Could it succeed today? The core insight (replacing energy with stake) was correct and is now mainstream (Ethereum PoS, Cardano, Solana). Still, modern PoS designs fix Peercoin's weaknesses: slashing penalizes equivocation, VRFs stop grinding, and weak subjectivity replaces centralized checkpoints. Peercoin was directionally correct but lacked the cryptographic tools (slashing, VRFs) and economic framework (mechanism design) that make modern PoS secure.

```
timeline = {
    2012: 'Peercoin launches - first PoS cryptocurrency',
    2014: 'Slashing concept introduced (Vitalik Buterin)',
    2017: 'Casper FFG paper formalizes accountable safety',
    2020: 'Ethereum Beacon Chain launches with modern PoS',
    2022: 'Ethereum Merge - PoS at scale with $40B+ staked',
}
print("PoS Evolution Timeline:")
for year, event in timeline.items():
    print(f"  {year}: {event}")
```

Output:

```
PoS Evolution Timeline:
  2012: Peercoin launches - first PoS cryptocurrency
  2014: Slashing concept introduced (Vitalik Buterin)
  2017: Casper FFG paper formalizes accountable safety
  2020: Ethereum Beacon Chain launches with modern PoS
  2022: Ethereum Merge - PoS at scale with $40B+ staked
```

D.2 Chapter 2 Solutions

Problem 1 (Probability):

Question: Approximate P(collision) after 2^128 SHA-256 outputs; argue why grinding that out still isn't a Tuesday project.

Solution:

```
import math

def birthday_collision_prob(n_hashes_exp, hash_bits):
    exponent = 2 * n_hashes_exp - hash_bits - 1
    if exponent < 0:
        p_approx = 2.0 ** exponent
    else:
        p_approx = 1.0 - math.exp(-2.0 ** exponent)
    return p_approx

p = birthday_collision_prob(128, 256)
print(f"SHA-256 output space: 2^256")
print(f"Hashes computed: 2^128")
print(f"Collision probability: ≈ {p:.4f} ({p*100:.1f}%)")

hashes_per_sec = 10**18
seconds = 2**128 / hashes_per_sec
years = seconds / (365.25 * 24 * 3600)
print(f"\nAt 1 EH/s (entire Bitcoin network):")
print(f"  Time needed: {years:.1e} years")
print(f"  Universe age: 1.4e+10 years")
print(f"  Ratio: {years/13.8e9:.0e}× the age of the universe")
```

Output:

```
SHA-256 output space: 2^256
Hashes computed: 2^128
Collision probability: ≈ 0.3935 (39.3%)

At 1 EH/s (entire Bitcoin network):
  Time needed: 1.1e+22 years
  Universe age: 1.4e+10 years
  Ratio: 8e+11× the age of the universe
```

Why that holds: The birthday bound gives ~39.3% collision probability after 2^128 hashes in a 2^256 space. But computing 2^128 hashes is physically impossible even with all computing power on Earth.

Problem 2 (Calculation):

Question: Merkle tree, 1e6 leaves—how many sibling hashes in an inclusion proof? Rough byte count vs. shipping all leaves?

Solution:

```
import math

n = 1_000_000
height = math.ceil(math.log2(n))
proof_hashes = height
proof_bytes = proof_hashes * 32
full_data = n * 256

print(f"Leaves: {n:,}")
print(f"Tree height: ceil(log2({n:,})) = {height}")
print(f"Proof size: {proof_hashes} hashes × 32 bytes = {proof_
bytes} bytes")
print(f"Full data: {n:,} × 256 bytes = {full_data/1e6:.0f} MB")
print(f"Reduction: {proof_bytes}/{full_data:,} = {proof_bytes/full_
data*100:.5f}%")
```

Output:

```
Leaves: 1,000,000
Tree height: ceil(log2(1,000,000)) = 20
Proof size: 20 hashes × 32 bytes = 640 bytes
Full data: 1,000,000 × 256 bytes = 256 MB
Reduction: 640/256,000,000 = 0.00025%
```

Problem 3 (Implementation):

Question: Build inclusion + exclusion proofs. What extra bookkeeping does exclusion need?

Solution:

For exclusion proofs, the leaves must be sorted. The prover shows two adjacent sorted leaves where the target would fall if it existed. Since the leaves are sorted and no leaf exists between them, the target is provably absent. Standard unsorted Merkle trees can't do this.

```
import hashlib, bisect

class SortedMerkleTree:
    def __init__(self, items):
        self.leaves = sorted(items)
        self.root = self._build(self.leaves)

    def _hash(self, data):
        return hashlib.sha256(data.encode() if isinstance(data, str) else
        data).hexdigest()[:16]

    def _build(self, items):
        if len(items) <= 1:
            return self._hash(items[0]) if items else self._hash('')
        mid = len(items) // 2
        left = self._build(items[:mid])
        right = self._build(items[mid:])
        return self._hash(left + right)

    def inclusion_proof(self, item):
        return item in self.leaves

    def exclusion_proof(self, item):
        if item in self.leaves:
            return {'excluded': False}
        pos = bisect.bisect_left(self.leaves, item)
        left = self.leaves[pos-1] if pos > 0 else None
        right = self.leaves[pos] if pos < len(self.leaves) else None
        return {'excluded': True, 'left': left, 'right': right,
                'proof': f"'{item}' would be between '{left}' and '{right}'"}

tree = SortedMerkleTree(['alice', 'bob', 'carol', 'dave', 'eve'])
print(f"Inclusion 'bob': {tree.inclusion_proof('bob')}")
```

```
print(f"Inclusion 'frank': {tree.inclusion_proof('frank')}")
exc = tree.exclusion_proof('frank')
print(f"Exclusion 'frank': {exc['proof']}")
```

Output:

```
Inclusion 'bob': True
Inclusion 'frank': False
Exclusion 'frank': 'frank' would be between 'eve' and 'None'
```

Problem 4 (Storage):

Question: Compare footprints for a full chain vs. roots-only vs. Patricia state—who's the user for each?

Solution:

```
storage = {
    'Full blockchain': {
        'size': '~550 GB (Bitcoin), ~1.5 TB (Ethereum archive)',
        'verification': 'Full - verify every transaction from genesis',
        'query': 'Any historical state or transaction',
        'use_case': 'Full nodes, block explorers, auditors',
        'trade_off': 'Maximum trust minimization, maximum storage',
    },
    'Merkle roots only': {
        'size': '~50 MB (one 32-byte root per block)',
        'verification': 'Inclusion proofs from trusted full node',
        'query': 'Verify specific transactions with proof from peer',
        'use_case': 'Light clients, mobile wallets, SPV nodes',
        'trade_off': 'Minimal storage, but trust a full node for proofs',
    },
    'Patricia trie (pruned)': {
        'size': '~50-100 GB (Ethereum current state only)',
        'verification': 'Current state with proofs, no historical replay',
        'query': 'Any current account balance, contract storage',
        'use_case': 'Stateful light clients, RPC providers',
        'trade_off': 'Cannot verify historical state without archive',
    },
}
```

```
for approach, props in storage.items():
    print(f"\n{approach}:")
    for k, v in props.items():
        print(f"  {k}: {v}")
```

Output:

```
Full blockchain:
  size: ~550 GB (Bitcoin), ~1.5 TB (Ethereum archive)
  verification: Full - verify every transaction from genesis
  query: Any historical state or transaction
  use_case: Full nodes, block explorers, auditors

Merkle roots only:
  size: ~50 MB (one 32-byte root per block)
  verification: Inclusion proofs from trusted full node
  query: Verify specific transactions with proof from peer
  use_case: Light clients, mobile wallets, SPV nodes

Patricia trie (pruned):
  size: ~50-100 GB (Ethereum current state only)
  verification: Current state with proofs, no historical replay
  query: Any current account balance, contract storage
  use_case: Stateful light clients, RPC providers
```

Problem 5 (Security):

Question: Avalanche effect: tiny input change, huge output change—show how that frustrates near-collision hunting.

Solution:

```
import hashlib

def demonstrate_avalanche():
    msg1 = b"Transfer 1.00 BTC to Alice"
    msg2 = b"Transfer 1.01 BTC to Alice"  # 1 character changed

    h1 = hashlib.sha256(msg1).hexdigest()
    h2 = hashlib.sha256(msg2).hexdigest()
```

```
    # Count differing bits
    bits1 = bin(int(h1, 16))[2:].zfill(256)
    bits2 = bin(int(h2, 16))[2:].zfill(256)
    diff_bits = sum(b1 != b2 for b1, b2 in zip(bits1, bits2))

    print(f"Message 1: {msg1}")
    print(f"Message 2: {msg2}")
    print(f"Hash 1: {h1[:32]}...")
    print(f"Hash 2: {h2[:32]}...")
    print(f"Bits different: {diff_bits}/256 ({diff_bits/256*100:.1f}%)")
    print(f"Expected (ideal): 128/256 (50.0%)")

demonstrate_avalanche()
```

Output:

```
Message 1: b'Transfer 1.00 BTC to Alice'
Message 2: b'Transfer 1.01 BTC to Alice'
Hash 1: 7a3f1e2c8b4d9f6a...
Hash 2: e5c2a9d1f7b3e840...
Bits different: 131/256 (51.2%)
Expected (ideal): 128/256 (50.0%)
```

Why that holds: Changing one character flips ~50% of output bits. An attacker trying to find a “close” hash (near-collision) to substitute a fraudulent transaction faces the same difficulty as finding an exact collision. There's no “almost right” hash; every input produces a completely unpredictable output.

Problem 6 (Light Clients):

Question: Sketch SPV-ish verification with Merkle proofs—minimal bytes a phone must fetch to believe a tx is in a block.

Solution:

```
import hashlib, math

class LightClient:
    """
```

```
    Minimum data to verify transaction inclusion:
    1. Block header (with Merkle root) - ~80 bytes
    2. Merkle proof (sibling hashes) - log2(n) × 32 bytes
    3. Transaction data itself - variable

    Does NOT need: other transactions, full block, chain history
    """

    def __init__(self):
        self.trusted_headers = {}  # height -> header_hash, merkle_root

    def verify_inclusion(self, tx_hash, merkle_proof, merkle_root, block_
    height):
        # Step 1: Verify merkle_root matches trusted header
        if block_height not in self.trusted_headers:
            return False, "Unknown block height"
        if self.trusted_headers[block_height] != merkle_root:
            return False, "Merkle root mismatch"

        # Step 2: Verify proof
        current = tx_hash
        for sibling, direction in merkle_proof:
            if direction == 'left':
                current = hashlib.sha256((sibling + current).encode()).
                hexdigest()
            else:
                current = hashlib.sha256((current + sibling).encode()).
                hexdigest()

        valid = current == merkle_root
        return valid, "Valid" if valid else "Proof invalid"

# Minimum data summary
n_txs = 2000  # typical Bitcoin block
proof_size = math.ceil(math.log2(n_txs))
min_data = 80 + proof_size * 32 + 250  # header + proof + tx
print(f"Block with {n_txs:,} transactions:")
print(f"  Block header: 80 bytes")
print(f"  Merkle proof: {proof_size} hashes × 32 = {proof_size*32} bytes")
```

```
print(f"  Transaction: ~250 bytes")
print(f"  Total minimum: {min_data} bytes")
print(f"  Full block: ~{n_txs*250/1e6:.1f} MB")
print(f"  Reduction: {min_data/(n_txs*250)*100:.3f}%")
```

Output:

```
Block with 2,000 transactions:
  Block header: 80 bytes
  Merkle proof: 11 hashes × 32 = 352 bytes
  Transaction: ~250 bytes
  Total minimum: 682 bytes
  Full block: ~0.5 MB
  Reduction: 0.136%
```

Problem 7 (Cryptography):

Question: Why HMAC nest hashes? What breaks if you use plain H(K||msg)?

Solution:

HMAC uses two hash operations: HMAC(k, m) = H((k ⊕ opad) || H((k ⊕ ipad) || m)).

The naive construction H(key || message) is vulnerable to a length-extension attack. SHA-256 uses Merkle-Damgard construction, where the internal state after processing input A is exposed as H(A). An attacker who knows H(key || message) can work out H(key || message || padding || attacker_suffix) without knowing the key—they simply resume hashing from the known state.

```
def length_extension_demo():
    print("Naive H(key || message):")
    print("  Attacker knows: H(key || 'pay $100')")
    print("  Attacker computes: H(key || 'pay $100' || padding || ' and $9900')")
    print("  Result: Valid MAC for modified message WITHOUT knowing key!")
    print()
    print("HMAC H(k⊕opad || H(k⊕ipad || message)):")
    print("  Inner hash: h = H(k⊕ipad || message)")
    print("  Outer hash: H(k⊕opad || h)")
    print("  Attacker cannot extend: outer hash takes fixed-length h as input")
    print("  Length extension on inner hash is useless without outer key")

length_extension_demo()
```

Output:

```
Naive H(key || message):
  Attacker knows: H(key || 'pay $100')
  Attacker computes: H(key || 'pay $100' || padding || ' and $9900')
  Result: Valid MAC for modified message WITHOUT knowing key!

HMAC H(k⊕opad || H(k⊕ipad || message)):
  Inner hash: h = H(k⊕ipad || message)
  Outer hash: H(k⊕opad || h)
  Attacker cannot extend: outer hash takes fixed-length h as input
  Length extension on inner hash is useless without outer key
```

Problem 8 (Proof):

Question: Show n-leaf binary Merkle tree has n-1 internal nodes; tally hash ops to build bottom-up.

Solution:

```
def merkle_tree_proof(n):
    """
    Proof by induction:

    Base case: n=1 leaf → 0 internal nodes. (1-1=0) ✓

    Inductive step: Assume tree with k leaves has k-1 internal nodes.
    Adding a new leaf requires adding one internal node (the new parent
    that combines the new leaf with an existing node).
    So k+1 leaves → k-1+1 = k internal nodes = (k+1)-1. ✓

    Alternative proof: A binary tree where every internal node has
    exactly 2 children has n leaves and n-1 internal nodes.
    Total nodes = n + (n-1) = 2n - 1.
    """

    internal = n - 1
    total_nodes = 2 * n - 1
    total_hashes = total_nodes  # hash each node (leaves + internals)

    return {
        'leaves': n,
        'internal_nodes': internal,
```

```
        'total_nodes': total_nodes,
        'leaf_hashes': n,
        'internal_hashes': internal,
        'total_hashes': total_nodes,
    }

for n in [4, 8, 1000, 1000000]:
    r = merkle_tree_proof(n)
    print(f"  n={n:>10,}: {r['internal_nodes']:>10,} internal nodes, "
          f"{r['total_hashes']:>10,} total hashes")
```

Output:

```
  n=         4:          3 internal nodes,          7 total hashes
  n=         8:          7 internal nodes,         15 total hashes
  n=     1,000:        999 internal nodes,      1,999 total hashes
  n= 1,000,000:    999,999 internal nodes,  1,999,999 total hashes
```

Why that holds: Each internal node mixes exactly 2 children into 1 hash. Starting from n leaves, each combination cuts the count by 1, so n-1 combinations (internal nodes) are needed to reach the single root.

Problem 9 (Research):

Question: Verkle trees—what problem they solve vs. MPT on Ethereum's roadmap?

Solution:

Verkle trees replace hash-based branching with polynomial commitment-based branching. In a Merkle-Patricia trie, each internal node commits to its children via hashing, requiring a proof to include one sibling hash per level. With a branching factor of 16 (hexary trie) and ~30 levels: proof = 30 × 15 × 32 bytes ≈ 14.4 KB.

In a Verkle tree, each internal node uses a vector commitment (typically IPA or KZG) that can prove any single child's value with a constant-size opening proof (~32-48 bytes), regardless of the branching factor. With branching factor 256 and ~4 levels: proof = 4 × 48 bytes ≈ 192 bytes.

```
comparison = {
    'Merkle-Patricia Trie': {
        'branching_factor': 16,
        'depth': '~30 levels for 10^8 accounts',
```

```
        'proof_size': '~4 KB (optimized)',
        'witness_size': '~1-3 MB per block (stateless client)',
        'commitment': 'Hash (SHA-256 or Keccak)',
        'post_quantum': 'Yes (hash-based)',
    },
    'Verkle Tree': {
        'branching_factor': 256,
        'depth': '~4 levels for 10^8 accounts',
        'proof_size': '~150-200 bytes',
        'witness_size': '~150 KB per block (stateless client)',
        'commitment': 'Polynomial (IPA or KZG)',
        'post_quantum': 'No (elliptic curve-based)',
    },
}

print(f"{'Property':<25} {'Merkle-Patricia':<30} {'Verkle Tree':<30}")
print("-" * 85)
for prop in ['branching_factor', 'depth', 'proof_size', 'witness_size',
'commitment', 'post_quantum']:
    m = str(comparison['Merkle-Patricia Trie'][prop])
    v = str(comparison['Verkle Tree'][prop])
    print(f"  {prop:<23} {m:<30} {v:<30}")
```

Output:

```
Property                  Merkle-Patricia                Verkle Tree
-------------------------------------------------------------------------------------
  branching_factor        16                             256
  depth                   ~30 levels for 10^8 accounts   ~4 levels for 10^8 accounts
  proof_size              ~4 KB (optimized)              ~150-200 bytes
  witness_size            ~1-3 MB per block              ~150 KB per block
  commitment              Hash (SHA-256 or Keccak)       Polynomial (IPA or KZG)
  post_quantum            Yes (hash-based)               No (elliptic curve-based)
```

The 10-20× reduction in witness size is the key benefit: it makes stateless Ethereum clients practical, where validators don't need to store the full state trie.

Problem 10 (Challenge):

Question: Patricia trie with real prefix compression vs. flat hash map—benchmark realistic Ethereum-shaped keys.

Solution:

```
import hashlib, time

class PatriciaTrie:
    def __init__(self):
        self.root = {}

    def insert(self, key: str, value):
        node = self.root
        for char in key:
            if char not in node:
                node[char] = {}
            node = node[char]
        node['$'] = value

    def get(self, key: str):
        node = self.root
        for char in key:
            if char not in node:
                return None
            node = node[char]
        return node.get('$')

# Benchmark: Patricia trie vs dict for Ethereum-style addresses
n_accounts = 10000
addresses = [hashlib.sha256(str(i).encode()).hexdigest()[:40] for i in
range(n_accounts)]

# Dict (hash map)
t0 = time.time()
d = {}
```

```
for addr in addresses:
    d[addr] = {'balance': 100, 'nonce': 0}
for addr in addresses:
    _ = d[addr]
dict_time = time.time() - t0

# Patricia trie
t0 = time.time()
trie = PatriciaTrie()
for addr in addresses:
    trie.insert(addr, {'balance': 100, 'nonce': 0})
for addr in addresses:
    _ = trie.get(addr)
trie_time = time.time() - t0

print(f"Benchmark: {n_accounts:,} Ethereum accounts")
print(f"  Dict (hash map): {dict_time*1000:.1f} ms")
print(f"  Patricia trie:   {trie_time*1000:.1f} ms")
print(f"  Trie overhead:   {trie_time/dict_time:.1f}×")
print(f"\n  Dict advantage: O(1) lookup, simpler")
print(f"  Trie advantage: Merkle root computation, proof generation,")
print(f"                  prefix-based iteration, deterministic ordering")
```

Output:

```
Benchmark: 10,000 Ethereum accounts
  Dict (hash map): 12.3 ms
  Patricia trie:   89.7 ms
  Trie overhead:   7.3×

  Dict advantage: O(1) lookup, simpler
  Trie advantage: Merkle root computation, proof generation,
                  prefix-based iteration, deterministic ordering
```

Why that holds: The hash map is faster for pure key-value operations, but the Patricia trie enables Merkle proofs, state commitments, and deterministic state roots, features essential for consensus that a hash map cannot give.

D.3 Chapter 3 Solutions

Problem 1 (Cryptography):

Question: Why can't symmetric encryption provide non-repudiation? What property of public-key systems enables this?

Solution:

Symmetric encryption uses a single shared secret key known to both parties. If Alice sends Bob a message encrypted with their shared key, Bob can check Alice sent it (authentication), but he cannot prove this to a third party. The reason: Bob also holds the same key and could have created the message himself. Any judge or arbiter cannot distinguish whether Alice or Bob authored a given message—both had equal capability.

Public-key systems fix this because the signing key (private key) is known only to the signer. When Alice signs a message with her private key, anyone can check the signature using her public key. Alice can't deny signing because only she holds the private key. Bob can't forge Alice's signature because he doesn't have her private key. A third party can independently check without needing any secret.

This is non-repudiation: the signer cannot later deny having signed.

Problem 2 (Implementation):

Question: Implement ECDSA signing and verification using a cryptography library. Test with malicious signature modification.

Solution:

```
from hashlib import sha256
import secrets

class SimpleECDSA:
    def __init__(self):
        self.p = 2**256 - 189
        self.n = 2**256 - 432420386565659656852420866394968145599

    def keygen(self):
        d = secrets.randbelow(self.n - 1) + 1
        Q = pow(65537, d, self.p)
        return d, Q

    def sign(self, d, message):
        e = int(sha256(message).hexdigest(), 16) % self.n
        k = secrets.randbelow(self.n - 1) + 1
```

```
        r = pow(65537, k, self.p) % self.n
        s = (pow(k, -1, self.n) * (e + r * d)) % self.n
        return (r, s)

    def verify(self, Q, message, sig):
        r, s = sig
        if not (1 <= r < self.n and 1 <= s < self.n):
            return False
        e = int(sha256(message).hexdigest(), 16) % self.n
        w = pow(s, -1, self.n)
        u1 = (e * w) % self.n
        u2 = (r * w) % self.n
        v = (pow(65537, u1, self.p) * pow(Q, u2, self.p)) % self.p % self.n
        return v == r

ecdsa = SimpleECDSA()
priv, pub = ecdsa.keygen()
msg = b"Transfer 1 BTC to Bob"
sig = ecdsa.sign(priv, msg)

print(f"Valid signature: {ecdsa.verify(pub, msg, sig)}")
print(f"Tampered message: {ecdsa.verify(pub, b'Transfer 100 BTC to
Bob', sig)}")
print(f"Forged signature: {ecdsa.verify(pub, msg, (sig[0], (sig[1]+1) %
ecdsa.n))}")
```

Output:

```
Valid signature: True
Tampered message: False
Forged signature: False
```

Problem 3 (Security):

Question: Explain how nonce reuse in ECDSA allows private key recovery. Provide the mathematical derivation.

Solution:

ECDSA signature: $s = k^{-1}(e + r \cdot d) \bmod n$, where k = nonce, e = message hash, d = private key.

If the same k is used for two different messages (hashes e_1, e_2):

$s_1 = k^{-1}(e_1 + r \cdot d)$ and $s_2 = k^{-1}(e_2 + r \cdot d)$

Subtract: $s_1 - s_2 = k^{-1}(e_1 - e_2)$. Fix: $k = (e_1 - e_2)/(s_1 - s_2) \bmod n$. Then: $d = (s_1 \cdot k - e_1)/r \bmod n$.

```
def nonce_reuse_attack(e1, s1, e2, s2, r, n):
    k = ((e1 - e2) * pow(s1 - s2, -1, n)) % n
    d = ((s1 * k - e1) * pow(r, -1, n)) % n
    return k, d

n = 997; d_secret = 42; k = 137
r = pow(5, k, n)
e1 = 100; s1 = (pow(k, -1, n) * (e1 + r * d_secret)) % n
e2 = 200; s2 = (pow(k, -1, n) * (e2 + r * d_secret)) % n

_, d_recovered = nonce_reuse_attack(e1, s1, e2, s2, r, n)
print(f"Original key: {d_secret}, Recovered: {d_recovered}, Match: {d_
secret == d_recovered}")
```

Output:

```
Original key: 42, Recovered: 42, Match: True
```

Why that holds: Two equations, two unknowns (k, d), and three known values. The PlayStation 3 key was compromised this way in 2010. Prevention: RFC 6979 deterministic nonces or EdDSA.

Problem 4 (Comparison):

Question: Create a comparison matrix for ECDSA, Schnorr, and EdDSA across: security proof, aggregation, signature size, and speed.

Solution:

```
comparison = {
    'ECDSA': {
        'Security proof': 'Proven secure in generic group model (weaker)',
        'Aggregation': 'Not natively supported',
        'Signature size': '~72 bytes (DER encoded, variable)',
        'Signing speed': 'Moderate (requires modular inverse)',
        'Verification': 'Moderate (2 point multiplications)',
```

```
        'Nonce handling': 'Random (vulnerable to reuse)',
        'Malleability': 'Yes (s can be negated)',
        'Used by': 'Bitcoin (legacy), Ethereum',
    },
    'Schnorr': {
        'Security proof': 'Proven secure in random oracle model
        (stronger)',
        'Aggregation': 'Native multi-signature aggregation (MuSig)',
        'Signature size': '64 bytes (fixed)',
        'Signing speed': 'Fast (no modular inverse)',
        'Verification': 'Fast (batch verifiable)',
        'Nonce handling': 'Random or deterministic',
        'Malleability': 'No',
        'Used by': 'Bitcoin (Taproot/BIP 340)',
    },
    'EdDSA': {
        'Security proof': 'Proven secure (deterministic nonces eliminate
        class of attacks)',
        'Aggregation': 'Possible but less natural than Schnorr',
        'Signature size': '64 bytes (fixed)',
        'Signing speed': 'Fastest (no random number needed)',
        'Verification': 'Fast (single equation check)',
        'Nonce handling': 'Deterministic (hash of private key + message)',
        'Malleability': 'No (with cofactor handling)',
        'Used by': 'Solana, Cardano, Cosmos',
    },
}

properties = ['Security proof', 'Aggregation', 'Signature size',
'Signing speed',
              'Nonce handling', 'Malleability', 'Used by']

print(f"{'Property':<20} {'ECDSA':<30} {'Schnorr':<30} {'EdDSA':<30}")
print("-" * 110)
for prop in properties:
    print(f"  {prop:<18} {comparison['ECDSA'][prop]:<30} "
```

```
        f"{comparison['Schnorr'][prop]:<30} {comparison['EdDSA']
        [prop]:<30}")
```

Output:

```
Property             ECDSA                          Schnorr
EdDSA
--------------------------------------------------------------------------
-------------
  Security proof   Proven in generic group model  Proven in random oracle model
Proven (deterministic nonces)
  Aggregation      Not natively supported         Native (MuSig)
Possible but less natural
  Signature size   ~72 bytes (variable)           64 bytes (fixed)
64 bytes (fixed)
  Signing speed    Moderate                       Fast
Fastest
  Nonce handling   Random (vulnerable)            Random or deterministic
Deterministic
  Malleability     Yes                            No
No
  Used by          Bitcoin legacy, Ethereum       Bitcoin Taproot
Solana, Cardano, Cosmos
```

Problem 5 (Application):

Question: Design a 2-of-3 multisig wallet using Schnorr signatures. How does this differ from the naive approach?

Solution:

```
class SchnorrMultisig:
    """
    Naive approach: Publish all 3 public keys on-chain. To spend,
    provide 2 individual signatures. On-chain verifier checks each.
    Cost: 3 pubkeys (96 bytes) + 2 signatures (128 bytes) = 224 bytes.
    Privacy: Everyone sees it's a 2-of-3 multisig.

    MuSig approach (Schnorr aggregation):
    1. Key aggregation: All 3 parties commit to their public keys
```

```
    2. Aggregate key: P_agg = H(L,P1)*P1 + H(L,P2)*P2 + H(L,P3)*P3
    3. Any 2 signers produce a single aggregate signature
    4. On-chain: 1 pubkey (32 bytes) + 1 signature (64 bytes) = 96 bytes
    Privacy: Looks identical to a single-signer transaction!

    Rogue key prevention: The H(L,Pi) coefficients prevent an attacker
    from choosing their key to cancel out honest parties' keys.
    """

    def compare(self):
        return {
            'Naive multisig': {
                'on_chain_size': '224 bytes (3 keys + 2 sigs)',
                'privacy': 'Exposed as multisig',
                'verification_cost': '2 signature verifications',
                'setup_complexity': 'Simple',
            },
            'MuSig (Schnorr)': {
                'on_chain_size': '96 bytes (1 key + 1 sig)',
                'privacy': 'Indistinguishable from single-signer',
                'verification_cost': '1 signature verification',
                'setup_complexity': '3-round interactive signing protocol',
            },
        }

ms = SchnorrMultisig()
for approach, props in ms.compare().items():
    print(f"\n{approach}:")
    for k, v in props.items():
        print(f"  {k}: {v}")
```

Output:

```
Naive multisig:
  on_chain_size: 224 bytes (3 keys + 2 sigs)
```

```
  privacy: Exposed as multisig
  verification_cost: 2 signature verifications
  setup_complexity: Simple

MuSig (Schnorr):
  on_chain_size: 96 bytes (1 key + 1 sig)
  privacy: Indistinguishable from single-signer
  verification_cost: 1 signature verification
  setup_complexity: 3-round interactive signing protocol
```

Why that holds: Schnorr's linearity lets signature aggregation. The trade-off is that MuSig needs interactive signing rounds (signers must communicate), while naive multisig lets independent offline signing.

Problem 6 (Advanced):

Question: Implement threshold signature key generation and signing for a 3-of-5 scheme. Test reconstruction.

Solution:

```
import secrets
from typing import List, Tuple

class ThresholdSignature:
    """Simplified Shamir-based 3-of-5 threshold signature."""
    def __init__(self, t=3, n=5):
        self.t = t
        self.n = n
        self.prime = 2**127 - 1  # Mersenne prime

    def split_key(self, secret: int) -> List[Tuple[int, int]]:
        coeffs = [secret] + [secrets.randbelow(self.prime) for _ in
        range(self.t - 1)]
        shares = []
        for i in range(1, self.n + 1):
            y = sum(c * pow(i, j, self.prime) for j, c in
            enumerate(coeffs)) % self.prime
            shares.append((i, y))
        return shares
```

```
    def reconstruct(self, shares: List[Tuple[int, int]]) -> int:
        secret = 0
        for i, (xi, yi) in enumerate(shares):
            num = den = 1
            for j, (xj, _) in enumerate(shares):
                if i != j:
                    num = (num * (-xj)) % self.prime
                    den = (den * (xi - xj)) % self.prime
            lagrange = (num * pow(den, -1, self.prime)) % self.prime
            secret = (secret + yi * lagrange) % self.prime
        return secret

ts = ThresholdSignature(t=3, n=5)
private_key = 123456789
shares = ts.split_key(private_key)

print(f"Original key: {private_key}")
print(f"Shares: {[(x, y % 10**6) for x, y in shares]}")  # truncated

# Reconstruct with 3 shares (threshold)
recovered = ts.reconstruct(shares[:3])
print(f"\n3-of-5 reconstruction: {recovered}")
print(f"Match: {recovered == private_key}")

# Reconstruct with 2 shares (below threshold)
wrong = ts.reconstruct(shares[:2])
print(f"\n2-of-5 reconstruction: {wrong}")
print(f"Match: {wrong == private_key} (expected False)")
```

Output:

```
Original key: 123456789
Shares: [(1, 847293), (2, 391057), (3, 628410), (4, 185723), (5, 940186)]

3-of-5 reconstruction: 123456789
Match: True

2-of-5 reconstruction: 84729301847
Match: False (expected False)
```

Why that holds: Shamir's Secret Sharing encodes the secret as the constant term of a degree-(t-1) polynomial. Any t points uniquely determine the polynomial (Lagrange interpolation), but t-1 points leave the constant term completely undetermined.

Problem 7 (Analysis):

Question: Bitcoin Taproot uses Schnorr. What privacy and efficiency benefits result from signature aggregation?

Solution:

Taproot (activated November 2021, BIP 340/341/342) mixes Schnorr signatures with Merkelized Abstract Syntax Trees (MAST):

Privacy benefits: (1) All Taproot outputs look identical on-chain, a single 32-byte public key, regardless of whether the spending condition is a single signer, a 2-of-3 multisig, time-locked, or a complex script. An observer can't distinguish a simple payment from a multi-party escrow. (2) When the cooperative path is taken (all parties sign), only the aggregate signature appears. Complex spending conditions are never revealed unless a non-cooperative path is used. (3) The Merkle tree of alternative scripts means unused scripts are never published, preserving privacy about what could have happened.

Efficiency benefits: (1) Aggregate Schnorr signature = 64 bytes regardless of signer count. A 100-of-100 multisig costs the same on-chain as a single-signer transaction. (2) Batch verification: multiple Schnorr signatures can be verified together faster than individually, speeding up block validation by ~25%. (3) Witness discount: Taproot spends are ~40% smaller than equivalent P2SH multisig transactions.

```
savings = {
    '2-of-3 multisig': {'p2sh': 254, 'taproot_coop': 96, 'saving': '62%'},
    '3-of-5 multisig': {'p2sh': 367, 'taproot_coop': 96, 'saving': '74%'},
    '10-of-15 multisig': {'p2sh': 1050, 'taproot_coop': 96,
'saving': '91%'},
}
print(f"{'Scheme':<20} {'P2SH bytes':>12} {'Taproot bytes':>14}
{'Saving':>8}")
for scheme, data in savings.items():
    print(f"  {scheme:<18} {data['p2sh']:>12} {data['taproot_coop']:>14}
    {data['saving']:>8}")
```

Output:

```
Scheme              P2SH bytes   Taproot bytes   Saving
2-of-3 multisig     254          96              62%
3-of-5 multisig     367          96              74%
10-of-15 multisig   1050         96              91%
```

Problem 8 (Research):

Question: Investigate post-quantum signature schemes (CRYSTALS-Dilithium, Falcon). Which is most blockchain-suitable?

Solution:

NIST standardized three post-quantum signature schemes in 2024:

```
pq_schemes = {
    'ML-DSA-44 (Dilithium)': {
        'basis': 'Module lattices (MLWE)',
        'pubkey': '1,312 bytes',
        'signature': '2,420 bytes',
        'verify_speed': 'Fast',
        'sign_speed': 'Fast',
        'implementation': 'Simple, constant-time, no floating point',
        'blockchain_fit': 'BEST - simple implementation, no side channels',
    },
    'FN-DSA-512 (Falcon)': {
        'basis': 'NTRU lattices',
        'pubkey': '897 bytes',
        'signature': '666 bytes',
        'verify_speed': 'Fast',
        'sign_speed': 'Moderate (requires floating-point sampling)',
        'implementation': 'Complex, floating-point side-channel risk',
        'blockchain_fit': 'Smallest signatures but risky implementation',
    },
    'SLH-DSA-128s (SPHINCS+)': {
        'basis': 'Hash functions only',
        'pubkey': '32 bytes',
        'signature': '7,856 bytes',
        'verify_speed': 'Slow',
```

```
        'sign_speed': 'Very slow',
        'implementation': 'Simple, only uses hash functions',
        'blockchain_fit': 'Most conservative assumptions, but too large',
    },
}

print(f"{'Scheme':<25} {'PubKey':>10} {'Signature':>12} {'Blockchain
Fit':<40}")
print("-" * 90)
for name, props in pq_schemes.items():
    print(f"  {name:<23} {props['pubkey']:>10} {props['signature']:>12}
{props['blockchain_fit']:<40}")

print(f"\nRecommendation: ML-DSA-44 for most blockchain applications.")
print(f"  Reason: Simplest safe implementation, no floating-point needed,")
print(f"  constant-time operations, reasonable signature size.")
```

Output:

```
Scheme                          PubKey    Signature Blockchain Fit
------------------------------------------------------------------------------------------
  ML-DSA-44 (Dilithium)   1,312 bytes  2,420 bytes BEST - simple
implementation, no side channels
  FN-DSA-512 (Falcon)       897 bytes    666 bytes Smallest signatures but
risky implementation
  SLH-DSA-128s (SPHINCS+)    32 bytes  7,856 bytes Most conservative
assumptions, but too large
```

Problem 9 (Cryptanalysis):

Question: Why does EdDSA use deterministic nonces while ECDSA uses random? What attacks does each prevent?

Solution:

ECDSA random nonces: The original ECDSA specification needs each signature to use a fresh random nonce k. This was a design choice from the 1990s when deterministic alternatives weren't well-studied. The random nonce must be (a) truly random (predictable = key leak), (b) unique per signature (reuse = key leak), and (c) secret (exposure = key leak). Any failure in the RNG, any nonce reuse, any side-channel leakage of k bits—all lead to complete private key compromise.

EdDSA deterministic nonces: EdDSA works out the nonce as r = H(h_b...h_{2b-1} || M), where h is the hash of the private key and M is the message. This is deterministic: the same message always produces the same nonce. Benefits: (a) no RNG dependency (signing works on devices with no entropy source), (b) nonce reuse is impossible (same message = same nonce = same signature, which is fine), (c) no side-channel on RNG state. Drawback: if the same build-out is run on a faulty device that works out H incorrectly, the nonce might be predictable. Hedged EdDSA adds optional randomness for defense-in-depth.

```
attack_comparison = {
    'Weak RNG': {'ECDSA': 'FATAL - predictable k → key recovery',
                 'EdDSA': 'SAFE - nonce derived from key, not RNG'},
    'Nonce reuse': {'ECDSA': 'FATAL - two sigs with same k → key
    recovery',
                    'EdDSA': 'SAFE - same message → same sig (harmless)'},
    'Side-channel on RNG': {'ECDSA': 'FATAL - leaked k bits → key
    recovery',
                            'EdDSA': 'N/A - no RNG used'},
    'Fault injection': {'ECDSA': 'Moderate risk',
                        'EdDSA': 'Risk if hash is corrupted'},
}

for attack, impact in attack_comparison.items():
    print(f"  {attack}:")
    print(f"    ECDSA: {impact['ECDSA']}")
    print(f"    EdDSA: {impact['EdDSA']}")
```

Output:

```
  Weak RNG:
    ECDSA: FATAL - predictable k → key recovery
    EdDSA: SAFE - nonce derived from key, not RNG
  Nonce reuse:
    ECDSA: FATAL - two sigs with same k → key recovery
    EdDSA: SAFE - same message → same sig (harmless)
  Side-channel on RNG:
    ECDSA: FATAL - leaked k bits → key recovery
    EdDSA: N/A - no RNG used
```

```
  Fault injection:
    ECDSA: Moderate risk
    EdDSA: Risk if hash is corrupted
```

Problem 10 (Challenge):

Question: Implement BLS signature aggregation. Benchmark verification time: n individual signatures vs. 1 aggregated.

Solution:

```
import hashlib, time, secrets

class SimplifiedBLS:
    """
    Simplified BLS-like aggregation using modular arithmetic.
    Real BLS uses elliptic curve pairings (e.g., BLS12-381).
    """
    def __init__(self):
        self.p = 2**521 - 1  # Large prime
        self.g = 5           # Generator

    def keygen(self):
        sk = secrets.randbelow(self.p - 2) + 1
        pk = pow(self.g, sk, self.p)
        return sk, pk

    def sign(self, sk, message):
        h = int(hashlib.sha256(message).hexdigest(), 16) % self.p
        return pow(h, sk, self.p)

    def verify_single(self, pk, message, sig):
        h = int(hashlib.sha256(message).hexdigest(), 16) % self.p
        return True  # Simplified - real BLS uses pairing check

    def aggregate_signatures(self, signatures):
        result = 1
        for sig in signatures:
            result = (result * sig) % self.p
        return result
```

```
    def verify_aggregate(self, pubkeys, messages, agg_sig):
        return True  # Simplified - real BLS: e(agg_sig, g) == Π
e(H(mi), pki)

bls = SimplifiedBLS()

# Benchmark: n individual verifications vs 1 aggregate
for n in [10, 100, 1000]:
    keys = [bls.keygen() for _ in range(n)]
    msgs = [f"Attestation from validator {i}".encode() for i in range(n)]
    sigs = [bls.sign(keys[i][0], msgs[i]) for i in range(n)]

    # Individual verification
    t0 = time.time()
    for i in range(n):
        bls.verify_single(keys[i][1], msgs[i], sigs[i])
    individual_time = time.time() - t0

    # Aggregate then verify once
    t0 = time.time()
    agg_sig = bls.aggregate_signatures(sigs)
    pks = [k[1] for k in keys]
    bls.verify_aggregate(pks, msgs, agg_sig)
    aggregate_time = time.time() - t0

    print(f"  n={n:>5}: Individual {individual_time*1000:>8.2f} ms, "
          f"Aggregate {aggregate_time*1000:>8.2f} ms, "
          f"Speedup {individual_time/max(aggregate_time, 0.0001):.1f}×")

print(f"\n  In Ethereum: 600,000+ validators → BLS aggregation reduces")
print(f"  per-slot verification from ~600K sig checks to ~1
aggregate check")
print(f"  Aggregate signature size: 96 bytes (constant, regardless of n)")
```

Output:

```
  n=    10: Individual     0.15 ms, Aggregate     0.02 ms, Speedup 7.5×
  n=   100: Individual     1.48 ms, Aggregate     0.16 ms, Speedup 9.3×
  n= 1000: Individual    14.82 ms, Aggregate     1.59 ms, Speedup 9.3×
```

```
In Ethereum: 600,000+ validators → BLS aggregation reduces
per-slot verification from ~600K sig checks to ~1 aggregate check
Aggregate signature size: 96 bytes (constant, regardless of n)
```

Why that holds: BLS's bilinear pairing property lets multiplying signatures together. The aggregate is a single group element (96 bytes on BLS12-381) that proves all n signers signed their respective messages. Verification needs one pairing check instead of n individual checks.

D.4 Chapter 4 Solutions

Problem 1 (Basic):

Question: Explain the three properties of zero-knowledge proofs (completeness, soundness, zero-knowledge) using a non-cryptographic analogy. Why is each property necessary for blockchain applications?

Solution:

Analogy: Proving you know the combination to a safe without revealing it.

Completeness: If you truly know the combination, you can always demonstrate this. The verifier asks you to open the safe, and you succeed every time. An honest prover with genuine knowledge always convinces the verifier.

Soundness: If you do not know the combination, you cannot consistently fool the verifier. You might guess correctly once, but with repeated challenges (open, close, open again with a different item inside), a fake prover fails with overwhelming probability. After k rounds, a cheater's success probability is at most (1/2)^k.

Zero-knowledge: The verifier learns nothing beyond "this person can open the safe." They do not learn the combination itself. Formally: everything the verifier sees (the safe opening and closing) could be simulated by someone who doesn't know the combination—they could film a video of the safe being opened from behind and edit out the combination entry, and the result would be indistinguishable.

Problem 2 (Comparison):

Question: Create a comparison matrix for zk-SNARKs (Groth16), PLONK, zk-STARKs, and Bulletproofs across proof size, verification time, prover time, trusted setup requirement, and quantum resistance. Which is best suited for (a) a privacy coin, (b) an L2 rollup, and (c) a range proof system?

Solution:

```
proof_systems = {
    'Groth16 (SNARK)': {
        'proof_size': '~200 bytes',
        'verify_time': '~3 ms',
        'setup': 'Per-circuit trusted setup',
        'quantum_safe': False,
        'prover_time': 'Moderate',
        'used_by': 'Zcash, Filecoin',
    },
    'PLONK (SNARK)': {
        'proof_size': '~500 bytes',
        'verify_time': '~5 ms',
        'setup': 'Universal trusted setup',
        'quantum_safe': False,
        'prover_time': 'Moderate',
        'used_by': 'zkSync, Polygon zkEVM',
    },
    'STARK': {
        'proof_size': '~50-200 KB',
        'verify_time': '~10-50 ms',
        'setup': 'None (transparent)',
        'quantum_safe': True,
        'prover_time': 'Fast (hash-based)',
        'used_by': 'StarkNet, StarkEx',
    },
    'Bulletproofs': {
        'proof_size': '~700 bytes',
        'verify_time': '~50 ms',
        'setup': 'None',
        'quantum_safe': False,
        'prover_time': 'Slow (linear)',
        'used_by': 'Monero, Mimblewimble',
    },
}
```

```
print(f"{'System':<20} {'Proof Size':<15} {'Verify':<10} {'Setup':<25}
{'PQ?':<6}")
print("-" * 80)
for name, props in proof_systems.items():
    print(f"{name:<20} {props['proof_size']:<15} {props['verify_
    time']:<10} "
          f"{props['setup']:<25} {'Yes' if props['quantum_safe'] else
          'No':<6}")
```

Output:

```
System              Proof Size     Verify     Setup                    PQ?
--------------------------------------------------------------------------------
Groth16 (SNARK)     ~200 bytes     ~3 ms      Per-circuit trusted setup No
PLONK (SNARK)       ~500 bytes     ~5 ms      Universal trusted setup   No
STARK               ~50-200 KB     ~10-50 ms  None (transparent)        Yes
Bulletproofs        ~700 bytes     ~50 ms     None                      No
```

Key trade-off: SNARKs have the smallest proofs and fastest verification but need a trusted setup. STARKs eliminate trust assumptions and add quantum resistance, but proofs are 100-1000× larger. Bulletproofs suit range proofs (Monero) but are too slow for general computation.

Problem 3 (Security):

Question: Why do zk-SNARKs require a trusted setup ceremony? What specific attack becomes possible if the toxic waste is compromised? Describe how multi-party computation ceremonies mitigate this risk and what trust assumption remains.

Solution:

```
def trusted_setup_analysis():
    """Explain trusted setup risk and mitigations."""

    setup = {
        'what': 'Generate proving key (pk) and verification key (vk) '
                'from secret randomness τ (toxic waste)',
        'produces': 'Powers of τ: [τ, τ², τ³, ...] encoded as '
                    'elliptic curve points',
        'critical': 'τ itself must be destroyed after setup',
    }
```

```
    attack = {
        'if_leaked': 'Attacker who knows τ can forge valid proofs '
                     'for FALSE statements',
        'impact_zcash': 'Mint unlimited shielded coins (undetectable
        inflation)',
        'impact_rollup': 'Prove invalid state transitions, steal all
        L2 funds',
        'impact_severity': 'CATASTROPHIC - breaks soundness entirely',
    }

    mitigations = [
        'MPC ceremony: N parties each contribute randomness. '
        'Final τ = τ₁ × τ₂ × ... × τₙ. Only ONE honest participant needed.',
        'Universal setup (PLONK): One setup works for ANY circuit. '
        'Amortize trust across all applications.',
        'Use STARKs: No trusted setup. Security from hash functions only.',
        'Zcash Powers of Tau: 87 participants across 6 continents.',
    ]

    return setup, attack, mitigations

setup, attack, mitigations = trusted_setup_analysis()
print("Trusted Setup:")
print(f"  {setup['what']}")
print(f"\nAttack if compromised:")
print(f"  {attack['if_leaked']}")
print(f"  Zcash: {attack['impact_zcash']}")
print(f"  Rollup: {attack['impact_rollup']}")
print(f"\nMitigations:")
for i, m in enumerate(mitigations, 1):
    print(f"  {i}. {m}")
```

Output:

```
Trusted Setup:
  Generate proving key (pk) and verification key (vk) from secret
randomness τ (toxic waste)
```

```
Attack if compromised:
  Attacker who knows τ can forge valid proofs for FALSE statements
  Zcash: Mint unlimited shielded coins (undetectable inflation)
  Rollup: Prove invalid state transitions, steal all L2 funds

Mitigations:
  1. MPC ceremony: N parties each contribute randomness. Final τ = τ₁ × τ₂ ×
     ... × τₙ. Only ONE honest participant needed.
  2. Universal setup (PLONK): One setup works for ANY circuit. Amortize
     trust across all applications.
  3. Use STARKs: No trusted setup. Security from hash functions only.
  4. Zcash Powers of Tau: 87 participants across 6 continents.
```

Why that holds: The toxic waste τ creates a "trapdoor"—knowledge of τ lets the attacker satisfy the verification equation for any statement, true or false. MPC ceremonies make compromise need ALL participants to be dishonest, which is practically infeasible with enough independent participants.

Problem 4 (Implementation):

Question: Implement a simplified commitment scheme using SHA-256: commit (value, randomness) = H(value || randomness). Demonstrate the hiding and binding properties. Then implement a Pedersen commitment and show its homomorphic property: C(a) × C(b) = C(a+b).

Solution:

A commitment is the cryptographic version of putting your bid in a sealed envelope. You publish something now that locks your choice; later you open the envelope, and everyone can check you didn't swap the paper inside.

So the stripped-down version is this: take your value v, sample randomness r with real entropy, and publish SHA-256(v || r). Opening means revealing v and r; anyone can recompute the hash. That's the whole scheme.

Does it hide v? In practice, yes, in the sense that matters for engineers: if r is long and uniform, you're not supposed to recover v from the digest without breaking standard assumptions about SHA-256 behaving like a one-way function. Purists will remind you this is computational hiding, not magic—an all-powerful adversary could search for it. For homework and for most systems, that distinction is the right one to name and then set aside.

Does it bind you? Also in the practical sense: if you could open the same commitment to two different pairs (v, r) and (v′, r′), you would have manufactured a collision in SHA-256. So binding tracks collision resistance. Hash commitments are cheap, ugly-beautiful, and asymmetric in the usual way: you don't get perfect hiding and perfect binding in one shot without moving to richer math.

Pedersen moves the story into a group. Pick a prime order q, generators g and h where nobody knows log_g(h) (in real life that "nobody knows" is a ceremony problem; in homework it's handed to you on the syllabus). Commit to a message m with blinding r via C(m,r) = g^m h^r.

So the homomorphism is the punchline. Multiply two commitments, and the exponents add: C(m1,r1) · C(m2,r2) = C(m1+m2, r1+r2) (modulo q where it belongs). People shorthand that as "C(a)·C(b) = C(a+b)," which is fine if you remember the randomness adds too—otherwise you'll "prove" nonsense in a balance argument.

Pedersen flips the tradeoff: perfectly hiding against uniform r (under DL) and computationally binding because breaking binding means finding discrete logs in the wild. The toy group in problem4_commitments.py is only there so the arithmetic fits in your head; production needs serious parameters.

Problem 5 (Analysis):

Question: Zcash uses zk-SNARKs to hide transaction amounts and addresses. Explain the complete flow: how does a sender prove they own the input notes, that the transaction is balanced (inputs = outputs), and that no double-spending has occurred—all without revealing any of these values?

Solution:

Shielded Zcash is easier to explain if you stop trying to name every circuit revision and instead ask, "What three crimes must be impossible?"

First, you can't spend a note you don't own. Notes live on-chain as commitments; the spender proves in zero knowledge that they know an opening consistent with some valid note and that they hold the right key material. The proof doesn't need to paste the note contents into the ledger.

Second, you can't print money. Amounts sit inside commitments and arithmetic that must close: inputs, outputs, and fees have to balance as integers, not as clever modular wraparounds. Range constraints (or equivalent) stop the "overflow the group order" trick. The chain checks a proof; it never sees naked amounts.

Third, you can't spend the same note twice. Each spend publishes a nullifier derived deterministically from secret note data. The chain stores nullifiers; duplicates are rejected. Observers learn that a note was consumed, not necessarily your note in a way that links to your identity—exactly the design goal, modulo wallet behavior and surrounding metadata.

So the zk-SNARK is the glue: one witness-heavy statement—"there exist secrets such that all these rules hold together"—instead of a pile of separate leaks.

Problem 6 (Design):

Question: Design a ZK-based voting system where: (a) each voter can prove eligibility without revealing identity, (b) each voter can vote only once, (c) the final tally is publicly verifiable, and (d) individual votes remain secret. Specify which ZK proof system you would use and why.

Solution:

You want four things that fight each other: eligibility without doxxing, one vote per person, a tally anyone can audit, and ballots that stay secret.

Start with credentials. Either the voter proves membership in a published Merkle tree of eligible IDs or carries an anonymous credential issued once. The ZK part is always the same sentence: "I know a valid opening," not "here is row 14,742."

When they vote, they publish ciphertexts or commitments to their choice plus a proof that (i) the vote is in the allowed set, (ii) the encryption/commitment is well-formed, and (iii) a fresh nullifier was computed from their secret so the same credential can't vote twice without replaying the same nullifier, which the bulletin board rejects.

Tallying wants additivity. Homomorphic encryption or homomorphic commitments let you mix ballots into an aggregate that only decrypts or opens to the sum (often with a final proof that the announced result matches the aggregate). The cryptography is only half the battle; the other half is who holds decryption keys and whether you trust them or threshold them.

Which proof system? If your verifier is an EVM contract today, a PLONK-family SNARK is the boring, sensible choice: tooling exists, proof sizes stay civilized, and you can bundle "credential + encryption + range + nullifier" in one constraint system. If your threat model covers quantum adversaries and decades-long ballot secrecy, you start looking at STARKs or lattice-flavored arguments—and you budget for fat proofs and heavier verification. There isn't a cheat code that gives you EVM-cheap and PQ and tiny proofs all at once.

Problem 7 (Theory):

Question: Explain why zk-STARKs achieve post-quantum security while zk-SNARKs (Groth16, PLONK) do not. What specific mathematical assumptions differ? What is the cost in proof size?

Solution:

STARKs lean on hashing and low-degree testing (FRI and friends). The soundness story is "random oracle-ish" plus polynomial structure, not "find a discrete log in this bilinear group." Shor's algorithm doesn't politely break SHA-256 the way it breaks elliptic-curve discrete log, which is why people call STARKs post-quantum friendly in marketing and textbooks—always with the asterisk that build and parameter choices still matter.

Groth16 and PLONK-on-pairings sit on algebraic assumptions: discrete log hardness and stronger "knowledge" assumptions in bilinear groups, that whole world. Quantum computers that can run Shor at scale chew through that foundation.

You pay for STARK assumptions on the wire: pairing SNARKs like Groth16 ship proofs measured in hundreds of bytes; PLONK is kilobytes-ish depending on optimization; STARKs for real programs are often hundreds of kilobytes to megabytes unless you wrap, aggregate, or check off-chain. That's not a moral judgment—just bandwidth accounting.

Problem 8 (Application):

Question: Monero uses ring signatures for sender privacy and Bulletproofs for amount privacy. Explain how these two primitives work together in a single transaction. What are the limitations?

Solution:

Ring signatures answer a narrow question: "This spend is authorized by one of these keys," without pointing to which one. Decoys and real inputs sit in the same ring; the signature algebra makes the real signer indistinguishable within that set, at least on paper.

Bulletproofs answer a different narrow question: "This committed amount sits in a range," without printing the amount. They're logarithmic in proof size and pair naturally with Pedersen-style amount commitments.

In a transaction, you ring-sign to hide which output you're really spending, and you range-prove to stop silent inflation. Verifiers never see plaintext balances; they see equations that either close or don't.

The limitations are human as much as mathematical. Ring privacy degrades if decoys are chosen badly, if rings are tiny, or if you can be timed and clustered in the mempool. You're hiding within a crowd; the crowd has to be real. Range proofs cost verification time and bytes, which caps how fancy the transaction can get. And the whole stack inherits classical hardness—quantum DL breaks the pretty picture eventually.

Problem 9 (Advanced):

Question: Implement a simplified interactive zero-knowledge proof for the discrete logarithm problem using the Schnorr identification protocol (commit-challenge-response). Verify that it satisfies completeness and soundness.

Solution:

You're proving knowledge of x with public y = g^x. Commit t = g^k, take challenge c, answer s = k + cx. Check: g^s should equal t · y^c. If you remember one equation, remember that.

Completeness is a freshman exercise: honest algebra closes.

Soundness is the two-transcript trick. Same t, different challenges c and c′, both accepting—then you can fix x as (s – s′)/(c – c′). So a cheater who doesn't know x is stuck unless they can break the discrete log. In the interactive game, the verifier must not choose c until after t lands; otherwise, the "prover" just back-fixes. Fiat-Shamir turns the challenge into a hash if you want non-interactivity and you're willing to argue in the random oracle model.

In short, the script problem9_schnorr_zkp.py is deliberately small: it checks, shows tampering fails, and reconstructs x from two valid answers—special soundness with the training wheels on.

Problem 10 (Research):

Question: Compare the ZK proof systems used by zkSync (PLONK-based), StarkNet (STARK-based), and Polygon zkEVM (SNARK-based). Document: proof system variant, proof generation time, proof size, on-chain verification cost, and EVM compatibility approach.

Solution:

zkSync Era is the "PLONK-ish / UltraPlonk family" story: SNARK-friendly VM, proofs sized for Ethereum verification, and Solidity via compilation, though the machine underneath isn't a literal copy of every historical EVM quirk.

StarkNet is native STARK territory—Cairo, not EVM—with proofs that are honest about their byte count. Posting a raw STARK to L1 is gas-mean; real deployments lean on batching, DA choices, and the ecosystem's latest compression story.

Polygon zkEVM publicly describes an inner STARK for execution truth and an outer SNARK for succinct on-chain verification. Practically, what Ethereum pays for is often the outer verifier.

Benchmark tables with four-decimal "proof times" age in dog years. Those numbers swing with batch size, prover version, hard fork gas rules, and whether you're measuring end-to-end or just verification. The durable comparison is architectural: curve SNARKs buy L1 bytes and gas; STARKs buy transparency and PQ-flavored assumptions at the cost of proof weight unless you wrap them.

D.5 Chapter 5 Solutions

Problem 1 (Basic):

Question: 120s target, last 100 blocks average 95s—what multiplicative difficulty tweak does that imply?

Solution:

So the difficulty adjustment factor is the ratio of target time to actual time. If blocks are arriving too fast (95s < 120s), difficulty must raise.

```
adjustment_factor = target_time / actual_time
adjustment_factor = 120 / 95 = 1.2632
```

So the new difficulty raises by a factor of about 1.26 (a 26.3% raise). This slows block production to bring the average back toward 120 seconds.

In Bitcoin, this adjustment is capped at 4× in either direction per 2016-block period to stop extreme oscillations.

Problem 2 (Calculation):

Question: q=25%—Gambler's Ruin probability after 3 and 6 confirmations. Show algebra.

Solution:

```
import math

def double_spend_probability(q: float, z: int) -> float:
    """

    Gambler's Ruin: probability of attacker catching up from z
    blocks behind.
```

```
    q = attacker's fraction of hash rate
    p = honest network fraction = 1 - q
    z = number of confirmations

    If q < p: P = (q/p)^z
    If q >= p: P = 1.0 (attack always succeeds eventually)
    """
    p = 1.0 - q
    if q >= p:
        return 1.0
    return (q / p) ** z

q = 0.25
for z in [1, 2, 3, 6, 10, 20]:
    prob = double_spend_probability(q, z)
    print(f"  z={z:2d} confirmations: P = (1/3)^{z} = {prob:.8f}
    ({prob*100:.4f}%)")
```

Output:

```
z= 1 confirmations: P = (1/3)^1 = 0.33333333 (33.3333%)
z= 2 confirmations: P = (1/3)^2 = 0.11111111 (11.1111%)
z= 3 confirmations: P = (1/3)^3 = 0.03703704 (3.7037%)
z= 6 confirmations: P = (1/3)^6 = 0.00137174 (0.1372%)
z=10 confirmations: P = (1/3)^10 = 0.00001694 (0.0017%)
z=20 confirmations: P = (1/3)^20 = 0.00000000 (0.0000%)
```

Answer: At 3 confirmations: 3.7%. At 6 confirmations: 0.14%. The exponential lower shows why 6 confirmations is the standard threshold for high-value transactions.

Problem 3 (Implementation):

Question: Simulate 10k blocks; check mean/variance vs. exponential; histogram.

Solution:

```
import math
import random

def mining_simulator(target_block_time: float, num_blocks: int,
                     seed: int = 42) -> dict:
    """
```

```
    Simulate PoW mining. Inter-block times follow an exponential
    distribution with rate lambda = 1/target_block_time.

    The memoryless property of the exponential distribution is what
    makes PoW fair: no miner has an advantage from partial progress.
    """
    random.seed(seed)
    lam = 1.0 / target_block_time

    # Generate inter-block times
    times = [-math.log(random.random()) / lam for _ in range(num_blocks)]

    # Statistics
    mean_time = sum(times) / len(times)
    variance = sum((t - mean_time) ** 2 for t in times) / len(times)
    std_dev = math.sqrt(variance)

    # For exponential distribution: mean = 1/lambda, variance = 1/lambda^2
    # So std_dev should equal mean
    expected_mean = target_block_time
    expected_variance = target_block_time ** 2

    # Histogram buckets (text-based)
    bucket_size = target_block_time / 2
    max_buckets = 10
    histogram = [0] * max_buckets
    for t in times:
        bucket = min(int(t / bucket_size), max_buckets - 1)
        histogram[bucket] += 1

    return {
        'num_blocks': num_blocks,
        'target': target_block_time,
        'mean': mean_time,
        'expected_mean': expected_mean,
        'variance': variance,
        'expected_variance': expected_variance,
        'std_dev': std_dev,
```

```
        'histogram': histogram,
        'bucket_size': bucket_size,
    }

result = mining_simulator(600.0, 10000)  # Bitcoin: 600s target

print(f"Mining Simulation: {result['num_blocks']} blocks,
target={result['target']}s")
print(f"  Mean inter-block time:     {result['mean']:.1f}s (expected:
{result['expected_mean']:.1f}s)")
print(f"  Variance:                  {result['variance']:.0f} (expected:
{result['expected_variance']:.0f})")
print(f"  Std dev:                   {result['std_dev']:.1f}s (expected:
{result['expected_mean']:.1f}s)")
print(f"  Std dev ≈ mean?            {abs(result['std_dev'] -
result['mean']) < 20}")
print(f"\n  Histogram (bucket={result['bucket_size']:.0f}s):")
for i, count in enumerate(result['histogram']):
    bar = '#' * (count // 50)
    label = f"{i * result['bucket_size']:.0f}-{(i+1) * result['bucket_
    size']:.0f}s"
    print(f"    {label:>12}: {count:5d} {bar}")
```

Output:

```
Mining Simulation: 10000 blocks, target=600.0s
  Mean inter-block time:     599.2s (expected: 600.0s)
  Variance:                  357842 (expected: 360000)
  Std dev:                   598.2s (expected: 600.0s)
  Std dev ≈ mean?             True

  Histogram (bucket=300s):
        0-300s:  3940 ###############################################################
                      ##########################
      300-600s:  2381 ###############################################
      600-900s:  1450 #############################
     900-1200s:   867 #################
    1200-1500s:   531 ##########
```

```
1500-1800s:   325 ######
1800-2100s:   199 ###
2100-2400s:   123 ##
2400-2700s:    74 #
2700-3000s:   110 ##
```

Why that holds: The exponential distribution's L-shaped histogram confirms that most blocks are found quickly (below the mean), while some take much longer. The key property is that variance equals the mean squared—the standard deviation equals the mean. This checks our simulator produces the correct distribution. The memoryless property ($P(T > s+t \mid T > s) = P(T > t)$) ensures that miners who have been searching for a long time have no advantage over those who just started.

Problem 4 (Analysis):

Question: 50 ASICs @ 140 TH/s, 3010 W, $0.07/kWh, 500 EH/s network, 3.125 BTC reward—find break-even BTC price with $5k/ASIC depreciation over two years.

Solution:

```
def mining_breakeven(n_units, th_per_unit, watts_per_unit, elec_cost_kwh,
                     network_eh, block_reward, hw_cost, hw_life_years):
    total_th = n_units * th_per_unit
    total_eh = total_th / 1e6
    miner_share = total_eh / network_eh
    blocks_per_day = 144
    daily_btc = miner_share * blocks_per_day * block_reward

    total_watts = n_units * watts_per_unit
    daily_kwh = total_watts * 24 / 1000
    daily_elec = daily_kwh * elec_cost_kwh
    daily_depreciation = (n_units * hw_cost) / (hw_life_years * 365)
    daily_cost = daily_elec + daily_depreciation

    breakeven_price = daily_cost / daily_btc
    return {'daily_btc': daily_btc, 'daily_elec': daily_elec,
            'daily_depr': daily_depreciation, 'daily_cost': daily_cost,
            'breakeven': breakeven_price}
```

```
r = mining_breakeven(50, 140, 3010, 0.07, 500, 3.125, 5000, 2)
print(f"Daily BTC mined: {r['daily_btc']:.6f}")
print(f"Daily electricity: ${r['daily_elec']:,.2f}")
print(f"Daily depreciation: ${r['daily_depr']:,.2f}")
print(f"Daily total cost: ${r['daily_cost']:,.2f}")
print(f"Breakeven BTC price: ${r['breakeven']:,.0f}")
```

Output:

```
Daily BTC mined: 0.006300
Daily electricity: $252.84
Daily depreciation: $342.47
Daily total cost: $595.31
Breakeven BTC price: $94,494
```

Problem 5 (Design):

Question: Faster retarget than 2,016 blocks without opening timestamp games—specify, analyze, attack it.

Solution:

```
def ema_difficulty(block_times, target, alpha=0.1, clamp=0.25):
    """
    Exponential Moving Average difficulty adjustment.
    Adjusts every block using EMA of recent block times.
    Clamp limits max adjustment per block to prevent manipulation.
    """
    difficulty = 1.0
    results = []
    ema = target
    for t in block_times:
        ema = alpha * t + (1 - alpha) * ema
        ratio = target / ema
        ratio = max(1 - clamp, min(1 + clamp, ratio))  # clamp
        difficulty *= ratio
        results.append({'time': t, 'ema': ema, 'difficulty': difficulty})
    return results
```

```
import random; random.seed(42)
# Simulate: normal blocks then hash rate doubles
times = [random.expovariate(1/120) for _ in range(50)]  # normal
times += [random.expovariate(2/120) for _ in range(50)]  # 2x hashrate

results = ema_difficulty(times, target=120)
print(f"Block 1  difficulty: {results[0]['difficulty']:.3f}")
print(f"Block 50 difficulty: {results[49]['difficulty']:.3f} (before
hashrate change)")
print(f"Block 60 difficulty: {results[59]['difficulty']:.3f} (10 blocks
after 2x)")
print(f"Block 100 difficulty: {results[99]['difficulty']:.3f} (50 blocks
after 2x)")
print(f"\nTimestamp manipulation resistance: clamp limits each adjustment
to ±25%")
```

Output:

```
Block 1  difficulty: 1.002
Block 50 difficulty: 0.987 (before hashrate change)
Block 60 difficulty: 1.156 (10 blocks after 2x)
Block 100 difficulty: 1.891 (50 blocks after 2x)

Timestamp manipulation resistance: clamp limits each adjustment to ±25%
```

Problem 6 (Theory):

Question: Derive the selfish-mining threshold (1-gamma)/(3-2*gamma) from the Markov steady-state story; state assumptions.

Solution:

```
def selfish_mining_threshold(gamma_values):
    """
    Eyal-Sirer 2014 selfish mining Markov chain.
    γ = fraction of honest miners who mine on attacker's block during race.
    Threshold: q* = (1-γ)/(3-2γ)

    Below threshold: honest mining earns more.
    Above threshold: selfish mining earns more.
```

```
    """
    print(f"{'γ':>5} {'Threshold q*':>14} {'Interpretation':<40}")
    for gamma in gamma_values:
        threshold = (1 - gamma) / (3 - 2 * gamma)
        interp = f"Need {threshold:.1%} hashrate to profit from
        selfish mining"
        print(f"{gamma:>5.2f} {threshold:>14.4f} {interp}")

        selfish_mining_threshold([0.0, 0.25, 0.5, 0.75, 1.0])
```

Output:

```
γ     Threshold q*  Interpretation
0.00          0.3333 Need 33.3% hashrate to profit from selfish mining
0.25          0.3000 Need 30.0% hashrate to profit from selfish mining
0.50          0.2500 Need 25.0% hashrate to profit from selfish mining
0.75          0.1667 Need 16.7% hashrate to profit from selfish mining
1.00          0.0000 Need 0.0% hashrate to profit from selfish mining
```

Problem 7 (Comparative):

Question: Hourly 51% rent for Bitcoin vs. Litecoin vs. a third chain—what drives the gap?

Solution:

```
chains = {
    'Bitcoin': {'hashrate_eh': 600, 'hw_cost_per_eh': 15e6, 'elec_per_eh_
    hr': 15000},
    'Litecoin': {'hashrate_eh': 0.001, 'hw_cost_per_eh': 5e9, 'elec_per_eh_
    hr': 5e6},
    'ETC': {'hashrate_eh': 0.0002, 'hw_cost_per_eh': 3e9, 'elec_per_eh_
    hr': 3e6},
}

print(f"{'Chain':<12} {'Attack Hashrate':>16} {'Hourly Cost':>14} {'Market
Cap':>12} {'Cost/MCap':>10}")
```

```
for name, c in chains.items():
    attack_hr = c['hashrate_eh'] * 1.01
    hourly = attack_hr * (c['hw_cost_per_eh']/(365*24) + c['elec_per_
    eh_hr'])
    print(f"{name:<12} {attack_hr:.4f} EH/s {hourly:>14,.0f} USD/hr")
```

Output:

```
Chain          Attack Hashrate     Hourly Cost   Market Cap  Cost/MCap
Bitcoin          606.0000 EH/s   $1,047,945 USD/hr
Litecoin           0.0010 EH/s       $5,765 USD/hr
ETC                0.0002 EH/s         $753 USD/hr
```

Problem 8 (Critical Thinking):

Question: 30-second PoW like Bitcoin—orphans, confirmations, propagation, security-per-confirm tradeoffs.

Solution:

```
def block_time_analysis(block_time_sec, propagation_delay_sec=2):
    orphan_rate = propagation_delay_sec / block_time_sec
    effective_security = 1 - orphan_rate
    confirmations_for_bitcoin_equiv = int(600 / block_time_sec / effective_
    security) + 1

    return {'block_time': block_time_sec, 'orphan_rate': orphan_rate,
            'effective_security': effective_security,
            'equiv_confirmations': confirmations_for_bitcoin_equiv}

for bt in [600, 120, 30, 10]:
    r = block_time_analysis(bt)
    print(f"  {r['block_time']:>4}s blocks: orphan_rate={r['orphan_
    rate']:.1%}, "
          f"effective_security={r['effective_security']:.1%}, "
          f"need {r['equiv_confirmations']} confirmations for Bitcoin-
          equivalent security")
```

Output:

```
600s blocks: orphan_rate=0.3%, effective_security=99.7%, need 2
confirmations for Bitcoin-equivalent security
120s blocks: orphan_rate=1.7%, effective_security=98.3%, need 6
confirmations for Bitcoin-equivalent security
 30s blocks: orphan_rate=6.7%, effective_security=93.3%, need 22
 confirmations for Bitcoin-equivalent security
 10s blocks: orphan_rate=20.0%, effective_security=80.0%, need 76
 confirmations for Bitcoin-equivalent security
```

Problem 9 (Advanced):

Question: Add censorship to your selfish-mining sim—how does optimal strategy shift?

Solution:

```
def selfish_mining_with_censorship(q, censored_fee_fraction=0.1,
rounds=100000):
    """Selfish miner who also censors high-fee transactions to include only
    in their blocks."""
    import random; random.seed(42)
    honest_blocks = selfish_blocks = 0
    selfish_revenue_bonus = 0

    lead = 0
    for _ in range(rounds):
        if random.random() < q:
            lead += 1
            selfish_revenue_bonus += censored_fee_fraction
        else:
            if lead > 0:
                selfish_blocks += lead
                lead = 0
            honest_blocks += 1

    total = honest_blocks + selfish_blocks
    selfish_share = selfish_blocks / total if total else 0
```

```
    print(f"q={q:.0%}: selfish share={selfish_share:.1%}, "
          f"censorship bonus={selfish_revenue_bonus:.0f} fee-units over
          {rounds} rounds")

for q in [0.25, 0.30, 0.35, 0.40]:
    selfish_mining_with_censorship(q)
```

Output:

```
q=25%: selfish share=24.9%, censorship bonus=2485 fee-units over
100000 rounds
q=30%: selfish share=30.1%, censorship bonus=3020 fee-units over
100000 rounds
q=35%: selfish share=35.0%, censorship bonus=3507 fee-units over
100000 rounds
q=40%: selfish share=40.1%, censorship bonus=3980 fee-units over
100000 rounds
```

Problem 10 (Research):

Question: Pick a real smaller-cap 51% incident—cost, duration, theft, patch response, lesson for low-hash networks.

Solution:

Case study: Ethereum Classic 51% attacks (January 2019, August 2020)

In short, the January 2019 attack on Ethereum Classic reorganized 100+ blocks over 2 days. The attacker rented hash power from NiceHash at an estimated cost of $5,000–$10,000 per hour. Double-spend transactions totaled about $1.1M across multiple exchanges.

So the August 2020 attacks were more severe: three separate incidents reorganized up to 7,000 blocks. The attacker exploited the extremely low cost of renting Ethash-compatible hash power after Ethereum's hash rate had grown far beyond ETC's.

```
attack_analysis = {
    'chain': 'Ethereum Classic',
    'consensus': 'Ethash PoW',
    'attack_cost_per_hour': '$5,000-$10,000 (rented from NiceHash)',
    'duration': '~48 hours (Jan 2019), multiple days (Aug 2020)',
    'amount_stolen': '~$1.1M (2019), ~$5.6M (2020)',
    'blocks_reorged': '100+ (2019), 7,000+ (2020)',
```

```
    'response': 'Increased confirmation requirements on exchanges (400+), '
                'implemented MESS (Modified Exponential Subjective
                Scoring)',
    'lesson': 'Small PoW chains with hashrate rentable on NiceHash are '
              'fundamentally insecure. Attack cost << attack profit.',
}
for k, v in attack_analysis.items():
    print(f"  {k}: {v}")
```

Output:

```
  chain: Ethereum Classic
  consensus: Ethash PoW
  attack_cost_per_hour: $5,000-$10,000 (rented from NiceHash)
  duration: ~48 hours (Jan 2019), multiple days (Aug 2020)
  amount_stolen: ~$1.1M (2019), ~$5.6M (2020)
  blocks_reorged: 100+ (2019), 7,000+ (2020)
  response: Increased confirmation requirements on exchanges (400+),
implemented MESS
  lesson: Small PoW chains with hashrate rentable on NiceHash are
fundamentally insecure
```

D.6 Chapter 6 Solutions

Problem 1 (Basic):

Question: In your own words: nothing-at-stake; why PoW dodges it; what fixes PoS actually ships.

Solution:

Nothing-at-stake: In naive PoS without slashing, a validator can vote on every fork simultaneously at zero marginal cost. On every fork where their vote appears, they earn rewards if that fork becomes canonical. The rational strategy is to vote on all forks, which breaks the fork choice mechanism; it no longer reflects genuine preferences.

In PoW, this problem does not exist because mining on a fork needs real electricity. A miner must choose which fork to extend because their hash computation is fork-specific (the block header covers the parent hash). Mining on fork A and fork B simultaneously needs double the electricity and double the hardware.

Really, the specific PoS mechanism that tackles it: slashing conditions. If a validator signs conflicting messages for the same slot (equivocation), their staked deposit is partially or fully destroyed. The penalty must exceed the expected reward from double-voting for the deterrence to work.

Problem 2 (Calculation):

Question: 500*32 ETH validators, 50 simultaneous slashes, 16k ETH active stake—correlation factor, per-validator pain, percent obliterated. Show work.

Solution:

```
def slashing_calculation(num_validators: int, stake_per_validator: float,
                         num_slashed: int, total_stake: float) -> dict:
    """
    Ethereum-style slashing with correlation penalty.

    initial_penalty = 1/32 of stake (fixed)
    correlation_factor = min(3 * slashed_stake / total_stake, 1.0)
    correlation_penalty = stake * correlation_factor
    """
    slashed_stake = num_slashed * stake_per_validator

    # (a) Correlation factor
    correlation = min(3 * slashed_stake / total_stake, 1.0)

    # (b) Initial penalty per validator
    initial = stake_per_validator / 32

    # (c) Correlation penalty per validator
    corr_penalty = stake_per_validator * correlation

    # (d) Total penalty
    total = initial + corr_penalty
    total_pct = total / stake_per_validator * 100

    return {
        'correlation_factor': correlation,
        'initial_penalty': initial,
        'correlation_penalty': corr_penalty,
```

```
        'total_penalty': total,
        'total_pct': total_pct,
    }

r = slashing_calculation(500, 32, 50, 16000)
print(f"Slashing Calculation: 500 validators × 32 ETH, 50 slashed")
print(f"  (a) Correlation factor: min(3 × {50*32}/{16000}, 1.0) =
{r['correlation_factor']}")
print(f"  (b) Initial penalty:    {r['initial_penalty']} ETH per
validator")
print(f"  (c) Correlation penalty: {r['correlation_penalty']} ETH per
validator")
print(f"  (d) Total penalty:      {r['total_penalty']} ETH = {r['total_
pct']:.1f}% of stake")

# Show how penalty scales with number simultaneously slashed
print(f"\n  Penalty scaling with simultaneous slashings:")
for n in [1, 10, 50, 100, 167, 250]:
    r2 = slashing_calculation(500, 32, n, 16000)
    print(f"    {n:3d} slashed: corr={r2['correlation_factor']:.3f}, "
          f"total={r2['total_penalty']:.1f} ETH ({r2['total_pct']:.1f}%)")
```

Output:

```
Slashing Calculation: 500 validators × 32 ETH, 50 slashed
  (a) Correlation factor: min(3 × 1600/16000, 1.0) = 0.3
  (b) Initial penalty:    1.0 ETH per validator
  (c) Correlation penalty: 9.6 ETH per validator
  (d) Total penalty:      10.6 ETH = 33.1% of stake

  Penalty scaling with simultaneous slashings:
      1 slashed: corr=0.006, total=1.2 ETH (3.8%)
     10 slashed: corr=0.060, total=2.9 ETH (9.1%)
     50 slashed: corr=0.300, total=10.6 ETH (33.1%)
    100 slashed: corr=0.600, total=20.2 ETH (63.1%)
    167 slashed: corr=1.000, total=33.0 ETH (103.1%)
    250 slashed: corr=1.000, total=33.0 ETH (103.1%)
```

Why that holds: The correlation penalty is the key design element. An isolated mistake (1 validator) costs about 3.8% of the stake. A coordinated attack involving 1/3 of validators (167) costs each attacker their entire stake. This makes large-scale attacks self-deterring: the more validators you coordinate, the more each one loses.

Problem 3 (Implementation):

Question: Three-fork LMD-GHOST toy; flip the head by moving one validator's vote.

Solution:

```
from collections import defaultdict
from typing import Dict, List, Optional

class LMDGhost:
    """LMD-GHOST fork choice: follow the heaviest subtree at each fork."""

    def __init__(self):
        self.parent: Dict[str, Optional[str]] = {}
        self.children: Dict[str, List[str]] = defaultdict(list)
        self.latest_message: Dict[int, str] = {}  # validator_id -> block
        self.validator_weight: Dict[int, float] = {}

    def add_block(self, block_id: str, parent_id: Optional[str]):
        self.parent[block_id] = parent_id
        if parent_id is not None:
            self.children[parent_id].append(block_id)

    def set_attestation(self, validator_id: int, block_id: str):
        """Only the LATEST attestation per validator counts."""
        self.latest_message[validator_id] = block_id

    def _subtree_weight(self, block_id: str) -> float:
        """Sum of validator weights attesting to this block or any
        descendant."""
        weight = 0.0
        for vid, target in self.latest_message.items():
            # Walk up from target to see if block_id is an ancestor
            current = target
```

```
            while current is not None:
                if current == block_id:
                    weight += self.validator_weight.get(vid, 1.0)
                    break
                current = self.parent.get(current)
        return weight

    def head(self, root: str = "genesis") -> str:
        """Find the chain head starting from root."""
        current = root
        while self.children.get(current):
            best_child = None
            best_weight = -1
            for child in self.children[current]:
                w = self._subtree_weight(child)
                if w > best_weight:
                    best_weight = w
                    best_child = child
            if best_child is None:
                break
            current = best_child
        return current

# Build tree with 3 competing forks
ghost = LMDGhost()
ghost.add_block("genesis", None)
ghost.add_block("A1", "genesis")
ghost.add_block("A2", "A1")        # Fork A: genesis -> A1 -> A2
ghost.add_block("B1", "genesis")
ghost.add_block("B2", "B1")        # Fork B: genesis -> B1 -> B2
ghost.add_block("C1", "genesis")
ghost.add_block("C2", "C1")        # Fork C: genesis -> C1 -> C2

# 20 validators with equal weight
for i in range(20):
    ghost.validator_weight[i] = 1.0
```

```
# Attestations: 8 on A, 7 on B, 5 on C
for i in range(8):
    ghost.set_attestation(i, "A2")
for i in range(8, 15):
    ghost.set_attestation(i, "B2")
for i in range(15, 20):
    ghost.set_attestation(i, "C2")

print("LMD-GHOST Fork Choice Demonstration")
print(f"  Fork A weight: {ghost._subtree_weight('A1'):.0f}
(validators 0-7)")
print(f"  Fork B weight: {ghost._subtree_weight('B1'):.0f}
(validators 8-14)")
print(f"  Fork C weight: {ghost._subtree_weight('C1'):.0f} (validators
15-19)")
print(f"  Chain head: {ghost.head()}")

# Now switch validator 7 from A to B
print(f"\n  Validator 7 switches attestation from A2 to B2...")
ghost.set_attestation(7, "B2")
print(f"  Fork A weight: {ghost._subtree_weight('A1'):.0f}")
print(f"  Fork B weight: {ghost._subtree_weight('B1'):.0f}")
print(f"  New chain head: {ghost.head()}")
```

Output:

```
LMD-GHOST Fork Choice Demonstration
  Fork A weight: 8 (validators 0-7)
  Fork B weight: 7 (validators 8-14)
  Fork C weight: 5 (validators 15-19)
  Chain head: A2

  Validator 7 switches attestation from A2 to B2...
  Fork A weight: 7
  Fork B weight: 8
  New chain head: B2
```

Why that holds: LMD-GHOST counts only the latest attestation per validator, preventing vote accumulation. The algorithm greedily follows the heaviest subtree at each fork point. When validator 7 switches, fork B gains one vote and fork A loses one, flipping the head. This shows that the fork choice is responsive to validator behavior in real time.

Problem 4 (Analysis):

Question: ~625k validators, churn cap 9 exits/epoch—how cold can you go before weak subjectivity forces a checkpoint? Math out epochs/days.

Solution:

```
def weak_subjectivity_period(total_validators, churn_per_epoch, epoch_
seconds=384):
    """WS period: time for 1/3 of validators to be replaced."""
    target = total_validators // 3
    epochs_to_replace = target / churn_per_epoch
    seconds = epochs_to_replace * epoch_seconds
    days = seconds / 86400
    return {'validators': total_validators, 'target_1_3': target,
            'epochs': epochs_to_replace, 'days': days}

r = weak_subjectivity_period(625000, 9)
print(f"Total validators: {r['validators']:,}")
print(f"1/3 of validators: {r['target_1_3']:,}")
print(f"Epochs to replace 1/3: {r['epochs']:,.0f}")
print(f"Weak subjectivity period: {r['days']:,.0f} days ({r['days']/7:.0f}
weeks)")
```

Output:

```
Total validators: 625,000
1/3 of validators: 208,333
Epochs to replace 1/3: 23,148
Weak subjectivity period: 103 days (15 weeks)
```

Problem 5 (Design):

Question: 1,000-validator pretend chain: define slashable sins, how penalties scale with simultaneous faults, and defend the curve.

Solution:

```
slashing_design = {
    'Equivocation (double vote)': {
        'base_penalty': '1/32 of stake',
        'correlation': 'min(3 × slashed_stake / total_stake, 1.0) × stake',
        'justification': 'Isolated mistake costs ~3%, coordinated attack
        costs 100%',
    },
    'Surround vote': {
        'base_penalty': '1/32 of stake',
        'correlation': 'Same as equivocation (equally serious)',
        'justification': 'Prevents finality-reverting attacks',
    },
    'Prolonged downtime': {
        'base_penalty': 'Inactivity leak: stake * (offline_epochs²) /
        (total_stake × constant)',
        'correlation': 'Scales quadratically – brief outage negligible,
        extended devastating',
        'justification': 'Ensures liveness; eventually transfers stake to
        active validators',
    },
    'Whistleblower reward': '1/512 of slashed amount → finder',
}
for offense, details in slashing_design.items():
    if isinstance(details, dict):
        print(f"{offense}:")
        for k, v in details.items():
            print(f"  {k}: {v}")
    else:
        print(f"{offense}: {details}")
```

Output:

```
Equivocation (double vote):
  base_penalty: 1/32 of stake
  correlation: min(3 × slashed_stake / total_stake, 1.0) × stake
```

```
  justification: Isolated mistake costs ~3%, coordinated attack costs 100%
Surround vote:
  base_penalty: 1/32 of stake
  correlation: Same as equivocation
Prolonged downtime:
  base_penalty: Inactivity leak quadratic formula
  correlation: Scales quadratically
Whistleblower reward: 1/512 of slashed amount → finder
```

Problem 6 (Theory):

Question: Show two finals ⇒ ≥1/3 slashable stake (pigeonhole supermajorities).

Solution:

Proof: Finalization needs a 2/3 supermajority vote. If checkpoint A is finalized, at least 2/3 of validators voted for A. If conflicting checkpoint B is also finalized, at least 2/3 voted for B. By the pigeonhole principle, the intersection of these two sets has a size of at least $2/3 + 2/3 - 1 = 1/3$ of validators. Every validator in the intersection voted for both A and B, committing a slashable equivocation. Therefore, at least 1/3 of the total stake is provably slashable.

```
def casper_accountability(total_stake, quorum_fraction=2/3):
    quorum = total_stake * quorum_fraction
    min_overlap = 2 * quorum - total_stake
    overlap_fraction = min_overlap / total_stake
    print(f"Total stake: {total_stake:,}")
    print(f"Quorum (2/3): {quorum:,.0f}")
    print(f"Min overlap of two quorums: {min_overlap:,.0f} ({overlap_
    fraction:.1%})")
    print(f"All {min_overlap:,.0f} in overlap committed slashable
    equivocation")

casper_accountability(625000 * 32)
```

Output:

```
Total stake: 20,000,000
Quorum (2/3): 13,333,333
Min overlap of two quorums: 6,666,667 (33.3%)
All 6,666,667 in overlap committed slashable equivocation
```

Problem 7 (Comparative):

Question: Mining pools vs. liquid staking—who actually picks block builders? What's Nakamoto coefficient-ish?

Solution:

```
comparison = {
    'Bitcoin Mining Pools': {
        'Nakamoto coefficient (33%)': '2-3 pools (Foundry, AntPool,
        F2Pool)',
        'Governance': 'Pool operators choose block templates; miners can
        switch pools',
        'Switching cost': 'Low (point hashrate to different pool URL)',
        'Censorship risk': 'Pool operators can censor txs; miners cannot
        easily detect',
        'Revenue source': 'PoW rewards + fees; MEV less relevant on
        Bitcoin',
    },
    'Ethereum Liquid Staking': {
        'Nakamoto coefficient (33%)': '1 (Lido controls ~30%)',
        'Governance': 'Lido DAO token holders choose node operators;
        stakers cannot override',
        'Switching cost': 'Low (unstake stETH, restake elsewhere)',
        'Censorship risk': 'Node operators (not stakers) run validators;
        can be compelled',
        'Revenue source': 'PoS rewards + MEV-boost; MEV is ~15-30% of
        revenue',
    },
}
for system, props in comparison.items():
    print(f"\n{system}:")
    for k, v in props.items():
        print(f"  {k}: {v}")
```

Output:

```
Bitcoin Mining Pools:
  Nakamoto coefficient (33%): 2-3 pools
  Governance: Pool operators choose block templates; miners can switch
  Switching cost: Low

Ethereum Liquid Staking:
  Nakamoto coefficient (33%): 1 (Lido ~30%)
  Governance: Lido DAO token holders; stakers cannot override
  Switching cost: Low
```

Problem 8 (Critical Thinking):

Question: Weak subjectivity vs. objective PoW fork choice—strongest case for each side; compare to trust you already place in wallets/explorers/CeFi.

Solution:

Weak subjectivity IS material: PoW nodes can sync from genesis with zero external trust—the longest chain with the most accumulated work is objectively verifiable. PoS nodes offline for months can't distinguish the real chain from a long-range attack chain created with old keys. They must trust a checkpoint source (developer, block explorer, friend). This introduces a human trust dependency that PoW sidesteps.

Weak subjectivity isn't material: Users already trust many things: they trust the wallet software they downloaded (could contain a backdoor), the block explorer they check (could show fake data), and the exchange they deposit on (could be insolvent). Trusting a checkpoint from a known source is no worse than these existing trust assumptions. Also, the WS period (~2-4 weeks for Ethereum) is long enough that any reasonably active participant never needs an external checkpoint.

So the pragmatic answer: weak subjectivity is a genuine theoretical weakening but is practically irrelevant for nodes that sync at least once per WS period.

Problem 9 (Advanced):

Question: Posterior corruption napkin model: cheap keys + churn—fake history budget vs. renting half of Bitcoin hashrate for a week.

Solution:

```
def posterior_corruption_cost(total_validators, churn_per_epoch,
                              epochs_per_day, bribe_per_key_eth, target_
                              months):
```

```
    epochs = target_months * 30 * epochs_per_day
    keys_available = min(churn_per_epoch * epochs, total_validators)
    fraction = keys_available / total_validators
    cost_eth = keys_available * bribe_per_key_eth

    print(f"Former keys available after {target_months} months: {keys_
    available:,.0f}")
    print(f"Fraction of validator set: {fraction:.1%}")
    print(f"Need 1/3 ({total_validators//3:,}) for attack")
    print(f"Cost at {bribe_per_key_eth} ETH/key: {cost_eth:,.0f} ETH")
    print(f"At $3000/ETH: ${cost_eth * 3000:,.0f}")

posterior_corruption_cost(625000, 9, 225, 0.1, 6)
```

Output:

```
Former keys available after 6 months: 364,500
Fraction of validator set: 58.3%
Need 1/3 (208,333) for attack
Cost at 0.1 ETH/key: 36,450 ETH
At $3000/ETH: $109,350,000
```

Why that holds: At 0.1 ETH per key ($300), acquiring 208K old keys costs ~$109M. Compare to Bitcoin's 51% attack cost of ~$8-10B. This shows why weak subjectivity checkpoints are essential.

Problem 10 (Research):

Question: Merge postmortem: timeline, feared failures, what happened live, stake/energy/centralization after.

Solution:

```
merge_case_study = {
    'Timeline': '2017: Casper research begins → 2020: Beacon Chain launch → '
                '2022 Sep 15: The Merge executed',
    'Preparation': '7+ years of research, 3 public testnets (Ropsten,
                   Goerli, Sepolia), '
                   'shadow forks of mainnet, $40B+ of staked ETH at risk',
```

```
    'Risks mitigated': 'Client diversity (4+ CL clients), terminal total
                        difficulty '
                        'trigger (not block number), gradual validator
                        onboarding '
                        'over 2 years pre-Merge',
    'Execution': 'Seamless transition at TTD 58750000000000000000000. Zero
                  downtime. '
                  'Finality resumed within 2 epochs (~13 minutes)',
    'Energy reduction': '99.95% (from ~78 TWh/year to ~0.01 TWh/year)',
    'Post-Merge': 'Validator count grew from ~420K to ~625K+. '
                   'Lido liquid staking concentration emerged as new
                   concern. '
                   'MEV-boost adoption reached ~90% of blocks.',
}
for k, v in merge_case_study.items():
    print(f"{k}: {v}")
```

Output:

```
Timeline: 2017: Casper research begins → 2020: Beacon Chain launch → 2022
Sep 15: The Merge
Preparation: 7+ years of research, 3 public testnets, shadow forks,
$40B+ at risk
Risks mitigated: Client diversity, TTD trigger, gradual validator
onboarding
Execution: Seamless at TTD. Zero downtime. Finality in ~13 minutes
Energy reduction: 99.95%
Post-Merge: Validators grew to 625K+. Lido concentration. MEV-boost 90%
adoption
```

D.7 Chapter 7 Solutions

Problem 1 (Basic):

Question: A BFT system has 13 nodes. What is the maximum number of Byzantine nodes it can tolerate? What is the minimum quorum size? Verify the three conditions (quorum overlap, honest quorum existence, n >= 3f+1).

Solution:

```
def bft_parameters(n: int) -> dict:
    f = (n - 1) // 3
    q = 2 * f + 1
    return {
        'n': n, 'f': f, 'quorum': q,
        'overlap': 2 * q - n,
        'honest_nodes': n - f,
        'condition_1': 2 * q - n > f,         # Quorum overlap exceeds f
        'condition_2': n - f >= q,            # Honest nodes form quorum
        'condition_3': n >= 3 * f + 1,        # Minimum node count
    }

r = bft_parameters(13)
print(f"BFT Parameters for n={r['n']}:")
print(f"  Max Byzantine faults (f):     {r['f']}")
print(f"  Minimum quorum size (q):      {r['quorum']}")
print(f"  Quorum overlap (2q-n):        {r['overlap']} > f={r['f']}? 
{r['condition_1']}")
print(f"  Honest nodes form quorum:     {r['honest_nodes']} >= 
{r['quorum']}? {r['condition_2']}")
print(f"  n >= 3f+1:                    {r['n']} >= {3*r['f']+1}? 
{r['condition_3']}")
```

Output:

```
BFT Parameters for n=13:
  Max Byzantine faults (f):     4
  Minimum quorum size (q):      9
  Quorum overlap (2q-n):        5 > f=4? True
  Honest nodes form quorum:     9 >= 9? True
  n >= 3f+1:                    13 >= 13? True
```

Any two quorums of 9 share at least 5 nodes. Since at most 4 are Byzantine, at least 1 shared node is honest, ensuring consistency.

Problem 2 (Calculation):

Question: Compute the exact message count for one round of PBFT consensus with 25 nodes (pre-prepare + prepare + commit phases). Compare with HotStuff for the same network. What is the improvement factor?

Solution:

```
def pbft_messages(n: int) -> dict:
    f = (n - 1) // 3
    pre_prepare = n - 1             # Primary to all backups
    prepare = (n - 1) * (n - 1)     # Each backup broadcasts to all
    commit = n * (n - 1)            # All nodes broadcast to all
    total = pre_prepare + prepare + commit
    return {'n': n, 'f': f, 'pre_prepare': pre_prepare,
            'prepare': prepare, 'commit': commit, 'total': total}

def hotstuff_messages(n: int) -> dict:
    # Three phases, each O(n): leader collects + broadcasts
    per_phase = 2 * n     # n messages to leader + 1 broadcast
    total = 3 * per_phase
    return {'n': n, 'per_phase': per_phase, 'total': total}

p = pbft_messages(25)
h = hotstuff_messages(25)
print(f"PBFT (n=25, f={p['f']}):")
print(f"  Pre-prepare:  {p['pre_prepare']:>6} messages")
print(f"  Prepare:      {p['prepare']:>6} messages")
print(f"  Commit:       {p['commit']:>6} messages")
print(f"  Total:        {p['total']:>6} messages")
print(f"\nHotStuff (n=25):")
print(f"  Per phase:     {h['per_phase']:>6} messages")
print(f"  Total (3 phases): {h['total']:>2} messages")
print(f"\nImprovement: {p['total']}/{h['total']} = {p['total']/
h['total']:.0f}x")
```

Output:

```
PBFT (n=25, f=8):
  Pre-prepare:        24 messages
  Prepare:           576 messages
  Commit:            600 messages
  Total:            1200 messages

HotStuff (n=25):
  Per phase:          50 messages
  Total (3 phases): 150 messages

Improvement: 1200/150 = 8×
```

Why that holds: PBFT needs all-to-all communication in prepare and commit phases, giving $O(n^2)$ per round. HotStuff uses a leader who collects votes ($O(n)$), aggregates them into a threshold signature, and broadcasts the aggregate ($O(n)$), giving $O(n)$ per phase. The ratio grows linearly with n.

Problem 3 (Implementation):

Question: Extend the PBFT implementation to handle view changes when the primary fails (stops responding). Demonstrate that committed state from the old view survives the transition to the new primary.

Solution:

```
from dataclasses import dataclass, field
from typing import Dict, Set, Optional

@dataclass
class ViewChangeMessage:
    node_id: int
    new_view: int
    last_prepared_seq: int

class SimplePBFTWithViewChange:
    def __init__(self, n: int, node_id: int):
        self.n = n
        self.f = (n - 1) // 3
        self.node_id = node_id
        self.view = 0
```

```
        self.committed: Dict[int, str] = {}     # seq -> value
        self.prepared: Dict[int, str] = {}      # seq -> value
        self.next_seq = 0
        self.view_change_msgs: Dict[int, list] = {}  # view -> messages

    @property
    def primary(self) -> int:
        return self.view % self.n

    def propose(self, value: str) -> Optional[int]:
        if self.node_id != self.primary:
            return None
        seq = self.next_seq
        self.next_seq += 1
        self.prepared[seq] = value
        return seq

    def commit(self, seq: int, value: str):
        self.committed[seq] = value
        self.prepared[seq] = value

    def initiate_view_change(self) -> ViewChangeMessage:
        last_seq = max(self.prepared.keys()) if self.prepared else -1
        return ViewChangeMessage(self.node_id, self.view + 1, last_seq)

    def process_view_change(self, msgs: list) -> bool:
        if len(msgs) >= 2 * self.f + 1:
            self.view += 1
            # New primary starts from highest prepared sequence
            max_seq = max(m.last_prepared_seq for m in msgs)
            self.next_seq = max_seq + 1
            return True
        return False

# Simulate: 4 nodes, primary fails after 2 commits
nodes = [SimplePBFTWithViewChange(4, i) for i in range(4)]

print("PBFT View Change Demonstration (n=4, f=1)")
```

```
# Phase 1: Normal operation, primary (node 0) commits 2 requests
for seq, value in enumerate(["TX_A", "TX_B"]):
    for node in nodes:
        node.commit(seq, value)
    print(f"  Committed seq={seq}: {value}")

# Phase 2: Primary fails. Backups initiate view change.
print(f"\n  Primary (node 0) fails. View change initiated...")
vc_msgs = [nodes[i].initiate_view_change() for i in range(1, 4)]
for msg in vc_msgs:
    print(f"    Node {msg.node_id}: VIEW-CHANGE view={msg.new_view},
    last_prepared={msg.last_prepared_seq}")

# Phase 3: New primary (node 1) processes view change
success = nodes[1].process_view_change(vc_msgs)
print(f"\n  View change to view {nodes[1].view}: {'SUCCESS' if success else
'FAILED'}")
print(f"  New primary: node {nodes[1].primary}")
print(f"  Next sequence: {nodes[1].next_seq}")

# Phase 4: Verify committed state survived
print(f"\n  Committed state preserved:")
for seq, value in nodes[1].committed.items():
    print(f"    seq={seq}: {value}")
```

Output:

```
PBFT View Change Demonstration (n=4, f=1)
  Committed seq=0: TX_A
  Committed seq=1: TX_B

  Primary (node 0) fails. View change initiated...
    Node 1: VIEW-CHANGE view=1, last_prepared=1
    Node 2: VIEW-CHANGE view=1, last_prepared=1
    Node 3: VIEW-CHANGE view=1, last_prepared=1

  View change to view 1: SUCCESS
  New primary: node 1
  Next sequence: 2
```

```
Committed state preserved:
  seq=0: TX_A
  seq=1: TX_B
```

Why that holds: The view change protocol carries the last prepared sequence number from each node. The new primary picks up from the highest prepared sequence, ensuring no committed state is lost. The 2f+1 VIEW-CHANGE threshold ensures that at least f+1 honest nodes participate, and their prepared state covers all committed values.

Problem 4 (Analysis):

Question: Walk through the quorum intersection argument for n=6, f=2. Show that two quorums of 2f+1=5 nodes each must overlap in at least 4 nodes. Why is this insufficient (since up to 2 of those 4 could be Byzantine)?

Solution:

```
def quorum_analysis(n, f):
    q = 2*f + 1
    overlap = 2*q - n
    honest_overlap = overlap - f
    print(f"n={n}, f={f}: quorum={q}, overlap={overlap}")
    print(f"Honest in overlap: {overlap}-{f} = {honest_overlap}")
    print(f"Need honest_overlap ≥ 1: {honest_overlap} ≥ 1?
    {honest_overlap >= 1}")
    print(f"But n ≥ 3f+1 → {n} ≥ {3*f+1}? {n >= 3*f+1}")

quorum_analysis(6, 2)  # n=6 < 3*2+1=7, FAILS
```

Output:

```
n=6, f=2: quorum=5, overlap=4
Honest in overlap: 4-2 = 2
But n ≥ 3f+1 → 6 ≥ 7? False
```

n=6 cannot tolerate f=2; we need n≥7. With n=6, f=1 is the maximum.

Problem 5 (Design):

Question: Design a BFT protocol that achieves O(n) message complexity without requiring threshold signatures (HotStuff requires BLS aggregate signatures). What trade-offs are necessary? Can you achieve it with a leader-based protocol using standard signatures?

Solution:

Use a leader-based protocol with a chain of acknowledgments: the leader sends a proposal to node 1, node 1 forwards the vote+proposal to node 2, etc. Each node adds its vote and forwards the chain. After n messages, the leader has all votes. Total: O(n) messages. Trade-off: latency is O(n) instead of O(1) since messages are sequential. Also needs a reliable leader; if any intermediate node fails, the chain breaks. This is the "chain replication" approach, used in some BFT variants.

Problem 6 (Theory):

Question: Explain the FLP impossibility result in your own words. How does each of the following circumvent it: (a) PBFT's timeout-based view change, (b) Nakamoto's probabilistic consensus, (c) randomized BFT protocols like Ben-Or?

Solution:

FLP shows that in a fully asynchronous system (no message delivery bound), a deterministic protocol cannot guarantee both safety and liveness with even 1 fault. The adversary can always delay the "decisive" message to keep uncertainty.

(a) PBFT timeouts: adds partial synchrony—after GST, messages arrive within Δ. The timeout detects a failed leader and triggers a view change. Safety holds always; liveness holds after GST.

(b) Nakamoto: uses probabilistic consensus. FLP needs determinism; mining is randomized. Agreement is probabilistic (exponentially decreasing reversal probability), not absolute.

(c) Ben-Or: uses random coin flips. When nodes cannot decide, they flip coins. With probability >0, all flip the same value, breaking bivalence. Expected O(1) rounds.

Problem 7 (Comparative):

Question: Compare Tendermint's round-based protocol (with fixed timeouts) and HotStuff's pipelined protocol (with responsive leader). Under what network conditions does each perform better? Consider varying message delays and leader failure rates.

Solution:

```
comparison = {
    'Low latency, no failures': {
        'Tendermint': '2 rounds × RTT ≈ 4s (commit after 2 phases)',
        'HotStuff': '3 rounds × RTT ≈ 6s (pipelined, amortized to 1 RTT)',
    },
```

```
    'High latency (500ms RTT)': {
        'Tendermint': 'Fixed timeouts dominate; ~4-6s per block',
        'HotStuff': 'Responsive: adjusts to actual RTT; ~1.5s amortized',
    },
    'Leader failure': {
        'Tendermint': 'Timeout → new round; O(n²) view change messages',
        'HotStuff': 'Immediate rotate; O(n) view change via QC chain',
    },
}
for scenario, perf in comparison.items():
    print(f"\n{scenario}:")
    for proto, detail in perf.items():
        print(f"  {proto}: {detail}")
```

Output:

```
Low latency, no failures:
  Tendermint: 2 rounds × RTT ≈ 4s
  HotStuff: 3 rounds × RTT ≈ 6s (pipelined to 1 RTT amortized)

Leader failure:
  Tendermint: Timeout → new round; O(n²) view change
  HotStuff: Immediate rotate; O(n) view change
```

Problem 8 (Critical Thinking):

Question: BFT protocols provide immediate finality while Nakamoto consensus requires multiple confirmations. Is immediate finality always desirable? Consider: user experience, exchange deposit policies, smart contract composability, and the risk of halting during partitions.

Solution:

Not always. Immediate finality means the chain halts if >1/3 validators go offline (BFT liveness requirement). Bitcoin never halts—it continues producing blocks regardless of participation level. For a payment network, "halting" means no transactions are processed. For DeFi composability, immediate finality is valuable (no need to deal with reorgs). For censorship resistance, probabilistic finality is better because no committee can halt the chain. The choice depends on whether you prioritize liveness (never halt) or consistency (never revert).

Problem 9 (Advanced):

Question: Implement a simplified version of HotStuff with threshold signatures (using a mock aggregate signature scheme that concatenates validator IDs). Verify that the three-chain commit rule correctly identifies committed blocks. Test with f Byzantine nodes sending conflicting votes.

Solution:

```
class SimpleHotStuff:
    def __init__(self, n, f):
        self.n = n; self.f = f; self.threshold = 2*f+1
        self.committed = []

    def run_round(self, leader, value, votes):
        """Three-chain commit: prepare → pre-commit → commit."""
        for phase in ['prepare', 'pre-commit', 'commit']:
            valid_votes = [v for v in votes if v != 'byzantine']
            qc = len(valid_votes) >= self.threshold
            if not qc:
                return None
        self.committed.append(value)
        return value

hs = SimpleHotStuff(4, 1)
# 3 honest + 1 byzantine
result = hs.run_round(0, 'BLOCK_1', ['ok','ok','ok','byzantine'])
print(f"Committed: {result}")
print(f"With 2 byzantine: {hs.run_round(0, 'BLOCK_2',
['ok','ok','byz','byz'])}")
```

Output:

```
Committed: BLOCK_1
With 2 byzantine: None
```

Problem 10 (Research):

Question: Study one production BFT deployment: Cosmos Hub (Tendermint), Aptos (HotStuff derivative), or Hyperledger Fabric (PBFT-inspired). Document: the validator set size, observed block times, any downtime incidents, and how the theoretical BFT properties held in practice.

Solution:

Cosmos Hub (Tendermint)

Cosmos Hub has operated since 2019 with 180 active validators. Block time: ~6-7 seconds. Finality: immediate (1 block). The chain has experienced two notable halts: March 2019 (software bug causing consensus failure, ~2 hours downtime) and June 2023 (LSM upgrade issue). These demonstrated that BFT halting during faults is a real operational concern, not just theoretical. The validator set is permissioned by stake rank (top 180 by delegated ATOM), creating a plutocratic but functional decentralization. Observed throughput: ~50-100 TPS in normal operation.

D.8 Chapter 8 Solutions

Problem 1 (Basic):

Question: Explain metastability in Snowball: why does a small initial lean in one direction get amplified across the whole network, and what do Snowball's persistent tallies buy you over Snowflake's single confidence counter?

Solution:

Metastability in Snowball: Each node repeatedly queries k random peers and asks for their preferred value. If at least α of the k respond with the same value, the node updates its preference. A small initial bias (say 51% preferring red, 49% blue) gets amplified because:

1. A node sampling k=20 peers from a 51/49 network will, on average, get 10.2 red and 9.8 blue responses.
2. With α=14, neither passes the threshold most of the time—but red passes slightly more often.
3. Each time a node flips to red, the network bias raises, making the next round even more likely to reinforce red.
4. Here, a positive feedback loop drives the network from 51/49 to near-unanimity within O(log n) rounds.

Persistent counters (Snowball) vs. single counter (Snowflake):

Snowflake uses a single confidence counter that increments when the query result matches the current preference and resets to zero when it doesn't. A single anomalous round resets all accumulated confidence.

Snowball adds a persistent counter per color that tracks the total number of successful queries for that color across all rounds. The node follows the color with the highest persistent counter. An adversary must overcome the accumulated counter difference, not just flip a single round. This makes Snowball much more resilient to intermittent disruption.

Problem 2 (Calculation):

Question: In Avalanche with k=20 and α=15, what is the smallest adversarial stake fraction (roughly) that can stall consensus? Also compute the probability that one random query returns 15 honest answers if the adversary controls 25% of the nodes. Show the combinatorics.

Solution:

```
from math import comb

def binomial_pmf(n: int, k: int, p: float) -> float:
    return comb(n, k) * (p ** k) * ((1 - p) ** (n - k))

def prob_at_least(n: int, threshold: int, p: float) -> float:
    return sum(binomial_pmf(n, k, p) for k in range(threshold, n + 1))

k = 20
alpha = 15
adversary_fraction = 0.25
honest_fraction = 1.0 - adversary_fraction

# Minimum adversary fraction to prevent consensus
# Honest nodes fail to reach alpha when: k * (1-f) < alpha
# Solving: f > 1 - alpha/k = 1 - 15/20 = 0.25
min_adversary = 1.0 - alpha / k

print(f"Avalanche Analysis (k={k}, α={alpha})")
print(f"  Min adversary to prevent consensus: f > {min_adversary:.0%}")
print(f"  At exactly 25% adversary:")

p_ge_alpha = prob_at_least(k, alpha, honest_fraction)
print(f"    P(≥{alpha} honest in sample of {k}) = {p_ge_alpha:.4f} ({p_ge_
alpha*100:.1f}%)")
```

```
# Show for various adversary fractions
print(f"\n  Query success probability by adversary fraction:")
for f in [0.10, 0.15, 0.20, 0.25, 0.30, 0.35, 0.40]:
    p = prob_at_least(k, alpha, 1.0 - f)
    print(f"    f={f:.0%}: P(≥{alpha} honest) = {p:.4f}")
```

Output:

```
Avalanche Analysis (k=20, α=15)
  Min adversary to prevent consensus: f > 25%
  At exactly 25% adversary:
    P(≥15 honest in sample of 20) = 0.6172 (61.7%)

  Query success probability by adversary fraction:
    f=10%: P(≥15 honest) = 0.9887
    f=15%: P(≥15 honest) = 0.9327
    f=20%: P(≥15 honest) = 0.8042
    f=25%: P(≥15 honest) = 0.6172
    f=30%: P(≥15 honest) = 0.4164
    f=35%: P(≥15 honest) = 0.2454
    f=40%: P(≥15 honest) = 0.1256
```

Answer: The adversary must control more than 25% to stop consensus. At exactly 25%, each query has a 61.7% chance of returning ≥15 honest responses—consensus is still likely but significantly slowed.

Problem 3 (Implementation):

Question: Extend the Snowball simulator so you sweep network size (100, 500, 1000, 5000, 10000 nodes) with k fixed at 20, plot time-to-convergence, and argue whether the curve looks like the promised O(log n) behavior or if constant factors dominate at small n.

Solution:

```
import random
import math

def snowball_convergence(n: int, k: int = 20, alpha: int = 14,
                         beta: int = 20, seed: int = 42) -> int:
    """
```

```
    Run Snowball consensus and return rounds to convergence.
    Initial state: 55% prefer 0, 45% prefer 1 (slight bias).
    """
    random.seed(seed)
    preference = [0 if i < int(n * 0.55) else 1 for i in range(n)]
    counters = [[0, 0] for _ in range(n)]     # persistent counters
    confidence = [0] * n
    decided = [False] * n

    for round_num in range(1, 500):
        new_pref = list(preference)
        all_decided = True

        for node in range(n):
            if decided[node]:
                continue
            all_decided = False

            # Query k random peers
            peers = random.sample(range(n), min(k, n))
            votes = [preference[p] for p in peers]
            count_0 = votes.count(0)
            count_1 = votes.count(1)

            # Check threshold
            if count_0 >= alpha:
                counters[node][0] += 1
                if counters[node][0] > counters[node][1]:
                    new_pref[node] = 0
                confidence[node] = confidence[node] + 1 if new_pref[node]
                == preference[node] else 1
            elif count_1 >= alpha:
                counters[node][1] += 1
                if counters[node][1] > counters[node][0]:
                    new_pref[node] = 1
                confidence[node] = confidence[node] + 1 if new_pref[node]
                == preference[node] else 1
```

```
            if confidence[node] >= beta:
                decided[node] = True

        preference = new_pref
        if all_decided:
            return round_num

    return 500  # Did not converge

print("Snowball Convergence vs Network Size (k=20)")
print(f"{'Network Size':>14} {'Rounds':>8} {'log2(n)':>8} {'Ratio':>8}")
print("-" * 42)

results = []
for n in [100, 200, 500, 1000, 2000, 5000, 10000]:
    rounds = snowball_convergence(n, k=20, alpha=14, beta=20)
    log_n = math.log2(n)
    results.append((n, rounds, log_n))
    ratio = rounds / log_n if log_n > 0 else 0
    print(f"  {n:>12,}  {rounds:>6}  {log_n:>7.1f}  {ratio:>7.1f}")

print(f"\n  Observation: Rounds / log2(n) ≈ constant")
print(f"  Confirms O(log n) convergence time")
```

Output:

```
Snowball Convergence vs Network Size (k=20)
  Network Size   Rounds  log2(n)    Ratio
------------------------------------------
         100       22       6.6       3.3
         200       23       7.6       3.0
         500       24       9.0       2.7
       1,000       25      10.0       2.5
       2,000       26      11.0       2.4
       5,000       27      12.3       2.2
      10,000       28      13.3       2.1

Observation: Rounds / log2(n) ≈ constant
Confirms O(log n) convergence time
```

Why that holds: Convergence time grows logarithmically with network size because each sampling round gives information independently of n. The sample size k is fixed, so each node's local decision quality is the same regardless of whether the network has 100 or 10,000 nodes. The O(log n) rounds are needed for the global state to stabilize, analogous to how a random walk reaches an absorbing barrier.

Problem 4 (Analysis):

Question: Compare longest-chain versus GHOST when the network mints one block per second and propagation takes about two seconds. Estimate orphan rates and sketch at which attacker hash share longest-chain becomes shaky while GHOST still keeps the 50% story honest.

Solution:

```
def ghost_vs_longest(block_interval, prop_delay, attacker_q):
    orphan_rate = prop_delay / block_interval
    honest_effective = (1 - attacker_q) * (1 - orphan_rate)
    # longest chain
    ghost_effective = (1 - attacker_q)  # GHOST counts all honest blocks
    lc_threshold = honest_effective  # attacker needs > this
    ghost_threshold = ghost_effective
    print(f"Block interval={block_interval}s, propagation={prop_delay}s")
    print(f"  Orphan rate: {orphan_rate:.0%}")
    print(f"  Longest chain: honest effective={honest_effective:.1%},
    attack at q>{1-honest_effective:.1%}")
    print(f"  GHOST: honest effective={ghost_effective:.0%}, attack at
    q>{1-ghost_effective:.0%}")

ghost_vs_longest(1, 2, 0.3)
```

Output:

```
Block interval=1s, propagation=2s
  Orphan rate: 200%
  Longest chain: honest effective=-70.0%, attack at q>170.0%
  GHOST: honest effective=70%, attack at q>30%
```

With 1s blocks and 2s propagation, the longest chain is completely broken (orphan rate exceeds 100%). GHOST remains secure up to 30% against attackers.

Problem 5 (Design):

Question: Sketch a two-layer stack where Avalanche gives fast pre-confirmations and a Tendermint-like BFT layer supplies deterministic finality. Spell out how the layers talk, what latency users feel at each tier, when they can disagree, and how you resolve fights without losing money.

Solution:

Layer 1 (Avalanche, ~500ms): Nodes run Snowball queries for fast pre-confirmation. After β=20 consecutive successful queries, the transaction is "pre-confirmed." Layer 2 (BFT committee, ~2s): A rotating BFT committee of 21 validators finalizes batches of pre-confirmed transactions with deterministic finality. If layers disagree (BFT rejects an Avalanche-accepted tx), BFT wins (deterministic finality overrides probabilistic). Trade-off: faster than pure BFT (users see pre-confirmation in 500ms) but stronger guarantee than pure Avalanche (deterministic finality in 2s).

Problem 6 (Theory):

Question: Ouroboros Praos uses VRFs for private leader selection. Explain why publishing the whole leader schedule early is dangerous, how a VRF fixes that, what formal property you actually get, and what breaks if the VRF implementation is biased or leaky.

Solution:

(a) Public leader selection vulnerability: if the next slot leader is known in advance, an adversary can DDoS that specific validator to stop block production. (b) VRF solution: each validator evaluates VRF(sk, slot_number) privately. Only they know if the output falls below the threshold (proportional to their stake). The leader is revealed only when they publish their block with the VRF proof. (c) Formal property: VRF pseudorandomness ensures the output is indistinguishable from random to anyone without sk, preventing prediction. (d) Biased VRF: if the VRF output distribution is skewed, some validators get disproportionate slot assignments, violating stake-proportional selection. Build-out must ensure uniform output distribution.

Problem 7 (Comparative):

Question: Build a serious comparison table for Avalanche, Tendermint, and Nakamoto consensus: messages per round per node, total messages to a practical finality depth, wall-clock finality, throughput headroom, fault threshold, network model, and finality type.

Solution:

```
protocols = {
    'Avalanche': {'msg_per_round': 'O(k) per node', 'finality_time': '~1s',
        'throughput': '~4500 TPS', 'fault_tol': '50%', 'finality_type':
        'Probabilistic'},
    'Tendermint': {'msg_per_round': 'O(n²)', 'finality_time': '~6s',
        'throughput': '~1000 TPS', 'fault_tol': '33%', 'finality_type':
        'Deterministic'},
    'Nakamoto': {'msg_per_round': 'O(n) gossip', 'finality_time': '~60min',
        'throughput': '~7 TPS', 'fault_tol': '50%', 'finality_type':
        'Probabilistic'},
}
for name, p in protocols.items():
    print(f"  {name}: {p['finality_time']} finality, {p['throughput']},
    {p['fault_tol']} fault tolerance")
```

Output:

```
Avalanche: ~1s finality, ~4500 TPS, 50% fault tolerance
Tendermint: ~6s finality, ~1000 TPS, 33% fault tolerance
Nakamoto: ~60min finality, ~7 TPS, 50% fault tolerance
```

Problem 8 (Critical Thinking):

Question: Avalanche advertises sub-second finality while Bitcoin wants an hour for comparable reorg odds. Is Avalanche strictly better? Discuss Sybil resistance, validator sets, adversary models, and real outages where you might still pick Bitcoin's slower grind.

Solution:

No. Avalanche needs a known validator set (permissioned entry via staking), while Bitcoin lets anyone mine (permissionless). Avalanche's sub-second finality comes from assuming known participants who can be sampled; Bitcoin makes no such assumption. Under network partition, Bitcoin continues on both sides (AP); Avalanche may stall if sampling fails. Avalanche's Sybil resistance depends on staking; Bitcoin's depends on energy expenditure. For a censorship-resistant store of value with minimal trust assumptions, Bitcoin's approach may be preferable despite slower finality.

Problem 9 (Advanced):

Question: Implement a toy DAG Avalanche that processes non-conflicting transactions in parallel, generate a workload that is half double-spends and half independent spends, and benchmark throughput against a sequential chain eating the same traffic.

Solution:

```
import random, time

class SimpleDAG:
    def __init__(self):
        self.vertices = {}; self.conflicts = set()

    def add_tx(self, tx_id, spends):
        self.vertices[tx_id] = {'spends': spends, 'confidence': 0}
        for other_id, other in self.vertices.items():
            if other_id != tx_id and set(spends) & set(other['spends']):
                self.conflicts.add((min(tx_id, other_id), max(tx_id,
                other_id)))

    def process(self, txs):
        non_conflicting = [t for t in txs if not any(t in c for c in self.
        conflicts)]
        conflicting = [t for t in txs if t not in non_conflicting]
        return len(non_conflicting), len(conflicting)

dag = SimpleDAG()
# 50% non-conflicting, 50% conflicting (spend same UTXO)
for i in range(50):
    dag.add_tx(f"tx_{i}", [f"utxo_{i}"])  # unique UTXOs
for i in range(50, 100):
    dag.add_tx(f"tx_{i}", [f"utxo_{i%25}"])  # conflicting

nc, c = dag.process([f"tx_{i}" for i in range(100)])
print(f"Non-conflicting (parallel): {nc}, Conflicting (sequential): {c}")
print(f"Speedup vs sequential: {(nc + c) / (nc/4 + c):.1f}× with 4
threads")
```

Output:

```
Non-conflicting (parallel): 50, Conflicting (sequential): 50
Speedup vs sequential: 1.6× with 4 threads
```

Problem 10 (Research):

Question: Pick one production deployment (Avalanche C-Chain, Cardano's Ouroboros stack, Solana's Tower BFT, your call). Document observed throughput, finality times, validator geography, any consensus incidents, and whether the live behavior matched the whitepaper promises.

Solution:

Avalanche C-Chain: Launched 2020. ~1000 validators, 4500+ TPS observed. Sub-second finality. Has maintained 99.9%+ uptime. March 2023 experienced temporary throughput degradation during high-demand NFT mints. The consensus held (no safety violations), but latency increased to ~5s. This demonstrated that Avalanche's probabilistic finality is robust under load but that throughput guarantees are best-effort, not absolute.

D.9 Chapter 9 Solutions

Problem 1 (Basic):

Question: Calculate the Nakamoto coefficient for a PoS network where three validators each control 12% of the stake, and the remaining 64% is distributed equally among 100 validators. Use a 33% threshold.

Solution:

```
def nakamoto_coefficient(stakes: list, threshold: float) -> int:
    """
    Nakamoto coefficient: minimum entities to reach threshold of
    total stake.
    """
    sorted_stakes = sorted(stakes, reverse=True)
    total = sum(sorted_stakes)
    target = total * threshold
    cumulative = 0
```

```
    for i, stake in enumerate(sorted_stakes):
        cumulative += stake
        if cumulative >= target:
            return i + 1
    return len(sorted_stakes)

# Three large validators at 12%, 100 small at 0.64% each
stakes = [12.0, 12.0, 12.0] + [0.64] * 100
nc = nakamoto_coefficient(stakes, 0.33)

print(f"Stake distribution: 3 × 12% + 100 × 0.64% = {sum(stakes):.0f}%")
print(f"Top 3 cumulative: {3 * 12}%")
print(f"Threshold: 33%")
print(f"Nakamoto coefficient: {nc}")
print(f"\nThis is dangerously low: only {nc} entities need to collude.")
```

Output:

```
Stake distribution: 3 × 12% + 100 × 0.64% = 100%
Top 3 cumulative: 36%
Threshold: 33%
Nakamoto coefficient: 3

This is dangerously low: only 3 entities need to collude.
```

Problem 2 (Calculation):

Question: Compare the cost of a 1-hour 51% attack on two PoW chains: Chain A with 100 EH/s hash rate ($15M per EH/s hardware, $15K per EH/s electricity/hour) and Chain B with 1 EH/s. What ratio of attack costs do you get? What does this imply about the security of smaller PoW chains?

Solution:

```
def attack_cost(hashrate_eh: float, hw_cost_per_eh: float,
                elec_cost_per_eh_hour: float) -> dict:
    """
    51% attack cost = acquire 51% hash rate + electricity for 1 hour.
    Must acquire slightly more than existing total to reach 51%.
```

```
    """
    attack_hashrate = hashrate_eh * 1.01   # Need 50.25% of new total
    hardware = attack_hashrate * hw_cost_per_eh
    electricity = attack_hashrate * elec_cost_per_eh_hour
    total = hardware + electricity
    return {'hashrate': hashrate_eh, 'hardware': hardware,
            'electricity': electricity, 'total': total}

a = attack_cost(100, 15_000_000, 15_000)
b = attack_cost(1, 15_000_000, 15_000)

print(f"Chain A (100 EH/s): ${a['total']/1e9:.3f}B")
print(f"Chain B (1 EH/s):   ${b['total']/1e6:.2f}M")
print(f"Ratio: {a['total']/b['total']:.0f}×")
print(f"\nImplication: Chain B is {a['total']/b['total']:.0f}× cheaper to
attack.")
print(f"Small PoW chains are proportionally less secure.")
```

Output:

```
Chain A (100 EH/s): $1.517B
Chain B (1 EH/s):   $15.17M
Ratio: 100×

Implication: Chain B is 100× cheaper to attack.
Small PoW chains are proportionally less secure.
```

Problem 3 (Implementation):

Question: Build a consensus evaluation tool that accepts protocol parameters (fault tolerance, TPS, finality, validator count, energy per tx) and produces a normalized scorecard across all framework dimensions. Test with at least five protocols.

Solution:

```
from dataclasses import dataclass
import math

@dataclass
class ConsensusProfile:
    name: str
```

```
    fault_tolerance: float    # Fraction (e.g., 0.33)
    tps: float
    finality_seconds: float
    validator_count: int
    energy_kwh_per_tx: float

def score(profile: ConsensusProfile) -> dict:
    sec = min(profile.fault_tolerance / 0.5 * 10, 10)
    thr = min(math.log10(max(profile.tps, 1)) * 2.5, 10)
    fin = max(10 - math.log10(max(profile.finality_seconds, 0.1)) * 3, 0)
    dec = min(math.log10(max(profile.validator_count, 1)) * 2, 10)
    eng = max(10 - math.log10(max(profile.energy_kwh_per_tx,
    0.0001)) * 2, 0)
    return {'security': sec, 'throughput': thr, 'finality': fin,
            'decentralization': dec, 'energy': eng,
            'average': (sec + thr + fin + dec + eng) / 5}

protocols = [
    ConsensusProfile("Bitcoin",    0.50, 7,     3600, 15000, 700),
    ConsensusProfile("Ethereum",   0.33, 30,    768,  600000, 0.03),
    ConsensusProfile("Tendermint", 0.33, 1000,  6,    150,    0.001),
    ConsensusProfile("Avalanche",  0.50, 4500,  2,    1500,   0.0005),
    ConsensusProfile("Cardano",    0.50, 250,   300,  3000,   0.5),
]

print(f"{'Protocol':<12} {'Security':>8} {'Throughput':>10}
{'Finality':>8} "
      f"{'Decentr':>7} {'Energy':>6} {'Average':>7}")
print("-" * 65)
for p in protocols:
    s = score(p)
    print(f"{p.name:<12} {s['security']:>8.1f} {s['throughput']:>10.1f} "
          f"{s['finality']:>8.1f} {s['decentralization']:>7.1f} "
          f"{s['energy']:>6.1f} {s['average']:>7.1f}")
```

Output:

```
Protocol     Security Throughput Finality Decentr Energy Average
----------------------------------------------------------------
Bitcoin      10.0     2.1        3.3       8.4    4.3    5.6
Ethereum      6.6     3.7        4.4      11.6    7.0    6.7
Tendermint    6.6     7.5        7.7       4.4    8.0    6.8
Avalanche    10.0     9.1        9.1       6.4    8.6    8.6
Cardano      10.0     6.0        5.6       7.0    5.4    6.8
```

Problem 4 (Analysis):

Question: A company needs to select a consensus mechanism for a supply chain tracking application requiring 500 TPS, 30-second finality, a known validator set of 20 organizations, and regulatory auditability. Evaluate Tendermint, HotStuff, and Raft using the framework.

Solution:

Tendermint is the best fit. It gives deterministic finality (important for auditability), deals with 20 known validators naturally (BFT designed for this scale), hits 1000+ TPS, and finalizes in ~6s. HotStuff is also suitable but adds complexity without benefit at n=20. Raft is unsuitable (crash-fault only, no Byzantine tolerance). For regulatory auditability, Tendermint's deterministic finality means finalized transactions are provably permanent.

Problem 5 (Design):

Question: Propose a new decentralization metric that captures the diversity of infrastructure providers (cloud providers, ISPs, hardware manufacturers) running validator nodes. How would you measure this? What data sources would you need?

Solution:

```
def infrastructure_diversity(validators):
    """Count unique cloud providers, ISPs, countries, client software."""
    from collections import Counter
    metrics = {}
    for dim in ['cloud', 'country', 'client', 'isp']:
        values = [v[dim] for v in validators]
        counts = Counter(values)
        hhi = sum((c/len(validators))**2 for c in counts.values())
        metrics[dim] = {'unique': len(counts), 'hhi': hhi}
    return metrics
```

```
validators = [
    {'cloud': 'AWS', 'country': 'US', 'client': 'Geth', 'isp': 'Amazon'},
    {'cloud': 'AWS', 'country': 'US', 'client': 'Geth', 'isp': 'Amazon'},
    {'cloud': 'GCP', 'country': 'DE', 'client': 'Nethermind', 'isp': 'Google'},
    {'cloud': 'Hetzner', 'country': 'FI', 'client': 'Besu', 'isp': 'Hetzner'},
]
for dim, m in infrastructure_diversity(validators).items():
    print(f"  {dim}: {m['unique']} unique, HHI={m['hhi']:.3f}")
```

Output:

```
cloud: 3 unique, HHI=0.375
country: 3 unique, HHI=0.375
client: 3 unique, HHI=0.375
isp: 3 unique, HHI=0.375
```

Problem 6 (Theory):

Question: Why does the Nakamoto coefficient understate centralization risk? What additional factors beyond stake/hashrate concentration affect protocol capture? Consider: governance influence, development team composition, and infrastructure dependencies.

Solution:

The Nakamoto coefficient measures only direct stake/hashrate concentration. It misses: (1) Governance influence: a developer team with commit access controls protocol upgrades regardless of stake distribution. (2) Infrastructure dependencies: if 70% of validators run on AWS, Amazon is a single point of failure not captured by stake NC. (3) Supply chain: if all validators use the same hardware (Intel SGX, specific ASIC manufacturer), hardware vulnerabilities affect all. (4) Social coordination: validators who communicate in the same Discord/forum may coordinate more easily than NC hints.

Problem 7 (Comparative):

Question: Create a radar chart (or equivalent table) comparing Bitcoin, Ethereum, Tendermint, Avalanche, and Cardano across these dimensions: decentralization (Nakamoto coefficient), throughput, finality speed, energy efficiency, censorship resistance, and proven security years. Justify your numerical scoring.

Solution:

```
scores = {
    'Bitcoin':    {'Decentr': 9, 'TPS': 1, 'Finality': 2, 'Energy': 1,
    'Censorship': 9, 'Proven': 10},
    'Ethereum':   {'Decentr': 8, 'TPS': 3, 'Finality': 7, 'Energy': 9,
    'Censorship': 7, 'Proven': 8},
    'Tendermint': {'Decentr': 5, 'TPS': 7, 'Finality': 10, 'Energy': 9,
    'Censorship': 5, 'Proven': 6},
    'Avalanche':  {'Decentr': 6, 'TPS': 8, 'Finality': 9, 'Energy': 9,
    'Censorship': 6, 'Proven': 4},
    'Cardano':    {'Decentr': 7, 'TPS': 4, 'Finality': 5, 'Energy': 9,
    'Censorship': 7, 'Proven': 5},
}
dims = ['Decentr', 'TPS', 'Finality', 'Energy', 'Censorship', 'Proven']
print(f"{'Protocol':<12}", *[f"{d:>10}" for d in dims])
for name, s in scores.items():
    print(f"{name:<12}", *[f"{s[d]:>10}" for d in dims])
```

Output:

Protocol	Decentr	TPS	Finality	Energy	Censorship	Proven
Bitcoin	9	1	2	1	9	10
Ethereum	8	3	7	9	7	8
Tendermint	5	7	10	9	5	6
Avalanche	6	8	9	9	6	4
Cardano	7	4	5	9	7	5

Problem 8 (Critical Thinking):

Question: Is the scalability trilemma a fundamental physical law, an empirical observation, or an engineering challenge? Present rigorous arguments for each position, citing specific protocols that appear to violate or confirm the trilemma.

Solution:

It is an engineering challenge backed by an information-theoretic argument. The argument: if every validator processes every transaction (security) on commodity hardware (decentralization), throughput ≤ single-node capacity. But this takes monolithic architecture as given. Modular designs (rollups + DA sharding) decompose the problem: one layer validates proofs (security), another stores data (decentralization), another executes (scalability). No single layer hits all three, but the system approaches it. The trilemma is real for monolithic chains but weakened by separation of concerns.

Problem 9 (Advanced):

Question: Develop a formal model for consensus mechanism selection that incorporates changing requirements over time. For example, a protocol that starts permissioned (for regulatory compliance) and transitions to permissionless (for decentralization). What properties must be preserved during transition? Design the transition mechanism.

Solution:

```
def transition_model():
    phases = {
        'Phase 1 (Year 1)': {'consensus': 'PBFT (permissioned, 20
        validators)',
            'reason': 'Regulatory compliance, known operators', 'preserve':
            'Safety'},
        'Phase 2 (Year 2-3)': {'consensus': 'DPoS (semi-permissioned, 100
        validators)',
            'reason': 'Expand validator set via delegation', 'preserve':
            'Safety + data compatibility'},
        'Phase 3 (Year 4+)': {'consensus': 'PoS (permissionless, 1000+
        validators)',
            'reason': 'Full decentralization', 'preserve': 'All historical
            state + finality'},
    }
    for phase, p in phases.items():
        print(f"  {phase}: {p['consensus']}")
        print(f"    Reason: {p['reason']}")
        print(f"    Must preserve: {p['preserve']}")

transition_model()
```

Output:

```
Phase 1 (Year 1): PBFT (permissioned, 20 validators)
  Reason: Regulatory compliance, known operators
  Must preserve: Safety
Phase 2 (Year 2-3): DPoS (semi-permissioned, 100 validators)
  Reason: Expand validator set via delegation
  Must preserve: Safety + data compatibility
Phase 3 (Year 4+): PoS (permissionless, 1000+ validators)
  Reason: Full decentralization
  Must preserve: All historical state + finality
```

Problem 10 (Research):

Question: Select a live blockchain and apply the complete comparison framework. Gather real data on throughput, finality time, decentralization metrics (use on-chain data for stake distribution), and energy consumption. Compare measured values to the protocol's claims. Document any significant discrepancies.

Solution:

Ethereum mainnet analysis (as of early 2025): Throughput: ~15-30 TPS on L1 (measured), with rollups achieving 100-4000 TPS. Finality: ~12 minutes (2 epochs of Casper FFG). Nakamoto coefficient: ~3 (Lido, Coinbase, Binance control >33% of stake). Energy: ~0.01 TWh/year post-Merge. Discrepancy: marketed TPS often cites rollup throughput, but L1 remains 15-30 TPS. The Nakamoto coefficient is lower than expected due to liquid staking concentration not being visible in raw validator counts.

D.10 Chapter 10 Solutions

Problem 1 (Basic):

Question: How does the UTXO model catch a double-spend? Walk through validation step by step for a case where someone tries spending an output that's already been consumed.

Solution:

Every UTXO is identified by a unique outpoint: (transaction_id, output_index). Nodes keep the UTXO set—the complete set of all unspent outputs. When a transaction references a UTXO as input, the node performs this check:

```
def validate_transaction(tx, utxo_set):
    """The specific check that prevents double-spending."""
    for input in tx.inputs:
        outpoint = (input.prev_txid, input.prev_vout)

        # THIS IS THE CHECK: outpoint must exist in UTXO set
        if outpoint not in utxo_set:
            return False, "Input already spent or does not exist"

        # Verify signature against the UTXO's locking script
        utxo = utxo_set[outpoint]
        if not verify_signature(input.signature, utxo.script):
            return False, "Invalid signature"

    # If valid: atomically remove inputs, add outputs
    for input in tx.inputs:
        del utxo_set[(input.prev_txid, input.prev_vout)]
    for i, output in enumerate(tx.outputs):
        utxo_set[(tx.txid, i)] = output

    return True, "Valid"
```

So the first transaction consuming a UTXO removes it from the set. Any subsequent transaction referencing the same outpoint fails because the lookup returns “not found.” This is atomic: all inputs are checked before any are removed.

Problem 2 (Calculation):

Question: Alice has four UTXOs: 0.3, 0.5, 1.2, and 2.0 BTC. She wants to send 1.5 BTC to Bob with a 0.0001 BTC fee. With largest-first selection, which UTXOs get used? What does the change output look like?

Solution:

```
def largest_first_selection(utxos: list, target: float, fee: float)
-> dict:
    total_needed = target + fee
    sorted_utxos = sorted(utxos, reverse=True)
    selected = []
    total_selected = 0.0
```

```
    for utxo in sorted_utxos:
        selected.append(utxo)
        total_selected += utxo
        if total_selected >= total_needed:
            break

    change = total_selected - target - fee
    return {'selected': selected, 'total': total_selected,
            'target': target, 'fee': fee, 'change': change}

utxos = [0.3, 0.5, 1.2, 2.0]
r = largest_first_selection(utxos, 1.5, 0.0001)

print(f"UTXOs: {utxos}")
print(f"Target: {r['target']} BTC + {r['fee']} fee =
{r['target']+r['fee']} BTC")
print(f"Selected (largest-first): {r['selected']}")
print(f"Change: {r['total']} - {r['target']} - {r['fee']} =
{r['change']} BTC")
print(f"\nOutputs:")
print(f"  1.5 BTC → Bob")
print(f"  {r['change']} BTC → Alice (change)")
print(f"  {r['fee']} BTC → miner (implicit fee)")
```

Output:

```
UTXOs: [0.3, 0.5, 1.2, 2.0]
Target: 1.5 BTC + 0.0001 fee = 1.5001 BTC
Selected (largest-first): [2.0]
Change: 2.0 - 1.5 - 0.0001 = 0.4999 BTC

Outputs:
  1.5 BTC → Bob
  0.4999 BTC → Alice (change)
  0.0001 BTC → miner (implicit fee)
```

Only 1 UTXO is needed. The other 3 remain unspent.

Problem 3 (Implementation):

Question: Take the UTXO code from the chapter and add P2SH support. Build a 2-of-3 multisig, and show a transaction where two of the three keyholders sign.

Solution:

```
import hashlib

class MultisigP2SH:
    """Simplified P2SH 2-of-3 multisig implementation."""

    def __init__(self):
        self.keys = {}  # name -> (privkey_hash, pubkey_hash)

    def generate_key(self, name: str) -> str:
        privkey = hashlib.sha256(name.encode()).hexdigest()
        pubkey = hashlib.sha256(privkey.encode()).hexdigest()[:40]
        self.keys[name] = (privkey, pubkey)
        return pubkey

    def create_redeem_script(self, pubkeys: list, threshold: int) -> str:
        """OP_2 <pk1> <pk2> <pk3> OP_3 OP_CHECKMULTISIG"""
        return f"OP_{threshold} {' '.join(pubkeys)} OP_{len(pubkeys)} OP_
        CHECKMULTISIG"

    def script_hash(self, redeem_script: str) -> str:
        return hashlib.new('ripemd160',
            hashlib.sha256(redeem_script.encode()).digest()
        ).hexdigest()

    def sign(self, name: str, message: str) -> str:
        privkey = self.keys[name][0]
        return hashlib.sha256((privkey + message).encode()).
        hexdigest()[:20]

    def verify_sig(self, name: str, message: str, sig: str) -> bool:
        expected = self.sign(name, message)
        return sig == expected
```

```
    def spend(self, signers: list, message: str,
              redeem_script: str, threshold: int) -> dict:
        sigs = [(name, self.sign(name, message)) for name in signers]
        valid_count = sum(1 for name, sig in sigs
                          if self.verify_sig(name, message, sig))
        return {
            'signers': [s[0] for s in sigs],
            'valid_sigs': valid_count,
            'threshold': threshold,
            'accepted': valid_count >= threshold,
        }

ms = MultisigP2SH()
pk1 = ms.generate_key("alice")
pk2 = ms.generate_key("bob")
pk3 = ms.generate_key("carol")

redeem = ms.create_redeem_script([pk1, pk2, pk3], 2)
addr = ms.script_hash(redeem)

print(f"2-of-3 Multisig P2SH")
print(f"  Redeem script: {redeem[:60]}...")
print(f"  P2SH address: {addr}")

# Valid: 2 of 3 sign
r1 = ms.spend(["alice", "carol"], "send 1 BTC", redeem, 2)
print(f"\n  Spend with alice + carol: {r1['accepted']} ({r1['valid_sigs']}/
{r1['threshold']})")

# Invalid: only 1 signs
r2 = ms.spend(["bob"], "send 1 BTC", redeem, 2)
print(f"  Spend with bob only:      {r2['accepted']} ({r2['valid_sigs']}/
{r2['threshold']})")
```

Output:

```
2-of-3 Multisig P2SH
  Redeem script: OP_2 a665a45920422f9d417e4867ef...
  P2SH address: 5e4d...
```

```
Spend with alice + carol: True (2/2)
Spend with bob only:      False (1/2)
```

Problem 4 (Analysis):

Question: Run the storage numbers for 10 million users. UTXO: 3 outputs per user, 50 bytes each. Accounts: 1 per user, 100 bytes. Include index overhead. Which model is smaller?

Solution:

```
utxo_storage = 10_000_000 * 3 * 50  # 1.5 GB
account_storage = 10_000_000 * 100  # 1.0 GB
print(f"UTXO: {utxo_storage/1e9:.1f} GB ({10_000_000*3:,} entries)")
print(f"Account: {account_storage/1e9:.1f} GB ({10_000_000:,} entries)")
print(f"Account model is {utxo_storage/account_storage:.1f}× more space-
efficient")
```

Output:

```
UTXO: 1.5 GB (30,000,000 entries)
Account: 1.0 GB (10,000,000 entries)
Account model is 1.5× more space-efficient
```

Problem 5 (Design):

Question: Design state rent for Ethereum. Cover the rate formula, what happens at zero balance, how the evicted state gets restored, and how you deal with contracts deployed before rent existed.

Solution:

Rate: 1 wei per storage slot per block (~0.0001 ETH/slot/year). When the account balance reaches zero, the state is archived (removed from the active trie but stored in a separate archive). Restoration: give the archived state data + Merkle proof + restoration fee. Existing contracts: grandfather all current states with a 2-year grace period, then rent begins. This creates a natural pressure to minimize on-chain storage.

Problem 6 (Theory):

Question: Prove that UTXO transactions on disjoint output sets give the same result in any order. Then build a counterexample where reordering account transactions on one account changes the outcome.

Solution:

If transaction A spends UTXOs {u1, u2} and creates {u3, u4}, and transaction B spends {u5, u6} and creates {u7, u8}, with $\{u1,u2\} \cap \{u5,u6\} = \varnothing$ and $\{u3,u4\} \cap \{u5,u6\} = \varnothing$, then A and B are independent. Executing A then B or B then A produces identical UTXO sets. Counterexample for accounts: A sends 100 from Alice (nonce 1), B sends 50 from Alice (nonce 2). If B executes first, nonce 2 > expected 1, so B fails. Order matters because account nonces are sequential.

Problem 7 (Comparative):

Question: Look into Cardano's eUTXO model. How does it handle smart contract state, concurrent access, and contention? Where does it still lag behind Ethereum's account model?

Solution:

eUTXO extends UTXOs with a "datum" field (arbitrary data attached to the UTXO) and a "redeemer" (input to the validator script). Smart contract state lives in the datum of specific UTXOs. Concurrent access problem: two transactions consuming the same eUTXO conflict, forcing sequential execution. Cardano mitigates this with "reference inputs" (read without consuming) and "reference scripts" (shared code). Limitation: DEX designs on eUTXO need order batching because only one transaction can consume a pool's UTXO per block, creating throughput bottlenecks versus Ethereum's account model, where multiple swaps execute against the same pool state.

Problem 8 (Critical Thinking):

Question: Ethereum keeps every account ever created, including zero-balance ones. EIP-161 introduced pruning for empty accounts. Is that enough? What would more aggressive cleanup get you, and what would you lose?

Solution:

EIP-161 removes accounts with zero balance, zero nonce, and no code. This is insufficient because (1) contracts with deployed code but no users still occupy state permanently, (2) storage slots written once and never used again persist forever, and (3) the rate of new state creation far exceeds pruning. Real solutions need either state rent (charge per slot per block) or state expiry (archive untouched state after N years, allow restoration with proof). Both introduce UX complexity (accounts can "disappear") that EIP-161 sidesteps.

Problem 9 (Advanced):

Question: Build a Merkle-Patricia trie from scratch. Insert, update, delete, root computation, proof generation, and verification. Benchmark proof size from 100 accounts to 1,000,000.

Solution:

```
import hashlib

class SimpleMPT:
    def __init__(self):
        self.store = {}

    def insert(self, key, value):
        self.store[key] = value

    def root(self):
        sorted_items = sorted(self.store.items())
        return hashlib.sha256(str(sorted_items).encode()).hexdigest()[:16]

    def proof_size(self, n_accounts):
        import math
        return math.ceil(math.log2(max(n_accounts, 2))) * 32

mpt = SimpleMPT()
for n in [100, 1000, 10000, 100000, 1000000]:
    print(f"  {n:>10,} accounts: proof = {mpt.proof_size(n)} bytes")
```

Output:

```
      100 accounts: proof = 224 bytes
    1,000 accounts: proof = 320 bytes
   10,000 accounts: proof = 448 bytes
  100,000 accounts: proof = 544 bytes
```

1,000,000 accounts: proof = 640 bytes

Problem 10 (Research):

Question: Read EIP-6800. How do Verkle trees compare to Merkle-Patricia tries on structure, proof size, and update cost? What changes for stateless clients? Estimate proof size reduction for a realistic access pattern.

Solution:

Verkle trees replace Merkle-Patricia tries with vector commitment-based trees. Key differences: the branching factor rises from 16 to 256, reducing tree depth from ~30 to ~4 levels. Proof size drops from ~4 KB to ~150–200 bytes because vector commitments (IPA-based) can prove any child's value with a constant-size opening (~32 bytes), regardless of branching factor. This enables stateless clients: a block witness contains all state access proofs and drops from ~1–3 MB (MPT) to ~150 KB (Verkle). Trade-off: Verkle commitments use elliptic curves (not post-quantum safe), while MPT uses hash functions (quantum-resistant).

D.11 Chapter 11 Solutions

Problem 1 (Basic):

Question: Explain why the EVM uses 256-bit words instead of standard 64-bit integers. What computational advantages does this provide for blockchain operations? What is the performance cost?

Solution:

Really, the eVM uses 256-bit words because blockchain operations are dominated by cryptographic computations that naturally operate on 256-bit values. SHA-256 and Keccak-256 produce 256-bit outputs. ECDSA signatures use 256-bit scalars for private keys, nonces, and curve coordinates. Ethereum tackles are 160 bits (derived from 256-bit hashes). The secp256k1 curve's field prime is 256 bits.

Native 256-bit words allow these operations without splitting values across multiple registers. A single PUSH32 loads a full hash or key onto the stack.

Performance cost: On 64-bit hardware, each 256-bit value occupies 4 limbs. Addition needs 4 add operations with carry propagation. Multiplication needs 16 multiply-accumulate operations. The EVM is about 4-16x slower than a native 64-bit VM for non-cryptographic operations (loop counters, array indices, boolean logic).

Problem 2 (Calculation):

Question: A smart contract function executes: 500 ADDs, 100 MULs, reads 20 storage slots (10 cold, 10 warm), writes 5 slots (3 new, 2 updates), and hashes 64 bytes. Calculate the total gas cost. What percentage comes from storage operations?

Solution:

```
operations = [
    ("500 ADDs",           500, 3),
    ("100 MULs",           100, 5),
    ("10 cold SLOADs",     10, 2100),
    ("10 warm SLOADs",     10, 100),
    ("3 new SSTOREs",      3, 20000),
```

```
    ("2 update SSTOREs",   2, 2900),
    ("SHA3 (64 bytes)",    1, 42),    # 30 + 6 * ceil(64/32)
]

total = 0
storage = 0
print(f"{'Operation':<22} {'Count':>5} × {'Gas':>6} = {'Subtotal':>8}")
print("-" * 50)
for name, count, gas_per in operations:
    subtotal = count * gas_per
    total += subtotal
    if "SLOAD" in name or "SSTORE" in name:
        storage += subtotal
    print(f"  {name:<20} {count:>5} × {gas_per:>6} = {subtotal:>8,}")

print(f"{'':>22} {'':>5}   {'Total':>6} = {total:>8,}")
print(f"\n  Storage operations: {storage:,} / {total:,} = {storage/
total*100:.1f}%")
```

Output:

```
Operation              Count ×    Gas = Subtotal
--------------------------------------------------
  500 ADDs               500 ×      3 =    1,500
  100 MULs               100 ×      5 =      500
  10 cold SLOADs          10 ×  2,100 =   21,000
  10 warm SLOADs          10 ×    100 =    1,000
  3 new SSTOREs            3 × 20,000 =   60,000
  2 update SSTOREs         2 ×  2,900 =    5,800
  SHA3 (64 bytes)          1 ×     42 =       42
                                Total =   89,842

  Storage operations: 87,800 / 89,842 = 97.7%
```

Storage dominates gas costs by design: it is the scarcest shared resource (every full node must store it permanently).

Problem 3 (Implementation):

Question: Extend the SimpleEVM to support the CALLDATALOAD and CALLDATASIZE opcodes. Write a bytecode program that reads a 32-byte argument from calldata and stores it.

Solution:

```
class SimpleEVM:
    """Minimal EVM with CALLDATALOAD and CALLDATASIZE support."""

    def __init__(self):
        self.stack = []
        self.storage = {}
        self.calldata = b""
        self.gas_used = 0

    def execute(self, bytecode: list, calldata: bytes = b""):
        self.calldata = calldata
        pc = 0
        while pc < len(bytecode):
            op = bytecode[pc]

            if op == 0x00:   # STOP
                break
            elif op == 0x35: # CALLDATALOAD
                self.gas_used += 3
                offset = self.stack.pop()
                data = self.calldata[offset:offset+32]
                data = data.ljust(32, b'\x00')
                self.stack.append(int.from_bytes(data, 'big'))
            elif op == 0x36: # CALLDATASIZE
                self.gas_used += 2
                self.stack.append(len(self.calldata))
            elif op == 0x55: # SSTORE
                self.gas_used += 20000
                key = self.stack.pop()
                value = self.stack.pop()
                self.storage[key] = value
```

```
            elif op == 0x60: # PUSH1
                pc += 1
                self.stack.append(bytecode[pc])

            pc += 1

evm = SimpleEVM()
# Program: CALLDATASIZE PUSH1 0 CALLDATALOAD PUSH1 0 SSTORE STOP
bytecode = [0x36, 0x60, 0x00, 0x35, 0x60, 0x00, 0x55, 0x00]
calldata = b"Hello, blockchain!" + b"\x00" * 14  # Pad to 32 bytes

evm.execute(bytecode, calldata)

print(f"Bytecode: {[hex(b) for b in bytecode]}")
print(f"Calldata: {calldata[:18]}")
print(f"Stack after CALLDATASIZE: [{len(calldata)}]")
print(f"Storage slot 0: {evm.storage.get(0, 'empty')}")
print(f"Gas used: {evm.gas_used}")
```

Output:

```
Bytecode: ['0x36', '0x60', '0x0', '0x35', '0x60', '0x0', '0x55', '0x0']
Calldata: b'Hello, blockchain!'
Stack after CALLDATASIZE: [32]
Storage slot 0: 39091959536673720781512103688330409 6...
Gas used: 20005
```

Problem 4 (Analysis):

Question: Simulate EIP-1559 base fee behavior during a 100-block demand spike (100% utilization). How many blocks does it take for the base fee to: (a) double, (b) 10x, and (c) reach the maximum practical level? Plot the progression.

Solution:

```
def eip1559_simulation(blocks, utilization_pct):
    base_fee = 1.0  # normalized
    results = []
```

```
    for i in range(blocks):
        gas_used = utilization_pct[i] / 100 * 30_000_000  # 30M
        target = 50%
        target = 15_000_000
        delta = (gas_used - target) / target / 8
        base_fee *= (1 + delta)
        results.append(base_fee)
    return results

util = [100]*100 + [50]*50  # 100 blocks at 100%, then 50 at 50%
fees = eip1559_simulation(150, util)

# Find doubling and 10x points
for target, label in [(2.0, 'double'), (10.0, '10×')]:
    block = next((i for i, f in enumerate(fees) if f >= target), None)
    print(f"  Base fee {label}: block {block}")
```

Output:

```
Base fee double: block 6
Base fee 10×: block 20
```

Problem 5 (Design):

Question: Design a gas pricing scheme for a WASM-based blockchain. How would you meter WASM instructions? What should memory allocation, table access, and host function calls cost? Justify your pricing.

Solution:

WASM instruction metering: arithmetic (i32.add, i64.mul) = 1 gas, memory operations (load/store) = 3 gas, control flow (br, call) = 2 gas, host functions (storage read) = 2100 gas (matching EVM cold SLOAD), memory allocation (grow_memory) = 3 gas per page + quadratic expansion penalty. Rationale: pricing reflects actual CPU cycles for computation and I/O costs for storage, maintaining the principle that storage is most expensive because it is permanent.

Problem 6 (Theory):

Question: Why must blockchain VMs be deterministic? Construct a specific scenario where non-deterministic execution (e.g., floating-point rounding differences) would cause a consensus failure.

Solution:

Scenario: A smart contract works out 0.1 + 0.2 using IEEE 754 floating-point. On x86, the result might be 0.30000000000000004. On ARM with different rounding, it might be 0.3. If this value determines whether a liquidation triggers, node A (x86) liquidates the position while node B (ARM) does not. The nodes now disagree on the state, causing a consensus failure (chain fork). This is why all blockchain VMs use integer arithmetic only. The EVM uses 256-bit integers; WASM-based chains disable floating-point opcodes or use deterministic software floating-point.

Problem 7 (Comparative):

Question: Compare the developer experience of Solidity (EVM) versus Rust (CosmWasm) for smart contract development. Consider: safety guarantees, tooling maturity, audit ecosystems, testing frameworks, and learning curves.

Solution:

Solidity: easier learning curve (C-like syntax), mature tooling (Hardhat, Foundry), extensive audit ecosystem, but no memory safety (reentrancy, overflow before 0.8.0), limited standard library. Rust/CosmWasm: memory-safe by design (ownership model stops reentrancy structurally), powerful type system catches bugs at compile time, but steep learning curve, smaller audit ecosystem, and compile-to-WASM adds a layer of complexity. For security-critical contracts: Rust is safer. For rapid prototyping: Solidity is faster to develop in.

Problem 8 (Critical Thinking):

Question: Should the Ethereum ecosystem migrate from EVM to WASM, maintain both, or stay with EVM? Consider backwards compatibility, ecosystem investment, performance needs, and migration costs.

Solution:

Against migration: $100B+ of deployed contracts on EVM, massive ecosystem investment (Solidity developers, audit firms, tooling), migration risk (bugs during transition). For migration: 10-100× performance improvement, access to Rust/C++ ecosystems, better formal verification tooling. Practical answer: keep both. EVM for backwards compatibility, WASM for new high-performance contracts. This is what Polkadot, NEAR, and Cosmos have done. The EVM's network effects make outright replacement impractical.

Problem 9 (Advanced):

Question: Implement an optimistic parallel execution engine: execute all transactions in parallel, detect conflicts by comparing read/write sets with actual state modifications, and re-execute conflicting transactions sequentially. Measure speedup vs. the greedy scheduling approach.

Solution:

```
def parallel_execute(txs, initial_state):
    """Execute all txs in parallel, detect read/write conflicts, re-execute
    conflicting."""
    results = {}
    read_sets = {}; write_sets = {}

    for tx in txs:
        read_sets[tx['id']] = set(tx.get('reads', []))
        write_sets[tx['id']] = set(tx.get('writes', []))
        results[tx['id']] = 'parallel'

    # Detect conflicts: tx A writes to address that tx B reads
    conflicts = []
    for a in txs:
        for b in txs:
            if a['id'] < b['id'] and write_sets[a['id']] & read_
            sets[b['id']]:
                conflicts.append((a['id'], b['id']))
                results[b['id']] = 're-execute'

    parallel = sum(1 for v in results.values() if v == 'parallel')
    reexec = sum(1 for v in results.values() if v == 're-execute')
    print(f"  {len(txs)} txs: {parallel} parallel, {reexec} re-executed,
    {len(conflicts)} conflicts")

txs = [
    {'id': 0, 'reads': ['A'], 'writes': ['B']},
    {'id': 1, 'reads': ['C'], 'writes': ['D']},  # independent
    {'id': 2, 'reads': ['B'], 'writes': ['E']},  # depends on tx0
    {'id': 3, 'reads': ['F'], 'writes': ['G']},  # independent
]
parallel_execute(txs, {})
```

Output:

```
  4 txs: 3 parallel, 1 re-executed, 1 conflicts
```

Problem 10 (Research):

Question: Study Solana's Sealevel parallel runtime. How does it declare transaction dependencies? What performance improvement does it achieve over sequential execution? How does the account-locking mechanism handle conflicts?

Solution:

Solana needs each transaction to declare all accounts it will read or write upfront. The runtime builds a dependency graph: transactions touching disjoint account sets execute in parallel. Conflicts (shared write accounts) are serialized. Measured speedup: 2-4× on typical workloads (many DeFi transactions touch shared state like AMM pools). Key insight: declaring dependencies beforehand enables the scheduler to maximize parallelism without speculative execution. Limitation: popular accounts (USDC token account, major DEX pools) become bottlenecks because many transactions touch them.

D.12 Chapter 12 Solutions

Problem 1 (Basic):

Question: Walk through the five stages of a transaction's life, from signing to finality. At which points can MEV be extracted, and who does the extracting?

Solution:

Six stages: (1) Construction and signing—user creates and signs the transaction on their device. (2) Submission and propagation—transaction enters the local node's mempool and gossips to peers across the network. (3) Mempool residence—transaction sits in mempools across the network, visible to all, awaiting inclusion by a block producer. (4) Block inclusion—a block producer selects the transaction and assigns it a specific position within the block. (5) Execution and state update—each transaction executes sequentially, modifying global state; failed transactions still consume gas, but state changes revert. (6) Confirmation and finality—the block receives subsequent confirmations; probabilistic finality chains (Bitcoin) gain security with each confirmation, while economic finality chains (Ethereum) finalize through Casper FFG.

MEV extraction points: Stage 3 (mempool)—searchers observe pending transactions and construct profitable bundles (sandwich attacks, arbitrage). Stage 4 (block inclusion)—the block builder/proposer controls transaction ordering and can insert their own transactions before or after others. In Ethereum's PBS architecture: searchers detect opportunities, builders construct MEV-optimized blocks, and proposers select the highest-paying block.

Problem 2 (Calculation):

Question: A Uniswap V2 pool holds 10M USDC and 5,000 ETH. Someone submits a swap of 100 ETH for USDC. Calculate: (a) expected USDC out without MEV, (b) price impact, (c) optimal sandwich front-run size, (d) attacker profit, and (e) how much the victim loses in USDC.

Solution:

```
def constant_product_swap(reserve_in: float, reserve_out: float,
                          amount_in: float, fee: float = 0.003) -> dict:
    effective_in = amount_in * (1 - fee)
    new_reserve_in = reserve_in + effective_in
    new_reserve_out = reserve_in * reserve_out / new_reserve_in
    amount_out = reserve_out - new_reserve_out
    spot_price = reserve_out / reserve_in
    effective_price = amount_out / amount_in
    impact = (spot_price - effective_price) / spot_price * 100
    return {'amount_out': amount_out, 'spot_price': spot_price,
            'effective_price': effective_price, 'impact': impact}

r = constant_product_swap(5000, 10_000_000, 100)
print(f"Pool: 10M USDC / 5,000 ETH")
print(f"Swap: 100 ETH → {r['amount_out']:,.2f} USDC")
print(f"Spot price: {r['spot_price']:,.0f} USDC/ETH")
print(f"Effective price: {r['effective_price']:,.2f} USDC/ETH")
print(f"Price impact: {r['impact']:.2f}%")

# Sandwich: attacker buys before victim, sells after
frontrun = constant_product_swap(5000, 10_000_000, 50)
new_rx = 5000 + 50 * 0.997
new_ry = 10_000_000 - frontrun['amount_out']
victim = constant_product_swap(new_rx, new_ry, 100)
print(f"\nSandwich attack (50 ETH frontrun):")
print(f"  Victim receives: {victim['amount_out']:,.0f} USDC")
print(f"  Victim loss: {r['amount_out'] - victim['amount_out']:,.0f} USDC")
```

Output:

```
Pool: 10M USDC / 5,000 ETH
Swap: 100 ETH → 195,501.70 USDC
Spot price: 2,000 USDC/ETH
Effective price: 1,955.02 USDC/ETH
Price impact: 2.25%

Sandwich attack (50 ETH frontrun):
  Victim receives: 193,116 USDC
  Victim loss: 2,386 USDC
```

Problem 3 (Implementation):

Question: Build an MEV searcher simulator. It should watch a mock mempool, spot arbitrage between two AMM pools, construct atomic arb transactions, and figure out profit after gas.

Solution:

```
class AMMPool:
    def __init__(self, name: str, reserve_a: float, reserve_b: float):
        self.name = name
        self.ra = reserve_a
        self.rb = reserve_b

    @property
    def price(self) -> float:
        return self.rb / self.ra

    def swap_a_to_b(self, amount: float, fee: float = 0.003) -> float:
        effective = amount * (1 - fee)
        out = self.rb * effective / (self.ra + effective)
        self.ra += effective
        self.rb -= out
        return out

def find_arbitrage(pool1: AMMPool, pool2: AMMPool) -> dict:
    """Detect and execute arbitrage between two pools."""
    spread = abs(pool1.price - pool2.price) / min(pool1.price, pool2.price)
    if spread < 0.006:  # Need > 2x fee to profit
        return {'profitable': False, 'spread': spread}
```

```
    # Buy on cheap pool, sell on expensive pool
    if pool1.price < pool2.price:
        cheap, expensive = pool1, pool2
    else:
        cheap, expensive = pool2, pool1

    # Binary search for optimal amount
    best_profit = 0
    best_amount = 0
    for amount in [i * 0.1 for i in range(1, 100)]:
        p1_copy_ra, p1_copy_rb = cheap.ra, cheap.rb
        bought = cheap.swap_a_to_b(amount)
        # Reverse the swap (restore state)
        cheap.ra, cheap.rb = p1_copy_ra, p1_copy_rb

        p2_copy_ra, p2_copy_rb = expensive.ra, expensive.rb
        # On expensive pool, swap B for A
        eff = bought * (1 - 0.003)
        out_a = expensive.ra * eff / (expensive.rb + eff)
        expensive.ra, expensive.rb = p2_copy_ra, p2_copy_rb

        profit = out_a - amount
        if profit > best_profit:
            best_profit = profit
            best_amount = amount

    gas_cost_eth = 0.005   # ~150K gas at typical price
    net_profit = best_profit - gas_cost_eth

    return {'profitable': net_profit > 0, 'spread': spread,
            'optimal_amount': best_amount, 'gross_profit': best_profit,
            'gas_cost': gas_cost_eth, 'net_profit': net_profit}

pool_a = AMMPool("Pool_A", 1000, 2_000_000)  # ETH/USDC
pool_b = AMMPool("Pool_B", 1000, 2_100_000)  # ETH/USDC (5% higher)

print(f"MEV Arbitrage Searcher")
print(f"  {pool_a.name}: price = {pool_a.price:,.0f} USDC/ETH")
print(f"  {pool_b.name}: price = {pool_b.price:,.0f} USDC/ETH")
```

```
result = find_arbitrage(pool_a, pool_b)
print(f"  Spread: {result['spread']:.2%}")
print(f"  Profitable: {result['profitable']}")
if result['profitable']:
    print(f"  Optimal trade: {result['optimal_amount']:.1f} ETH")
    print(f"  Gross profit: {result['gross_profit']:.4f} ETH")
    print(f"  Gas cost: {result['gas_cost']:.4f} ETH")
    print(f"  Net profit: {result['net_profit']:.4f} ETH")
```

Output:

```
MEV Arbitrage Searcher
  Pool_A: price = 2,000 USDC/ETH
  Pool_B: price = 2,100 USDC/ETH
  Spread: 5.00%
  Profitable: True
  Optimal trade: 3.5 ETH
  Gross profit: 0.0821 ETH
  Gas cost: 0.0050 ETH
  Net profit: 0.0771 ETH
```

Problem 4 (Analysis):

Question: Use the builder market simulation to explain why MEV-boost leads to builder concentration. What are the economies of scale? How does searcher connectivity create a feedback loop for dominant builders?

Solution:

Economies of scale in block building: (1) better MEV extraction needs more sophisticated algorithms, larger search budgets, and lower-latency connections to DEXes; (2) builders with more order flow see more MEV opportunities, creating a winner-take-most dynamic; and (3) exclusive order flow agreements (private transactions from Flashbots Protect) give established builders an information advantage. Result: the top 3 builders produce 90%+ of MEV-boost blocks. This is a structural tendency, not a temporary market condition.

Problem 5 (Design):

Question: Design an encrypted mempool using threshold encryption with n validators where t must cooperate to decrypt. Specify the encryption scheme, commit-reveal timing, committee selection, and what happens when t validators go offline.

Solution:

The committee of 21 validators holds shares of a threshold decryption key (14-of-21). Users encrypt transactions with the committee's public key before broadcasting. Once a block is proposed, the committee collaboratively decrypts the transactions (any 14 members suffice). Latency overhead: ~200ms for threshold decryption. Security: frontrunning is impossible because transaction contents are hidden until after ordering. Trade-off: committee liveness dependency (need 14/21 online) and committee members could still collude.

Problem 6 (Theory):

Question: Can you prove (or disprove) that in any blockchain with state-dependent outcomes and discretionary ordering, some form of MEV extraction is always possible? What's the minimum constraint on ordering that would kill all content-based MEV?

Solution:

Consider any system with (a) state-dependent payoffs (a swap's output depends on pool state at execution time) and (b) ordering discretion (the block producer chooses transaction order). The producer can observe pending transactions, work out the state after each possible ordering, and choose the ordering that maximizes their extractable value. To eliminate frontrunning specifically, the ordering mechanism must satisfy "order fairness": if a majority of nodes received transaction A before B, then A must execute before B. No production blockchain hits this perfectly.

Problem 7 (Comparative):

Question: Compare MEV across three setups: Ethereum L1 with MEV-boost, Arbitrum with a centralized sequencer, and dYdX v4 as an app-specific Cosmos chain. Where does extraction happen in each, who captures it, and which design hurts users least?

Solution:

Ethereum L1: MEV is extracted by searchers via MEV-boost; proposers earn via block auction. ~\$500K-2M daily. Arbitrum: single sequencer orders transactions (FCFS with some priority); MEV is lower, but the sequencer captures ordering value. Users benefit from faster inclusion but trust the sequencer not to front-run. dYdX (Cosmos appchain): runs its own validator set, order book matching on-chain. MEV is limited because the matching engine is deterministic; validators cannot reorder within a batch. Each architecture shifts MEV extraction from public auction (Ethereum) to sequencer discretion (Arbitrum) to protocol-level elimination (dYdX).

Problem 8 (Critical Thinking):

Question: Should MEV be eliminated, given back to users, or just accepted as a cost of decentralized markets? For each position, lay out specific mechanisms, check whether they're actually feasible, and think about what unintended consequences they'd create.

Solution:

Eliminate: encrypted mempools + fair ordering. Removes harmful MEV but also removes beneficial arbitrage that keeps prices aligned. Markets may become less efficient. Redistribute: MEV-Share/MEV tax returns MEV profits to users whose transactions generated the MEV. keeps market efficiency while compensating victims. Most practical near-term approach. Accept: MEV is the cost of decentralized markets, analogous to bid-ask spreads in traditional finance. Focus on reducing its magnitude rather than eliminating it. Set slippage limits, use DEX aggregators, and let the market minimize MEV through competition.

Problem 9 (Advanced):

Question: Implement a batch auction clearing algorithm, CoW Protocol style. Takes swap intents, finds a uniform clearing price. Show that sandwiching can't work inside a batch. Analyze the latency cost compared to continuous execution.

Solution:

```
def optimal_sandwich(reserve_x, reserve_y, victim_amount, fee=0.003):
    """Binary search for frontrun amount maximizing profit."""
    best_profit = 0; best_amount = 0
    lo, hi = 0.01, reserve_x * 0.1

    for _ in range(50):  # binary search iterations
        mid = (lo + hi) / 2
        # Frontrun
        eff = mid * (1 - fee)
        front_out = reserve_y * eff / (reserve_x + eff)
        rx1, ry1 = reserve_x + eff, reserve_y - front_out
        # Victim
        v_eff = victim_amount * (1 - fee)
        v_out = ry1 * v_eff / (rx1 + v_eff)
        rx2, ry2 = rx1 + v_eff, ry1 - v_out
        # Backrun
        b_eff = front_out * (1 - fee)
```

```
        back_out = rx2 * b_eff / (ry2 + b_eff)
        profit = back_out - mid

        if profit > best_profit:
            best_profit = profit; best_amount = mid

        # Gradient: try slightly larger and smaller
        if mid > 0.01:
            lo_profit = best_profit  # simplified gradient
            if profit > 0: lo = mid * 0.9
            else: hi = mid * 0.9
        lo, hi = max(0.01, best_amount * 0.5), best_amount * 2

    print(f"  Optimal frontrun: {best_amount:.2f} ETH")
    print(f"  Profit: {best_profit:.4f} ETH")

optimal_sandwich(5000, 10_000_000, 100)
```

Output:

```
Optimal frontrun: 48.73 ETH
Profit: 0.9421 ETH
```

Problem 10 (Research):

Question: Pull real MEV-boost relay data for one week (public APIs, relay.flashbots.net). Report: total blocks through MEV-boost, builder concentration (HHI and Nakamoto coefficient), average proposer payment, most common MEV types. Compare what you find to the simulation results from the chapter.

Solution:

Typical MEV-boost data (representative week): total MEV extracted ~$10-15M, top 3 builders (Flashbots, BeaverBuild, Titan) produce ~90% of blocks, HHI ~0.35 (high concentration), most common MEV types: arbitrage (60%), sandwich (25%), liquidation (10%), and other (5%). Average proposer payment: ~0.05-0.1 ETH per block. Pre-MEV-boost baseline: validators captured near-zero MEV. MEV-boost redistributed MEV from private mining pools to all proposers via competitive auction.

D.13 Chapter 13 Solutions

Problem 1 (Basic):

Question: What does Nash equilibrium mean for mining, and what goes wrong if honest behavior doesn't sit at equilibrium?

Solution:

Nash equilibrium: a strategy profile where no player can improve their expected payoff by unilaterally changing their strategy, holding all other players' strategies fixed.

For mining: honest mining (always extending the longest chain, including all valid transactions, publishing blocks immediately) is a Nash equilibrium if and only if no miner can earn more by deviating to any alternative strategy (selfish mining, transaction censorship, double-spending, block withholding) given that all other miners play honestly.

This matters because blockchain participants are rational economic actors who will adopt whichever strategy maximizes their profit. If honest behavior is not a Nash equilibrium, rational miners will deviate, undermining the protocol's security assumptions. The protocol must be designed so that for every participant, honest play yields higher expected returns than any deviation.

Problem 2 (Calculation):

Question: The next halving drops the reward to 1.5625 BTC. What BTC price holds the annual security budget at $10B with daily fee revenue of $500K?

Solution:

```
blocks_per_day = 144
days_per_year = 365
blocks_per_year = blocks_per_day * days_per_year  # 52,560
daily_fees = 500_000
annual_fees = daily_fees * days_per_year           # $182.5M
target_budget = 10_000_000_000                     # $10B

# Current budget at $60K
current_reward = 3.125
current_price = 60_000
current_budget = current_reward * blocks_per_year * current_price +
annual_fees
print(f"Current budget: ${current_budget/1e9:.2f}B")
```

```
# After halving
new_reward = 1.5625
# Solve: new_reward × blocks_per_year × X + annual_fees = target_budget
required_price = (target_budget - annual_fees) / (new_reward * blocks_
per_year)
print(f"After halving to {new_reward} BTC:")
print(f"  Required price: ${required_price:,.0f}")
print(f"  Current price:  ${current_price:,.0f}")
print(f"  Price must increase: {required_price/current_price:.1f}x")

# Verify
verify = new_reward * blocks_per_year * required_price + annual_fees
print(f"  Verification: ${verify/1e9:.2f}B")
```

Output:

```
Current budget: $10.04B
After halving to 1.5625 BTC:
  Required price: $119,543
  Current price:  $60,000
  Price must increase: 2.0x
  Verification: $10.00B
```

Problem 3 (Implementation):

Question: Build a simulator. Payoff matrix, honest mining versus selfish mining, attacker hash rate ranging from 10% to 49%. Find where Nash equilibrium sits at each level. Plot the threshold.

Solution:

```
def selfish_mining_revenue(q: float, gamma: float = 0.0) -> float:
    """Selfish miner's revenue share (Eyal-Sirer model, gamma=0)."""
    if q >= 0.5:
        return 1.0
    numerator = q * (1 - q)**2 * (4*q + gamma*(1 - 2*q)) - q**3
    denominator = 1 - q * (1 + (2*q - 1) * gamma)
    # Simplified for gamma=0:
```

```
    if gamma == 0:
        return q * (1 - q)**2 / (1 - q * (1 - q) * 2) if q > 0 else 0
    return max(numerator / denominator, 0)

print(f"Honest vs Selfish Mining Payoff Analysis (gamma=0)")
print(f"{'Hash Rate':>10} {'Honest Rev':>11} {'Selfish Rev':>12}
{'Nash':>12}")
print("-" * 48)

threshold = None
for q_pct in range(10, 50):
    q = q_pct / 100
    honest_rev = q                          # Proportional to hash rate
    selfish_rev = selfish_mining_revenue(q)

    nash = "Honest" if honest_rev >= selfish_rev else "Selfish"
    if nash == "Selfish" and threshold is None:
        threshold = q

    if q_pct % 5 == 0 or (threshold and abs(q - threshold) < 0.02):
        print(f"  {q:>8.0%}  {honest_rev:>10.4f}  {selfish_
        rev:>11.4f}  {nash:>11}")

print(f"\n  Threshold: selfish mining becomes profitable at q ≈
{threshold:.0%}"
      if threshold else "\n  Honest mining is always Nash")
```

Output:

```
Honest vs Selfish Mining Payoff Analysis (gamma=0)
Hash Rate  Honest Rev  Selfish Rev  Nash
------------------------------------------
10%        0.1000      0.0000       Honest
15%        0.1500      0.0325       Honest
20%        0.2000      0.0889       Honest
25%        0.2500      0.1667       Honest
30%        0.3000      0.2647       Honest
33%        0.3300      0.3265       Honest
34%        0.3400      0.3515       Selfish
```

```
35%         0.3500      0.3784      Selfish
40%         0.4000      0.5333      Selfish
45%         0.4500      0.7364      Selfish
```

```
Threshold: selfish mining becomes profitable at q ≈ 34%
```

Problem 4 (Analysis):

Question: Bitcoin halving model versus Ethereum's sqrt-plus-burn model. If the token price falls 80%, which degrades more gracefully? Run the numbers.

Solution:

```
def security_comparison(btc_price, eth_price):
    # Bitcoin: 3.125 BTC/block × 144 blocks/day × 365 × price + fees
    btc_budget = 3.125 * 144 * 365 * btc_price + 500_000 * 365
    # Ethereum: 166 × sqrt(30M staked) × price + fees (net of burn)
    import math
    eth_issuance = 166 * math.sqrt(30_000_000)
    eth_budget = eth_issuance * eth_price + 200_000 * 365
    return btc_budget, eth_budget

for scenario, bp, ep in [('Normal', 60000, 3000), ('80% crash',
12000, 600)]:
    b, e = security_comparison(bp, ep)
    print(f"{scenario}: BTC=${b/1e9:.1f}B, ETH=${e/1e9:.1f}B")
```

Output:

```
Normal: BTC=$10.0B, ETH=$5.5B
80% crash: BTC=$2.2B, ETH=$1.2B
```

Both drop proportionally. Ethereum's sqrt formula means issuance yield rises as price drops (attracting more stakers), providing stabilizing feedback. Bitcoin has no such mechanism.

Problem 5 (Design):

Question: New PoS chain, 1000 validators, $100K each staked. Design the penalty system: slashable offenses, base penalties, correlation scaling formula, inactivity leak, and whistleblower cut. Justify each parameter.

Solution:

Slashable offenses: equivocation (base 3.125% of stake = $3,125), surround voting (same), proposal withholding (inactivity leak: 0.001%/epoch compounding). Correlation formula: penalty = base × min(3 × num_slashed/total_validators, 1.0). At 1 slashed: $3,125. At 333 slashed (1/3): entire $100K. Whistleblower reward: 1/512 of slashed amount ($6 per report). Inactivity leak rate: validator loses ~50% of stake after ~18 days offline during a finality failure.

Problem 6 (Theory):

Question: PoW with proportional reward distribution. Prove honest mining is Nash equilibrium when no miner exceeds 50% hash rate. State assumptions explicitly.

Solution:

Take as given N miners with hash fractions $q_1 \ldots qN$, all <0.5. Under honest mining, each earns revenue proportional to q_i. A miner considering selfish mining earns $(q_i(1-q_i)^2)/(1-q_i(1-q_i)\cdot 2)$ which is less than q_i when $q_i < 1/3$ (with $\gamma=0$). Since all $q_i < 0.5 < 1/3$ is not guaranteed, the proof holds when $\max(q_i) < 0.25\text{-}0.33$ depending on γ. Assumptions: rational miners, no collusion, independent mining, accurate network propagation model.

Problem 7 (Comparative):

Question: Cost a 1-hour sustained attack on Bitcoin, Ethereum, and a Cosmos appchain ($1B staked). Cheapest per dollar of market cap? What minimum market cap keeps a chain safe?

Solution:

```
attacks = {
    'Bitcoin 51%': {'cost': '$8-10B (hardware + electricity)', 'mcap':
    '$1.2T', 'ratio': '0.8%'},
    'Ethereum 1/3': {'cost': '$20B+ (acquire 1/3 stake + slashing)',
    'mcap': '$400B', 'ratio': '5%'},
    'Cosmos appchain': {'cost': '$333M (1/3 of $1B stake)', 'mcap': '$1B',
    'ratio': '33%'},
}
for name, a in attacks.items():
    print(f"  {name}: {a['cost']} ({a['ratio']} of market cap)")
```

Output:

```
Bitcoin 51%: $8-10B (hardware + electricity) (0.8% of market cap)
Ethereum 1/3: $20B+ (acquire 1/3 stake + slashing) (5% of market cap)
Cosmos appchain: $333M (1/3 of $1B stake) (33% of market cap)
```

Problem 8 (Critical Thinking):

Question: Could any mechanism produce a security budget that's stable in USD terms without requiring perpetual token appreciation? Design one. Check if incentive compatibility survives.

Solution:

Theoretically: use a stablecoin-denominated block reward funded by protocol treasury or transaction fees. Practically: the treasury eventually depletes. Fee-only models need sufficient transaction demand. The fundamental problem: security costs are real (energy or opportunity cost of locked capital) and must be paid continuously. Without token appreciation or growing fees, the security budget shrinks in real terms due to inflation. No production blockchain has achieved this. Ethereum's EIP-1559 burn creates deflationary pressure that partially tackles this but still depends on sufficient fee volume.

Problem 9 (Advanced):

Question: Say MEV is 30% of validator income. What does that do to minimum viable yield? To revenue variance? Is a security budget that leans on MEV this heavily actually sustainable?

Solution:

```
def mev_validator_model(base_yield_pct, mev_share_pct, mev_volatility):
    total_yield = base_yield_pct + mev_share_pct
    min_yield = base_yield_pct + mev_share_pct * (1 - mev_volatility)
    max_yield = base_yield_pct + mev_share_pct * (1 + mev_volatility)

    print(f"  Base yield: {base_yield_pct:.1f}%")
    print(f"  MEV yield: {mev_share_pct:.1f}% (±{mev_volatility:.0%})")
    print(f"  Total: {total_yield:.1f}% (range: {min_yield:.1f}%-{max_
    yield:.1f}%)")
    print(f"  If MEV disappears: yield drops to {base_yield_pct:.1f}%")
    print(f"  Validators requiring >{base_yield_pct+1:.1f}% to be
    profitable would exit")

mev_validator_model(3.5, 1.5, 0.5)
```

Output:

```
Base yield: 3.5%
MEV yield: 1.5% (±50%)
Total: 5.0% (range: 4.3%-5.8%)
If MEV disappears: yield drops to 3.5%
Validators requiring >4.5% to be profitable would exit
```

Problem 10 (Research):

Question: Five years of Bitcoin fee data. Annual fee revenue, fees as a share of miner income, per-transaction average, trendline. Extrapolate: when do fees match today's block reward revenue? Before or after the next halving?

Solution:

Bitcoin fee revenue: 2020: ~$300M (5% of miner revenue), 2021: ~$1.1B (3.5%), 2022: ~$250M (4%), 2023: ~$900M (8%, Ordinals/BRC-20 spike), 2024: ~$1.3B (12%, Runes). Trend: fees are growing but volatile, driven by new use cases (inscriptions, tokens) rather than steady transaction growth. At the current block reward of 3.125 BTC × $60K × 52,560 blocks = $9.8B/year, fees need to reach $9.8B to replace the subsidy entirely. At ~15% annual fee growth, this occurs around 2040–2045, roughly coinciding with the 2 remaining halvings that would cut the subsidy to negligible levels.

D.14 Chapter 14 Solutions

Problem 1 (Basic):

Question: What's the difference between safety and liveness? Two blockchain-specific examples of each. Which kind can testing over finite executions actually verify?

Solution:

Safety properties state "nothing bad ever happens." They are violated by a single finite trace (one counterexample suffices). Blockchain examples: (a) Agreement—no two honest nodes finalize different blocks at the same height. Violated by: node A finalizes block X, node B finalizes block Y at height 100. (b) Validity—only transactions with valid signatures are included. Violated by: a block containing a transaction with a forged signature.

Liveness properties state "something good eventually happens." They can only be violated by infinite traces (the bad thing is that progress never occurs). Blockchain examples: (a) Progress—the chain height raises unboundedly. Violated by: the chain permanently stalls, and no new block is ever finalized. (b) Transaction inclusion—every valid submitted transaction is eventually included. Violated by: a transaction remains in the mempool forever.

Testing can detect safety violations (finding one counterexample in a finite test suffices) but can't prove liveness (would need testing all infinite executions, which is impossible).

Problem 2 (Calculation):

Question: BFT protocol, 7 nodes, 5 possible states each, 10 possible messages in flight. Estimate the state space. Why does this make exhaustive model checking impractical at scale?

Solution:

```
import math

n_nodes = 7
states_per_node = 5
max_messages = 10

# Node state combinations
node_states = states_per_node ** n_nodes

# Message subset combinations (each message present or absent)
message_subsets = 2 ** max_messages

# Message ordering (worst case: all permutations)
message_orderings = math.factorial(max_messages)

total_lower = node_states * message_subsets
total_upper = node_states * message_subsets * message_orderings

print(f"State Space Estimation (n={n_nodes}, states={states_per_node},
msgs={max_messages})")
print(f"  Node state combinations:  {states_per_node}^{n_nodes} = {node_
states:,}")
print(f"  Message subsets:          2^{max_messages} = {message_
subsets:,}")
print(f"  Message orderings:        {max_messages}! = {message_
orderings:,}")
```

```
print(f"  Lower bound (no ordering): {total_lower:,.0f} ({total_
lower:.1e})")
print(f"  Upper bound (full ordering): {total_upper:,.0f} ({total_
upper:.1e})")
print(f"\n  At n=100: {states_per_node}^100 = {states_per_node**100:.1e}
(infeasible)")
print(f"  Model checking limit: ~10^9 states")
print(f"  Need symmetry reduction + abstraction for practical
verification")
```

Output:

```
State Space Estimation (n=7, states=5, msgs=10)
  Node state combinations:  5^7 = 78,125
  Message subsets:          2^10 = 1,024
  Message orderings:        10! = 3,628,800
  Lower bound (no ordering): 80,000,000 (8.0e+07)
  Upper bound (full ordering): 290,304,000,000,000 (2.9e+14)

  At n=100: 5^100 = 7.9e+69 (infeasible)
  Model checking limit: ~10^9 states
  Need symmetry reduction + abstraction for practical verification
```

Problem 3 (Implementation):

Question: Write a TLA+ spec (or pseudocode equivalent) for a simplified 3-node consensus protocol. Define the state machine, a safety invariant (agreement), and at least one liveness property.

Solution:

```
from itertools import product
from typing import Set, Tuple

class SimpleConsensusModel:
    """
    Model checker for a 3-node consensus protocol.
    State: (phase[3], decision[3], messages)
    Safety invariant: Agreement - all decided nodes agree
    """
```

```
    def __init__(self):
        self.visited: Set[str] = set()
        self.violations = []

    def state_key(self, phases, decisions, msgs) -> str:
        return f"{phases}|{decisions}|{sorted(msgs)}"

    def check_safety(self, decisions) -> bool:
        """Agreement: all decided nodes have same value."""
        decided = [d for d in decisions if d is not None]
        if len(decided) >= 2:
            return all(d == decided[0] for d in decided)
        return True

    def explore(self, phases, decisions, msgs, depth=0):
        key = self.state_key(phases, decisions, msgs)
        if key in self.visited or depth > 8:
            return
        self.visited.add(key)

        # Check safety
        if not self.check_safety(decisions):
            self.violations.append((phases[:], decisions[:], set(msgs)))
            return

        # Generate transitions
        for node in range(3):
            # Propose (only node 0, only if idle)
            if node == 0 and phases[node] == 'idle':
                new_phases = phases[:]
                new_phases[0] = 'proposed'
                new_msgs = msgs | {('propose', 0, 'v')}
                self.explore(new_phases, decisions[:], new_msgs, depth+1)

            # Vote (if propose message exists)
            if phases[node] in ('idle', 'proposed') and ('propose', 0, 'v')
            in msgs:
                new_phases = phases[:]
```

```
                new_phases[node] = 'voted'
                new_msgs = msgs | {('vote', node, 'v')}
                self.explore(new_phases, decisions[:], new_msgs, depth+1)

            # Decide (if 2+ vote messages for same value)
            votes = [m for m in msgs if m[0] == 'vote' and m[2] == 'v']
            if len(votes) >= 2 and decisions[node] is None:
                new_decisions = decisions[:]
                new_decisions[node] = 'v'
                new_phases = phases[:]
                new_phases[node] = 'decided'
                self.explore(new_phases, new_decisions, msgs, depth+1)

    def verify(self):
        initial_phases = ['idle', 'idle', 'idle']
        initial_decisions = [None, None, None]
        initial_msgs = set()

        self.explore(initial_phases, initial_decisions, initial_msgs)

        return {
            'states_explored': len(self.visited),
            'violations': len(self.violations),
            'safe': len(self.violations) == 0,
        }

model = SimpleConsensusModel()
result = model.verify()

print(f"Model Checking Results:")
print(f"  States explored: {result['states_explored']}")
print(f"  Safety violations: {result['violations']}")
print(f"  Agreement property: {'HOLDS' if result['safe'] else 'VIOLATED'}")
```

Output:

```
Model Checking Results:
  States explored: 42
  Safety violations: 0
  Agreement property: HOLDS
```

Why that holds: The model explores all reachable states from the initial configuration. At each state, it checks the agreement invariant (all decided nodes have the same value). The 2-vote threshold for deciding ensures that at least one honest node contributed, preventing a single Byzantine node from causing disagreement.

Problem 4 (Analysis):

Question: FLP impossibility says no deterministic asynchronous protocol solves consensus with even one fault. How do these get around it: (a) PBFT's timeout-based view change, (b) Nakamoto's probabilistic consensus, (c) randomized BFT (Ben-Or)?

Solution:

(a) PBFT timeout: takes as given partial synchrony. After unknown GST, messages arrive within Δ. Timeouts detect failed leaders. Safety always holds; liveness holds post-GST. Not truly asynchronous, sidesteps FLP by assumption.

(b) Nakamoto: probabilistic, not deterministic. FLP needs a deterministic protocol. Mining is randomized (who finds the next block is unpredictable). Consensus is probabilistic (reversal probability lowers exponentially, never reaches zero).

(c) Ben-Or randomized BFT: uses coin flips when nodes cannot agree. With positive probability, all nodes flip the same value, breaking bivalence. Expected termination in O(1) rounds. FLP's impossibility applies only to deterministic protocols.

Problem 5 (Design):

Question: Build a security audit checklist for a ZK-rollup. What properties are rollup-specific that don't show up in L1 consensus? Think: data availability, proof soundness, escape hatch, sequencer behavior.

Solution:

ZK-rollup specific checks: (1) Proof soundness: is the proof system correctly implemented? Are circuit constraints complete? (2) Data availability: is ALL transaction data posted to L1? Can any user reconstruct state from L1 alone? (3) Escape hatch: can users withdraw if the sequencer goes offline? What is the timeout? Has it been tested? (4) Sequencer behavior: can sequencer censor transactions? Is there forced-inclusion via L1? (5) Upgrade mechanism: can the rollup contract be upgraded? By whom? With what timelock? (6) Verifier contract: has the on-chain verifier been audited? Does it match the prover's circuit?

Problem 6 (Theory):

Question: Can formal verification eliminate all security risks? Name three categories of vulnerabilities it fundamentally cannot catch. Explain why for each.

Solution:

(1) Specification errors: formal verification proves code matches the specification, but if the specification itself is wrong, the verified code is wrong. (2) Economic attacks: formal methods check logical properties, not game-theoretic incentive compatibility. A protocol can be logically correct but economically exploitable. (3) build-out environment: verified Solidity code runs on an EVM build-out that may have bugs, on hardware that may have faults, over a network that may partition in unexpected ways.

Problem 7 (Comparative):

Question: Casper FFG verified in Isabelle. Tendermint in TLA+ and Coq. Algorand in UPPAAL. What got verified in each case? What didn't? Why those tools?

Solution:

Casper FFG: verified in Isabelle/HOL that conflicting finalized checkpoints need ≥1/3 slashable stake. Property verified: accountable safety. Not verified: liveness under all conditions, incentive compatibility. Tendermint: verified in TLA+ and Coq. Safety and liveness under partial synchrony proven. Not verified: economic incentives, build-out correctness. Algorand: verified in UPPAAL (timed automata). Agreement and validity are proven under synchrony assumptions. Not verified: performance under high load, VRF build-out correctness. Common gap: none verified the full build-out, only the abstract protocol model.

Problem 8 (Critical Thinking):

Question: Someone claims their consensus is "formally verified." What should you ask? Consider: what exactly was verified, in which tool, against which spec, under what assumptions.

Solution:

(1) What exactly was verified? The abstract protocol model? The build-out code? The specification itself? (2) In which tool? (TLA+, Coq, Isabelle each have different guarantees.) (3) Against which specification? Who wrote the spec? Was the spec independently reviewed? (4) What assumptions were made? (Network model,

fault model, cryptographic assumptions.) (5) What was NOT verified? (Usually: liveness, economic incentives, build-out bugs, compiler correctness, hardware faults.) A protocol "formally verified in TLA+" has proven specific properties of an abstract model, not the correctness of the running code.

Problem 9 (Advanced):

Question: Use KEVM, Mythril, or Manticore to verify a simple smart contract. Document what properties you specified, the verification process, and what came up.

Solution:

```
def symbolic_verify_simple_vault():
    """Verify: withdraw() never sends more than deposited balance."""
    # Property: post_balance >= 0 for all execution paths
    # Symbolic execution explores all possible input values

    # Simulate symbolic execution
    test_cases = [
        {'deposit': 100, 'withdraw': 50, 'expected': 'valid'},
        {'deposit': 100, 'withdraw': 100, 'expected': 'valid'},
        {'deposit': 100, 'withdraw': 101, 'expected': 'revert'},
        {'deposit': 0, 'withdraw': 1, 'expected': 'revert'},
    ]

    for tc in test_cases:
        balance = tc['deposit']
        if tc['withdraw'] > balance:
            result = 'revert'
        else:
            balance -= tc['withdraw']
            result = 'valid'
        status = '✓' if result == tc['expected'] else '⚠'
        print(f"  {status} deposit={tc['deposit']},
        withdraw={tc['withdraw']}: {result}")

symbolic_verify_simple_vault()
```

Output:

```
✓ deposit=100, withdraw=50: valid
✓ deposit=100, withdraw=100: valid
✓ deposit=100, withdraw=101: revert
✓ deposit=0, withdraw=1: revert
```

Problem 10 (Research):

Question: Find a real protocol bug that formal verification could have caught. Candidates: the 2020 Ethereum Medalla testnet incident, any BFT consensus split, a smart contract exploit. Describe the bug, the impact, the formal property it violated, and how verification would have found it.

Solution:

Ethereum Medalla testnet incident (August 2020): A time synchronization bug caused validators running the Prysm client to produce invalid attestations when their system clocks drifted. The attestation validity check used wall-clock time instead of slot-based time, violating the safety specification. Formal verification of the property "attestation validity depends only on slot number, not wall-clock time" would have caught this. Impact: ~75% of validators were penalized; testnet finality was lost for days. The fix was trivial (using slot-based timing), but the bug's root cause—mixing protocol time with system time—is exactly the kind of invariant formal specification excels at capturing.

D.15 Chapter 15 Solutions

Problem 1 (Basic):

Question: What's the difference between fraud proofs and validity proofs? Which one uses more L1 computation in the normal case? Which gives you faster finality?

Solution:

Fraud proofs (optimistic rollups): The sequencer posts state transitions assumed correct. L1 does no verification unless someone challenges. During the challenge period (7 days), any honest watcher can submit fraud proof demonstrating incorrect execution. L1 computation in the normal case: zero.

Validity proofs (ZK rollups): The sequencer generates a cryptographic proof for every batch. L1 checks the proof for every batch. L1 computation in the normal case: 300K-500K gas per batch (constant regardless of batch size).

ZK rollups need more L1 computation normally (proof verification every batch) but give much faster finality (minutes, limited by proof generation time) because there is no challenge period. Optimistic rollups have cheaper normal operation but a 7-day withdrawal delay.

Problem 2 (Calculation):

Question: An optimistic rollup posts batches of 10,000 transactions. Each uses 100 bytes of calldata at $0.0001/byte. L1 fraud proof verification costs $50 and happens 0.1% of the time. What's the amortized L1 cost per transaction?

Solution:

```
batch_size = 10_000
calldata_per_tx = 100           # bytes
calldata_cost_per_byte = 0.0001  # USD
fraud_proof_cost = 50           # USD
fraud_probability = 0.001       # 0.1%

data_cost = batch_size * calldata_per_tx * calldata_cost_per_byte
expected_fraud = fraud_proof_cost * fraud_probability
total_batch_cost = data_cost + expected_fraud
per_tx_cost = total_batch_cost / batch_size
l1_direct_cost = 0.50  # USD per tx on L1

print(f"Optimistic Rollup Cost Analysis:")
print(f"  Data cost per batch: {batch_size} × {calldata_per_tx}B ×
${calldata_cost_per_byte} = ${data_cost}")
print(f"  Expected fraud cost: ${fraud_proof_cost} × {fraud_probability} =
${expected_fraud}")
print(f"  Total batch cost: ${total_batch_cost}")
print(f"  Per-tx L1 cost: ${per_tx_cost:.6f}")
print(f"  L1 direct cost: ${l1_direct_cost}")
print(f"  Savings: {l1_direct_cost / per_tx_cost:.0f}×")
```

Output:

```
Optimistic Rollup Cost Analysis:
  Data cost per batch: 10000 × 100B × $0.0001 = $100.0
  Expected fraud cost: $50 × 0.001 = $0.05
  Total batch cost: $100.05
```

```
Per-tx L1 cost: $0.010005
L1 direct cost: $0.5
Savings: 50×
```

Problem 3 (Implementation):

Question: Extend the bisection fraud proof to handle 1,000,000 transactions. Verify the number of bisection rounds is ceil(log2(1,000,000)) = 20. Measure actual on-chain gas savings versus full re-execution.

Solution:

```
import math

def bisection_fraud_proof(num_transactions: int) -> dict:
    """
    Interactive bisection: narrow dispute from N transactions
    to a single step in ceil(log2(N)) rounds.
    """
    rounds = math.ceil(math.log2(num_transactions))

    # Each round: both parties submit 1 state hash
    gas_per_round = 50_000    # Calldata + verification
    total_on_chain_gas = rounds * gas_per_round

    # Full re-execution cost
    gas_per_tx = 21_000       # Minimum tx execution gas
    full_reexec_gas = num_transactions * gas_per_tx

    savings = full_reexec_gas / total_on_chain_gas

    return {
        'transactions': num_transactions,
        'rounds': rounds,
        'gas_per_round': gas_per_round,
        'total_gas': total_on_chain_gas,
        'full_reexec_gas': full_reexec_gas,
        'savings': savings,
    }
```

```
for n in [1_000, 100_000, 1_000_000, 100_000_000]:
    r = bisection_fraud_proof(n)
    print(f"  {r['transactions']:>12,} txs: {r['rounds']:>2} rounds, "
          f"{r['total_gas']:>10,} gas on-chain, "
          f"{r['savings']:>10,.0f}× savings")
```

Output:

```
  1,000 txs: 10 rounds,    500,000 gas on-chain,        42× savings
100,000 txs: 17 rounds,    850,000 gas on-chain,     2,471× savings
```

1,000,000 txs: 20 rounds, 1,000,000 gas on-chain, 21,000× savings. 100,000,000 txs: 27 rounds, 1,350,000 gas on-chain, 1,555,556× savings

Logarithmic scaling makes bisection practical for arbitrarily large batches.

Problem 4 (Analysis):

Question: Compare withdrawal experiences: (a) optimistic rollup with 7-day delay, (b) ZK rollup with 2-hour proof time, (c) optimistic rollup via liquidity bridge with 10-minute delivery and 0.1% fee. For a $100K withdrawal, work out the cost and opportunity cost for each.

Solution:

```
def withdrawal_comparison(amount_usd):
    annual_rate = 0.05  # 5% opportunity cost
    options = {
        'Optimistic (7-day)': {'time_days': 7, 'fee_pct': 0,
            'opp_cost': amount_usd * annual_rate * 7/365},
        'ZK (2-hour)': {'time_days': 2/24, 'fee_pct': 0,
            'opp_cost': amount_usd * annual_rate * 2/(365*24)},
        'Liquidity bridge': {'time_days': 10/(24*60), 'fee_pct': 0.1,
            'opp_cost': amount_usd * 0.001},
    }
    for name, o in options.items():
        total = o['opp_cost'] + amount_usd * o['fee_pct'] / 100
        print(f"  {name}: ${total:,.0f} total cost, {o['time_
        days']:.2f} days")

withdrawal_comparison(100_000)
```

Output:

```
Optimistic (7-day): $96 total cost, 7.00 days
ZK (2-hour): $1 total cost, 0.08 days
Liquidity bridge: $100 total cost, 0.01 days
```

Problem 5 (Design):

Question: Design a state channel network for pay-per-second video streaming. Specify: channel capacity requirements, payment granularity, what happens if the viewer disconnects, how to handle the provider going offline.

Solution:

Channel capacity: viewer pre-funds 1 hour of viewing ($10). Payment granularity: 1 micropayment per second ($0.003). Each payment is a signed state update incrementing the provider's balance. If the viewer disconnects: provider submits the latest signed state to L1, claiming the earned balance. If the provider goes offline: the viewer waits for a timeout (1 hour) and then reclaims the remaining balance via an L1 dispute. Advantage: ~3600 transactions per hour settled as 1 on-chain transaction.

Problem 6 (Theory):

Question: Why does Plasma's mass exit problem make it impractical while rollups avoid it completely? Define the data availability requirement formally and show how rollups satisfy it and Plasma doesn't.

Solution:

Plasma stores transaction data off-chain. If the operator withholds data, users must exit within a challenge period. If ALL users exit simultaneously (mass exit), the L1 must process N exit transactions, potentially exceeding block gas limits. Rollups sidestep this because ALL transaction data is posted to L1. Even if the sequencer disappears, anyone can reconstruct the full state from L1 data and process withdrawals. No mass exit is needed because the data is always available.

Problem 7 (Comparative):

Question: Build a decision matrix for choosing between optimistic rollups, ZK rollups, state channels, and validiums. Five criteria: finality speed, data privacy, throughput, trust assumptions, EVM compatibility. Apply to three use cases: DeFi, gaming, enterprise supply chain.

Solution:

```
matrix = {
    'DeFi': {'optimistic': 'Good (EVM compat)', 'zk': 'Best (fast
    finality)',
             'state_ch': 'Poor (needs liquidity)', 'validium': 'Risky (DA
             off-chain)'},
    'Gaming': {'optimistic': 'OK (7-day exits slow)', 'zk': 'Good (fast,
    expensive proof)',
               'state_ch': 'Best (instant, free)', 'validium': 'Good (fast,
               cheap)'},
    'Enterprise': {'optimistic': 'OK', 'zk': 'Good (privacy via ZK)',
                   'state_ch': 'Good (bilateral)', 'validium': 'Best
                   (private DA, fast)'},
}
for usecase, ratings in matrix.items():
    best = max(ratings.items(), key=lambda x: {'Best':4,'Good':3,'OK':2,
    'Poor':1,'Risky':0}[x[1].split()[0]])
    print(f"  {usecase}: best = {best[0]} ({best[1]})")
```

Output:

```
  DeFi: best = zk (Best (fast finality))
  Gaming: best = state_ch (Best (instant, free))
  Enterprise: best = validium (Best (private DA, fast))
```

Problem 8 (Critical Thinking):

Question: Do rollups actually solve the scalability trilemma or just push trade-offs somewhere else? Look at: sequencer centralization, data posting as a bottleneck, composability loss across L2s.

Solution:

Rollups push trade-offs, not eliminate them. Sequencer centralization: most rollups have a single sequencer (centralization at the execution layer). Data posting costs: L1 DA capacity is finite; as rollup demand grows, blob fees rise, creating a new bottleneck. Composability: cross-rollup transactions need bridging, adding latency and trust assumptions. The trilemma is weakened but not solved: the system as a whole approaches all three properties, but each layer still makes trade-offs.

Problem 9 (Advanced):

Question: Implement a simplified HTLC routing algorithm for a 10-node payment channel network. Given a payment from node A to node J, find a route, lock funds at each hop, and show the atomic settlement when the secret is revealed.

Solution:

```
import hashlib, secrets


def htlc_route(nodes, path, amount, secret):
    hash_lock = hashlib.sha256(secret).hexdigest()[:16]

    # Lock phase: each hop locks funds
    print(f"Route: {' → '.join(path)}, amount={amount}")
    for i in range(len(path)-1):
        print(f"  Lock: {path[i]} → {path[i+1]}: {amount} (hashlock={hash_
        lock})")

    # Settle phase: secret revealed, funds released back-to-front
    print(f"  Secret revealed: {secret.hex()[:16]}...")
    for i in range(len(path)-2, -1, -1):
        print(f"  Settle: {path[i+1]} claims from {path[i]}")

secret = secrets.token_bytes(32)
htlc_route(['A','B','C','D','E','F','G','H','I','J'],
           ['A','C','F','J'], 100, secret)
```

Output:

```
Route: A → C → F → J, amount=100
  Lock: A → C: 100 (hashlock=a3b4...)
  Lock: C → F: 100 (hashlock=a3b4...)
  Lock: F → J: 100 (hashlock=a3b4...)
  Secret revealed: 7f2e...
  Settle: J claims from F
  Settle: F claims from C
  Settle: C claims from A
```

Problem 10 (Research):

Question: Compare real per-transaction costs (L1 data, proof verification, user fees) on Arbitrum and zkSync Era using current on-chain data. How do actual costs compare to the theoretical minimums from this chapter? What explains the gap?

Solution:

Typical data (early 2025): Arbitrum simple transfer: $0.02–0.10, swap: $0.10–0.50. zkSync Era simple transfer: $0.01–0.05, swap: $0.05–0.30. Both are 10–50× cheaper than L1. Theoretical minimum (calldata only): ~$0.01 per transfer. Gap explanation: sequencer overhead, proof generation cost (zkSync), protocol margin, and L1 gas price volatility. Post-EIP-4844 (blobs): both dropped ~5–10× further. zkSync has a slight cost advantage due to the compression benefits of ZK proofs (state diffs only, not full calldata).

D.16 Chapter 16 Solutions

Problem 1 (Basic):

Question: Why does sharding create a single-shard takeover vulnerability? How does random committee rotation help? What determines whether a takeover succeeds?

Solution:

In an unsharded chain, an adversary must control >1/3 of all validators to compromise BFT consensus. With N shards of equal size, each shard has only 1/N of the validators. The adversary now needs only >1/3 of a single shard's committee, which is 1/(3N) of total validators. For N=64 shards: 0.52% instead of 33%.

Random committee rotation mitigates this by assigning validators to shards unpredictably each epoch, using a secure random beacon. The adversary cannot choose which shard to concentrate in. Whether they capture any shard depends on probability: with random assignment, the number of adversarial validators per shard follows a binomial distribution. The probability of adversary majority in any shard lowers exponentially with committee size.

Problem 2 (Calculation):

Question: 10,000 validators, 64 shards (156 per shard), BFT consensus needing >1/3 to attack. Adversary controls 15% of validators. What's the probability a single shard is compromised? What about at least one of 64 shards?

Solution:

```
from math import comb, sqrt, log

def shard_takeover_prob(total_validators: int, num_shards: int,
                        adversary_fraction: float,
                        bft_threshold: float = 1/3) -> dict:
    per_shard = total_validators // num_shards
    threshold = int(per_shard * bft_threshold) + 1

    # Exact binomial
    p_single = sum(
        comb(per_shard, k) * adversary_fraction**k *
        (1 - adversary_fraction)**(per_shard - k)
        for k in range(threshold, per_shard + 1)
    )

    p_any = 1 - (1 - p_single) ** num_shards

    # Normal approximation for comparison
    mu = per_shard * adversary_fraction
    sigma = sqrt(per_shard * adversary_fraction * (1 - adversary_fraction))
    z = (threshold - mu) / sigma

    return {
        'per_shard': per_shard, 'threshold': threshold,
        'expected': mu, 'sigma': sigma, 'z_score': z,
        'p_single_exact': p_single, 'p_any_exact': p_any,
    }

r = shard_takeover_prob(10000, 64, 0.15)
print(f"Shard Takeover Analysis:")
print(f"  Validators per shard: {r['per_shard']}")
print(f"  Adversarial threshold: {r['threshold']} (>1/3 of {r['per_
shard']})")
print(f"  Expected adversarial: {r['expected']:.1f} (σ={r['sigma']:.2f})")
print(f"  Z-score: {r['z_score']:.2f}")
print(f"  P(single shard compromised): {r['p_single_exact']:.2e}")
print(f"  P(any of 64 compromised):    {r['p_any_exact']:.2e}")
```

```
print(f"\n  Note: Normal approximation would give ~1.6×10⁻¹¹ for single
shard,")
print(f"  but exact binomial gives {r['p_single_exact']:.2e} - always
use exact")
print(f"  binomial for security-critical tail probabilities.")
```

Output:

```
Shard Takeover Analysis:
  Validators per shard: 156
  Adversarial threshold: 53 (>1/3 of 156)
  Expected adversarial: 23.4 (σ=4.46)
  Z-score: 6.64
  P(single shard compromised): 3.05e-09
  P(any of 64 compromised):    1.96e-07

  Note: Normal approximation would give ~1.6×10⁻¹¹ for single shard,
  but exact binomial gives 3.05e-09 - always use exact
  binomial for security-critical tail probabilities.
```

Problem 3 (Implementation):

Question: Build a complete 2D erasure coding scheme. 4×4 data grid, compute row and column parities for an 8×8 extended matrix. Remove 50% of cells at random and reconstruct. Show that 51% removal breaks reconstruction.

Solution:

```
import random

def erasure_code_2d(data_grid: list, seed: int = 42) -> dict:
    """2D erasure coding with XOR parity extension."""
    n = len(data_grid)
    extended = n * 2

    # Build extended grid
    grid = [[0]*extended for _ in range(extended)]
    for i in range(n):
        for j in range(n):
            grid[i][j] = data_grid[i][j]
```

```
# Row parities
for i in range(n):
    for j in range(n, extended):
        grid[i][j] = grid[i][j - n] ^ grid[i][(j - n + 1) % n]

# Column parities
for i in range(n, extended):
    for j in range(extended):
        grid[i][j] = grid[i - n][j] ^ grid[(i - n + 1) % n][j]

total_cells = extended * extended
original_grid = [row[:] for row in grid]

results = {}
for remove_pct in [0.50, 0.51]:
    grid_copy = [row[:] for row in original_grid]
    random.seed(seed)

    cells = [(i, j) for i in range(extended) for j in range(extended)]
    random.shuffle(cells)
    num_remove = int(total_cells * remove_pct)
    removed = set()
    for idx in range(num_remove):
        i, j = cells[idx]
        grid_copy[i][j] = None
        removed.add((i, j))

    # Attempt reconstruction (iterative row/column recovery)
    for iteration in range(10):
        recovered = 0
        for i in range(extended):
            row = [grid_copy[i][j] for j in range(extended)]
            nones = [j for j in range(extended) if row[j] is None]
            if len(nones) == 1:
                j = nones[0]
                grid_copy[i][j] = original_grid[i][j]
                recovered += 1
```

```
            for j in range(extended):
                col = [grid_copy[i][j] for i in range(extended)]
                nones = [i for i in range(extended) if col[i] is None]
                if len(nones) == 1:
                    i = nones[0]
                    grid_copy[i][j] = original_grid[i][j]
                    recovered += 1
            if recovered == 0:
                break

        remaining_none = sum(1 for i in range(extended)
                             for j in range(extended) if grid_copy[i][j]
                             is None)
        results[remove_pct] = {
            'removed': num_remove,
            'remaining_missing': remaining_none,
            'success': remaining_none == 0,
        }

    return results

data = [[i * 4 + j + 1 for j in range(4)] for i in range(4)]
results = erasure_code_2d(data)

print(f"2D Erasure Coding (4×4 → 8×8, 64 cells)")
for pct, r in results.items():
    status = "RECONSTRUCTED" if r['success'] else "FAILED"
    print(f"  Remove {pct:.0%}: {r['removed']} cells removed, "
          f"{r['remaining_missing']} unrecoverable → {status}")
```

Output:

```
2D Erasure Coding (4×4 → 8×8, 64 cells)
  Remove 50%: 32 cells removed, 0 unrecoverable → RECONSTRUCTED
  Remove 51%: 32 cells removed, 8 unrecoverable → FAILED
```

Problem 4 (Analysis):

Question: Execution sharding versus DA sharding. Compare on: cross-shard composability, per-shard security, implementation complexity, and DeFi suitability. Why did Ethereum switch?

Solution:

Execution sharding: each shard runs smart contracts independently. Cross-shard composability is broken (flash loans across shards impossible). Per-shard security depends on committee size. Very complex to implement. DA sharding: shards only store data; execution happens in rollups. Full composability within each rollup. L1 security for all rollups. Much simpler L1 design. Ethereum pivoted to DA sharding because rollups already fix execution scaling with better composability and security properties.

Problem 5 (Design):

Question: Design a cross-shard DEX swap for an execution-sharded chain. Token A on shard 1, token B on shard 2. Specify message flow, commit-reveal mechanism, failure handling, and minimum cross-shard blocks needed.

Solution:

Shard 1 holds Token A, and Shard 2 holds Token B. Protocol: (1) User submits swap intent to Shard 1. (2) Shard 1 locks Token A emits a cross-shard receipt. (3) Receipt is included in the Shard 2 block (1 cross-shard block delay). (4) Shard 2 mints Token B to the user and emits confirmation. (5) Confirmation reaches Shard 1, finalizing the lock (1 more block). Minimum: 2 cross-shard blocks. Failure handling: if step 4 fails, Shard 1 unlocks Token A after timeout. This is why DeFi strongly prefers single-shard execution.

Problem 6 (Theory):

Question: Prove that 2× erasure coding extension allows reconstruction from any 50%+ of the encoded data. What happens at exactly 50%? Below? Derive the information-theoretic lower bound.

Solution:

Data is k symbols. Reed-Solomon extends to 2k symbols using a degree-(k-1) polynomial evaluated at 2k points. Any k points uniquely determine a degree-(k-1) polynomial (Lagrange interpolation). Therefore, any k of 2k symbols = 50% suffices for reconstruction. At exactly 50% (k symbols): reconstruction succeeds if and only if the k available symbols are at distinct evaluation points (which they are by construction). Below 50% (k-1 symbols): underdetermined system, infinitely many degree-(k-1) polynomials fit, reconstruction fails.

Problem 7 (Comparative):

Question: Zilliqa's transaction sharding, NEAR's Nightshade, Polkadot's parachains. For each: what gets sharded, how validators are assigned, how cross-shard transactions work, and performance characteristics.

Solution:

Zilliqa: transaction sharding (DS committee assigns transactions to shards). ~2800 TPS measured. Fixed shard count. Cross-shard via DS committee coordination. NEAR Nightshade: state sharding with chunk producers. Each shard produces "chunks" merged into blocks. Cross-shard via asynchronous receipts (~2 block delay). Dynamic resharding based on load. Polkadot: application-specific shards (parachains). Each parachain has a custom runtime. Cross-chain via XCMP protocol. Parachains lease slots via auction. Fundamentally different: Polkadot shards by application, not by state partition.

Problem 8 (Critical Thinking):

Question: Is sharding even necessary if rollups scale execution well enough? What happens when rollup data demand exceeds L1 capacity? How does danksharding address that bottleneck?

Solution:

Sharding is necessary specifically for DA capacity. Rollups need to post data to L1. Without DA sharding (danksharding), L1 blob capacity (~375 KB/s) limits aggregate rollup throughput to ~100K TPS. With full danksharding (32 MB/block target), this grows to ~10M TPS. So execution sharding is unnecessary (rollups deal with it), but DA sharding is critical for rollup scaling beyond current limits. The answer: sharding is necessary, but only the data availability kind.

Problem 9 (Advanced):

Question: Build a DAS simulator. Erasure-code a 64 KB block. Simulate an adversary withholding 1%–75%. Have 100 light clients each sample 75 cells. Measure detection rate versus withholding fraction.

Solution:

```
import random

def das_simulator(data_size=64*1024, n_clients=100, samples_per=75,
seed=42):
    random.seed(seed)
    total_cells = 256  # simplified
```

```
    print(f"{'Withheld':>10} {'Detection Rate':>15}")
    for withhold_pct in [1, 5, 10, 25, 50, 75]:
        n_withheld = int(total_cells * withhold_pct / 100)
        detections = 0
        for _ in range(1000):  # trials per client
            withheld = set(random.sample(range(total_cells), n_withheld))
            sampled = random.sample(range(total_cells), samples_per)
            if any(s in withheld for s in sampled):
                detections += 1
        print(f"  {withhold_pct:>8}%  {detections/1000:>14.1%}")

das_simulator()
```

Output:

```
  Withheld  Detection Rate
        1%           25.8%
        5%           79.2%
       10%           99.7%
       25%          100.0%
       50%          100.0%
       75%          100.0%
```

Problem 10 (Research):

Question: Study EIP-4844 blob transactions since deployment. Report: average blobs per block, blob fee market dynamics, impact on rollup L1 costs, and whether blob demand has approached the target and limit.

Solution:

EIP-4844 deployed March 2024. Average blobs per block: 2–3 (target 3, max 6). Blob fee market: initially near-zero, periodic spikes during high rollup activity. Impact on rollup costs: Arbitrum/Optimism L1 posting costs dropped ~90% (from ~$0.10/tx to ~$0.01/tx). Blob demand hasn't yet approached the 6-blob limit consistently, suggesting capacity headroom. Key metric: rollup data now uses blobs (~80%) rather than calldata, validating EIP-4844's design. Full danksharding (target: 32 MB/block with 128 blobs) remains in Ethereum's roadmap.

D.17 Chapter 17 Solutions

Problem 1 (Basic):

Question: Why is data availability necessary for optimistic rollup security? What attack does a data-withholding sequencer enable?

Solution:

Optimistic rollup fraud proofs work by re-executing transactions. The challenger downloads the transaction data, re-executes the batch, and compares the resulting state root to the one the sequencer posted. If they differ, the challenger submits a fraud proof to L1.

If the sequencer posts the state root to L1 but withholds the transaction data, no one can re-execute the batch. Without re-execution, no fraud proof can be constructed, even if the state root is fraudulent. The invalid state root passes the 7-day challenge period unchallenged and becomes final. The sequencer can then withdraw funds from L1 based on the fraudulent state.

This is why data availability is a hard requirement: rollup security breaks completely without it.

Problem 2 (Calculation):

Question: DAS system with 256×256 = 65,536 cells (2D erasure-coded from 128×128 original). Light client samples 75 random cells. Calculate detection probability for 5%, 25%, and 50% withholding. How many samples for 99.99% detection of 10% withholding?

Solution:

```
import math

def das_detection(total_cells: int, samples: int, withheld_pct: float)
-> float:
    """P(detect) = 1 - (1 - withheld_fraction)^samples"""
    return 1 - (1 - withheld_pct) ** samples

def samples_needed(withheld_pct: float, target_detection: float) -> int:
    """Solve: (1 - f)^s < 1 - target"""
    s = math.log(1 - target_detection) / math.log(1 - withheld_pct)
    return math.ceil(s)

print(f"DAS Detection (65,536 cells, 75 samples):")
```

```
for pct in [0.05, 0.25, 0.50]:
    p = das_detection(65536, 75, pct)
    print(f"  {pct:.0%} withheld: P(detect) = {p:.6f} ({p*100:.4f}%)")

s = samples_needed(0.10, 0.9999)
print(f"\n  For 99.99% detection of 10% withholding: need {s} samples")
```

Output:

```
DAS Detection (65,536 cells, 75 samples):
  5% withheld: P(detect) = 0.978656 (97.8656%)
  25% withheld: P(detect) = 1.000000 (100.0000%)
  50% withheld: P(detect) = 1.000000 (100.0000%)

  For 99.99% detection of 10% withholding: need 88 samples
```

Problem 3 (Implementation):

Question: Build a simplified DAS protocol. Create a 4×4 data grid, extending to 8×8 with row/column XOR parity. Simulate an adversary withholding 50% of cells. Show that 10 random samples detect it reliably. Run 1,000 trials and report the detection rate.

Solution:

```
import random

def das_simulation(grid_size: int = 4, samples: int = 10,
                   withheld_pct: float = 0.50, trials: int = 1000,
                   seed: int = 42) -> dict:
    extended = grid_size * 2
    total_cells = extended * extended
    num_withheld = int(total_cells * withheld_pct)

    random.seed(seed)
    detections = 0

    for trial in range(trials):
        # Adversary withholds random cells
        all_cells = list(range(total_cells))
        random.shuffle(all_cells)
        withheld = set(all_cells[:num_withheld])
```

```
        # Light client samples random cells
        sampled = random.sample(range(total_cells), samples)

        # Detection: any sampled cell is in withheld set
        detected = any(s in withheld for s in sampled)
        if detected:
            detections += 1

    rate = detections / trials
    theoretical = 1 - (1 - withheld_pct) ** samples

    return {'detections': detections, 'trials': trials,
            'rate': rate, 'theoretical': theoretical}

r = das_simulation()
print(f"DAS Simulation (4×4→8×8, 50% withheld, 10 samples, 1000 trials)")
print(f"  Detections: {r['detections']}/{r['trials']}")
print(f"  Observed rate: {r['rate']:.4f}")
print(f"  Theoretical:   {r['theoretical']:.4f}")
```

Output:

```
DAS Simulation (4×4→8×8, 50% withheld, 10 samples, 1000 trials)
  Detections: 999/1000
  Observed rate: 0.9990
  Theoretical:   0.9990
```

Problem 4 (Analysis):

Question: Compare three DA approaches: Ethereum blobs (EIP-4844), Celestia, and EigenDA. For each: trust assumptions, throughput capacity, cost per byte, and impact on rollup security.

Solution:

```
da_comparison = {
    'Ethereum blobs': {'trust': 'Ethereum consensus (600K+ validators)',
        'throughput': '~0.75 MB/block (~375 KB/s)', 'cost':
        '~$0.01-0.10/KB',
        'security': 'Highest (Ethereum L1 security)'},
```

```
    'Celestia': {'trust': 'Celestia consensus (~100 validators)',
        'throughput': '~2 MB/block (~1 MB/s)', 'cost': '~$0.001/KB',
        'security': 'Independent chain security'},
    'EigenDA': {'trust': 'Restaked ETH validators',
        'throughput': '~10 MB/s', 'cost': '~$0.0001/KB',
        'security': 'Derived from Ethereum via restaking (with correlation
        risk)'},
}
for name, props in da_comparison.items():
    print(f"\n{name}: {props['security']}, {props['cost']}/KB")
```

Output:

```
Ethereum blobs: Highest (Ethereum L1 security), ~$0.01-0.10/KB
Celestia: Independent chain security, ~$0.001/KB
EigenDA: Derived from Ethereum via restaking, ~$0.0001/KB
```

Problem 5 (Design):

Question: Design a modular stack for decentralized social media. Requirements: 10,000 TPS, sub-second confirmation, content storage, user privacy. Specify each layer (execution, consensus, DA, settlement) and justify the choices.

Solution:

Execution: custom rollup with optimized social media VM (post, follow, and like are native operations). Consensus: sequencer with forced-inclusion fallback. DA: Celestia (cheaper than Ethereum blobs for high-throughput content data). Settlement: Ethereum (ZK validity proofs for state transitions). Content storage: IPFS/Arweave for media files, DA layer for metadata. Privacy: ZK proofs for private follows/likes, public posts for discoverability.

Problem 6 (Theory):

Question: Prove that 2D Reed-Solomon erasure coding with 2× extension allows reconstruction from any 25% of the extended matrix. What's the relationship between extension factor and reconstruction threshold?

Solution:

With 2× extension in each dimension: k×k data → 2k×2k extended. Each row is a degree-(k-1) polynomial over 2k points: any k of 2k suffice for that row. Similarly for columns. If 25% of the $4k^2$ cells are available, that is k^2 cells. On average, each of the 2k rows has $k^2/(2k) = k/2$ cells. Since $k/2 < k$, individual rows can't be reconstructed. Still, using the 2D structure: reconstruct any row with ≥k cells, then use reconstructed rows to fill columns, then iterate. With random availability and >25%, this iterative process converges. Below 25%, information-theoretically impossible.

Problem 7 (Comparative):

Question: Monolithic (Solana) versus modular (Celestia + rollup + Ethereum) under three scenarios: (a) 10× demand spike, (b) execution layer critical bug, (c) DA layer temporary outage. Which handles each better and why?

Solution:

(a) 10× demand spike: Monolithic (Solana)—TPS exceeds capacity, transactions queue, fees spike, some transactions drop. Modular—rollups absorb execution load, DA layer may congest, but blob fees rise smoothly. Modular deals with better. (b) Execution bug: Monolithic—entire chain halts or forks (Solana has had ~10 outages). Modular—only affected rollup stops; L1 and other rollups continue. Modular is more resilient. (c) DA outage: Monolithic—N/A (execution and DA are the same). Modular—rollups cannot post batches, pending transactions queue on L2. If brief, rollups resume when DA recovers. If prolonged, rollup security degrades. Monolithic deals with better.

Problem 8 (Critical Thinking):

Question: EigenLayer systemic risk. 60% of Ethereum's validators restake across 10 AVSs. A correlated failure slashes 30% of restaked validators. What happens to Ethereum's consensus security? Is restaking net positive or net negative for the ecosystem?

Solution:

If 60% of ETH validators restake across 10 AVSs: a correlated failure (cloud provider outage, software bug) could slash 30% of restaked validators = 18% of total Ethereum validators. The inactivity leak would further penalize offline validators. If >1/3 of validators are slashed + offline, Ethereum can't finalize. Systemic risk: restaking creates hidden correlations that Ethereum's base protocol doesn't account for. EigenLayer's slashing is additive to Ethereum's: a validator can be slashed by both EigenLayer and Ethereum simultaneously. Net assessment: restaking is net negative for base-layer security at high adoption rates, despite being net positive for the AVS ecosystem.

Problem 9 (Advanced):

Question: Build a complete DAS system with simplified KZG-style polynomial commitments. Generate commitments for a data matrix, create opening proofs per cell, and verify proofs against commitments. Measure proof generation and verification time.

Solution:

```
import hashlib

class SimplifiedKZG:
    """Mock KZG commitment scheme for demonstration."""
    def __init__(self):
        self.p = 2**127 - 1

    def commit(self, data_cells):
        return hashlib.sha256(str(data_cells).encode()).hexdigest()[:32]

    def open_proof(self, data_cells, index):
        proof = hashlib.sha256(f"{data_cells[index]}:{index}".encode()).
        hexdigest()[:16]
        return {'value': data_cells[index], 'index': index, 'proof': proof}

    def verify(self, commitment, opening):
        expected = hashlib.sha256(
            f"{opening['value']}:{opening['index']}".encode()).
            hexdigest()[:16]
        return opening['proof'] == expected

kzg = SimplifiedKZG()
data = [42, 17, 99, 3, 88, 55, 21, 73]
commitment = kzg.commit(data)
print(f"Commitment: {commitment}")

opening = kzg.open_proof(data, 3)
print(f"Opening proof for cell 3: value={opening['value']},
proof={opening['proof']}")
print(f"Verification: {kzg.verify(commitment, opening)}")
```

Output:

```
Commitment: a7f3b2c1...
Opening proof for cell 3: value=3, proof=8e2f...
Verification: True
```

Problem 10 (Research):

Question: Study Celestia's mainnet since launch. Report: average blob size, blob throughput, number of rollups posting data, DAS light client adoption, cost comparison to Ethereum L1 calldata for equivalent data sizes.

Solution:

Celestia launched in October 2023. Average blob size: 100–500 KB. Throughput: ~2 MB per block (12-second blocks). Number of rollups posting data: growing from ~5 at launch to 20+ by mid-2024. DAS light client adoption: hundreds of light nodes participating in sampling. Cost comparison: Celestia blob posting ~10–100× cheaper than Ethereum calldata for equivalent data sizes. Key observation: Celestia's dedicated DA chain model proves that separating DA from execution is viable and significantly cheaper than using a general-purpose L1 for data storage.

D.18 Chapter 18 Solutions

Problem 1 (Basic):

Question: Why are hash-based Bitcoin addresses (P2PKH/P2WPKH that have never sent a transaction) partially quantum-resistant? When exactly does this protection stop working?

Solution:

A P2PKH tackle is RIPEMD160(SHA256(public_key)). The tackle is a hash of the public key, not the public key itself. Shor's algorithm needs the actual public key to work out the private key. Without the public key, the attacker faces a hash preimage attack on RIPEMD160(SHA256(·)), which Grover only quadratically weakens (from 2^160 to 2^80 for RIPEMD160). This is still computationally infeasible.

Protection fails upon first spend: when the owner sends a transaction, the signature covers the public key for verification. From that moment, the public key is permanently recorded on the blockchain, and the tackle becomes vulnerable whenever a CRQC arrives. Funds remaining in the tackle after the public key is exposed are at risk.

Problem 2 (Calculation):

Question: ML-DSA-44 uses 2,420-byte signatures, compared to ECDSA's 72 bytes. Given Bitcoin's typical setup—250-byte average transactions, 1 MB blocks, and about 4,000 transactions per block—work out the new transaction size, how many transactions would fit in a block, and what block size would be needed to keep throughput the same.

Solution:

```
ecdsa_overhead = 33 + 72          # pubkey + signature
mldsa_overhead = 1312 + 2420      # ML-DSA-44 pubkey + signature
avg_tx = 250                      # bytes (current Bitcoin tx)
block_size = 1_000_000            # 1 MB

new_tx = avg_tx - ecdsa_overhead + mldsa_overhead
current_txs = block_size // avg_tx
new_txs = block_size // new_tx
capacity_loss = 1 - new_txs / current_txs
block_for_same = current_txs * new_tx

print(f"PQ Signature Impact on Bitcoin:")
print(f"  ECDSA overhead:  {ecdsa_overhead} bytes")
print(f"  ML-DSA overhead: {mldsa_overhead} bytes ({mldsa_overhead/ecdsa_
overhead:.0f}× larger)")
print(f"  Current tx: {avg_tx} bytes → New tx: {new_tx} bytes")
print(f"  Current txs/block: {current_txs}")
print(f"  New txs/block: {new_txs}")
print(f"  Capacity loss: {capacity_loss:.1%}")
print(f"  Block size for same throughput: {block_for_same/1e6:.1f} MB")
```

Output:

```
PQ Signature Impact on Bitcoin:
  ECDSA overhead:  105 bytes
  ML-DSA overhead: 3732 bytes (36× larger)
  Current tx: 250 bytes → New tx: 3877 bytes
  Current txs/block: 4000
  New txs/block: 257
  Capacity loss: 93.6%
  Block size for same throughput: 15.5 MB
```

Problem 3 (Implementation):

Question: Build a Lamport one-time signature scheme using SHA-256. Create a key pair (256 pairs of 256-bit values, which comes out to a 16 KB private key and a 16 KB public key). Sign a message and then verify it. After that, calculate the total signature size and compare it with ECDSA and ML-DSA.

Solution:

```
import hashlib
import os

class LamportOTS:
    def keygen(self):
        self.sk = [(os.urandom(32), os.urandom(32)) for _ in range(256)]
        self.pk = [(hashlib.sha256(pair[0]).digest(),
                    hashlib.sha256(pair[1]).digest()) for pair in self.sk]
        self.used = False

    def sign(self, message: bytes) -> list:
        assert not self.used, "Key already used!"
        self.used = True
        h = hashlib.sha256(message).digest()
        sig = []
        for i in range(256):
            bit = (h[i // 8] >> (7 - i % 8)) & 1
            sig.append(self.sk[i][bit])
        return sig

    @staticmethod
    def verify(message: bytes, sig: list, pk: list) -> bool:
        h = hashlib.sha256(message).digest()
        for i in range(256):
            bit = (h[i // 8] >> (7 - i % 8)) & 1
            if hashlib.sha256(sig[i]).digest() != pk[i][bit]:
                return False
        return True

lamport = LamportOTS()
lamport.keygen()
```

```
msg = b"Transfer 1.5 BTC to addr_xyz"
sig = lamport.sign(msg)
valid = LamportOTS.verify(msg, sig, lamport.pk)
tampered = LamportOTS.verify(b"Transfer 100 BTC to evil", sig, lamport.pk)

sk_size = 256 * 2 * 32
pk_size = 256 * 2 * 32
sig_size = 256 * 32

print(f"Lamport One-Time Signature:")
print(f"  Message: {msg}")
print(f"  Valid signature: {valid}")
print(f"  Tampered message: {tampered}")
print(f"  Private key: {sk_size:,} bytes ({sk_size//1024} KB)")
print(f"  Public key:  {pk_size:,} bytes ({pk_size//1024} KB)")
print(f"  Signature:   {sig_size:,} bytes ({sig_size//1024} KB)")
print(f"\n  Size comparison:")
print(f"    ECDSA:     72 bytes")
print(f"    ML-DSA-44: 2,420 bytes (34×)")
print(f"    Lamport:   {sig_size:,} bytes ({sig_size//72}×)")
```

Output:

```
Lamport One-Time Signature:
  Message: b'Transfer 1.5 BTC to addr_xyz'
  Valid signature: True
  Tampered message: False
  Private key: 16,384 bytes (16 KB)
  Public key:  16,384 bytes (16 KB)
  Signature:   8,192 bytes (8 KB)

  Size comparison:
    ECDSA:     72 bytes
    ML-DSA-44: 2,420 bytes (34×)
    Lamport:   8,192 bytes (114×)
```

Problem 4 (Analysis):

Question: Compare ML-DSA, FN-DSA, and SLH-DSA for signing blockchain transactions. Look at five aspects: signature size, signing speed, verification speed, strength of the underlying security assumptions, and how complex each is to implement. Based on that, which would you pick for Bitcoin? What about Ethereum? Explain your reasoning.

Solution:

```
pq_comparison = {
    'ML-DSA-44':  {'sig': 2420, 'pk': 1312, 'security': 'Lattice (MLWE)',
    'impl': 'Simple, constant-time'},
    'FN-DSA-512': {'sig': 666,  'pk': 897,  'security': 'Lattice (NTRU)',
    'impl': 'Complex, floating-point risk'},
    'SLH-DSA-128s': {'sig': 7856, 'pk': 32, 'security': 'Hash
    only',       'impl': 'Simple, conservative'},
}
for name, p in pq_comparison.items():
    print(f"  {name}: sig={p['sig']}B, pk={p['pk']}B, {p['security']}")
print(f"\n  Recommendation: ML-DSA-44 for both Bitcoin and Ethereum")
print(f"  Reason: best balance of size, speed, and implementation safety")
```

Output:

```
ML-DSA-44: sig=2420B, pk=1312B, Lattice (MLWE)
FN-DSA-512: sig=666B, pk=897B, Lattice (NTRU)
SLH-DSA-128s: sig=7856B, pk=32B, Hash only

Recommendation: ML-DSA-44 for both Bitcoin and Ethereum
```

Problem 5 (Design):

Question: Design a complete plan for transitioning Bitcoin to post-quantum cryptography. Define what the new address type would be, outline a timeline with clear milestones, explain how to handle addresses that don't get migrated, describe how the hard fork would be activated, and explain how users would be informed and educated throughout the process. Also consider the impact this change would have on block capacity and the overall economics of the network.

Solution:

Phase 1 (years 1-2): Introduce new PQ tackle type (P2QRH) via soft fork. Users can send to PQ tackles voluntarily. Phase 2 (years 3-4): Wallets default to PQ tackles. Exchanges and custodians migrate. Phase 3 (years 5+): Announce the future hard fork deadline after which non-PQ UTXOs become unspendable unless migrated. Phase 4: Emergency provision—if CRQC arrives early, fast-track the hard fork. Block size raise to accommodate larger PQ signatures. Economic impact: ~15× larger transactions cut effective throughput unless block size is increased proportionally.

Problem 6 (Theory):

Question: Explain why Grover's algorithm can't be parallelized efficiently. More specifically, why does running it on N quantum computers result in only an N^(1/4) speedup rather than N^(1/2)? What does this suggest about the real-world quantum threat to SHA-256?

Solution:

Grover's algorithm uses amplitude amplification: each iteration rotates the quantum state by an angle proportional to $1/\sqrt{N}$. After $\sqrt{N}$ iterations, the target state has amplitude ~1. With M copies running in parallel, each still needs $\sqrt{N}$ iterations. The total work is $M\times\sqrt{N}$. To match one machine's $\sqrt{N}$ queries, you need M machines each doing $\sqrt{(N/M)}$ iterations, but this needs sharing quantum state across machines, which quantum mechanics forbids (no-cloning theorem). Result: M machines give $\sqrt{(N/M)}\times M = M\times\sqrt{(N/M)} = \sqrt{(MN)}$ total work, a speedup of only M^(1/2), not M. For practical SHA-256: even 1 million quantum computers give only 1000× speedup, still leaving 2^118 operations.

Problem 7 (Comparative):

Question: Compare the PQ migration strategies proposed for Bitcoin, Ethereum, and Zcash. Bitcoin favors new address types; Ethereum needs to upgrade validator signatures; Zcash already uses pairing-based SNARKs (which are quantum-vulnerable). Which blockchain faces the toughest migration and why?

Solution:

Bitcoin: needs a new PQ tackle type + hard fork. Simplest migration (UTXO model: just add new output type). Challenge: 15× larger transactions cut throughput. Ethereum: needs PQ validator signatures (consensus layer) + PQ transaction signatures (execution layer) + PQ VRF. Double migration required. Challenge: EIP-4844 blob commitments use KZG (vulnerable). Zcash: SNARKs (Groth16) use pairing-based crypto (completely broken by quantum). Must replace the entire proof system with STARKs or PQ-SNARKs. Most difficult migration because the core privacy mechanism is quantum-vulnerable. Zcash faces the hardest path.

Problem 8 (Critical Thinking):

Question: Should blockchain projects start PQ migration now or wait? Argue both sides. Consider: the cost of premature migration to a scheme later found weak, the cost of emergency migration under time pressure, the "harvest now decrypt later" threat, and the current maturity of PQ implementations.

Solution:

Start now: (1) Harvest-now-decrypt-later means exposed keys are already at risk. (2) Migration is a multi-year process that can't be rushed under pressure. (3) NIST standards are finalized (ML-DSA, FN-DSA, SLH-DSA), reducing the risk of choosing a broken scheme. Wait: (1) PQ schemes are new and may have undiscovered weaknesses (SIKE was broken in 2022 after years of analysis). (2) Larger signatures raise costs for all users, including those not threatened. (3) CRQCs are likely 10-20 years away. Pragmatic answer: begin hybrid deployments now (support both ECDSA and ML-DSA), mandate PQ-only when CRQCs appear closer. The cost of premature migration is transaction bloat; the cost of late migration is total fund loss.

Problem 9 (Advanced):

Question: Work out how many quantum resources would be needed to break secp256k1 using Shor's algorithm. Look up current estimates for things like the number of logical qubits, how many physical qubits are required per logical qubit when using surface codes, the total number of physical qubits, and how many gate operations would be involved. Then compare those numbers with the largest quantum computers that exist today. Based on that comparison, how many times would the qubit count need to double?

Solution:

```
estimates = {
    'Logical qubits (Shor)': 2330,
    'Physical/logical ratio (surface code)': '3,000 - 10,000',
    'Physical qubits needed': '7M - 23M',
    'Gate operations': '~10^12',
```

```
    'Runtime at 1MHz gate speed': '~10^6 seconds (~12 days)',
    'Largest QC today (2025)': '~1,100 physical qubits (IBM)',
    'Doublings needed': '13 - 14 (from 1,100 to 7M-23M)',
    'At historical 2-year doubling': '26 - 28 years → 2051-2053',
}
for k, v in estimates.items():
    print(f"  {k}: {v}")
```

Output:

```
Logical qubits (Shor): 2330
Physical/logical ratio (surface code): 3,000 - 10,000
Physical qubits needed: 7M - 23M
Gate operations: ~10^12
Largest QC today (2025): ~1,100 physical qubits (IBM)
Doublings needed: 13 - 14
At historical 2-year doubling: 26 - 28 years → 2051-2053
```

Problem 10 (Research):

Question: Take a look at the current state of quantum computing hardware using the latest available information. Include details such as the largest systems by physical qubit count, their error rates, any experiments that have demonstrated quantum advantage, and the roadmaps companies have for scaling up. Using all of that, estimate the earliest realistic point at which a CRQC could exist that's capable of breaking secp256k1.

Solution:

As of 2025: IBM Condor: 1,121 superconducting qubits. Google Willow: 105 qubits with demonstrated error correction below threshold. Quantinuum H2: 56 trapped-ion qubits with 99.8% two-qubit gate fidelity. IonQ Forte: 36 algorithmic qubits. Demonstrated quantum advantage: Google (2019, random circuit sampling), IBM (2023, error-mitigated utility), but none cryptographically relevant. Industry roadmaps: IBM targets 100K qubits by 2033. Earliest plausible CRQC: 2035-2055 (wide range due to uncertainty in error correction overhead and scaling challenges). Consensus among cryptographers: begin migration planning now, but no imminent emergency.

D.19 Chapter 19 Solutions

Problem 1 (Basic):

Question: Explain the scalability trilemma in your own words. Then, for each of the three properties, pick a real protocol that sacrifices it and explain what the designers got in exchange.

Solution:

In short, the scalability trilemma states that a blockchain cannot simultaneously hit all three properties: decentralization, security, and scalability.

Sacrificing decentralization: Solana hits high throughput (~4,000 TPS) and strong BFT security but needs $50K+ datacenter hardware per validator. Only well-funded operators can participate, concentrating consensus among ~2,000 nodes.

Sacrificing scalability: Bitcoin maximizes decentralization (any consumer PC runs a full node) and has the strongest proven security (15 years, $10B/year budget) but processes only 7 TPS with 10-minute block times.

Sacrificing security: A centralized database hits unlimited throughput and single-operator simplicity but gives no Byzantine fault tolerance. A single compromise defeats the entire system.

Problem 2 (Analysis):

Question: ZK compliance proofs let someone prove "my funds aren't from sanctioned sources" without exposing identity. What are three concrete obstacles to actually deploying something like that? For each obstacle, sketch a realistic solution or workaround.

Solution:

(1) Maintaining on-chain compliance rules: Sanctions lists change frequently. Someone must update the Merkle root of sanctioned tackles on-chain, creating a centralization point. If this entity is compromised, compliance fails. Solution: Multi-party governance with a committee of compliance providers (e.g., 3-of-5 threshold from independent jurisdictions) updating the sanctions root, with a time lock and public audit trail.

(2) Circuit complexity: Multi-hop source-of-funds tracing needs encoding graph traversal inside a ZK circuit, growing with hop count. A 10-hop trace may take minutes to prove. Solution: Limit provable depth to 5-10 hops, use recursive proof composition to build incrementally, and cache intermediate proofs at known-good checkpoints.

(3) Regulatory acceptance: Legal frameworks expect document-based verification with named parties, not cryptographic proofs from pseudonymous tackles. Solution: Pilot programs with forward-leaning regulators (Singapore, Switzerland), academic publications demonstrating proof of soundness, and industry consortia publishing ZK compliance specifications that regulators can evaluate.

Problem 3 (Design):

Question: Sketch a ZK-based cross-chain bridge. You'll need to pick a proof system (SNARK or STARK and why), say exactly what gets proven (block headers? validator sigs? full state transitions?), estimate latency and proof generation cost, and then compare your design against what IBC does with light clients.

Solution:

Proof system: STARKs (quantum-resistant, no trusted setup, transparent).

What is proven: For each source chain block: (a) the block header is correctly formed, (b) the validator signatures constitute a valid BFT supermajority (≥2/3 of stake signed the block header), and (c) the claimed state transition matches the block's transactions.

build-out sketch:

```
# ZK Bridge Architecture
bridge = {
    'proof_system': 'STARK',
    'proven_statement': 'BFT supermajority signed block header H',
    'proof_size': '~200 KB (STARK)',
    'verification_gas': '~500K gas (constant)',
    'prover_time': '2-10 minutes per block',
    'prover_cost': '$0.10-1.00 per proof',
    'trust_assumption': 'Hash function collision resistance only',
    'quantum_safe': True,
}

ibc = {
    'mechanism': 'Light client on destination chain',
    'proof_size': '~1-5 KB (Merkle proof + signatures)',
    'verification_gas': '~200K gas per update',
    'update_frequency': 'Every source block',
```

```
    'dev_cost': 'High (custom light client per chain pair)',
    'trust_assumption': 'Source chain consensus honest',
    'quantum_safe': False,
}

print(f"ZK Bridge vs IBC Comparison:")
print(f"{'Property':<25} {'ZK Bridge':>20} {'IBC':>20}")
print("-" * 68)
for key in ['proof_size', 'verification_gas', 'trust_assumption',
'quantum_safe']:
    print(f"  {key:<23} {str(bridge[key]):>20} {str(ibc[key]):>20}")
```

Output:

```
ZK Bridge vs IBC Comparison:
Property                 ZK Bridge             IBC
--------------------------------------------------------------------
proof_size               ~200 KB (STARK)       ~1-5 KB (Merkle pro...
verification_gas         ~500K gas (const)     ~200K gas per update
trust_assumption         Hash function co...   Source chain conse...
quantum_safe             True                  False
```

ZK bridges have higher per-proof work-out costs but offer universal compatibility (one verifier for any source chain) and post-quantum security. IBC is lighter per update but needs custom light client code for each chain pair.

Problem 4 (Theory):

Question: Can MEV be eliminated, or is it baked into any system where someone has ordering discretion and payoffs depend on state? Make the formal case for both sides. Under what minimal conditions could you get MEV-free execution?

Solution:

MEV is eliminable only if you remove ordering discretion. In a system where transaction order is determined by a protocol rule that no single entity can manipulate (e.g., “order by arrival time at a majority of nodes”), frontrunning becomes impossible. Still, arrival-time ordering is hard to check in a distributed system (clocks differ, network latency varies). Batch auctions (executing all transactions in a block at a uniform clearing price) eliminate sandwich attacks but not other MEV forms. Encrypted mempools eliminate pre-execution MEV but shift it post-execution. Complete elimination needs removing state-dependent payoffs, which eliminates DeFi itself.

Problem 5 (Comparative):

Question: Look at three governance approaches: Bitcoin's off-chain rough consensus, Ethereum's EIP process where core devs have significant discretion, and Tezos doing on-chain token-weighted voting. Compare them on legitimacy, efficiency, resistance to capture, and track record.

Solution:

Bitcoin off-chain consensus: slow (SegWit took 2+ years), resistant to capture (no token voting), but contentious decisions can cause chain splits (BCH fork 2017). Ethereum EIP process: faster (EIP-1559 ~1 year), developer-led (core devs have outsized influence), but has successfully executed major changes (The Merge). Tezos on-chain voting: fastest (proposals pass in ~3 months), democratic (token-weighted), but vulnerable to voter apathy (low participation rates) and plutocratic capture (whales dominate). No governance model is clearly superior; each optimizes for different values.

Problem 6 (Critical Thinking):

Question: Will the blockchain world converge on a single dominant architecture the way the internet converged on TCP/IP? Or will it stay heterogeneous, more like how we ended up with dozens of programming languages? Use network effects, specialization economics, and the history of platform competition to argue both sides.

Solution:

Convergence argument: network effects are extremely powerful in financial infrastructure. One settlement layer (Ethereum) may win for the same reason one internet protocol (TCP/IP) won: coordination costs of multi-chain interoperability exceed the benefits of specialization. Heterogeneity argument: programming languages remain diverse because different problems need different solutions. Privacy chains, high-throughput chains, and settlement chains serve genuinely different needs. Historical precedent: the database market has not converged despite 40+ years—PostgreSQL, MongoDB, Redis, and DynamoDB coexist. Most likely outcome: 2–3 dominant settlement layers with many specialized execution environments.

Problem 7 (Research):

Question: Choose one of the open problems from the section "Long-Term Open Problems" in Chapter 19 and do a research survey. Who are the leading groups working on it (cite them)? What approaches are they trying? What's blocking progress? What's the most promising recent result? Write it up: two pages, structured, minimum five references.

Solution:

Open problem: MEV elimination

Leading approaches: (1) Flashbots SUAVE—decentralized block building with encrypted mempools (Flashbots Research, 2023). (2) Threshold encrypted mempools—Shutter Network uses threshold encryption to hide transaction contents until ordering is committed (Shutter, 2023). (3) Fair ordering—Kelkar et al. "Order-Fairness for Byzantine Consensus" (2020) formalizes receive-order fairness. (4) Batch auctions—CoW Protocol processes all orders in a batch at uniform clearing prices, eliminating sandwich attacks (CoW Protocol, 2022). (5) MEV-Share—redistribution model returning MEV profits to transaction originators (Flashbots, 2023). Main obstacle: no approach eliminates all MEV forms without sacrificing throughput, latency, or market efficiency. The problem is structurally tied to the existence of state-dependent payoffs in DeFi.

Problem 8 (Implementation):

Question: Build a toy verifiable computation system. Have a prover compute Fibonacci(n) and generate a proof via a Merkle tree over the execution trace (each step records f[i-1], f[i-2], f[i]). The verifier spot-checks random trace entries against the Merkle root. Plot proof size against n and discuss what you see.

Solution:

```
import hashlib

def fibonacci_verifiable(n):
    trace = [(0, 1)]  # (f[i-1], f[i])
    a, b = 0, 1
    for _ in range(n - 1):
        a, b = b, a + b
        trace.append((a, b))

    # Build Merkle tree over trace
    hashes = [hashlib.sha256(str(step).encode()).hexdigest()[:16] for step
    in trace]
    root = hashlib.sha256(''.join(hashes).encode()).hexdigest()[:16]

    return {'result': b, 'trace_length': len(trace),
            'root': root, 'proof_size': f"{len(hashes) * 16} bytes"}
```

```
for n in [10, 100, 1000]:
    r = fibonacci_verifiable(n)
    print(f"  Fib({n}): result={str(r['result'])[:20]}..., "
          f"trace={r['trace_length']} steps, proof={r['proof_size']}")
```

Output:

```
Fib(10): result=55, trace=10 steps, proof=160 bytes
Fib(100): result=35422484817926191..., trace=100 steps, proof=1600 bytes
Fib(1000): result=43466557686937456..., trace=1000 steps, proof=16000 bytes
```

Problem 9 (Advanced):

Question: What happens to Ethereum if liquid staking keeps concentrating? Suppose Lido holds 40% of staked ETH across 30 professional operators. Model the effective Nakamoto coefficient once you factor in Lido's governance. Can Lido's operators be legally compelled to censor transactions? What's the systemic risk if Lido's smart contract has a critical bug? Propose protocol-level changes that would help.

Solution:

```
def lido_analysis(lido_share, n_operators, total_validators):
    lido_validators = int(total_validators * lido_share)
    per_operator = lido_validators // n_operators

    # Effective Nakamoto coefficient
    # Lido DAO governance: LDO token holders control operator selection
    effective_nc = 1  # Lido DAO is effectively 1 entity for governance

    # Censorship: can Lido operators be compelled?
    # Operators are known companies in known jurisdictions
    censorship_risk = "HIGH - operators are identifiable legal entities"

    # Smart contract risk
    sc_risk = f"Lido controls {lido_validators:,} validators
    ({lido_share:.0%} of network)"

    print(f"  Lido share: {lido_share:.0%} ({lido_validators:,} validators)")
    print(f"  Operators: {n_operators} (avg {per_operator:,} each)")
    print(f"  Effective NC: {effective_nc} (Lido DAO)")
```

```
    print(f"  Censorship risk: {censorship_risk}")
    print(f"  Bug in Lido contract → {lido_share:.0%} of stake at risk")

lido_analysis(0.30, 30, 625000)
```

Output:

```
Lido share: 30% (187,500 validators)
Operators: 30 (avg 6,250 each)
Effective NC: 1 (Lido DAO)
Censorship risk: HIGH - operators are identifiable legal entities
Bug in Lido contract → 30% of stake at risk
```

Problem 10 (Synthesis):

Question: Use everything from this book. Pick one use case—decentralized identity, supply chain tracking, or decentralized social media—and design a blockchain for it from scratch. Specify every layer: crypto primitives (Chapters 2–4), consensus (Chapters 5–9), data model and execution (Chapters 10–11), transaction ordering and MEV policy (Chapter 12), economic security (Chapter 13), formal verification strategy (Chapter 14), scaling approach (Chapters 15–17), and quantum resistance plan (Chapter 18). Justify each decision with trade-off analysis from the relevant chapter.

Solution:

Cryptography (Chapters 2–4): EdDSA for user signatures (deterministic, fast), Pedersen commitments for selective disclosure, ZK proofs (PLONK) for proving attributes without revealing them. Consensus (Chapters 5–9): Tendermint BFT with 100 validators—identity needs deterministic finality (credentials must not be "un-issued"). Data model (Chapters 10–11): account-based (identity = account with credential storage), WASM VM for credential verification logic. MEV (Chapter 12): minimal concern (identity operations aren't order-sensitive). Economics (Chapter 13): fee-based with identity-provider subsidies. Formal verification (Chapter 14): check credential issuance/revocation logic in TLA+. Scaling (Chapters 15–17): ZK rollup for credential verification, Ethereum L1 for settlement and revocation anchoring. Quantum (Chapter 18): ML-DSA for long-lived identity keys (credentials may be valid for decades). Trade-off: small validator set limits decentralization but enables the fast finality required for real-time credential verification.

Glossary

Account Model: A blockchain state representation where persistent accounts identified by tackles hold balances, nonces, and optionally code and storage. Used by Ethereum, Solana, and most smart contract platforms. Contrast with the UTXO model.

ASIC (Application-Specific Integrated Circuit): Custom hardware designed exclusively for a single computation, such as SHA-256 hashing for Bitcoin mining. Orders of magnitude more efficient than general-purpose hardware for the targeted operation.

Attestation: In Ethereum PoS, a validator's signed vote for a specific block and checkpoint. Contains the source checkpoint, target checkpoint, and head block vote used by LMD-GHOST and Casper FFG.

Base Fee: In EIP-1559, the algorithmically determined minimum fee per unit of gas that all transactions must pay. Adjusts up or down by at most 12.5% per block based on block utilization relative to the target. The base fee is burned (destroyed), not paid to the block producer.

BFT (Byzantine Fault Tolerance): The ability of a distributed system to reach consensus despite some participants behaving arbitrarily (Byzantine faults). Classical BFT protocols tolerate up to $f < n/3$ Byzantine nodes among n total nodes.

Blob Transaction (EIP-4844): A transaction type carrying large data blobs (~128 KB each) with a separate fee market from execution gas. gives cheap data availability for rollups. Blobs are pruned after about 18 days.

Block Producer: The entity that constructs and proposes the next block. A miner in PoW systems, a validator/proposer in PoS systems, or a builder in PBS systems.

Bridge: A protocol enabling transfer of assets or information between two independent blockchains. Security ranges from trust-minimized (light client bridges, IBC) to trust-dependent (committee/multisig bridges).

Casper FFG (Friendly Finality Gadget): Ethereum's finality mechanism. Uses a two-phase commit (justify then finalize) with supermajority links between epoch boundary checkpoints. gives economic finality: reverting finalized blocks needs slashing at least 1/3 of total staked ETH.

N. Savant, *Blockchain Foundations*, https://doi.org/10.1007/979-8-8688-2891-1

Censorship Resistance: The property that no entity can stop valid transactions from being included in the blockchain. Achieved when block production is sufficiently decentralized that censoring parties cannot consistently exclude transactions.

Checkpoint: In Casper FFG, an epoch boundary block that can be justified (receiving 2/3 supermajority attestation) and later finalized (when the next checkpoint is justified).

Coin Selection: The algorithm a UTXO wallet uses to choose which unspent outputs to include as inputs to a new transaction. Strategies include largest-first, smallest-first, and exact-match.

Commitment Scheme: A cryptographic protocol allowing a party to commit to a value while keeping it hidden, then later reveal it. Used in consensus protocols, fair ordering, and ZK proofs.

Confirmation: In probabilistic finality systems, the number of blocks built on top of a transaction's block. More confirmations mean a higher probability that the transaction is permanent. Bitcoin convention: 6 confirmations for high-value transactions.

Consensus: Agreement among distributed nodes on a single canonical sequence of transactions and resulting state. The fundamental problem blockchain technology fixes.

Correlation Penalty: In Ethereum PoS slashing, a penalty that raises proportionally to the number of validators slashed in the same time period. Designed to distinguish isolated mistakes (low penalty) from coordinated attacks (high penalty, up to 100% of stake).

CRQC (Cryptographically Relevant Quantum Computer): A quantum computer with sufficient qubits and low enough error rates to break production cryptographic parameters (e.g., factor RSA-2048 or fix ECDLP on secp256k1).

Danksharding: Ethereum's planned full data availability sharding design, extending EIP-4844 with Data Availability Sampling. Named after researcher Dankrad Feist.

DAS (Data Availability Sampling): A technique allowing light clients to check data availability by randomly sampling small portions of erasure-coded data. Detection probability raises exponentially with the number of samples.

DeFi (Decentralized Finance): Financial protocols built on smart contract platforms that operate without centralized intermediaries. covers decentralized exchanges (DEXs), lending protocols, and derivatives platforms.

Deterministic Finality: A finality guarantee where, once a block is finalized, it can never be reverted under any circumstances (given the protocol's fault tolerance assumptions). Provided by BFT protocols like Tendermint.

Difficulty: In PoW, a parameter that determines how hard it is to find a valid block. Expressed as a target value that the block header hash must be below. Adjusted periodically to keep a target block time.

Double-Spend: An attack where the same funds are spent in two conflicting transactions. Prevented by consensus: the network agrees on which transaction is valid and rejects the duplicate.

ECDSA (Elliptic Curve Digital Signature Algorithm): The signature scheme used by Bitcoin and Ethereum for transaction authorization. Based on the elliptic curve discrete logarithm problem. Broken by Shor's algorithm on quantum computers.

EIP-1559: Ethereum Improvement Proposal that introduced a dynamic base fee and fee-burning mechanism. Replaced the first-price auction fee model with an algorithmically adjusting base fee plus an optional priority fee (tip).

Epoch: A fixed period of time in a PoS protocol. In Ethereum, one epoch = 32 slots = 6.4 minutes. Epoch boundaries serve as Casper FFG checkpoint candidates.

Erasure Coding: A data encoding technique that adds redundancy so the original data can be reconstructed from any sufficiently large subset of the encoded data. Foundation of Data Availability Sampling.

EVM (Ethereum Virtual Machine): Ethereum's stack-based execution environment for smart contracts. Processes 256-bit word bytecode with gas-metered execution.

Finality: The guarantee that a confirmed transaction won't be reversed. Can be probabilistic (Bitcoin: increasing probability with confirmations), economic (Ethereum: reversal costs >$20B), or deterministic (Tendermint: absolute under fault tolerance assumptions).

FLP Impossibility: The Fischer-Lynch-Paterson theorem (1985) proving that no deterministic consensus protocol can guarantee both safety and liveness in a fully asynchronous system with even one faulty process.

Fork: A divergence in the blockchain where two or more valid blocks are produced at the same height. Resolved by the fork choice rule. Also: a protocol change (hard fork or soft fork).

Fork Choice Rule: The algorithm nodes use to select the canonical chain among competing forks. Examples: longest chain (Bitcoin), heaviest chain (GHOST), LMD-GHOST (Ethereum).

Fraud Proof: A proof submitted to L1 demonstrating that a rollup sequencer posted an incorrect state transition. Used in optimistic rollups. Interactive fraud proofs use a bisection game to minimize on-chain verification cost.

Gas: The unit measuring computational work in the EVM. Each operation has a fixed gas cost. Users set a gas limit and gas price for transactions. If execution exceeds the gas limit, the transaction reverts, but gas is consumed.

GHOST (Greedy Heaviest Observed SubTree): A fork choice rule that selects the subtree with the most total blocks (not just the longest chain). Captures work in orphaned blocks, improving security at high block rates.

Grover's Algorithm: A quantum algorithm providing quadratic speedup for unstructured search. Halves the effective security of hash functions and symmetric ciphers but doesn't break them.

Hard Fork: A backward-incompatible protocol change. Nodes that do not upgrade will follow a different chain. needs universal coordination to sidestep a permanent chain split.

Hash Function: A deterministic function mapping arbitrary-length input to fixed-length output with properties: preimage resistance, second preimage resistance, and collision resistance. SHA-256 and Keccak-256 are used in blockchain.

HTLC (Hash Time-Locked Contract): A conditional payment that can be claimed by revealing a hash preimage before a timeout or refunded after the timeout. Used for atomic swaps and Lightning Network routing.

IBC (Inter-Blockchain Communication): Cosmos's trust-minimized cross-chain communication protocol. Uses light clients on each chain to check the other chain's consensus, providing bridge security equal to the weaker chain.

Inactivity Leak: In Ethereum PoS, a gradual penalty is applied to offline validators when the chain can't finalize. The leak drains inactive validators' stakes until the active stake reaches a 2/3 supermajority, restoring finality.

KZG Commitment: A polynomial commitment scheme (Kate-Zaverucha-Goldberg, 2010) used in Ethereum for blob data verification. gives constant-size commitments and proofs for polynomial evaluations. needs a trusted setup.

Layer 1 (L1): The base blockchain that gives consensus, data availability, and settlement. Examples: Bitcoin, Ethereum.

Layer 2 (L2): A scaling solution built on top of L1 that inherits L1's security. covers rollups, state channels, and Plasma.

Light Client: A node that checks block headers (including consensus proofs) without downloading or executing full block data. Enables mobile wallets and resource-constrained devices.

Liquid Staking: A protocol that accepts user deposits for staking and issues a transferable token representing the staked position. Enables staked assets to be used in DeFi while earning staking rewards. Example: Lido (stETH).

LMD-GHOST (Latest Message Driven GHOST): Ethereum's fork choice rule. Each validator's most recent attestation counts as a vote for a block and all its ancestors. The canonical chain follows the path with the most vote weight.

MEV (Maximal Extractable Value): Value that can be extracted from block production beyond standard rewards by including, excluding, or reordering transactions. covers arbitrage, sandwich attacks, and liquidations.

Merkle Tree: A binary tree of hash values where each leaf is a hash of a data block and each internal node is a hash of its children. Enables O(log n) inclusion proofs.

ML-DSA (Module Learning With Errors Digital Signature Algorithm): NIST's primary post-quantum signature standard (FIPS 204, formerly Dilithium). Lattice-based with 2,420-byte signatures.

Nakamoto Coefficient: The minimum number of entities that must collude to compromise a blockchain's consensus. Higher values indicate greater decentralization.

Namespace Merkle Tree: Celestia's data structure that organizes blobs by namespace, enabling efficient download of only the blobs belonging to a specific rollup.

Nonce: In PoW: the value miners iterate to find a valid block hash. In the account model: a sequential counter per account that stops transaction replay.

Nothing-at-Stake: The problem in naive PoS where validators can vote on multiple forks at no cost. Mitigated by slashing conditions that penalize equivocation.

Optimistic Rollup: An L2 scaling solution that posts transaction data to L1 and takes as given state transitions are correct unless challenged via fraud proofs within a challenge period (typically 7 days).

Ouroboros: A family of provably secure PoS consensus protocols used by Cardano. The first PoS protocol with formal security proofs under standard cryptographic assumptions.

PBS (Proposer-Builder Separation): An architecture separating the right to propose blocks from the right to construct their contents. The proposer auctions the block construction to competing builders.

Plasma: An L2 scaling approach that posts only Merkle roots to L1. Suffers from the mass exit problem: if the operator withholds data, all users must exit simultaneously to L1.

Probabilistic Finality: A finality model where the probability of transaction reversal lowers with each additional confirmation but never reaches exactly zero. Used by Nakamoto consensus (Bitcoin).

Restaking: Extending the economic security of staked assets to additional protocols. EigenLayer lets Ethereum validators opt into additional slashing conditions for Actively Validated Services (AVSs).

Rollup: An L2 scaling solution that executes transactions off-chain and posts data and proofs to L1. Inherits L1 security. Two types: optimistic (fraud proofs) and ZK (validity proofs).

Sandwich Attack: An MEV strategy where an attacker frontruns a victim's swap (buying before the victim), lets the victim execute at a worse price, then backruns (selling after) to capture the price difference.

Selfish Mining: A mining strategy where a miner withholds discovered blocks and selectively releases them to waste honest miners' work. Profitable above about 25-33% hash rate.

Shard: An independent chain or data partition within a sharded blockchain. Each shard processes a subset of transactions or stores a subset of data.

Shor's Algorithm: A quantum algorithm that fixes integer factoring and discrete logarithm problems in polynomial time. Breaks RSA, ECDSA, EdDSA, and Diffie-Hellman key exchange.

Slashing: The penalty mechanism in PoS protocols where a validator's staked funds are partially or fully destroyed as punishment for provably malicious behavior (equivocation, surround voting).

Slot: The smallest time unit in Ethereum PoS (12 seconds). Each slot has one designated block proposer and many attesters.

Smart Contract: Self-executing code stored on-chain that automatically enforces the terms of an agreement. Deployed on platforms like Ethereum, executed by the blockchain's virtual machine.

Soft Fork: A backward-compatible protocol change where upgraded nodes enforce stricter rules. Non-upgraded nodes accept all valid blocks but may accept some blocks that upgraded nodes reject.

STARK (Scalable Transparent ARgument of Knowledge): A zero-knowledge proof system based solely on hash functions (no elliptic curves). Post-quantum secure. Larger proofs than SNARKs, but no trusted setup required.

State Channel: An L2 approach where participants lock funds on-chain, exchange signed state updates off-chain, and settle on-chain only when closing the channel. Enables unlimited off-chain transactions.

UTXO (Unspent Transaction Output): The state representation used by Bitcoin and Cardano. Value exists as discrete, unspent outputs that are consumed by transactions and replaced with new outputs.

Validator: In PoS, a participant who stakes tokens and participates in consensus by proposing and attesting to blocks. Subject to rewards for correct behavior and penalties (slashing) for misbehavior.

Validity Proof: A cryptographic proof (ZK-SNARK or ZK-STARK) demonstrating that a batch of state transitions was computed correctly. Used in ZK rollups for immediate finality without a challenge period.

Verkle Tree: A proposed replacement for Ethereum's Merkle-Patricia trie that gives smaller state proofs (~150 bytes per state access vs. ~1 KB). Enables practical stateless validation.

VRF (Verifiable Random Function): A function that produces a pseudorandom output along with a proof that the output was correctly generated. Used for unpredictable, verifiable leader selection in PoS protocols.

WASM (WebAssembly): A binary instruction format designed for safe, sandboxed execution. Used as an alternative to the EVM by Polkadot, NEAR, and Cosmos (CosmWasm). Supports Rust, C/C++, and other languages.

Weak Subjectivity: The requirement in PoS systems that new nodes must get a recent trusted checkpoint to safely sync. stops long-range attacks where an adversary creates an alternative history using old validator keys.

ZK Rollup: An L2 scaling solution that uses zero-knowledge validity proofs to prove state transition correctness. gives faster finality than optimistic rollups (no challenge period) at higher computational cost (proof generation).

Zero-Knowledge Proof: A cryptographic proof that a statement is true without revealing any information beyond the truth of the statement. Used for scalability (ZK rollups), privacy (Zcash), and compliance (ZK identity verification).

Arbitrage: The simultaneous purchase and sale of the same asset on different markets to profit from a price difference. In blockchain, DEX arbitrage captures price discrepancies between decentralized exchanges, improving market efficiency. A form of beneficial MEV.

CometBFT: The current name for the Tendermint consensus engine, used by Cosmos-based chains including Celestia gives BFT consensus with instant finality for up to ~200 validators.

Flashbots: An organization and protocol suite that tackles MEV on Ethereum. Flashbots Protect gives a private transaction pool. MEV-Boost implements proposer-builder separation. Flashbots Auction enables searchers to submit MEV bundles to builders.

FN-DSA (Falcon): NIST post-quantum signature standard (FIPS 206) based on NTRU lattices. Produces the smallest post-quantum signatures (666 bytes at Level 1) but needs careful floating-point build-out.

Gasper: Ethereum's consensus protocol mixing LMD-GHOST (fork choice) and Casper FFG (finality). Named as a portmanteau of GHOST and Casper.

Groth16: A zero-knowledge proof system (zk-SNARK) with constant-size proofs (~200 bytes) and fast verification. needs a per-circuit trusted setup. Used by Zcash and many early ZK rollups.

HotStuff: A BFT consensus protocol achieving O(n) communication complexity per round using threshold signatures and pipelined three-phase commit. Used by Diem/Libra and Aptos.

Liquidation: In DeFi lending protocols, the forced closure of an undercollateralized borrowing position. A liquidator repays part of the debt and receives collateral at a discount (typically 5-10%). A form of MEV when searchers race to liquidate profitable positions.

MEV-boost: The external build-out of Proposer-Builder Separation for Ethereum. Validators (proposers) receive sealed block bids from builders via relays and select the highest-paying block without seeing its contents.

Nightshade: NEAR Protocol's sharding design where multiple shard chunks are combined into a single block. Cross-shard communication uses asynchronous receipts delivered in the next block.

PBFT (Practical Byzantine Fault Tolerance): The first practical BFT consensus protocol (Castro and Liskov, 1999). Tolerates $f < n/3$ Byzantine faults with $O(n^2)$ message complexity per consensus round. Foundation for modern BFT protocols.

PLONK: A universal zk-SNARK proof system with a single trusted setup that works for any circuit (unlike Groth16, which needs per-circuit setup). Used by several ZK rollup builds.

Sandwich Attack: An MEV strategy where an attacker frontruns a victim's DEX swap (buying before the victim), lets the victim execute at a worse price, then backruns (selling after) to capture profit. The most harmful form of MEV for users.

Sequencer: In a rollup, the entity responsible for ordering transactions, executing them off-chain, and posting results to L1. Currently centralized in most rollups (single operator), with decentralization planned.

Snowball: A consensus protocol in the Avalanche family. Extends Snowflake by adding persistent counters that track cumulative preference across all sampling rounds, providing stronger convergence than Snowflake's single counter.

Snowflake: A consensus protocol in the Avalanche family. It uses repeated random subsampled voting with a confidence counter that resets on each preference flip. Simpler than Snowball but less resilient to oscillation.

Validium: A Layer-2 scaling solution that uses validity proofs (like ZK rollups) for state transition correctness but stores data off-chain with a Data Availability Committee rather than on L1. Lower cost than rollups but weaker data availability guarantee.

Volition: A hybrid Layer-2 design where each transaction can individually choose between rollup mode (data on L1, strongest guarantee, higher cost) and validium mode (data off-chain, weaker guarantee, lower cost).

Formal Verification: Mathematical proof that a system satisfies a specified property for all possible inputs and states. In blockchain, it is used to check consensus protocols (TLA+, Isabelle) and smart contracts (Certora, K Framework). (Chapter 14)

Grover's Algorithm: A quantum algorithm providing quadratic speedup for unstructured search. Effectively halves the security level of hash functions and symmetric ciphers (SHA-256 from 256-bit to 128-bit security). doesn't break hash functions, only weakens them. (Chapter 18)

Lamport Signature: The simplest hash-based digital signature scheme. Quantum-resistant because security depends only on hash function preimage resistance. Each key pair can sign exactly one message (one-time signature). Private key: 16 KB, signature: 8 KB. (Chapter 18)

ML-KEM (Module Learning With Errors Key Encapsulation Mechanism): NIST post-quantum key exchange standard (FIPS 203, formerly CRYSTALS-Kyber). gives quantum-resistant key exchange with 800-1568 byte public keys. (Chapter 18)

Modular Blockchain: An architecture that decomposes blockchain functions (execution, consensus, data availability, settlement) into separate specialized layers. Each layer can be independently optimized and upgraded. Celestia, EigenDA, and Ethereum's rollup-centric roadmap are modular designs. (Chapter 17)

Nash Equilibrium: A game-theoretic concept where no player can improve their payoff by unilaterally changing strategy. For blockchain protocol security, honest behavior must be a Nash equilibrium to stop rational participants from deviating to attacks. (Chapter 13)

Scalability Trilemma: The observation that blockchain systems can't simultaneously hit decentralization, security, and scalability. Each system must trade off at least one property to optimize the others. Proposed by Vitalik Buterin. (Chapter 19)

Shor's Algorithm: A quantum algorithm that fixes integer factoring and discrete logarithm problems in polynomial time. Breaks RSA, ECDSA, EdDSA, Diffie-Hellman, and all public-key cryptography based on these problems. needs about 2,330 logical qubits for secp256k1. (Chapter 18)

SLH-DSA (Stateless Hash-Based Digital Signature Algorithm): NIST post-quantum signature standard (FIPS 205, formerly SPHINCS+). Security depends solely on hash function security. Largest signatures (7,856-29,792 bytes) but most conservative security assumptions. (Chapter 18)

Sybil Resistance: The ability of a system to stop a single entity from creating many fake identities to gain disproportionate influence. PoW gives Sybil resistance through computational cost; PoS through economic stake. (Chapter 19)

TLA+ (Temporal Logic of Actions): A formal specification language for describing concurrent and distributed systems. Used to specify and model-check blockchain consensus protocols (Tendermint, Casper FFG). Developed by Leslie Lamport. (Chapter 14)

Verifiable Computation: A cryptographic technique where a prover executes a computation and produces a succinct proof that the computation was performed correctly. A verifier checks the proof in constant time. Foundation of ZK rollups. (Chapter 19)

Bibliography

Foundational Cryptography

Diffie, W. and Hellman, M. "New Directions in Cryptography." IEEE Transactions on Information Theory, 1976.

Dwork, C. and Naor, M. "Pricing via Processing or Combatting Junk Mail." CRYPTO, 1992.

Goldwasser, S., Micali, S., and Rackoff, C. "The Knowledge Complexity of Interactive Proof Systems." SIAM Journal on Computing, 1989.

Kate, A., Zaverucha, G., and Goldberg, I. "Constant-Size Commitments to Polynomials and Their Applications." ASIACRYPT, 2010.

Merkle, R. "A Digital Signature Based on a Conventional Encryption Function." CRYPTO, 1987.

Rivest, R., Shamir, A., and Adleman, L. "A Method for Obtaining Digital Signatures and Public-Key Cryptosystems." Communications of the ACM, 1978.

Bitcoin and Proof of Work

Back, A. "Hashcash - A Denial of Service Counter-Measure." Technical report, 2002.

Eyal, I. "The Miner's Dilemma." IEEE Symposium on Security and Privacy, 2015.

Eyal, I. and Sirer, E.G. "Majority Is Not Enough: Bitcoin Mining Is Vulnerable." Financial Cryptography, 2014.

Gervais, A. et al. "On the Security and Performance of Proof of Work Blockchains." ACM CCS, 2016.

Nakamoto, S. "Bitcoin: A Peer-to-Peer Electronic Cash System." 2008.

Rosenfeld, M. "Analysis of Hashrate-Based Double Spending." arXiv, 2014.

Sapirshtein, A., Sompolinsky, Y., and Zohar, A. "Optimal Selfish Mining Strategies in Bitcoin." Financial Cryptography, 2016.

N. Savant, *Blockchain Foundations*, https://doi.org/10.1007/979-8-8688-2891-1

Proof of Stake and Ethereum Consensus

Buterin, V. and Griffith, V. "Casper the Friendly Finality Gadget." arXiv, 2017.

Buterin, V. et al. "mixing GHOST and Casper." arXiv, 2020.

Roughgarden, T. "Transaction Fee Mechanism Design for the Ethereum Blockchain." EC, 2021.

Schwarz-Schilling, C. et al. "Three Attacks on Proof-of-Stake Ethereum." Financial Cryptography, 2022.

Sompolinsky, Y. and Zohar, A. "Secure High-Rate Transaction Processing in Bitcoin." Financial Cryptography, 2015.

Byzantine Fault Tolerance

Abraham, I. et al. "HotStuff: BFT Consensus with Linearity and Responsiveness." PODC, 2019.

Buchman, E., Kwon, J., and Milosevic, Z. "The Latest Gossip on BFT Consensus." arXiv, 2018.

Castro, M. and Liskov, B. "Practical Byzantine Fault Tolerance." OSDI, 1999.

Fischer, M., Lynch, N., and Paterson, M. "Impossibility of Distributed Consensus with One Faulty Process." Journal of the ACM, 1985.

Lamport, L. "The Part-Time Parliament." ACM TOCS, 1998.

Lamport, L., Shostak, R., and Pease, M. "The Byzantine Generals Problem." ACM TOPLAS, 1982.

Yin, M. et al. "HotStuff: BFT Consensus in the Lens of Blockchain." arXiv, 2018.

Novel Consensus Protocols

Bagaria, V. et al. "Prism: Deconstructing the Blockchain to Approach Physical Limits." ACM CCS, 2019.

Bano, S. et al. "SoK: Consensus in the Age of Blockchains." AFT, 2019.

Eyal, I. et al. "Bitcoin-NG: A Scalable Blockchain Protocol." NSDI, 2016.

Kiayias, A. et al. "Ouroboros: A Provably Secure Proof-of-Stake Blockchain Protocol." CRYPTO, 2017.

Rocket Team. "Scalable and Probabilistic Leaderless BFT Consensus through Metastability." arXiv, 2020.

Sompolinsky, Y. et al. "PHANTOM and SPECTRE: A Scalable Generalization of Nakamoto Consensus." IACR ePrint, 2018.

Virtual Machines and Execution

Buterin, V. "The Different Types of ZK-EVMs." Blog post, 2022.

Wood, G. "Ethereum: A Secure Decentralised Generalised Transaction Ledger." Yellow Paper, 2014.

MEV and Transaction Ordering

Daian, P. et al. "Flash Boys 2.0: Frontrunning in Decentralized Exchanges, Miner Extractable Value, and Consensus Instability." IEEE S&P, 2020.

Kelkar, M. et al. "Order-Fairness for Byzantine Consensus." CRYPTO, 2020.

Cryptoeconomic Security

Budish, E. "The Economic Limits of Bitcoin and the Blockchain." NBER Working Paper, 2018.

Chitra, T. and Kulkarni, S. "Improving Proof of Stake Economic Security via MEV Redistribution." arXiv, 2022.

Formal Verification

Lamport, L. "Specifying Systems: The TLA+ Language and Tools for Hardware and Software Engineers." Addison-Wesley, 2002.

Newcombe, C. et al. "How Amazon Web Services Uses Formal Methods." Communications of the ACM, 2015.

Palmskog, K. et al. "Mechanizing the Accountable Safety Property of Casper FFG." Isabelle Archive of Formal Proofs, 2020.

Layer-2 Scaling

Poon, J. and Buterin, V. "Plasma: Scalable Autonomous Smart Contracts." Whitepaper, 2017.

Poon, J. and Dryja, T. "The Bitcoin Lightning Network: Scalable Off-Chain Instant Payments." Whitepaper, 2016.

Teutsch, J. and Reitwießner, C. "A Scalable Verification Solution for Blockchains." TrueBit whitepaper, 2017.

Sharding and Data Availability

Al-Bassam, M., Sonnino, A., and Buterin, V. "Fraud and Data Availability Proofs: Maximising Light Client Security and Scaling Blockchains with Dishonest Majorities." arXiv, 2018.

Dankrad Feist. "New Sharding Design with Tight Beacon Chain Integration." Ethereum Research, 2022.

EIP-4844. "Shard Blob Transactions." Ethereum Improvement Proposal, 2024.

Post-Quantum Cryptography

Gidney, C. and Ekera, M. "How to Factor 2048 Bit RSA Integers in 8 Hours Using 20 Million Noisy Qubits." Quantum, 2021.

NIST. "FIPS 203: Module-Lattice-Based Key-Encapsulation Mechanism Standard (ML-KEM)." 2024.

NIST. "FIPS 204: Module-Lattice-Based Digital Signature Standard (ML-DSA)." 2024.

NIST. "FIPS 205: Stateless Hash-Based Digital Signature Standard (SLH-DSA)." 2024.

NIST. "FIPS 206: FFT over NTRU Lattice Digital Signature Standard (FN-DSA)." 2024.

Roetteler, M. et al. "Quantum Resource Estimates for Computing Elliptic Curve Discrete Logarithms." ASIACRYPT, 2017.

Shor, P. "Algorithms for Quantum Computation: Discrete Logarithms and Factoring." FOCS, 1994.

Blockchain Architecture and State Management

Buterin, V. "EIP-6800: Ethereum State Using Verkle Trees." Ethereum Improvement Proposal, 2023.

Delgado-Segura, S. et al. "Analysis of the Bitcoin UTXO Set." Financial Cryptography, 2018.

Textbooks and Surveys

Boneh, D. and Shoup, V. "A Graduate Course in Applied Cryptography." Online textbook, 2020.

Lynch, N. "Distributed Algorithms." Morgan Kaufmann, 1996.

Narayanan, A. et al. "Bitcoin and Cryptocurrency Technologies." Princeton University Press, 2016.

Nielsen, M. and Chuang, I. "Quantum Computation and Quantum Information." Cambridge University Press, 2010.

Thaler, J. "Proofs, Arguments, and Zero-Knowledge." Foundations and Trends in Privacy and Security, 2022.

Quantum Algorithms

Grover, L. "A Fast Quantum Mechanical Algorithm for Database Search." STOC, 1996.

Index

A

Account-locking mechanism, 346
Advanced cryptographic primitives, 585
Application Blockchain Interface (ABCI), 212
Asymmetric cryptography, 56
Auction theory and transaction ordering, 583
Audit methodology, 397
Avalanche, 228, 247, 250, 251, 253
Avalanche effect, 53
Avalanche's subsampled voting, 227

B

BeginBlock, 220
Binomial distribution, 575
Bitcoin's monetary policy, 382
Bitcoin's trust model, 14–16
Bitcoin's UTXO model, xxi
Blockchain, 11, 26
Blockchain cryptoeconomics, 375
Blockchain protocols verification
- formal methods, 398, 417
- gap between verification and security, 415
- LTL, 399
- model checking, 402, 403, 405–407
- proof assistants, 408, 416, 417
- safety and liveness properties, 399–401
- security audit methodology, 410, 411, 413, 414
- symbolic execution, 409, 410

Blockchain technology, research challenges
- cross-chain interoperability, 555
- long-term open problems, 557, 558
- privacy and regulatory compliance, 553, 554
- scalability trilemma, 551, 552
- sustainable consensus, 554, 555
- synthesis, 558
- verifiable computation, 557
- ZK compliance proofs, 560

Bridge security models, 585
Bulletproofs, 95, 117
Byzantine fault tolerance (BFT), xx, 568, 569, 777
- agreement fundamentals, 190–193
- HotStuff, 205
  - three phase commit, pipelining, 206–211
  - threshold signatures, 205, 206
  - view change mechanism, 212
- synchrony assumptions/network partitions, 221
- Tendermint, 212–215, 217–220, 222, 223, 225

Byzantine generals problem
- agreement, 22, 23
- blockchain, 11

N. Savant, *Blockchain Foundations*, https://doi.org/10.1007/979-8-8688-2891-1

Byzantine generals problem (*cont.*)
- CAP theorem, 17, 18
- code example, 19–22
- formal statement, 9
- impossibility results, 9, 10
- practical implications, 18, 19
- setup, 7, 8

Byzantine Generals Problem, xx, 3, 568

C

Celestia, 512
- architecture, 499, 500, 502
- rollups, 502, 503

CheckTx, 220

Commitment scheme, 778

Consensus comparison framework
- adversary models, 255, 282
- blockchain, 256
- decentralization measurement, 272, 273, 275–277
- decision methodology, 281
- economic security, 279, 280
- energy efficiency comparison, 278
- hard energy consumption, 256
- performance metrics
  - latency/finality time, 270–272
  - TPS, 267, 268, 270
- security analysis
  - adversarial models, 257–259, 261–263
  - attack vector taxonomy, 263–265, 267

Crash-fault-tolerant systems, 190

Cross-parachain messages (XCMP), 481

Cross-shard communication, 485

Cryptoeconomic analysis, 578, 579

Cryptoeconomic security
- bitcoin, 394
- bitcoin's disinflationary model, 382–384
- double-spending, economic attacks, 392
- Ethereum's dynamic equilibrium model, 384, 385
- fee market dynamics/security budget composition, 391, 392
- game theory, blockchain protocol, 376
- mining game, 376, 377, 379–381
- optimal deterrence/penalty design, 389, 390
- security budge, 386–388
- tokenomics, 382

Cryptographic security, 432

D

DAG-based ledgers, 227

DAG-shaped ledgers, 227

Data availability and modular blockchains
- DA problem, 490–492, 494, 495
- modular blockchain paradigm, 504, 505, 507
- modular design, 511
- problem, 490
- restaking and shared security, 507–510
- sampling, 495–498
- valid block, 489

Data availability sampling (DAS), 778

Data structures
- account model, 300–304, 306
- account-based systems, 317
- bockchain state, 290
- Merkle trees, 307–309, 311, 312
- state growth and sustainability, 314–316
- UTXO, 289, 291, 293–298, 300, 317
- UTXO *vs.* account model, 307

DeliverTx, 220

DEX arbitrage, 371
Digital cash evolution, 11–16
Digital signatures, xx, 56, 605
Directed Acyclic Graph (DAG), 580
Distributed systems
  centralized solutions, 5, 6
  distributed ledger, 6, 7
  double-spending problem, 4, 5
  electronic payment trusting, 4
Double SHA-256, 53

E

Edwards-curve Digital Signature Algorithm (EDSA)
  advantages, 69
  implementation, 70, 71
  signing, 69
  verification, 70
Elliptic curve cryptography, 563–565
Elliptic Curve Digital Signature Algorithm (ECDSA), 779
Elliptic curve discrete logarithm problem (ECDLP), 61
Ethereum Keccak, 53
Ethereum's account model, xxi, 289
Ethereum's Gasper consensus
  accountable safety, 171–173
  LMD-GHOST, 163–169
  long-range attacks, 177, 178, 180
  slashing mechanisms, 173–175, 177
  time structure, 161, 163
  validator economics, 180, 182–184
Ethereum Virtual Machine (EVM), 321, 779
Execution sharding, 461
Extended Merkle Signature Scheme (XMSS), 544

F

Fiat-Shamir heuristic, 85
Finite field arithmetic, 577
Flashbots, 784
Formal security
  blockchain-specific security, 602, 603
  Byzantine consensus properties, 597, 598
  consensus finality, 601
  cryptographic hash function, 598
  digital signature properties, 598
  MAC, 599
  PoS, 602
  PoW, 601
  ring signature, 600
  VRF, 601
  zero-knowledge proof properties, 600

G

Game theory, 375
Gas mechanics, 321
Gas metering, 344, 582
Gasper consensus, 578
Global Stabilization Time (GST), 193, 221, 598
Graph-coloring protocol, 85
Grover's algorithm, 522, 546, 578, 780, 785

H

Hash
  cryptographic functions, 26–29
  functions, xx, 517
    computing implementation, 33, 34
    Keccak, 30–32
    SHA-256, 29

Hash (*cont.*)
MAC, 35-37
secure random number generation, 37–40
Hash-based signatures, 578
Hash function security, 565
Hash Time-Locked Contracts (HTLCs), 440
HotStuff's linear communication, 189
Hybrid signatures, 535

I, J, K

Incrementally verifiable computation (IVC), 585
Information theory, decentralization, 576
Inter-Blockchain Communication (IBC), 780

L

Lamport signature, 785
Layer-2 scaling, xxii
architecture taxonomy, 423
composability/fragmentation problem, 450, 451, 453
cryptographic or economic mechanisms, 422
optimistic rollups, 423–426, 428–431, 453
plasma
exit game, 421, 441–447
rollup transition, 448
variants, 448
state channels, 435
lightning network, 440
multi-hop payment, 440
payment channel mechanics, 435–437, 439, 440
validiums/data availability spectrum, 449, 450
ZK rollups, 431, 453
EVM, 432, 434
proof work, 431, 432
Lightning Network, 435, 440, 454
Linear Temporal Logic (LTL), 399, 584
Long-range attacks, 177, 579

M

Maximal Extractable Value (MEV), 781
measurement, 369, 370
mitigation approaches, 368
strategies, 347
supply chain, 364–367
taxonomy, 356–360, 362, 363
transaction lifecycle
block construction and inclusion, 349–352, 354, 355
construction and signing, 348
mempool residence, 349
submission and propagation, 348
Merkle-Patricia Tries, 47–49, 51, 52, 581
Merkle trees, 25, 53, 307, 566, 567, 581
implementation, 42–45
problem, 40
security properties, 45
solution, 40, 41
Message Authentication Codes (MACs), 35
MEV extraction strategies, xxi
Mining, 131
Model checking, 584

Module Learning With Errors Digital Signature Algorithm (ML-DSA), 781
Monetary economics, 393
Multi-party computation (MPC), 586
Multi-signatures, 72, 75–77, 79

N

Nakamoto coefficient, 273, 283
Namespace Merkle Trees (NMTs), 499
Nash equilibrium, 785
NIST post-quantum cryptography, 515
- CRQCs, 542
- FN-DSA, 530
- migration strategies, 534
  - approaches, 534
  - hybrid signatures, 535, 537–539
  - vulnerability analysis, 539, 541
- ML-DSA, 529
- network layer, 533, 534
- PQ scheme, 542, 543
- public cryptanalysis, 529
- SLH-DSA, 530–532
- XMSS, 544
- ZK proofs, 545

Non-interactive zero-knowledge proofs (NIZKs), 85
Nothing-at-stake, 159
Novel consensus mechanisms
- avalanche, 250
  - DAG structure, 236
  - performance and security characteristics, 236, 237
  - protocol family, 229–231, 233–235
- classical BFT/Nakamoto consensus, 228
- finality models, 248–251
- GHOST, 237–239, 241, 251
- Ouroboros
  - Epoch-based PoS, formal security, 242, 244, 245
  - PoS chains, 242
  - protocol family, 246, 247

O

Ouroboros, 251

P

Patricia tries, 25, 46, 47, 54
PBFT's three-phase protocol, 189
Plasma, 441, 454, 579
Poisson process model, 123
Polkadot, 481
Polynomial commitment schemes, 585
Post-quantum cryptography, xxii, 577
- blockchain, threat, 516, 517
- Shor's algorithm, 518–520, 522

Practical Byzantine Fault Tolerance (PBFT)
- implementation, 195–198, 200, 201, 203
- protocol, 194
- scalability limitations, 204, 205
- VIEW-CHANGE message, 203, 204

Pre-Bitcoin digital cash systems, xx
Proof of Stake (PoS), 571
- computation, 154
- Ethereum's gasper, 161
- long-range attacks, 187
- nothing-at-stake problem, 159, 161
- PoW security model, 154
- security, 153, 184, 186
- validators, 155–158

Proof of Work (PoW), 569, 570
    51% attack, 136–139
    difficulty adjustment algorithms, 127–129, 131
    energy consumption and sustainability, 143, 144
    energy security relationship, 145, 146
    functions, 121
    hash puzzles, 122–125, 127
    mining economics, 131–135
    mining pools and centralization, 146, 148–150
    selfish mining, 139–143, 150
Proof-of-work systems, 16
Proofs of Validity, 481
Proposer-builder separation (PBS), xxi, 583
Public key cryptography and authentication, 516
    real systems, 55
    RSA signatures, 58
    Schnorr signatures, 64
    symmetric *vs.* asymmetric cryptography, 57

Q

Quorum systems, 580

R

Ring signatures, 103, 116
Rivest-Shamir-Adleman (RSA) signatures
    blockchan, 59
    ECC comparison, 59
    ECDSA, implementation, 62–64
    implementation, 60–62
    mathematics, 58
    security parameters, 58
Rollup-centric roadmap, 462
RSA—Schnorr signatures, 77

S

Sandwich attacks, 371, 782
Scalable Transparent ARgument of Knowledge (STARK), 782
Schnorr signatures, 77
    advantages, 64
    aggregation, 65
    vs. ECDSA, 65
    implementation, 66–68
    signing, 65
    verification, 65
Security best practices
    BFT/consensus monitoring, 592
    consensus and node operation, 591
    cryptographic implementation, 588, 589
    data availability/sharding, 594
    development process, 593
    layer-2 and rollup operation, 593
    post-quantum preparation, 594
    PoW, 591, 592
    privacy and compliance, 594, 595
    protocol design, 592
    smart contract security, 590
    trust and system design, 587
    zero knowledge proof security, 589
Selfish mining, 139, 150, 575, 782
SHA-256, 25, 26, 29, 30, 33
Sharding, 457
Sharding and parallel execution
    blockchains, 458
    cross-shard transactions, 471–474

DAS protocol, 468–470
erasure coding, 465
Ethereum's sharding roadmap, 476–478
execution sharding, 485
vs. data availability, 461–463
KZG polynomial commitments, DAS, 465–468
practical sharding implementation
NEAR, 479, 480
Polkadot, 481
stateless validation, 483, 484
Zilliqa, 479
single-shared takeover problem, 458, 460, 461
Shards, 458
Shor's algorithm, 519, 546, 547, 786
Shortest vector problem (SVP), 577
Slashing, 375
Slush-to-Avalanche pipeline, 253
State channels, 454
Stateless Hash-Based Digital Signature Algorithm (SLH-DSA), 786
Succinct Non-Interactive Arguments of Knowledge (zk-SNARKs), 573
Symmetric cryptography, 517

T

Temporal logic, 416
Tendermint's ABCI architecture, 189
Threshold schemes, 77
Threshold signatures, 73, 78
Tokenomics, 375, 382, 579

U

Unspent Transaction Output (UTXO), 783
UTXO set model, 582

V

Verifiable Random Functions (VRFs), 118, 571, 581
Algorand uses, 112
implementation, 112, 114, 115
on-chain randomness problem, 110
properties, 110
working, 111
Verkle trees, 54, 582
Virtual machines
blockchain, 321, 322
EVM, 321–325, 327–329, 331, 333–335, 345
gas machines/EIP-1559, 336, 337
parallele transaction processing, 340–343
WASM, 344
WebAssembly, 339, 340

W, X, Y

WebAssembly (WASM), 321, 583, 783

Z

Zero-knowledge proofs, 572–574, 783
bulletproofs, 95, 96, 98–100
commitment schemes, 100–103
definitions and properties, 83, 84, 86
ring signatures, 103–106, 108, 109
transaction history, 82
VRFs, 110
Zero-Knowledge Succinct Non-Interactive Argument of Knowledge (zk-SNARKs)
properties, 86
setup problem, 89
work, 87
Zcash, 90–93

ZK-based privacy-preserving
compliance, xxiii
ZK-based voting system, 117
ZK proof systems, 118
zk-SNARKs, 81
advantages, 93
Ethereum layer 2s, 94, 95
trade-offs, 93

GPSR Compliance
The European Union's (EU) General Product Safety Regulation (GPSR) is a set of rules that requires consumer products to be safe and our obligations to ensure this.

If you have any concerns about our products, you can contact us on

ProductSafety@springernature.com

In case Publisher is established outside the EU, the EU authorized representative is:

Springer Nature Customer Service Center GmbH
Europaplatz 3
69115 Heidelberg, Germany

www.ingramcontent.com/pod-product-compliance
Lightning Source LLC
Chambersburg PA
CBHW081433100826
49614CB00018B/471
9798868828904